THE ENLIGHTENMENT WORLD

The Enlightenment World offers an informed, comprehensive and up-to-date analysis of the European Enlightenment (circa. 1720-1800) as both an historical epoch and a cultural formation. This richly illustrated collection begins with the intellectual origins of the Enlightenment and progresses through a wide range of topics in an exploration of an era of sweeping changes and transformations.

The chapters are written by 39 leading international experts and presented in non-technical and accessible language. Chapters cover areas as diverse as government, fashion, craftsmanship and artisans, philanthropy, cross cultural encounters, feminism, censorship, science and education, and contemporary and modern critics of the Enlightenment.

This critically acclaimed volume provides essential reading for all students of the Enlightenment.

Martin Fitzpatrick was formerly Senior Lecturer and Senior Research Associate at the Department of History and Welsh History, the University of Wales, Aberyswyth. He is co-editor of Enlightenment and Dissent.

Peter Jones is Professor Emeritus of Philosophy and was Director of the Institute for Advanced Studies in the Humanities at the University of Edinburgh.

Christa Knellwolf is affiliated to the Austrailian National University and co-editor (with Christopher Norris) of 'The Cambridge History of Literary Criticism, vol.9.'

Iain McCalman is the Director of the Humanities Research Centre at the Australian National University and general editor of An Oxford Companion to the Romantic Age: British Culture 1776-1832'

The Routledge Worlds

THE ENLIGHTENMENT WORLD

Edited by
Martin Fitzpatrick, Peter Jones,
Christa Knellwolf and Iain McCalman

Routledge
Taylor & Francis Group

LONDON AND NEW YORK

First published 2007
by Routledge
2 Park Square, Milton Park, Abingdon, Oxon OX14 4RN

Simultaneously published in the USA and Canada
by Routledge
270 Madison Avenue, New York, NY 10016

Routledge is an imprint of the Taylor & Francis Group, an informa business

© 2007 Martin Fitzpatrick, Peter Jones, Christa Knellwolf and Iain McCalman

Typeset in Garamond by
Keystroke, High Street, Tettenhall, Wolverhampton
Printed and bound in Great Britain by
The Cromwell Press, Trowbridge, Wiltshire

British Library Cataloguing in Publication Data
A catalogue record for this book is available from the British Library

Library of Congress Cataloging in Publication Data

ISBN10: 0–415–40408–8

ISBN13: 978–0–415–40408–2

CONTENTS

———•◦•———

III   THE HIGH ENLIGHTENMENT

IV   POLITE CULTURE AND THE ARTS

— Contents —

— *Contents* —

VII TRANSFORMATION AND EXPLORATIONS

VIII THE ENLIGHTENMENT AND ITS CRITICS: THEN AND NOW

ILLUSTRATIONS

Edited by Georgina Fitzpatrick

CONTRIBUTORS

Hugh Dunthorne teaches History at the University of Wales, Swansea. Besides writing on the Enlightenment, he has published on Anglo-Dutch relations through-out the early modern period and is currently completing a book on the Revolt of the Netherlands and its impact on seventeenth-century Britain.

James Dybikowski, Professor Emeritus of Philosophy at the University of British Columbia, is a specialist in Greek and eighteenth-century philosophy, with particular reference to civil and political liberty and the free-thinkers. This last reflects his perennial fascination with intellectual mavericks. Dybikowski is the author of *On Burning Ground* (1993), a book on the eighteenth-century deist, political theorist and educational experimentalist David Williams. He is preparing an edition of the correspondence of Anthony Collins. He co-edits the journal *Enlightenment and Dissent* and co-edited *Scepticisme, clandestinité et libres pensées* (2002).

Frances Ferguson is the author of *Wordsworth: Language as Counter-Spirit, Solitude and the Sublime: Romanticism and the Aesthetics of Individuation*, and *Pornography: The Theory*, as well as numerous essays on the eighteenth century and Romanticism. She teaches at Johns Hopkins University, where she holds the Mary Elizabeth Garrett Professorship in Arts and Sciences.

Martin Fitzpatrick, formerly Senior Lecturer, Department of History and Welsh History, University of Wales, Aberystwyth, is a founder and co-editor of the journal *Enlightenment and Dissent*. He contributed the essay on 'Enlightenment' to *An Oxford Companion to the Romantic Age*, and the chapters, 'Enlightenment and Conscience', in John McLaren and Harold Coward (eds), *Religious Conscience, the State and the Law: Historical Contexts and Contemporary Significance* (1998); and 'The Enlightenment and Toleration', in Ole P. Grell and Roy Porter (eds), *Toleration in Enlightenment Europe* (2000).

Tom Furniss is a Senior Lecturer in the Department of English Studies at the University of Strathclyde in Glasgow. He is the author of *Edmund Burke's Aesthetic Ideology* (1993) and of a number of articles and essays on Burke, Paine and Wollstonecraft. He is currently completing a book about the discourse of radical nationalism.

Aaron Garrett teaches philosophy at Boston University. He is the author of a book on Spinoza and the editor of volumes on the history of animal rights, a critical edition of Hutcheson's *Essay on the Passions with Illustrations on the Moral Sense* and forthcoming volumes of the works of John Millar. In addition he has written on Locke, Hume, Jefferson, Scottish anthropology, and a lengthy article on 'Human Nature' for the *Cambridge History of Eighteenth Century Philosophy*.

David Garrioch teaches at Monash University in Australia and has published mainly on the history of eighteenth-century Paris. His most recent book is *The Making of Revolutionary Paris* (2002). He is currently working on a comparative social history of Paris, Milan, and Stockholm in the eighteenth century.

Eckhart Hellmuth is Professor of Modern History, University of Munich and has written extensively on eighteenth-century Germany and Britain. His publications include: editor, *The Transformation of Political Culture: England and Germany in the late Eighteenth Century* (1990); 'Why Does Corruption Matter? Reforms and Reform Movements in Britain and Germany in the Second Half of the Eighteenth Century', in T. C. W. Blanning and Peter Wende (eds), *Reform in Great Britain and Germany 1750–1850* (1999); with Michael Trauth and Immo Meenken (eds), *Zeitenwende? Preußen um 1800: Festgabe für Günter Birtsch zum 70. Geburtstag* (1999); with John Brewer (eds), *Rethinking Leviathan – The Eighteenth-Century State in Britain and Germany*; 'Criticising the Constitution: or, How to Talk about the Liberty of the Press in the 1790s', in Uwe Böker and Julie A. Hibbard (eds), *Sites of Discourse – Public and Private Spheres – Legal Culture* (2002); with Wolfgang Piereth, 'Germany, 1760–1815', in Hannah Barker and Simon Burrows (eds), *Press, Politics and the Public Sphere in Europe and North America, 1760–1820* (2002).

John Henry is a Senior Lecturer in the History of Science at the University of Edinburgh. He specializes in the early modern period but has published widely on the history of science, medicine and philosophy from the Renaissance to the nineteenth century. He is the author of *Moving Heaven and Earth: Copernicus and the Solar System* (2001); and *Knowledge is Power: Francis Bacon and the Method of Science* (2002); and *The Scientific Revolution and the Origins of Modern Science* (2nd edn, 2002).

Carla Hesse is Professor of History at the University of California, Berkeley. She is the author, most recently, of *The Other Enlightenment: How French Women Became Modern* (2001), and is a member of the editorial board of the journal *Representations*.

Ian Hunter is an Australian Professorial Fellow and Associate Director of the Centre for the History of European Discourses at the University of Queensland. He is the author of several works on early modern philosophical, religious and political thought, most recently *Rival Enlightenments: Civil and Metaphysical Philosophy in Early Modern Germany* (2001).

Clare Jackson is Lecturer and Director of Studies in History at Trinity Hall, Cambridge. She is the author of *Restoration Scotland 1660–1690: Royalist Politics, Religion and Ideas* (2003) as well as a range of articles on the history of ideas in early modern Britain.

Margaret C. Jacob is Professor of History at UCLA and before 1998 she taught at the University of Pennsylvania and the New School of Social Research. Her first book, *The Newtonians and the English Revolution* (1976) won the Gottschalk Prize from the American Society for Eighteenth Century Studies and in 1996 she served as its president. Her research interests began with the nature of Newtonian science, its relationship to religion and the state, and then extended to the transmission of English science to Continental Europe. From those topics came her general interest in the European Enlightenment and the role of science in early industrial development. Her books include: *The Radical Enlightenment: Pantheists, Freemasons and Republicans* (1981; 2nd edn, 2003); *The Cultural Meaning of the Scientific Revolution* (1986) and its sequel, *Scientific Culture and the Making of the Industrial West* (1997). She has a new book forthcoming, co-authored with Larry Stewart, *The Impact of Newton's Science, 1687–1851*. She is a member of the American Philosophical Society.

Peter Jones was Director of the Institute for Advanced Studies in the Humanities from 1986 to 2000, and Professor of Philosophy in the University of Edinburgh from 1984 to 1998. He is an expert on the work of David Hume and the author or editor of twelve books and a hundred articles and reviews on eighteenth-century British philosophy, culture and the arts, including *Philosophy and the Novel* (1975), *Hume's Sentiments* (1982), *Adam Smith Reviewed* (1992), *The Reception of David Hume in Europe* (2005), *Kames's Elements of Criticism* (2005) and *Ove Arup: Master Builder of the Twentieth Century* (2006). In 1995 he was Gifford Lecturer at the University of Aberdeen. He has held many visiting professorships and Fellowships, and is a Fellow of the Royal Society of Arts, the Society of Antiquaries of Scotland, and the Royal Society of Edinburgh – of which he has served on the governing council. He is a member of UNESCO and government panels and seminars and a trustee of several foundations.

Jonathan Lamb is Professor of English at Vanderbilt University. Author of numerous books and articles, his publications include: *The Rhetoric of Suffering* (1995); *Voyages and Beaches: Europe and the Pacific 1769–1840* (1999); *Exploration and Exchange: British and American Narratives of the Pacific 1680–1900* (2000); and *Preserving the Self in the South Seas, 1680–1840* (2001), for which he was awarded the John Ben Snow Prize in 2002.

Johnson Kent Wright is Associate Professor of History at Arizona State University. He is the author of *A Classical Republican in Eighteenth-Century France: The Political Thought of Mably* (1997), and essays on French political thought, eighteenth-century historiography and twentieth-century historiography of the Enlightenment.

Christa Knellwolf is a Research Fellow affiliated to the Australian National University. Author of a book on Alexander Pope, *Representations of Women in the Poetry of Alexander Pope* (1998), she is also an editor (with Christopher Norris) of *The Cambridge History of Literary Criticism*, vol. 9: *Twentieth-Century Historical, Philosophical and Psychological Perspectives* (2001); and an editor (with Robert Maccubbin) of a special issue of *Eighteenth-Century Life, Exoticism and the Culture of Exploration* (2002). She has published widely on eighteenth-century literature and culture and is working on a book about the cultural representation of discovery and exploration.

Iain McCalman was Director of the Humanities Research Centre at the Australian National University, Canberra, from 1995 to 2003, and Deputy Director of the Centre for Cross Cultural Research, also at the ANU. He is a specialist in British and European cultural history of the late Enlightenment and Romantic periods. He is author of *Radical Underworld: Prophets, Revolutionaries and Pornographers in London, 1795–1840* (1993); general editor of *An Oxford Companion to the Romantic Age: British Culture, 1776–1832* (1999); co-editor of *Barnaby Rudge* for Oxford World's Classics (2003); and author of *The Seven Ordeals of Count Cagliostro: Count Cagliostro, Master of Magic in the Age of Reason* (2003). Professor McCalman is President of the Australasian and Pacific Association for Eighteenth Century Studies. He has recently been awarded a five-year Commonwealth Fellowship to develop a book and multi-media re-enactment charting the life and spectacles of the artist and stenographer Philippe Jacques de Loutherbourg.

Randall McGowen, Professor of History, University of Oregon, is the co-author of *The Perreaus and Mrs. Rudd: Forgery and Betrayal in Eighteenth-Century London* (2001). He has written numerous articles on the criminal law and penal policy in eighteenth- and nineteenth-century Britain.

Darrin M. McMahon is the Ben Weider Associate Professor of History at Florida State University, author of *Enemies of the Enlightenment: The French Counter-Enlightenment and the Making of Modernity* (2001) and the forthcoming *Happiness: A History*.

Peter McNeil is a design historian whose research interests include eighteenth-century English and French masculine dress, consumption and the city, and the caricature print as a genre of visual culture. He holds an Australian Research Council Large Grant for a study of eighteenth-century male fashionability with a focus on the macaroni and the *petit-maître*. He has published articles in journals including *Art History*, *Journal of Design History* and *Fashion Theory*.

Jon Mee is Margaret Candfield Fellow in English at University College, Oxford. His most recent book is *Romanticism, Enthusiasm, and Regulation: Poetics and the Policing of Culture in the Romantic Period* (2003). He has written widely on literature, print culture and politics in the Romantic period with a special interest in William Blake and the popular radicalism of the 1790s. He was also on the editorial board of *An Oxford Companion to the Romantic Age* (1999).

Martin Mulsow gained his Habilitation in Philosophy at the University of Munich and is now a member of the Institute for Advanced Study, Princeton. His numerous books on the intellectual history of early modern Europe include: *Renaissance to Enlightenment: Frühneuzeitliche Selbsterhaltung* (1998) winner of the Premio Luigi de Franco, Italy; *Monadenlehre, Hermetik und Deismus* (1998); *Die drei Ringe* (2001); *Moderne aus dem Untergrund* (2002). He is editor or co-editor of: *Johann Lorenz Mosheim* (1997); *Skepsis, Providenz, Poyhistorie* (1998); *Georg Schade: Die unwandelbare Religion* (1999); *Die Praktiken der Gelehrsamkeit in der frühen Neuzeit* (2001); *The Berlin Refuge* (2002); *Das Ende des Hermetismus* (2002); *Socinianism and Cultural Exchange* (2003); *Secret Conversions to Judaism in Early Modern Europe* (forthcoming).

Alexander Murdoch is the author of *The People Above: Politics and Administration in Mid-Eighteenth-Century Scotland* (1980); and *British History 1660–1832: National Identity and Local Culture* (1998). He was co-editor, with John Dwyer and Roger A. Mason, of *New Perspectives on the Politics and Culture of Early Modern Scotland* (1982). A graduate of George Washington University, Washington, D.C. and the University of Edinburgh, currently he is a Senior Lecturer in Scottish History at the University of Edinburgh, having previously taught at what is now University College Northampton.

Karen O'Brien is Reader in English and American Literature at the University of Warwick. She is the author of *Narratives of Enlightenment: Cosmopolitan History from Voltaire to Gibbon* (1997); and *Feminist Debate in Eighteenth-Century Britain* (forthcoming).

Dorinda Outram is the first holder of the Franklin W. and Gladys I. Clark Chair of History, University of Rochester. She has written on women in science, the French Revolution, the Enlightenment and on the naturalist Georges Cuvier. Her books include: *George Cuvier: Vocation, Science and Authority in Post-Revolutionary France* (1984); editor with Pnina G. Abir-Am, *Uneasy Careers and Intimate Lives: Women in Science, 1789–1979* (1987); *The Body and the French Revolution: Sex, Class and Political Culture* (1989); and *The Enlightenment* (1995).

Geraint Parry was W. J. M. Mackenzie Professor and is now Emeritus Professor of Government at the University of Manchester. His research and teaching interests are the history of political ideas, democratic theory and practice and political sociology. He is the author of *Political Elites* (1969); *John Locke* (1978); and, with G. Moyser and N. Day, *Democracy and Political Participation in Britain* (1992). He has edited *Participation in Politics* (1972); *Democracy, Consensus and Social Contract* (1978, with P. Birnbaum and J. Lively); *Democracy and Democratization* (1994, with M. Moran),; and *Fundamentals in British Politics* (1999, with I. Holliday and A. Gamble). He is currently working on the history of the relationship between political theory and educational theory. He has been editor of *Government and Opposition*, the international journal of comparative politics, and is a former President of the Political Studies Association of the UK.

Mark Philp is Chair of the Department of Politics and International Relations, University of Oxford, and Fellow and Tutor at Oriel College. He has written widely on late eighteenth-century political thought and social movements, with books and edited collections of William Godwin and Thomas Paine. His most recent research has been divided between contemporary work on political corruption and standards in public life and a project on Napoleon and the invasion of Britain, 1797–1815.

Jane Rendall is a Senior Lecturer in the History Department and the Centre for Eighteenth Century Studies at the University of York. She is interested in eighteenth- and nineteenth-century British and comparative women's history, and particularly in Scottish women's history. Her publications include: *The Origins of Modern Feminism* (1985); *Women in an Industrializing Society: England 1750–1880* (1990); and, with Catherine Hall and Keith McClelland, *Defining the Victorian Nation* (2000). She has also edited: *Equal or Different: Women's Politics 1800–1914* (1987); jointly with Karen Offen and Ruth Roach Pierson, *Writing Women's History: International Perspectives* (1991); and, with Mark Hallett, *Eighteenth-Century York: Culture, Space and Society* (2003). She is currently working on a study of the gendered legacies of the Enlightenment in Scotland.

Nicholas Rogers is a Professor of History at York University, Toronto, and the co-editor of the *Journal of British Studies*. He is the author of *Crowds, Culture and Politics in Georgian Britain* (1998) and, with Douglas Hay, of *Eighteenth-Century English Society* (1997). He recently completed a cultural history of Halloween. His next book will be a study of British naval impressment in the long eighteenth century.

Peter Schouls is an Adjunct Professor at both Simon Fraser University (Graduate Liberal Studies) and the University of British Columbia (Philosophy). He was a Professor of Philosophy at the University of Alberta and has, in addition, held academic positions at Auckland University, the Free University of Amsterdam, Massey University and the University of Toronto. His philosophical interests are in early modern as well as Enlightenment philosophy. Two of his books are *Reasoned Freedom: John Locke and Enlightenment* (1992) and *Descartes and the Possibility of Science* (2000).

Luisa Simonutti is a Research Fellow at the National Research Council in Milan and Professor of the History of Renaissance Philosophy in Ferrara. A specialist in the history of modern philosophy and in the political doctrines of the sixteenth and seventeenth centuries, she has published numerous essays on the thought of John Locke in relation to the Dutch and Continental philosophy of the period. She has also studied various aspects of the work of Spinoza, and analysed the emergence and consolidation of the concept of toleration in the modern age. She has edited a number of articles and books, including *Dal necessario al possibile: Determinismo e libertà nel pensiero anglo-olandese del XVII secolo* (2001).

Larry Stewart is Professor of History in the University of Saskatchewan, and co-editor of the *Canadian Journal of History/Annales canadiennes d'histoire*. His main research interest is in the social implications of scientific advancement. His publications include: *The Rise of Public Science: Rhetoric, Technology and Natural Philosophy in Newtonian Britain* (1992); 'Global Pillage: Science, Commerce and Empire in the Eighteenth Century', in Roy Porter (ed.), *The Cambridge History of Science*, vol. 4: *Science in the Eighteenth Century* (2001); and 'Putting on Airs: Science, Medicine and Polity in the Late Eighteenth Century', in T. H. Levere and G. L'E Turner (eds), *Discussing Chemistry and Steam: The Minutes of a Coffee House Philosophical Society, 1780–1787* (2002). He is co-author with Margaret C. Jacob of *The Impact of Newton's Science, 1687–1851*, forthcoming.

Kathryn Sutherland is Professor of Bibliography and Textual Criticism at Oxford University and a Fellow of St Anne's College. Her edition with critical commentary of Adam Smith's *An Inquiry into the Nature and Causes of the Wealth of Nations* appeared in 1993. She edited with Stephen Copley *Adam Smith's Wealth of Nations: New Interdisciplinary Essays* (1995).

John Sweetman is an art historian and artist (especially in acrylic and drawing media). He was Reader in the History of Art, Southampton University, until retirement in 1990. Previously Keeper of Temple Newsam House, Leeds; Curator, Barlow Collection (Chinese Ceramics) and Senior Visiting Research Fellow, Sussex University 1974–85; and editor of *Oriental Art*, 1982–9. Publications include: *The Oriental Obsession* (1988); *The Enlightenment and the Age of Revolution 1700–1850* (1998); *The Artist and the Bridge 1700–1920* (2000); 'Bridges and the Engineer: The Artist's View', in exhibition catalogue *La Ingeniería Civil en la Pintura*, Academy of San Fernando, Madrid (forthcoming). He has contributed to *Europa 1700–1992* (1992) and to numerous dictionaries, art historical catalogues and journals.

Cynthia Verba is a Lecturer in the Harvard University Extension School, and Director of Fellowships of the Graduate School of Arts and Sciences, also at Harvard University. An expert on Enlightenment musical thought in France, she is author of *Music and the French Enlightenment: Reconstruction of a Dialogue, 1750–1764* (1993).

Howard Williams is Professor of International Politics at the University of Wales, Aberystwyth, and has been has been a visiting scholar at the universities of Berlin Humboldt, Wilfrid Laurier, Frankfurt, Munich, Mainz. Author of numerous books and articles over a wide range of subjects, he is, in particular, an expert on Kant and Hegel. His works include: *Kant's Political Philosophy* (1983), *Concepts of Ideology* (1988), *Hegel, Heraclitus and Marx's Dialectic* (1989), *International Relations in Political Theory* (1991), *International Relations and the Limits of Political Theory* (1996), with D. Sullivan and Gwynn Matthews, *Francis Fukuyama and the End of History* (1997), and *Kant's Critique of Hobbes: Sovereignty and Cosmopolitanism* (2003).

Susan Wilson is a Lecturer in Drama at Anglia Polytechnic University in Cambridge. Her teaching and research interests are in twentieth-century drama and literature, particularly Samuel Beckett's plays and prose, postmodernism and critical theory.

Richard Yeo is an Australian Professorial Fellow in the Faculty of Arts, Griffith University, Brisbane. He has written on the history of eighteenth- and nineteenth-century science, and his books include: *Defining Science: William Whewell, Natural Knowledge and Public Debate in Early Victorian Britain* (1993) and *Encyclopaedic Visions: Scientific Dictionaries and Enlightenment Culture* (2001).

PREFACE

———•◦•———

From some perspectives, it can be argued there was a unity to the Enlightenment: as a movement, which gave many writers, thinkers, reformers and readers a sense of identity; as a set of philosophical assumptions about man and society; as a set of scientific assumptions about the natural world; or as a generalized attitude of mind. From other perspectives, however, it can be argued that there were several enlightenments. There are, of course, contexts in which reference to *the* Enlightenment is justifiable; but we have often avoided the definite article, in order to signal the variety of ways in which the term can be used.

Our authors were free, within a general framework, to explore familiar and unfamiliar themes of their own choosing, but even in a large book there are many contexts, themes and ideas to which no reference is made, and many individuals who are never mentioned. This book concentrates on contexts, because they provide necessary conditions for understanding what was happening, what was said, and the significance of complex past events. Modern readers occupy different and multiple contexts, from which different interpretations necessarily result. New perspectives, new enquiries and new findings will continually challenge and supplement the findings and suggestions of our authors.

In 1803 John Bristed, while writing about a tour of the Scottish Highlands, remarked that there is no 'book by which the jargon may be learned'. To make this book accessible to as many readers as possible, the editors have compiled a brief glossary to explain some of the terminology fashionable in the eighteenth century or even today. In addition, each part has been introduced by an editor, who explains the background and concerns of the chapters in that part.

The links between a person's ideas and actions, and the ways in which ideas can be transformed by subsequent interpretation or actions, are matters of endless enquiry and debate: final judgement on the significance of such variations is rare, if not impossible. The contributors to this book have clearly demonstrated these truths in their explorations of enlightenment themes.

ACKNOWLEDGEMENTS

The editors have incurred numerous debts during the course of their labours. First, they wish to acknowledge and thank the following institutions for invaluable financial and administrative support: The Humanities Research Centre of the Australian National University; the Australian Research Council, for the Discovery Grant; King's College, University of Aberdeen; the Foundation for Advanced Studies in the Humanities, Edinburgh.

Special thanks are due to the University of Aberdeen, its Principal and Vice-Chancellor, Professor C. Duncan Rice, and the Dean of Arts and Divinity, the Very Rev. Professor Iain Torrance, for hosting and funding The Enlightenment World Symposium in April 2002, which enabled the editors and contributors to present and discuss draft chapters. In addition, we thank Professor John Dunkley for his participation and assistance.

We thank Georgina Fitzpatrick for her tireless and enthusiastic support in tracing and editing the illustrations. Thanks are also due to Eckhart Hellmuth, Alison Kennedy and Pamela Clemit for help with illustrations and reproductions, Owen Larkin for editorial assistance, and David Garrioch and Jean Jones for invaluable support and advice.

Martin Fitzpatrick and Peter Jones wish to thank the Humanities Research Centre for Fellowships and warm hospitality, which made their editorial work in Canberra so enjoyable. In addition Martin Fitzpatrick is grateful for the support of Professor Aled Jones and the Department of History and Welsh History, University of Wales, Aberystwyth. Christa Knellwolf gratefully acknowledges Fellowship support from the Swiss National Science Foundation.

Illustrations are reproduced with grateful thanks to: ANU Photography, Australian National University; Bancroft Library, University of California, Berkeley; Bibliothèque Nationale de France, Paris; Bodleian Library, University of Oxford; British Library; British Museum; Derby Museum and Art Gallery; Gemeentearchief Amsterdam [Municipal Archives]; Guildhall Library, Corporation of London; Herzog August Bibliothek, Wolfenbüttel; Hunterian Art Gallery, University of Glasgow; Humanities Research Centre, Australian National University; Huntington Library, Art Collections and Botanical Gardens, San Marino, California; Koninklijke Bibliotheek, The Hague; Mitchell Library, Glasgow; Musée d'Art et d'Histoire,

Geneva; Musée de la Révolution Française, Vizille; Musée Carnavalet, Paris; National Library of Australia; National Portrait Gallery, London; Philadelphia Museum of Art; Photothèque des Musées de la Ville de Paris; Princeton University Library; Thomas Jefferson Foundation Inc.; Sir Thomas Browne Institute, University of Leiden; Wallace Collection, London.

Thanks also to the following for prints: Martin Fitzpatrick; Peter Jones; Peter McNeil; Barbara Peacock; Nicholas Rogers.

Further thanks to the following institutions, which waived fees on reproduction rights: Bancroft Library, University of California, Berkeley; British Library; Derby Museum and Art Gallery; Guildhall Library, Corporation of London; Huntington Library, Art Collections and Botanical Gardens, San Marino, California; Koninklijke Bibliotheek, The Hague; Mitchell Library, Glasgow; Musée de la Révolution Française, Vizille; National Library of Australia; Princeton University Library; Thomas Jefferson Foundation Inc.; Sir Thomas Browne Institute, University of Leiden.

BIBLIOGRAPHICAL NOTE

To convey as accurately as possible the dating of primary works mentioned in the text, the date after the author's name in the reference within the text is normally the date of the original publication of that work. This is then followed by a reference, usually a page reference, to the edition used, the full details of which are in the reference section at the end of the chapters. There are sometimes bibliographical complexities: the date of completion of a work may differ from the date of publication, and the date of publication itself may be misleading. In such cases, the date in the reference within the text is the date given for the work in the edition used by the contributor.

PART I

INTELLECTUAL ORIGINS
OF ENLIGHTENMENT

INTRODUCTION

———◆·◆·◆———

Peter Jones

No single idea, belief or practice unites all of the writers associated with Enlightenment thought; no one meaning informed even the banners under which dispute was sustained; no one definition embraces the ways in which the most self-consciously used terms were employed – terms such as 'science', 'republic', 'scepticism', 'Christian', 'atheist'. This does not render such labels useless, because they function as maps, simultaneously reflecting and requiring inter-pretation. No one map, and no single label, can represent everything that could be represented; each must be drawn up on a certain scale, and all can be misread. An analogy with maps was popular among writers of the time who were keen to signal the challenges of interpreting unfamiliar contexts. Richard Bentley (1662–1742), the first Boyle lecturer, in 1692 was worried by the fact that we can only view the topography of the past as if from a mountain top: the very real obstacles confronting travellers on the ground are flattened out: 'All the Inequality of Surface would be lost to his View; the wide Ocean would appear to him like an even and uniform Plane (uniform as to its Level, though not as to Light and Shade) though every Rock of the Sea was as high as the *Pico* of *Teneriff*' (Boyle's Lecture Sermons 1739: vol.1, 84). Moreover, as Anthony Collins (1676–1729) forcefully stated in 1710, maps 'are not designed to represent *Mountains, Valleys, Lakes and Rivers*, to those who have no Ideas of them. Maps suppose Men to have these Ideas before-hand' (Collins 1710: 36).

Many writers were aware of the importance of contexts in determining both what to do and how to understand the past. The discipline, familiar to all educated people in the seventeenth and eighteenth centuries, which placed context at the centre was rhetoric, underpinned by grammar. Bishop Berkeley (1685–1753), in 1709, captures the thought, by then almost commonplace, illustrating a point made by Dybikowski (Chapter 3), that remarks deemed unexceptionable from a bishop's pen are perceived as subversive from a freethinker's: 'A word pronounced with certain circumstances, or in a certain context with other words, hath not always the same import and signification that it hath when pronounced in some other circumstances, or different context of words' (Berkeley 1732: para. lxxiii).

Rhetoric was supposed to be concerned with effective public communication, but practical success explicitly presupposed many things, above all transparency in

3

meaning: this did not assume that anything was self-evident, but rather that everything required interpretation. Ephraim Chambers (1680–1740), in 1728, echoed an idea trumpeted by almost everyone since Francis Bacon (1561–1626): that wilful obscurity should be condemned because it gives a reader the spurious freedom to invent whatever meaning he wishes, and with it the seductive illusion of ownership. The human mind, he says, 'in apprehending what was hid under a veil, fancies itself in some measure the author of it' (Chambers 1728: '*Mixed* Fables'). He recognized, of course, that the more a study of rhetoric was confined within institutions, the more it declined into scholastic formalities.

> There is something arbitrary and artificial in all writings: they are a kind of draughts, or pictures, where the aspect, attitude, and light, which the objects are taken in, though merely arbitrary, yet sway and direct the whole representation. Books are, as it were, plans or prospects of ideas artfully arranged and exhibited, not to the eye, but to the imagination; and there is a kind of analogous perspective, which obtains in them, wherein we have something not much unlike points of sight, and of distance. An author, in effect, has some particular view or design in drawing our his ideas . . . The case amounts to the same as the viewing of objects in a mirror; where, unless the form of the mirror be known, viz. whether it be plain, concave, convex, cylindric, or conic, etc., we can make no judgement of the magnitude, figure, etc. of the objects.
>
> (Chambers 1728: vol. I, xvi)

Clarity of expression was everyone's declared goal, but the frequency with which it was asserted indicated the extent of the struggle. Too often writers failed to define their central terms, or to abide by their definitions. And, as D'Alembert acidly observed in 1751, when it came to acknowledgements, 'the common practice is to refer to sources or to make citations in a way that is vague, often unreliable, and nearly always confused' (Diderot and D'Alembert 1751: xxxvii). Moreover, two theoretical problems seemed to make the tasks of communication intractable: first, the puzzling relations of language to the world; and second, the ubiquitous implications of change. D'Alembert, no doubt reflecting on Chambers, declared that:

> It is almost as if one were trying to express (a) proposition by means of a language whose nature was being imperceptibly altered, so that the proposition was successively expressed in different ways representing the different states through which the language had passed. Each of these states would be recognized in the one immediately neighbouring it; but in a more remote state we would no longer make it out.
>
> (Diderot and D'Alembert 1751: viii–ix)

He fears, in other words, that across separated points in time, and in the absence of an intervening medium, we may be unable to work out what was being said. The meaning of many everyday expressions might change independently of any changes in what they described. Action-at-a-distance might be doubtful; meaning-at-a-distance impossible.

To grasp the import of such insights, let us consider briefly some of the differences between, say, 1759 and today. In that year Handel died, and the Seven Years War (1756–63) was raging to no one's benefit. In that year, too, Voltaire (1694–1778) published *Candide*, Samuel Johnson (1696–1772) his moral tale *Rasselas*, and Adam Smith (1723–90), *Theory of Moral Sentiments*. With the eighth volume about to be published, the great *Encyclopédie* of Diderot (1713–84) and D'Alembert (1717–83) was banned by order of King Louis XV, along with *De l'Esprit* of Helvétius (1715–71). In chapter 30 of Johnson's melancholy novel, Rasselas and his sister declare themselves to have little interest in history. They are firmly rebuked: 'To see men we must see their works, that we may learn what reason has dictated, or passion has incited, and find what are the most powerful motives of action. To judge rightly of the present we must oppose it to the past; for all judgement is comparative, and of the future nothing can be known.'

Such a view had been gathering support for over a century, and in 1759 had been conspicuously exemplified in the newly published Tudor volumes of David Hume's *History of England*. Hume (1711–76) had already identified one unavoidable challenge: historians of the past know the outcome and consequences of actions, but not the intentions necessary for understanding them. The original agents, on the other hand, know their own intentions when they set out, but not the outcome. But there are other kinds of challenge: for example, almost no statistics were available. In 1752 Hume stated, 'We know not exactly the numbers of any European kingdom, or even city, at present' (Hume 1752: vol. 1, 414). Yet, in 1759 no one can be said, in a defensible modern sense, to have known:

- anything about forms of energy other than light and heat;
- anything about the composition of air or water;
- anything about the nature of fire, breathing or procreation;
- anything about the age of the earth or the size of the universe;
- anything about the nature of stars or the origins of life;
- anything about the evolution of animals or genetic inheritance.

There were, of course, 'opinions' about such matters, and within a dozen years or so some recognizably modern views were being formulated; but we have beliefs about these things, with varying degrees of assurance, and such beliefs irradiate all our assumptions and attitudes. To enter the minds of 1759, as it were, we would have to *un-think* what we know, in order to understand what we do not believe. Can it be done?

Alongside conceptual challenges of this kind, a second point about context and method should be underlined. There are huge differences over time in what is admitted, by whom, to be a proper question; and in what count as the proper methods for reaching acceptable answers to it. Hume was not the first to insist that scientific and religious views may be understood by ordinary people, and may affect their lives in ways quite other than philosophers acknowledge – this was a fairly standard observation by Deists. The elements of abstract theories that might be translated into common life were always unpredictable, even if detectable. Moreover, an increasing number of writers from the mid-seventeenth century onwards, including Claude Perrault (1613–88) and Fontenelle (1657–1757) in France, and Hume and Adam Ferguson (1723–1816) in Britain, argued that most people were simply not motivated by theories of any kind, and most definitely not purely by reason. Following Bacon, they all held that fact, not doctrine or untestable speculation, was the goal of enquiry. Echoing French contemporaries such as Bayle and Fontenelle, and citing their classical mentor Cicero, the unidentified author of *The Spectator*, 408, in 1712 (often thought to have been Alexander Pope) prominently declared, 'Reason must be employed in adjusting the Passions, but they must ever remain the Principles of Action' (*Spectator*, 408).

Contemporaries can be as puzzled by terminology as later historians. There was, of course, censorship, and writers might need to disguise what they meant; but readers could also suspect subversive texts where none was intended. In the first two parts we read how writers variously understood such terms as 'Newtonianism', or 'scepticism', and how they employed what today we regard as 'sceptical' arguments in surprisingly selective contexts. Garrett (Chapter 4) emphasizes that many writers influenced by, or even adopting, sceptical arguments did not see themselves as sceptics, nor as addressing sceptical challenges. Indeed, like other labels, including 'republican' and 'Christian', the ideas encompassed under them vary almost to the point of self-contradiction. Overall, however, the goal of many prominent writers accused, or even boasting, of a sceptical approach to knowledge was to promote rigorous, repeatable, experience-based enquiry. That such a goal strikes a modern reader as hardly worthy of comment demonstrates the total success of the approach – and the difficulty of understanding contexts in which such views were vigorously challenged.

In Chapter 2 Schouls explains how, for thinkers of the early modern period, tradition was rejected as a principal source of truth and wisdom: both the criteria and objects of certainty lay within individuals themselves. And although neither Descartes nor Locke discarded God from his philosophy, they had established the means by which their immediate followers could, and would, do so. Indeed, in 1753 Turgot (1727–81) surmised that Descartes dared not admit the irrelevance of God to his philosophical position because of the solitude it entailed. The demand and search for certainty may seem incomprehensible to a modern reader, but society itself appeared to be under threat as the authority of those who had claimed knowledge collapsed: was everyone equally ignorant? What were the criteria of justified belief; what warranted the acceptance of other people's claims; how should prejudice be identified and replaced? Prejudice was an important notion because, as Milton (1608–74) stated in his *Areopagitica*, if a man 'beleeve things only because his Pastor says so . . . without knowing other reason, though his belief be true, yet the very truth he holds, becomes his heresie' (Milton 1644: 38–9).

Such anxieties meant that the nature of education had to be addressed, with emphasis on individual effort and achievement, and rejection of the mechanical repetition of traditional methods and ideas. Insistence on thinking and judging for oneself soon led to the view that one's knowledge is essentially made – not passively imbibed, not inherited, not divinely vouchsafed. In his *Novum Organum* (I.xcv) of 1620, Bacon had famously claimed:

Those who have handled sciences have been either men of experiment or men of dogmas. The men of experiment are like the ant; they only collect and use; the reasoners resemble spiders, who make cobwebs out of their own substance. But the bee takes a middle course; it gathers its material from the flowers of the garden and the field, but transforms and digests it by a power of its own. Not unlike is the true business of philosophy.

Thereafter, most thinkers up to Condorcet (1743–94) said something about education. Benjamin Franklin in 1749 tells his readers to study Milton, Locke, Hutcheson, Obadiah Walker, Charles Rollin and George Turnbull. The earlier writers, such as Milton and Descartes, initially dismissed tradition, culture and community as irrelevant, but even they soon reabsorbed all three notions into their emerging moral, social and political philosophies. Locke, followed by Hume and his Scottish contemporaries, insisted that knowledge and its pursuit could not be merely individual endeavours: for one thing, no one has enough personal experience to ensure even minimal security in a hostile world. Indeed, knowledge must be regarded as an essentially social phenomenon, requiring the presence of others from whom to learn, and among whom to test one's own ideas. Moreover, Hume, arguably inspired as much by Descartes's successors such as Malebranche (1638–1715) as by Locke, insisted that we cannot understand the nature of the present without some notion of its roots in the past. This required a grasp of the culture and tradition from which the present emerged, and awareness of the often complex causal connections that occurred. Only with such awareness can anyone in the present decide what needs revision or rejection in the repertoire of ideas and practices they have inherited; and only with such awareness can anyone hope to build on past successes and avoid past errors. Obvious: once it has become obvious.

By the mid-seventeenth century there had developed a recognition that even if scholastic philosophical and theological obscurities could be successfully shamed into dissolution, the increasingly specialized new enquiries – later labelled as 'scientific' – were generating new obstacles to mutual understanding. Ephraim Chambers, writing only a year after the death of Isaac Newton (1642–1727), deplored the fact that in the modern world people 'of the same profession, no longer understand one another . . . [and] our knowledge is grown into little other than that of peoples misunderstandings or misapprehensions of one another' (Chambers 1728: xvii).

An indication of the extent to which the new, moderately sceptical, experience-based enquiries had permeated most areas of study by the time of the French Revolution in 1789 can be gauged from two brief quotations. In the first, William Robertson, leader of the Moderate clergy in Edinburgh, and Principal of the university there, objects to the ways in which missionary priests had projected their own views on to the peoples whom they wished to convert:

They study to reconcile the institutions, which fall under their observations, to their own creed, not to explain them according to the rude notions of the people themselves. They ascribe to them ideas which they are incapable of forming, and suppose them to be acquainted with principles and facts, which it is impossible that they should know.

(Robertson 1777: vol. 2, 133)

Adopting a similar tone, and writing at the beginning of the Revolution, J.-M.-A. Servan (1741–1808), a distinguished French lawyer, observed that in conjectures about the future one cannot guess the intervening crevasses that might impede progress towards distant mountains – a metaphor that by now had lasted more than a century:

> No matter how much we study we shall never learn more than a little of the present, far less of the past, and almost nothing, perhaps even nothing at all, of the future . . .
>
> History, in short, provides warning signals; it is a light that alerts us to the dangers of a reef ahead, but it is not a clear chart and compass.
>
> (Servan quoted by Bongie 1965: 76)

Although Enlightenment ideas did influence subsequent thought in so many ways, it is easy to forget one of their central social insights. It is this. Everyone learns and absorbs ideas from other people, from the contexts in which they live and from the traditions with which they become familiar. Very rarely have even the best-known thinkers originated the ideas for which they are famous; typically, what distinguishes them are the ways in which they mould, develop or emphasize existing ideas, make new syntheses and interpret their own context. Countless philosophers before David Hume, for example, reflected on the how and why of change, and thus on the nature of causation, including his immediate predecessors discussed in this book, such as Malebranche, Locke, Descartes and Bacon – quite apart from Aristotle, whose famous distinction in *Poetics*, II.8, between causal connection and mere temporal sequence, was known to everyone. A rather small group of Hume's contemporaries agreed with his analysis of causation, but it is subsequent interpreters and historians who have singled out his work as peculiarly influential on later thought. Contemporaries and posterity judge authors by different standards and from different perspectives.

Most of the discussions in this book refer to activities and ideas of an exceptionally small minority of the total populations: they were the people who held or aspired to power, and who possessed or had access to resources which enabled them to pursue or promote enquiry and implement change. The social benefits of their influence were most marked in the educational opportunities that gradually became available to more people, accompanied by decreasing poverty, and the eventual participation of more people in decisions which affected their own lives. It would be a mistake to think, however, that the names or achievements of those whom we discuss were known to more than a handful of their contemporaries or their descendants.

REFERENCES

Bacon, F. (1620) *Novum Organum*, in *The Philosophical Works of Francis Bacon*, ed. John M. Robertson, trans. Ellis and Spedding (1905) London: Routledge.

Berkeley, G. (1732) *An Essay towards a New Theory of Vision* [1709], 4th edn, in (1975) *Philosophical Works*, introduction by M. R. Ayers, London: Dent.

Bongie, L. L. (1965) *David Hume Prophet of the Counter-revolution*, Oxford: Clarendon Press.

[Boyle's Lecture Sermons] (1739) *A Defence of Natural and Revealed Religion: Being a Collection of the Sermons Preached at the Lecture Founded by the Honourable Robert Boyle, Esq. (From the Year 1691 to the Year 1732)*, London.

Chambers, Ephraim (1728) *Cyclopaedia: or an Universal Dictionary of the Arts and Sciences*, 2nd edn, 2 vols (1738) London.

[Collins, Anthony] (1710) *A Vindication of the Divine Attributes . . .* , London.

Diderot, D. and D'Alembert, J. (1751) 'Discours Préliminaire des Editeurs', in *Encyclopédie ou Dictionnaire Raisonné Des Sciences, Des Arts et Des Métiers*, Paris.

Hume, D. (1752) 'Of the Populousness of Ancient Nations', in *Political Discourses*, Edinburgh; quoted in *Essays and Treatises on Several Subjects* (1764) London.

[Johnson, S.] (1759) *The History of Rasselas, Prince of Abissinia: A Tale*, London.

Milton, J. (1644) *Areopagitica*, ed. John W. Hales (1894) Oxford: Clarendon Press.

Robertson, William (1777) *The History of America*, Dublin.

CHAPTER ONE

SCIENCE AND THE COMING OF ENLIGHTENMENT

————— ·•◆•· —————

John Henry

The seminal influence of the new philosophy, or (as we would say) the new science, of the seventeenth century upon the leading Enlightenment thinkers is so unanimously acknowledged in all the literature on the 'long eighteenth century' that it is in danger of being taken for granted. Because science is such a powerful cultural force in modern life, and since the Enlightenment has been be seen as the beginning of modernity, it is all too easy for us to leave unexamined the powerful influence of seventeenth-century natural philosophy on eighteenth-century thinkers. It is important to realize that it was only in the eighteenth century that scientific knowledge acquired the cultural kudos in the West which it has ever since enjoyed; and only then that science began to be recognized as the supreme cognitive authority, the intellectual system to which all others should defer.

This new recognition of the intellectual power of scientific knowledge was not merely a matter of eighteenth-century intellectuals waking up to an obvious, previously unrecognized, truth. There was nothing inevitable about the rise of science. On the contrary, it was the Enlightenment's *philosophes* who took up the science of the preceding age and helped to establish it as the dominant force in Western culture. They would not have done so had there not been something about the science of that preceding age which profoundly impressed them. It is the aim of this chapter, therefore, to look more closely at the science of the period before the Enlightenment, with a view to understanding what it was that so impressed the intellectuals of the late eighteenth century, and made them believe that, thanks in large measure to recent developments in science, they were living in an age of enlightenment.

We will be concerned with developments in the period known to historians as the Scientific Revolution, roughly from the middle of the sixteenth century to the early decades of the seventeenth. This was a period when the finite spherical and earth-centred universe of pre-modern times was replaced by the notion of a sun-centred solar system in an infinite expanse of space. What's more, these changes in cosmology were accompanied by numerous astronomical discoveries, including new stars, satellites and the magnetic nature of the earth. There were numerous advances in the knowledge not only of human anatomy, but also of the anatomy of insects and plants. Knowledge of physiology also improved with the discovery of the circulation of the blood in animals and sexual generation in plants, and life processes in general came to be seen not as the result of the special influence of souls or other vital principles but merely the result of physical and chemical processes. Ancient beliefs in inherent purposes and qualities in things gave way to ideas of cause and effect based merely on the physical interactions of bodies. The idea that bodies were made of four elements having their own characteristic qualities gave way to the belief that all bodies and their properties were simply the result of invisibly small particles of matter in characteristic arrangements. It was also a time when it was first accepted that knowledge of nature and its processes could best be understood by close observation and by mathematical analysis, and when it was first realized that the operations of nature followed precise law-like rules.

It might seem, even from a rapid survey like this, that these achievements speak for themselves; that we only have to go through each of them in more detail to understand why the leading *philosophes* were so impressed. There is no denying the cumulative impact of all these achievements, but the real legacy of the Scientific Revolution was not simply a bundle of newly established knowledge. Its importance was to show how yet more discoveries might be made, and how new truths about the world and everything in it could be established and understood. In short, the Scientific Revolution pointed the way to progress, and the new methodology of science became a major factor in the development of Enlightenment optimism.

In what follows, therefore, I do not attempt to consider the manifold achievements of the Scientific Revolution in any detail (there are, after all, many books on the period which are readily available). I simply focus on those aspects of the Scientific Revolution which caused Enlightenment thinkers to believe that knowledge of the natural world, what we would call 'scientific knowledge', should be seen as paradigmatic of all knowledge claims, and, if correctly pursued, would lead to the irresistible progress of mankind. My concern, therefore, is not so much with specific scientific achievements as with what is called 'scientific method'. It was what they perceived to be the new methodology of science which had the most profound influence upon Enlightenment thinkers. The specific achievements of the Scientific Revolution amply demonstrated the efficacy of the new scientific method. For the intellectuals of the succeeding age, therefore, it was simply a matter of bringing that method to bear on other aspects of life and thought.

THE NEW PHILOSOPHY, OR NEW PHILOSOPHIES?

Late seventeenth-century natural philosophers frequently referred to something called 'the new philosophy', which they contrasted to the old scholastic philosophy, traditionally taught in the universities. It is evident, however, that there was not just one new philosophy. As Voltaire (1694–1778) made plain in his *Philosophical Letters*, there was a vigorous rivalry, for example, between English and French new philosophies:

> A Frenchman arriving in London finds quite a change in philosophy as in all else. Behind him he left the world full; here he finds it empty. In Paris one sees

the universe composed of vortices of subtle matter; in London one sees nothing of the sort. With us it's the pressure of the moon that causes the rising of the tide; with the English it's the sea gravitating toward the moon; so that when you [French] think the moon ought to give us a high tide, these gentlemen think it ought to be low.

(Voltaire 1734: Letter Fourteen, 60)

Here, and in the rest of this letter, Voltaire is comparing the rival new philosophies of the great French thinker René Descartes (1596–1650), founder of the so-called 'mechanical philosophy', and the supreme English mathematician and experimental philosopher Isaac Newton (1642–1727). According to Descartes, the world was full, and according to Newton it must be empty. Voltaire writes in an entertaining way, straying even into facetiousness (he suggests that the only way we could decide who was right about the moon's effect on the tides would require seeing the state of affairs at 'the first moment of creation'), but he was fully aware of the far-reaching significance of these and the other 'tremendous contrarieties' that he mentioned.

Voltaire, true to his *anglomanie*, was one of the first Frenchmen to acknowledge the superiority of Newtonian science over Cartesian mechanical philosophy. His *Philosophical Letters* played a part not only in convincing other Frenchmen that Newtonianism should be taken more seriously, but also in raising the profile of natural philosophy in general as a prime means of discovering the truth about the way things are, and therefore as a major source of intellectual authority, capable even of supplanting ecclesiastical authority.

The astonishing wider impact of these philosophies of nature almost certainly stemmed from the fact that they seemed to offer so much promise in discovering the truth. To begin with, Cartesianism seemed so superior to scholastic natural philosophy that it became immensely influential in spite of numerous difficulties. Those difficulties, however, led other natural philosophers to develop refinements or alternatives to the Cartesian system which eventually culminated in the mathematical physics of Isaac Newton's *Principia Mathematica* (1687). Although quickly accepted in England by the majority of natural philosophers, on the Continent Newtonianism seemed to deviate too far from sound Cartesian principles to be acceptable. But it was gradually recognized that Newtonianism could be used to advance beyond Cartesianism, giving rise in the eighteenth century to a newer natural philosophy. Indeed, post-Cartesian and post-Newtonian science became a major factor in Enlightenment optimism.

To understand why these new philosophies inspired such optimism, one needs to know how they came to be amalgamated so successfully.

CARTESIANISM

Inspired partly by the Renaissance revival of knowledge about ancient atomism, the earlier work of Galileo Galilei (1564–1642), and the innovative work of his erstwhile friend and collaborator Isaac Beeckman (1588–1637), Descartes developed a natural philosophy in which all physical phenomena could be explained in terms of matter in motion. Descartes's great advance over his precursors was to develop a complete system of philosophy in which there were no unexplained, or inexplicable, phenomena. Assuming that all bodies were composed of invisibly small particles in various combinations and arrangements, Descartes explained all change in terms of the motion and therefore rearrangement of the constituent particles.

The crucial difference between Descartes's philosophy and ancient atomism, or even the contemporary 'physico-mathematics' of Beeckman, was the claim that all the required motions could be explained in terms of the working of specific laws of nature. Taking it as axiomatic that motion could never be lost from the world system, but must always remain at a constant level, these laws stipulated how motions were transferred in collisions from one particle to another. Where ancient atomists, or their Renaissance revivers, sometimes invoked unexplained principles of motion to account for the new motions of atoms, Descartes only allowed transfer of motion from one part of the system to another, in accordance with his rules of collision. At least, that's how it was in principle.

It followed from this that Descartes was committed to a universe in which nothing could be allowed to hinder the lawlike transfer of motion from one particle to another. There could thus be no empty spaces between particles (spaces which might absorb the vibratory motions of a particle, for example, without passing the motion on to adjacent particles). This is why a Frenchman, according to Voltaire, thinks the world is full. A full universe, however, as the ancient atomists pointed out long ago, was in danger of being a universe locked in stasis. How could anything move if every possible space to move into was already occupied? Descartes avoided this by insisting upon a kind of instantaneous fluidity in the universe, so that as soon as one particle moved, its place was immediately filled by another (to avoid formation of a vacuum), and its place in turn was filled by another, and so on. This process did not have to go on *ad infinitum*, however. According to Descartes, such movements were locally confined, so that there was a kind of circular displacement initiated by the movement of one particle but closed by completion of a circle of displacement. Such circular displacements could be large or small but they always acted instantaneously, in the sense that there could never be a moment when there was a vacuum left where a particle once had been. These circular displacements, required essentially as part of Descartes's metaphysics, came to play a role in his physics, being invoked to account for the circular motions of the planets and other cosmic phenomena. The name given to such a whirlpool of matter was 'vortex', and this is what Voltaire had in mind in his letter 'On Descartes and Newton', when he wrote that 'In Paris one sees the universe composed of vortices of subtile matter' (Voltaire 1734: Letter Fourteen, 60).

Descartes was sufficiently confident of the explanatory power of his new system of philosophy that he was able to claim, at the end of his *Principia philosophiae* (1644), the fullest account of his system, 'that no phenomena of nature have been omitted by me in this treatise', and that 'there is nothing visible or perceptible in this world that I have not explained' (Descartes 1644: Part IV, §199, 282–3). The claim was not meant to be taken literally, but as a statement of principle.

The advantages of this system over the traditional version of Aristotelian philosophy which had become enshrined in university curricula throughout Western

Europe were evidently sufficient to ensure its influence. New discoveries and new theories, such as the astronomical theory of Copernicus and the theory of motion of Galileo, not only seemed to undermine Aristotelianism but exposed the unsatisfactory way Aristotelian philosophers defended their traditional positions. Increasingly, Aristotelianism was seen to rely merely on its own definitions of how things are. Copernicus must be wrong, Aristotelians insisted, because the 'natural place' of the earth is at the centre of the world system. One of the most derided of such Aristotelian concepts was the notion of so-called 'substantial forms'. Growing out of Aristotle's original claim that bodies cannot consist simply of matter, since matter can only be understood if it is formed into a particular shape, substantial forms accounted for all of a body's qualities. A piece of matter in the shape of a cube might turn out, on inspection, to be a cube of wood or a cube of iron. Since Aristotle claimed all unformed matter was the same, what makes wood differ from iron? His answer: the (substantial) form. But what this meant was that any poorly understood, or downright inexplicable, phenomena could simply be 'explained' in terms of the substantial form of the body or bodies in question. This was becoming something of a philosophical scandal.

The mechanical philosophy did away with the concept of substantial forms at a stroke. Matter, still always the same, was held to exist in countless numbers of particles of different sizes and shapes, but always smaller than could be detected by human senses. It was the combination of these particles, in particular arrangements, or their movements in particular ways, which gave rise to the bodies (wood, iron, etc.) and other phenomena of everyday life. Explanations in these terms (essentially still current in modern science) were considered by converts to the mechanical philosophy to be more intelligible and more plausible than explanations in terms of Aristotelian substantial forms or other scholastic concepts.

Nevertheless, there were serious disadvantages to the Cartesian system. In spite of its author's boldly expressed confidence in the unassailable nature of its explanations, it was perfectly clear that the whole system was based entirely upon speculation; given that all explanations depended upon the behaviour of imperceptible movements and particles, there was no accessible evidence for any of the explanations, much less any certainty. Moreover, some well-known physical phenomena seemed very hard to reconcile with Cartesian principles. Many everyday phenomena could be understood in terms of the transfer of motions in collisions, although usually a willing suspension of disbelief was urgently called for, but there were others which seemed inexplicable in Cartesian terms. How can gunpowder send a heavy cannonball flying at high speed and over a great distance just because it is tickled by the gentle motion of a flame? Contrary to Cartesian principles, this looks like the generation of new motion, rather than the transfer of motion from one thing (the flame) to another (the cannonball). Efforts to suggest that the required kind of vigorous motion must somehow be trapped in the gunpowder during its manufacture did not seem convincing – nothing in the making of gunpowder required that the ingredients be implosively brought together in a way that mirrored its subsequent explosiveness. For many, therefore, the Cartesian system seemed merely fantastic – the result of an ingenious imagination, perhaps, but entirely lacking in support. For Voltaire, the problem was that Descartes 'gave himself up to the systematizing spirit. From then on his philosophy was no more than an ingenious romance, at best seeming probable to the ignorant' (Voltaire 1734: Letter Fourteen, 64).

Voltaire was condemning Descartes for the very thing that had made his philosophy seem so powerful to many seventeenth-century thinkers. By the early decades of the seventeenth century it was becoming increasingly obvious that Aristotelian philosophy was seriously flawed, maybe even untenable. In spite of the innovations of Copernicus, Galileo and others, however, it was all too clear that there was nothing capable of replacing the fully comprehensive system of Aristotle. Acceptance of Copernican astronomy, or the Galilean theory of motion, immediately raised innumerable questions about other aspects of physics which were simply never addressed by Copernicus or Galileo. What was required was a complete system of natural philosophy, able to offer an account of *all* phenomena – this was precisely what the Aristotelian system provided. Descartes was the first philosopher ever to provide a coherent, all-embracing system that could replace the Aristotelian system, lock, stock and barrel. For many, this had been the major strength of the Cartesian system. Voltaire, however, was an admirer of English philosophy, where the 'systematizing spirit' was treated with suspicion, if not outright disdain.

ENGLAND AND THE EXPERIMENTAL PHILOSOPHY

Nowhere, it seems, were philosophers more suspicious of the Cartesian romance than in seventeenth-century England. By mid-century there was already a strong tradition of empiricism in England; a belief that knowledge could be established only by an experience dependent ultimately on sense perceptions. Consequently, even those natural philosophers who immediately recognized the superiority of Cartesianism over scholastic Aristotelianism (and there were many) considered it only as a starting point for thinking about the natural world, not as the final word.

The suggested reform of natural philosophy put forward by Francis Bacon (1561–1626), statesman and man of letters, can be seen as both symptomatic of English attitudes and influential in reinforcing them. The emphasis on empiricism was at least partly the result of English experiences following the Henrician Reformation. Being the only Reformation initiated on non-doctrinal grounds, it gave rise to protracted religious disputes between those who wished to remain Anglo-Catholic and those who sought more radical reform. This in turn led to what came to be seen as characteristically English attempts to reach compromise positions to reconcile opposed factions. Since entrenched doctrinal positions were always defended on supposedly well-reasoned grounds, English intellectuals tended to distrust claims based on 'reason' and looked for compromise in more pragmatically based positions. Bacon grew to maturity as the famous 'Elizabethan compromise', based on the supposedly conciliatory Thirty-Nine Articles of the Anglican Church, was being promoted. Against this background, especially of the outdated Aristotelian natural philosophy of the scholastics, it is not surprising that Bacon's work, from the outset, was empiricist and hostile to premature system-building. (He lived too early

Figure 1.1 *Instauratio Magna*, Francis Bacon, frontispiece from his (1730) *Opera Omnia*, vol. 2, London: M. Gosling. By permission of the National Library of Australia.

to oppose the Cartesian system but dismissed earlier anti-Aristotelian systems developed by BernardinoTelesio (1509–88), Francesco Patrizi (1529–97) and others.)

Although Bacon was never able to reform natural philosophy in the way that he envisaged, he outlined his methodological prescriptions in a number of published works which proved immensely influential, especially in England. Although Bacon was an empiricist, and a champion of experiment as a way of reaching an understanding of natural processes, his method was uniquely different from other experimentalists. In particular, Bacon was opposed to what he saw as the common practice of performing experiments in order to confirm what one already believed. For Bacon, this was simply another example of what he called 'anticipations of nature', rather than an unbiased means of discovering the truth. It was all too easy, Bacon believed, to design an experiment to prove what you wanted it to prove. For Bacon, experiments should be designed merely to establish facts, to establish precisely what happens in a given set of circumstances. This approach went hand in hand with Bacon's generally natural historical approach; that is to say, his emphasis on gathering natural histories, or catalogues of natural data. Indeed, Bacon spoke often of the need to gather 'natural and experimental' histories. In his most famous book, the *Novum Organum* (*New Organon*, or *New Instrument*, 1620), Bacon described in detail how such empirical data should be set out in what he called 'Tables of Discovery'. The crucial point here was Bacon's belief that the search for explanatory causes, to account for the phenomena listed in the tables, should follow the gathering of data, not precede it. This was the right kind of disciplined approach, Bacon believed, to avoid jumping to unsubstantiated conclusions. 'The understanding', he wrote in the *New Organon*, 'must not therefore be supplied with wings, but rather hung with weights, to keep it from leaping and flying' from particulars to remote axioms, or principles (Bacon 1620: Book I, Aphorism 104).

Bacon's ambition to reform natural philosophy could hardly fail to attract international attention at a time when Aristotelianism was seen to be in terminal decline, but it was undoubtedly in England where he had the most influence. His ideas seemed especially congenial to leading natural philosophers after the Restoration of the monarchy in 1660. Seeing the Civil War and Interregnum periods as times of religious fanaticism (or enthusiasm, as it was usually called), many among the educated classes turned once again to religious compromise as a way of damping controversy. Latitudinarianism became a prominent movement within the newly restored Anglican Church. Taking inspiration from earlier efforts at compromise during the reign of Edward VI (1547–53), Latitudinarians insisted only upon a few fundamental doctrines, which would be acceptable (they hoped) to all Christians. Other points of religion were held to be indifferent to one's salvation, and therefore believers could hold their own view until the truth should be revealed on the Last Day. In this religious atmosphere Baconianism began to flourish even more.

The Baconian emphasis upon compiling natural histories and avoiding commitment to particular theoretical points of view until the time was ripe (when all the relevant data was deemed to have been made available) was seen as a way of avoiding controversy in natural philosophy, analogous to the method of Latitudinarian churchmen. This was important because Aristotelian natural philosophy, traditionally regarded as a 'handmaiden' to the 'Queen of the sciences' (theology), was now seen (particularly after the Galileo affair) as a bolster to Roman Catholicism. Similarly, other rival versions of new philosophies could be associated with sectarian enthusiasm, or with atheism (widely perceived in the seventeenth century to be a new and highly dangerous threat to stable societies). For a leading group of natural philosophers in Restoration England, the way to avoid such charges of ideological bias in natural philosophy was to claim to be dealing only with matters of fact. Bacon provided the philosophical justification for such an approach.

The leading scientist in late seventeenth-century England, certainly as far as European onlookers were concerned, was Robert Boyle (1627–91), and nobody exemplified the Baconian method better. The majority of Boyle's publications can be seen as 'natural and experimental histories' in the Baconian mould. Furthermore, Boyle's method was described and justified to natural philosophers all over Europe by his secretary, Henry Oldenburg (*c.* 1620–77). When Oldenburg became secretary of the Royal Society his correspondence expanded greatly, giving him greater opportunities to promote the new version of Baconianism throughout Europe. Indeed, the Royal Society itself came to be seen abroad as a Baconian institution.

Founded in the year of the Restoration, the Royal Society was a new kind of institution, explicitly devoted to the experimental and experiential investigation of nature. Its Baconian antecedents were proudly proclaimed and many of its fellows engaged in the kind of collaborative gathering of data for natural histories which Bacon had insisted was an essential prerequisite for his reform of natural philosophy. The Society was more than once likened to Salomon's House, an imagined research institute devoted to natural philosophy, which Bacon described in his posthumously published Utopian fable, the *New Atlantis* (1627). In case the significance of the Baconian antecedents of the Royal Society was missed, the leading fellows commissioned and supervised a kind of manifesto of the Society which insisted that the fellows were engaged not upon promoting a particular natural philosophy (which might be construed as a handmaiden to a particular religious faction), but merely upon the gathering of facts, based upon a theoretical (or doctrinal) minimalism. Under a suitably Baconian title, *The History of the Royal Society of London* (1667), Thomas Sprat (1635–1713), an up-and-coming man of letters, told his readers that the Society pursued the Baconian version of the experimental method, that it had 'wholly omitted doctrines', and was committed only to the gathering of 'matters of fact'. Their aim, therefore, was 'not to lay the Foundation of an English, Scottish, Irish, Popish, or Protestant Philosophy; but a Philosophy of Mankind' (Sprat 1667: Part II, Section VI, 63) Having said this, however, Sprat could not resist drawing the analogy between the method of the Royal Society and the irenic method of the Latitudinarian Church of England: 'Though I cannot carry the Institution of the Royal Society many years back, yet the seeds of it were sown in King Edward the Sixth's, and Queen Elizabeth's Reign . . . The Church of England therefore may justly be styl'd the Mother of this sort of Knowledge' (Sprat 1667: 372).

The importance of these English developments is that they contribute forcefully to what has been called the 'prehistory of objectivity' (Daston 1991; Henry 1992). Although the notion of 'objectivity' was yet to be coined, the idea that scientific knowledge is the supreme form of objective knowledge, free from prejudice and partiality, has its beginnings among the Baconian philosophers of Restoration

England. Due to their recent collective experience of the political and religious upheaval of the Interregnum, they were the only natural philosophers to whom it seemed important to claim ideological neutrality. The general significance of this was not lost on the intellectuals of the Enlightenment.

It is important to note, however, that the Baconianism professed by the leading fellows of the Royal Society was, to a large extent, rhetorical. As a means of persuading contemporaries that their natural philosophy was certain and reliable, being based only on matters of fact gathered by philosophers with no preoccupations about the way things should be, the rhetoric worked well. In practice, however, the natural philosophers of Restoration England often deviated from the methodological precepts of their mentor. This was most noticeable in their fairly unanimous commitment to one version or another of the mechanical philosophy. The philosophical advantages of Cartesianism were recognized even in a would-be Baconian England. The resulting tension between these two philosophical approaches gave rise to what was often called the 'experimental philosophy'.

In effect, this was a version of the mechanical philosophy, in which physical phenomena were assumed to be explicable in terms of the motions and interactions of invisible particles or corpuscles (as they were usually designated). What set it apart from Cartesianism, however, was the way in which its claims were justified. Where Descartes had based his claims on a long chain of reasoning starting from initial premises which he took to be indubitable, the English philosophers referred back as often as they could to supposedly empirical supports for their claims. More often than not, the so-called empirical or experiential evidence for English claims was nothing of the sort. Consider, for example, the standard claim that acids are composed of invisibly small particles shaped like needles. The empirical evidence for this is the sensation that acids seem to prick the tongue. Is this undeniably how we experience the taste of an acid? Or did Boyle and his contemporaries think this way because they already believed the action of an acid must be based on the shape of its constituent particles.

With hindsight it seems hard to believe that anyone could have accepted there were genuine empirical grounds for believing in the mechanical philosophy. Almost as hard as it is to believe anybody could have accepted Descartes's rational, but (to us) highly implausible, account of the workings of magnetism, gravity, human emotions and numerous other aspects of his philosophy. To understand the powerful influence of these philosophies, we need continually to remind ourselves of the perceived need to come up with something capable of replacing *in toto* the intellectually bankrupt Aristotelian system.

ISAAC NEWTON, BACONIAN

For a long time, the supreme exponent of the experimental philosophy was Robert Boyle. He, more than anyone else, pursued the Baconian ideal of gathering data. If he did not quite compile his findings in 'tables of discovery', he was able to show his contemporaries how his findings could be construed as empirical support for the 'corpuscular philosophy', as he called his version of the mechanical philosophy.

Teaching Baconian experimental philosophy by example, Boyle's writings played a valuable role in throwing doubt on Cartesian dogmas. A less acute thinker might have insisted that the experiments he performed with the newly invented air-pump, for example, proved the Cartesian plenum was false. Boyle knew that the various unusual phenomena he could bring about in the chamber of his air-pump were the result of the partial evacuation of the air, but he also knew there was still some air in there, to say nothing of light (which, unlike sound, was unaffected by the operation of the pump), or of other invisible effluvia or subtle spirits that might remain in the chamber. True to his Baconianism, therefore, Boyle did not claim to have refuted Cartesianism, nor even to have established the possibility of a vacuum. For the convenience of discussing his experimental results, he referred to the state of affairs within the air-pump as a *vacuum Boylianum*, but made no further claims as to the wider significance of this. Nevertheless, Boyle's intellectual modesty and cautious empiricism made their marks (Shapin and Schaffer 1985). Long before Voltaire, Cartesianism seemed increasingly to be revealed as an 'ingenious romance', while Boyle continued to base everything on experimentally verified matters of fact.

The intellectual development of Isaac Newton was profoundly shaped not just by Robert Boyle, but also by the entire background of English Baconianism (Dear 1985). One of the most significant outcomes of Newton's education was that he was able to exploit in his work the possibility that bodies could attract one another at a distance. Where a Cartesian would have to seek a mechanical explanation, based upon the assumption of direct contact, or a chain of such contacts, Newton could simply point to gravitational attraction as an undeniable 'matter of fact'. Gravity can easily be established experimentally (you could hold this book a few feet above the ground and then let go of it, for example). What's more, in the hands of a Newton it can be analysed mathematically. Newton was a supremely gifted mathematician and was able to compare the fall of a body on earth to the force of attraction required to keep the moon in its orbit. As he put it: 'I . . . compared the force requisite to keep the Moon in her Orb with the force of gravity at the surface of the earth, and found them answer pretty nearly' (Newton *c*. 1715, quoted in Westfall 1980: 143). This was sufficient for a Baconian like Newton to base his physics upon the assumption that attractive forces between bodies at a distance were undeniable matters of fact (Voltaire 1734: Letter Fifteen, 72–4; Gabbey, Garber, Henry and Joy 1998).

For a mechanical philosopher in the Cartesian mould, the notion of action at a distance was completely unacceptable. We can see this in the response of one of the leading Continental natural philosophers, G. W. Leibniz (1646–1716). According to Leibniz, Newton had failed to complete the account of planetary motions in his *Principia mathematica* (1687) because he had offered no physical explanation of how the attractive forces he had described mathematically were transmitted from one body to another. What Leibniz had in mind, of course, was a typically mechanistic account involving the movement of streams of particles between the 'attracting' bodies which then somehow caused the bodies to move towards one another. Newton was able to call upon the tradition of English Baconianism to give this objection short shrift. He made it clear that he was dealing in his *Principia mathematica* with matters of fact, and that, unlike Cartesian mechanical philosophers, he did not dabble in unsubstantiated hypotheses:

Figure 1.2 *Sir Isaac Newton*, Edward Hodges Bailly after Roubiliac. By courtesy of the National Portrait Gallery, London.

I have not as yet been able to deduce from phenomena the reason for these properties of gravity, and I do not feign hypotheses. For whatever is not deduced from the phenomena must be called a hypothesis; and hypotheses, whether metaphysical or physical, or based on occult qualities, or mechanical, have no place in experimental philosophy.

(Newton 1713: General Scholium, 943)

21

What we see in the work of Isaac Newton, then, is the triumphant culmination of English Baconianism. Newton was a mechanical philosopher, but one who tempered his mechanistic worldview with a Baconian concern for matters of fact and avoidance of hypothesis or unsubstantiated speculation. There could be no better vindication of the Royal Society's way of doing natural philosophy than Newton's *Principia mathematica*, still universally acknowledged as one of the greatest achievements of the human mind.

THE COMING OF ENLIGHTENMENT

In the *Preliminary Discourse to the Encyclopaedia* (1751), Jean D'Alembert (1717–83) admitted that, while Newton's genius had been quickly accepted in Britain, 'at that time it would have taken a good deal to make Europe likewise accept his works'. D'Alembert went on to portray a France still dominated by scholastic Aristotelianism when Newton 'had already overthrown Cartesian physics' (D'Alembert 1751: 88). Although this was generally true, D'Alembert plays down the extent to which the leading natural philosophers in late seventeenth-century France, no less than in Holland, were committed to Cartesianism. By the end of the seventeenth century those in the vanguard of natural philosophy on Continental Europe were for the most part Cartesian mechanists, and it was the prominent use by Newton of action-at-a-distance which led them to dismiss his new philosophy.

Indeed, Descartes's influence was so strong that a cultural commentator like Voltaire thought it necessary to teach eighteenth-century Continental philosophers about the philosophy of Francis Bacon before they could be expected to accept Newtonianism. It was no doubt for this reason that Voltaire preceded his discussion of Newton in *Philosophical Letters* with a letter 'On Chancellor Bacon' (Bacon had been Lord Chancellor of England, 1618–21). Voltaire began by describing Bacon as the 'father of the experimental philosophy' and the experimental method as 'a hidden treasure of which Bacon had some expectations and which all the philosophers, encouraged by his promise, laboured to unearth' (Voltaire 1734: 48, 49). But he also portrayed Bacon as pointing the way to the discovery of Newtonian gravitation. 'What has surprised me most', he wrote, 'has been to find in explicit terms in his book that novel theory of attraction which Mr Newton is credited with inventing' (Voltaire 1734: 49).

Bacon also figured prominently in the history of recent science recounted by D'Alembert in the *Preliminary Discourse*. Tempted to regard him as 'the greatest, the most universal, and the most eloquent of the philosophers', D'Alembert noted Bacon's hostility to philosophical systems and his ambition to catalogue 'what remained to be discovered' (D'Alembert 1751: 74, 75). The *Encyclopaedia* itself was in many ways a Baconian enterprise; a vast textual equivalent of the kind of collaborative knowledge-gathering advocated by Bacon and professed as part of their aim by the fellows of the Royal Society. In organizing the entries for their *Encyclopaedia* Diderot and D'Alembert developed an 'encyclopaedic tree' of knowledge closely modelled upon the division of the sciences drawn up by Bacon in his *De Dignitate et Augmentis Scientiarum* (*On the Proficiency and Advancement of the Sciences*, 1623) (D'Alembert 1751: 76–7, 159–64; Darnton 1984).

But if Bacon pointed the way forward, so did Descartes. In spite of their harsh criticism of the founder of the mechanical philosophy, both Voltaire and D'Alembert acknowledged his importance in the brief histories of science they presented in *Philosophical Letters* and the *Preliminary Discourse*. For Voltaire, Descartes 'gave sight to the blind' by teaching us how to reason. 'He who has set us on the road to truth', he wrote, 'is perhaps as worthy as he who since then has gone on to the end of it' (Voltaire 1734: 64). Similarly, for D'Alembert, Descartes pointed philosophers in the right direction: 'He can be thought of as a leader of conspirators who, before anyone else, had the courage to arise against a despotic and arbitrary power and who, in preparing a resounding revolution, laid the foundation of a more just and happier government, which he himself was not able to see established' (D'Alembert 1751: 80).

It was Newton, however, who succeeded in combining the rational, mathematical approach of Descartes with the experimental method of Bacon and, as D'Alembert said, 'gave philosophy a form which apparently it is to keep' (D'Alembert 1751: 81). Like British philosophers before them, Enlightenment *philosophes* saw Newtonianism as the new method of doing science. The achievement of the *Principia mathematica*, and of Newton's second great book, the *Opticks* (1704), seemed to stand out above all the other achievements of the Scientific Revolution. Clearly, Newton had success- fully combined the methods extolled by Bacon and Descartes, and demonstrated how natural philosophy should henceforward be pursued. There was a genuine optimism that it was now only matter of time before all truths would be discovered.

Newton's influence was dominant in both physics and chemistry, of course, and to a lesser extent in the biomedical sciences (Brown 1987; Guerlac 1981; Hankins 1985; Schofield 1970), but most remarkable was his influence in the new 'human sciences'. Newton himself, perhaps unwittingly, contributed to this general trend. In the closing paragraph of his book on the nature of light, *Opticks*, arguably more influential on eighteenth-century science than the *Principia* itself, Newton wrote: 'And if natural Philosophy in all its Parts, by pursuing this Method, shall at length be perfected, the Bounds of Moral Philosophy will be also enlarged' (Newton 1704: 405). Newton was a deeply religious thinker and went on to say that our duty towards God, 'as well as that towards one another, will appear to us by the Light of Nature'. For the faithful, Newton showed the importance of the study of nature for revealing the existence and attributes of God, for more secular thinkers it was an easy matter to dismiss the religious gloss and focus on the possibility of a naturalistic ethics.

John Locke (1632–1704) saw his *Essay Concerning Human Understanding* (1690) as a kind of tidying-up, clarifying the workings of the human mind in order better to understand the truths of nature uncovered by Newton and other natural philo- sophers (Locke 1690: Epistle to the Reader, xxxv). David Hartley (1705–57) paraphrased Newton's account of scientific method and insisted upon its use in morality and religion in his *Observations on Man* (1749: 6):

The proper method of philosophizing seems to be, to discover and establish the general laws of action, affecting the subject under consideration, from certain select, well defined and well attested phaenomena, and then to explain and predict the other phenomena by these laws. This is the method of analysis and synthesis recommended and followed by Sir Isaac Newton . . . It is of the utmost consequence to morality and religion that the Affections and Passions should be analysed into their simple compounding parts, by reversing the steps of the Associations which concur to form them.

The newly conceived psychological phenomenon, the association of ideas, was seen by David Hume (1711–76) as 'a kind of attraction, which in the mental world will be found to have as extraordinary effects as in the natural, and to show itself in as many and as various forms' (Hume 1739: Book I, Part I, Section IV). Hume, like many contemporary physicists and chemists, followed Newton's suggestion that all natural phenomena 'may depend on certain forces by which the particles of bodies, by causes not yet known, either are impelled toward one another . . . or are repelled from one another and recede' (Newton 1687: Preface, 382–3). The attempt to explain human behaviour in terms of two opposing principles, self-love (we would say selfishness) and reason (or common sense), was also largely Newtonian in inspiration. These were the moral equivalents of attraction and repulsion. Any excessive tendency to selfishness would be tempered by our 'rational' or 'experimental' discovery that we could optimize our chances of gaining pleasure and avoiding pain by co-operation with others. When Alexander Pope, in his *Essay on Man* (1733–4) asked, 'Could he [Newton], whose rules the rapid Comet bind,/Describe or fix one movement of his Mind?' He answered in the affirmative. Properly applied, the Newtonian method reveals that:

> Two Principles in human nature reign;
> Self-love to urge, and Reason to restrain . . .
> Self-love, the spring of motion, acts the soul;
> Reason's comparing balance rules the whole.
>
> The same Self-love, in all, becomes the cause
> Of what restrains him, Government and Laws . . .
> Self-love forsook the path it first pursu'd,
> And found the private in the public good . . .
> So two consistent motions act the Soul;
> And one regards itself, and one the Whole.
> Thus God and Nature link'd the gen'ral frame,
> And bade Self-love and Social be the same.
>
> (Pope 1733–4: Epistles II and III)

The same 'Newtonian' moral principles can be seen to have inspired Adam Smith's *Wealth of Nations* (1776), and a host of other contributions to the 'science of man'. After all, as Condorcet pointed out, at the beginning of his predictions for man's future progress in the 'Tenth Epoch':

> The sole foundation for the belief in the natural sciences is this idea, that the general laws directing the phenomena of the universe, known or unknown, are

necessary and constant. Why should this principle be any less true for the development of the intellectual and moral faculties of man than for the other operations of nature?

(Condorcet 1795)

There can be little doubt that Enlightenment thinkers were optimistic about the possibilities of establishing true and certain principles in the social and political sciences because they were inspired by the astonishing success of the new science. For many, that new science owed its success principally to the triumvirate of Bacon, Descartes and Newton. The inspiration was not so much the science itself as the new method, which seemed so potent and successful. Furthermore, that method might be variously interpreted by different thinkers. Some took a more professedly Baconian line than others, while some continued to praise reason and took a more Cartesian line. Some might be said to be genuinely Newtonian in their approach, while others might decry Newton while still employing some Newtonian precepts. It is clear, for example, that both Hume and Hartley were inspired by Newton, but Hume's Newtonianism was secular and lacked the theological dimensions of Hartley. Enlightenment thought was not straightforwardly Newtonian, but Newton, alongside Bacon and Descartes, embodied the scientific method which proved so influential.

However loosely conceived, the influence of Newtonianism beyond the physical sciences into what we now call the social sciences shows the crucial importance of scientific developments in the origins of Enlightenment thinking. It also tends to confirm the recent observation that Enlightenment *anglomanie* was not a precondition for the appreciation of English natural philosophy, but an outcome of it (Israel 2001: 518).

It is undeniable that Enlightenment thinkers were greatly inspired by the seventeenth-century Scientific Revolution. They saw it as the outcome of a scientific method, in which a supremely rational approach was checked and confirmed by experimental investigations, conducted in an entirely impartial and unprejudiced way. It is hardly surprising that they should regard this as the legacy principally of Bacon, Descartes and Newton, the three thinkers most responsible for forging the new scientific method.

REFERENCES

Bacon, Francis (1620) *New Organon* [*Novum Organum*], in *The Works*, 7 vols, J. Spedding, R. L. Ellis and D. D. Heath (eds) (1857–61) London, vol. IV.

Brown, Theodore M. (1987) 'Medicine and the Principia', *Journal of the History of Ideas*, 48: 629–48.

Condorcet, Marie Jean Antoine Nicolas Caritat, Marquis de (posth. 1795) *Esquisse d'un tableau historique des progrés de l'esprit humain*, trans. June Barraclough with intro. Stuart Hampshire (1955) *Sketch for a Historical Picture of the Progress of the Human Mind*, London: Weidenfeld & Nicolson.

D'Alembert, Jean Le Ronde (1751) *Preliminary Discourse to the Encyclopaedia of Diderot*, trans. Richard N. Schwab (1995) Chicago: University of Chicago Press.

Darnton, Robert (1984) 'Philosophers Trim the Tree of Knowledge: The Epistemological Strategy of the Encyclopédie', in *The Great Cat Massacre and Other Episodes in French Cultural History*, New York: Basic Books.

Daston, Lorraine (1991) 'Baconian Facts, Academic Civility, and the Prehistory of Objectivity', *Annals of Scholarship*, 8: 337–63.

Dear, Peter (1985) *'Totius in verba*: Rhetoric and Authority in the Early Royal Society', *Isis*, 76: 145–61.

Descartes, René (1644) *Principles of Philosophy* [*Principia philosophiae*], trans. Valentine Rodger Miller and Reese P. Miller (1983) Dordrecht: D. Reidel.

Gabbey, Alan, Garber, Daniel, Henry, John and Joy, Lynn (1998) 'New Doctrines of Body and Its Powers, Place and Space', in *The Cambridge History of Seventeenth-Century Philosophy*, D. Garber and M. Ayers (eds) Cambridge: Cambridge University Press.

Guerlac, Henry (1981) *Newton on the Continent*, Ithaca: Cornell University Press.

Hankins, Thomas L. (1985) *Science and the Enlightenment*, Cambridge: Cambridge University Press.

Hartley, David (1749) *Observations on Man, his Frame, his Duty, and his Expectations*, 5th edn (1810), London.

Henry, John (1992) 'England', in *The Scientific Revolution in National Context*, Roy Porter and Mikulas Teich (eds), Cambridge: Cambridge University Press.

Hume, David (1739) *A Treatise of Human Nature*, ed. P. H. Nidditch (1978) Oxford: Clarendon Press.

Israel, Jonathan I. (2001) *Radical Enlightenment: Philosophy and the Making of Modernity, 1650–1750*, Oxford: Oxford University Press.

Locke, John (1690) *An Essay Concerning Human Understanding*, ed. John W. Yolton (1961) London: J. M. Dent & Sons Ltd.

Newton, Isaac (1687/1713) *Mathematical Principles of Natural Philosophy*, trans. I. B. Cohen and Anne Whitman (1999) Berkeley: University of California Press.

—— (1704) *Opticks*, 2nd edn (1717) London.

Pope, Alexander (1733–4) *Essay on Man*, London.

Schofield, Robert E. (1970) *Mechanism and Materialism: British Natural Philosophy in an Age of Reason*, Princeton: Princeton University Press.

Shapin, Steven and Schaffer, Simon (1985) *Leviathan and the Air-Pump: Hobbes, Boyle and the Experimental Life*, Princeton: Princeton University Press.

Sprat, Thomas (1667) *History of the Royal Society of London*, ed. Jackson I. Cope and Harold W. Jones (1966) London: Routledge & Kegan Paul.

Voltaire (1734) *Philosophical Letters*, trans. Ernest Dilworth (1961) Indianapolis and New York: Bobbs-Merrill Company, Inc.

Westfall, R. S. (1980) *Never at Rest: A Biography of Isaac Newton*, Cambridge: Cambridge University Press.

CHAPTER TWO

THE QUEST FOR PHILOSOPHICAL CERTAINTY

Peter Schouls

CERTAINTY, TRADITION AND TRANSCENDENCE

Among the portraits on Jean D'Alembert's walls were those of Voltaire, Frederick II and Descartes. The first, the most erudite and satirical attacker of both secular and religious hierarchies, and the second, a royal patron of Enlightenment culture, form excellent company for this philosopher–mathematician and encyclopaedist. But why Descartes, who, in his *Meditations* (1641), deems it important to prove God's existence not once but twice, and whose correspondence with Princess Elizabeth of Bohemia as well as his final year of life at the court of Queen Christina of Sweden would seem to indicate an obsequious attitude to royalty and authority? Would not John Locke, champion of individual rights, have been a better choice? For Locke's likeness in a private dwelling we have to go to Ireland, to the home of William Molyneux. When Molyneux requested him to sit for this portrait, Locke displayed characteristic diffidence: 'Painting was designed to represent the gods, or the great men that stood next to them.' Molyneux agreed and presciently pointed Locke to the place which eighteenth-century Enlightenment thinkers were to assign him: '"Painting, it is true, was designed to represent the gods, and the great men that stand next them;" and therefore it was, that I desired your picture' (Locke 1823: vol. 9, 12 and 26 September 1696, 386, 391).

Those troubled by Descartes's inclusion in the Enlightenment's pantheon underestimate his formative influence on Enlightenment thinkers. In their quest for knowledge and certainty, neither Descartes nor Locke sought the relevant tools or criteria for this search in civil or ecclesiastical powers; neither of them looked for the objects of certainty to a Platonic Good or to an Augustinian God's revelation; both located criteria for and objects of certainty within individual searchers for truth. This departure from Greek and medieval dependence on what transcended the human situation was the radical move – in which Descartes was the leader and Locke a critical and innovative follower – which made possible the eighteenth century's revolutionary conception of the nature of human beings and of their relationships, especially in the realm of politics. In the Cartesian project the prominence of God is chiefly a device to reveal the absolute trustworthiness of human reason as the tool to achieve certainty in knowledge and, through its application in

Figure 2.1 *René Descartes*, Lucien Butavard after Frans Hals. By courtesy of the National Portrait Gallery, London.

the affairs of human life, amelioration of humanity's lot. For Europe's great medieval universities, the founding vision was that truth and certainty derive from God in whose light only can we see light – as intimated through Oxford's motto *Deus illuminatio mea*. For founders of the intellectual origins of the Enlightenment, truth, wisdom and certainty are to be found, created and established by a humanity whose autonomy requires rejection of tradition. True, Descartes argues that an atheist cannot develop systematic knowledge that may be legitimately stamped as 'immutable and certain' unless he recants his atheistic stance and 'recognizes that he has been created by a true God who cannot be a deceiver' (1985: vol. 2, 289). But, unlike eighteenth-century thinkers, Descartes does not recognize that atheists can consistently be Cartesians, that in some way they can be better Cartesians than Descartes himself. Consider the argument through which Descartes believes he establishes the absolute certainty of human knowledge, an argument best known from its formulation in the first three of his *Meditations*.

Human knowledge, Descartes there argues, has three possible sources: sensation, sensation combined with reason, and reason working alone. If we want to establish absolute certainty, then any item that is a candidate for knowledge will have to prove itself impervious to all possible doubt, no matter how slight or far-fetched such doubt may appear to be. Because of the possibility of sensory illusion or delusion, no sense-based knowledge can withstand this test. Even the most trusted set of sensations, the set that we believe gives us our knowledge of our current position and activity, is not absolutely certain; for there is the possibility, slight though it may be, that we are dreaming. Hence sense-based knowledge fails the test, as does knowledge derived from sensation and reason combined – as in the applied sciences – because it involves the senses. So there remains reason working on its own. Can its pronouncements be deemed absolutely certain? The test which sensation could not pass does not invalidate reason, for whether I am awake or asleep two plus three equals five. But suppose there exists an omnipotent god who, rather than being good, is thoroughly evil and consistently tricks me with respect to what I have always taken to be absolutely certain, such as the judgements I make in arithmetic. On the slight chance that this hypothesis of a deceiving god turns out to be true, I can no longer take the judgements of reason as absolutely certain. There is one exception: no matter how hard he tries, this god cannot make it uncertain or false that I exist when I think I exist – for if I think, then I exist: *cogito ergo sum*. And there is no doubt about the fact that I now think, for else I could not even entertain the hypothesis; hence there is no doubt that I now exist. From this absolute certainty of the *cogito* Descartes proceeds to demonstrate that the hypothesis is invalid because self-contradictory, that a good god exists, that reason is absolutely trustworthy and its edicts therefore certain, and that reason can demonstrate to what extent the senses can be trusted.

Atheists can be better Cartesians than Descartes because they can entertain the hypothesis that an omnipotent *deceiving* god exists and show that, on Descartes's grounds, this hypothesis is self-contradictory. They share Descartes's conclusion that his argument refutes the possibility which the hypothesis of the deceiving god advances – including the crucial role of the individual's consciousness as expressed in the *cogito* – but only the atheist recognizes that Descartes's position on certainty does not depend on proof of the existence of a *veracious* god. Mere faith or hope in the trustworthiness of reason's edicts and their efficacy to ameliorate humanity's condition once enacted becomes a certainty through the absolute trustworthiness of human reason demonstrated in the *cogito*'s limitation of the omnipotent deceiver's power: even if God exists and is against rather than for me, reason remains trustworthy and its edicts absolutely certain. In effect, Descartes's argument entails the non-existence of a deceiving god (because 'divinity' and 'deception' cannot co-exist in the same being) as well as the irrelevance of a veracious god (both because the limitation of omnipotence is a contradiction in terms and because reason can now establish its own trustworthiness and that of the senses). So Pascal's complaint was to the point: 'I cannot forgive Descartes. In all of his philosophy he would have been quite willing to dispense with God' (1670: 26). And Turgot may have been right as well when he surmised that Descartes dared not admit the irrelevance of God even to himself because 'he was frightened by the solitude in which he had put himself' (1753: 94).

UNWARRANTED AND WARRANTED CERTAINTY

The seventeenth century's quest for philosophical certainty provided important contents and contours for Enlightenment thought and action. Because they were convinced that the certainties of the past were unwarranted and enslaving, those engaged upon it experienced the quest for certainty as a matter of urgency. Commitment to unwarranted certainty and conformity to it in the affairs of daily life were deemed irrational, hence subhuman action, the kind of action which could never improve the human condition but would always tend to physical and intellectual bondage. Although many seventeenth-century thinkers decried such action, Descartes and Locke stand out among them because they were the most radical in their opposition to it and because their articulation of the new principles proposed for thought and action were widely accepted in the eighteenth century as liberating humanity from its yoke and placing it firmly on the path of indefinite progress. So, when eighteenth-century thinkers looked to the past, Descartes and Locke loomed large. About Descartes, Condorcet wrote that he 'gave men's minds that general impetus which is the first principle of a revolution in the destinies of the human race' for, because of Descartes, 'man could proclaim aloud his right, which for so long had been ignored, to submit all opinions to his own reason'; while Locke, he said, 'grasped the thread by which philosophy should be guided; he showed that an exact and precise analysis of ideas, which reduces them step by step to other ideas of more immediate origin or of simpler composition, is the only way to avoid being lost in that chaos of incomplete, incoherent and indeterminate notions which chance presents to us at hazard and we unthinkingly accept' (Condorcet 1795: 147–8, 136, 132–3). Because of their radically novel stance and the eighteenth century's widespread celebration of this novelty, I limit myself to Descartes and Locke in my discussion of the quest for philosophical certainty as one important origin of Enlightenment thinking.

Achievement of certainty requires suitable preparation. It demands ability to discern unwarranted certainty for what it is, understanding the process by means of which unwarranted certainty is obtained, and power to erase acquired unwarranted certainty and to forestall subsequent infestation with it. For these preparatory activities, Descartes and Locke took human reason and freedom, working in tandem, as the necessary and sufficient tools. Unwarranted is anything accepted as certain without reason's authorization; only reason's authorization warrants acceptance. Since, as we shall see, the reason in question must be that of each individual, achievement of certainty becomes entirely dependent on individual action, so that reason's opposing prejudice is the individual's opposing external authority. By educating the individual to avoid reliance on unwarranted certainty and to rely only on warranted certainty, Descartes and Locke prepare the ground for Condorcet's utopian vision: 'The time will therefore come when the sun will shine only on free men who know no other master but their reason' because they have learned 'how to recognize and so to destroy, by force of reason, the first seeds of tyranny and superstition' (Condorcet 1795: 179). In Descartes and Locke we begin to discern Kant's formulation of the Enlightenment's challenge as well as of its central aim. Although 'rules and formulas . . . are the shackles of a permanent immaturity' making it 'difficult for any individual man to work himself out of the immaturity that has all but become his nature', it is nevertheless 'each person's calling to think for himself'. Hence Kant's 'motto of enlightenment': 'Have courage to use your own understanding!' Reject 'guidance from another' and so 'emerge' from what is after all 'self-imposed immaturity' (Kant 1784: 41–2).

PREJUDICE AND UNWARRANTED CERTAINTY

Descartes and Locke used various terms and phrases to label beliefs people hold without reason's authorization. Chief among these, for Descartes, is what we tend to translate as 'bias', 'prejudgement' or 'prejudice', words which render Descartes's *prévention*, *préjugement* or *praejudicium*. Their use indicates the doctrine that, as rational beings, we ought not to take any judgement as certain before reason has authorized it as such, that if we neglect such authorization, we act prematurely in prejudgement of what we have no right to judge at that time. Locke uses 'prejudice' in exactly this way but adds phrases pointing to an explanation of our tendency to prejudge matters and attach certainty to such prejudgements, phrases like 'common opinions', 'received hypotheses', 'well-endowed opinions in fashion', 'ill habits'. For both, prejudice arises from uncritically absorbed experience and, given the nature of human beings – 'we were all children before being men and had to be governed for some time by our appetites and our teachers' (Descartes 1985: 117) – experience in general and education in particular have riveted prejudices to the mind so securely that the will to examine is often hard to come by. As Descartes's *First Meditation* states, even when we 'sincerely and freely' examine them, 'ancient and commonly held opinions still revert frequently to my mind, long and familiar custom having given them the right to occupy my mind against my inclination and rendered them almost masters of my belief'.

Locke is equally insistent on the power of prejudice. 'Habits have powerful charms . . . Fashion and the common Opinion having settled wrong Notions, and education and custom ill habits, the just values of things are misplaced' (1690: 2.21.69); thus, many if not most, people 'firmly embrace falsehood for truth . . . because . . . blinded as they have been from the beginning' by their upbringing, they do not have the freedom or 'vigour of mind able to contest the empire of habit' (1706: para. 41). And, although 'natural reason' is the 'touchstone', 'every man carries about him . . . to distinguish truth from appearances', its 'use and benefit . . . is spoiled and lost . . . by assumed prejudices, overweening presumption, and narrowing our minds' (1706: para. 3).

Later, Enlightenment thinkers echo these statements. There is Condorcet, who, like Descartes and Locke, is keenly aware of the vulnerability of youth. These years he characterizes as a time when 'the flexible intelligence and uncertain, pliant soul can be shaped at will', with 'teaching . . . everywhere in a state of bondage and everywhere exercising a corrupting influence, crippling the minds of children with the weight of religious prejudices and stifling the spirit of liberty in older students with political prejudices'. Like Descartes and Locke, he holds that crippled minds and stifled spirits are not easily liberated or rehabilitated 'because men retain the prejudices of their childhood, their country and their age, long after they have discovered all the truths necessary to destroy them' (Condorcet 1795: 118–19, 163, 11). There is Condillac: 'While we are yet in the state of childhood . . . we fill our heads with such ideas and maxims as chance and education offer. When we come to an age in which the mind begins to arrange its thoughts, we continue to see only those things with which we have been long acquainted' (Condillac 1754: 301). And there are Rousseau's inimitable words painting a broader picture: 'Our wisdom is slavish prejudice, our customs consist in control, constraint, compulsion. Civilised man is born and dies a slave. The infant is bound up in swaddling clothes, the corpse is nailed down in his coffin. All his life long, man is imprisoned by our own institutions' (Rousseau 1762: 10). Rational people fear prejudice because it curtails reason's efficacy. But because – as Descartes's *Meditations* demonstrate – reason can destroy prejudice's unwarranted certainty and shake the comfort of the uncritical life to its very foundations, the person prejudiced from childhood on is loath to relinquish its certainty and takes flight in ceaseless invention of ruses to prevent the confrontation of prejudice and reason. Locke's vignette of the 'learned Professor' comes to mind:

> And who ever by the most cogent arguments will be prevailed with, to disrobe himself at once of all his old Opinions, and Pretences to Knowledge and Learning, which with hard study, he hath all this Time been labouring for; and turn himself out stark naked, in quest a-fresh of new Notions? All the arguments that can be used will be as little able to prevail, as the wind did with the traveller to part with his cloak, which he held only the faster.
>
> (Locke 1690: 4.20.11)

Was not enlightened Thomas Paine saying just that of conservative Edmund Burke? 'Under how many subtleties, or absurdities, has the divine right to govern been imposed on the credulity of mankind! Mr Burke has discovered a new one' (Paine 1791: 43).

METHOD AND WARRANTED CERTAINTY

Descartes (with respect to all knowledge) and Locke (with respect to general knowledge) share a single method coupled with a single set of criteria which serve both to overcome prejudice and to attain and develop the knowledge to which they attached warranted certainty. Since I have presented them elsewhere (Schouls 1992: ch. 1.4), it is not necessary to rehearse the grounds for holding that as far as it concerns *general knowledge* – which is knowledge founded on universal concepts which the mind creates through abstraction from everyday experience, as in the mathematical and moral sciences – Locke's method is Cartesian. But two things are necessary: first, a brief sketch of this common method; and, second, an indication of the grounds Descartes and Locke share for holding this method to be absolutely trustworthy. For it is this method and the grounds for its trustworthiness which lead them – as well as many later Enlightenment thinkers – to their conviction that warranted certainty is within human grasp, that it can be recognized as such when attained, that it can be developed systematically, and that action on the resulting systematic knowledge will ameliorate humanity's condition.

My sketch of the method I interweave with the role of *clarity and distinctness*, the criteria Descartes articulates for all knowledge and Locke adopts for general knowledge. Their most explicit statement is in Principle 45 of Descartes's *Principles of Philosophy*, which stipulates that anything is clear only when *all* of what pertains to the item in question is before the mind, and distinct when we are aware of *nothing but* what pertains to that item. The connection between clarity and distinctness, on the one hand, and warranted certainty, on the other, is strongest at the foundation of a science where we deal with the simplest of concepts, those irreducible concepts out of which a science is generated. Since such irreducible concepts are a science's simplest parts, no mistakes are possible in our comprehending any one of them: for, if it is before the mind at all, all of it is before the mind and then it cannot but be understood, and is known with certainty.

When, in the second part of the *Discourse on the Method*, Descartes articulates the four rules required to reach and develop certainty, he places them in the context of everyday experience. Since whatever we initially experience is interrelated with other experiences, hence characterized by complexity rather than simplicity, such items cannot be clear and distinct to us. Thus our experience initially always presents us with problems, with situations in which we must doubt the certainty of whatever presents itself. The first rule therefore instructs us not to judge precipitously, to avoid prejudice through always letting our reason be the final judge on any issue that confronts us. The second rule states that, with respect to any matter or question we seek to understand, allowing reason to judge demands that we divide the problem into as many parts as possible. Through a question such as 'Is that which I now experience clear and distinct to me?' it is doubt that propels division of the problem until we reach its clear and distinct parts (if it has any such clear and distinct parts). Then, third, beginning with our knowledge of these clear and distinct simplest parts, we relate them to form more complex knowledge, always taking care that each step in this (re)construction is clear and distinct. Fourth, when we believe that this (re)construction is complete, we review all the steps taken to make certain that nothing relevant was omitted (here we again meet the criterion of clarity) and (dictated by the criterion of distinctness) that nothing irrelevant was included.

Condorcet sometimes ascribes this method's origin to Descartes, sometimes to Locke. Whoever he may have believed to have been its source, of its effect he had no doubt: it 'for ever imposed a barrier between mankind and the errors of its infancy, a barrier that should save it from relapsing into its former errors under the influence of new prejudices, just as it should assure the eventual eradication of those that still survive unrecognized' (Condorcet 1795: 134). Turgot waxes eloquent on the method's effects: 'What mortal dared to reject the insights of all past ages, and even the ideas he believed most certain? . . . Great Descartes, if it was not always given to you to find the truth, you did at least destroy tyranny and error' (Turgot 1808–11: 89).

Second, what, according to Descartes and Locke, are the grounds which warrant the trust we place in this method's efficacy for leading us to knowledge and certainty? There are two main grounds, one concerning the relation of this method to human reason, the other pertaining to the nature of humankind and of the world. Both grounds were widely accepted by eighteenth-century thinkers. I shall deal with them in turn.

CERTAINTY, LOGIC AND REASON

The method is to be adopted with absolute confidence in its efficacy because it is the articulation of the way reason goes about its business in its pursuit of knowledge and certainty. Thus a statement of proper procedure is in effect a definition of the function of reason, and since it is reason that presents the definition, this statement of method is reason's self-portrait. Descartes emphasizes that without method we cannot obtain certainty about anything (as in the *Principles* 1: 13, 42 and 43); for general knowledge, Locke echoes this doctrine (as in 1690: 4.12.7; 4.17.2, 3, 4 and 17). Traditionally, it was 'logic' which indicated the workings of reason. It is then no wonder that in the seventeenth century we meet a juxtaposition of new and old logics, new and old definitions of reasoning. Those who objected to Descartes's mode of procedure and its results are mistaken, says Descartes, because they remain enmeshed in an old form of thinking which is 'of no use whatever to those who wish to investigate the truth of things' (as *Regulae* 10). So when Gassendi accuses Descartes of prejudice in the way he used the *cogito* as his Archimedean point, Descartes replies that 'the most important mistake our critic makes here is the supposition that knowledge of particular propositions must always be deduced from universal ones, following the same order as that of a syllogism' (as in scholastic logic), and he dismisses Gassendi's criticism as that of a person who has succeeded only in displaying 'how little he knows of the way in which we should search for the truth', being ignorant of the fact that 'it is certain that if we are to discover the truth, we must always begin with particular notions in order to arrive at general ones later' (Descartes 1985: vol. 2, 271). Descartes's work was widely accepted as a new logic or a new way of thinking. When, in 1662, Antoine Arnauld published *La Logique, ou l'art de penser*, he acknowledged that parts of it were copied from the manuscript of Descartes's *Rules for the Direction of the Mind*.

Locke's *Essay Concerning Human Understanding*, from the beginning, was also recognized as presenting a new mode of reasoning or a new logic. In terms evoking Descartes's titles, Molyneux spoke of Locke as one who 'delivered more profound Truths . . . for the Direction of Man's mind in the Prosecution of knowledge, (which I think may be properly term'd *Logick*) than are to be met with in all the Volumes of the Antients' (Locke 1976–88: vol. 4, 479). Locke agrees with Molyneux's characterization of his work (Locke 1976–88: vol. 5, 351). This identification of 'method' and 'logic' became commonplace in the eighteenth century, and the logic in question was expected to have its use across a wide spectrum of human endeavour and experience. The full title of a work Isaac Watts published in 1726 illustrates this well: *Logick: or, The Right Use of Reason in the Enquiry after Truth, with a Variety of Rules to Guard against Error, in the Affairs of Religion and Human Life, as well as in the Sciences*. In language evoking doctrines of both Descartes and Locke, Condillac insists that 'Our first aim, which we ought never to lose sight of, is the study of the human understanding; not to discover its nature, but to know its operations; to observe . . . how we ought to conduct them, in order to acquire all the knowledge of which we are capable' (1754: 5–6). Throughout this work, Condillac reiterates that method is nothing but a functional definition of reason. And, in Condorcet's words, Descartes's 'method for finding and recognizing truth' was not limited 'to the mathematical and physical sciences'; he gave 'mankind that general guidance of which it seemed to stand in need' as he extended 'his method to all the subjects of human thought; God, man and the universe'; and so 'he commanded men to shake off the yoke of authority, to recognize none save that which was avowed by reason' (1795: 122).

Both Descartes and Locke understood that to advocate a new logic is one thing, to have it recognized and adopted as authoritative quite another. They used identical tactics to make this logic recognized and accepted as the one and only way to certainty. Their shared tactics amounted to shared fundamental principles about education or re-education of children and adults. This tactic involved no abstract set of rules that might be taught, memorized and mechanically applied. Instead, both insisted that only practice in arguments themselves constructed through the use of the new logic would make it familiar and established, for in this exercise reason would come to recognize itself as authoritatively at work. Both believed that everyone must think for her- or himself, that none can think for others or have others think for them. For both, therefore, education – in getting to know the method as well as in its subsequent application – amounts in the end not to being taught by others, but to being placed in positions that allow each person to become self-taught. So Descartes insists: 'I never wanted to force anyone to follow my authority. On the contrary, I pointed out in several places that one should allow oneself to be convinced only by quite evident reasonings' (1985: vol. 2, 272). Locke is no less emphatic: 'we may as well rationally hope to see with other Mens Eyes, as to know by other Mens Understandings' for 'the floating of others Mens Opinions in our brains makes us not one jot the more knowing, though they happen to be true' (1690: 1.4.23). This 'thinking for oneself' concerns all possible areas of human experience, including that of faith, where, for Descartes, Locke and later Enlightenment thinkers, imposition of others' thought and hence the rule of prejudice traditionally weighed heaviest on humanity. 'Even with respect to the truths of faith', says Descartes, 'we should perceive some reason which convinces us that they have been revealed by God, before deciding to believe them' (1985: vol. 2, 272–3). And Locke, more pointedly, writes: 'In all things . . . reason is the proper judge; and revelation . . . cannot . . . invalidate its decrees. Faith . . . can have no authority against the plain and clear dictates of reason' (1690: 4.18.6).

The ground for the authoritative nature of reason or the trustworthiness of the method therefore needs to be authenticated by each person individually. To that end, Descartes attaches to the *Discourse* treatises on geometry, optics and meteorology, which, he holds, could not have been developed without the method and whose certainty depends on the method, for it is 'method which gives certainty to mathematics' and to all disciplines which the human mind is capable of developing (as he writes in the paragraph following that which articulates the four rules of the method). The *Meditations'* exposition is quite deliberately in first-person-singular language to bring home the point that all will have to make this journey for and by themselves because each can know only for her- or himself. And study of the *Principles* 'will accustom people little by little to form better judgements about all the things they come across, and hence will make them wiser' (1985: vol. 7, 188). Reflection on their reason's progress through these writings will make each reader conscious of the procedures of reason. And whereas the usefulness of the method is established through the results achieved in these treatises, its absolute trustworthiness is established in the *Meditations*: application of the most excessive doubt imaginable through the hypothesis that God exists and does all he can to deceive me in my reasoning establishes the full trustworthiness of method as the process of reasoning and of the certainty of its conclusions.

With reason located in each individual, Descartes ascribes the search for knowledge to each individual. Such autonomy precludes the possibility of others thinking for me, because it places me under the compulsion to think for myself if I want to be human at all; it is an autonomy that makes tradition, culture or community irrelevant for warranted certainty. We now reach certainty through individually exercised freedom to pursue the proper method. No matter how wise or certain some beliefs may be proclaimed to be, all attempts to impose them violate the individual. Wisdom and certainty now have their roots in egocentricity. Since neither wisdom nor certainty comes about except through each individual's uprooting all acquired prejudice and submitting only to the newly acquired dictates of one's own reason, they in effect depend on newly established selves of which each individual is her or his own creator. As Locke puts this in the *Conduct of the Understanding*, 'The result of our own judgment upon . . . Examination is what ultimately determines the Man, who could not be free if his will were determin'd by any thing, but his own desire guided by his own Judgment' (1706: para. 71). In Condorcet's pithy statement, everyone must 'refashion his own intelligence' (1795: 119). Thus warranted certainty grows in the soil of individual enquiry. Knowledge and certainty are no longer imparted or received, but made; and for all human beings it now holds that each is the maker of her or his own knowledge and certainty.

CERTAINTY, AUTONOMY AND NON-RELATIVISM

Relativism is not entailed by this position because of two of its underlying assumptions. The first of these concerns the nature of human beings, the second the nature of the world in which humanity finds itself.

Descartes believes that wherever the faculty of reason is found, it works in the same way and that reason 'is naturally equal in all men' (1985, vol. 1, 111). Locke shares these assumptions about uniformity and egalitarianism: 'I think the intellectual faculties are made, and operate alike in most men', he writes to Stillingfleet (Locke 1823: 4, 139; 1690: 1.1.5 and 6, and 2.11.16). He also agrees with Descartes about the necessity of the individual search for knowledge, on the uselessness of rules (as is clear from the *Education* para. 66, as well as from the *Conduct* paras 2 and 4), and on the importance of disciplines following the correct method. Two passages from the *Conduct*, the first from its sixth paragraph and the next from its seventh, are among the clearest statements of these points:

> Would you have a man reason well, you must use him to it betimes, exercise his mind in observing the connexion of ideas, and following them in train. Nothing does this better than mathematics, which, therefore, I think should be taught all those who have the time and opportunity; not so much to make them mathematicians, as to make them reasonable creatures . . .

And:

> having got the way of reasoning, which that study necessarily brings the mind to, they might be able to transfer it to other parts of knowledge, as they shall have occasion. For, in all sorts of reasoning, every single argument should be managed as a mathematical demonstration.

Through 'reflection' or introspection that makes a person's reason 'its own Object' as it proceeds in a science like mathematics, one reaches legitimate conclusions about 'the Original, Certainty, and Extent of humane Knowledge' (Locke 1690: 1.1.1 and 2). Locke is more explicit and critical at this point than is Descartes. Introspection allows infallible knowledge of the workings of one's own mind, but such certainty does not extend to one's knowledge of the workings of other minds, for 'I can but speak of what I find in my self'. There is, however, a 'nevertheless': 'if we will examine the whole course of Men in their several Ages, Countries, and Educations', they 'seem to depend on those foundations which I have laid, and to correspond with this Method, in all the parts and degrees thereof' (1690: 2.11.1).

Those whom Locke influenced in the eighteenth century tended to replace his tentativeness with certainty on a ground we find in Descartes, Locke and many others both before and after them. That ground is the belief that each person's acts of reasoning, including that of turning one's reason upon itself in introspection, is activity carried out by universal (or, if they retained theological commitments, divine) reason which is present in each individual. 'Turn on it self thy Godlike Reason's Ray/Thy Mind contemplate, and its Power survey', writes Sir Richard Blackmore (1712: 202–3). Introspection is taken to provide knowledge of the universal sameness of reason's mode of operation. And so D'Alembert (1751) writes that Locke, having reflected on the procedures of his own mind, was able to hold up to humankind the mirror in which all can see the operations of their own minds reflected.

The second ground for confidence in the trustworthiness of reason and in the certainty of the results that its operations engender is a doctrine about the nature of the world or of the universe as the context of humankind. This doctrine permeates the history of Western philosophy. We meet it in Augustine, in Aquinas, and in seventeenth-century Cambridge Platonists like Ralph Cudworth. It is the definitive presence of rationality in each person as well as in humanity's divinely created context. For Descartes, on the premise that a rational god created a rational universe with rational beings in it, his argument takes the following form: if human beings use their reason to understand whatever they experience of the world, the knowledge they have thereby acquired is certain. That is why Descartes can say that 'I showed what the laws of nature were, and . . . that they are such that, even if God created many worlds, there could not be any in which they failed to be observed' (1985: vol. 1, 132). Locke employs it in the area of general knowledge, as when, in the *Second Treatise*, he writes about the 'State of Nature' that 'has a Law of Nature to govern it', and since it is 'Reason, which is that law' therefore the 'Law of Nature' is 'plain and intelligible to all Rational Creatures' (1823: paras 6 and 124). In the form of the possibility of knowledge of 'the constancy of the laws of nature' it is part of the ground on which the Enlightenment thinkers based their hopes for 'the progress reserved for future generations' (e.g. Condorcet 1795: 9).

CERTAINTY AND ITS LIMITS

Since I have focused on origins of Enlightenment quests for certainty, I stressed affinities instead of differences between various thinkers I take to belong to the Enlightenment movement in the broad sense, stretching from Descartes and Locke to Kant and Condorcet. It remains to indicate some differences concerning the nature and extent of certainty. Enlightenment thinkers often praise Locke for recognizing the limitations of human understanding and castigate Descartes for having been uncritical about the extent of reason's province and as a consequence having fallen into dogmatism. Two examples will suffice.

First, Locke's commendation derives from his insistence on two kinds of certainty: the absolute certainty achievable in mathematics and morals, that is, in areas of general knowledge; and the probable certainty of the physical sciences, which is the area of knowledge of particular things. It derives, as well, from his modesty in metaphysics – a realm in which he is satisfied that little if anything is known with certainty. His minimalist commitments in metaphysics make Locke adamant about our ignorance concerning the true nature or essences of physical objects, with a result that knowledge about them depends on inductive generalizations whose results are characterized by probability rather than absolute certainty. Descartes is reprimanded because he posits absolute certainty in both mathematics and metaphysics, and the latter therefore allows no Lockean limits to reason which would entail a distinction between general knowledge and knowledge of the particulars of nature, between the absolute certainty of mathematics and the probability of physics.

Second, for Descartes, the metaphysical doctrine of mind–body dualism is so fundamental and certain that without it there cannot be human freedom as distinct from natural causality, a distinction he deems necessary for the possibility of science, of progress, and of the amelioration of humanity's condition. Locke, more modest, remained agnostic about dualism and points out that it is as difficult to comprehend that there is spatially extended substance that thinks as it is that there is thinking substance which is spatially non-extended. Because we have no certain knowledge about the truth of either of these possibilities, either one of them may be false – or true. But he believes it to be of no great consequence that 'our Faculties cannot arrive at demonstrative Certainty . . . about the immateriality of the Soul', for 'All the great Ends of Morality and Religion, are well enough secured, without philosophical Proofs of the Soul's Immateriality' (Locke 1690: 2.23.23 and 4.3.6). Enlightenment thinkers approved of Locke's metaphysical modesty, in this second case not the least because it allowed them grounds for deism or atheism. For if it were to be true that extended matter thinks, then God and the universe could be one and the same thing; and that position, even as a mere possibility, indicates that the certainty claimed for religious dogma is unwarranted.

So how do Enlightenment thinkers relate to Descartes when, in the name of reason, he asserts so much more as certain than does Locke? Rather than wholesale rejection, they reprimand Descartes for having overstepped the bounds of reason by conflating reason and imagination while assigning to the latter the certainty that properly attaches only to the former. Such conflation, for D'Alembert, is 'bad taste'. For Condorcet it constitutes the main difference between Descartes and Locke: 'Descartes had brought philosophy back to reason; . . . however, his impatient imagination snatched it from the path he had traced for it . . . Locke, finally, was the first man who dared set a limit to the human understanding, or rather to determine the nature of the truths that it can come to know' (Condorcet 1795: 132–3; see also 122).

Descartes, nevertheless, remained one of the Enlightenment's great progenitors. Most members of the Enlightenment did not claim that reason would reveal everything, but they all claimed that reason has the right to question everything. When Descartes intrinsically connected rational analysis with the doubt of questioning or criticism, so opposing reason to prejudice and credulity, and made this new form of reasoning definitive of each individual's human nature, he taught the Enlightenment that questioning is not just a right but a duty of each individual: to be human is to be a critic. Whether directly or by way of Locke, Descartes's questioning stance helped to shape the Enlightenment's contours to the extent that it strove for independence from tradition through rejection of unwarranted certainty, and for founding warranted certainty on personal autonomy.

REFERENCES

Blackmore, Sir Richard (1712) *The Creation*, London.

Condillac, Etienne Bonnot de (1754) *Essai sur l'origine des connaissances humaines*; trans. and ed. Thomas Nugent (1756) *An Essay on the Origin of Human Knowledge*, repr. with intro. by James H. Stam (1974) New York: AMS Press.

Condorcet, Marie Jean Antoine Nicolas Caritat, Marquis de (posth. 1795) *Esquisse d'un tableau historique des progress de l'esprit humain*; trans. June Barraclough (1955) as *Sketch for a Historical Picture of the Progress of the Human Mind*, Westport: Hyperion Press.

D'Alembert, Jean Le Rond (1751) *The Encyclopédie: Discours Preliminaire*, trans. and ed. John Lough (1971) London: Longman.

Descartes, René (1985) *The Philosophical Writings of Descartes*, vols 1 and 2, trans. and ed. John Cottingham, Robert Stoothoff and Dugald Murdoch, Cambridge: Cambridge University Press.

Kant, Immanuel (1784) *An Answer to the Question: What is Enlightenment?* in Ted Humphrey (trans. and ed.) (1983) *Immanuel Kant, Perpetual Peace and Other Essays*, Indianapolis: Hackett.

Locke, John (1690) *An Essay Concerning Human Understanding*, ed. Peter H. Nidditch (1975) Oxford: Clarendon Press.

—— (1706) *Of the Conduct of the Understanding*, in *Works of John Locke* (1823) *op. cit.*

—— (1823) *Works of John Locke*, 10 vols, London; repr. (1963) Aalen.

—— *The Correspondence of John Locke*, 8 vols, ed. E. S. de Beer (1976–88) Oxford: Clarendon Press.

Paine, Thomas (1791) *Rights of Man*, notes Henry Collins (1969), intro. Eric Foner (1984) Harmondsworth: Penguin.

Pascal, Blaise (posth. 1670) *Pensées*, trans. and ed. H. S. Thayer (1965) New York.

Rousseau, Jean Jacques (1762) *Emile*, trans. and ed. Barbara Foxley (1976) London and New York: Everyman.

Schouls, Peter (1992) *Reasoned Freedom: John Locke and Enlightenment*, Ithaca and London: Cornell University Press.

Turgot, Anne Robert Jacques (1753) in Ronald L. Meek (1973) *Turgot on Progress, Sociology and Economics*, Cambridge: Cambridge University Press.

—— (1808–11) *Oeuvres*, vol. 2, Paris.

CHAPTER THREE

THE CRITIQUE OF CHRISTIANITY

———•—•———

James Dybikowski

EXTERNAL AND INTERNAL CRITIQUES OF CHRISTIANITY

It is useful to distinguish between external and internal critiques of Christianity's claims to truth and certainty as founded on a special and unique revelation from God. Good examples of external critiques are Spinoza's *Tractatus Theologico-Politicus* and the clandestine manuscripts that circulated under such titles as *L'Esprit de Spinosa* or *Traité des trois imposteurs* (Charles-Daubert 1999). These last were collages drawn from many sources, including Spinoza (1632–77) and Hobbes (1588–1679). The depth of their hostility not only to Christianity but to religion generally was shocking. For them, Jesus was an impostor whose religion made its way in the world by deceit, and whose moral ideas had nothing to recommend them not already present in the writings of other ancient authors. External critics evaluate Christianity from a perspective outside it. For Spinoza, that perspective was his metaphysical system.

Internal critics divide into two kinds. The first consists of Christian apologists who acknowledged Christianity's vulnerabilities, but believed that exposing and answering them would secure its foundations. Examples include the Catholic biblical critic and historian Richard Simon (1638–1712); the Remonstrant theologian Jean Le Clerc (1657–1736); and the English latitudinarians, who included Samuel Clarke (1675–1729) and John Locke (1632–1704). The second and for present purposes more significant class of internal critics consists of those who largely adopted their premises from Christian writers, but, variously, laid the foundations for, hinted at, suggested or drew conclusions that weakened or undermined Christianity. For prudential reasons, they did not always make their intentions clear. Like classical sceptics, they often drew premises from one sect to expose the weakness of its rival, while using the strength of the rival to expose the weakness of its opposition. They weakened and undermined Christianity from within rather than from without and included freethinkers such as Anthony Collins (1676–1729), John Toland (1670–1722), Matthew Tindal (1657–1733) and the 3rd Earl of Shaftesbury (1671–1713). While they differed from one another in the style and depth of their critiques of Christianity and in their philosophical views, they were bound together by a common commitment to freedom of thought. In drawing on Christian writers, they frequently lavished praise on them and expressed agreement with certain Christian teachings, although they agreed with qualifications, and their critics regularly classed them with Spinoza and Hobbes, on the basis of their supposed intentions rather than their methodology. For that matter, even the boundary between the two sorts of internal critics is not sharp. Simon was seen as a threat to Catholics and Protestants alike; Le Clerc and Clarke were accused of preparing the way for deism; while Locke was at times classed with the freethinkers and at others sharply distinguished from them.

Shaftesbury brilliantly illustrated the method of argument to which freethinkers were partial (Shaftesbury 1711: vol. 2, 352–60). An assembled company, cornering a sceptical freethinker, try to force him to concede that Holy Scripture is a sufficient rule to achieve unity of thought, an objective he claims to be neither possible nor desirable. The freethinker responds to the pressure with a question: what does 'Scripture' mean? He cites variant readings, apocryphal and lost books, uncertainties in textual transmission and opportunities for tampering with the text's integrity. He catalogues the difficulties in interpreting the text, whether literally or figuratively, the innumerable commentaries on it as different from one another as the commentators themselves and similarly for the translations. The company is incensed with him as 'a preacher of pernicious doctrines' who is armed with an anti-religious agenda that might seduce the ignorant and the vulgar. What shock they experience when the freethinker reveals he has only been quoting from a great Protestant bishop Jeremy Taylor (1613–67). Remarks scarcely noticed when they emerged from the bishop's pen are perceived as dangerous and subversive when they come from the freethinker's mouth. Taylor only intended his catalogue of difficulties to justify liberty of judgement and a reluctance to allow others to prescribe one's religious opinions. As the company observes, however, when his message is delivered without the reassurance of a bishop's mitre, it does this by raising serious doubt whether Holy Scripture really can provide a clear and secure rule of faith.

My focus is largely directed to these freethinkers, whose method of argument made them effective critics. They were familiar with and influenced by the work of Pierre Bayle (1647–1706), Le Clerc, Simon and Spinoza, as well as many other Continental European writers. They also had greater influence in Continental Europe than in Britain, where their ideas were made known initially through Huguenot journalists, such as Pierre Des Maizeaux (*c.* 1672–1745), who has been seen as a predecessor of Voltaire in making English thought available to the French literary public, and journals. It is necessary to consider them, however, in the light of the apologetic exercises off which they fed, as well as the external critiques that helped provoke the apologetic efforts. While the freethinkers knew these last well, they generally refrained from citing them, even when their arguments followed similar paths.

SAMUEL CLARKE AND THE LATITUDINARIANS

I begin in Protestant England in January 1704, when Samuel Clarke delivered the first of sixteen Boyle lectures at St Paul's Cathedral (Clarke 1738: vol. 2, 513–758). Then only twenty-eight and a rising star, Clarke was Cambridge educated and an ordained minister in the Church of England identifying with the latitudinarians (Rivers 2000: vol. 2, 15). Intellectually precocious and versatile, he was well versed in and deeply influenced by natural philosophy, Newtonianism in particular. He argued that Newton's system, far from threatening Christianity, powerfully supported it. Clarke would have agreed with the declarations of an earlier latitudinarian, Simon Patrick (1626–1707), that 'True *Philosophy* can never hurt sound *Divinity*' and that 'nothing is true in Divinity, which is false in Philosophy, or, on the contrary' (Patrick 1662: 24, 11). One and the same faculty, reason, judges everything, whether nature, divine revelation or historical fact.

Locke expressed much the same point when he characterized reason as natural revelation, and revelation as natural reason enlarged by God's communication (Locke 1700: IV.19.§4). Spinoza claimed much the same, but with a different intention, when he remarked that all natural knowledge is God's revelation, differing from what ordinarily goes by the name in being commonly accessible to all men and, consequently, less highly valued (Spinoza 1670: ch. 1). Latitudinarianism rejected all traditional authority that set itself beyond the scope of criticism, whether Aristotle's, Rome's or a bishop's, in favour of a new and free philosophy (Patrick 1662: 14, 19ff.). It advocated a wider liberty of conscience and rational enquiry. Far from endangering religion, this was the way to free it from the 'scorn and contempt' to which it was otherwise liable (Patrick 1662: 24).

It was clear to Clarke that Christianity had as much to fear from its internal quarrels and divisions as from external enemies, but his focus, by the terms of Boyle's bequest, was on infidelity, whether open or disguised. His lectures were intended to defend Christianity on a rock-solid foundation of natural religion against atheists and deists. The power of his position turned on his claim that even they must grant his premises. When he considered atheists, he named names: Hobbes, Spinoza and their contemporary followers, including the intellectual maverick and freethinker John Toland, whose scepticism about the New Testament canon occasioned one of his earliest publications, *Some Reflections on a Book Called Amyntor* (Clarke 1738: vol. 3, 917–26). For Clarke, since God's existence and attributes can be established with demonstrative certainty, atheism is impossible. Its attraction is attributable to stupidity and libertinism.

When he turned to the deists, Clarke was less forthcoming, identifying them doctrinally, not by name. He lavished special attention on those who, while they seemingly conceded God's existence, the objectivity of morals and a future state of rewards and punishments, baulked at accepting the Christian revelation. For Clarke, the evidence for revelation, while not demonstrative, shows it to be so morally certain that only a hardened sceptic would reject it. Like William Chillingworth (1602–44), one of latitudinarianism's progenitors, Clarke neither claimed nor demanded assent stronger than the evidence warranted (Chillingworth 1638: II.154). That said, to persist in rejecting it, in view of the combined evidence of miracles, prophecy, history and reason, was to be an atheist in disguise. Unaided reason is not only consistent with scripture and scriptural morality, but can even prove as morally certain that there would be a divine revelation to human beings in their weak and fallen state. It also can show that there will be a future state of rewards and punishments to compensate for the ill usage of the virtuous in this life. For Clarke, Christianity's external enemies reduce to one: atheists. Since reason and natural philosophy show that atheism is untenable, the more serious threats arise from its internal divisions and a reluctance to embrace reason as an ally or return to Christianity's uncorrupted primitive beginnings.

For Clarke, scripture alone – not the oral traditions to which Catholics and High Church Anglicans appealed or the Pope's infallibility – is the rule of Christian doctrine, although, like other latitudinarians, he respected the Church Fathers for the light they could shed on the canon. Some revealed truths are not discoverable by human reason, although consistent with and supported by it, while the intellectual perspectives opened by revelation cause the discovery of truths that themselves require no other foundation than human reason. How else is the advance of scientific knowledge, natural religion and systematic morality over anything in the ancient and non-Christian world explainable? On this point Clarke's position is similar to that of Locke, who claimed that before Christ's revelation there was no 'full and sufficient Rule for our direction' (Locke 1695: 153). Revelation was necessary not only to discover what unaided reason had not discovered and still could not establish on proper foundations, but also to strengthen human will against the passions.

Christian faith, for Clarke, makes few and readily accessible doctrinal demands; Christianity is largely about moral virtue whose foundations are independent of and binding on God's will and to which positive religious duties are subordinate. He was well disposed to a wide-ranging Christian toleration and liberty of examination. He opposed setting limits on what counted as Christianity so narrowly that they could only be satisfied by a particular sect.

Still there were certain metaphysical doctrines that Clarke argued are incompatible with Christianity because they are inconsistent with God's existence and attributes as established by natural religion. The doctrine on which he placed most weight is the freedom of the will. For him, if the supreme cause of the universe is necessitated to act as it does, it cannot be identified as God and, a fortiori, as the Christian God, since it can be neither intelligent nor moral. It follows, on his view of matter's essential passivity, that Christianity and materialism are incompatible. Few eighteenth-century Christians challenged this claim, Joseph Priestley (1733–1804) being one of the few who did. Clarke was also confident he could prove the soul's immortality by demonstrating its immateriality. Anthony Collins would challenge these arguments, taking pleasure in showing that Clarke's metaphysics excluded many devout Christians, such as Jansenists and Calvinists, from the Christian fellowship (Clarke 1738: vol. 3, 873). He followed Locke in arguing that it is beyond the power of natural reason to demonstrate the soul's immateriality, but, contrary to Locke, he claimed that available evidence generally supports its materiality. Nevertheless, Clarke articulated a comprehensive Christian metaphysical system exuding self-confidence. It was an intellectual high-water mark in Protestant Christian apologetics.

COLLINS, LOCKE AND FREETHINKING

Over Christmas of 1703 and through the early days of the New Year, as Clarke turned his mind to his inaugural Boyle lecture, Collins, also Cambridge educated and a year his junior, was visiting Locke, whom he had befriended the year before. Locke, impressed by Collins's intellectual promise, took him into his confidence and treated him as a son. Their intimacy was seminal to Collins's philosophical coming of age. At the time Collins also counted among his friends the notorious freethinkers John Toland and Matthew Tindal, but he was still finding his philosophical identity, while Clarke already possessed settled opinions on the leading questions of philosophy and religion. The dominant theme of Collins's friendship with Locke is the love of truth pursued along tracks not beaten down by others and with indifference about whom it pleases. Locke claimed that the best test of its presence is the refusal to entertain propositions with greater assurance than their proofs warrant (Locke 1700: IV.19.§1). This was a basic premise of freethinking, the idea that pervades Collins's thought: for critics like Clarke, however, freethinking was in reality a pretext for being anti-Christian, a deist or, at its logical conclusion, an atheist.

Collins defined freethinking as the impartial use of the understanding to:

(a) determine the meaning of propositions;
(b) assess the evidence for and against them; and
(c) judge their truth or falsity, their probability or improbability on the apparent strength or weakness of that evidence (Collins 1713: 5).

Each element in this account is anchored in Locke's *Essay*, especially its seminal discussion of faith and reason. Collins defended freethinking so defined as not only a universal human right, but also, in religion, a duty. For him, freethinking is a condition of knowledge and demands a healthy scepticism, particularly in the examination of received ideas. Such a sceptical disposition he was proud to claim in the assessment of historical as well as philosophical claims, but, in religion, he found the clergy had far too little of it. He confided to a correspondent that clerics were oblivious how weak the foundations were for doctrines of the utmost consequence for them.

Locke defined faith, as against knowledge, as the mind's assent to a proposition based on its probability (Locke 1700: IV.15.§§2–3). For this reason, Hume later described him as 'the first Christian who ventured openly that faith was nothing but a species of reason' (Hume 1779: Part I), although Locke could easily trace his view to, among others, Chillingworth, who characterizes faith as the understanding's assent proportional to the evidence (Chillingworth 1638: Preface, §2; II.§48). For traditional revelation, Locke added that faith was the assent conferred 'upon the Credit of the Proposer, as coming from God'. Few could legitimately claim to be recipients of an immediate revelation and those who did solely on the basis of an inner light were dismissed by him as enthusiasts who divorced faith from reason to the cost of both (Locke 1700: IV.19). Any proposition clearly attributable to God possesses the highest certainty, since God is no deceiver (Locke 1700: IV.16.§14). Its meaning as well as its attribution to God, however, must be judged by reason on principles applicable to the assessment of any testimony.

Locke argued that when a revealed truth is also discoverable by natural reason and thereby constitutes *clear* knowledge, there is no need for revelation (Locke 1700: IV.17.§4). Natural reason should be our guide, with knowledge trumping faith. When there is *clear* revelation and natural reason yields only probable conjectures, however, revelation properly carries the day (Locke 1700: IV.18.§8). Since the greater evidence outweighs the lesser, this condition obtains only if the evidence for revelation is more compelling than natural reason on its own, as Locke claimed it was for Christianity (Locke 1695: 145). For him, Christ's mission was plainly established by his miracles, while the truth of his teaching was conformable to reason (Locke 1695:153). Locke's principles, accordingly, specify when claims of revelation should, but, more importantly, when they should not determine judgement, even if evidence that supports revelation is available. Although it was not his intention, he effectively identified conditions that could be used to sideline revelation without openly denying its truth. The freethinkers took advantage of this opening.

Viewed either as a right or a duty, freethinking opposed restraints on reason, particularly when imposed by 'priestcraft', that is, by the clergy. Among these restraints was the encouragement of fearfulness about the exercise of individual reason because one might embrace views that would result in damnation. Freethinkers and latitudinarians alike defended the innocence of error attributable to an honest effort to use God-given reason. It is morally inconceivable, they argued, that God would punish those who err in this way. This, freethinkers alone emphasized, no matter how far the inquirer falls short of the truth: 'God is not like an Egyptian task-master. He does not require brick, where he gives no straw, and expects not equal knowledge and belief from men of unequal abilities' (Collins 1726b: 426).

A further restraint freethinkers identified arose from the notion that Christianity demands the understanding's submission to propositions it cannot grasp. Mysteries, such as the Trinity or Transubstantiation, were said to be 'above reason' to comprehend. For the freethinkers, however, if a claim is incomprehensible, whatever the text or tradition on which it is founded, it has no claim to assent. The proper course is to suspend judgement. There is much one does not understand, they agreed, but to agree with this is not to assent to an idea one does not understand. For them, such doctrines serve only the interest of priests. This attack on the mysteries lies within a Lockean framework, although he sounds a different note. Locke accepted that there are truths 'above reason', but he defined them as truths not *discovered* by natural reason alone. His standard illustration is not the Trinity, but the Resurrection: an occurrence for which he believed reason could form an idea, but not prove (Locke 1700: IV.17.§23; Collins 1707: 24). For Christian critics, however, the freethinkers' rejection of the mysteries was a clear sign that they opposed the attitude of submission to an all-powerful creator necessary for the acceptance of religion.

By the same token, freethinkers rejected Bayle's fideist claim that when reason is baffled by difficulties apparently insuperable to it, such as the problem of evil, it should keep close to scripture and allow itself to be captivated by the obedience of faith. Collins applauded Bayle's acumen in his relentless exposure of the difficulties barring a solution to the problem of evil within a Christian framework, but not the moral he appeared to draw from it (Collins 1710: 7–10).

Freethinkers likewise opposed the institutional claims of Churches and their clergy to authority. They rejected their claims to an independent authority held by divine right. Freethinking was Erastian through and through. They showed a tendency, moreover, to go farther. Collins denied that an established religion is necessary to maintain the public peace (Collins 1713: 111–15). Religion, he argued, is 'a matter purely personal', a thesis pointing in the direction of secularism (Collins 1726b: 435). He also denied that priests rightly commanded deference to their expert authority (Collins 1713:107–11). For not only did their differences on nearly every issue undermine such a claim, so did the doctrinal undertakings they gave as a condition of holding office. As the Huguenot editor, translator and natural law theorist Jean Barbeyrac remarked, the history of the science of morals owed scarcely any of its progress to ministers of religion, and nearly everything to the laity (Barbeyrac 1712: esp. i–xii). Anticlericalism is not anti-Christianity, but the notion of 'priestcraft' offered freethinkers a story of how Christianity sustained itself when its rational credentials were as weak as they claimed. In their view, Christianity had too often used its institutional power to limit and discourage the exercise of reason in order to block exposure of weaknesses that would threaten its position.

COLLINS AND CLARKE

Why start with Collins and Clarke? The short answer is that while freethinkers such as Collins were seen as dangerous critics of Christianity, many charged Clarke and the latitudinarian tradition with preparing the way for them (Berkeley 1732: 34). Freethinkers were partial to quoting latitudinarians and their predecessors, Chillingworth and John Hales (1584–1656), in particular. Collins listed Archbishop John Tillotson (1630–94), one of Locke's closest friends, as 'Head' of the English freethinkers, provocatively placing him in his chronological catalogue of freethinkers directly after Hobbes (Collins 1713: 171). Collins admired the latitudinarians' commitment to reason and the right to think for oneself. He applauded their acceptance of the innocence of error and their subordination of the positive duties of revealed religion to moral virtue, their theological minimalism and their defence of natural religion as an indispensable foundation to revealed religion (Collins 1713: 34, 75–6 and 171–6; Hill 2001).

Where Clarke's strategy was to argue from principles acceptable to atheists, Collins argued from principles accepted by clerics. He and his fellow freethinkers claimed that Christianity's resources – its texts, and traditions, their meanings and its proofs from miracles and prophecies – fell short of the moral certainty Clarke and Locke claimed for them. At the same time, the freethinkers argued that criticism of Christianity entailed neither atheism nor moral libertinism and scepticism, as Clarke had insisted. Any true principles espoused by Christianity were available with greater clarity, comprehensiveness and certainty to natural reason. If so, the greater evidence ought to be preferred to the lesser.

THE BIBLE

Some incautious remarks from Chillingworth set the stage. His bedrock principle is: 'God hath said so, therefore it is true.' The freethinkers did not quarrel with the inference, only with the antecedent. For Chillingworth, God's Word is in a Bible that constitutes a self-sufficient and perfect rule of faith: 'Propose me any thing out of this Book, and require whether I believe or no, and seem it never so incomprehensible to human reason, I will subscribe it with hand and heart, as knowing no Demonstration can be stronger than this, God hath said so, therefore it is true.' (Chillingworth 1638: VI.§56) While parts of the Bible are open to interpretation and debate, much needs neither interpretation nor interpreters. A judge is needed to remedy defects of law with principles of reason. The Bible, however, 'is a perfect Rule of Faith, and therefore needs no supply of the defects of it . . . all necessary points of Religion are plain and easie, and consequently every man in this cause [is] a competent Judg [sic] for himself' (Chillingworth 1638: II.§§14 and 16). The point about incomprehensibility to human reason has already been dealt with, but the Bible as God's Word and as a perfect rule of faith has not.

Spinoza was not as charitably disposed towards the Bible as was Chillingworth. He argued that much of it cannot plausibly be regarded as revelation, since it conveys no sure knowledge God might have revealed to human beings. Its interpretation, which he set out to examine as methodically as the interpretation of nature, demonstrates the necessity of separating religion from philosophy. Philosophy aims at truth; religion, by contrast, at obedience and just so much doctrine – that is to say, very little – as is absolutely necessary to support this objective. The test of religion is not truth, of which it contains little, but effectiveness in moving human beings to devotion by engaging their imaginations. Scriptural prophecies are adapted to their audiences, but, as importantly, they also reflect the limitations of prophets, who are distinguished not by any knowledge they possess; only by their piety. Many of their claims are neither divinely inspired nor true, and it is a mistake to make them so by ingenious metaphorical interpretation. To unite the God of scripture with the God of philosophy is a misguided project to convert scripture into philosophy. In what sense, then, can God be claimed as the Bible's author? Spinoza's answer is that it is 'not because God willed to confer on men a set number of books, but because of the true religion that is taught therein' (Spinoza 1670: 153). True religion consists in the teaching of true moral doctrine and this alone establishes the work's divinity (Spinoza 1670: 90). That the moral doctrine is true, however, is known by natural investigation (Spinoza 1670: 158).

Richard Simon agreed that scripture can be properly understood only by an historical analysis of the language and meaning of texts and a grasp of their historical development. He openly acknowledged there had been 'great alterations' in the original texts of the Old Testament, as Spinoza argued in his analysis of the Pentateuch (Spinoza 1670: ch. 8). Simon also argued that the Gospel was established in Churches well before any written text existed, but he denied that such a history undermined the Bible's claim to being inspired. While he opposed some of Spinoza's claims, he vigorously argued that the history of the texts thoroughly undermined the Protestant claim that they are plain and reliable as expressions of God's Word without reference to any further principle. In particular, their claim to divine inspiration depends on the authority of tradition: 'if we join not Tradition with the Scripture, we can hardly affirm any thing for certain in Religion. We cannot be said to quit the word of God by joining therewith the Tradition of the Church, since he who refers us to the Holy Scriptures has also refer'd us to the Church whom he has trusted with his holy pledge' (Simon 1680: author's preface). The freethinkers admired Simon's scholarship. There are dozens of references to him and his works in Collins's works, for example. The freethinkers agreed that if oral tradition carries no authority, there would be no religious certainty. Unlike Simon, however, they affirmed the antecedent. The critical examination of the history of the New Testament canon casts doubt over its claim to divine authority. It was established centuries after the events it relates 'by weak, fallible, factious, and interested men' (Collins 1724: 17).

The rejection of oral tradition as a reliable foundation for religious truth pervades freethinking writings. Not only did they argue for the uncertainty of tradition and the existence of false traditions, but they claimed that tradition is characteristically projected backwards from the present. A notable example was the projection of the Christian conception of the Messiah back on to the Old Testament, 'thereby explaining former passages by modern faith and notions' (Collins 1726b: 68). The Old Testament's Messiah was a victorious, temporal figure, not the spiritual Messiah of Christianity (Collins 1726b: 83). Such arguments, Collins noted, had been used to justify the doctrine of transubstantiation, since no other explanation, it was claimed by its supporters, could satisfactorily explain the depth and pervasiveness of the belief in it. Such arguments, however, prove too much by relying on the obviously false historical thesis 'that no error can be generally introduced' (Collins 1726b: 70). Far from infallibly transmitting truths across time, tradition does not even continue the same. Even a single individual can not preserve the same notions and practices over a lifetime, let alone a people from one generation to the next (Collins 1726b: 67–91). Tradition, accordingly, cannot bear the weight Simon expected it to carry.

Jean Le Clerc, another of Locke's close friends, defended the Protestant cause against Simon, but he did so only after conceding that much of the Bible was neither inspired nor pretended to be. Christianity ought not to saddle itself with indefensible positions. The internal contradictions in the Bible show this, and much of it is and can claim to be no more than historical or eyewitness narrative, although no less morally certain for all that. Even where it is inspired, however, its authors should not be regarded as 'Secretaries of [the] Spirit' (Le Clerc 1690: 30). What matters is the substance of their teaching, not the language in which that teaching is conveyed. Only what is directly attributable to Christ can be claimed as infallible; not even the Apostles when they receive the spirit of miracles and tongues (Le Clerc 1690: 64–5, 71). It is a concession that weakens the inferences that can be legitimately drawn from miracles. Even the Old Testament's claim to being inspired depends on Christ's general approval and authorization of it (Le Clerc 1690: 104, 114). Collins would reply that since Jesus' claim to be the Messiah depends on the Old Testament being inspired, Christianity is saddled with circularity. The New Testament being inspired depends on the Old, but *its* being inspired depends on the New. We are a long way from the proposition that since the Bible is God's Word, it must be true. On the contrary, the way is open to doubt whether God's Word, strictly speaking, is to be found in it at all. Doubts about the text, its history and interpretation, helped to reinforce scepticism about traditional arguments for the truth of Christianity, those from miracles and fulfilled prophecies, in particular.

MIRACLES

This is obviously true for Spinoza, whose exposure of the weakness of traditional claims made on behalf of the biblical text surrounds his notorious analysis of miracles. He argues that if miracles are identified as events that contravene nature's order – that is to say, God's order – then, far from supporting God's existence, they cast doubt on it. If, on the other hand, they are merely unusual works beyond the known powers of human agents, they reflect rather on human ignorance. From their occurrence, there is no warranted inference to God's nature or even His existence. In short they cannot show what only philosophy, which has no dependence on revelation, can. They offer no independent support of the truth of revealed religion, serving only as testimonials to the preconceived beliefs of those who rely on them.

Although he did as much to distance himself from Spinoza's philosophy as he possibly could, Clarke agreed that God's works as revealed through an investigation of nature were reasons as compelling of God's existence and nature as miracles. He viewed it as careless thinking not to acknowledge as much. Such arguments, however, belong to natural religion and provide no evidence for Christianity as such. Accordingly, he continued to defend the value of miracles as evidence, while he conceded that their attribution to God depends on the goodness of the doctrine to which they testify. Collins would have none of this. As extraordinary works, he argued in keeping with Spinoza, miracles may attest to a being's power, not to its veracity, infallibility or identity. This would be so even if they were performed by Jesus, as long as his claim to be the Messiah is not independently established (Collins 1724: 32). But even if miracles are attributable to God due to the content of the doctrine to which they attest, the doctrine serves to prove the miracle, not the miracle the doctrine (Collins 1726a: 26; 1727: 92–3).

THE ARGUMENT FROM PROPHECY

For Collins, as for Locke and Hobbes, among others, a central and critical claim of Christianity is Jesus' identity as the Messiah. It follows, for him, that Jesus' miracles play only a secondary role in showing he fulfils the Old Testament prophecies. No matter how well authenticated the miracles, they, of themselves, cannot establish his identity. There is, however, an apparent lack of fit between the Old Testament prophecies and their fulfilment in Jesus. The Messiah expected by the Jews was a victorious, not a spiritual Messiah. The prophecies by which the New Testament writers tried to establish Jesus' identity as the Christ, such as the virgin birth, appeared in any case to apply to events closer at hand and not to Jesus. Clarke's eccentric friend, William Whiston (1667–1752), argued that the lack of fit between the Old and New Testaments is to be explained by the deliberate corruption of the Old Testament text. Collins agreed that there was compelling evidence, as Simon and others had argued, that the text had been considerably altered over time, but argued that there was none to support Whiston's theory of how it had been altered (Collins 1724: 112). The alterations, indeed, posed a question whether many of the prophecies were recorded in scripture after the prophesied event, like prophecies in Virgil's *Aeneid* (Collins 1724: 137).

For Whiston, it was crucial that Christ should uniquely and literally fulfil the prophecies. If he only fulfilled them in a secondary or typical or mystical way, prophecy, he conceded, would not support the truth of Christianity. For then there could be multiple fulfilments, but there could be only one Messiah. Christianity would be exposed to ridicule (Whiston 1708: vol. 2, 268–73). Once again, the response of the freethinkers was to accept the inference, but to agree with the Dutch humanist Hugo Grotius (1583–1645) and the tradition of interpretation he represented that the only way to reconcile the Old and New Testaments was by reading their texts in a double sense. Interpretation could reconcile the texts, but, in doing so, it undermined the value of prophecy as evidence for the truth of Christianity.

REASON AND MORALS

The freethinkers viewed human reason as more limited in certain respects than Clarke had claimed, since they argued that it could not demonstrate the soul's immateriality or immortality. They were more confident than Clarke or Locke about what it could achieve in morals, for them the heart of religion. Tindal's provocative *Christianity as Old as the Creation*, which rebuts Clarke's claim that Christianity rendered any coherent form of deism impossible, clearly illustrates this. Since Christianity only republishes the religion of nature, although in a language more obscure and allegorical, and less comprehensive in its findings, and since it depends on a corrupt and translated text, there is no reason to pay heed to anything other than the religion of nature. Other religions, for that matter, could equally claim to be further editions of the same text. It is an argument that resulted in the deistic worship introduced by David Williams (1738–1816) at the Margaret Street Chapel in London, based on universal principles shared by all religions.

Tindal argued that no scriptural rules can possibly stipulate what should be done in all of life's circumstances. Any such rules would have to be supplemented, interpreted and judged against the light of nature, the fundamental standard of human action. This is true, Tindal added, even for Christ's moral precepts. Plainer they may be, but, literally interpreted, they commit the believer to 'monstrous Absurdities'. Those precepts, he argued, 'are for the most Part deliver'd either so hyperbolically, that they would lead Men astray, were they govern'd by the usual Meaning of Words; or else express'd in so loose, general, and undermin'd a Manner, that Men are as much left to be govern'd by the Reason of Things, as if there were no such Precepts' (Tindal 1730: 338). Where Clarke and Locke insisted that

Figure 3.1 *Matthew Tindal*, from James Granger (1769–74) *A Biographical History of England*, vol. XXXI, p. 32a. By permission of the Huntington Library, San Marino, California.

Figure 3.2 *John Locke*, engraving after G. Kneller, from *Memoirs of the Life and Writings of John Gray*, vol.1, p.158. By permission of the Huntington Library, San Marino, California.

revelation is necessary to remedy the shortcomings of human reason, Tindal claimed the reverse: the defects of revelation must be remedied by natural reason (Tindal 1730: 201). Revealed religion, accordingly, is not a self-sufficient and perfect rule requiring no interpreters.

Locke made concessions to such a view in his *Essay*:

> Since then the Precepts of Natural Religion are plain, and very intelligible to all Mankind, and seldom come to be controverted; and other revealed Truths, which are conveyed to us by Books and Languages, are liable to the common and natural obscurities and difficulties incident to Words, methinks it would become us to be more careful and diligent in observing the former, and less magisterial, positive, and imperious, in imposing our own sense and interpretation on the latter.
>
> (Locke 1700: III.9.§23)

The freethinkers, however, thought that a much stronger conclusion was warranted than the tolerationist one Locke draws. Since natural religion yields knowledge of human duty and virtue while revelation yields probabilities and obscurities, Tindal asked: 'must not Faith be swallow'd up by Knowledge; and Probability by Demonstration?' (Tindal 1730: 369–70) How can the lesser and obscurer evidence outweigh the greater and clearer?

Tindal expressed confidence in natural reason precisely where Clarke and Locke supposed it to be weak and ineffective. In Clarke's appeal to a fallen state from which mankind was extricated only by special revelation, Tindal located a deep ambivalence about human reason. How could Clarke claim, on the one hand, that a future state of rewards and punishments is 'in general deducible, even demonstrably, by a Chain of clear, and undeniable Reasoning' (Tindal 1730: 358) and, on the other, complain about deists who were prepared to rely on his argument? Not, of course, that the deists felt compelled to accept that morality requires justification by reference to a future state. Against the thesis of a fallen state, Tindal counterposed the notion that human beings are 'created in a State of Innocence, capable of knowing, and doing all God requires of them' (Tindal 1730: 375). For him, reason and freethinking actualize this capacity. To judge human reason defective on issues central to living virtuously is to attribute a moral defect to God for providing His creation with means that fall short of the intended end (Tindal 1730: 378).

It is all part of the Enlightenment project of liberating the understanding from the chains that restrain and enslave it. For Locke, Clarke, Le Clerc and the latitudinarians, the liberation of the understanding was consistent with and, indeed, required Christianity; for the freethinkers, Christianity and revealed religion generally stood in the way. Some Christians concluded that if the argument was framed in this way, the contest was one in which religious faith could not do well. They shifted the basis for faith away from the setting in the theory of knowledge in which Locke and the latitudinarian tradition had located it. From the opposite direction, French atheists, such as the Baron d'Holbach (1723–89) and Jacques André Naigeon (1738–1810), had little patience for the method of argument of those like Collins, which they misunderstood as based on authority rather than as being situated in the sceptical tradition (Naigeon 1791–2: I. 858). For them, Collins spent too much of his considerable philosophical force on arguments with Christian theologians in whose views no person of sound mind would still take any interest and which belonged with the debris of history (Naigeon 1791–2: I.858). For them, his real significance was the systematic defence of the possibility of materialism and the necessity of human action in his metaphysical encounters with Clarke. The refutation of the principles of natural religion on which Christianity was taken to rely obviated any need to concern oneself with the authenticity or meaning of scripture.

REFERENCES

Barbeyrac, J. (1712) *Le Droit de la nature et des gens*, trans. and ed. Samuel Pufendorf, Amsterdam: Pierre de Coup.

Berkeley, G. (1732) *Alciphron, or the Minute Philosopher*, London: J. Tonson; David Berman (ed.) (1993) *George Berkeley: Alciphron, or the Minute Philosopher in Focus*, London and New York: Routledge.

Charles-Daubert, F. (1999) *Le 'Traité des trois imposteurs' et 'L'Esprit de Spinosa': Philosophie clandestine entre 1678 et 1768*, Oxford: Voltaire Foundation.

Chillingworth, W. (1638) *The Religion of Protestants, a Safe Way to Salvation*, Oxford: L. Lichfield; repr. (1972) Menston: Scolar Press.

Clarke, S. (1738) *The Works of Samuel Clarke*, 4 vols, London: John and Paul Knapton; repr. (1978) New York: Garland Publishing.

[Collins, A.] (1707) *An Essay Concerning the Use of Reason in Propositions the Evidence whereof Depends upon Human Testimony*, London; repr. (1984) in vol. 2 of Peter A. Schouls (ed.) *The Philosophy of John Locke*, New York and London: Garland Publishing.

—— (1710) *A Vindication of the Divine Attributes*, London: A. Baldwin.

—— (1713) *A Discourse of Free-Thinking*, London; repr. (1965) ed. Günter Gawlick, Stuttgart-Bad Cannstatt: Friedrich Frommann Verlag.

—— (1724) *A Discourse of the Grounds and Reasons of the Christian Religion*, London; repr. (1976) New York: Garland Publishing.

—— (1726a) *A Letter to the Author of the Discourse of the Grounds and Reasons of the Christian Religion*, London: A. Moore [*sic*].

—— (1726b) *The Scheme of Literal Prophecy Considered*, London [*sic*]: T[homas] J[ohnson] for the booksellers of London & Westminster.

—— (1727) *A Letter to the Reverend Dr Rogers*, London.

Hill, H. (2001) 'Christianity and Natural Religion: John Tillotson', *Anglican and Episcopal History*, 70: 169–89.

Hume, D. (1779) *Dialogues Concerning Natural Religion*, London; repr. (1988) ed. Richard H. Popkin, 2nd edn, Indianapolis and Cambridge: Hackett Publishing.

Le Clerc, J. (1690) *Five Letters Concerning the Inspiration of the Holy Scriptures*, trans. John Locke (?), [London]; excerpted from Richard Simon (1685) *Sentimens de quelques Theologiens de Hollande sur l'histoire critique du Vieux Testament*, Amsterdam: Henri Desbordes and (1686) *Défense des Sentimens de quelques théologiens de Hollande*, Amsterdam: Henri Desbordes.

Locke, J. (1700) *An Essay Concerning Human Understanding*, 4th edn, London; ed. Peter H. Nidditch (1975) Oxford: Clarendon Press.

—— (1695) *The Reasonableness of Christianity as Delivered in the Scriptures*, ed. John C. Higgins-Biddle (1999) Oxford: Clarendon Press.

Naigeon, J. A. (1791–2) *Encyclopédie methodique. Philosophie ancienne et moderne*, 3 vols, Paris: Panckoucke.

[Patrick, S.] (1662) *Brief Account of a New Sect of Latitude-Men*, London; repr. (1963) Los Angeles: William Andrews Clark Memorial Library.

Rivers, Isabel (1991 and 2000) *Reason, Grace and Sentiment: A Study of the Language of Religion and Ethics in England, 1660–1780*, 2 vols, Cambridge: Cambridge University Press.

Shaftesbury, A. A. C., 3rd Earl (1711) *Characteristics of Men, Manners, Opinions, Times*, London: John Darby; ed. John M. Robertson (1900), 2 vols, London: Grant Richards.

Simon, R. (1680) *Histoire critique du Vieux Testament*, Paris; trans. H. D. [Henry Dickinson] (1682) *A Critical History of the Old Testament*, London: Walter Davis.

Spinoza, B. (1670) *Tractatus Theologico-Politicus*, Hamburg: Henricum Künraht [*sic*]; trans. Samuel Shirley (1998) *Theological-Political Treatise*, Indianapolis and Cambridge: Hackett Publishing.

Tindal, M. (1730) *Christianity as Old as the Creation*, London; repr. (1999) Bristol: Thoemmes Press.

Whiston, W. (1708) *The Accomplishment of Scripture Prophecies*; rev. and repr. (1739) in *A Defence of Natural and Revealed Religion*, 3 vols, London: D. Midwinter.

CHAPTER FOUR

ENQUIRY, SCEPTICISM AND ENLIGHTENMENT

Aaron Garrett

In this chapter I shall develop some general considerations about scepticism in the mid- to late seventeenth century and early eighteenth century, concentrating on the relation between scepticism and philosophical enquiry. Following the eminent scholar Richard Popkin, I understand scepticism not as a unified movement, but rather as the employment of arguments and strategies derived from Sextus Empiricus and Renaissance sceptics for undermining positive knowledge claims in various areas of human enquiry. Above all, it was the use of Sextus' ten modes from the *Outlines of Pyrrhonism*, together with arguments taken from Montaigne and his followers. Consequently, I do not mean that there are knowledge claims which can be shown to be neither true nor false, as claimed by some twentieth-century advocates of 'epistemic scepticism'. Bayle's arguments against our access to the religious beliefs of others, and portions of Hume's 'sceptical argument' at the close of the first book of the *Treatise*, are sceptical in this sense. As a general definition, though, it is unduly restrictive. Furthermore, loose definition is consistent with the sometimes intentionally vague ways that seventeenth- and eighteenth-century authors discussed scepticism.

In the wake of Popkin's highly original research, further work by him and others has identified many varieties of scepticism from Sanchez, Montaigne and Charron to Bayle, Nicole, Hume and beyond. Moreover, he argued for a sceptical counter-tradition existing both alongside and in opposition to some of the most influential anti-sceptical views of early modern philosophers, especially among Cartesians. Renaissance and early modern revivals of scepticism were co-extensive with the rise of the new science and philosophy, as well as the rise of Enlightenment intellectual cultures throughout Europe. Furthermore, there were a number of advocates of scepticism – Gassendi and Nicole are obvious examples – who were important contributors to the new science and new philosophy. The history of the Enlightenment or Enlightenments and the history of scepticism are clearly intertwined, and form a theme of Popkin's great work, *The History of Scepticism from Erasmus to Spinoza*.

I will start from a rather different premise: that many of the most important early modern philosophers – Bacon, Descartes, Arnauld, Locke, Boyle – were not sceptics in a strong sense and did not normally identify themselves as such. This list is not meant to be exhaustive. Others who were considered sceptics (Gassendi), or who were criticized for being sceptical in particularly controversial ways (Hobbes and Spinoza), drew on sceptical arguments in some regions of their philosophies and found them unproblematic in others.

I will consider five basic categories of scepticism employed by seventeenth- and eighteenth-century philosophers, or more properly five different ends to which sceptical argument is put. This list is not meant to be exhaustive. For example, scepticism was often taken to be primarily about religion, but I will touch on this only tangentially as it has already been discussed in Chapter 3 of this volume. We can distinguish:

1 Pragmatic scepticism about the limits of human knowledge in the service of the new science (Glanvill, Locke, Bacon, Boyle, and all the others); also used by some opponents of the new science to argue for Aristotelianism.
2 Scepticism about the relation between knowledge and belief, interconnected with issues of religious toleration, as in Bayle and Voltaire.
3 Closely connected with this was scepticism about the grounding of moral principles, for example in Bayle, Spinoza, Hume, Gibbon, Mandeville, Nicole.
4 Deflationary scepticism as in Bayle, Sanchez, Montaigne, Hume, and so on.
5 Cartesian *a priori* extreme scepticism about the grounds of knowledge as such.

Strictly speaking, these distinctions signal two domains in which scepticism operates – those of knowledge and moral principles – and three overlapping forms in which it was pursued – extreme, deflationary and pragmatic. For example, Hume's arguments about animal reasoning seek to deflate assumptions about man's superiority over other animals by showing that all share the same fundamental passions: the pride of a peacock is the same as that of man. Hume's arguments are ultimately derived from Montaigne's *Apologie pour Raimond Sebond*, similar claims in Mandeville's *Fable of the Bees* and Bayle's article 'Rorarius' in the *Dictionnaire*. Montaigne insisted that at best we are no better than other animals. Hume, combining elements of both scepticism and Epicureanism in Mandeville, used such scepticism to limit the power of reason. A single explanation in terms of natural causes suffices for both human and animal passions, because there is no detectable difference between them.

With the obvious exception of Descartes, most authors did not take general *a priori* scepticism very seriously. Particular arguments, however, were taken seriously within particular contexts: Were there unshakeable principles in morality? Was there a definitive argument for or against Copernicanism? Was our experience trust-worthy? But the subversive arguments of Sextus or Montaigne were employed in the service of positive knowledge claims far more often than they were used to argue for a thoroughgoing scepticism. Even many of the self-identified sceptics, as I will discuss in a moment, pursued their scepticism in tandem with positive knowledge claims.

Spinoza is one of many philosophers who, while using limited forms of scepticism, did not take extreme Cartesian doubt seriously. His attention centres on Descartes's *Principles* and the *Discourse on Method*, which certainly discussed scepticism, but not to the extent of the *Meditations*. Indeed, in his central work, *The Ethics*, Spinoza hardly mentions doubt, in spite of his debts to Descartes. Attempting to draw limits around cognition, Spinoza argued that many philosophical errors arise from failing to distinguish what we can know from what we cannot. He was deeply sceptical about the authority of revealed religion. This 'on again–off again' attitude towards scepticism was the norm. Many thinkers affected by sceptical arguments neither saw themselves as sceptics nor addressed sceptical challenges. Rather, they used them to emphasize the subjective character of belief and the uncertainty of knowledge. Locke, for example, holding that Aristotle's views were an obstacle to scientific advancement, denied that knowledge of the real essence of things is possible. In Pyrrhonian fashion, he argues that real essences are unknowable: using traditional vocabulary to distinguish ways of approaching the issue, he holds that we can know a subject only by means of its predicates, a substance by means of its qualities, and the real essence of something by means of the nominal essences actually experienced in the world. For example, all we can know about sheep is derived from our experiences of them, which include their shape, their wool, their number of legs and so on. Such experiential knowledge, nevertheless, does not reveal the real essence of sheep or their underlying substance – if there is one.

Locke emphasizes that such knowledge, strictly speaking, is imprecise or incomplete. But it is all that we have got, and should not be set aside under the persistent pressure of sceptical doubt. Berkeley is another philosopher who used sceptical arguments negatively and positively simultaneously: his arguments against the existence of material objects were used to support an argument from design and for the benign providence of God.

One might say that scepticism was somewhat like republicanism, an idea in many minds but one that few, if any, seemed to advocate wholesale. Just as there were many mixed monarchy theorists in the eighteenth century with republican sentiments, so there were many neo-Epicureans, neo-Stoics, Cartesians, Royal Society members and others in the seventeenth century who drew on sceptical ideas in order to attack dogmatism but not necessarily to advocate full-blooded scepticism – by which I mean a way of life advocated by Sextus Empiricus or by Bayle and Montaigne. Sceptical argument is certainly at the heart of early modern and Enlightenment scientific and philosophical enquiry, but normally in a selective way. For example, the prominent self-proclaimed sceptic Joseph Glanvill, author of *The Vanity of Dogmatizing*, on most issues was no more sceptical than Locke, and, on some issues, far less. Like Locke, he accepted the basic methods of the Royal Society, and favoured toleration in matters of religion. He also distinguished types of sceptic:

> [T]he *Free Philosophers* are by others accounted *Scepticks* from their way of enquiry, which is not to continue still poring upon the Writings and Opinions of Philosophers, but to seek Truth in the Great Book of Nature; and in that search to proceed with wariness and circumspection . . . This, among others, hath been the way of those Great Men the Lord Bacon, and Des-Cartes; and is now the method of the Royal Society of London . . . This is *Scepticism* with some; and if it be so is indeed, 'tis such Scepticism, as is the only way to sure and grounded knowledge, to which confidence in uncertain Opinions is the most fatal Enemy . . . I am absolved from being a *Sceptick*, in the ill sense; for I neither derogate from Faith, nor despair of Science; and the Opinion of

those of that character are directly destructive of the one, and everlasting discouragements of the other.

(Glanvill 1676: 44–5)

Glanvill clearly thought that there was a well-founded distinction between ill or destructive sceptics – those 'desperate Renegados whose intellects are . . . debauched by Vice' and enquirers who seek to use scepticism to combat dogmatism. For Glanvill, there was no reason why scepticism should in and of itself lead to the destruction of faith or knowledge: well-founded scepticism is consistent with both faith and liberal toleration. And, as for knowledge,

If I should say, we are to expect no more from our Experiments and Inquiries, than great likelihood, and such degrees of probability, as might deserve hopeful assent; yet thus much of diffidence and uncertainty would not make me a *Sceptick*; since *They* taught, That no one thing was *more probable* than an *other*; and so with-held assent from all things.

(Glanvill 1676: 44–5)

Scepticism is as capable of deforming into dogmatism as are other sorts of human knowledge, a point well made by Hume.

Non-dogmatic scepticism, for Glanvill, was consistent with the Royal Society agenda in the sciences in a way also found in Locke's and in Boyle's criticisms of the doctrine of forms. The dogmatic sceptic assumes that anything we can know is either certain or not certain, whereas the non-dogmatic sceptic grants that the more or less probable is sufficient for science; in particular a science emphasizing scientific instruments, natural history, experiment and intervention in the tradition of Bacon and Boyle. The emphasis on well-founded judgements from probability was common among many with sceptical leanings, such as Pierre-Daniel Huet, Simon Foucher and Pierre Gassendi. The basic mistake of the sceptical dogmatist is to become dogmatically committed and overly 'enthusiastic' about sceptical argumentation. A temperate scepticism leads in quite a different direction, towards the expansion of useful probable knowledge.

Gassendi was in many ways the paradigm of this sort of temperate scepticism, and of how the temperate sceptic may also be an agitator for a different non-sceptical position. On the one hand, in the *Excitationes Paradoxicae adversus Aristoteleos* (1624), the *Syntagma Philosophicum* (1658) and many other works he laid out powerful sceptical arguments, both specific arguments against many Aristotelian and Cartesian doctrines and general catalogues of sceptical argument strategies. Yet Gassendi was interested in using his sceptical arguments to promote a probabilistically based Epicurean empiricism, which was consistent with his own devout and fideistic Christianity. Hence he also wrote *Philosophiae Epicuri Syntagma* (1658), as well as many other works that emphasized both a physics and a theory of the passions in an Epicurean tradition. His consistent position seems to have been that, although 'we cannot be admitted into the very inner shrines of nature, we can still live among certain of the outer altars' (Gassendi 1658: I.2.5; Brush 1972: 327) – Epicureanism provided positive knowledge which satisfied this desire.

This was already a current in the work of the Renaissance sceptic Francisco Sanchez, author of *Quod Nihil Scitur* (1581) – *That Nothing Is Known*. Together with Montaigne's *Essays*, Sanchez's work is central to early modern scepticism. Like Gassendi after him, Sanchez offered a series of powerful Pyrrhonian arguments against Aristotelian natural science, and an encouragement to philosophers to think for themselves. Although it is unclear whether he was an Epicurean when it came to the physical sciences, it is clear that like Gassendi, his main purpose was to clear the way for the new science.

So, in Glanvill, Sanchez, Gassendi and others, there are forms of scepticism, derived from different sources, but all serving to promote the quest for knowledge. We can see this in the work of Montaigne's popularizer, Pierre Charron, whose widely disseminated work *De la Sagesse* (1601) fused moderate scepticism and stoicism.

This point is made most clearly by the greatest of all modern British sceptics, David Hume. In 1742 Hume published, in his second volume of *Essays, Moral and Political*, a quartet of essays each presenting a character type associated with one of the major schools of ancient philosophy: 'The Epicurean', 'The Platonist', 'The Stoic' and 'The Sceptic'. The last of these was nearly as long as the other three combined. Hume's four essays are useful for analysing general tendencies in early modern philosophy, and also offer insight into how modern sceptics thought about scepticism and its alternatives. There were many neo-Stoics in the seventeenth and eighteenth centuries, including Justus Lipsius, Spinoza, Shaftesbury and Hutcheson. For Hume, Stoics are seeking an undisturbed state of mind, which should result from their questioning, while maintaining their belief in providence. There were also many Platonists, immediately before and up to the time of Hume, including Descartes, Arnauld, Henry More, Cudworth and Berkeley. Finally, there were many Epicureans, arguing for atomism, efficient causes and chance: Gassendi, Hobbes, Toland, Walter Charleton, Saint Evremond, Collins, Mandeville and, shortly, Helvétius, Diderot and D'Holbach. Hume's character types, therefore, helpfully signal modern trends of thinking, if not schools in a strict sense.

Although the voice of the sceptic is mostly Hume's own, there are many features in the essays on 'The Epicurean' and 'The Stoic' that were also integral to his philosophy. Unlike the Epicurean, the moderate sceptic does not believe that there is a natural man to be uncovered, superior to artifice. Unlike the Stoic, he does not believe that passions should be extirpated. And unlike the Platonist, he does not believe in a realm of universals with its concomitant realist assumptions. But the moderate sceptic agrees with both the Epicurean and the Stoic that natural explanations of human passions and *mores* are possible. He is a reductionist, like the Epicurean, but agrees with the Stoic that human artifice is a key for understanding man. Essentially, however, the moderate sceptic strives to avoid any hint of dogmatism. Hume is concerned that the sceptic carries his arguments too far and fails to acknowledge that we can all acquire stable moral principles.

Hume's moderate scepticism, derived from so many different sources, is entirely commonplace among philosophers of his own and the previous generation. All were selective in their use of sceptical arguments and none was consistently sceptical in all contexts. There is the Hobbesian-Cartesianism of Velthuysen, Spinoza and Pufendorf; the Scholastico-Cartesianism of Clauberg and Geulincx; the Sceptico-

Epicureanism of Gassendi; the Sceptico-Stoicism of Charron; and the Sceptico-Platonism of Shaftesbury.

It may well be true that Montaigne and Bayle are themselves only moderate sceptics, like everyone else. In the seventeenth century the former's thought was often presented in a form which revealed Epicurean and Stoic elements, but it is not necessary to discuss it further here. Bayle, however, requires comment because of his profound influence on eighteenth-century writers. He offered a compelling argument for the independence of religion and morality as well as for the natural status of morality. His arguments on these matters, and against superstition in *Reflections on the Comet* (1682), in his discussion of Spinoza in that volume and in the *Dictionnaire* (1696), were often taken to be a defence of morality independent of revelation, but consistent with toleration. Shaftesbury, for example, was deeply influenced by Bayle, and used his arguments to support a neo-Roman natural morality of a kind that Bayle would probably not have approved. Diderot's *Letter on the Blind* (1749) blends elements from Bayle with an empiricism derived from Condillac. If all knowledge is derived from the senses, and morality is naturally acquired, then morality will differ as the senses differ; and the moral codes of the blind will differ from ours. Diderot's goal, probably not shared by Bayle, was to deflate the pretensions of moralists and to render plausible the Epicurean theory of man.

There were a number of important thinkers who cannot be viewed as sceptics in any helpful sense, quite aside from the Cambridge Platonists or neo-Scholastics. Three noted materialist philosophers of mind – David Hartley, Joseph Priestley and Anthony Collins – might fit Hume's account of the Epicurean. Yet, although Hartley occasionally uses sceptical strategies, it would be implausible to class this most earnest advocate of the theology of love as a sceptic. Similarly for Joseph Priestley: his attacks on Hume, Gibbon and other sceptics were completely consistent with his own variant of materialism. Indeed, he consciously identified himself as a bulwark against the loathsome scepticism of the age. By contrast, a third materialist philosopher, Anthony Collins, was sceptical in all of the first four senses listed at the beginning of this chapter.

I have already mentioned many philosophers who were prepared to use sceptical arguments in some contexts but refused to do so on the topics of religion and morality. Jesuits, for example, used arguments about the relative character of morality in support of the revealed status of religion. A number of writers have been interpreted as fideists, notably Bayle and Montaigne, and it is indubitable that Johann Georg Hamann, inspired by Hume's *Dialogues Concerning Natural Religion*, also used sceptical arguments to support fideism. Conversely, critics of established religion, such as Shaftesbury, used sceptical strategies to criticize it but also held a fairly rigid, naturalistic and universalistic theory of morals.

Scepticism, though, was particularly important in the creation of one of the great positive achievements of all the national Enlightenments: movements for religious toleration. Bayle and Spinoza both developed important arguments for toleration, built on our lack of access to other minds and the impossibility of certainty about others' beliefs. In the *Tractatus Theologico-Politicus* (1670) Spinoza held that since the state could not control the thought of its citizens, attempts to do so were not only fruitless but undermined state security. This enabled him to formulate a pragmatic argument for freedom of speech. Bayle developed more radical arguments, perhaps derived in part from Spinoza. In the *Philosophical Commentary* (1686/7) (a copy of which Thomas Jefferson kept in his library) Bayle criticized the parable of the feast (Luke 14, 12–24), in which a rich man, unable to fill places at his table, instructed his servant to compel strangers to come in. The words 'compel them to come in' were notoriously used by the French Catholic Church in its persecution of the Huguenots. At the heart of his commentary, Bayle, himself a Huguenot in exile, argues that not only can we never be sure of another person's beliefs, but we cannot change them even by force. Each individual alone has access to his own beliefs and the sole ability to change them. The only way to deal with persecutors and bigots is to try to help them to see for themselves, and to accept that their own views have no special standing.

Figure 4.1 *Pierre Bayle*, medal S387, Jean Dassier. By permission of the Trustees of the Wallace Collection, London.

Bayle provided a powerful case for toleration and his arguments were taken up by Voltaire without embracing the radical sceptical consequences. More importantly the sceptical solution 'know yourself', 'think for yourself', and change yourself accordingly, became a *leitmotif* of the French and German Enlightenments. This was rarely presented as the consequence of the radical sceptical argument. Instead, it was erected on very different grounds. Yet Enlightenment and radical sceptics shared an inheritance, even if the former normally rejected the arguments of the latter and reached safer conclusions.

Finally, I would like to consider scepticism about the foundation of morals, which was a driving force in moral philosophy throughout the seventeenth and eighteenth centuries, and many of the central claims related to matters of virtue: the claim ascribed to Hugo Grotius that there might be a stable natural morality independent of revealed religion; Hobbes's arguments that morality arises with the Common-wealth and derives from self-interest; Bayle's radicalization of Grotius in arguing that virtue might be independent of all religion; Mandeville's claim in the *Fable of the Bees* that vice was intrinsic to successful and stable societies. Such arguments naturally provoked legions of authors: Richard Cumberland, Samuel Pufendorf,

Samuel Clarke, Joseph Butler, Francis Hutcheson and many others. Among the many responses to the sceptics and their associates were those of Hutcheson who attempted to establish an unshakeable moral sense and show benevolence to be intrinsic to our moral judgement, and Clarke who argued that there were real 'fitnesses' between things, providing a secure backing for morals.

From the middle of the eighteenth century a group of philosophers, beginning with David Hume, attempted to set their account of human morals and practices in a historical context, while also arguing for a set of stable human dispositions which express themselves differently at different times. Hume, in his *History of England* (1754–62) and many essays, and Gibbon, in his *The Decline and Fall of the Roman Empire* (1776–88), presented a range of character types who behave differently over time. Adam Smith, in most of his works, and John Millar, in *The Origin of the Distinction of Ranks* (1771), argued for the shape that moral and customary associations might take. In different ways, therefore, they all attempted to historicize moral philosophy, and applied their restrained scepticism creatively to the development of the 'science of man'. Thus, as Popkin and others have suggested, the rise of the human and moral sciences, together with philosophical history, can be understood as one of the most profound legacies of scepticism in the Enlightenment.

REFERENCES

Brush, C. (ed. and trans.) (1972) *The Selected Works of Pierre Gassendi*, New York: Johnson Reprint Corp.

Gassendi, P. (1658) *Opuscula Philosophica*, 6 vols, Lyon: Annisson.

Glanvill, J. (1676) *Essays on Several Important Subjects in Philosophy and Religion*, London.

Hume, David (1742) *Essays, Moral and Political*, in *Essays, Moral, Political, and Literary* (1777), rev. edn ed. E. F. Miller (1985) Indianapolis: Liberty Fund.

Popkin, R. H. (1960) *The History of Scepticism from Erasmus to Descartes*, Assen: Van Gorcum.

CHAPTER FIVE

THE HUGUENOT DEBATE
ON TOLERATION

Luisa Simonutti

Huguenot thought, particularly its political-religious aspects, contributed to the delineation of a number of concepts which became central to the early Enlightenment and also to the mature development of the same philosophy. The discussion about religion and the possibility of concord or toleration in relation to the problem of different faiths existing within the same territory or the confines of the same nation; debate about the role of the monarchy and the concept of despotism within the political-religious sphere; the shift from the idea of political sovereignty as a concession of privileges to the idea of sovereignty as an acquisition of rights; these were some of the questions which exercised Huguenot thinkers in the early days of the modern age. During the sixteenth and seventeenth centuries, the circulation of this complex of matters for debate was not limited to France, but expanded to England, and also to the rest of Continental Europe. It gained a particularly strong foothold in Holland, as a result of the experience of the Refuge and the contribution of the Huguenots, who became particularly active in the circulation of ideas through the publication of books and pamphlets, as well as through their personal correspondence; and, above all, through some of the major European scholarly reviews which flourished in the second half of the seventeenth century and the early decades of the eighteenth.

RECONCILIATION AND LIBERTY OF CONSCIENCE

From the 1530s on, the Calvinist Reformation had to obtain a foothold within a realm where the inhabitants were already convinced of being a Christian people enjoying special divine protection, and whose king was known by the epithet *très chrétien*. The King of France was traditionally honoured by this title as a result of the oath taken at both the anointing and the coronation, sacred rituals which ensured absolute devotion and endowed him with miraculous powers (see Crouzet 1996).

The period in which the initial political-religious conflicts emerged with increasing asperity between Huguenots and Catholics was one of particular economic and social difficulty in France. A significant rise in the population coincided with an agricultural crisis and a lowering of living standards, which prejudiced attempts at social concord or at overcoming the political and religious tensions.

The edicts of pacification and the policy of reconciliation pursued by Catherine de Medici – which were to culminate in the Edict of Nantes – were followed by several decades of coexistence between the two creeds, both on a strictly theological level and in terms of the political order and state organization. This regime of coexistence and civil concord, achieved after forty years of political and religious struggles and accompanied by a widespread pamphlet literature, proved to be impermanent. The seventeenth century witnessed a progressive hardening of attitudes on the part of the Gallican clergy and of the representatives of the crown. The result was to bring to light the legislative and textual difficulties inherent in the, supposedly tolerant, Edict of Nantes, showing up its ambiguities and limitations, both political and social. The edict represented a crucial point in the formulation of a policy of toleration in the early modern age, but what came to be increasingly emphasized, especially in Catholic quarters, was not the natural and social rights which had been effectively achieved for all subjects but the special circumstances in which it was granted and the particular privileges it conferred. The ascent to the throne of Louis XIV marked a further alteration in the condition of the French Protestants: a progressive reduction of their political representation and an increasing limitation of their religious liberty (see Daussy 2002; Jouanna 1996; Jouanna *et al*. 1998).

During the reign of Henry IV, and in the course of the seventeenth century, the demand for the legitimization of Protestantism in France had found its principal argument in the political and military support which the Huguenots had supplied to the King, their recognition of his absolute sovereignty and loyalty to the crown. This military support, juridical assent and allegiance to the monarchy were reaffirmed during the period of the Fronde. But in the years of the persecution perpetrated by the Sun King, until the Revocation, religious coercion and social repression led to a critical reconsideration of this consensus and provoked comparison with other European political experiences, especially those of England and Holland.

However, the political concepts of the Huguenots were not marked by a complete and passive acceptance of absolutism; on the contrary, in the 1570s and 1580s there was a flourishing controversial literature which brought into question the origins of the power of the monarch and his absolute authority in religious and political spheres, issues which were to be debated with renewed vigour at the time of the Revocation of the Edict of Nantes.

THE RIGHT OF RESISTANCE AND RELIGIOUS COEXISTENCE IN THE REIGN OF HENRY IV

During the Wars of Religion, through their words and deeds, the Chancellor Michel de L'Hospital and Philippe Duplessis-Mornay sought through the coexistence of the 'two religions' a means of conciliating the rival creeds each with its imperative of conversion. A similar approach had, in other countries, such as the kingdom of Poland, calmed the political tumult and given rise to a regime of toleration. The proposed solution to the problems of conversion and coexistence was undermined by its incompatibility with the underlying conviction of each creed that it alone was true. Besides, the presence of the 'two religions' on French soil was felt by the Catholic exponents to be counter to the concept of national unity, while for the Huguenots the difference in faith made a complete political and cultural identification with the central government difficult. This ensured that confessional strife invaded the specific sphere of politics.

In seeking a solution to such problems, the figure of Duplessis-Mornay was emblematic. Actively committed to the defence of the Reformed religion from the attacks of the Catholics and from the polemics of the Reformed Church itself, the Huguenot thinker played a leading role in ensuring the support and loyalty of the Reformed subjects for the peaceful policy of Henry IV, on the one hand, thus distancing himself from suspicion of sedition, and, on the other, standing warranty himself among his co-believers for the political credibility of the monarch, regardless of the latter's religious choices. Contrary to any policy designed to '*asservir la conscience d'autruy*', and at the same time concerned to maintain a distinction between the spheres of politics and religion, in his writings and public letters he consistently underlines the advantages for the nation of social concord (Duplessis-Mornay 1585: 2–3). He exhorts the King to support a conciliatory project inspired by ideals opposed to those expressed at the notorious Council of Trent. In spite of his commitment to religious coexistence, the ideals of religious liberty expounded by Duplessis-Mornay were limited by the pre-eminent requirement to protect the legitimacy of the Reformed creed from Protestant and Catholic polemic, and by the effort to achieve the unification of all the Reformed brethren.

A contemporary Catholic defender of coexistence, Michel de L'Hospital was convinced that, after years of political weakness and court conflicts, the only way to reinforce the authority of the monarch was through liberty and concord. In his writings and public addresses the Chancellor of State sought to open the eyes of the *parlement* and of the King himself to the fact that the liberal coexistence of the two religions would not weaken the power of the King over his subjects, nor his authority in relation to neighbouring states. In the address he made at Poissy in 1561 before the prelates of France, he warned his listeners not to brand the Reformed as seditious. They had shown themselves to be loyal subjects on every possible occasion. Since the King was responsible for the care of consciences and the salvation of souls, in this crucial assignment it was in his interests to choose 'the most gentle and indulgent way possible of resolving the conflicts' (de L'Hospital 1561). It was, he argued, a requisite for national stability that a pacific agreement be reached with the Reformed subjects and aristocrats as they represented an extensive and authoritative segment of the population. Seditious movements which had developed among certain sectors of the population had been provoked by resentment for the offences suffered and by political and economic maltreatment. He also emphasized the very nature of Christian preaching, founded on the persuasive force of words and example, not on that of arms and coercion. Chancellor de L'Hospital proved to be equally determined in his denial of any right of resistance on the part of the subjects, and in his affirmation of the illegality of tyrannicide, thus distancing himself from the formulations of the ancient Greek and Roman worlds.

Although acknowledging the deep social roots of religious conflict, he was unwilling to subordinate religion to political reason, remaining a convinced supporter of the humanistic ideal of Christian concord which finds its roots in the universalist matrix of the medieval Church. He was moved by an ecumenical spirit in which the theological roots of toleration are to be found in the Christian precepts of a charitable forbearance of those in error, not unrelated to a commitment to convert the Reformed to the true faith through a persevering proselytism based on biblical precepts and right reason. For de L'Hospital, civil peace constituted an essential political goal in the government of the nation, to be achieved only by conciliation. His calls for a national council to assuage and resolve the religious conflicts were overruled by the clergy and the Catholic members of the *parlement*, and by monarchist policy.

Although on opposite sides, the political and religious ideals expressed by Duplessis-Mornay and by de L'Hospital, inspired by a common religious zeal and directed towards proselytism, subordinated abstract rights of toleration to a policy of religious coexistence. These remained lively ideals in French society, along with the 'poetic concept of liberty of conscience' which characterized the related public addresses and speeches of the Catholic and Huguenot pamphleteers in the following the decades. In the work of de L'Hospital, exhortations to lay one's trust in the judgement of God, to call a universal council, the metaphor of the French nation as a ship which requires a strong crew or sound government in order to confront the storm, and finally another metaphor of the King as a good doctor who cures the sick body of the state, avoiding remedies which are too radical, and seeking to prevent the onset of maladies, constituted an effective rhetorical use of traditional figures which were to return as stock themes in the numerous writings that animated the political debate at the time of the civil wars.

However, at the end of the sixteenth century, the question which the moderate exponents of both the Catholic and Protestant factions wished to settle, by pacific means, was not only that of the unity of creed, but also of the conformity of the religion of the King with that of the rest of the country. The anonymous author of the *Discours sur une question d'estat de ce temps* (1591) added his voice to those of the Gallican humanists of the late sixteenth century. Having recalled the Christian princes to their role as defenders of the universal Church, he concluded his reflections by assigning to the members of a general and supranational conference the task of agreeing and resolving all controversies in a public and general confession of faith, requesting all representatives religiously and inviolably to maintain that which the assembly should decree.

On the part of the Reformed, the anonymous author of *De la Concorde de l'Estat par l'observation des Edicts de Pacification* (1599) emphasized the need to maintain *la toleration e le libre exercice* of the Reformed religion promulgated by the edicts. While being convinced that religious concord is a desirable end and one of great benefit to the good of the state, he did not consider that it was a prerequisite for the functioning of civil society. Civil concord nonetheless represented an essential feature of any peaceful and prosperous society, and for that religious concord also was necessary (Anon. 1599: 83; see Turchetti 1998).

In spite of the dramatic political instability following the Saint Bartholomew's Day Massacre (1572), there were many ready to assert with conviction that '*Legalité est la première partie de l'equité*' (Anon. 1574). The guarantees of justice on the part of the magistrates and the King would conduct the vessel of state towards a safe harbour far from the storms of civil war and internal sedition, bringing all the people to strive for the public good (Anon. 1599: 40). But, in spite of many moderate writings, the majority of texts proclaimed one or other of the rival views as mutually exclusive (see Yardeni 1971).

Through the diverse proposals for political and religious stability there ran the conviction that the horrors of the Wars of Religion had not favoured the cause of religion but rather had encouraged atheism, libertinism and Epicureanism. Nonetheless, theological–dogmatic confrontation remains central in these writings, thus protecting the integrity of the doctrine, be it Catholic or Reformed, not only from the opposite ranks, but also from those who propose a Nicodemus-type behaviour, against which both sides are vociferous in invoking an open declaration of faith and an active proselytism. Similarly opposed was an eirenic strategy aimed at reuniting all Christians around a fundamental nucleus of dogmas, a solution which was unpopular with the Catholics and the Reformed alike, both of whom clung to their own doctrine and dogmas, and who saw this as opening the floodgates to religious indifference and atheism. In the last years of the century, the hardening of the attitudes of both Churches, deaf to the appeal to follow the teachings of the ancient Fathers of the Church, led to the failure of the conciliatory attempt to achieve ecclesiastical peace, promoted at length by the influential Huguenot pastor Jean de Serres.

The doctrinal difficulties which obstructed the debate regarding the rights of conscience, together with the pressure of historical events, contributed to accentuate the political dimensions of toleration. Not only in minor literature, but also in more authoritative Huguenot writings, such as the *Discours politiques et militaires* (1587) by de la Nouë, the proposed concord and toleration between the two religions increasingly becomes a political rather than a religious goal. After having pointed out the damage caused by false zeal on the one hand and by the true enemies of the republic – that is the supporters of civil war – on the other, de la Nouë exhorts the King and the government pragmatically to follow the easiest road: that of peaceful coexistence and political concord. This was a conviction which was shared by the Catholic pamphleteers. The anonymous author of the *Remonstrance des Catholiques pacifiques, pour la paix* (1585), after having declared his commitment to *reunir* and not *ruiner*, stated that the Reformed and the Catholics were in agreement on the principal aspects of salvation. Yet he calls for prudence, reminding that the remedy must not be so drastic as to cause the death of the patient.

In the writings examined so far, the idea of the authority of the King and the divine origin of monarchical power remained unquestioned. However, the recognition of the Catholic prince as the guarantor and intermediary between God and the people, and as prime mover towards the consolidation of the 'two religions' in France, highlighted issues concerning the foundations and limitations of sovereign power, especially in relation to matters of faith. Huguenot politicians and theologians, such as de la Boétie, Innocent Gentillet and the author (Junius Brutus) of *Vindiciae contra tyrannos*, were already reflecting critically on the foundations and limits of regal authority.

Alongside the monarchist pamphlets which sustained the typical absolutist theories, emphasizing in particular the divine right of kings and the sacred bond which bound the subjects to their sovereign – pamphlets which evoked and reworked Bodin's ideas in more generic terms – there were also numerous pamphlets which gave voice to a question frequently brought up in the anti-absolutist political literature of the second half of the sixteenth century: how far should the authority of the sovereign legitimately extend. The principal themes of de la Boétie were exhortation to satisfy man's natural desire for freedom and encouragement to resist a sovereign who impoverishes his people and enslaves their consciences. His work became a landmark of Huguenot pamphleteering in the 1570s. While, in the course of his brief life, de la Boétie moulded his political commitment on the conciliatory policy of Chancellor de L'Hospital, his *Discours de la servitude volontaire* expressed with all its radical force his conviction of the moral obligation of every subject to rediscover and defend his neglected liberties, including the religious.

FROM PRIVILEGE TO RIGHT:
THE APPEAL TO TOLERATION IN THE REIGN
OF LOUIS XIV

It was, above all, the Huguenot pamphleteers who in the second half of the seventeenth century were to draw inspiration from the historic events and the writings which circulated in France at the time of the Wars of Religion. This was an epoch which effectively found an extraordinary epilogue in the promulgation of the Edict of Nantes on the part of Henry IV, an edict which was based upon the theories and politico-philosophical thinking of the major Huguenot humanists – Hotman, Languet and Duplessis-Mornay – and anti-monarchist thinkers of the sixteenth century. While in the minor writings which are the main subject of this study the flavour of polemic and appropriate retort prevails, in the works of the more important exponents, both Reformed and Catholic, there emerges the requirement to define an ethics and a policy which, distancing itself from prejudice and faction, can effectively be proposed as the connective tissue of this redesigned social order.

While limited here to an analysis of certain aspects of the Huguenot pamphleteering activities of the late Renaissance and the seventeenth century, we should nevertheless bear in mind that this type of literary production was a widespread phenomenon of vast cultural and social relevance. This was the case not only in France, but throughout the Protestant countries, where questions relating to toleration, liberty of conscience and the definition of the duties and limitations of political power could not be eluded (see Solé 1997). These pamphlets extended over a broad theoretical range, but were above all expressed in numerous *discours*, *exhortations*, *lettres*, *remonstrances*, *propositions* and *harangues*, frequently anonymous.

The most complete and well-expressed formulation of these polemical views appear in the famous debate between Bayle and Jurieu, and in the writings of Claude and others which are the culmination of debates provoked by over a century of religious wars and persecution. In January 1685, a few months before the Revocation of the Edict of Toleration, Claude – the major interpreter of contemporary Huguenot ideas – addressed to Louis XIV a petition in defence of the Reformed religion, reminding him of past history and the obligatory laws which had been passed by previous monarchs. A year later he published *Les Plaintes des Protestants* (1686), in which, albeit indirectly, he once again addressed himself to the King. He recalled the inviolable loyalty of the Protestants during the revolts of the Fronde and underlined the immutable nature of the laws of the state. The positions which he adopted, which were of an increasingly political nature, were taken up in various articles and pamphlets. In 1688 Charles Ancillon, basing his arguments on the principle of natural right and the rights of the people, defended the contractarian foundations of the state and the irrevocability of the Edict of Nantes against the deceptive glory promised to the King and the nation by the clergy and the persecutors. This latter theme was to be amply developed in the slightly later essay (attributed to Ancillon), *La France interessée a rétablir l'Edit de Nantes*.

At the beginning of the 1680s, and in particular when the first persecutions began to make themselves felt, appeals and remonstrances in defence of the Reformed religion addressed directly to the person of the sovereign were fairly frequent. As a result, the *Lettre au Roy Tres-Chrestien*, which appeared in 1683, assigned to Louis XIV the role of settling the various wars which tormented the Continent, and of putting himself forward as the new emperor who would guarantee the civil and religious peace of all peoples. A similar allegiance to the laws and figure of the sovereign is explicitly confirmed in a brief pamphlet, published several years later, entitled *Très-humbles remonstrances à toutes les puissances Protestantes, reformées et evangéliques, sur le rétablissement des Eglises Protestantes de France*. The anonymous author calls for the annulment of the orders contained in the Revocation of the Edict of Nantes and for the foreign powers of Protestant faith to declare themselves guarantors of the irrevocability of Henry IV's edict. Significantly, however, the author, unlike more zealous apologists, does not entertain any hope of intervention by the Protestant powers against the sovereign and the Catholic clergy.

In 1685, Elie Merlat finally completed and published *Traité de pouvoir absolu des souverains*. Condemning all forms of republic, he declares that temporal sovereigns may enjoy unlimited and absolute power, to which their subjects may offer no resistance whatsoever on pain of falling into sin. He holds that the political subjection of the human race, and the need to delegate to the absolute power of the magistrates and the prince the guidance of society, is the fruit of the Fall. In this condition man has lost his original innocence, along with liberty and equality, and is falling prey to passions, reciprocal oppression, self-love and so on. Merlat identifies ten sources for the origins of absolute power, starting with the 'primary cause' (God) and going on to list the 'secondary causes' consequent upon the corruption of the human race. Only absolute power can prevent the destruction of the human race and the decline into anarchy. Merlat analyses various forms of government where the power of the sovereign is limited, demonstrating their inadequacy. In his account of absolute power, the people are left with no legislative power or control over the operation of the King, nor have they the right to resist a tyrant or a sovereign professing a different religion. Nevertheless, Merlat accepts that if the sovereign were to attack their own religion, it is preferable to obey God rather than the sovereign: while legitimizing absolute power, he concedes the liberty of the internal conscience.

In the second part of his book, Merlat does not restate this position. On the contrary, he frequently distances himself from it: true religion exists in the conscience of men, and it is for God alone, the magistrate of kings and princes, to judge, punish and oust tyrants. Merlat explains Louis's persecution of Huguenots in terms of his relations with the Gallican clergy and with Rome. Accordingly, he follows other Huguenot writers in urging a return to the fundamental laws of the French state, towards which they had always been and continued to be loyal. Merlat acknowledges that in many respects he was adopting the political but not the moral philosophy of Thomas Hobbes. Indeed, man's self-love and wickedness, which Hobbes regards as natural, he regards as resulting from the Fall, and not as intrinsic to man's nature. He holds that absolute power is not an end in itself, but merely the extreme remedy to render men sociable and to establish a civil society based on reason and free will.

As well as being a significant text illustrating the moderate Huguenot tradition, contrary to the political theory of popular sovereignty, Merlat's work is also an explicit testimony of how this strand of thought came to be enriched by more recent political theories – in particular those of Hobbes – and succeeded in gathering themes and arguments from these in spite of the general reprobation with which they were greeted upon their appearance (see Grandjean and Roussel 1998).

THE REFUGE

In March 1686, a few months after the Revocation, there appeared an impassioned pamphlet by Pierre Bayle, *Ce que c'est que la France toute Catholique*, and, shortly afterwards, the first two parts of his *Commentaire philosophique*. In these two writings he resumes his earlier defence of Protestant doctrine against the Jesuit arguments of Maimbourg in *Critique générale de l'histoire du Calvinisme*. He extends his defence of atheist society in his own *Pensées diverses* to embrace paganism and the errant conscience and argues that religious diversity is immaterial to development. In *Avis important aux réfugiés* he defends the absolute power of the sovereign against every form of participatory government with the precise purpose of guaranteeing the ideals of liberty of conscience and civil toleration. His views represented a level of elaboration which was fairly advanced for the period, even in relation to the proponents of civil toleration, such as Locke and, much later, Voltaire. In his essay *Ce que c'est que la France toute Catholique* Bayle pointed to English society as an example of the political coexistence of different religions where the medieval principle by which subjects had to adapt themselves to the religion of the sovereign did not hold (James II was Catholic, while his subjects were, for the most part, Protestant). Faith in a specific religion, or any other choices related to the inner conscience, must be neither required of nor imposed on subjects. Heresy is merely error, and even the persistence in error – invincible ignorance – cannot be punished by the laws of the state or by the secular arm.

For Bayle, the Protestants should not infringe the laws of the French state, hoping, in the wake of the events in England (1688/9), for the overthrow of the tyrannical King, possibly with the assistance of foreign powers. Like Merlat, Bayle argues that Huguenots should not lay themselves open to the accusation of sedition, but rather should appeal to the King for the annulment of the Revocation of the Edict, and the recall of exiles and refugees. What in Merlat's work was only hinted at in Bayle becomes the fundamental condition for civil toleration, namely, the separation of the divine sphere from the temporal.

According to Bayle, only moderate behaviour, devoid of any republican sympathy, could make the King well disposed towards the reinstatement of the Edict. Nor did he consider feasible either the overthrow or conversion of Louis XIV (as Jurieu had at one point hoped). So, in the *Avis* Bayle directs his polemic not only against contemporaries, notably Jurieu, but also against anti-monarchist theories (by which Jurieu seems to be directly inspired) and against the *Vindiciae contra tyrannos*, which had defended the sovereignty of the people and the legitimacy of tyrannicide. Bayle takes over the political theories of the supporters of the absolute power of the sovereign. Replying to the accusations of Jurieu contained in *Des Droits des deux souverains en matière de Religion*, written to refute the *Commentaire philosophique*, he raises the argument to an impassioned *querelle* which would last until his death. Jurieu presents himself as a supporter of William of Orange, and defender of the Glorious Revolution, to which he frequently turns his attention in the course of the *Lettres pastorales*.

For Jurieu, toleration necessarily leads to religious indifference and, like the majority of his contemporaries, he draws no distinction between civil toleration and religious toleration: his erastianism and his anti-absolutist political stance represent a means of achieving a more liberal political order and contained the implicit aspiration that the King would embrace Protestantism. In this sense he is closer to the political-religious ideals of the Catholic champion Jacques-Bénigne Bossuet than to the thought of Bayle and Locke.

Affairs in England in the late 1680s strengthened opposition to absolutism and became a matter of contention among Jurieu and his contemporaries. Bayle and others accused Jurieu and Protestants who shared his views of the most extreme anti-monarchist ideals, especially as regards the sovereignty of the people. In 1691 Jurieu replied to the accusations, summarizing the central themes of his political and religious thought. He agrees with Bayle's argument in the *Avis* that in order to set up an organized society the people must necessarily place their sovereignty in the hands of a monarch or of a number of governors, but immediately distances himself from the promoters of absolute royal power by maintaining that, at times, the people may legitimately preserve privileges or rights which are inalienable under any form of monarchy.

Several authors attempted to discover a middle way between the theories of Bayle and Jurieu. Elie Saurin, a pastor of the Walloon church of Utrecht, in an extensive essay of 1697 distanced himself from both indifference in questions of religion to which Bayle's ideas naturally led, and from the intolerant epilogue which was the outcome of those of Jurieu. Aubert de Versé also emphasized the risks of Protestant zeal. In *Le Protestant pacifique* he argued that, for the coexistence of all the Christian sects, including the Socinians, the Arminians, the Anabaptists and the Quakers, society must be founded on civil toleration and religious peace. The dictates of faith are taught to us by the Christian religion, and, by following the principles of reason, we are free to choose our religious creed, which cannot be forced. It follows that the guarantor of religious liberty has to be a state in which the power of the king and the magistrates is limited by law. For supporters of toleration, social order typically requires the limitation of the power of the sovereign and magistrates, but essentially requires a distinction between the religious and political spheres, thereby avoiding ambiguity in the concepts of toleration and a confessional state detectable in the thought of Jurieu, in whose work he finds an indirect justification of persecution (Guggisberg *et al.* 1991).

And so the doctrine of civil toleration finds its greatest development not among the ranks of the most zealous Protestants (such as Jurieu and Claude), but among thinkers such as Bayle and de Versé; that is, among the supporters of the principle that the toleration of all religions does not constitute a threat to the political order of a state, whether it be based on a royalist, oligarchic or democratic regime. It is significant that the doctrines of toleration of Locke and Voltaire were based on these same principles, and they were moreover concepts which were widespread in the political-religious thought of the second half of the seventeenth century. A further example is furnished by the essay *Traité de la liberté de religion*, published in London in 1678, but which refers principally to the French situation. This text, analysing the need to grant liberty of conscience to the heretics, focuses on the fact that the latter are no more dangerous than the infidels, the pagans or believers in other Christian faiths. Moreover, it is pointless to persecute or exile them, since, as had happened in other countries, such measures serve only to consolidate and confirm their religious convictions. The only option open to the Catholics is that of pacific coexistence within civil society, as was taught by the Fathers of the Church. The anonymous author of the *Traité* deliberately does not dwell on the ways in which religious concord should be achieved or implemented, but devotes the entire work to a demonstration of how heretics can live in peace and observe the laws of civil society by, like all other citizens, obeying the rules which regulate the social order. The author also maintains that the heretics cannot be punished when they err out of ignorance, a concept which was to become central to the thought of Bayle.

Within the sphere of Huguenot thought, there were numerous promoters of religious toleration, including D'Huisseau, Isaac Papin and Gédéon Huet. These writers maintained the possibility of distinguishing between fundamental and inessential doctrines of the Christian religion. Accordingly, believers should come together on essentials and be tolerant of disagreement over non-essentials. Such suggestions provoked strong reactions on the part of the 'zealots'; Jurieu accused these critics of Socinianism or even atheism.

As early as 1667, in his *Essay on Toleration*, John Locke had outlined the framework for a liberal and tolerant society. But after his exile in Holland, when he came into contact with Huguenot and Dutch Protestant thought, he elaborated his views in *Two Treatises of Government* and *A Letter Concerning Toleration*. Some credit for his more sustained analysis is due to the extensive, and often clandestine, Huguenot pamphleteers whose work we have discussed.

A GLANCE AHEAD

In 1763, outraged by the judicial murder of the Huguenot Jean Calas, Voltaire, in his *Traité sur la tolérance*, returns to one of his favourite themes: civil toleration. Familiar with Huguenot pamphlets, but above all with the extensive arguments of Bayle, he adopts Locke's arguments for civil toleration and subordination of religious matters to the authority of the magistrate. The only limitation to toleration concerns defence of public order, and each sect should uphold the political structure of society at large. In spite of being obliged to adopt a more cautious tone than the Protestants, he analysed aspects of ancient and pagan history and the customs of Middle Eastern peoples in relation to their creeds. In many respects, Voltaire is closer to Bayle than to Locke in the extent to which he upholds toleration. He recognizes that Christians themselves had promoted intolerance. In spite of his moderate tone, his work goes beyond the professions of faith by which Bayle and Locke felt themselves to be bound, even bringing into question the dogmatic heritage of Christianity and the possibility of a natural religion devoid of fanaticism (see Laursen and Nederman 1996 and 1998). Such reflections, elaborated both in his own works and those of his contemporaries, were indissolubly linked to the development of civil liberty and the progress of Enlightenment.

REFERENCES

Ancillon, Charles (1688) *L'Irrévocabilité de l'edit de Nantes*, Amsterdam.

[Ancillon, Charles attrib.] (1690) *La France interessée a rétablir l'Edit de Nantes*.

—— (1574) *Declaration des causes qui ont meu ceux de la Religion à reprendre les armes pour leur conservatio*, Montauban.

—— (1585) *Remonstrance des Catholiques pacifiques, pour la paix*.

—— (1591) *Discours sur une question d'estat de ce temps*.

—— (1599) *De la Concorde de l'Estat par l'observation des Edicts de Pacification*.

—— (1678) *Traité de la liberté de religion*, London.

—— (1683) *Lettre au Roy Tres-Chrestien*.

Bayle, Pierre (1682) *Critique générale de l'histoire du Calvinisme de Mr Maimbourg*, Amsterdam.

—— (1683) *Pensées Diverses, ecrites a un Docteur de Sorbonne, a l'occasion de la Comete qui parut au mois de Decembre 1680*, Rotterdam.

—— (1686) *Ce que c'est que la France toute Catholique*, Amsterdam.

—— (1686) *Commentaire philosophique sur ces paroles de Jesus-Christ contrain-les d'entrer*, Amsterdam.

—— [and Larroque, Daniel de ?] (1690) *Avis important aux réfugiés sur leur prochain retour en France*, The Hague.

—— (1697) *Dictionnaire historique et critique*, Rotterdam.

Boétie, Estienne de la (1577) *Discours de la servitude volontaire*.

[Brutus, Junius, pseud.] (1579) *Vindiciae contra tyrannos*, Edinburgh.

—— (1581) *De la puissance legitime du prince sur le peuple, et du peuple sur le prince. Traité tres-utile et digne de lecture en ce temps, escrit en Latin par Estienne Junius Brutus*.

Crouzet, Denis (1996) *La Genèse de la Réforme française 1520–1562*, Paris: SEDES.

Daussy, Hugues (2002) *Les Huguenots et le Roi: Le Combat politique de Philippe Duplessis-Mornay (1572–1600)*, Geneva: Droz.

Duplessis-Mornay, Philippe (1574) *Exortation à la paix aux Catholiques François*, Poitiers.

—— (1585) *Lettres particulieres envoyez au Roy, par un gentilhomme françoy*.

Gentillet, Innocent (1574) *Remonstrance au Roy Tres Chrestien Henry III. de ce nom, Roy de France et de Pologne, sur le faict des deux Edicts de sa Maiesté donnés a Lyon, l'un du X. de Septembre, et l'autre du XIII. d'Octobre dernier passé, présente année 1574: Touchant la nécessité de la paix, et moyens de la faire*, Frankfurt.

—— (1576) *Discours sur le moyens de bien gouverner et maintenir en bonne paix un Royaume ou autre Principauté, divisez en trois partes à savoir du Conseil, de la Religion et Police, que doit tenir un Prince: Contre Nicolas Machiavel Florentin*.

Grandjean, Michel and Roussel, Bernard (eds) (1998) *Coexister dans l'intolérance*: L'Edit de Nantes, 1598, 'Histoire et Société', 37, Geneva: Labor et Fides.

Graverol, Jean (1687) *Instructions pour les Nicodemites, où après avoir convaincu ceux qui sont tombez de la grandeur de leur crime, on fait voir qu'aucune violence ne peut dispenser les hommes de l'obligation de professer la verité*, Amsterdam.

Guggisberg, Hans R., Lestringant, Frank and Margolin, Jean-Claude (eds) (1991) *La Liberté de conscience XVIe–XVIIe siècles*, Actes de Colloque de Mulhouse et Bâle, 1989, *Etudes de Philologie et d'Histoire*, 44, Geneva: Droz.

L'Hospital, M. de (1561) *Proposition et harangue faite par Monsieur le Chancelier de France, sur le fait de la religion, en la ville de Poissy . . . Imprimé nouvellement*.

Jouanna, Arlette (1996) *La France du XVIe siècle 1483–1598*, Paris: Presses Universitaires de France.

Jouanna, Arlette, Boucher, Jacqueline, Biloghi, Dominique and Le Thiec, Guy (eds) (1998) *Histoire et dictionnaire des guerres de religion*, Paris: Robert Laffont.

[Jurieu, Pierre] (1686) *Lettres pastorales aux fidèles de France*, Rotterdam.

—— (1687) *Des Droits des deux souverains en matière de religion*, Rotterdam.

—— (1691) *Examen d'un libelle contre la religion, contre l'état et contre la revolution d'Angleterre. Intitulé: 'Avis important aux réfugiés sur leur prochain retour en France'*, The Hague.

Laursen, John Christian and Nederman, Cary J. (eds) (1996) *Difference and Dissent: Theories of Toleration in Medieval and Early Modern Europe*, Lanham, Md. and London: Rowman & Littlefield.

—— (eds) (1998) *Beyond the Persecuting Society: Religious Toleration before the Enlightenment*, Philadelphia: University of Pennsylvania Press.

Locke, John (1667) *Essay on Toleration*.

—— (1689) *A Letter Concerning Toleration*, London.

—— (1690) *Two Treatises of Government*, London.

Merlat, Elie (1685) *Traité de pouvoir absolu des Souverains, pour servir d'instruction, de consolation et d'apologie aux Eglises Reformées de France qui sont affligees*, Cologne.

Noüe, François de la (1587) *Discours politiques et militaires*, Basle.

Papin, Isaac (1687) *La Foy réduite à ses veritables principes et renfermée dans ses justes bornes*.

Saurin, Elie (1697) *Réflexions sur les droits de la conscience*, Utrecht.

Serres, Jean (1597) *Voeu pour la prospérité du Roy et du Royaume, l'an mil cin cens nonantes sept*, Paris.

Solé, Jacques (1997) *Les Origines intellectuelles de la Révocation de l'Edit de Nantes, Saint-Etienne: Publications de l'Université de Saint-Etienne*.

Turchetti, Mario (1998) 'L'arrière-plan politique de l'édit de Nantes, avec un aperçu de l'anonyme "De la concorde de l'Estat. Par l'observation des Edicts de Pacification"', in Grandjean, Michel and Roussel, Bernard (eds) *Coexister dans l'intolérance, op. cit.*: 93–114.

Versé, Aubert de (1684) *Le Protestant pacifique*, Amsterdam.

—— (1687) *Traité de la liberté de conscience ou de l'autorité des souverains sur la religion des peuples*, Cologne.

Voltaire (1763) *Traité sur la tolérance*, Geneva.

Yardeni, Myriam (1971) *La Conscience nationale en France pendant les guerres de religion (1559–1598)*, Publication de la Faculté des lettres et sciences humaines de Paris-Sorbonne, Série Recherches, t. 59; Travaux du Centre de recherches sur la civilisation de l'Europe moderne, facs. 8; Louvain: Editions Nauwelaerts; Paris: Béatrice-Nauwelaerts.

PART II

ASPECTS OF ENLIGHTENMENT FORMATIONS

INTRODUCTION

Martin Fitzpatrick

One way of viewing the Enlightenment is to see it as a movement which originated in the leading Protestant countries of Europe, England and the United Provinces, spilled over into neighbouring countries, and moved decisively into France during the period of the regency of Philip of Orleans. Thereafter, with Montesquieu and Voltaire at its head, the French assumed leadership of the movement which they never relinquished. This interpretation would appear to be persuasive, explaining Enlightenment origins and later the key position of France. It is certainly true that almost all the leading figures in early Enlightenment thought were English, Dutch or lived for some time in England or the United Provinces: for example, Grotius, Descartes, Bacon, Locke, Newton and Bayle. Shaftesbury, with his notion of Enlightenment as a movement casting light from the more enlightened nations to the less, and his euphoric expectation that it would 'spread itself over the whole world', captured the sense of Enlightenment leadership emanating from that part of Europe.

Shaftesbury was writing at a time when the achievements of Newton and Locke were beginning to make a considerable impact, but it was the Dutch republic which set the early example. As Hugh Dunthorne (Chapter 6) shows, the republic stood for liberty and independence. The Dutch prided themselves on the fact that self-government, unlike foreign tyranny, was good government. It made for a prosperous nation and society. The rule of law, equality before the law, religious toleration and the humane treatment of citizens were virtues also associated with prosperity. Such arguments were fortified by the success of the Dutch in wars against Spain and France, by their advanced financial systems and commercial dominance which made the republic the envy of Colbert. Dutch society was respectful of new knowledge and receptive to new ideas. Press freedom, albeit at times haphazard, made it attractive to authors and 'the intellectual entrepôt of Europe'. The number of printers and publishers in Amsterdam was astonishing at that time, as was the range of works published. No wonder so many French writers published their works in Amsterdam, many of which subsequently circulated clandestinely in less free countries, including their own.

The complex mix of freedom and repression which could be found in Europe at this time was a factor in assisting the success of the idea of a cosmopolitan republic of letters. Enlightenment thinkers often had more in common with writers, correspondents and readers in other countries than with the other social groups in their own. It is significant that Huguenots, who had experienced repression (French) and freedom (Dutch), played such a significant part in the creation and development of the republic of letters, so deliberately fostered by Pierre Bayle. They also played a crucial role in ensuring that the language of the Enlightenment would be French – it is doubtful whether this would have happened without them, whatever the contemporary belief of the French that their language and culture were superior to all others. Yet it was not a French émigré but a Portuguese Jew, Spinoza, who added a further dimension to Dutch Enlightenment. His works were highly influential, but were so offensive to the authorities and conventional thinkers that they had to be distributed in secret. He proved a key figure in the development of a clandestine Enlightenment which existed and overlapped with public Enlightenment. Its existence allowed Enlightenment thinkers to express themselves in different ways, including clandestine manuscripts for the advanced few, clandestine publications for the enlightened cognoscenti and expurgated works for the literate many. The cosmopolitan network of enlightened thinkers would also be furthered by the development of Freemasonry.

The fact that Enlightenment had a clandestine aspect to it qualifies Shaftesbury's notion of it as a mighty light. Alexander Murdoch (Chapter 7) shows how a diffusionist view of Enlightenment is simplistic, both in terms of chronology and geography. Within Britain there were Enlightenments with different emphases, national or provincial, rural or urban, with complex interconnections both within Britain and between Britain and the Continent. London could be a generator for Enlightenment elsewhere (as Paris would for distant parts of France) and an exporter of ideas, yet it could also receive ideas from the Continent not only directly from Holland or France but also via Scottish thinkers. Scotland, of course, was not only receptive to Enlightenment ideas coming directly from the Continent but to the new Newtonian science from south of the border. Scots were among the first to teach Newtonian mathematics; one of the best expositions of Newtonian science for the educated layman was written by a Scot, Colin Maclaurin.

Martin Mulsow's (Chapter 8) investigation of the early Enlightenment in Germany is indicative of the diversity within Enlightenment thought at this time. In Germany this mirrored the variety of political structures within the Holy Roman Empire. The development of Enlightenment, as elsewhere, reflected in part political needs. As Germany recovered from the Thirty Years war there was a need for an educated elite capable of transforming the fortunes of their countries. At the same time as German states were drawn into the conflict between Louis XIV, the United Provinces and Britain, they were also increasingly influenced by early Enlightenment thinking in those countries. Stolle and his companions were travelling through Prussia and Hanover when they were both at war with the France of Louis XIV. It does not seem to have affected their perambulations. The anti-French coalition forces under the Duke of Marlborough were operating in southern Germany. Further north, Stolle could sample all the trends in early Enlightenment culture. A key aspect of his quest was to find a suitable religion for new enlightened times. While eclecticism was the order of the day and would indeed continue to find favour in the Enlightenment, partly because it was associated with a non-partisan approach to knowledge, the constituents of Enlightenment thought needed to have a degree of consistency. Old attitudes towards the Bible, heresy, persecution, witchcraft, the devil and all his works were being challenged. Proponents of new thinking, such as Thomasius, were operating on the boundaries of acceptability, and part of their skill was to express their ideas in such a way as to make prosecution difficult, but their meaning clear. The intellectual journey often had unusual twists and turns, as well as unpredictable endings, such as Speeth's conversion to Judaism. Mystical and spiritualist traditions mixed with new ideas on the reasonableness of Christianity influenced by the new science. Enthusiasm and reason found unusual combinations at the beginning of the Enlightenment as they did at the end.

Both Dutch and British societies were freer and more tolerant than the larger monarchical kingdoms of Europe. Commercial society and toleration were felt to go hand in hand, and foreign commentators agreed. The belief that what was right was also beneficial became a commonplace of enlightenment thought. In 1744 Lord Chief Justice Willes ruled that treating infidels as perpetual enemies was contrary to 'common sense and common humanity' as well as to scripture. He went on to declare, 'besides the irreligion of it, it is a most impolitic notion and would at once destroy all that trade and commerce from which this nation reaps such great benefits' (Salbstein 1982: 31). When the Danish city of Altona sought to rival Hamburg, it introduced a policy of toleration in order to encourage trade and prosperity. As I note (Chapter 9), Voltaire contrasted the toleration in England favourably with French intolerance. Toleration would become a defining feature of Enlightenment campaigning to improve society. It would be so, because absolute monarchs proved reluctant to accept enlightened arguments. Toleration was associated with freedom of thought which was subversive of the social order. Divine right absolutism, moreover, viewed the state as a religious entity, the king as God's lieutenant on earth, and not only regarded Protestantism as heretical, but thought toleration would lead to even more subversive ideas. Enormous effort was invested in preventing the circulation of ideas critical of orthodox religion and that included those which did not accord with the dominant religious currents at court. When censorship was reorganized in France in 1699 and the Abbé Bignon became director of the book trade (see Chapter 22), over half of the sixty or so censors under his control spent their time checking religious works. Works of piety were subject to policing, as were less orthodox works, and the policy continued even in the regime of Malesherbes, friend of the *philosophes*, who ventured to suggest that the works of Father Quesnel might have been more harmful that those of Spinoza.

Toleration was also associated with societies which enjoyed Addisonian sociability, societies in which intellectual life had moved beyond the academies and universities to the clubs and coffee houses. This was a deliberate strategy on Addison's part, for he wrote:

> It was said of Socrates that he brought philosophy down from heaven, to inhabit among men; and I shall be ambitious to have it said of me, that I have brought Philosophy out of the closets and libraries, schools and colleges, to dwell in clubs and assemblies, at tea-tables and in coffee-houses.
>
> (*Spectator*, 10, 12 March 1710/11)

The *Spectator* and the *Tatler* would be imitated all over Europe. They came to be viewed as essential ingredients in Enlightenment culture. If the pretensions of their editors now seem overblown, if not ridiculous, they are indicative of that Enlightenment optimism expressed by Shaftesbury. In the prospectus for the Edinburgh weekly *The Bee*, James Anderson outlined his editorial ambitions thus:

> The world *at large* he considers as the proper theatre for literary improvements, and the whole human race, as constituting but one great society, whose general advancement in knowledge must tend to augment the prosperity of all its parts.
> (*The Bee* 1790: viii; cited by Klancher 1987: 25)

While rulers could be drawn down the route of encouraging journals – and perhaps none more so than Catherine the Great of Russia – the sociability they encouraged could be a cause for concern. Margaret C. Jacob (Chapter 17) notes how Catholic authorities equated polite sociability with licence and irreligion, and the concern of the Inquisitions in Italy, Spain and Avignon about the social mixing of Christian and Jew. Court-sponsored institutions were much safer. Thus Philip V (1700–46), the first Bourbon king of Spain, would follow the example of his grandfather Louis XIV in such matters. He established academies of language (1713), medicine (1734) and history (1738). Versailles set the pattern and pace for other rulers, too, for almost all rulers from the highest to the lowest felt that they had to follow Louis XIV and demonstrate their power and significance by living in courtly magnificence. The cultural adornment of power was an essential part of the process, but although politeness was essential for courtiers, critical thinking was not. One should not, however, think of the court in the narrow sense of those who surround monarchs in their palaces. The court set the standard for the elite in society who maintained loyalty to monarchy even as they queried some of its values. For all the significance of the Dutch and English/British examples, the French pattern of Enlightenment established at the very outset of Louis XIV's personal reign, especially through the efforts of Colbert, would eventually become dominant.

Courts did not exist in isolation; they were invariably in or nearby capital cities, notably Berlin, Vienna, Madrid, St Petersburg and, of course, Paris. Just as Versailles provided the supreme example for court culture, Paris set the example followed by other cities within and outside France. It is worth bearing in mind that France, with a population of about 20 million, was the largest and most populous country in Europe, and during the eighteenth century the population would increase by some 5–7 million people. Although London was almost double the size of Paris (the population of which was about 600,000 at the end of the century), there were more substantial cities in France than in Britain – Bordeaux, Lyon, Marseille and Rouen. These would have their academies and libraries, salons and clubs. Perhaps most important of these were the provincial academies. Daniel Roche estimates (1993: 438–9) that three-quarters of the cities with populations of over 20,000 had academies and that there were roughly forty cities in the category. Following the pattern established in Paris in Louis XIV's reign, they 'everywhere saw their link to the monarchy as the justification for their existence'. Yet they did develop a critical spirit and increasingly became progenitors of schemes for the public good. Their membership would include the names of leading *philosophes*, and although exclusive (about 6,000 were involved) they would increasingly reach out to the public.

Among monarchies, the great exception to this paradigm was Britain, where the monarchy was limited and the court was different in character from that in the rest of Europe. The Hanoverians did not live in palatial splendour, nor did they surround themselves with innumerable courtiers. The city rather than the court determined the pattern of Enlightenment. Of course, there were patrons in eighteenth-century Britain, including politicians seeking to influence the political nation and wealthy patrons wishing to show off their Enlightenment credentials, but the monarch was just one among them, and the market to a considerable extent was the major factor in cultural and intellectual exchange. Addison had deliberately encouraged Enlightenment in the public spaces provided by town and cities. Although he attempted to lay down the parameters for polite conversation, in comparison with formal institutions such as universities and academies, these informal urban developments challenged court-sponsored Enlightenment. If the practices of the British, Dutch and some of the German states could not be completely replicated elsewhere, primarily because of their freer political structures, the development of sociability and with it a wider public for enlightened ideas would create strains not only in the cultural formation of court societies but also in the relationship between the writers, their patrons, their institutional affiliations and their public. Yet not even the more liberal societies could accept all of the challenging new ideas, especially those relating to religion.

Writers in the early days of the Enlightenment tried to find appropriate ways of communicating with very different audiences. They were quite capable of speaking with several voices. Newton kept his millenarian and Socinian ideas out of his published works. Thomas Burnet confined the full exposition of his millenarian ideas to the original Latin edition of his *Sacred Theory of the Earth* (Part II, 1689; English trans., 1690). The Dutch Calvinist minister Balthasar Bekker attacked witchcraft in his *De Betoverde Weereld* (1691) – *The World Bewitched*, but carefully omitted the anti-Catholic passages from the French translation, *Le Monde enchanté*. Only clandestine works, such as the *Three Impostors*, took no account of the sensitivities of the audience, or rather enjoyed speaking their mind to the fortunate few. There are about 200 catalogued copies of the manuscript treatise, considerably more than any other clandestine work of the early Enlightenment period. That gives some indication of the size of the audience and the nature of its influence.

Writers had to make their own compromises, dependent on the society in which they lived, the source of their livelihood and their own personalities. The Curé Meslier was an atheist and yet remained in the Church all his life. He was imprisoned in 1716 for subversive preaching, but for the most part he kept his radical thoughts to himself, leaving on his death three copies of *Mémoire* of his thoughts. Extracts circulated clandestinely and were known to Voltaire, who published one. The subterfuges employed concerning religion would later in the eighteenth century be used more dangerously in relation to politics. Yet, as this part demonstrates, many of the tensions which proved so creative when Enlightenment was at its height were present at the outset.

REFERENCES

Klancher, Jon P. (1987) *The Making of English Reading Audiences, 1790–1832*, Madison and London: University of Wisconsin Press.

Roche, Daniel (1993) *La France des Lumières*, Paris: Fayard; trans. Arthur Goldhammer (1998) as *France in the Enlightenment*, Cambridge, Mass., and London: Harvard University Press.

Salbstein, M. C. N. (1982) *The Emancipation of the Jews in Britain. The Question of the Admission of the Jews to Parliament, 1828–1860*, Toronto and London: Associated University Presses.

CHAPTER SIX

THE DUTCH REPUBLIC

'That mother nation of liberty'

Hugh Dunthorne

One of the earliest allusions to the dawning of an Age of Enlightenment in Europe occurs in a letter of the philosopher 3rd Earl of Shaftesbury, written in 1706 to the theologian and journalist Jean Le Clerc. 'There is a mighty light,' Shaftesbury observes, 'which spreads itself over the whole world, especially in those two free nations of England and Holland, on whom the affairs of all Europe now turn' (Gay 1967: 11). As a way of describing the growth and diffusion of knowledge and ideas, the metaphor of light was to become increasingly familiar. But why did Shaftesbury apply it particularly to Holland, the country in which he had been living a couple of years earlier and where Le Clerc spent most of his adult life? Was he conscious of a specifically Dutch Enlightenment? And how might he have defined the role of the Netherlands in the wider European Enlightenment of these early years?

PROPAGANDA AND PUBLIC INTEREST

Any attempt to answer these questions must begin with the Dutch Republic itself, 'that mother nation of liberty', as Shaftesbury called it on another occasion (Haley 1988: 179). Around 1700 it was still a relatively new state, one which had emerged only a century earlier out of the flames of the Low Countries' rebellion against Spanish misrule and which had quickly acquired an enviable reputation for good government, economic prosperity and freedom. That reputation was largely of the Hollanders' own making. Fighting Spain had forced them to become propagandists as well as soldiers, and during the course of the war (1568–1648) and for some time afterwards reams of material were produced by the printing presses of the Netherlands in order to justify their cause and trumpet their successes. This propaganda was successful, too. Europeans became fascinated by the story of the rise of the Dutch Republic as well as by what they saw when they visited the country, as, in growing numbers, they did. And by the later seventeenth century (the period which historians now call the early Enlightenment), foreigners as well as native Netherlanders were writing and publishing works on the recent history and present state of the Dutch Republic. One of the earliest and most perceptive of these accounts was Sir William Temple's

Observations upon the United Provinces of the Netherlands, first printed in London in the spring of 1673. It is a work worth exploring briefly for what it can tell us about the reputation that the Netherlands state and society enjoyed in the late seventeenth century, and indeed continued to enjoy for much of the eighteenth.

At the time when he wrote the *Observations*, Temple was best known as a diplomat, having served during the 1660s as Charles II's ambassador in the Spanish Netherlands, as well as in the Dutch Republic. But he was also a man of the Enlightenment (though the term itself was not yet current) and he was soon to be numbered among Britain's leading freethinkers. He was influenced by the new scientific mentality of his time and was in some senses a political scientist, a pioneer of what later generations would call the 'science of man'. Anticipating Montesquieu, he paid attention to factors like climate and physical geography. Like the philosophical historians of the next century, he held that 'most national customs are the effect of some unseen, or unobserved, natural causes or necessities' (Temple 1673: 81). And, as Voltaire was to do in his *Letters Concerning the English Nation* (1733), Temple approached his subject in the belief not only that it was interesting in itself but also that lessons could be learned from his analysis by the rulers of other countries, including his own.

A STATE TO BE EMULATED

Temple was an admirer of the Netherlands; but he was not uncritical, being concerned to correct certain received opinions and popular misconceptions about the country. In analysing the Dutch Revolt, for example, he argued that the Netherlanders' hatred of Spanish misrule had been a stronger motive for rebellion than 'love for their liberties', pointing out that the rule of their own magistrates under the new Republic was hardly less 'absolute' than that of the hated Spaniards which it replaced (Temple 1673: 34–6). The difference lay not in the extent of the government's power but rather in the quality of those who now rose to high office and in the fact that those in authority did not exploit their public position for private gain. Government by assembly or committee, which existed at all levels in the Dutch Republic, was in Temple's opinion an effective way of enabling the ablest administrators and policy-makers to emerge. And, although the regime was oligarchical not democratic, its members could not afford to ignore the country's active and well-informed public opinion (Temple 1673: 68–9, 70–2). Dutch laws might be harsh, but they treated everyone impartially; and although taxes were high, they were accepted because they were used to promote the welfare of the whole community – for example, in the various charitable institutions which Temple admired (as did many other visitors to the Low Countries), though he was aware that they also served as a means of social control (Temple 1673: 86–8). Temple's affinities with the Enlightenment are no less apparent in his chapter on the religious life of the Netherlands, providing both an analysis of the system of religious toleration for which the Dutch Republic had already become famous (or notorious, depending on one's point of view) and a demonstration of the benefits which he believed such a system brought. Like John Locke's later writings on toleration, Temple's argument was more practical than theological. Tolerance of those who dissented from the state Church was desirable, he believed, because it ensured 'civil peace' and social harmony, allowing people to live together as the Dutch themselves did – 'like citizens of the world, associated by the common ties of humanity and by the bonds of peace . . . with equal encouragement of all art and equal freedom of speculation and enquiry' (Temple 1673: 106–7). Toleration was good for business too, since it encouraged immigration into the country and so increased its density of population, which Temple considered one of the two pillars of Dutch economic prosperity. The other pillar was the rule of law, as distinct from arbitrary rule. Trade would flourish, he believed, only where government was trusted and property secure – and both conditions were fulfilled in the Dutch Republic (Temple 1673: 109–15).

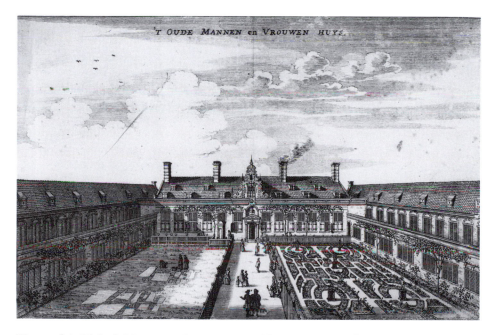

Figure 6.1 *'T Oude Mannen en Vrouwen Huys*, old people's home from Dapper's *Historische beschryving der stadt Amsterdam*. During the seventeenth and eighteenth centuries the towns of the Dutch Republic were widely admired for their institutions of social welfare. This print, from a description of Amsterdam published in 1663, shows the old men's and old women's home on the Oudezijdsvoorburgwal. It accommodated citizens over fifty years of age who were unable to live alone; in return, their own property was forfeited to the institution. By permission of Gemeentearchief (the Municipal Archives), Amsterdam.

Temple's account of Dutch government and society, summarized here, was by no means the only book of its kind. Others soon followed, including several works by Huguenot refugees, such as François Michel Janiçon's *Etat présent de la République des Provinces-Unies* (1729). Yet, for all its imitators, Temple's book proved the most enduring of these accounts – and probably the most influential. Between its initial publication in 1673 and the mid-eighteenth century, it went through no fewer than eight English editions, besides being translated into French and Dutch. It provided David Hume and other Scots writers with most of what they knew about the growth of the Dutch economy, while it supplied the founding fathers of the American Republic with insights into federalism. The English deist Anthony Collins quoted Temple at length on the political and social advantages of religious liberalism (Collins 1724: xxxi–xxxiv). Nor is it surprising that Temple's concluding *bon mot* on this subject – 'Religion may possibly do more good in other places, but it does less hurt here' (Temple 1673: 107) – should have proved irresistible to Diderot, who reproduced it word for word (without acknowledgement) in his 'Voyage de Hollande' (Diderot 1773: 432).

By the time Diderot visited the country in 1773, Temple was in some respects decidedly out-of-date. The Dutch Republic was no longer the great power that it had been a century earlier. Its economy was partially in decline, and corruption was seeping into its government. Yet, however idealized, the image of the Netherlands which Temple and others had projected – of a free nation, well governed, educated, tolerant and prosperous – continued to be valued precisely because it *was* an ideal, and thus an inspiration to rulers and policy-makers in an age of enlightened reform. Dutch ways of doing things continued to be emulated, from commercial and industrial techniques to policies of toleration, education and penal justice. In the middle decades of the eighteenth century, for example, British advocates of penal reform, from Bishop Berkeley to John Howard, repeatedly referred to the Dutch houses of correction as models of humane and effective punishment and urged the adoption of a similar penal regime in Britain (Berkeley 1735–7: 109; Howard 1777: 44–6) – a process eventually set in motion with the passing of the Penitentiary Act in 1779 (Beattie 1986: 549–54, 568–76).

IMMIGRATION AND INTERNATIONAL PUBLISHING

One important part of Holland's role in the early Enlightenment, then, was to set an example to Europe, to show how a well-administered state could flourish. Moreover, the early reputation of the Dutch Republic as a model community had practical consequences which allowed it to contribute to European intellectual life in a second and more direct way. For good government and prosperity were qualities that did more than attract attention and encourage emulation. They also attracted thousands of immigrants, including a significant number of writers, printers and booksellers.

Many of those who came to the Dutch Republic were fleeing from religious persecution at home – Calvinists from the Spanish Netherlands, such as the printer Louis Elsevier; Bohemian and Moravian Protestants, among them Comenius, the educationalist; Socinians (i.e., Unitarians) from Poland and dissenters of various kinds from France, including the Jansenist Antoine Arnauld and the Huguenot Pierre Bayle. Other newcomers were political refugees. During and after the English Civil War royalists like Bishop John Bramhall and the London bookseller Samuel Browne moved to the Netherlands (Keblusek 2001: 151–8), as did members of the Whig opposition, including John Locke and Gilbert Burnet, in the 1680s. Others again were victims of public criticism, as in the case of Anthony Collins, who retreated to Holland in 1713 following the publication of his controversial *Discourse of Free-Thinking*.

Yet, whatever the varying circumstances which drove these émigrés out of their own countries, the conditions which attracted them to the Dutch Republic were always much the same. As René Descartes remarked of the society in which he lived for twenty years, the Hollanders were 'a great people' who offered the scholar 'repose as well as liberty' (Schama 1981: 59). And liberty meant not only freedom of thought and of conscience but also freedom of the press. This is not to say that publishing in the Netherlands was entirely unrestricted. Especially at times of domestic or international tension, publications on religion or politics that were considered blasphemous or seditious could be banned by provincial or municipal authorites and fines could be imposed on authors and publishers. Yet, thanks to the uncentralized character of the Dutch state and to the commercial priorities of its rulers, controls of this kind were haphazardly imposed, allowing the press much greater latitude than it had elsewhere in Europe. It is thus unsurprising that the province of Holland, where most of the country's printers were based, should have been called 'the Mecca of authors' by a French writer in 1687 (Groenveld 1987: 63), nor that a modern scholar should describe the Dutch Republic of the seventeenth and eighteenth centuries as 'unquestionably the intellectual entrepôt of Europe' (Gibbs 1971: 323). For, just as Dutch merchants and seafarers had established their pre-eminence by the mid-seventeenth century as the commercial carriers of Europe and Dutch towns had become the great commodity market of the Continent, where goods and services of every kind were bought and sold, so by the 1660s those same towns had won an unrivalled position in the international publishing industry and Dutch booksellers were making themselves indispensable as traders in print to Europe's republic of letters. In Holland in 1600 there were 55 printing presses; by 1675 this had increased to 203, with more than half of that number in Amsterdam alone. Some 230 booksellers are recorded as doing business in the city between 1680 and 1710.

What these presses printed and what Dutch booksellers and their agents abroad distributed was extremely varied, ranging from Bibles to newspapers and embracing, according to a German traveller in Holland, 'all literary tongues known to Europe' (Barbour 1963: 65). Good modern editions of Latin and Greek texts appeared, often in the cheap duodecimo format which the Dutch helped to pioneer. There were works in Oriental languages – Arabic, Hebrew, Aramaic and Syriac – for which the necessary type was at this time manufactured only in the Netherlands. Ancient and modern histories were published, alongside medical and other scientific treatises. And there were works of a radical or polemical kind, known in France as *livres de Hollande*, which had to be printed in the Netherlands because it was thought too dangerous to publish them in the country of their origin. Among philosophers who at one time or another found it necessary to publish their work in the Dutch entrepôt were Richard Simon, Fontenelle, Montesquieu, Voltaire, Holbach, La Mettrie and Rousseau. What is more, wherever sufficient sources survive to allow the activities of individual printers or booksellers to be reconstructed, that evidence invariably reveals the variety and geographical breadth of their business. Pieter van der Aa, for

Figure 6.2 *Huguenot Bookshops in Amsterdam*, from [Johannes Phoonsen] (1715) *Les Loix et les coutumes de change*, trans Jean Pierre Ricard, Amsterdam: E. Roger. Taken from the title-page of an early eighteenth-century guide to commercial exchange rates in Holland, this print shows the Amsterdam bookshops of François l'Honoré and Jaques Desbordes, two of the many Huguenot publishers who sought refuge in the Dutch Republic during the last quarter of the seventeenth century. Desbordes was the nephew of Pierre Bayle's printer, Henry Desbordes, and he continued the tradition of publishing French-language literary and political journals. By permission of Koninklijke Bibliotheek, The Hague.

example, heir to the Elsevier publishing dynasty at Leiden and from 1715 printer to the university, had contacts with fellow-booksellers in Berlin, Venice and Paris, as well as through the annual Frankfurt book fairs. He built up a catalogue of scholarly publications, ranging from the complete works of Erasmus (edited by Le Clerc) to Christiaan Huygens's treatise on the wave theory of light, and for the popular side of the market he produced a series of pocket-sized travel books covering Italy, Spain and Portugal, Britain and Ireland, ancient and modern Rome, and Switzerland. He supplied medical treatises and Latin classics to a leading London bookseller, published the voluminous geographical and geological studies of the Zurich professor Johann Jakob Scheuchzer, and provided the imperial library at St Petersburg with atlases and other works of reference (Hoftijzer 1992: 169–84).

A NEW KIND OF JOURNALISM

It could be argued that entrepreneurs such as van der Aa, for all their aggressive commercialism, were simply extending and expanding activities which had been undertaken in earlier times by members of the Venetian and German book trades. Yet, in one respect at least, the printers of the Netherlands and the authors whom they served were unquestionably pioneers. This was in developing, if not inventing, the new medium of the monthly literary and scientific journal, offering critical book reviews, scholarly news and occasional articles, all tailored to an international readership. The earliest of these journals, with the inspired title *Nouvelles de la République des Lettres*, was founded in 1684 by Pierre Bayle, in its first three years, largely written by him, and printed in Amsterdam by a fellow-Huguenot refugee, Henry Desbordes. Bayle's aim was to create a forum of ideas and information with the broadest possible appeal – moderate in opinion, informal and accessible in style, varied in content. Religion and theology were most noticed in its pages, but there was room also for history and literature, science and medicine. And good taste was carefully observed. If a piece was thought likely to prove shocking to some readers – as in the case of Antonij van Leeuwenhoek's letters on human reproduction – then it appeared decently clothed in Latin. Though banned in France after 1685, the journal continued to circulate there through the post and by other, more surreptitious means. And wherever French was understood it found a ready market – in the Low Countries and Italy, among Catholics and Protestants, scholars and amateurs.

Where Bayle and Desbordes led, others quickly followed. In 1686 Jean Le Clerc and a group of Amsterdam publishers launched the *Bibliothèque Universelle et Historique*, the journal in which the exiled Locke was persuaded to make his first forays into print. And over the next thirty years a dozen or so similar periodicals appeared in Holland, the majority edited by Huguenots and written in French, though several were in the hands of Dutch publishers, and one – Pieter Rabus's *Boekzaal van Europe*, founded in 1692 – was a wholly Dutch venture. Taken together, these Franco-Dutch journals performed an invaluable service, enabling readers across western Europe to keep abreast of new publications and new ideas, even if they lacked the means to acquire the books for themselves. It is the kind of service that we take for granted today, but in the 1680s it was quite new.

SPINOZISM AND TOLERATION

Besides setting an example to other states, then, the Dutch Republic also served the early Enlightenment by putting its ideas into print and distributing them across Europe and giving asylum to exiles of every kind. In Bayle's well-known phrase, Holland was 'the great ark of the refugees' (Bayle 1697: 2.255, 'Kuchlin'): 'the fatherland of philosophers', as a French émigré of the next generation called it (d'Argens 1737: 308). Yet, indispensable as these services were, they also raised doubts. Wasn't there something rather passive and menial about the role of the Dutch as middlemen in the international republic of letters? The Netherlanders seemed to be the artisans rather than the architects of the Enlightenment, its protectors rather than its protagonists. Where were the Dutch *philosophes* – the Dutch Montesquieu or the Dutch Hume? Was there no distinctively Dutch *intellectual* contribution to the early Enlightenment?

One way of answering these questions would be to point to the looming figure of Benedict de Spinoza, the pioneer of historically informed biblical criticism, the advocate of democratic republicanism as 'the most natural form of state', the pantheist who identified God with Nature and who denied the possibility of miracles because 'nothing . . . can happen in Nature to contravene her own universal laws' (Spinoza 1670: XVI, 243; VI, 126). Born into the Amsterdam community of Sephardic Jews, Spinoza did all his philosophical work in Holland, mixing with ecumenical Dutch Collegiants and even counting a few members of the Republic's political élite among his friends and protectors. Yet, for all that, it is difficult to see him as a representative figure in Dutch intellectual life. For one thing, Spinoza's work met with an overwhelmingly hostile reception in his own country. Condemned as 'utterly pestilential', 'profane, blasphemous and atheistic' (Israel 2001: 276, 292), both his *Tractatus Theologico-Politicus* (1670) and his *Opera Posthuma* (1677) were banned in Holland and Utrecht and had to be distributed in secret (with considerable success, it should be said). Second, though he attracted small circles of associates and followers in the towns of Holland and Overijssel – they included the lexicographer Lodewijk Meyer and the academic physicist Burchardus de Volder in Amsterdam, the jurist Abraham Johannes Cuffeler at The Hague and the liberal Calvinist minister Frederik van Leenhof in Zwolle – the 'radical Enlightenment' which his philosophy spawned was essentially a European movement rather than a Dutch one. In Holland, the clandestine cultivation of Spinoza's ideas had passed its peak by the 1720s (Israel 2001: 308). As the leading Netherlands historian of the Enlightenment has pointed out, 'a creative Dutch Spinozism . . . did not emerge before the nineteenth century' (Mijnhardt 1992: 204).

Yet, if Spinoza's radicalism placed him outside the mainstream of Dutch intellectual life, he did make an important contribution to one of its central debates. This was over religious toleration, which accompanied the gradual emergence of a practical system of confessional coexistence in the Netherlands. Such a sytem was not achieved easily; nor did it satisfy everyone. How far toleration should go, whether freedom of conscience implied freedom of public worship, whether it should embrace freedom of expression and even equality of civil status – these were always matters of intense controversy in the Dutch Republic. There, as elsewhere in Europe, the most eloquently argued pleas for tolerance often came from 'the disappointed' or 'the dispossessed' (Pettegree 1996: 198). Thus, around 1580, as militant Calvinists tightened their grip on Holland's towns and sought to have Catholicism banned, it was the Christian humanist Dirck Volckertsz Coornhert who defended liberty of conscience and of worship and upheld the freedom to publish on religious matters. The Bible, he pointed out, provided no authority for persecuting heretics. And since no one except God could be certain what was heresy and what was true religion, it was better to avoid all 'faction, dispute, condemnation, banishment and persecution' (Gelderen 1992: 243–56). Similarly, after the National Synod of Dordrecht in 1618–19 had upheld Calvinist orthodoxy and condemned liberal Arminianism, it was the Arminian Simon Episcopius who renewed Coornhert's plea. Challenging the conventional wisdom that religious uniformity was essential to a country's political and social stability, his *Vrije Godes-Dienst* (*Free Religion*; 1627) argued that permitting differences of opinion and of practice within and between coexisting Churches not only encouraged fruitful theological enquiry but also eliminated the feelings of resentment which would otherwise build up. A state offering its citizens religious freedom would earn their loyalty, though he conceded that a special oath of loyalty would be required from Dutch Catholics (Israel 1997: 19–20). And again, in the wake of anti-Socinian laws passed in Holland during the 1650s, it was Spinoza (among others) who took up the case for tolerance once more, stung into action by the death in prison of his fellow-radical Adriaen Koerbagh, whose crime was to have written books rejecting the doctrine of the Trinity and asserting that Jesus was not God but only a great teacher. Spinoza argued for religious toleration, of course. Anticipating Rousseau, he proposed a dominant ecumenical civil religion, with more modest Churches for dissenters. But his prime concern, set out in the *Tractatus Theologico-Politicus*, was to make the broader case for intellectual toleration. Implicit in man's inalienable 'freedom to judge and think as he pleases' was the right to publish, provided what was published did not conflict directly with the constitution of the state; and any attempt by confessional 'agitators' to restrain that right could only cause social discord (Spinoza 1670: XX, 291–9).

The Netherlands' debate over toleration – intellectual and religious – continued intermittently during the eighteenth century. Orthodox Calvinist attempts to ban the distribution of La Mettrie's materialist tract *L'Homme Machine* (1747), for example, prompted the book's Leiden publisher, Elie Luzac, to write a vigorous *Essai* (1749) in defence of 'freedom of expression' (Velema 1993: 6–22); while clerical objections to the appearance of Voltaire's *Traité sur la Tolérance* in Dutch translation (1764) provoked dissenters and liberal Calvinists into attacking the whole privileged position of the Dutch Reformed Church. They demanded a 'mutual toleration' that would have amounted to equality – and that was eventually achieved with the separation of Church and state under the new Batavian Republic in 1796 (Wall 2000: 115–27).

As the comparison of Spinoza with Rousseau suggests, there were affinities between the arguments for tolerance voiced by Netherlands writers of the seventeenth and eighteenth centuries and those used by writers in other countries. Reviewing Locke's first *Letter Concerning Toleration* (1689), Le Clerc pointed out how much it reflected Arminian teaching (Colie 1960: 126). And Bishop William Warburton

(1698–1779), writing in 1771, went further. For him, the Arminians of Holland were the 'Heroes' to whom 'this enlightened Age' was 'principally indebted' (Wall 2000: 125). Yet, it would be a mistake to regard the arguments of Coornhert, Episcopius and their successors as peculiarly Dutch. They were part of a common stock of more or less liberal ideas that stretched back to ancient times. What gave Dutch versions of these ideas greater force was the social context in which they took shape. For in the Netherlands, more than in any other European country, confessional coexistence had become an everyday experience, a workable and profitable way of life. It was this way of life, observed during his years of exile in the Netherlands, that caused Bishop Burnet to become 'much in love with toleration', and which he found more persuasive than any amount of speculative theory (Burnet 1724: 93–4).

ENLIGHTENED EDUCATION

Perhaps, then, we should look for a distinctively Dutch intellectual contribution to the early Enlightenment not in the ideas of a single philosopher, however radical, nor in those of a group of writers, however influential, but rather in the institutions which shaped Dutch society and culture. And no institutions were more formative than those which made up the Republic's system of education, from basic schooling up to university instruction. For this was a highly educated society – by the late seventeenth century perhaps the most literate and numerate in Europe. During the previous hundred years the northern Netherlands (and especially the maritime provinces of Holland, Friesland and Zeeland) had undergone something of an educational revolution, stimulated both by the Protestantization of the country and by the combined demands of commercial development and modern scientific warfare. In village after village during the late sixteenth century, the establishment of the first Calvinist minister was quickly followed by the installation of the first school-master 'to educate the children in reading, writing and reckoning and the catechism' (Vries 1974: 211). And in the towns, besides the common schools funded by the municipality, private commercial schools were soon springing up to teach arithmetic and book-keeping, as well as technical institutes such as the so-called Duytsche Mathematique, established at Leiden in 1600 to train surveyors and military and civil engineers, and Rotterdam's Collegium Mechanicum, founded in 1626. One symptom of the twin processes of education and commercialization was the early decline in the northern Netherlands of belief in witchcraft (Holland's last formal witchcraft trial, ending in acquittal, took place in 1614), for this was a society – it has been argued – whose mathematical conception of causality left little room for fears of sorcery and the supernatural (Waardt 1991: 201–8). Thus, when in 1691 the Cartesian Balthasar Bekker published *De Betoverde Weereld* (*The World Bewitched*), denying the devil's power to influence human life and the natural world, his views, for all the fuss that they caused among orthodox Calvinists, were not revolutionary or original but broadly in line with a developing popular tradition of reasoned scepticism.

The Dutch Republic's institutions of higher learning, and especially its five universities, were also characterized by trends in more sophisticated reasoning. Like the state itself, the universities were new institutions, founded between 1575 and 1636 at Leiden, Franeker (in Friesland), Harderwijk (in Gelderland), Groningen and Utrecht. Unimpeded by past scholastic traditions, they were able to explore new fields of study, such as physics and other natural sciences, and to develop new ways of teaching old disciplines, as with clinical instruction in medicine and post-mortem anatomy demonstrations. They were also well endowed financially, reflecting the wish of municipal and provincial authorities that the universities should be a means of winning international prestige for the young republic. Thus botanical gardens were planted; anatomy theatres, astronomical observatories and physics and chemistry laboratories were built, and equipped with growing collections of scientific instruments; and a cosmopolitan professoriate was appointed. At Groningen, for example, more than half the professors employed during the seventeenth century were foreigners. Since teaching was conducted in Latin, the result was to attract students from across Europe and – more importantly – to open the universities to currents of international thought. Despite initial disapproval from the authorities in Church and state, Cartesian rationalism was absorbed into the Dutch universities during the middle decades of the seventeenth century, and by 1700 the inductive experimental method associated with Robert Boyle and Isaac Newton was being assimilated, too. Willem 's Gravesande, professor of mathematics at Leiden, did more than anyone to introduce Newtonian science to Continental Europe – partly through the *Journal Littéraire*, which he edited from 1713 with Justus van Effen and the French émigré Prosper Marchand, partly through his lectures at the university (which Voltaire himself attended during the winter of 1736–7), and partly through publishing the first textbook on Newton's physics with detailed engravings of the instruments which he used in his lecture-demonstrations, a book whose original Latin text was quickly translated into various modern European languages ('s Gravesande 1720/1; Israel 1995: 1042).

Herman Boerhaave, 's Gravesande's older colleague, also lectured on Newton, notably in his rectorial address *De comparando certo in physicis* (*On the Achievement of Certainty in Physics*; Leiden, 1715). Moreover, he applied Newton's inductive method to his own fields of medicine, chemistry and botany, further strengthening the Leiden medical faculty's international reputation as a progressive centre of clinical teaching and empirical research. It was, indeed, as an inspiring teacher that Boerhaave was most widely known. His textbooks – *Institutes of Medicine* (1708), *Aphorisms on the Diagnosis and Treatment of Diseases* (1708) and *Elements of Chemistry* (1732) – were endlessly reprinted, pirated and translated, even into non-European languages such as Turkish and Japanese. And his students, the majority of whom came from outside the Netherlands and who included major figures, such as Albrecht von Haller (1708–77), Gerhard van Swieten (1700–72) and Alexander Monro (1697–1767), went on to found medical schools on the Leiden pattern in Berlin, Göttingen, Vienna and Edinburgh. At Leiden itself, ironically, the practice of clinical teaching was allowed to lapse for half a century after Boerhaave's death in 1738. But elsewhere in the Netherlands his legacy was sustained, notably in the work in clinical surgery and comparative anatomy undertaken at Groningen by one of his last pupils, Petrus Camper.

Figure 6.3 *Boerhaave Delivering a Rectorial Address on Newton*, engraving from the frontispiece of *Boerhaave's Orations* (1983) Leiden: Leiden University Press. The title-page of Boerhaave's *De comparando certo in physicis*, this engraving shows him giving his rectorial address to the University of Leiden on 8 February 1715, the first occasion on which the principles of Newtonian science were expounded to a Continental audience. A popular lecturer and a pioneer in the clinical teaching of medicine, Boerhaave continued to sustain Leiden's international reputation for more than twenty years. By permission of the Sir Thomas Browne Institute, University of Leiden. Photograph by permission of the National Library of Australia.

SCIENCE, RELIGION AND THE PROFESSIONS

The absorption into Dutch universities of first Cartesian and then Newtonian ideas did not mean that science was to be separated from religion. On the contrary, 's Gravesande, Boerhaave and their followers stressed the presence of divine providence in nature and contributed through their teaching to the growth of a Dutch tradition of 'physico-theology'. This was a term coined by the English scientist William Derham in his Boyle Lectures of 1711–12. But the idea which it conveyed, of nature as a form of divine revelation, was already current in the Netherlands. It underlay the entomological work of Jan Swammerdam in the later 1670s: 'the Almighty Finger of God', he believed, could be seen even 'in the anatomy of a louse, in which you will find wonder piled upon wonder and God's Wisdom clearly exposed in one minute particle' (Cook 1992: 140–1). And it found its most influential exponent in Bernard Nieuwentijt, physician and burgomaster of Purmerend in northern Holland. His *Regt Gebruick der Wereltbeschouwingen* (1715), translated into English as *The Religious Philosopher; or the Right Use of Contemplating the Works of the Creator . . . Designed for the Conviction of Atheists and Infidels* (1718) quickly became a best-seller not only in the Netherlands and Britain but in France and Germany too.

Moreover, while academics and members of the political elite sought to reconcile science and religion, the very structure of the faculties in the universities of the Netherlands also helped to link the new sciences to more traditional areas of the curriculum. Study in the arts faculty was regarded as a necessary preliminary to the professional education provided by the higher faculties of theology, law and medicine. And since it was in the arts faculty that mathematics and philosophy (including natural philosophy, or physics) were taught, many clergymen, lawyers and doctors went from university into their professional careers with more than a passing interest in the mathematical and natural sciences (Hackmann 1975: 96). It is thus not as incongruous as it might seem that the physicist and astronomer Christiaan Huygens should have begun by taking a law degree at Leiden, nor that Swammerdam should have been a graduate in medicine. Neither man went on to practise the profession for which he had been trained. But many who did – members of Holland's large professional middle class – were able to combine their ordinary duties with a lively taste for scientific enquiry. This explains the popularity of public scientific lectures, pioneered by Daniel Gabriel Fahrenheit in Amsterdam from 1718. And it explains, too, the fashion for exploring the natural history of the Netherlands and its overseas empire in illustrated books and collections of 'rarities'. In 1699 the German émigré artist Maria Sibylla Merian left Holland for Surinam, where she spent two years studying the insects and plants depicted in her *Metamorphosis insectorum Surinamensium* (Amsterdam 1705); while from the East Indies a decade later the missionary François Valentijn returned home to Dordrecht with a celebrated collection of Moluccan seashells and the idea of setting up a society of conchologists. When he did so in 1714, scientific societies were rare in the Netherlands. But the later eighteenth century would see them proliferate to an astonishing extent, from a minority of semi-official bodies like the Holland Society of Science (founded at Haarlem in 1752) to a much larger number of less formal local groups. By 1778

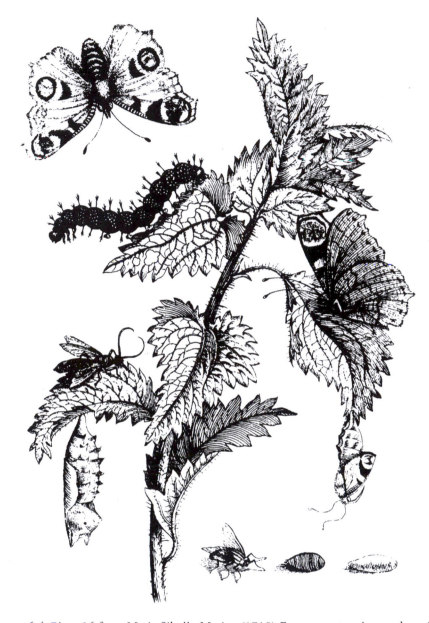

Figure 6.4 Plate 26 from Maria Sibylla Merian (1718) *Erucarum ortus*, Amsterdam; from facs. edn, *The Wondrous Transformation of Caterpillars* (1978) London: Scolar Press. Painter, engraver and pioneering entomologist, Maria Sibylla Merian did much to establish the study of plants and insects as a fashionable pastime during the eighteenth century. This plate, showing a peacock butterfly, an ichneumonid (below left) and a tachinid fly (below right) around a common nettle, comes from her earliest work, a study of European insects, originally published at Nuremberg in 1679 and later reissued in Dutch, Latin and French editions. It laid the foundations for her more famous book on the entomology of Surinam.

Haarlem had a second society, too, established on the initiative of the merchant Pieter Teyler van der Hulst. Known as Teyler's Museum, its collections can still be seen in the town today, housed and displayed much as they were in the 1780s.

TOWARDS THE LATER ENLIGHTENMENT

This chapter has suggested some of the ways in which the Dutch contributed to the early European Enlightenment: as members of an exemplary state and society, as intellectual entrepreneurs, and as enlightened educators. In all three capacities, their conduct was energetic, confident and forward-looking. Yet, by 1730 a change of direction is discernible, and with it a loss of confidence that was to darken the middle and later years of the eighteenth century. For, while foreign observers continued to think of the Dutch Republic much as Temple had described it in 1673, the Dutch themselves were uneasily aware of their country's decline – of its loss of international standing and growing burden of public debt, of moral corruption, social and religious tension and natural disasters. In the European war crisis of 1733 the republic retreated into diplomatic neutrality, partly for financial reasons, while other disasters loomed on the domestic front. Scarcely had Dutch self-esteem recovered from the 'sodomite scandal' and subsequent executions of 1730–1 than it was rocked by outbursts of anti-popery, the spread of cattle plague and reports that the country's sea-defences were being destroyed by a lethal and previously unknown species of pile-worm.

Signs of the growing anxiety caused by such developments can be found in the pages of a new literary journal, *De Hollandsche Spectator*, founded in 1731 by Justus van Effen as a Dutch imitation of the English *Spectator* of Joseph Addison. In some ways its tone was conventional enough. Socially conservative, it recommended reason and moderate religion as the guides to virtuous conduct. Yet, woven into van Effen's writing was a new concern about the republic's difficulties, and especially its waning international position. The cause of decline, he believed, was moral. Native Dutch virtue was being sapped by French manners and vices. The remedy lay in reviving the commercial culture of the seventeenth-century Dutch Republic. His message, in other words, was that the present must be reformed by looking to the past.

Van Effen was not alone in taking this view. It was a theme that was to be repeated with increasing conviction in Dutch public debate for much of the remainder of the eighteenth century, and it lent a retrospective and self-obsessed quality to the later years of the Dutch Enlightenment.

REFERENCES

Argens, J. B. de Boyer d', Marquis (1737) *Mémoires de Monsieur le Marquis d'Argens*, 2nd edn, 'Londres' [Amsterdam?].

Barbour, V. (1963) *Capitalism in Amsterdam in the Seventeenth Century*, Ann Arbor: University of Michigan Press.

Bayle, P. (1697) *Dictionnaire Historique et Critique*, Rotterdam: R. Leers.

Beattie, J. M. (1986) *Crime and the Courts in England 1660–1800*, Oxford: Clarendon Press.

Berkeley, G. (1735–7) *The Querist, Containing Several Queries Proposed to the Consideration of the Public*, ed. T. E. Jessop (1953) *Works of George Berkeley Bishop of Cloyne*, Edinburgh: Thomas Nelson.

Burnet, G. (1724) *A Supplement to Bishop Burnet's History of My Own Time*, ed. H. C. Foxcroft (1902) Oxford: Clarendon Press.

[Collins, A.] (1724) *A Discourse of the Grounds and Reasons of the Christian Religion*, repr. (1976) New York: Garland.

Colie, R. L. (1960) 'John Locke in the Republic of Letters', in J. S. Bromley and E. H. Kossmann (eds) *Britain and the Netherlands: Papers Delivered to the Oxford–Netherlands Historical Conference 1959*, London: Chatto & Windus.

Cook, H. J. (1992) 'The New Philosophy in the Low Countries', in R. Porter and M. Teich (eds) *The Scientific Revolution in National Context*, Cambridge: Cambridge University Press.

Diderot, D. (1773) 'Voyage de Hollande', in J. Assézat and M. Tourneux (eds) (1876) *Oeuvres complètes de Denis Diderot*, Paris: Garnier.

Gay, P. (1967) *The Enlightenment: An Interpretation: The Rise of Modern Paganism*, London: Weidenfeld & Nicolson.

Gelderen, M. van (1992) *The Political Thought of the Dutch Revolt 1555–1590*, Cambridge: Cambridge University Press.

Gibbs, G. C. (1971) 'The Role of the Dutch Republic as the Intellectual Entrepôt of Europe in the Seventeenth and Eighteenth Centuries', *Bijdragen en Mededelingen betreffende de Geschiedenis der Nederlanden*, 86: 323–49.

Gravesande, W. J. 's (1720/1) *Mathematical Elements of Natural Philosophy, Confirm'd by Experiments; or an Introduction to Sir Isaac Newton's Philosophy*, trans. J. Th. Desaguliers, London: J. Senex and W. Taylor.

Groenveld, S. (1987) 'The Mecca of Authors? State Assemblies and Censorship in the Seventeenth-century Dutch Republic', in A. C. Duke and C. A. Tamse (eds) *Too Mighty to be Free: Censorship and the Press in Britain and the Netherlands* (Britain and the Netherlands, 11), Zutphen: De Walburg Pers.

Hackmann, W. D. (1975) 'The Growth of Science in the Netherlands in the Seventeenth and Early Eighteenth Centuries', in M. Crosland (ed.) *The Emergence of Science in Western Europe*, London: Macmillan.

Haley, K. H. D. (1988) *The British and the Dutch: Political and Cultural Relations through the Ages*, London: George Philip.

Hoftijzer, P. G. (1992) 'The Leiden Bookseller Pieter van der Aa (1659–1733) and the International Book Trade', in C. Berkvens-Stevelinck, H. Bots, P. G. Hoftijzer and O. S. Lankhorst (eds) *Le Magasin de l'Univers: The Dutch Republic as the Centre of the European Book Trade*, Leiden: Brill.

Howard, J. (1777) *The State of the Prisons in England and Wales, with . . . an Account of Some Foreign Prisons*, 4th edn (1792), London: J. Johnson, C. Dilly and T. Cadell.

Israel, J. I. (1995) *The Dutch Republic: Its Rise, Greatness, and Fall, 1477–1806*, Oxford: Oxford University Press.

—— (1997) 'The Intellectual Debate about Toleration in the Dutch Republic', in C. Berkvens-Stevelinck, J. Israel and G. H. M. Posthumus Meyjes (eds) *The Emergence of Tolerance in the Dutch Republic*, Leiden: Brill.

—— (2001) *Radical Enlightenment: Philosophy and the Making of Modernity 1650–1750*, Oxford: Oxford University Press.

Keblusek, M. (2001) 'The Exile Experience: Royalist and Anglican Book Culture in the Low Countries (1640–60)', in L. Hellinga *et al.* (eds) *The Bookshop of the World: The Role of the Low Countries in the Book-trade 1473–1941*, 't Goy-Houten, Netherlands: Hes & De Graaf.

Mijnhardt, W. W. (1992) 'The Dutch Enlightenment: Humanism, Nationalism and Decline', in M. C. Jacob and W. W. Mijnhardt (eds) *The Dutch Republic in the Eighteenth Century*, Ithaca: Cornell University Press.

Pettegree, A. (1996) 'The Politics of Toleration in the Free Netherlands, 1572–1620', in O. P. Grell and B. Scribner (eds) *Tolerance and Intolerance in the European Reformation*, Cambridge: Cambridge University Press.

Schama, S. (1981) 'The Enlightenment in the Netherlands', in R. Porter and M. Teich (eds) *The Enlightenment in National Context*, Cambridge: Cambridge University Press.

Spinoza, B. de (1670) *Tractatus Theologico-Politicus*, ed. S. Shirley (1989) Leiden: Brill.

Temple, Sir William (1673) *Observations upon the United Provinces of the Netherlands*, ed. Sir G. Clark (1972) Oxford: Clarendon Press.

Velema, W. R. E. (1993) *Enlightenment and Conservatism in the Dutch Republic: The Political Thought of Elie Luzac (1721–1796)*, Assen/Maastricht: Van Gorcum.

Vries, J. de (1991) *The Dutch Rural Economy in the Golden Age 1500–1700*, New Haven, Conn.: Yale University Press.

Waardt, H. de (1991) *Toverij en Samenleving: Holland 1500–1800*, The Hague: Stichting Hollandse Historische Reeks.

Wall, E. van der (2000) 'Toleration and Enlightenment in the Dutch Republic', in O. P. Grell and R. Porter (eds) *Toleration in Enlightenment Europe*, Cambridge: Cambridge University Press.

CHAPTER SEVEN

A CRUCIBLE FOR CHANGE: ENLIGHTENMENT IN BRITAIN

Alexander Murdoch

INTRODUCTION

There are three aspects of early Enlightenment formations in Britain which will receive particular emphasis in this chapter. First, it is a mistake to perceive early Enlightenment formations in Britain as interchangeable with the spread of English cultural influence elsewhere in the archipelago. 'Britain' was a term and an idea that came into use during the early formation of the Enlightenment in the British Isles, as older national traditions in England, Wales, Scotland and Ireland came into contact with Enlightenment ideas. Second, there was an insular element to British participation in a more cosmopolitan European Enlightenment. Many of the Enlightenment ideas perceived as distinctly British were in origin imported from the humanist culture of northern Europe and beyond (Porter 2000; Allan 2000). Third, recent research has demonstrated in compelling detail the 'urban renaissance' in late seventeenth- and early eighteenth-century England which provided the forum for the development of the Enlightenment in Britain (Borsay 1989; Sweet 1997). Later they would provide the crucible for the transformation of British public life in the eighteenth century as being British became less about Enlightenment toleration, human liberty and confidence in the power of scientific knowledge and more about the issues of British empire which came to preoccupy public discourse (Money 1977; Wilson 2002).

NEWTON AND ENLIGHTENMENT IN BRITAIN

The personification of the early Enlightenment in Britain was Sir Isaac Newton (1643–1727), whose image became a defining symbol of the growing influence of science, knowledge and an educated public who appreciated their virtues. Science, knowledge, reason, freedom and liberty all became linked in a manner that suggested that the very formation of Britain was a result of the Enlightenment. As Pope wrote in the couplet intended originally for Newton's monument at Westminster Abbey:

All nature and its laws lay hid in night
God said: Let Newton be: and all was light.

Newton's career lay at the centre of the spread of ideas of Enlightenment in Britain during the reigns of the restored Stuart kings, Charles II and his brother James II, and their successors, Mary and her husband William of Orange. The amazing advances in scientific knowledge that Newton and his associates achieved by the time of his death in 1727 appeared to many in Britain to presage equally important discoveries regarding the laws governing the politics and economics of human society.

The very term 'Glorious Revolution' reflected the public influence of the scientific culture personified by Newton, implying that the movement of monarchs in response to complex forces could mirror the movement of the planets as they revolved within the solar system. This idea began to change after 1688, but the elements of continuity with early Enlightenment formations under the restored Stuart monarchs were just as important as the dynamic for change unleashed in 1688; 'glorious' in England, but violent and contested in the rest of what became Britain between 1707 and 1801. The formation of the Royal Society in London under charter from Charles II in 1662 occurred two years after his restoration. The charter brought no royal income, but the subscription money raised from those eager for the status of Fellows of the Royal Society helped to pay for the publication of the *Philosophical Transactions*, in which Newton published seventeen papers from 1672 to 1676, thereby establishing his reputation as a scientist of genius. The Society was not able to raise funds to publish Newton's *Principia* in 1686, but it authorized their president to license the printing of the book, which Newton dedicated to the Society. The eventual replacement of Pepys as President by Newton demonstrated the changing politics of public science. Pepys resigned at the time of the revolution of government in 1688, and Newton's subsequent election to the council of the Society in 1697 and to the presidency in 1703 marked the gradual change from aristocratic patronage to the patronage of the public in early Enlightenment Britain. 'Newton thus rescued the Society from the distractions of the *virtuosi* rather than succeeding in establishing it as a major centre of scientific research' (Gjertsen 1986: 535).

Newton's presidency of the Royal Society marked his place in the public pantheon of early Enlightenment Britain as the symbol of its achievements. If his mathematics and physics were not widely understood, the popularization of his ideas in terms of discovery of hitherto unknown laws governing the physical universe had an enormous impact in eighteenth-century Britain, particularly through events such as the Boyle Lectures in London. As provincial learned and scientific societies began to establish themselves in British towns in imitation of the Royal Society, their members aspired to do as Newton had done in his Royal Society papers of 1672–4: they hoped to launch new ideas into the world through the transactions of their societies and receive public acknowledgement (and reward) of their contribution to the advancement of knowledge and progress.

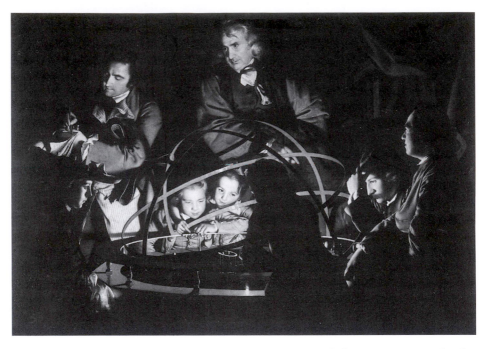

Figure 7.1 *A Philosopher Giving that Lecture on the Orrery, in which a Lamp is Put in the Place of the Sun,* Joseph Wright of Derby. A famous representation of the popularization of Newton's discoveries through public lectures in English provincial towns. By permission of the Museum and Art Gallery, Derby.

THE HUGUENOTS AND EUROPEAN INFLUENCE ON THE EARLY ENLIGHTENMENT IN BRITAIN

Sir Isaac Newton was no John Bull, but in many respects he was quintessentially English. He spent his entire life in the eastern counties of England, from Lincoln-shire to Cambridge. Yet the public world in which he operated as Master of the Mint and President of the Royal Society in London was becoming less purely English and casting its net ever wider. An important part of early Enlightenment culture in Britain came from northern Europe even before the restoration of the Stuart monarchy in 1660. French Huguenots had been seeking refuge in the south-east of England since the religious wars of the sixteenth century and by the time of the Revocation of the Edict of Nantes were well established in London, having been encouraged to immigrate even before 1685 by the Stuart monarchy. They flourished in all trades associated with fashion, such as cabinet-making, textiles (especially silk) and silversmithing. They brought a Calvinistic element to London life that reinforced the impact of the Scottish Covenanters (who owed much to French Calvinism) during the middle of the seventeenth century. Of course, the Huguenots also migrated to Scotland, Wales and, especially, Ireland, and on the Continent many settled in Holland, Prussia and Switzerland. Some also went to British North America. This dispersal helped create international networks of correspondents.

The Huguenots played an important role in establishing the direct communication between London and Amsterdam that became a major axis for cultural, political and economic exchange throughout the period of the early Enlightenment. Prominent among the Huguenot refugees in the Netherlands was Pierre Bayle, whose 'use of scepticism as an instrument of study, which he had acquired from Descartes . . . was broadcast throughout Europe by his influential *Historical and Critical Dictionary* of 1695–7' (Gwynn 1985: 84–5). John Locke's exile in Amsterdam during the latter days of the Stuart regime, his acquaintance with Huguenot intellectuals such as Bayle and, later, Molyneux in Dublin, and his key role in constructing the ideological basis of the change of political regime and British constitution in 1688 all make him almost the equal of Newton as a personification and icon of the early Enlightenment. Ideas of England and British liberty were then exported throughout Europe by an international network of northern European intellectuals in which the Huguenots loomed large, but which also included the Dutch and many Germans. The arrival in what had become Britain by 1707 of a Hanoverian king, whose mother, Sophie, was a patron of advanced ideas in Germany (Israel 2001), consolidated the hold of early Enlightenment culture in Britain as much as it consolidated the British state formed by the union of the parliaments of England and Wales and Scotland in 1707.

THE REVOLUTION OF 1688

The revolution of 1688 was a multiple British revolution, or rather it marked a dramatic shift in the relation of the separate kingdoms within Britain, which resulted in the creation of the British state, drawing on the long-standing idea of a strong Protestant Britain as guarantor of cultural and political change in northern Europe (Harris 1999; Williamson 1982). It was 'Britain' rather than England which emerged as the principal opponent of the French Bourbon project for a universal monarchy. In essence Britain was created because the Dutch, Huguenot and German soldiers in the service of William of Orange, with some English, Welsh, Scottish and Protestant Irish support, undermined the military edifice supporting the monarchy of James II and went on to secure military victory in contested territory in Scotland and Ireland.

The political and constitutional transformation in Britain after 1688, though perhaps not as glorious nor as revolutionary as it has sometimes been represented, still marked a significant departure in European history by establishing a regime which, in England at least, shared executive authority with a parliament containing all of the nobility and elected representatives of landowners and urban property-holders. Voltaire's admiring account of British liberties under the Hanoverian monarchy circulated widely in Europe and was often read as an implicit criticism of absolute monarchy. With the lapse in 1695 of the Licensing Act introduced under Charles II after his restoration, the content and availability of the culture of print expanded significantly (Fox 2000: 392–4). The courts of law were less subject to government interference (although not quite as free from it as admirers of British liberties sometimes thought) (Connolly 1992; Prest 1998). The monarchy survived the early death of James II's daughter Mary as joint monarch despite William of Orange's preoccupation with Continental war. Under William's sister-in-law and cousin, Anne, the project of parliamentary union with Scotland was achieved by co-option of key members of the Scottish nobility and the promise of the continued establishment of Presbyterianism in the Church of Scotland. Britain was thus an idea long before it became a political reality, but the achievement of an agreement, in law if not in practice, marked early Enlightenment culture in Britain. This was illustrated in the career of Daniel Defoe, a government spy in Edinburgh during the union negotiations of 1707, and propagandist for the completion of the union in his *A Tour through the Whole Island of Great Britain* (1724–7). David Gregory, the Newtonian astronomer, and John Arbuthnott, writer and future physician of the royal family, similarly participated in early metropolitan Enlightenment by migrating from Scotland to London. Stability, peace and consolidation arrived with the end of the war in Europe (1713), the peaceful succession to the British throne of the Elector of Hanover as George I in 1714, and the defeat of a major Jacobite rebellion in Scotland (with the help of Dutch troops provided under a treaty of mutual British/Netherlands defence) in 1715.

The example of the United Provinces and the important role of the Dutch in establishing the Williamite regime in Britain fostered the idea that political and constitutional change was associated with broader changes in society and culture, which came to be perceived in Britain as part of the Enlightenment. Adam Smith, for example, wrote in 1760 of the beneficial effects of the union on Scotland, despite its early unpopularity: the disaffection of Scotland was excusable, as the immediate effect of British union 'was to hurt the interest of every single order of men in [Scotland]', although in time 'infinite Good had been derived' there (Smith 1977). What kind of 'Good' did he mean? Economic development and an increase of wealth, naturally, but also social and cultural development, as more wealth reached more people, and reduced the dependence of the many upon the wealthy few that had characterized early modern Scottish society. Culturally these ideas were often associated with tolerance, and with the liberalization of English society which made the development of an expanding commercial economy possible in England and in Britain more generally.

THE GROWTH OF TOLERATION IN BRITAIN

Toleration of a Presbyterian Church in Scotland under the terms of the parliamentary union was matched by growing acceptance of Protestant dissenters in England and Wales as entitled to participation in the public culture of the country. This toleration was never complete. Increasingly, dissenters became integrated into English society, and commerce and the use of leisure for social activity became more important than religious orthodoxy. Although the English Toleration Act of 1689 failed to extend full civil rights to English Protestants who were not members of the Church of England, it did create the impression to foreigners, such as Voltaire, of a tolerant and pluralistic society. This was further reinforced by the peaceful accession to the British throne in 1714 of the Lutheran Elector of Hanover as King George I, a British king who never spoke English, who maintained a Lutheran established Church in his German electorate, and who supported and conformed to the Episcopalian Church of England.

At the same time, George accepted a Presbyterian Church of Scotland which declared its loyalty to his regime when faced with the threat of restoration of the Roman Catholic Stuart dynasty at the time of the rebellion of 1715. This 'Jacobite' rebellion was supported by the large number of Scottish Episcopalians in the Highlands and north-east Scotland, who, despite some shared principles of church government with the Church of England, remained loyal to the Stuart dynasty. Despite the misfortunes of the Jacobites, the strides made by the Protestant dissenting academies of England and Presbyterian colleges of Scotland in pioneering new developments in education epitomized the country's religious plurality. Ironically, the 'Church of England' came to play a key role in the revival of Welsh-speaking culture in Wales during the eighteenth century. Sermons in Welsh were given more frequently over the course of the century, and the Church encouraged the publication of more books and the scriptures in the language. Thus, the Church of England, by embracing the vernacular, brought the Welsh language into print, and laid the basis for important changes in Welsh culture which preserved that culture into modern times (Davies 1993: 295–8).

By the 1770s, the unthinkable was countenanced, with public relief for the rights of Roman Catholics in England and Wales. And although parliamentary legislation failed Scotland in 1779, the leaders of the legal and ecclesiastical establishments there were known to favour it. Jacobitism and its discontents appeared to die in 1766 with the 'Old Pretender', the putative James VIII, rather than linger until the death of his eldest son Charles Edward in 1788. By the 1770s, Roman Catholics in Ireland and the Highlands of Scotland were important sources of military manpower for the prosecution of the war against the rebellious colonies in America. There was, therefore, a certain pragmatism in the British government's sponsorship of Catholic relief. This provoked considerable public hostility, leading to the Anti-Popery riots in Scotland in 1779 and the Gordon Riots in London in 1780, both of which witnessed the deeply unenlightened spectacle of the burning of books. The mob burned the library of the Roman Catholic Bishop of Scotland, in Edinburgh, and the library of the judge William Murray, Earl of Mansfield, in London. From a Perthshire Jacobite family, Mansfield (whom even Scottish-hating Dr Johnson admired) fell suspect of encouraging authoritarian tendencies in the British monarchy. Catholic relief was seen by some as a plot to allow the army to acquire troops which would support executive rather than parliamentary privilege: Enlightenment interest in toleration encouraged the government to defend it. The measure was extended in 1791 to give Roman Catholics the same status as Protestant dissenters, and indeed in Ireland to give many Roman Catholic tenant farmers the vote.

THE RISE OF THE PUBLIC

As religious loyalties became less overt in Britain, public culture came to be associated less with religion than with leisure and social intercourse. Public life developed in which culture could be seen to be about consumption and display, as much as ideas and toleration. The coffee-house culture of late seventeenth-century London, which spawned the journalism of Addison and Steele and the triumphs of *The Spectator* and the *Tatler* became less political early in the eighteenth century, though this trend was later reversed. A small group of writers clustered around John Dryden (1631–1700), Alexander Pope (1688–1744), Joseph Addison (1672–1719) and Jonathan Swift (1667–1745), described their age as 'Augustan', claiming that it possessed the same cultural excellence as the supposedly golden age of intellectual achievement during the reign of the Roman Emperor Augustus (27 BC – AD 14). The Augustan England of the early British Enlightenment gave way to a commercial, urban, middle-class culture of paternalistic Whig elites, presiding over an expanding urban commercial society. This was a world which witnessed the triumph of the medium of print, in the form of books, pamphlets, broadsheets, prints and newspapers. Print, no longer the preserve of a metropolitan and aristocratic elite, brought about a continuous expansion of production that generated the popular triumph of the writers of England's Augustan age (approx. 1690–1740). The development of publication by subscription enabled Alexander Pope to live comfortably from his publications, but he could be scathing about such writers as Defoe, who wrote for a less discriminating audience. This is an indication of the many possibilities which opened up through the expansion of printing and readership.

Print also made possible the establishment of more localized cultures, as in the revival of Welsh, the resurgence of Scots song and poetry, and the emergence of regionally distinct English poets and working-class artists such as Stephen Duck, John Clare and Thomas Bewick. Public culture extended into public participation in local dancing assemblies, musical societies, scientific and philosophical associations and committees established to promote the foundation of medical infirmaries, turnpike roads, canals and other civic and regional amenities.

A rich store of local studies also charts the spread of Enlightenment ideas to many urban areas in eighteenth-century Britain. In Halifax in 1774 a group of manufacturers advertised their intent to raise a subscription to build a cloth hall in the town. The result was the formation of a voluntary association dominated by wealthy merchants and 'manufacturers' (in fact, merchants who paid other people to make things and assemble them). Artisans were excluded by the level of financial subscription required for the Halifax Piece Hall, but when it opened in 1779 they were included as members of a celebratory procession which paraded before the subscribers, described as 'ladies and gentlemen'. Decisions of the subscription association had been taken by ballot of the subscribers, and there was no aristocratic patronage. Instead, pride was expressed by subscribers in the 'elegant simplicity' adopted for the design of the hall, created manifestly as a place for trade and utility rather than pleasure and entertainment (Smail 1994: 142–4). 'Civic improvement' became the rage. Medieval town gates were removed, streets and bridges were widened, markets were moved to increase the public amenity of the central areas of towns which they had formerly occupied (Clark 1984: 41). Poor houses, infirmaries and 'bedlams' (lunatic asylums) were constructed in increasing numbers across urban communities in Britain to accommodate, or perhaps control, those less fortunate. In

Figure 7.2 *Painting Room of the Foulis Academy*, *c*. 1760. David Allan. Robert and Andrew Foulis extended their activities as booksellers and publishers to establishing a collection to support public instruction in fine art in Scotland. By permission of the Mitchell Library, Glasgow.

this growing public sphere, women found a role as readers and purchasers of the expanding volume of printed books, including the novel, and as guests or members of local assemblies, musical societies and public lectures sponsored by scientific and philosophical societies. While denied political and legal rights, women gained access to the public culture of the Enlightenment in Britain through membership of the audience which made possible the expansion of public performance, social interaction and the availability of printed literature (see Chapter 16 of this volume.)

AN EXPANDING ECONOMY

The government of Sir Robert Walpole (Prime Minister: 1720–44) brought a period of peace. Its policy of state participation in the economy created the wealth and leisure that enabled the public culture of the Enlightenment to expand so dramatically in Britain over the course of the eighteenth century. With Walpole's fall from power over the issue of war with Spain from 1739, and the subsequent outbreak of war with France, government involvement in London's financial markets became ever more entrenched. At the same time the links forged with the Dutch Republic after 1688 began to loosen. As the British state became involved in wars of empire, so those with a financial interest in its continued expansion grew in numbers. Likewise, the mercantile world of London became more diverse as Scots, German, Huguenot, Dutch and Jewish immigrants all increased their participation (Brewer 1989). Expansion of London's financial markets led to greater debate over the respective cultural merits of metropolis and province, which in turn drew Enlightenment culture away from London and its parliamentary politics towards smaller, expanding urban centres in the provinces – in Britain, Ireland or British North America. This increased cultural confidence in the English regions and Scotland, and fostered the expansion of the British union to Ireland in the United Kingdom, established in 1801, even as it also generated grievances in more distant urban centres in British North America. Dissatisfaction with the perceived corruption of the British monarchy and Parliament produced the first secession from Britain in 1783 by English colonies, increasingly developing societies which were more diverse than those on the island of Britain itself. As the Philadelphian Benjamin Franklin wrote to a fellow British provincial, the Scottish judge Henry Home, Lord Kames, in 1767, 'Scotland and Ireland are differently circumstanced. Confined by the sea, they can scarcely increase in numbers, wealth and strength, so as to overbalance England.' But, to Franklin, America was a very different proposition in terms of Britishness, 'an immense territory, favoured by Nature with all advantages of climate, soil, great navigable rivers, and lakes &c must become a great country, populous and mighty' (Franklin 1970: 69–70). The failure of British efforts to retain America provoked a re-examination of the institutions of the British state, which reflected the influence of Enlightenment ideas of utility, public debate and moral accountability. Recent scholarship has emphasized that this debate contributed to the cultural developments which recreated Britain as an imperial state in the early nineteenth century, led by an elite schooled in the public culture of the British Enlightenment which sought moral and public regeneration in Britain even as it turned its back on political reform (Colley 1992).

THE EXTENSION OF ENGLISHNESS

If there was a British Enlightenment, was it merely the result of an expansion of English culture into other areas of Britain? If Franklin saw a British union as inevitably dominated by England through force of numbers and influence of wealth, there were Scots, Irishmen and kindred spirits in provincial England and Wales who looked to reinvent Britain as something more dynamic than the extension of English culture and institutions to provincial societies. What has come to be called the Scottish Enlightenment was no less than a project by leaders of the Scottish professional middle classes to reinvent their ancient country as a dynamic part of a modern and expanding British polity which would give Scots access to expanding world markets through the economies of scale and the protection of a powerful British navy. It would also open up opportunities for public advancement and cultural achievement by Scots at many levels – through the modernization of their

Church as a national institution of instruction and debate; the evolution of the universities from ecclesiastical seminaries into secular academies of the liberal arts on the model of the Dutch colleges; a readjustment of the law to the needs of modern commercial society. Franklin's correspondent Henry Home played a full role in this endeavour (Phillipson 1981: 19–40). If the Dutch had helped bring English ideas to a Continental audience, the Scots came to mediate between a modern anglophone Enlightenment of economic and social enquiry and a European audience for the works of the British Enlightenment. Scots played a vigorous role in introducing the ideas of Rousseau, Goethe and many other Europeans into anglophone discourse (Oz-Salzberger 1995) through the first *Edinburgh Review* in the 1750s to the second, founded in 1802, and the impact of Sir Walter Scott's Romantic poetry and prose in the early nineteenth century. They generated the idea of Britishness as an umbrella of constitutional stability, personal liberty and commercial culture which could be made available to all who wished access to it. This was demonstrated by the role of Scots, such as James Murray (first British governor of Quebec), Lord Mansfield and Alexander Wedderburn, in the formulation of British policy towards the French-speaking Roman Catholic population which came under its authority in 1763. The Quebec Act (1774) which recognized local institutions that were not 'British' in the interests of long-term integration echoed the Scottish experience of 1707. Many Scots perceived Britishness as an important part of Enlightenment.

THE URBAN RENAISSANCE

An expanding urban Enlightenment featured many recruits from younger members of gentry families (Borsay 1989). Provincial mercantile elites in cities such as Birmingham or towns like Halifax drew on the cultural life of the local gentry based on the county town as well as on London metropolitan examples. This process allowed a middle class to create its own culture by following earlier practices of public protest and challenging elite culture (Murdoch and Sher 1988; Smail 1994). The Scottish Enlightenment may be seen as a mediation of French thought and culture into the commercial world of the eighteenth century. It did not invent the modern world, as some of its most enthusiastic supporters have claimed; it represented an accommodation of locality and province to the state in a manner which preserved the vigour and distinctiveness of a variety of cultures within one polity (Sher 1985). There were no large-scale urban markets in the Highlands, as there were none in most of Wales and in many localities of England, though smaller markets were prevalent in all these areas, and urbanization in provincial England became a crucible of early Enlightenment culture (Clark and Houston in Clark (ed.) 2000). Much of this occurred through the clubs and societies which began to proliferate in English towns during the early Enlightenment. The model of Addison's *Spectator* was a major influence, but this was not a development which involved imitation of metropolitan culture in a provincial setting. There was a dynamic in which toleration and the pursuit of knowledge became important civic values at a time when the 'middling sorts' were acquiring access to increased leisure and disposable income. If the urban renaissance began in metropolitan London, its legacy was the vigour of Enlightenment culture in English provincial towns over the course of the eighteenth century (Borsay 1989: 257–83). There was a symbiotic cultural relationship between London and the provincial town, with periodicals from London achieving national circulation and booksellers in the towns importing a steady stream of London publications that spread Enlightenment values through their customers and their localities. However, this was not a one-way process, and as the eighteenth century progressed, so provincial elites gained confidence in their ability to participate in the mainstream of Enlightenment culture.

CLUBS AND SOCIETIES

Enlightenment ideas were fostered within the culture of clubs which, over the course of the eighteenth century, became national social institutions in Britain (Clark 2000: 60–93). Several contrasting developments in British public life showed this tendency to move away from formal politics and towards social networking and cultural activity. This period saw the growth of Freemasonry and of more specialized learned societies concerned with scientific or antiquarian expertise. Freemasonry, having long ceased to be specific to a trade, instead developed social rituals which attracted new recruits from a less hierarchical urban middle-class sector interested in social intercourse rather than public display. The constitution published by the Grand Lodge of London in 1723 became immensely influential in Britain and through translated editions appearing across Europe. The Grand Lodge influenced the development of Freemasonry across Britain, where it became part of the public culture of the urban middle class who were the shock troops of the Enlightenment (see Chapter 17 of this volume).

The scientific societies of Enlightenment Britain owed much to the example of the Royal Society (see above) and proliferated in their hundreds across the country. If their scientific and artistic achievements seldom matched their sense of self-regard, they nevertheless acted as the medium through which the public culture of the coffee house and the club became more serious. This emphasis on learning may have come at the expense of an earlier convivial vitality found in, for example, the 'Easy Club' of Edinburgh, led by the poet Allan Ramsay early in the eighteenth century, and Samuel Johnson's literary 'Club', recorded later by James Boswell.

CONCLUSION

The early Enlightenment in Britain went hand in hand with an expansion of urban culture which, by the middle of the eighteenth century, had transformed Bristol, Birmingham, Buxton and many other provincial urban centres. This expansion provided the students for the dissenting academies and Scottish universities. Britain as a concept was a product and creation of the early Enlightenment period. It can be seen in the parliamentary union of Scotland and England in 1707 which created a kingdom of Great Britain for the first time, and in the determination of a king (George III) of German descent to announce at his coronation in 1761 that he 'gloried in the name of Briton', only to find himself denounced as a dupe of the Scots by suspicious political opponents in England. This was a Britain which excluded Ireland and eventually most of 'British' North America as well. The subsequent incorporation of the former was a response to the lessons of conflict with the second, although in the long term this proved unsuccessful. The new Britain was one in which the Welsh in Wales and London could claim cultural precedence as the descendants of the first Britons. The Scot Tobias Smollett, whose grandfather had been one of the Scots who negotiated the parliamentary union of 1707, made the principal narrator of his novel *Humphrey Clinker* the Welsh gentleman Matthew Bramble, in another literary effort to complete the British union. The reinvention of Welsh culture and identity by the Welsh of eighteenth-century London was an important and neglected aspect of the development of Enlightenment culture in Britain. Enlightenment interest in cultural diversity led to the discovery of new worlds within Britain as well as beyond Europe.

REFERENCES

Allan, D. (2000) *Philosophy and Politics in Later Stuart Scotland*, East Linton: Tuckwell Press.

Borsay, P. (1989) *The English Urban Renaissance: Culture and Society in the Provincial Town, 1660–1770*, Oxford: Clarendon Press.

Brewer, J. (1989) *Sinews of Power*, London: Unwin Hyman.

Broadie, A. (2001) *The Scottish Enlightenment*, Edinburgh: Birlinn.

Clark, P. (1984) *The Transformation of English Provincial Towns*, London: Hutchinson.

—— (2000) *British Clubs and Societies, 1580–1800*, Oxford: Clarendon Press.

—— (ed.) (2000) *The Cambridge Urban History of Britain: Volume II, 1540–1840*, Cambridge: Cambridge University Press.

Colley, L. (1992) *Britons*, London: Yale University Press.

Connolly, S. J. (1992) *Religion, Law and Power: The Making of Protestant Ireland 1660–1760*, Oxford: Clarendon Press.

Davies, J. (1993) *A History of Wales*, London: Penguin.

Dunthorne, H. (1987) '"An Inseparable Alliance"? Scotland and Holland in the Age of Improvement', *Documentatieblad 18E EEUW*, 19: 157–70.

Fitzpatrick, M. (2001) 'Natural Law, Natural Rights and the Toleration Act in England and Wales, 1688–1829', unpublished paper.

Fox, A. (2000) *Oral and Literate Culture in England 1500–1700*, Oxford: Oxford University Press.

Franklin, B. (1970) *Papers of Benjamin Franklin*, vol. 14, ed. L. Labaree, London: Yale University Press.

Gjertsen, D. (1986) *The Newton Handbook*, London: Routledge.

Gwynn, R. (1985) *Huguenot Heritage: The History and Contribution of the Huguenots in Britain*, London: Routledge.

Harris, T. (1999) 'The People, the Law and the Constitution in Scotland and England', *Journal of British Studies*, 38: 28–58.

Israel, J. I. (2001) *Radical Enlightenment: Philosophy and the Making of Modernity, 1650–1750*, Oxford: Oxford University Press.

Jenkins, P. (1983) *The Making of a Ruling Class: The Glamorgan Gentry 1640–1790*, Cambridge: Cambridge University Press.

Melton, J. (2001) *The Rise of the Public in Enlightenment Europe*, Cambridge: Cambridge University Press.

Money, J. (1977) *Experience and Identity: Birmingham and the West Midlands*, Manchester: Manchester University Press.

Murdoch, A. (1980) *'The People Above'*, Edinburgh: John Donald.

Murdoch, A. and Sher, R. (1988) 'Literary and Learned Culture', in T. M. Devine and R. Mitchison (eds) *People and Society in Scotland: Volume I, 1760–1830*, Edinburgh: John Donald.

—— (1999) *British History 1660–1832*, Basingstoke: Macmillan (now Palgrave).

Neeson, J. (1993) *Commoners: Common Right, Enclosure and Social Change in England 1700–1820*, Cambridge: Cambridge University Press.

Oz-Salzberger, F. (1995) *Translating the Enlightenment*, Oxford: Clarendon Press.

Phillipson, N. (1981) 'The Scottish Enlightenment', in R. Porter and M. Teich (eds) *The Enlightenment in National Context*, Cambridge: Cambridge University Press.

Porter, R. (2000) *Enlightenment: Britain and the Creation of the Modern World*, London: Penguin.

Prest, W. (1998) *Albion Ascendant: English History 1660–1815*, Oxford: Oxford University Press.

Sher, R. (1985) *Church and University in the Scottish Enlightenment*, Edinburgh: Edinburgh University Press.

Smail, J. (1994) *Origins of Middle-class Culture: Halifax, Yorkshire, 1660–1780*, London: Cornell University Press.

Smith, A. (1977) *Correspondence of Adam Smith*, ed. E. Mossner and I. Ross, Oxford: Clarendon Press.

Sweet, R. (1997) *The Writing of Urban Histories in Eighteenth Century England*, Oxford: Clarendon Press.

Williamson, A. (1982) 'Scotland, Antichrist and the Invention of Great Britain', in J. Dwyer *et al.* (eds) *New Perspectives on the Politics and Culture of Early Modern Scotland*, Edinburgh: John Donald.

Wilson, K. (2002) *Island Race: Englishness, Empire and Gender in the Eighteenth Century*, London: Routledge.

CHAPTER EIGHT

THE ITINERARY OF A YOUNG INTELLECTUAL IN EARLY ENLIGHTENMENT GERMANY

Martin Mulsow

The Early Enlightenment in Germany was not a unified movement. Although launched at the University of Halle, founded in 1694, with Christian Thomasius as its most prominent figure, its impetus came from all directions, and its dissemination throughout the Holy Roman Empire brought it to a variety of milieux: urban bourgeoisie, universities of different traditions and confessions, small states and their courts. It developed along several alternative lines. The leading professors lent it a liberal Protestant reforming character, with different accents depending on whether the protagonists were theologians, scientists or jurists, and some underground authors gave it a note that was radically critical of religion or radically spiritualistic. The German intellectual scene of the eighteenth century was marked by different types: there were Pietists, scholarly sceptics, courtly secular gallants, prolific polymaths, erudite merchants and millenarian ministers, cunning schoolmasters and young, adventurous globe-trotters. The fact that, on the one hand, 'Germany' was a patchwork of small states, kingdoms, duchies and principalities, and, on the other hand, it had a multi-faceted intellectual scene made it both weak and strong. There may have been territories that firmly clung to old traditions, but there were many others in which innovation was a possibility. If you wanted to carry through your interests you had to know how to handle all those rivalries and differences and how to use relevant networks and connections.

The Thirty Years War claimed more than a third of Germany's population. In 1648 there were hardly 10 million inhabitants left, and up to the 1680s we are talking about a post-war society. There were exceptions, of course, as there had always been, in this 'monster' called the Holy Roman Empire. Different denominational shades within Lutheranism, Calvinism and Catholicism would still fundamentally colour society. For a long time, Germany tried hard to catch up with the rapid cultural developments in France, Britain and the Netherlands, but the means were lacking. The situation changed with the advent of the new movement in the 1690s. People resumed reading the journals and writings that came across the borders from Western Europe, and there were fresh ideas and approaches again. Everyone read them differently, and drew different conclusions. Let us follow the itinerary of a young intellectual in order to get an idea of the plurality of views in Germany in the early eighteenth century.

SETTING OUT FOR A JOURNEY
THROUGH GERMANY

Halle, April 1703: three young men prepare for a journey. They want to get to know Germany and the Netherlands; they want to travel to university towns and courts; they want to talk to scholars and people who know about life and the world. Gottlieb Stolle, a Silesian from Liegnitz, who studied in Leipzig and Halle and reached the age of thirty in February, is the leader of the trio. Stolle was badly off: for the last few years in Halle, he had lived off nothing but stale bread. To him, it was of such great concern to be at the centre of Germany's intellectual resurrection, later to be called the 'early Enlightenment', that he put up with these privations.

A few years before, Halle had still been a sleepy place of 5,000 inhabitants. There had been a university for nine years, and in this short span of time thousands of students, predominantly of law, but also of theology, had moved into the town, because the university had earned the reputation of being the most progressive in Germany. It belonged to Brandenburg (which had lately become Prussia), and was mainly designed to educate the ruling elite. Since the seventeenth century, there had been a growing demand in the territorial states for officials qualified as jurists. New disciplines such as Public Law of the Empire ('Reichspublicistik') and Cameralism and Study of the European State System ('Staatenkunde'), which were essential for the operation of the state, were emerging. In Halle, these disciplines were cultivated and developed. And, of course, it suited the university well that its fame attracted students from all countries.

Thomasius was the crowd-puller of the institute. In 1687, when he was still in Leipzig, he caused a sensation when he announced a lecture, the first ever to be delivered in German, not Latin, on *How Far to Imitate the French in Everyday Life and Situations*. The question was how Germany could take advantage of the innovative impetus from France without becoming dependent on French culture. Afterwards, Thomasius was successful with his *Monatsgespräche*, a monthly magazine containing reviews in German. At the same time, he had drawn up a programme for a courtly philosophy. This would adopt the secular ideals of conversation, and develop the critical self-confidence to challenge the pedantry of the existing Aristotelian university system. These aims and objectives stirred Stolle and drew hundreds of enthusiastic students to the city.

'If you go to Halle,' people in German cities would say, 'you will return as a Pietist or as an atheist'; Pietist because of the orphanage (*Waisenhaus*) founded by August Hermann Francke, which in the course of the eighteenth century became one of the leading centres of educational theory and practice. Thomasius himself, at least in the 1690s, was attracted to Pietism and shared its desire for reformation, for a simple and undogmatic piety and for its rejection of 'scholastic' teachings.

The Halle early Enlightenment was primarily a movement of jurists. The spiritualist Friedrich Breckling agreed with Thomasius 'that God will finally choose the jurists to wreck many a *theologo* [Breckling's expression for the theologians] and to integrate that kind of *extravagantes* with the rules *juris humani*' (Breckling to Thomasius, Ms. Sup. Ep. 4,33). That was the objective: to 'integrate', that is, to stop theological encroachment on civil life by means of jurisprudence and to draw clear

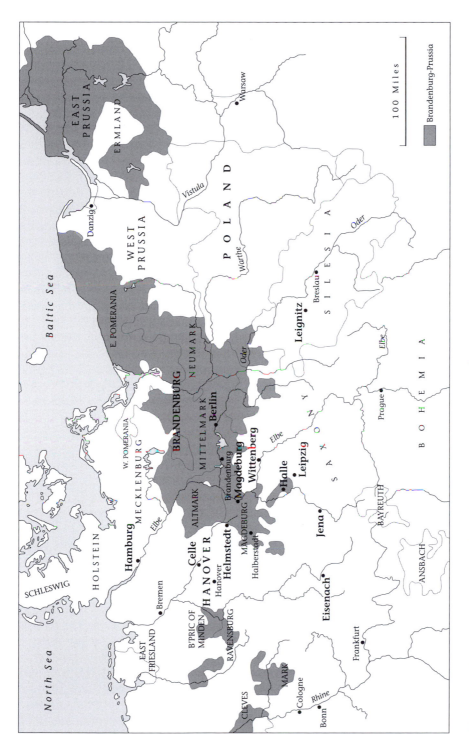

Figure 8.1 Germany in the early eighteenth century, illustrating the places Stolle visited.

Figure 8.2 *Christian Thomasius*. By permission of the Staatliche Graphische Sammlung, Munich.

and definite lines between secular law on the one hand and private convictions on the other. Many traditionalists already called this 'atheism'. These lines of demarcation concerned the divorce laws, the persecution of heretics and political reason (*politische Klugheit*). Pufendorf's *De habitu religionis ad vitam civilem* of 1687 was the decisive work, although some cunning jurists attempted to surpass it with a polemic entitled *De habitu superstitionis ad vitam civilem*, which reproached religion for being potentially superstitious and subversive of the civil order.

The majority of the supporters of the early Enlightenment were not anti-religious. *Superstitio* was associated with Catholicism, partly also with 'papist' excesses within Lutheran orthodoxy, but the identity of the Lutheran Reformation and its links with original, pre-Constantine Christendom was still strong enough to allow Thomasius and his friends to see themselves as Christians. They had a basically moral conception of Christendom, but the fundamental concepts of their philosophy were theological. In Thomasius's view, for instance, the deprivation of the will by the Fall characterizes the *conditio humana*, and yet he believed that an appropriate life could be achieved through *charitas ordinata*, that is, reasonable love.

However, when Thomasius talks about natural state and the Fall of man, he does not only mean theology, but also the Hippocratic teaching of the four humours and Samuel Pufendorf's natural law. The early Enlightenment in Germany is unthinkable without Pufendorf. His most important work, *De jure naturae et gentium* of 1672, contained the teaching of human *Socialitas*, that is, the predisposition of man to society. It allowed him to set up a system of social ethics rooted in anthropology and based on reason rather than revelation.

The doctrine of the four humours, which Thomasius outlined in his *Ausübung der Sittenlehre* of 1696, was central to his anthropology. It provided psychological ideas for the evaluation of behaviour, national character, political types and moral tendencies, and even literary and philosophical works. Whenever Stolle describes his interlocutors in his travel diary, he does it by using the terminology he had been taught by Thomasius: so, for instance, a man who has a melancholic and sanguine temperament tends to have the prejudice of 'precipitation', or he tends to be precise and conceited, since he is choleric.

IN RENGER'S BOOKSHOP IN HALLE

When, in the days prior to his departure, Stolle was strolling past Renger's bookshop in the basement of the town hall on the marketplace, he could see in the window the latest writings printed in Halle, such as, for example, the second edition of *Fundamenta Medicinae*, the textbook by the medical professor Friedrich Hoffmann, a mechanist and the academic opponent of his colleague Georg Ernst Stahl, who had a vitalistic conception of the human body. They were both regarded as leading German medical authorities. Next to the textbook lay some impudent books written in German, which sold well, such as *Sieben böse Geister welche heutigen Tages guten Theils die Küster, oder so genannte Dorff-Schulmeister regieren* (*Seven Evil Spirits that Nowadays Often Rule over the Vergers or So-called Village Schoolmasters*), written in the style of the reformist writings of the satirical theologian Johann Balthasar Schupp

Figure 8.3 *A Shop in Germany*, from Andreas Rüdiger (1711) *Philosophia synthetica*.

from the middle of the previous century. Its author was Johann Georg Zeidler, who earned his living as a prolific writer and translator of a great variety of works. He was, after all, one of those in Halle who tried to breathe new life into the decrepit structures of Church and education.

Another work in the window was the seventh and latest issue of the periodical *Observationes selectae ad rem litterariam spectantes*. The *Observationes* contained short, scholarly essays by Halle professors such as Thomasius, Budde, Gundling, Stahl and several others. In comparison to the *Acta eruditorum*, a magazine edited by Otto Mencke in Leipzig and established throughout Europe, this one was of marginal importance. It was still significant as all its essays were presented anonymously. Whenever a new issue was out, Stolle and his friends would try to puzzle out who might be the authors of the new contributions. Anonymity allowed authors to advance controversial theses. Thomasius made extensive use of these periodicals to publish materials from his father Jakob's estate. In this way, he filled a large part of the issues from 1700 to 1703. The latest issue, the one lying in the window, included contributions on Church law, literary conversations and metal refining.

Almost all of the authors of the *Observationes* had been teachers of Stolle. Nikolaus Hieronymus Gundling was hardly older than Stolle. He was studying for a doctorate in law, and would give lectures in that very year. In his writing, he was as bold as Thomasius, and courageous enough to broach philosophical and historical topics. Budde's latest work *Elementa philosophiae instrumentalis*, published by the orphanage, was not, however, displayed in Renger's shop. In this book, Budde, like Thomasius, proposed a reformed logic and methodology, focusing on the term 'eclectics'. This was a vogue word among the Halle professors, meaning an undogmatic digest of convictions, compiled after a thorough examination of all knowledge that was available, regardless of faction or 'sect'. Independent thinking and freedom to decide were what mattered. As early as 1691, Thomasius had put forth a *Vernunftlehre* ('theory of reason') which opposed an eclectic sensualism to the metaphysics, which still predominated at that time. When in the years following 1700 French and Latin translations made John Locke's *Essay Concerning Human Understanding* better known in Halle, a number of similarities between the two approaches would be revealed.

The book of one of Stolle's former fellow-students was for sale, too: *Unterschiedliche Schrifften vom Unfug des Hexen-Proceßes, zu fernerer Untersuchung der Zauberey* (*Various Writings on the Injustice of Witch Trials and on the Examination of Witchcraft*). The editor was Johann Reiche, whose doctorate with Thomasius two years earlier had been followed with close interest by Stolle and many others. In a big lecture hall (which had to be rented since the university did not have a building of its own) Thomasius and Reiche disputed *De criminae magiae* and deplored the witch trials, which had ravaged seventeenth-century Germany and still took place. In general, Thomasius used these disputes to wage his campaigns against prejudice and superstition. He let his students take the lead, some of whom, such as Theodor Ludwig Lau, were to become yet more radical than he.

The year before, the witchcraft dispute had enabled some theologians openly to suspect that Thomasius no longer believed in the devil's existence. So, at the beginning of the winter semester, Thomasius put up notices at the entrance of the lecture halls, reading:

Just as I – firstly – believe in the devil and I – secondly – believe he is the general root of all evil and thus – thirdly – also for the Fall of man; I – fourthly – also believe that there are sorcerers and witches . . . But I still deny constantly, since I cannot believe it, that the devil has horns, hooves and claws, that he looks like a Pharisee, a monk, or a monster, or any other way he is generally depicted. I cannot believe that he can take any form and appear to people in any of these or in whatever form.

(Thomasius: 177f.)

In view of such theses, it is small wonder that the seeds of the conflict with the theologians had been sown. Even the moderate Halle theologians were sometimes tough customers.

Stolle earned his living by giving private lessons. In these lessons, he read with his students Johann Gottfried Arnold's *Unpartheiische Kirchen- und Ketzer-Historie* (*An Impartial History of the Church and of its Heretics*), which was published in 1699 and 1700 in two large volumes. Thomasius had recommended it as 'the most important book after the Bible'. This work, like Bayle's *Dictionnaire*, published in Rotterdam, contained contributions by numerous intellectuals, constituting a 'counter-history': the history of the persecuted and suppressed 'heretics' who, according to Arnold, were merely searching for the truth. In such ways Pietists and the supporters of the early Enlightenment created a history for themselves.

RESTLESS SEARCHERS:
PIETISTS AND RADICAL SUPPORTERS OF THE EARLY ENLIGHTENMENT

On 27 April, Stolle and his friends arrive at Helmstedt. The university, during the times of the quarrel on syncretism in the first half of the seventeenth century, had been a leading institution and symbol of moderate Lutheranism. Although it no longer provided such stimulation, having become rather petty, Stolle nonetheless gains valuable information here. For example, Hermann von der Hardt, an expert in Oriental studies, tells him about Johann Peter Speeth, a Protestant from Augsburg who became a Catholic, reverted to Protestantism, gravitated towards Socinianism and Quakerism, and finally converted to Judaism in Amsterdam. 'As he found nobody', von der Hardt told Stolle, 'who agreed with him but always somebody whose opinion was contrary to that of the other, he finally decided: *omnia esse incerta, nisi hoc: unum scilicet esse Deum* [everything is uncertain except this: there is only one God], and thus he converted to Judaism in order to satisfy his conscience.'

Speeth's story reveals the networks of the spiritualists and Pietists (still quite a vague term at that time). In Germany distances were considerable, but letters and conversations with itinerant students, friends or visitors facilitated the spread of ideas. There emerged, as it were, a physical and intellectual map marked out by the great unorthodox religious authorities of that time. One key symbol on the map stands for the theologian Philipp Jakob Spener, originally from Frankfurt, principal court chaplain in Dresden (1686–91) and now in Berlin (1691 on), the first man to organize Pietistic conventicles and a proponent of a reformed piety. Another symbol stands for Gottfried Arnold, former professor in Gießen, author of the *Ketzerhistorie* and now living as a preacher in Saxony-Eisenach. Others were Johann Wilhelm Petersen and his wife, spiritualistic advocates of chiliasm and of the 'Apokatastasis panton' ('universal salvation'). Petersen was superintendent in Lüneburg and had lived a secluded life on an estate near Magdeburg since 1692. Last but not least there was Friedrich Breckling, head of the spiritualists and administrator of their tradition. Breckling ran his activities from Amsterdam.

As befits a searcher, Speeth had all their addresses in his notebook. He called on Spener, Breckling and Petersen in his quest for his true self, a quest driven by deep anxiety about his spiritual welfare and his fate after death, and often informed by mystical speculations. In 1700 Jakob Böhme's books were still quite well known, and within Pietist and spiritualistic networks in particular he was considered a special authority. But, despite this interest in the mystical tradition, the Pietist network was also a source of reforms and radical views. Maybe one could even call it a 'theosophic' kind of early Enlightenment – an expression that is not as paradoxical as it seems. For example, Franciscus Mercurius van Helmont moved in the circles of Benjamin Furly, Philipp van Limborch and John Locke. He opposed the doctrine of eternal torments of hell and had mapped out plans to reform education; or the Hermeticist Johann Konrad Dippel, who wrote under the pseudonym 'Christianus Democritus', and made discoveries in chemistry and secularized thinking about redemption. As for Speeth, his return to Judaism embraced at the same time a progressive biblical criticism, the historical criticism of the Platonic influence on Christian thought and anti-Trinitarian rationalism.

Speeth had died in 1701, and rumour had it that other Jews from Amsterdam had poisoned him because he did not want to believe in the 'rabbinic yarns'. In his last years he had got to know Johann Georg Wachter, a young German, who felt he had to denounce him as a supporter of the Kabbalah and Spinozism. Wachter even held the opinion that the Kabbalah and Spinozism were almost the same in their idolatrous glorification of the world. However, Wachter had got Speeth completely wrong. The latter had long since dissociated himself from van Helmont's Kabbalistics and he had nothing to do with Spinoza, either. Wachter himself, though, became increasingly embroiled in this world, and, during his stay in Amsterdam in 1699/1700, became a Kabbalistic Spinozist. He thinks that the Jewish tradition is the first formulation of the view that the world had one origin, by means of a spiritual mediator, which, in Wachter's view, Spinoza described in a purely rational way. Even Trinitarian Christology could be interpreted in the light of this tradition of ideas.

In 1702 Wachter had set down this theory in *Elucidarius cabalisticus*, but neither Stolle nor anybody else knew the text, since Wachter still hesitated to publish it. When he finally did so in 1706, because he combined elements of opposing views, he satisfied neither the spiritualistic radicals nor the anti-Trinitarian radicals (including some atheists). In retrospect it is more evident than it could ever have been to a contemporary such as Stolle that there were several routes to Enlightenment. Some took the simple path of reason, preferring anti-Trinitarian, Jewish and Socinian arguments; others followed a more complex path and used Platonic,

Kabbalistic or Hermetic bases for their 'reasonable' religion beyond Revelation. The first line may be associated with Locke, Collins, Lau or Speeth; the second with Cudworth, Wachter or – years later – Herder.

CONTINUING THE TRADITION

Stolle roams a world in which absolute regimes are well established; but also one in which intellectual and religious ideas were in a state of flux – at least behind the façade of orthodoxy. Stolle notes a 'dissimulation' in many scholars, for instance in Leibniz. Although Leibniz goes to church from time to time to take part in the festivities of the Holy Communion, Stolle considers him a 'naturalist'. He speaks of professors who love 'contradiction' and who follow Hobbes, and of others who deny entry to their libraries, for the 'paradoxical' writings they keep there. In order to avoid his being 'denounced as a heretic from the pulpit', von der Hardt asks his students to keep his lectures to themselves in case his views may be misconstrued. Often it was important to use the relations and connections one had to the prince to counter the distrust of other theologians. But sometimes just the opposite was true: one needed to bring the various faculties together in order to stand up to the court. After the appearance of the Pietists it had become even more difficult to maintain such a 'private prudence' (*Privatklugheit*), because they often drew attention to themselves. Stolle understands that in Hanover a Pietist had grabbed the wig off a courtier's head. In Celle, he meets a mint master who bears private, heretical thoughts in his heart, namely that the Father as well as the Son would come to earth and become human. People wrote refutations, but they did so secretly and without publishing anything. They wanted to avoid attention and trouble.

Since the Reformation, such 'enthusiastic' variations had occurred time and again in Germany. But now, around 1700, they could include 'Enlightenment' ideas. Examples were not only Speeth or Wachter, but Matthias Knutzen, who as early as the 1670s had started to connect Bible criticism and anticlericalism with missionary ambitions which one could compare to those of the Baptists. Once the *Tractatus theologico-politicus* by Spinoza and the *Leviathan* by Hobbes had been read, such hybrid connections were possible in Germany.

Not far away from Helmstedt, about seventy miles to the east, there was the University of Wittenberg, which in the early eighteenth century was still the home of Lutheran orthodoxy. There, the journal *Unschuldige Nachrichten* (*Innocent News*) was closely monitoring 'enthusiastic', 'naturalistic' or Socinian dangers. The 'enthusiastic' followers of Böhme and Weigel were still considered the biggest threat, although the perspective has changed in the meantime. 'Platonism', including Hermeticism and Kabbalah, which they considered the political basis for effusive heretical thoughts, was now regarded by some as the foundation of Spinoza's dangerous ideas.

It is by no means possible simply to juxtapose 'orthodox' environments such as that in Wittenberg with environments of the early Enlightenment in Halle. There existed connections between Thomasians and Pietistic and spiritual networks. Sceptical scholars, too, could be found in Wittenberg, such as the jurist Johann Georg Heber, who took a critical position towards pedantic attitudes and worked with Thomasius. Moreover, there were students, such as Hoelmann, Gerhardt and Burghardt, all Silesians, like Stolle, who wrote poems directed against metaphysical ideas. These were published by Benjamin Neukirk in an anthology of lyrics. One rhyme read: '*Ein Metaphysicus und Alchymist,/Die sonsten weiter nichts mehr seyn/Die treffen wohl in vielen ueberein;/Der will aus allem fast die besten kraeffte zwingen/Und jener alles unter eine decke bringen.*' This speaks of a metaphysician and an alchemist who have quite a lot in common. One wants to get the best out of everything, the other wants to combine everything!

On 23 August 1704, one such student, Urban Gottfried Bucher, was to play the role of an opponent in a medical disputation on the subject of the immortality of the souls of animals. In Wittenberg it was common formally to oppose Cartesian mechanism by emphasizing the immaterial souls in humans and animals. Bucher boldly opposed such views with a radical mechanistic argument. He said that if you can tackle the problem why animals react in a certain way without considering a soul, would not then a soul be unnecessary in men as well? In his view, animal reactions were indeed explicable without reference to a soul. In 1704, this was still bold advocacy but uncertain theory. Bucher's own doubts were soon resolved through reading, in the *Unschuldige Nachrichten*, about Coward and the English debates on the mortality of the soul, and researching local traditions in Wittenberg, such as, for example, Melanchthon's emphasis on the close connection between the body and the soul with its various emotions. According to that theory, there was no substantial soul in *man*, and therefore nothing that would survive the death of the mortal part. Bucher formulated his thoughts in correspondence with his professor. When the professor died, the correspondence was published without Bucher's permission as *Zweier guten Freunde vertrauter Brief-Wechsel vom Wesen der Seelen* (*Letters of Two Good Friends on the Subject of the Nature of the Soul*). In this way, not only had excessive orthodoxy turned into heterodoxy, but also a 'freethinker' who had never wanted to articulate more than private doubts was created. Who then published these *letters* in Jena in 1713? Possibly Gottlieb Stolle?

URBANITY, POETRY AND SCIENCE

On 17 May, Stolle arrives at Hamburg, a huge seaport with 80,000 inhabitants. Although at the time there was no university there, just an 'academic secondary school', the town boasted numerous scholars of distinction. This made Hamburg an attractive place to visit. Here everything came together: trade, cosmopolitan attitudes, urbanity and philological thoroughness. Only Frankfurt am Main during the book fair and Leipzig had similar features. In Germany, a search for a 'conservative Enlightenment' in the sense of a theology based on physical evidence (*Physiko-theologie*), the upholding of commerce and sociability, and the connection between science and revelation normally brought you to Hamburg. The port was the German gate to English culture. People went to the opera, would imitate the letters of the English *Spectator* in the journal *Patriot*, have meetings in the drawing rooms of Jewish merchants or in the fashionable 'coffee houses'; there was a form of 'public sphere' in which a refinement of good taste could evolve.

A figurehead of this kind of Enlightenment was Johann Albert Fabricius, a Greek and Latin scholar with a huge library. Stolle visits him immediately, just as the patrician Zacharias Konrad von Uffenbach from Frankfurt would do eight years later, when he comes through Hamburg during his *peregrinatio*. Apparently, Fabricius could – without any problem – combine the humanist heritage with an eye for criticism and progressive natural sciences. His friend Barthold Hinrich Brockes expressed in rhyme theological ideas based on physical science, drawing on *Irdisches Vergnügen in Gott* (*Earthly Pleasure through God*), a popular multi-volumed work that had been in print since the 1620s. Fabricius and Brockes performed a necessary role as conciliators. In the 1690s, the argument between Pietism and orthodoxy had escalated in Hamburg: there had been riots and street violence, although the situation was now calmer. However, hatred against orthodox Lutherans and their power in the city had prepared the ground for many heterodox activities. For example, two years after Stolle had left Hamburg, an anonymous author called 'Alethophilus' published a translation of the *Corpus Hermeticum* (based on the Dutch version). By doing that, he wanted to support the opposition. Not far from Hamburg, the young Peter Friedrich Arpe spent his time writing a work in which he defended the assumed arch-atheist Giulio Cesare Vanini. Fabricius himself, one of Arpe's mentors, told Stolle that there were no 'atheistic views' in Vanini's writings, although he had been burned for his atheism. So one could pick up diverse heterodox ideas from Arnold of Brescia, Bayle or Thomasius and hopefully view the burning of a philosopher for atheism as an act of barbarism of times now past.

Stolle noticed that in Hamburg

> everyone is tolerated, whatever his beliefs, as long as he lives silently. Apparently, there are not just Reformed Christians, Jews and Pietists here, but also Catholics, Quakers, Mennists, Boehmists and Indifferentists. But none of these sects holds public divine services here in Hamburg. The Reformed Christians, the Catholics, the Mennists, Quakers and Jews go to church in Altona.

Altona was a Danish settlement outside Hamburg, in which a policy of tolerance was pursued in order to draw people and commerce away from the city.

The religious diversity, and at the same time the strong position of Lutheran orthodoxy, had bizarre consequences in which heterodoxy and satire combined in strange ways. Just a few blocks away from where Fabricius lived, in the house of the orthodox pastor Johann Friedrich Mayer, there was, for example, a Latin manuscript with the title *De imposturis religionum*. The few people who had seen it thought that it might be the legendary writing *De tribus impostoribus*, of which rumours had circulated since the Middle Ages. In fact, this work, in which Moses, Jesus and Mohammed were called religious political imposters, had never existed. But in 1688 Mayer's friend Johann Joachim Müller started – secretly – to write it (as a forged original version). He then passed it on anonymously to the pastor. The reason for that was that Mayer, the opponent of the Pietists, was – as were many of his colleagues – very fond of tracking down atheistic writings. Müller then wanted to fool him with his *De imposturis religionum* and, with that, present him with new evidence in his crusade against atheists. But the very evidence which Müller compiled, including Hobbes, Herbert of Cherbury and many other heterodox sources, could be responsible for undermining orthodoxy. In the course of the eighteenth century, this compilation became one of the most widely read clandestine writings of the Enlightenment.

HUGUENOTS, ALCHEMISTS, SOCINIANS

From Hamburg, Stolle goes to the Netherlands, apart from England the most progressive and liberal country in Europe. Stolle and his friends stay there for several months. Thomasius had given them the advice to 'be aware of the Spinozists'. The monism of the Dutch Jew was considered a danger for their own reformatory projects in Halle.

But Stolle is far too curious to heed Thomasius's warning. Very often his first question is whether somebody had known Spinoza, or whether somebody knew something of him. On his way back from Holland, Stolle comes to Berlin. There he spends the winter of 1703/4. In January, Leibniz comes from Hanover to Berlin – as he often does – for two weeks to speak with his friend, the Prussian Queen Sophie Charlotte, and to promote the project of an 'Academy of Sciences' modelled after the academies in England and France. It had been authorized for about three years as a small '*Societät*', but it was not until 1711 that it became a real *Academie*. Leibniz was by then already famous throughout Europe, but not much was known about his philosophy, apart from a few articles. The *Theodicée* was published in 1710, the *Nouveaux Essais* against Locke only posthumously in 1765, and a great part of his writings only in the nineteenth century. Christian Wolff can claim responsibility for making Leibniz's thinking influential, although in his own version.

In March, Leibniz contacts the King's new librarian, the Frenchman Mathurin Veyssière La Croze. He had fled to Prussia from the Parisian monastery of Saint Germain des Prés because he could no longer approve of Louis XIV's religious policy. In Berlin he became part of the considerable colony of Huguenots. Following the Revocation of the Edict of Nantes in 1685 the Great Elector had encouraged the fleeing French Protestants to settle. La Croze and other scholars in this colony, such as Jaquelot, Beausobre, Barbeyrac, Ancillon and Lenfant, combined francophone with German ideas. Barbeyrac in particular made French Enlightenment thinkers familiar with Pufendorf's work on *The Law of Nature and Nations*.

Leibniz, when he was in Berlin, spoke with La Croze about medieval writings, the Chinese language, Socinianism and much else besides, but possibly not the dogmatic niceties of theologians. In this year, 1704, Johann Konrad Dippel, the Hermetic doctor, also comes to Berlin. In Hesse he had fallen into debt because of his experiments and was hoping to find support from the court in Berlin. Unfortunately, Dippel had some 'inconvenient' views. For him, as for Knutzen, the only authority was conscience, and he believed in personal salvation through the 'inner light'.

Spener urged him to come immediately for a visit and to have a conversation about common Pietistic views. Despite a friendly reception, Dippel's connections with Berlin did not last. At the beginning of 1707, he was put in jail, but would later flee in Swedish disguise. He reached Frankfurt via Kösteritz, and afterwards found a safe haven in Holland.

Back to Spener: at that time he was working on a voluminous book directed against the Socinians. These anti-Trinitarian followers of a radical Reformation were, after having been expelled from Poland, tolerated in some areas in Prussia. Most people shunned them, but free-minded intellectuals like La Croze were by no means timid: time and again he had meetings with Samuel Crell, a Socinian theologian. Crell could report on his journeys through western Europe, on his contacts with Locke, Newton, Le Clerc, Bayle and Shaftesbury. La Croze held that it had been a mistake to persecute the Socinians, although they might be wrong in their beliefs. Spener, on the other hand, considered Socinianism a danger. Their movement could, in his eyes, lead to rationalism and deism, as in Holland and England. A scandal of this nature had occurred even in Berlin 1692: the son of the court chaplain, Stosch, had become a Spinozist, perhaps because he originally belonged to Reformed circles sympathetic to Socinianism.

ERUDITION AND SCEPTICISM

In April 1704, Stolle is back in Halle. Thomasius is meanwhile working on his *Fundamenta Juris Naturae et Gentium*, in which he will express a pessimistic anthropology and argue for strict separation between law, morality and decorum; Gundling is writing a historic and critical revision of the origins of philosophy; Budde, as rumours have it, is about to become Professor of Theology in Jena. When this happens in1706, Stolle follows him there, staying for the several years, except for short interruptions. On Saturdays between two and four o'clock he probably attended the small discussion group which had been founded by Burkhard Gotthelf Struve. Meeting in Struve's house, they discussed newly published books and writings as well as current topics of interest. Among those who attended was Ephraim Gerhard, a student who composed poetry; years later, he would be the first and only scholar in Germany to apply Locke's *Second Treatise on Government* to the imperial context.

Struve inaugurated this group with a lecture on the 'Scholar as an Atheist'. An important issue for all who attended, he addressed the speculation surrounding those suspected of atheism, including naturalists such as Pomponazzi and Vanini and 'politicians' such as Machiavelli. This topic gave the young German scholars goose pimples, but at the same time it held an irresistible fascination for them. What secularizing potential was to be found in erudition and science? Was it not possible to oppose a specific 'Christian' form of erudition to this tendency?

Even Christian Thomasius had to endure a personal crisis on account of such questions. He undertook an intense study of the contemporary mystic Pierre Poiret, who established a Christian *eruditio solida*, opposed to the *eruditio superficiaria* and *falsa*. Many young scholars, including Struve, Reimmann and even Stolle, underwent such a crisis, and in the process reread the mystics of the late Middle Ages, notably Thomas à Kempis.

What followed from this crisis of scholars? Was one to become a Pietist or a sceptic? Such possibilities were not necessarily contradictory; St Paul had already warned of the stupidity of secular knowledge. This scepticism, however, could lead to a fideistic rejection of philosophy, as was the case with the Pietist Joachim Lange, but it could also lead to a moderate scepticism, which purported to cleanse traditional views of error by means of a historical criticism. Reading the *Dictionnaire* by Bayle, or the writings of the French libertines Naudé and La Mothe Le Vayer added to the crisis. When Stolle was away in 1703, Joachim Lange visited his friend Jakob Friedrich Reimmann in his house in Halberstadt to talk with him about the two directions of scepticism. They could not reach an agreement. Lange accused Reimmann of being a godless philosopher (which, of course, was not true), who associated the biblical Solomon with the libertine scepticism of Le Vayer. Reimmann, on the other hand, insisted that the best form of eclecticism incorporated a sceptical approach.

Other students of Thomasius, such as Friedrich Wilhelm Bierling and Christoph August Heumann, adopted a moderately sceptical erudition compatible with secular knowledge. While Stolle was travelling, Bierling, a professor in Rinteln, wrote *De iudicio historico*, in which Pyrrhonist doubts were raised about many historical claims. Later, Heumann became a professor in Göttingen, and a founder of a critical historiography: there were so many tales and legends about history and alleged oriental wisdom that one had to destroy!

Until the 1740s, the great historiographic *historia literaria* collections of Struve, Heumann, Gundling and Reimmann or Jakob Brucker would greatly influence the form of German erudition: a polymathic erudition with a great number of footnotes and digressions. In the middle of the eighteenth century this kind of erudition was criticized as exaggeratedly meticulous, and in the course of a few years almost all footnotes disappeared from such works. At the time, however, scholars considered themselves as being very modern and enlightening by avoiding seemingly timeless speculation. Reimmann very bluntly demanded professorial chairs for *historia literaria* instead of metaphysics.

SCIENCES

Metaphysics would regain its vogue in Germany in the 1720s and 1730s but before then its adherents saw themselves as under siege. Stolle, returning briefly to Halle from Jena, met Christian Wolff, the mathematician and philosopher, who had arrived there the previous year from Leipzig. Unfortunately, his mathematical and mechanical ideas did not appeal to those in Thomasius's circle, and Gundling, among others, was quick to attack him. Only the physician Friedrich Hoffmann found his ideas congenial.

Followers of Thomasius were not on good terms with supporters of Cartesian or Boyleian approaches to the natural sciences. In *Versuch vom Wesen des Geistes* (1699), Thomasius committed himself to a search for the spiritual essence of physical science. Wolff found just a few allies in favour of his mechanistic views: Tschirnhaus in Saxony, who was associated the development of Dresden porcelain; and his own patron, Leibniz, in Hanover. A robust defender of metaphysics, Leibniz provided a counterpoise to the movement in Halle. Attributing the radicalizing and secularizing tendencies of the early Enlightenment to the school of natural law, he suggested that 'Pufendorf and the Messieurs Thomasius and Gundling opened the door to exaggerated freedom way too far' (Leibniz 1716: 516).

Wolff would adopt the tradition of experimental physics, which had been developed by Johann Christoph Sturm in Altdorf, a German form of the sceptical science of Robert Boyle. Altdorf had the necessary environment for experimental physics. As the university of the Free Imperial Town of Nuremberg, it had the background of a citizenry with a tradition of *societates curiosae*; favourable to experiments and their practical consequences. Following correspondence between Boyle, Hoffman and Sturm, the latter's *Philosophia eclectica* of 1686 proclaimed eclecticism as essential for the promotion of empirical investigations and tolerance among the community of scientists.

The scene changed again in the 1720s and 1730s, when Wolff's philosophy became successful and started its triumphant progress throughout Germany. Wolff was a systematician. In the voluminous edition of his complete works, written in German and Latin, he spoke of virtually all disciplines: ontology, ethics, natural law, mathematics and physics. A number of the 'scholastic' Aristotelian elements discarded by Thomasius re-emerged and were connected with ideas formulated by Leibniz. This was the first time that a philosophical reform spread beyond the boundaries of the university to the educated citizenry. The followers of Thomasius had concentrated on the reform of the practical and moral disciplines, but now 'Enlightenment' in all domains was required. Many of the old obstacles remained, however. Like Thomasius before him, Wolff came under suspicion from the theologians. In 1723, he had to leave Halle because of accusations formulated by the Pietists, and only after Frederick the Great became King in 1740 could he return. By now the period of the early Enlightenment was over and a new phase had begun.

REFERENCES

Breckling's letters to Christian Thomasius, Supellex Epistolica Uffenbachii et Wolfiorum, University Library of Hamburg.

Gierl, Martin (1997) *Pietismus und Aufklärung: Theologische Polemik und die Kommunikationsreform der Wissenschaft am Ende des 17. Jahrhunderts*, Göttingen: Vandenhoeck & Ruprecht.

Hammerstein, Notker (1972) *Jus und Historie: Ein Beitrag zum historischen Denken an den deutschen Universitäten im späten 17. und 18. Jahrhundert*, Göttingen: Vandenhoeck & Ruprecht.

Hochstrasser, Tim (2000) *Natural Law Theories in the Early Enlightenment*, Cambridge: Cambridge University Press.

Kemper, Hans-Georg (1991) *Deutsche Lyrik in der frühen Neuzeit*, vols 5/I and 5/II, Tübingen: Niemeyer.

Leibniz, Gottfried Wilhelm (1716) 'Letter to la Croze, 29 May', in vol. 5 of (1768) *Opera omnia*, ed. Louis Dutens, 6 vols, Geneva.

Mulsow, Martin (2002) *Moderne aus dem Untergrund: Radikale Frühaufklärung in Deutschland 1680–1720*, Hamburg: F. Meiner.

Pott, Martin (1992) *Aufklärung und Aberglaube: Die deutsche Frühaufklärung im Spiegel ihrer Aberglaubenskritik*, Tübingen: Niemeyer.

Schilling, Heinz (1994) *Höfe und Allianzen: Deutschland 1648–1763*, Berlin: Siedler Verlag.

Schneiders, Werner (1971) *Naturrecht und Liebesethik: Zur Geschichte der praktischen Philosophie im Hinblick auf Christian Thomasius*, Hildesheim and New York: G. Olms.

Simons, Olaf (2001) *Marteaus Europa oder Der Roman, bevor er Literatur wurde*, Amsterdam: Rodopi.

Stolle, Gottlieb (1703/4) *Reise dreyer vertrauter Freunde durch Holland und einen Theil Deutschlands*, Ms. Cod. IV oct. 49 und Ms. R 766, Biblioteka Uniwersytecka, Wrocław.

Thomasius, Christian (1970) *Deutsche Schriften*, ed. Peter von Düffel, Stuttgart: Reclam.

CHAPTER NINE

THE AGE OF LOUIS XIV AND EARLY ENLIGHTENMENT IN FRANCE

Martin Fitzpatrick

The purpose of this chapter is to discuss not so much early Enlightenment intellectual trends as the broad social and political context in which they found expression. It will argue that Enlightenment in France began within the court society of Louis XIV and remained within its ambit in the eighteenth century even while growing increasingly critical of such a society. The Regency, which is often taken to signal the moment when Enlightenment forces in France become irresistible, will be examined briefly to show the elements of continuity from Louis XIV's time and the new trends which favoured the development of a spirit of criticism.

LOUIS XIV AND THE AGE OF REASON

In 1751, Voltaire published his *Le Siècle de Louis XIV*. The work had taken him some twenty years to write. Around the time he began writing his study of the century of Louis XIV he published his *Letters on England* (1733), published subsequently as the *Lettres philosophiques* (1734), in which he was deeply critical of French government and society, notably for their lack of freedom, religious tolerance and social recognition for the arts and sciences:

> It seems to me that at the present time the taste at Court is far removed from letters. Perhaps in a short time the fashion for using one's mind will come back – a king has only to have the will and he makes what he likes of a nation. In England as a rule people think, and literature is more honoured than in France. This advantage is a natural outcome of the form of their government. In London there are some eight hundred people with the right to speak in public and uphold the interests of the nation; about five or six thousand aspire to the same honour in their turn, all the rest set themselves to sit in judgement on these, and anybody can print what he thinks about public affairs.
>
> (Voltaire 1733: Letter 20, 101)

Almost twenty years later, he painted a more positive picture in *Le Siècle de Louis XIV*. He still thought that the English were superior to the French in their achievements in philosophy, but those of his countrymen were not to be ignored. Colbert, jealous of the English Royal Society (founded in 1662) had established an Academy of Science in 1666. By offering large cash incentives, he attracted leading scientists of the day to work in the Academy: Domenico Cassini from Italy, Huygens from Holland and Roemer from Denmark. Nonetheless, Voltaire conceded 'the philosophy of reason did not make such great progress in France as in England' (Voltaire 1751: 357). It was in language and literature that France eclipsed other nations and set new standards of good taste. Whereas in his *Letters on England* he had been very critical of the French Academy, notably for the reams of eulogistic addresses which it published (Voltaire 1733: Letter 24, 116–18), in his *Siècle* he attributed the growing refinement and standardization of the French language to 'the French Academy and above all to Vaugelas' – his *Translations of Quintus Curtius* (1646). He noted, too, of the leading writers of the age – Corneille, Racine, Boileau, Molière, Quinault – that 'all these great men . . . were protected by Louis XIV, with the exception of La Fontaine' (Voltaire 1751: 358, 367). He argued that, through its literary achievement (in history, works 'of reflection, and light literature') France set the pattern for enlightening Europe, and its achievements were carried abroad through the agency of the French writers, especially Huguenots, and instanced Pierre Bayle, Rapin de Thoyras, Saint Evremond, the Duchesse de Mazarin and Mme d'Olbreuses (later the Duchess von Zell). He concluded:

> Of all the nations, France has produced the greatest number of such works. Its language has become the language of Europe . . . The social spirit is the natural heritage of the French; it is a merit and a pleasure of which other nations have felt the need. The French language is of all languages that which expresses with the greatest of ease, exactness and delicacy all subjects of conversation which can arise among gentlefolk; and it thus contributes throughout all Europe to one of the most agreeable diversions of life.
>
> (Voltaire 1751: 371)

For Voltaire, that was the summit of French achievement, but it was not the sum total, for he praised French excellence in music, architecture, sculpture, painting, engraving and the art of surgery. Royal patronage played a key role in many of these achievements. Although *Le Siècle de Louis XIV* which Voltaire recounted, 'began in the time of Richelieu, and ended in our days', it was above all the kingship of Louis XIV which led to French cultural ascendancy. The age marked 'the progress of the human spirit' and, were it to be eclipsed by a more enlightened age, it would 'remain the model of more fortunate ages, to which it will have given birth' (Voltaire 1751: 375).

Voltaire's divided opinions will form the basis of our discussion of the early Enlightenment in France. Indeed, it was the combination of the cultural brilliance of France and the ascendancy of the French language set against the failings of absolutism, and the existence of an alternative set of values and practices across the Channel, which would shape the very nature of the Enlightenment in France and the rest of Europe.

LOUIS XIV

In 1661, the personal rule of Louis XIV began after the death of his chief minister, Cardinal Mazarin. He inherited a bankrupt state, one which had suffered the civil wars of *La Fronde* (1648–53). At the time there had been a flood of scurrilous literature directed against Mazarin, who on his death left the greatest fortune ever accumulated in *ancien régime* France. Mazarin recommended to Louis that his own personal intendant of affairs, Jean Baptiste Colbert, should become his chief minister. Louis ignored the advice. He was determined to assert his own role as king and to be his own chief minister, informing his courtiers that he would 'personally administer the finances with the aid of loyal men acting under me' (Lossky 1967: 341). Mazarin had offered to leave his enormous fortune to Louis while cleverly inviting him to make the magnanimous gesture of turning it down. Louis duly obliged (Dessert 1987: 225–8). He did, however, choose to inherit Mazarin's trusty servant, Colbert, who sorted out the tangle of financial mismanagement which had begun with the death of Cardinal Richelieu in 1643. In time Colbert would become first minister in all but name. He sought to build up French economic power through mercantilist policies, namely protectionism and the patronage of French industry, especially the production of luxuries. Although not as bellicose as Louvois, Minister of War, he was just as anxious to promote French ascendancy in Europe. His mercantilism was warfare by other means and, if it failed, then war became almost inevitable. His protective tariffs proved to be a major cause of the war with the Dutch, 1672–8. Colbert accepted that at the heart of Bourbon absolutism was the pursuit of *la gloire*. Writing to the King in 1666, he suggested it is a 'beautiful maxim that it is necessary to save five *sous* on unessential things, and to pour out millions when it is a question of your glory' (Cole 1939: vol. 1, 292).

ABSOLUTE MONARCHY AND *LA GLOIRE*

When Louis began his personal rule he could draw on theorists of absolutism who stressed his unique power and responsibility. Cardinal Richelieu, in his *Testament politique*, likened the position of the king to that of God. He ruled through sovereign authority which stood above all particular interests of individuals and groups, and his role was to ensure that the public interest prevailed. In Richelieu's ideal state the monarch would order and govern his earthly territory as effectively as God was able to order and govern His universe. But, although his vision of government was one of power and control emanating from the centre, he accepted that force alone could not ensure the smooth running of government and society: For that, it was necessary to supplement force with reason: 'authority constrains men to obedience, but reason persuades them to do it' (*Testament politique* quoted in Keohane 1980: 177).

The public interest as understood by Richelieu had little to do with the humanistic notion of public well-being. For him it meant strengthening the power of the monarch, both within his state and in relation to other states. Schooled by Mazarin, Louis shared the same vision. It was a lesson he readily imbibed, for he was a child of the Fronde. His own description of the situation which he inherited

Figure 9.1 *The Celebration of Louis celebrated*, Louis Simonneau after a drawing by Noel Coypel, frontispiece of *Medailles sur les principaux evénements du regne de Louis le Grand* (1702). This handsome volume, published by the royal press, provided a medallic history of Louis XIV's reign. It was indicative of the continuing concern to record the great moments of his reign and to provide a permanent record and reminder of his glorious achievements. By permission of the British Library.

was bleak: serious internal instability which limited the effective prosecution of the war with Spain and in his own court 'little fidelity without personal interest' (Louis's *Mémoires* quoted in Wolf 1970: 61).

With such a background, Louis XIV knew that there was a huge gulf between absolutist theory and the actual authority which he was able to exercise. Churchmen were particularly prone to elevate the king's authority above all worldly things. The notion of the divine right of kings became especially powerful during the late sixteenth century and the seventeenth. The term 'absolute monarch' was popularized by Jean Bodin, in his *Six Books of the Republic* (1576), in which he argued that the king was not subject to human laws, but only to natural, divine and fundamental law. Symbolic of this monarch's power was his right to pardon criminals, especially at his coronation. On *his* coronation in 1654, Louis XIV pardoned a range of offences, some of which might be construed as contrary to natural, divine and fundamental law – such as premeditated murder and duelling. Yet the growing tendency to deify the monarchy was such that the distinction between the king being subject to divine law and the king as a source of divine law could easily become blurred. In an ode composed by the Jesuits for Louis's coronation, he was placed alongside Jesus Christ as 'God-given'. When Bishop Bossuet, in a much-cited sermon of 1662, said of kings that 'you are gods', he was only repeating a declaration of the Assembly of the Clergy of 1625 (Jackson 1984: 108–12, 206–20). Nonetheless, absolutist propaganda reached its zenith in Louis XIV's reign and divine right theory found its supreme exponent in Bossuet's *Politics Founded on Holy Scripture*, written for the edification of the Dauphin.

If the propaganda of Louis XIV's monarchy was not original, it was supremely powerful. The melding of classical with Christian symbolism, pagan gods with Christian divinity, Christian kingship with Roman imperialism, had occurred in the late sixteenth century and was strongly present at the coronation entry into Reims of Louis XIII in 1610. The myth that the Franks were descended from the Trojans who founded Rome provided the justification for much of the symbolism, but there were other dimensions to it. At the coronation, solar symbolism played a major role. Louis XIV and his propagandists, however, proved to be supreme in combining classical with Christian imagery to create a shining vision of monarchical power. At his coronation in 1653, he chose the sun as his personal symbol. His bedroom at Versailles faced east to enable him to witness the rising of the sun, and his *lever* and *coucher* imitated sunrise and sunset (Jackson 1984: 148–54, 180–85, 213).

Louis and his ministers created a notion of kingship with many dimensions. Imagery supplemented and arguably transcended absolutist theory. The King appeared as the father of his people, as their protector, and as the focus of their affections, as a saint with divine attributes who healed divisions and unified the nation, as the almighty King without equal in the world, who would brook no opposition (Pommier 1992: 299). He was both a pagan god of mythic powers, and His Most Christian Majesty. All this seems very contradictory, but it was undoubtedly a potent mixture drawing on well-established traditions (Wolf 1970: 460–2). The ultimate aim was to create the sense that monarchical power was irresistible. Despite Richelieu's emphasis on supplementing force with reason, the symbolic embellishment of power made subordination much more attractive than the cold logic and the threat of force. Indeed, Richelieu (just after the passage cited earlier, in which he talked of reason supplementing force) wrote of *insensibly* winning over men's wills. The pursuit of *gloire* undoubtedly facilitated the monarch's task of giving unity and coherence to a country which was more like a federation than a unitary state (Shennan 1969: 22).

Of course, the theory of absolutism and its symbolism had to bear an approximate relation to reality in order not to be undermined by scepticism and ridicule. One can only imagine what many thought when extensive use was made of solar imagery at the coronation of Louis XVI in 1775. One image had the accompanying verse attached to it: 'I regulate the seasons, I divide the days; the universe embellishes itself with my prolific light, and faithful to the law that governs my heart, I am the benefactor of the world' (Jackson 1984: 184). By that time, there was a rival Enlightenment which believed it could serve the world through its own exertions and not that of the monarch. Long before then, however, Enlightenment thinking in France would develop as a result of both the desire of the monarchy to enhance its *gloire* through cultural means and the failings of that enterprise towards the end of Louis XIV's reign.

Louis XIV was fortunate enough to inherit a kingdom which was much stronger internally and externally than it had been at the accession of his father. Some of the baroque complexity of the state was being resolved, although government and society were shot through with privileges regarded by many as rights. A major obstacle to the reform of the state was the fact that most offices were purchased, and the cost of buying out office-holders was prohibitive – Colbert estimated it would cost 419.6 million livres to do so, almost four times the cost of Versailles (Bonney 1978: 450, n. 2; Wolf 1970: 444). They would, however, be made to pay for their privileges through taxation. At the same time, institutional rights and privileges which stood in the way of the exercise of kingly authority would be modified. The most notable instance of this was the withdrawal in 1673 of the right of the *parlements* to hold up royal edicts by refusing to register them immediately and remonstrating against them. This did not prevent opposition to some royal edicts, but by 1683 all parts of the kingdom had their own royal provincial intendants, officials directly answerable to the King, who often took on groups of the privileged within the provinces in order to secure royal wishes, and to protect the interests of the more vulnerable members of the community. Theory and practice were therefore not too out of joint, and the idea of the Sun King whose rays illuminated his kingdom did not seem at all ridiculous.

THE COURT

The centre of the King's social and political authority was the court. Blaise Pascal noted, 'People go away and hide themselves for eight months in the country so they can shine for four months at Court' (Pascal 1670: Additional *Pensée* 7, 358). Louis XIV's new palace at Versailles, substantially completed by 1688, became the symbolic centre of his power, the actual centre of his government, the focus of social aspirations and a model for imitation at home and abroad. Every aspect – the buildings, the gardens, the furnishings, the paintings and tapestries – was designed to impress the elite with the brilliance of the King's authority and to remind them of the values of serving him.

But the court was not a static hierarchy; rather, individuals and groups jostled for precedence, rather like the Soviet generals at Chairman Andropov's funeral. Versailles provides a good example of the nature of French monarchy. Norbert Elias has argued that the court was 'a complex of interdependent groups competing with each other and holding each other in check' (Elias 1983: 270–4). The King dominated this system and made creative use of the conflicts and tensions within his own court. There was huge scope for such a role, for distinctions of all sorts, within families as well as between orders, were endless, including rank and birth, as well as merit and wealth (Le Roy Ladurie 1997: 23–61). Louis XIV proved to be a master of the art of manipulation, and had a genius for inducing others to do what he wanted them to do (Campbell 1993: 110; Levron 1976: 133–4; Revel 1992: 92–6). Government operated in the kingdom in a similar way. If the King was ultimately sovereign, it was always better to achieve one's ends through the power of one's reputation and the creation of a deferential public, rather than through the exercise of physical power. He wrote early on in his career, 'A king need never be ashamed of seeking fame, for it is a good that must be ceaselessly and avidly desired, and which alone is better able to secure success of our aims than any other thing. Reputation is often more effective than the most powerful armies' (quoted in Wolf 1970: 241). He kept to his own advice rather more in the early years of his personal reign than later. That is the period when he unleashed the energies of Colbert to create court-sponsored Enlightenment.

The institutions he and his associates created not only served to add to the prestige of the Sun King but also provided opportunities for fame for philosophers and writers. The list is impressive. In 1663 Colbert established the Petite Académie, with the purpose of glorifying the King. It dealt with everything connected with *belles-lettres*, and co-operated with Charles Lebrun in arbitrating on matters of taste. In 1696 it became an independent academy with the title of the Académie Royale des Médailles et Inscriptions. The title was changed again in 1701, and finally in 1717, first to the Académie des Inscriptions et Médailles and then to Académie des Inscriptions et Belles Lettres. In 1663–4 the Académie Royale de Peinture et de Sculpture, founded in 1648, was reorganized and handsomely funded. With Lebrun as its chancellor (1661–90), it was extremely influential at court, and all artists working for the King were required to be members. The reorganization was followed by the creation of the Académie Française de Rome (1666), providing the elite of its students with an opportunity to study in Rome: it offered three-year bursaries for a dozen young French artists. In 1671 the Académie d'Architecture was established, as was the Académie d'Opera, although the latter was replaced in the following year by the Académie Royale de Musique. An Académie des Spetacles was founded in 1674 but never registered (Burke 1992: esp. 50–1; Parker 1983: 132–3; Friedman 1990: 211, 214).

These academies ensured that artistic and intellectual life focused on the court, that the elevation of the image of the monarch was constantly in mind, and that cultural control was exercised in a whole variety of ways. Here, we shall focus primarily on two key institutions and two leading individuals associated with them. One of the institutions, the Académie Française, had been established by Cardinal Richelieu in 1635.

INSTITUTIONS OF EARLY ENLIGHTENMENT

In 1672, Louis XIV became the protector of the Académie Française. He was the first king to assume this role. The academy had been established in order to purify and standardize the French language and make it comprehensible to all. The core of academicians had gathered informally since 1629, and Richelieu's intention in formalizing the academy was to subvert the development of private cultural circles and to harness the men of letters in service to the state (Maland 1970: 96). They, in turn, benefited from the prestige he conferred on them. Indeed, they were deemed the 'immortals' (from the device 'to Immortality' on the seal given to the academy by Richelieu).

The academicians – there were initially twenty-seven and subsequently forty, elected by their peers – decided that, in order to fulfil their purpose, they needed to compose 'a comprehensive dictionary and a most precise grammar' (Maland 1970: 99–100). Claude Favre, Seigneur de Vaugelas, praised by Voltaire, played a major role in purifying and standardizing the language. His concept of *bon usage* illustrates the fusion of court standards with those of men of letters, for he defined it as 'the manner of speech of the most sensible men at court with the manner of writing of the soundest authors of the time' (Maland 1970: 101). He also especially commended the unselfconscious language of aristocratic women.

The compilation of the dictionary proceeded slowly and it was not published until the height of Louis's reign, in two volumes in 1694. A second edition was published in 1718 and two further editions followed before the end of the *ancien régime*. As Voltaire noted, during this period French became the premier language of Europe, thus fulfilling one of Richelieu's aspirations. Moreover, the value of linguistic uniformity within France was not lost on the servants of Louis XIV, many of whose subjects were not even French speaking (Goubert 1969: 273, 277–8; Roche 1993: 239–40). The language of the academy, however, was not the French of the common people, but that of the court and polite society – of Versailles and Paris, as Vaugelas made clear: '*le bon [usage] . . . est composé, non pas de la pluralité, mais de l'élite des voix*' (quoted in Lough 1954: 247). The dominant language for Enlightenment thought was the aristocratic and self-consciously modern language of the age of Louis XIV (Lough 1954: 251–5).

Patronage of the arts and letters was just one aspect of absolutist policy designed to encourage unity and engender loyalty to the King and pride in his country, especially among the governing elite, whose loyalty in the mid-century had been in doubt. Through his manifold activities, Colbert founded a veritable 'department of glory' which controlled the image of the King and presented the events of his reign to the public (Burke 1992: 58–9). Academies held competitions for the best construction of appropriate aspects of Louis's *gloire*. Relying on specialists for concrete suggestions, notably Jean Chapelain (literature), Charles Lebrun (painting and sculpture) and Claude Perrault (architecture), Colbert's organization spanned the spectrum of cultural activity. 'Artists, writers, and scholars' were all mobilized 'in the service of the king' (Burke 1992: 50): recipients of Louis's pensions and *gratifications* in a single year included three theologians, eight linguists, twenty-five French and three foreign 'men of letters', five historians, one painter, one lawyer, six students of physics, four surgeons and medical men, one botanist and one mathematician. Men of the distinction of Molière, Racine, Perrault, Boileau, Tellemont, Godefroy and de La Croix were supported in this way (Wolf 1970: 455) and considerable sums of money were lavished on their academies (King 1949: 287–9). The policy was a great success and institutions created and patronized by the crown provided a secure livelihood for a 'high proportion' of men of letters (Waller 1977). The resulting self-confidence permeated French intellectual society and played a significant role in the emergence of Enlightenment thought.

Charles Perrault (1628–1703) is a good example of the opportunities which royal service provided and of the confidence in the age which a successful career engendered. Trained as a lawyer, he began his career as a clerk, entered the service of Colbert in 1663, then became in 1665 chief clerk at the department of buildings of the royal household. In 1667 he supervised the building of the Royal Observatory, using the plans of his brother Claude, also a beneficiary of royal patronage. Although Charles had written an ode to the King which attracted some attention, he had written little when elected to the Académie Française in 1671. The following year he was elected chancellor of the academy and a year later its librarian. He had achieved these distinctions before he wrote his long narrative poem *Le Siècle de Louis le Grand* (1687), in which the age of Louis is seen as worthy of comparison with that of Augustus, foreshadowing Voltaire's homage to the age. For Perrault, the greatness of Louis and his people provided 'the necessary foundation for great literary achievement' (DeJean 1997: 43), and in his subsequent *Parallèle des anciens et des modernes, en ce qui regard les arts et les sciences* (1688–97), he made the case for the superiority of the achievements of the moderns and reanimated a controversy that had been raging for about a century. Not all agreed that the modern age was superior to that of the ancients, but those engaged in the controversy agreed that knowledge of natural philosophy and the applied sciences (including military technology) had progressed, and all celebrated the age of Louis XIV (DeJean 1997: 43; Sonnino 1990: 201).

Colbert's role in the creation of this self-confidence was crucial. Naturally, he made sure that those who benefited from royal patronage rendered appropriate service to the King, but his real importance lay in his broad understanding of the contribution of all the arts and sciences to the glory of Louis and the systematic way he went about achieving such ends. Thus the Académie Royale des Sciences, established in 1666 on his initiative, was not set up just in imitation of the Royal Society in England (as Voltaire later maintained); rather, it formed part of an ambitious scheme for the creation of *la Grande Académie*, which would be divided into four sections: *belles-lettres*, history, philosophy and mathematics. This was successfully opposed by the Académie Française and other corporate interests, leaving the Académie Royale des Sciences as an institution devoted primarily to mathematics and natural philosophy (see Briggs 1991: 42).

Yet, out of the compromises Colbert was forced to make by the competing interests in the state, a new form of scientific organization was born. It had arisen not from the demands of the practitioners of the new science, for they had their own patrons; rather, this new institution for early Enlightenment thought had grown out of the imperatives of the court society of Louis XIV. With its establishment, private patronage of the new science was superseded, which suited Colbert well (Lux 1991: 191–4). He regarded the patronage of scientific research as providing a new dimension to a king's *gloire* and as being of great potential service to the state, especially in military and naval affairs. Sebastién le Clerc engraved the King visiting the recently established Académie Royale des Sciences as the frontispiece for Claude Perrault's *Mémoires pour l'histoire naturelle des animaux* (1671), even though the King never made such a visit (Burke 1992: 54 and plate 18). He had limited interest in science (see Stroup 1992: 225–7; Hahn 1992: 196–7). He visited the academy in 1681 and the Royal Observatory the following year, apparently his only visit (King 1949: 290; Wolf 1970: 456; Stroup 1992: 226).

In 1699, the academy was reorganized. It received new letters patents and its official status was enhanced. Colbert's vision of a mutually beneficial relationship between science, the monarchy and the state remained the inspiration, notably for Bernard le Bovier de Fontenelle. Already a member of the Académie Française, he owed his appointment as its perpetual secretary in 1697 to his reputation as a popularizer of science, and he lived up to it. From 1699 to 1740 he produced an annual *Histoire de l'Académie des Sciences* in which his literary skills were employed in making new science accessible to the Parisian elite (Niklaus 1985:165). His *éloges* of great scientists – he composed sixty-nine during his long time in office – summed up their achievements in non-technical language and created a genre that outlasted him and informed an educated public throughout the Enlightenment period. He also set a pattern and style imitated by later Enlightenment writers. He was the inspiration for the encyclopaedists and an early *philosophe* (Niklaus 1985). Fontenelle admired Colbert greatly and, like him, saw no conflict between service to the crown and intellectual activity. Moreover, the public to which many *philosophes* appealed had already developed in Louis XIV's reign, and that indeed accounts for Fontenelle's style – he aimed to explain difficult scientific truths to 'an assembly of *honnêtes hommes* and *femmes*' (Paul 1980: 18), a matter of some importance since the academies were all masculine institutions.

Fontenelle possessed all the necessary qualities for a *philosophe* living under an absolutist regime. He was socially and intellectually deft, knowing how to dress up dangerous ideas in polite and entertaining ways, how to divorce social criticism from social conformity and broadly to please his masters and retain their patronage while maintaining intellectual freedom, a not inconsiderable achievement and one which few *philosophes* matched (Sonnino 1990: 203–4). Thus he was one of the few to criticize the persecution leading to the revocation of the Edict of Nantes, in a fictional letter from Borneo. Yet, even Pierre Bayle, who published the letter, was slow to decode its covert criticism. When the message did sink in, Fontenelle's career was not immediately impeded because he took out an insurance on his orthodoxy by translating Latin allegorical verses into French, which could be construed as supporting the revocation. They were intended as a backdrop for the occasion of a panegyric to be delivered on the revocation by Père Quartier (Adams 1991: 25–7). Although ashamed of the price he had to pay on this occasion for his intellectual freedom, Fontenelle nonetheless succeeded in setting the pattern for *philosophes* by which ideas could be popularized through entertaining writing, and 'vulgarisation could be made more effective' paradoxically 'by appealing to the "happy few", the more intelligent and discerning reader' (Niklaus 1985: 172–3).

In this way, he propagated early Enlightenment thinking, possessing the unusual ability simultaneously to absorb the ideas of others, enhance their subversive scepticism, and disguise their force: his *Histoire des Oracles* (1687) and *De L'Origine des Fables* (1724) well illustrate this skill. It was not complete proof against his critics and he also needed powerful protectors at court. According to Voltaire, his *Histoire des Oracles* got him into hot water at the end of Louis's reign. The work popularized the ideas of the Dutch scholar Anthonie van Dale (1638–1708). In 1713, the King's confessor, the Jesuit Le Tellier, accused Fontenelle of atheism. He would have been stripped of 'his pension, his office, and his freedom' had not the Marquis d'Argenson intervened on his behalf (Voltaire 1764: art. *Philosophe*, 423; Israel 2001: 359–61, 370–1). Nor had the letter from Borneo been forgotten: it contributed to the danger he was in at that time (Adams 1991: 26).

Fontenelle, however, continued to tread the fine line between conformity and criticism, for he was the only member of the Académie Française to protest against the expulsion of the Abbé de Saint-Pierre for his *Polysnodie*, in which he recommended the administrative regime initially adopted by the Regency in reaction to that of Louis XIV. This was the academy's first notable act under the Regency, and it was a sign that it would not move with the times, but would seek to preserve the reputation and ideals of the Sun King (Brunel 1884: 9–11)

FREEDOM AND CONTROL

The skills of a Fontenelle were at a premium because the position of an intellectual under absolutism was fraught with contradiction and difficulty. There was a sense in which philosophers saw themselves as apart from society, and free to think their own thoughts. When the Académie Française in its first dictionary, published in 1694, listed *philosophe*, it offered three definitions:

1 A student of the sciences (in the language of the late seventeenth century this meant someone seeking certain knowledge, usually with a mathematical basis).
2 A wise man who lives a quiet life.
3 A man who by freethinking puts himself above the ordinary duties and obligations of civil and religious life.

The full original phrasing is: '*un homme, qui, par libertinage d'esprit, se met au dessus des devoirs et des obligations ordinaires de la vie civile et chrétienne. C'est un homme qui ne se refuse rien, qui ne se contraint sur rien, et qui même une vie de Philosophe*' (Smith 1934: 309–10; Commager 1977: 236–45; Beales 1985: 169–70).

Taken together, these present the picture of a learned, disinterested thinker who places himself apart from the ordinary strains and stresses of life; this was indeed

Fontenelle's ideal (Rappaport 1981: 226). At the same time there is the implication that the thoughts and behaviour of the *philosophe* were unsuitable for society at large. Here lurked a potential danger, for, although 'dictionaries record innovations only after due deliberation' (Ozouf 1988: S2), even at the time there was perhaps an element of wishful thinking in these definitions. Already in the late seventeenth century the notion that the *philosophe* was a critic of ordinary values was beginning to imply that he should play a public role in attempting to ameliorate some of the excesses of superstition, dogmatism and prejudice. Moreover, the man of letters, whatever his inclination, could not afford to ignore completely the world around him, for he almost invariably depended on patronage for his position. That came at a price, for patrons were interested in the opinions of their clients. Thus the situation of the *philosophes* was fraught with ambiguity. Although they regarded themselves as members of an intellectual community of equals, they were also, as members of institutions of 'Enlightenment' fostered by the government, expected to serve the government, for their pensions were not sinecures (King 1949: 293).

The national academies and their counterparts in the provinces had one central purpose: the enhancement of the *gloire* of the King. Between 1669 and 1695 six provincial academies modelled on the Académie Française were established – at Arles, Soissons, Nîmes, Angers, Villefranche and Toulouse; three were founded on the model of the Académie Royale des Sciences – at Caen, Montpellier and Bordeaux; and an opera house and an academy of music on the Parisian model was set up in Marseille in 1684 (Burke 1992: 155). These were institutions which needed nurturing *and* controlling. The latter extended from the regulation of their manner of proceeding – Colbert set out the precise number of hours that the Académie Française should meet and gave its members a very expensive pendulum clock to ensure that they kept to time – to the quest for the most suitable recipients of patronage (Chapelain wrote reports on ninety writers), and finally to the control of publications and ideas (Burke 1992: 53, 58). Indeed, the 'degree of government control' exercised over 'the entire spectrum of artistic and intellectual activity' was 'unsurpassed before the twentieth century' (Parker 1983: 131–2).

From the time peace was restored after the Fronde, the government had been anxious to prevent the circulation of seditious ideas. In 1652 and 1653 measures were announced in the official *Gazette* for restoring control over the press and preventing the publication of 'any posters or books and slanderous tracts with a seditious tendency' (Rossel 1982: 108–9). New philosophical ideas might appear to be several stages removed from such things, but it was vitally important that the elites in society learned new ideas in acceptable forms, especially those which did not upset received religious orthodoxy, on which it was felt the moral and political order rested. The absolute state was deeply sensitive to anything which might encourage religious dissidence. It also took for granted its right to control opinion. The weekly *Journal des Savants*, founded in 1665, contained obituaries of scholars, information about experiments and reviews of books. In spreading news of the world of learning it also advertised the King's patronage. Published by the royal press, it was edited by creatures of Colbert, although the first editor, Denis de Sallo, overstepped the mark and was replaced by the Abbé Gallois (Rossel 1982: 33–4; Maland 1970: 290).

The fall of Foucquet, who had maintained an extravagant lifestyle at his chateau at Vaux le Vicomte, was an indication that the King would brook no rivals as a modern Maecenas, and after the conclusion of his trial in 1667, when Louis overruled the judges to increase his sentence from exile to perpetual imprisonment, censorship was tightened. This was supervised by the newly appointed lieutenant of police, La Reynie. As the reign progressed the *Journal des Savants* was subject to increasing official control (Vittu 1994: 108). In 1699, through the creation of the office of overseer of books, an attempt was made to collate information on authors, printers and booksellers. Authors, rather like academics applying for support today, were required to provide written justifications for their publications (Parker 1983: 145). The elevated status granted to the Académie Royale des Sciences included giving its members the powers of censorship (Chapin 1990: 188).

As in other spheres, instruments intended for the sustenance of absolutism contained the potential for its subversion. The *Journal des Savants*, in providing a model for other journals devoted to the latest ideas, helped to foster the republic of letters which spread ideas critical of the intellectual apparatus of absolutism (Rossel 1982: 34). Censorship encouraged writers not only to seek clandestine methods of publication but also to find new and ingenious ways of expressing their ideas. Irony and satire, key elements in the weaponry of the *philosophes*, were increasingly used against official orthodoxies. At the same time readers grew more sophisticated (and sceptical) in their reading. The Parisian intelligentsia became used to reading texts in a knowing way, in the expectation that writers, constrained by censorship, would present their views in a covert or restrained manner. Elisabeth Labrousse has argued that the Parisian intelligentsia, reading Pierre Bayle during the Regency, viewed him as anti-Christian rather than anti-Catholic because they assumed that his message was more subversive than the surface appearance of the text. They failed to appreciate that Bayle could write almost as he wished in the much more liberal environment of Holland (Labrousse 1987: 11; see also Niklaus 1985: 172).

The judgement of the authorities could also be affected by the climate of suspicion which the desire to control created. The loyalty of the Huguenots was felt to be suspect when the evidence suggested otherwise, at least since the Peace of Alais of 1629. Similarly, the piety of the Jansenists was felt to have a dangerously critical dimension. When Quesnel's pietistic *Moral Reflections on the New Testament* (1678) was condemned by the papacy, as a result of French pressure, in the Bull Unigenitus (1713), it included in the condemnation Quesnel's injunction that all must read scripture (McManners 1975: 260; Maire 1992: 308). Yet, for all the hazards of the enterprise, the monarchy had little choice but to attempt to cultivate and shape opinion. Lacking representative institutions which might have provided support for the policies of the monarchy and the political theology of absolutism, the King had to woo and cajole the influential (Parker 1983: 146).

PUBLIC OPINION

It was a fairly common notion among the educated in the early modern period that opinion was 'queen of the world'. Blaise Pascal noted that power needed to appeal to the imagination to make itself effective, although, curiously, he exempted the monarchs from this rule, for 'they do not wear the trappings, they simply have the power'. He died in 1662, before he could witness how effectively Louis XIV wore the trappings (Pascal 1670: 41). The queen of the world needed to be courted in order to make the reign of force less obvious. Although this helped to tame the seditious tendencies in society, especially of the nobility, opinion was not viewed as an independent force; rather, it was seen as something diffused through different sectors of a hierarchically organized society. France lacked representative institutions to give authenticity to the notion of public opinion as an independent force which could restrain as well as incite governmental action.

In Britain, opinion first came to be seen as an independent force operating on government, rather than as a force shaped by government, (Gunn 1983: 265). For that notion to be plausible, one needed institutions which were responsive to the public, and opinion had to be free from censorship, or censorship had to be either weak or ineffective, and there had to be a fairly large reading public. These conditions were first fulfilled in the relatively liberal British and Dutch societies. In France public opinion would not emerge as a result of a straightforward process of liberalization. It was believed that opinion needed to be shaped rather than consulted, for, left to its own devices, it was often prejudiced and ignorant. Yet, as the reading public grew, and as rival groups and authorities – the monarchy, the *parlements*, the Jansenists and then the *philosophes* – sought to win it over, it was increasingly treated as an independent force. Although *philosophes* liked to emphasize their role in 'creating' or 'shaping' public opinion, they were in fact doing just what the monarchy itself had been doing for some considerable time. At the same time, institutions which had been intended in the seventeenth century to promote the *gloire* of the King, in the mid-eighteenth century began to take on the role of enlightening the public. Indeed, it is significant that the friend and protector of the *philosophes*, Malesherbes, traced the birth of public opinion to the establishment of the Académie Française (Ozouf 1988: S6–7).

In Louis XIV's reign, through the development of the system of royal provincial intendants, the monarchy became much more aware of local opinions, problems and grievances. In the closing decades of his reign, the government began to communicate its official decisions in a different way. The standard means had been through public criers, posters and the reading of edicts from the pulpit. Now the government began to use commercial publication for edicts and information, and sent copies to all officials with an interest in public order. This, Daniel Roche notes, created two publics: the general public, who heard of decisions in the old way, or were prepared to buy news-sheets; and an elite public of nobles and bourgeoisie who were 'integrated into the management of affairs'. The former were passive, the latter active. They formed part of a living court society which 'was held up as a model of political participation for regulating differences between the state and its constitutive *corps*' (Roche 1993: 269–70). The value of print in creating an *esprit de corps* was a lesson that would not be lost on the *philosophes*. Nor could the 'passive' public be ignored. The government needed to know what was politically possible.

Moreover, the government became interested in public opinion in new ways as part of what can be described as the development of government as a science; that is, government which based its decisions on systematic empirical data. The great inspiration for the development of a more informed and professional government was Colbert, but in the eighteenth century the government would test opinion in ways which were inconceivable in his time. The most important example of this comes from 1745 when Orry, the *contrôleur general*, deliberately tested public opinion by circulating a rumour about a rise in taxation (Ozouf 1988: S8). Orry's purpose was to ascertain the attitude of the public to a rise in taxes during a time of war. Public opinion came thus to be viewed as a tribunal, and one in which the *philosophes* themselves put their case.

In Louis XIV's reign, an experiment like Orry's would have risked serious popular disturbances. Maybe such an experiment would not have been possible even had it been deemed wise, for Mona Ozouf has suggested that 'there was no public opinion under Louis XIV for the brilliance of the monarchy outshone it' (Ozouf 1988: S10). Certainly public culture in the reign of Louis XIV was inseparable from absolutism since it was shaped by the ambitions of the Sun King, and by the superb orchestration of the arts and sciences. Royal patronage ensured that public culture looked upwards to the King and not outward to a wider audience. New ideas could be accepted so long as they could be enlisted in the cause of an absolutist vision of a hierarchical society in which individuals and corporate institutions knew their place. Thus Fontenelle's *Entretiens sur la pluralité des mondes* (1686) presented Cartesian natural philosophy as 'the cosmic justification for the *status quo*' (Jacob 1987: 268), though it is worth noting that Fontenelle managed to write the work without mentioning God (Niklaus 1985: 170). A wider and more fluid public sphere did develop in the eighteenth century, yet few writers freed themselves from patronage, and nor did they uniformly embrace the notion of an unregulated public sphere. Their public sphere was outside neither the state nor civil society, but was one in which it was implicitly accepted that 'opinion' could be used as a lever for change. The growing failures of Louis XIV's kingship in the closing decades of his reign were crucial in altering the relationship between writers and the state (Rothkrug 1965: 372–469). The public culture, which in the early decades of Louis XIV's reign had successfully served the needs of absolutism, began to break up. Although it would not be until the mid-eighteenth century that writers began to address a wider audience and to break through the restrictions of patronage and court control (Simon 1995: 6–7), the transition began in the closing years of Louis's reign. Since his reign witnessed the growing ascendancy of French culture in Europe, conditions were also being created for the assumption of leadership of Enlightenment by *philosophes* deeply critical of the status quo (Fumaroli 1992: 602).

CONTINUITY AND CHANGE

In a famous study of the changes in European thought between 1680 and 1720, Paul Hazard declared that 'One day the French people, almost to a man were thinking like Bossuet. The day after they were thinking like Voltaire' (Hazard 1935: 7). Hazard's emphasis was on the intellectual changes which occurred in the period, but it is significant that he chose Bossuet as representative of the old order of thinking.

Although Bossuet used the words '*propres paroles*' in the title of his *Politics Founded on the Very Words of Holy Scripture* (*Politique tirée des propres paroles de l'Ecriture Sainte*), he was less concerned with the true meaning of scripture than with maintaining its authority as a foundation for divine right absolutism (Kearns 1979: 123). This left him vulnerable not only to enlightened biblical critics who questioned his interpretation of scripture but also to those who wondered whether such absolutism actually performed the Christian role he ascribed to it.

In 1685 Louis XIV, by the Edict of Fontainebleau, revoked the Edict of Nantes, which since 1598 had given Huguenots a measure of toleration. This was the last of a series of intolerant actions against the Huguenots and it forced them into maintaining their faith in a clandestine way or going into exile. Some 200,000 left France and found a haven in Protestant Europe and America. Few in France regretted the action at the time. Bossuet supported the execution of the new penal legislation in its full force and praised the 'moderation' of the chancellor, Le Tellier, who revoked the edict. He was untroubled by the fact that he had argued that the King should protect all his subjects, should be solicitous for the welfare of the weak, should use his power wisely and rationally, and should persuade rather than compel his subjects into obedience (Kearns 1979: 124; Adams 1991: 22–3). Although some thought it was irrational to repress some of France's most industrious subjects, most, like Bossuet, regarded Protestantism as sinful and worthy of separate treatment.

The same could not be said of movements within the Catholic Church which the monarchy also regarded as dissident. The repression of Quietism, a spiritual movement which took Bossuet's concern for the King's subjects too literally, and of Jansenism, which was subject to particularly brutal treatment (Sedgwick 1998: 236–7), led many to call into question the professed ambitions of absolutism. Jansenism, which was initially rather like a puritan movement within the Catholic Church, Augustinian in theology, spiritually ascetic and morally strict, became politicized by Louis XIV's actions. With influential supporters among the *parlement* of Paris, enthusiastic support among the lower clergy, though decreasingly among the episcopate, it was a thorn in the side of the monarchy under Louis XV. Jansenists maintained the most successful clandestine publication in eighteenth-century France, the weekly *Nouvelles ecclésiastiques* (Coward 1981; Maire 1992: 317). It eluded all the efforts of the police to track it down. In seeking papal support for the repression of the Jansenists, culminating in the disastrous Bull Unigenitus (1713), Louis had departed from the monarch's traditional policy of supporting the rights of the Gallican Church against the papacy. The submissive culture of absolutism in the heyday of his reign would never be recreated; a climate of criticism began to develop, and in the mid-eighteenth century the bickering of Jesuits, Ultramontains, Gallicans and Jansenists diverted attention from the more dangerous ideas emerging from the *philosophes* and fortified anticlericalism (McManners 1975: 270–3).

Criticism did not develop solely because of Louis XIV's intolerance. The aspirations of the Sun King had captured the imagination of France's 'spiritual and intellectual elite' and they were 'eager collaborators' in his policy of intolerance, celebrating it in art, poetry and prose. The Académie Française offered prizes for works which celebrated the elimination of heresy (Adams 1991: 19, 30). From the first, however, dissident voices were heard and these would grow stronger as the wider ambitions of Louis XIV suffered setbacks in the War of the League of Augsburg (1688–97) and then defeat in the War of the Spanish Succession (1701–13). It is in the context of the crumbling of these ambitions that criticism began to coalesce, constituting something like an enlightened alternative set of values to those of divine right absolutism. Critics attacked the appropriation of Christian values by absolutism, the authoritarian nature of French mercantilism, the inadequacies of the French fiscal system, the inequity of taxation, the financial chaos caused by the cost of warfare, and the huge fortunes accumulated by speculators. The monarchy was also criticized for events beyond its control (the famines of the 1690s and the hunger caused by the 'great winter' of 1708–9), a sure sign that it was losing its aura (Perry 1990: 53).

THE REGENCY

The criticism which had emerged before the end of Louis XIV's reign demonstrates that the Regency of Philippe, Duc d'Orleans, does not represent a sharp break with Louis's reign, although it does represent a break with some of the latter's practices. The Regency period seemed to be opening the way to a more liberal and tolerant regime, and it did lead to the bold financial and economic experiments of John Law, which, had they succeeded, would have modernized the economy and established a state bank. Freed from reliance on private finance for public purposes and on venal office-holders (sale of offices was suspended during the Regency), the state and the social order may have been liberalized in other ways. But Law's experiments failed, and that had an inhibiting effect on future reform.

Still, there were other grounds for viewing the Regency as a liberal regime. Louis XIV had been powerless to prevent the circulation of radical works from abroad, especially those stemming from the Huguenot community in exile, but in 1720 the Regent actually accepted the dedication of an edition of Bayle's *Dictionnaire*, arguably the most important of the subversive books. More than a decade before Voltaire fixed the English model of liberal constitutionalism in the enlightened imagination through his *Lettres philosophique*, the Regent was being instructed in the workings of the House of Commons. Furthermore, reform ideas patterned on the notion of the restoration of Christian aristocratic values were being replaced by more fundamental suggestions for change based on new philosophical ideas (Roche 1993: 457).

The prospect of the Regent carrying through liberal constitutional reform proved chimerical. His task was to preserve the inheritance of the young Louis XV. He acted more like a nascent enlightened absolutist than a nascent constitutional monarch. Voltaire saw the inside of the Bastille during his rule and Montesquieu was not confident enough in the liberality of the regime to put his own name to the *Persian Letters* (1721), in which he satirized the pretensions of divine right absolutism. The *philosophes* had some way to go before they formed a confident party intent on changing things. Their attitude remained in many ways defensive (Fletcher 1985: 24) and their emphasis was on spreading ideas among an elite rather than addressing a wider audience directly. Their location was in the academies and the salons; that is, within the parameters of court society.

Nonetheless, court society did lose some of its coherence in the Regency period. In 1715 the court moved to Paris, and, although it returned to Versailles in 1723, it never regained the dominance which had been its feature in the heyday of Louis XIV. The Regent's mother complained bitterly about the collapse of court society and what she saw as a bourgeois takeover. Parisian society, however, provided a welcome home for Enlightenment sociability, notably in the salons.

SALONS

Salon society in the late seventeenth century was characteristically aristocratic, organized in the salons of Parisian town houses (*hôtels*) by women of special charm and ability. In their salons, men of letters from the third estate learned to control the disputatiousness of the French scholarly tradition and to adopt the social graces necessary for conversing with the great, for, in the salons, as in the academies, all were on an equal intellectual footing. Although there were tensions between aristocrat and bourgeois – one dispute led Voltaire to seek exile in England – generally salon society from the Regency onwards came to provide an enlightened forum to rival the masculine academies. If it was not until the 1740s, with Madame Geoffrin's salon, that the model enlightened salon was finally established (Goodman 1994: 91), by 1720 there were salons in Paris to cater for different interests and tastes.

Salon settings often represented a reaction to the classicism of Louis XIV's reign, which self-consciously displayed order, reason and discipline. Rococo style, which became the rage in the Regency, created agreeable surroundings for public conversation in private surroundings, appropriate for salon society rather than for a court (Goodman 1994: 84–9). It was especially suitable for the Parisian *hôtels* of the aristocracy and would reach its apogee in the oval salons installed about 1735 by Germain Boffrand and painted by Charles Natoire in the *Hôtel de Soubise*, the splendid home of the Prince and Princess of Soubise (Tadgel 1978: 133–7). Of course, rococo would be adopted by the French court, but its ethos was far removed from the grandeur of classicism. Indeed, it is noteworthy that Colbert had opposed Le Vau's idea of an oval salon. Yet if, as Dena Goodman has suggested, the salons represented a rival to the court and the academies and belonged to a republic of letters antipathetic to *ancien régime* society, they were not simply a reaction to the ideals of Louis XIV. They also represented a combination of privilege and Enlightenment familiar in his reign. As she herself has noted, 'Upon entering the Republic of Letters, the philosophes did not leave Old Regime France. Even on their own ground, they still found themselves acting and speaking like Old Regime Frenchmen' (Goodman 1994: 98–9). The domination of the court had been 'provisional' and with the Regency it lost its cultural hegemony. Indeed, a new definition of culture was already emerging in Louis XIV's reign, as a 'form of commerce between . . . respectable people', and the salons were eminently respectable (Revel 1992: 113–16).

As the court lost its centrality as a repository for all cultural values, opportunities occurred for Enlightenment ways of thinking. Charles Perrault could declare without irony that 'no sooner' would a prince declare, '"let there be a palace" than an admirable palace rose from the earth' (Revel 1992: 108). This type of veneration of the sovereign by intellectuals did not survive the Regency and would be lampooned in Montesquieu's *Persian Letters*. However, the break with the age of Louis XIV was far from complete. Indeed, perhaps the best way to envisage the period of the Regency is as a period of 'thaw' (Ladurie 1997: 344–5), or 'the beginning of a period of "conservative transition"' (Roche 1993: 453). The form and structure of the early Enlightenment remained roughly the same but relationships were more relaxed than under the Sun King. France continued to be a society of privilege, patronage and individual and corporate liberties.

CONCLUSION

Although the role of court society weakened during the eighteenth century, no coherent alternative emerged. The *philosophes* liked to think that they were leading society in an enlightened direction, but, like absolutism itself, they were caught in the cusp of change. Voltaire's alternative English model was more useful for its critique of *ancien régime* France than as a serious proposal for a more liberal constitutional structure and a different set of social values. The court society of the Sun King, given canonical expression in *Le Siècle de Louis XIV*, was a lasting source of pride and an exemplar of French refinement and cultural ascendancy (Revel 1992: 72–3). The sense of nostalgia for a period of matchless perfection may have been more acute as a result of the intuition that the institutional forms of Enlightenment which developed under Louis could not cope with the new more democratic world of public opinion which they helped to create.

Louis XIV aimed to appeal to the imagination, the *philosophes* to reason, but force lay behind the brilliance of Versailles, and the general public was treated as passive. The *philosophes* thought they could replace the appeal of absolutism, and that they required no force other than that of reason. But in cultivating opinion and trying to use it as an instrument for change, they played a key role in creating an active public sphere in which opinions could be expressed beyond their control, in ways which were less than polite, and some of them would come to be viewed as creatures of a discredited regime (Darnton 1971).

If the Enlightenment formations of the age of Louis were less than appropriate in the age of democratic revolution, many of the rich characteristics of Enlightenment in France arose through the ambivalences of being a citizen of the republic of letters and a subject of absolute monarchy.

ACKNOWLEDGEMENTS

I am grateful to David Garrioch, Peter Jones and Hugh Fitzpatrick for comments on earlier drafts of this chapter.

REFERENCES

Adams, Geoffrey (1991) *The Huguenots and French Opinion 1685–1787: The Enlightenment Debate on Toleration*, Waterloo, Ontario: Wilfrid Laurier University Press.

Beales, D. (1985) 'Christians and *Philosophes*: The Case of the Austrian Enlightenment', in D. Beales and G. Best (eds) *History, Society and the Churches: Essays in Honour of Owen Chadwick*, Cambridge: Cambridge University Press.

Bonney, Richard (1978) *Political Change in France under Richelieu and Mazarin 1624–1661*, Oxford: Oxford University Press.

Briggs, Robin (1991) 'The Académie Royal des Sciences and the Pursuit of Utility', *Past and Present*, 131: 38–88.

Brunel, Lucien (1884) *Les Philosophes et L'Académie Française au Dix Huitième Siècle*, Paris: Librairie Hachette.

Burke, Peter (1992) *The Fabrication of Louis XIV*, New Haven, Conn., and London: Yale University Press.

Campbell, Peter Robert (1993) *Louis XIV, 1661–1715*, London and New York: Longman.

Chapin, Seymour L. (1990) 'Science in the Reign of Louis XIV', in Paul Sonnino (ed.) *The Reign of Louis XIV*, New Jersey and London: Humanities Press International.

Cole, Charles Woolsey (1939) *Colbert and a Century of French Mercantilism*, 2 vols, New York: Columbia University Press.

Commager, Henry Steele (1977) *The Empire of Reason: How Europe Imagined and America Realized the Enlightenment*, New York: Anchor Press/Doubleday.

Coward, D. A. (1981) 'The Fortunes of a Newspaper: The *Nouvelles ecclésiastique* 1728–1803', *British Journal for Eighteenth-Century Studies*, 4, 1: 1–27.

Darnton, Robert (1971) 'The High Enlightenment and the Low-Life of Literature in Prerevolutionary France', *Past and Present: A Journal of Historical Studies*, 51, May: 81–115; repr. in Robert Darnton (1982) *The Literary Underground of the Old Regime*, Cambridge, Mass., and London: Harvard University Press.

DeJean, Joan (1997) *Ancients versus Moderns: Culture Wars and the Making of a Fin de Siècle*, Chicago and London: University of Chicago Press.

Dessert, Daniel (1987) *Fouquet*, Paris: Fayard.

Elias, Norbert (1983) *Die höfische Gesellschaft/The Court Society*, trans. Edmund Jephcott, Oxford: Blackwell.

Fletcher, Dennis (1985) 'Guides, Philosophers and Friends: The Background of Voltaire's *Discours vers sur l'homme*', in R. J. Howells, A. Mason, H. T Mason and D. Williams (eds) (1985) *Voltaire and his World: Studies Presented to W. H. Barber*, Oxford: Voltaire Foundation.

Friedman, Ann (1990) 'The Art History of the Reign', in Paul Sonnino (ed.) *The Reign of Louis XIV*, New Jersey and London: Humanities Press International.

Fumaroli, Marc (1992) 'The Genius of the French Language', in *Les Lieux de mémoire, sous la direction de Pierre Nora*, Paris: Gallimard; repr. and trans. (1998) as *Realms of Memory*, vol. III: *Symbols*, ed. Lawrence D. Kitzman, trans. Arthur Goldhammer, New York: Columbia University Press.

Goodman, Dena (1994) *The Republic of Letters: A Cultural History of the French Enlightenment*, Ithaca and London: Cornell University Press.

Goubert, Pierre (1969) *L'Ancien régime*: tome 1, *La société*, Paris: Armand Colin; trans Steven Cox (1973) *The Ancien Régime: French Society 1600–1750*, London: Weidenfeld & Nicolson.

Gunn, J. A. W. (1983) *Beyond Liberty and Property: The Process of Self-Recognition in Eighteenth-century Political Thought*, Kingston and Montreal: McGill-Queen's University Press.

Hahn, Roger (1992) 'Louis XIV and Science Policy', in David Lee Rubin (ed.) *Sun King: The Ascendancy of French Culture in the Reign of Louis XIV*, Washington, London and Toronto: Folger Books.

Hazard, Paul (1935) *La Crise de la conscience européene*, Paris; trans. J. Lewis May (1953) *The European Mind 1680–1715*; repr. (1964) Harmondsworth: Penguin Books.

Israel, Jonathan I. (2001) *Radical Enlightenment: Philosophy and the Making of Modernity 1650–1750*, Oxford: Oxford University Press.

Jacob, Margaret C. (1987) 'The Crisis of the European Mind: Hazard Revisited', in Phyllis Mack and Margaret C. Jacob (eds) *Politics and Culture in Early Modern Europe: Essays in Honour of H. G. Koenisberger*, Cambridge: Cambridge University Press.

Jackson, Richard A. (1984) *Vive le Roi: A History of the French Coronation from Charles V to Charles X*, Chapel Hill and London: University of North Carolina Press.

Kearns, Edward John (1979) *Ideas in Seventeenth-century France: The Most Important Thinkers and the Climate of Ideas in which They Worked*, Manchester: Manchester University Press.

Keohane, Nannerl O. (1980) *Philosophy and the State in France: The Renaissance to the Enlightenment*, Princeton: Princeton University Press.

King, James E. (1949) *Science and Rationalism in the Government of Louis XIV 1661–1683*, Chapel Hill: Johns Hopkins University Press; repr. (1972) New York: Octagon Books.

Labrousse, Elisabeth (1987) 'Reading Bayle in Paris', in Alan C. Kors and Paul J. Korshin (eds) *Anticipations of the Enlightenment in England, France and Germany*, Philadelphia: University of Pennsylvania Press.

Le Roy Ladurie, E. with Jean Francois Fitou (1997) *Saint Simon et le Système de la Cour*; trans. Arthur Goldhammer (2001) *Saint Simon and the Court of Louis XIV*, Chicago and London: University of Chicago Press.

Levron, J. (1976) 'Louis XIV's Courtiers', in Ragnhild Hatton (ed.) *Louis XIV and Absolutism*, London and Basingstoke: Macmillan.

Lossky, Andrew (ed.) (1967) *The Seventeenth Century, 1600–1715*, vol. VII: *Sources in Western Civilization*, gen. ed. Herbert H. Rowen, New York: Free Press.

Lough, John (1954) *An Introduction to Seventeenth Century France*, repr. (1960) London: Longmans.

Lux, David S. (1991) 'The Reorganization of Science 1450–1700', in Bruce T. Moran (ed.) *Patronage and Institutions: Science, Technology, and Medicine at the European Court 1500–1700*, Rochester, NY, and Woodbridge: The Boydell Press.

Maire, Catherine (1992) 'Port-Royal: The Jansenist Schism', in *Les Lieux de mémoire, sous la direction de Pierre Nora*, Paris: Gallimard; repr. and trans. (1996) *Realms of Memory*, vol. I: *Conflicts and Divisions*, ed. Lawrence D. Kitzman, trans. Arthur Goldhammer, New York: Columbia University Press.

Maland, David (1970) *Culture and Society in Seventeenth-century France*, London: B. T. Batsford.

McManners, John (1975) 'Jansenism and Politics in the Eighteenth Century', in Derek Baker (ed.) *Church, Society and Politics: Studies in Church History*, 12.

Niklaus, Robert (1985) 'Fontenelle as a Model for the Transmission and Vulgarisation of Ideas in the Enlightenment', in R. J. Howells, A. Mason, H. T. Mason and D. Williams (eds) *Voltaire and his World: Studies presented to W. H. Barber*, Oxford: Voltaire Foundation.

Ozouf Mona (1988) '"Public Opinion" at the end of the Old Regime', *Journal of Modern History*, 60, 3, September: Supplement.

Parker, David (1983) *The Making of French Absolutism*, London: Edward Arnold.

Pascal, Blaise (1670) *Pensées*, trans. with intro. by A. J. Krailsheimer (1966) Harmondsworth: Penguin Classics.

Paul, Charles B. (1980) *Science and Immortality: The 'Eloges' of the Paris Academy of Sciences (1699–1791)*, Berkeley, Los Angeles and London: University of California Press.

Perry, Mary Elizabeth (1990) 'The Popular History of the Reign', in Paul Sonnino (ed.) *The Reign of Louis XIV*, New Jersey and London: Humanities Press International.

Pommier, Edouard (1992) 'Versailles', in *Les Lieux de mémoire, sous la direction de Pierre Nora*, Paris: Gallimard; repr. and trans. (1998) *Realms of Memory*, vol. III: *Symbols*, ed. Lawrence D. Kitzman, trans. Arthur Goldhammer, New York: Columbia University Press.

Rappaport, Rhoda (1981) 'The Liberties of the Paris Academy of Sciences 1716–1785', in Harry Woolf (ed.) *The Analytic Spirit: Essays in the History of Science*, Ithaca and London: Cornell University Press.

Revel, Jacques (1992) 'The Court', in *Les Lieux de mémoire, sous la direction de Pierre Nora*, Paris: Gallimard; repr. and trans. (1996) *Realms of Memory*, vol. II: *Traditions*, ed. Lawrence D. Kitzman, trans. Arthur Goldhammer, New York: Columbia University Press.

Roche, Daniel (1993) *La France des Lumières*, Paris: Fayard; trans. Arthur Goldhammer (1998) as *France in the Enlightenment*, Cambridge, Mass., and London: Harvard University Press.

Rothkrug, Lionel (1965) *Opposition to Louis XIV: The Political and Social Origins of the French Enlightenment*, Princeton: Princeton University Press.

Rossel, André (1982) *Le Faux Grand Siècle (1604–1715)*, Paris: Presses de la Cromo-Litho.

Sedgwick, Alexander (1998) *The Travails of Conscience: The Arnauld Family and the Ancien Régime*, Cambridge, Mass., and London: Harvard University Press.

Shennan, J. H. (1969) *Government and Society in France, 1441–1661*, London: Allen & Unwin; New York: Barnes & Noble.

—— (c. 1979) *Philippe, Duke of Orléans: Regent of France, 1715–1723*, London: Thames & Hudson.

Simon, Julia (1995) *Mass Enlightenment: Critical Studies in Rousseau and Diderot*, Albany: State University Press of New York.

Smith Preserved (1934) *A History of Modern Culture*, vol. II: *The Enlightenment, 1687–1776*, New York: Holt, Rinehart & Winston; repr. (1962) New York: Collier Books.

Sonnino, Paul (1990) 'The Intellectual History of the Reign', in Paul Sonnino (ed.) *The Reign of Louis XIV*, New Jersey and London: Humanities Press International.

Stroup, Alice (1992) 'Louis XIV as Patron of the Parisian Academy of Sciences', in David Lee Rubin (ed.) *Sun King: The Ascendancy of French Culture in the Reign of Louis XIV*, Washington, London and Toronto: Folger Books.

Tadgell, Christopher (1978) 'France', in Anthony Blunt (ed.) *Baroque and Rococo: Architecture and Decoration*, London: Paul Elek; repr. (1988) Ware: Wordsworth Editions.

Van Horn Melton, James (2001) *The Rise of the Public in Enlightenment Europe*, Cambridge: Cambridge University Press.

Vittu, Jeanne-Pierre (1994) '"Le people est fort curieux de nouvelles": l'information périodique dans la France des années 1690', in Haydn Mason (ed.) *Pour Encourager les Autres: Studies for the Tercentenary of Voltaire's birth 1694–1994*, Oxford: Voltaire Foundation.

Voltaire (1733) *Letters on England*, trans. with intro. by Leonard Tancock (1980) Harmondsworth: Penguin Books.

—— (1751) *The Age of Louis XIV*, trans. Martyn P. Pollack with pref. by F. C. Green (1961) London: Dent; New York: Dutton.

—— (1764) *Philosophical Dictionary*, trans. with intro. and glossary by Peter Gay (1962) New York: Harcourt, Brace & World.

Waller, Richard (1977) 'The Situation of the Man of Letters in English and French Society 1700–1730', *British Society for Eighteenth-Century Studies, Newsletter*, 11, February: 31–3.

Wolf, John B. (1968) *Louis XIV*, London, Gollancz; repr. (1970) London: Panther Books.

PART III

THE HIGH
ENLIGHTENMENT

INTRODUCTION

Martin Fitzpatrick

The Enlightenment has often been viewed exclusively as a philosophic movement operating in a rarefied intellectual climate. This approach was called into question in the last decades of the twentieth century. Robert Darnton argued, 'we should question the overly highbrow, overly metaphysical view of intellectual life in the eighteenth century' (Darnton 1971: 2). He went further in suggesting that by the time of Voltaire's death the ideas associated with this rarefied High Enlightenment could be considered as 'relatively tame' (Darnton 1971: 40). Although he did not deny the influence of High Enlightenment ideas in the early days of the Revolution, his purpose was to contrast its ideas with the more subversive ones emerging from literary low life in pre-revolutionary France. This book takes to heart his plea for the contextualization of ideas and his strictures against rarefied intellectual history, but there is still a place for the careful examination of some of the key concerns of the *philosophes* and their contemporaries. There is considerable variation in their ideas, and their impact is not always obvious. They did not, after all, come in a neat package. But they shaped profoundly the world in which they lived and left a permanent legacy. Indeed, that is what they were intended to do. Although there were varying degrees of commitment to the power of ideas to change ways of thinking and of behaving, the sense expressed by Shaftesbury (see Chapter 6 above) that there was a 'mighty light' bringing a new understanding to fundamental aspects of existence was increasingly shared by philosophers and their audience.

The metaphor of light was ancient but still potent. It was particularly associated with the idea of revelation – in the religious context, divine revelation. From the Renaissance and particularly from Erasmus onwards, there was a tradition of attempting to reconcile reason and revelation. During the Scientific Revolution there was not so much a separation of science and religion as a complex process of readjustment between natural philosophy and theology, in which many sought to reconcile reason and revelation. Reason could be likened to a divine light. Taking his text from Proverbs 20.27, Nathaniel Culverwell, in his *Discourse of the Light of Nature*, declared 'the understanding of man *is* the Candle of the Lord' (1699: 1). Locke, too, viewed reason in a similar way (see Chapter 10). Shaftesbury, who was tutored by Locke, was a deist who had no time for revelation, but still viewed the light of the

Enlightenment as both rational and divine. While Enlightenment ideas could be hostile to Christianity, and can be seen as an alternative to it, they were framed by Christian concerns: What is truth? What is the relationship between God and man ('man' is used here in the generic sense)? What is the purpose and end of existence? What is the cause of evil in the world? What is man's true nature? What obligations do we owe to fellow men? How can we improve ourselves? The thinkers of the High Enlightenment were not all Christians, but, as the chapters in this part show, they were offering new answers to old questions.

While it is helpful to see Enlightenment ideas as cast within a broad framework of Christian concerns, it would be false to think that the light of reason did not cause problems for traditional believers. Some rejected revelation altogether and abandoned Christianity, but those Enlightenment thinkers who remained within the Christian framework had to adapt their Christianity to the new ways of thinking. Not surprisingly, many, like Newton and Locke, were unorthodox Christians. Locke's *tabula rasa* psychology (see especially Chapters 10 and 14) was contrary to the notion of original sin. The light of the Enlightenment was not innate, nor an inner personal revelation, nor the will of God as revealed in the Bible, but came from thought and reflection. Despite the many attempts to reconcile the Bible with natural philosophy, creating 'physico-theologies' which synthesized Newtonian science with biblical teaching, reasoned belief was to be taken as the criterion of a genuine revelation. William Whiston was a follower of Newton who expressed in public heterodox ideas of the sort which Newton kept to himself. In his popular *New Theory of the Earth* (1696), Whiston declared as axiomatic, 'That which is clearly accountable in a natural way, is not without reason to be ascrib'd to a Miraculous Power' (Whiston 1696: 48). The phrase 'in a natural way' is indicative of the confidence derived from the success of the new science in demonstrating nature's laws. Voltaire described Newton's theory of gravitation as 'sublime'. In contrast with Aristotelian science, Newton had shown how the whole of the universe was subject to the same laws. These were simple, even if the mathematics behind them was beyond the comprehension of most enlightened thinkers. Moreover, Newton suggested that the inductive method of experimental philosophy could provide new answers to many Christian preoccupations. He wrote in his *Opticks*:

> And if Natural philosophy in all its parts, by pursuing this method, shall at length be perfected, the bounds of Moral Philosophy will also be enlarged. For so far as we can know by Natural Philosophy what is the First cause, what power he has over us, and what benefits we receive from him, so far our duty towards him, as well as that towards one another, will appear to us by the light of Nature.
>
> (Newton 1704: 151)

Newton believed that 'this most beautiful system of the sun, planets and comets' could not proceed from 'mere mechanical causes' (Newton 1687: 143). Others disagreed (see Chapter 10), yet believers and unbelievers all accepted the uniformity and regularity of the laws of nature. When combined with an enlightened version of the Christian belief that man's nature was essentially the same throughout time, we can see how enlightened thinkers felt able to study man as part of nature, and sought to discover the underlying natural laws of society. In many ways they deified nature. That left them with some awkward questions to answer. If nature was so beneficent, why didn't men live in harmony with one another? If man was not innately sinful, why did he behave so badly? If empirical reasoning had been so successful in explaining the workings of the universe, why had it cast so little light upon man's history and his existing circumstances? These were challenges which were taken up by Enlightenment thinkers, and their answers are explored in the following chapters. Enlightenment, as Kant argued, gave man a chance to come of age. New understanding could lead to a Baconian renovation of the world. As D'Alembert pointed out in his Preliminary Discourse to the *Encylopédie*, Bacon had conceived of philosophy 'as being only that part of our knowledge which should contribute to making us better and happier' (1751: 132). Enlightenment thinkers set about that task with relish.

It would be easy to sum up the High Enlightenment in triumphalist terms: the emergence of an idea of progress, of clearly articulated plans for the future, of public education and of an enlightened public sphere, of a secular understanding of the stages of human history, and of a science of man. But that would be to simplify. Enlightenment thinkers welcomed the challenge of public debate, which they saw as potentially strengthening their ideas, but many were equally aware of the limitations of some of their views. For example, the Marquis de Condorcet singled out Richard Price as one of the first proponents of the doctrine of the indefinite progress of the human species (Condorcet 1795: 166). Yet Price, a Christian thinker, albeit of an unorthodox kind, recognized that

> The highest point of knowledge to which we can attain is knowledge of our own ignorance . . . The more we study the constitution of nature, and the dispensations of Providence, the more we must be convinced that they are above our faculties and the causes of the most familiar appearances are unknown to us.
>
> (Price 1816: Sermon ix, 176)

Condorcet's idea of progress was entirely secular (see Chapter 11) and he did not share Price's reservations. He closed his *Esquisse d'un tableau historique des progrès de l'esprit humain* (1795) with a discussion of the future tenth epoch, in which many of the failings of man will be remedied, and the progress of one generation (including moral and physical progress) would be passed on to the next. Yet, at the very end of his discussion of the indefinite progress of humankind, he chose, in his final sentence, to dwell on the consolations provided by the achievement of irreversible progress and on the 'asylum' offered by the thought of 'man re-established in his rights as well as in the dignity of his nature'. In this situation, the *philosophe* 'forgets the man whom avarice, fear, or envy torments and corrupts. Then he truly is with his equals in an Elysium which his reason has been able to create and which his love for humanity embellishes with the purest joys'.

Condorcet's indebtedness to a religious world view is obvious. Perhaps the High Enlightenment's indebtedness to religion sharpened its critical edge, tempered its claims, made it more aware of the dangers of faith in reason. The experimental method also, to a degree, ensured that truth was not taken on trust, but needed to be put to the test, for experiment required repetition and verification, and that in turn led to the extension of the scientific community and the growth of public knowledge of science (see Chapter 15). It also led to considerable debate, since experiments could not always be easily repeated. Joseph Priestley, who worried about the problem, nonetheless thought that the experimental method could be applied to many other spheres, not least government (Priestley 1768: 108–9). Yet there was danger in the Enlightenment advocacy of rapid change based solely on reason. Free enquiry was not always candid; some were impatient with the obstacles to progress and were deaf to opinions which they considered unenlightened. Many enlightened thinkers were aware of these potential drawbacks. The Swiss writer Isaak Iselin called for the 'toleration of superstition' despite his concern to maximize public happiness (Im Hof 1993: 160, 269). Educationalists worried about giving the state the power to create model citizens. Hume not only drew attention to the dangers of religious enthusiasm but also to the limitations of reason (see Chapter 12). Adam Smith and Adam Ferguson worried about the effect of commercial society (see Chapter 13).

In sum, the High Enlightenment was a vibrant, varied and often self-critical movement. André Maurois's description of Voltaire's *Philosophical Dictionary* (1764) as a 'chaos of clear ideas' could be applied also to the thought of many of his contemporaries (Maurois 1962: ix). These chapters provide valuable insight into their intellectual world.

REFERENCES

Culverwell, Nathaniel (1669) *An Elegant and Learned Discourse of the Light of Nature with Several Other Treatise*, Oxford.

Condorcet, Jean-Antoine-Nicolas Caritat, Marquis de, *Esquisse d'un tableau historique des progrès de l'esprit humain* (posth.1795) ed. O.H.Prior (1933), new edn. presented by Yvon Belaval (1970), Paris: Librairie Philosophie J. Vrin.

D'Alembert (1751) *Preliminary Discourse to the Encyclopaedia*, trans. R. N. Schwab (1963) in vol. 2, Simon Eliot and Beverley Stern (eds) (1979) *The Age of Enlightenment*, 2 vols, New York: Barnes & Noble.

Darnton, Robert (1971) 'The High Enlightenment and the Low Life of Literature in Prerevolutionary France', *Past and Present*, 51 (May): 81–115; repr. in Darnton, Robert (1982) *The Literacy Underground of the Old Regime*, Cambridge, Mass., and London: Harvard University Press.

Im Hof, Ulrich (1993) *Das Europa der Aufklärung*, Munich: Beck; trans. William E. Yuill (1994) *The Enlightenment: An Historical Introduction*, pbk edn (1997) Oxford: Blackwell.

Maurois, André (1962) 'Preface', in *Voltaire: Philosophical Dictionary*, trans. with introduction by Peter Gay, New York: Harcourt, Brace & World.

Newton, Isaac (1687) *Principia Mathematica* and *Opticks* (1704) in Andrew Lossky (ed.) (1967) *Sources in Western Civilization: The Seventeenth Century*, New York: Free Press.

Price, Richard (1816) *Sermons on Various Subjects*, ed. William Morgan, London.

Priestley, Joseph (1768) *An Essay on the First Principles of Government*, 2nd edn (1771); repr, in Peter Miller (ed.) (1993) *Joseph Priestley: Political Writings*, Cambridge: Cambridge University Press.

Whiston, William (1696) 'Introductory Discourse', in *A New Theory of the Earth*; quoted in James E. Force (1985) *William Whiston, Honest Newtonian*, Cambridge: Cambridge University Press.

CHAPTER TEN

PURSUING AN ENLIGHTENED GOSPEL

Happiness from deism to materialism to atheism

———◆◆◆———

Darrin M. McMahon

When men and women of the Enlightenment set out in search of happiness, what did they hope to find? The question is straightforward, but far from easy to answer. For, though happiness was a central term in enlightened vocabularies, it remains to this day difficult to define, let alone to capture. As the wag has said, if there is a secret to happiness, then surely it is well kept.

Enlightened authors did their best to reveal the secret, as well as to expound the term, writing more about happiness than any previous period in western history. In doing so, they hoped to break with all previous norms, dispelling the mystery and mystique that had surrounded the concept of happiness for centuries. Whereas earlier ages had cloaked it in religion or fate, Enlightenment authors would unveil it in its natural purity, its naked state. And whereas previous ages had searched for happiness in faith, Enlightened observers would aim to see it clearly in its own right, with unobstructed eyes. Neither the reward of the next world nor the gift of good fortune or the gods, happiness was above all an earthly affair, to be achieved in the here and now through human agency alone. Ironically, however, in spreading this revolutionary gospel, this modern good news, Enlightenment thinkers put forth a faith of their own.

IN THE BEGINNING

The word for happiness in every Western language is cognate with luck or fate. The early Middle English (and Old Norse) *happ*, in this respect – chance, fortune, what *happens* in the world – is perfectly consistent with the Mittelhochdeutsch *Glück*, still the modern German word for happiness and luck. It is consistent, too, with the Old French *heur* (luck, chance), root of *bonheur* (happiness); the Portuguese *felicidade*; the Spanish *felicidad*; and the Italian *felicità* – all derived ultimately from the Latin *felix* (fate). And it is consistent, finally, with the ancient Greek *eudaimonia*, from *eu* (good) and *daimon* (god or spirit). Those who were happy enjoyed the favour of an indulgent deity, a fortunate position, to say the least. One could expand the list, but the point would remain the same: in the language families of Europe, the modern words for happiness took root in the soil of chance.

Which is not to say that there was anything random about the process, or anything new. On the contrary, the fact that these words sprouted up during the late Middle Ages and early modern period in climates that invariably linked happiness to God is testimony to the tremendous endurance of an older, pre-Christian tradition that tied one's fortune in the world to forces beyond one's control. The position of the stars, the spinning of the Fates, the caprice of the gods – these are the explanations to which traditional cultures frequently turn in their effort to understand the seemingly chaotic events that rain down upon mere mortals. Why does one woman suffer? Why does another man experience fleeting joy or pain? Regardless of the immediate answers, in this 'tragic' view of the world, the larger forces that drive our fate are always beyond our control. To be happy is to be fortunate. And to be happy for too long is always to tempt the gods. With good reason, then, did the Greek chorus sing, 'Call no man happy until he is dead.'

This view of the world was given its purest expression in the West in the great tragic plays – the tragedies – of Aeschylus, Sophocles and Euripedes in the fifth century BC. However, although, as is clear from the later words for happiness themselves, vestiges of these playwrights' views on happiness, human agency and fate far outlived them, it is also clear that their perspective was subjected, virtually from the start, to a powerful critique of no less lasting influence. Indeed, as Martha Nussbaum has shown, it was precisely *against* the troubling notion that one's fortune was a matter of fortune – that one's happiness was contingent on luck or fate – that classical Greek philosophy openly rebelled (Nussbaum 1996). Beginning with Socrates in the fifth century BC, and following his lead for centuries well into the Hellenistic period, the four great schools of Athens sought to hedge humanity's bets, restricting the space in which luck could rule our lives. For Plato and the Platonists, Aristotle and the Aristotelians, Zeno and the Stoics, and Epicurus and the Epicureans, happiness (*eudaimonia*) was not the plaything of the gods, but the reward of virtue, the product of a life well lived. When human beings ordered their constitutions in an appropriate manner – cultivating, in Aristotle's famous phrase, the 'activity of the soul that expresses virtue' – they could be reasonably confident of exercising control over the course of their lives (Aristotle: 1098a). The natural human end – our *telos* – was happiness, and getting there was largely our own responsibility.

Of course, like their Roman successors, the Greeks disagreed among themselves over the nature of virtue, just as they disagreed over whether the role of luck in happiness could entirely be overcome. Some did in fact take this line, arguing with the Roman Stoics, Cicero and Epictetus, that the virtuous sage could be happy even while undergoing torture. Most, however, remained more sensitive to the uncertainties of life, to the chance occurrences and twists of fate that threatened always to topple the fortress of even the strongest moral constitution, making a mockery of our pretensions to happiness. Try as they might, even the ancients could not escape the dictates of fortune. A bit of the *daimon* remained embedded in *eudaimonia*.

Indeed, it was precisely this inability to root out the vagaries of life completely that rendered pagan thought susceptible to the third of the major influences shaping happiness prior to the Enlightenment: Christianity. Admittedly, happiness does not always spring to mind when one contemplates the Christian tradition, steeped, as it is, in the central narrative of suffering, of God and humanity alike. And yet the *promise* of happiness was absolutely crucial to the development of the faith. 'Rejoice and be glad,' Christ commands throughout the Gospels, 'for great is your reward in heaven' (Matthew 5: 12). The prospect of a better world, and the unavoidable suffering of this one here below, drove the tradition from the start. With reason does that patriarch of patriarchs St Augustine entitle his first work, penned immediately upon his conversion, *De Beata Vita* (*The Blessed (or Happy) Life*). A classical dialogue regarding the ultimate classical quest, the work concludes that our search for happiness will end in death. Earthly pilgrims, men and women, in the meantime are condemned to wander in vain, awaiting that great moment when they will 'come home', expiring to see God, as St Paul has promised, 'face to face' (1 Corinthians 13: 12). Only then can we hope to be happy, for happiness is God.

In elaborating this doctrine of what he came to call the 'happiness of hope', Augustine provided the early Church with a powerful explanation for the futility of the pagan quest. 'True happiness . . . is unattainable in our present life,' he argued at length in his magnum opus, the *City of God*, due to our very nature (Augustine: Book XIV, ch. 25). Having forsaken perfect paradise through their own fault, Adam and Eve bequeathed congenital sin to all posterity. Permanently damaged, fundamentally flawed, human beings now sought in vain to find peace.

The *City of God*, like early Christian theology as a whole, was directed 'against the Pagans'. Yet Augustine, and his many successors, proved remarkably adept at tilling conquered soil. In a process that would reach its apotheosis only in the late Renaissance, Christian philosophers grafted the teachings of the classical schools on to the main trunk of the faith, producing flowerings of Christian Platonism, Christian Aristotelianism, Christian Stoicism and even of Christian Epicureanism (Trinkaus 1940). Despite their great difference, and their common insistence that true felicity resided only in death, these hybrids nonetheless helped to keep happiness forever on the Western landscape. And lest anyone be led too far from the pilgrim's path, a host of other writers, religious and lay, were ready to remind them of the wisdom of the tragic tradition. 'And thus does Fortune's wheel turn treacherously/And out of happiness bring men to sorrow,' the Monk warns in that classic of Christian pilgrimage, Chaucer's *Canterbury Tales* (1387–1400: 'The Monk's Tale', II, 509–10). The *happ* of happiness was quickly subsumed into the narrative of Christian providence.

Three distinct traditions, each internally complex, yet each wound about the other in ways more complex still. This brief sketch can only provide the barest of outlines. But it must serve here as the broad backdrop against which thinkers of the Enlightenment rehearsed their own understandings of happiness, as they prepared to proclaim them to the world.

DEISM: THE TRUE LIGHT OF THE WORLD

In the Christian and tragic traditions, then, the nature of human beings combined with the nature of the world to deny lasting happiness on earth. Inscrutable, daunting, opaque, the universe resisted comprehension and control, just as God resisted any detailed understanding of his Master plan beyond what He had deigned to reveal.

At the same time, our very natures – marked at birth by a sickness unto death, tossed about by conflicting emotions, driven by rapacity, greed and all manner of sin – refused the *summum bonum*, the highest good, that would come only in heaven, if it all. Were human beings to imagine happy lives on earth, they would first have to conceive of themselves and their universe in new ways.

The work of forging this new conception was of course a collective enterprise, elaborated slowly over the course of centuries. But for many Enlightenment thinkers, two men stood head and shoulders above the rest. The first, Isaac Newton, was a 'great genius', declared Jean Le Rond D'Alembert in that Bible of the Enlightenment, the French *Encyclopédie*, a man who gave to philosophy the form 'which apparently it is to keep'. The second, John Locke, 'undertook and successfully carried through what Newton had not dared to do . . . It can be said that [Locke] created metaphysics, almost as Newton had created physics' (D'Alembert 1751: 81–3). D'Alembert may have exaggerated, but his views were widely shared.

More than any other pioneer, Newton seemed to the men and women of the Enlightenment to have proved that the universe was constituted according to ordered, predictable laws. And as he showed in his *Principia Mathematica* of 1687, these laws could be discerned through reason and experiment, and described mathematically, which was, of course, the key. For, though many before him – from Aristotle to Descartes – had claimed to understand the nature of matter and motion, or to discern laws in the world, no thinker had so convincingly demonstrated their existence. In the Newtonian system, every particle in the universe attracted every other with a force that varied directly according to the product of their masses and inversely according to the square of the distance between them. Planets in their orbits and apples falling to earth were drawn by an identical force. Gazing up at the heavens, one witnessed the same harmonious system that operated here below.

Newton thus restored the *cosmos* to its fundamental sense (from the Greek *kosmos*, 'order'), demonstrating like no other before him the principles on which it ran. The universe was not random, God's laws were not inscrutable. We could know our place in the world. For Newton himself, a pious, if unorthodox, Christian, who denied the Trinity but steadfastly maintained his faith, none of this implied that the universe was a self-operating system, a self-governing machine. On the contrary, Newton believed that the cosmos required the periodic intervention and constant oversight of its creator, a belief that was quickly put to use in the service of religious apology. 'Newtonianism', when presented in this light, served as scientific proof for a theory of providential design, displaying the blueprints of a universe drawn up and maintained by a rational, benevolent creator.

Yet others were willing to push what they saw as the logic of Newton's system a step further, asking whether this finely calibrated universe really required a spirit in its works, a ghost in its machine. Was it not possible, they asked, to conceive of a cosmos that ran smoothly on its own? A creator may have set the works in motion. But now that they were up and running, did God really need to intervene? At the very least, Newton's system seemed to deny the miraculous upheavals and dramatic interventions of the Old Testament God. And perhaps, more radical minds were prepared to speculate, the creator had created the world, and then left it alone to run its own course?

In the decades following the publication of the *Principia* Newton's thought summoned such speculation among men and women who came to be known as 'deists', proponents of natural or rational religion. The work of Newton's contemporary and friend John Locke inspired similar conjecture. Although the precise role of the one's influence on the other is complex and contested, it is clear that Locke's theory of the mind appeared to many to offer the perfect complement to Newton's theory of the cosmos. Whereas Newton demonstrated the universal laws that governed the motion of the universe, Locke revealed the universal laws that governed the workings of thought. Taken together, the two presented a portrait of nature that convinced their more radical interpreters that, when allowed to run as it should, the world was leading us on a happy course.

Locke presented his part of this picture most forcefully in the work for which he earned his international reputation, the *Essay Concerning Human Understanding*. Begun as early as 1671, though not published until December 1689, the *Essay* argues at length against the received belief that the mind is born into the world with fixed notions or innate ideas. Our brains do not come pre-loaded with software; they are not inscribed with the code of conscience or the law of God. On the contrary, the human mind at birth, to use Locke's own metaphors, is like an 'empty cabinet' or a 'white piece of paper'. This is the famous *tabula rasa*, the blank slate, and in the bulk of the *Essay* Locke strives to show how the world writes upon it, imprinting itself on our minds through the complex mechanics of the motion of thought.

From the perspective of the history of the theory of knowledge, this discussion is fascinating in itself. But from the perspective of the history of happiness, two other salient points come to the fore. In the first place, the *tabula rasa* effectively wipes our slate free of sin. A Calvinist by birth who never completely renounced his faith, Locke himself, it is true, always retained a healthy understanding of the human potential for egotism and self-regard. Nonetheless, his theory of the mind dealt a crushing blow to the view that individuals were marked at birth, inherently deficient, tending naturally towards corruption. And if not impeded by original sin, what was to prevent them from successfully pursuing happiness?

This, in fact, is the second major point, presented by Locke in the critical chapter 'Power', in Book 2 of the *Essay*, a chapter in which he employs the monumental phrase 'the pursuit of happiness' no fewer than four times. Throughout the chapter, Locke makes use of Newtonian metaphors – speaking of stones that fall, tennis balls hit by racquets, and billiard balls struck by cues – to describe the way in which human beings are propelled, and propel themselves, through the space of their lives. But what is the force that moves them, the power that draws them near? 'I answer happiness and that alone,' Locke responds. The 'general *Desire* of Happiness operates constantly and invariably' upon all human beings, keeping them forever in motion (Locke 1689: 258, 283).

Likening happiness to a universal force – a sort of human, emotional gravity – Locke describes the mechanics of this operation. If it is happiness that moves desire, it is 'uneasiness' that moves our will. Locke's blanket term for 'all pain of the body', and 'disquiet of the mind', uneasiness, in fact, is invariably accompanied by desire, which is 'scarce distinguishable from it'. When we experience the uneasiness of pain, we desire to be free of it. And when we experience the uneasiness of an absent good, we desire the pleasure of its possession (Locke 1689: 250–4). To be uneasy, then, is to be restless, kinetically dissatisfied, to desire movement or change. Continually attracted to pleasure, we are continually repulsed by pain. '*Happiness* then in its full extent is the utmost Pleasure we are capable of, and *Misery* the utmost pain' (Locke 1689: 258).

Although there were echoes of Aristotle and other Greek philosophers here, this was revolutionary stuff for the time. Whereas Christian moralists had argued for centuries that pleasure was dangerous, and pain was our natural lot, Locke stood this proposition on its head. God in his infinite wisdom had designed men and women to seek pleasure and flee pain naturally, he claimed. And this was as it should be. '[P]leasure in us, is that we call *Good*, and what is apt to produce Pain in us, we call *Evil*' (Locke 1689: 259). In Locke's divinely orchestrated universe, pleasure was providential. It helped lead us to God.

This is not to say that Locke was an apologist for all manner of indulgence, any more than it is to suggest that he conceived of human beings as without the freedom to resist 'gravitational' pull. On the contrary, he placed our liberty precisely in the ability to make wise decisions about wherein true pleasures lay. Through reason – the 'true candle of the Lord' – Locke believed that men and women could be persuaded to take a long view of their happiness, abjuring fleeting pleasures or undergoing short-term pain for the sake of greater goods to come. And whatever the revolutionary nature of his thought in other respects, he continued to see the highest happiness, the greatest good, as that of the world to come.

> To him, I say, who hath a prospect of the different State of perfect Happiness or Misery, that attends all men after this Life, depending on their Behavior here, the measures of Good and Evil, that govern his choice, are mightily changed. For since nothing of Pleasure and Pain in this Life, can bear any proportion to endless Happiness, or exquisite Misery of an immortal Soul hereafter, Actions in his Power will have their preference, not according to the transient Pleasure, or Pain that accompanies them here; but as they serve to secure that perfect durable Happiness hereafter.
>
> (Locke 1689: 274)

Thus Locke, in the end, like Newton, was unable to dispense with the Christian doctrine of ultimate rewards. In fact, he saw clearly the consequences of so doing. Were one to deviate from the order of goods that marked out the path to heaven, the road to happiness would branch off into as many byways as there were feet to travel. 'Were all the Concerns of Man terminated in this Life,' Locke observed, then 'why one followed Study and Knowledge, and another Hawking and Hunting; why one chose Luxury and Debauchery, and another Sobriety and Riches' would simply be 'because their *Happiness* was placed in different things'. Pleasure, in a word, would become an end in itself. 'If there be no Prospect beyond the Grave, the inference is certainly right, *Let us eat and drink*, let us enjoy what we delight in, *for tomorrow we shall die*' (Locke 1689: 268–70).

Yet, despite their ultimate intentions, both Newton and Locke had prepared the ground for taking strides in precisely this direction. While Newton's physics suggested to some the prospect that nature was a self-governing machine, running smoothly on its own, Locke's metaphysics pointed to the possibility that human beings were drawn to happiness, naturally, on earth. It was not long before critics were drawing these conclusions, walking beyond the borders where these two great pioneers had stopped.

MATERIALISM: THE WORD MADE FLESH

For much of the eighteenth century, a controversy raged in England and on the European Continent as to whether Locke was a 'materialist', one who maintained, that is, that matter could think (Yolton 1991). In a celebrated passage of the *Essay Concerning Human Understanding* (IV.3), Locke had speculated that God *could* super-add the power of thought to matter, so throwing into question the long-held orthodox distinction between matter and mind. Although Locke emphasized that he did not believe God had actually taken this step, his willingness to entertain the thought helped sustain the controversy well into the eighteenth century. At the same time, as Jonathan Israel has recently shown (2001), the tremendous influence of the Dutch philosopher Baruch Spinoza was a central force in prompting materialist speculation in Europe, particularly in the first half of the eighteenth century.

These sources – and there were others – helped prepare the way for the great materialist debates of mid-century and thereafter. But the work of one man in particular, Julien Offray de La Mettrie, helped spark the uproar that transformed materialism from an underground controversy into a public scandal.

Born in France in 1709, La Mettrie, like Locke, studied to be a doctor, completing his training under Hermann Boerhaave at Leyden. He served as a surgeon in the French army before being expelled from France for publishing unorthodox views. Taking refuge in Holland, where he lived in exile in 1746–7, he was eventually hounded from there, too, and forced to flee east to the court of the philosophically radical, and religiously tolerant, Frederick the Great of Prussia. There, La Mettrie consolidated his reputation as a scandalous man before dying, prematurely, in 1751.

What was so scandalous about La Mettrie? A great deal: with a penchant for satire, a poisonous tongue and a taste for living large, the young doctor managed to offend in myriad ways. But it was above all his contention that the soul was 'an empty word to which no idea corresponds' that horrified the great majority of his detractors (La Mettrie 1747: 59). The contention was shocking because it threatened to collapse what Western culture had separated for centuries: matter and mind, body and soul. For the majority of Greeks and Romans, as for their Christian heirs, the two substances were separate, the one inferior to the other. To contend that our highest essence – the immortal breath blowing through our mortal bodies – was only so much gristle and bone was thus a radical claim. In effect, it was to blur the distinctions between animal, plant and human, hinting that all were self-generating machines.

La Mettrie makes this dramatic claim in his most famous work, the aptly entitled *L'Homme Machine* (*Man a Machine*), first published in late 1747. 'The human body is a self-winding machine,' he observes there, 'a living representation of perpetual motion.' Well-tuned clocks, 'contraptions of springs', men and women are sophisticated models of animals and plants. 'Man is not moulded out of more precious clay than they,' La Mettrie writes. 'Nature employed the same dough for both man and animals, varying only the leaven.' And given that 'the transition from man to animal is not abrupt', it follows that we should think of ourselves as part of a fluid continuum that has evolved from below. 'An ape full of intelligence is just a little man in another form' (La Mettrie 1747: 32, 65, 50, 41, 75).

Organic machines composed of matter endowed with the ability to think, human beings were more advanced than animals and plants, but not different in kind. It followed from this, La Mettrie argued, that we should consider our human activities accordingly. Just as plants extended their roots in search of the natural nutrients that gave them life; just as animals constantly roamed in search of ways to fulfil their natural desires; human beings should follow the dictates of nature's demands. And what, La Mettrie asked, was more natural than pleasure? Was not pleasure our most fundamental response to the stimulus of the world? All who taught otherwise – all philosophers who counselled conditioning to pain, all theologians who warned of the dangers of delight – were charlatans who turned us aside from our natural course. When rightly considered, human beings were simple machines intended for happiness:

> Our organs are capable of feeling or being modified in a way that pleases us and makes us enjoy life. If the impression created by this feeling is short it constitutes pleasure; if longer, sensuality and if permanent, happiness. It is always the same feeling; only its duration and intensity differ . . . The more long-lasting, delicious, enticing, uninterrupted and untroubled this feeling is, the happier one is.
>
> (La Mettrie 1750: 120)

In making these claims, La Mettrie, like Locke before him, was drawing self-consciously on the tradition of the Greek philosopher Epicurus, to which he paid repeated and open homage in such works as *The System of Epicurus*; *The Art of Enjoying Oneself*; *The School of Sensual Pleasure*; and *The Anti-Seneca* (also entitled *The Discourse on Happiness*). Defying the more general classical tendency to separate matter and mind, Epicurus, and more explicitly his Roman successor Lucretius, had taught that the world was a swirling mass of atoms which comprised both body and soul. The soul, in other words, was not a substance apart; nor was it intended for an afterlife. When one accepted this basic truth, Epicurus argued, one could dispel the false fears of divine punishment or eternal damnation that caused us continual anxiety and pain, allowing us to focus instead on the more enlightened goal of attaining pleasure in this world.

In these respects, La Mettrie was faithful to the Epicurean system. Yet there was a crucial and essential difference between the ancient and modern man. For all his endorsement of pleasure, Epicurus was no hedonist, but rather an ascetic, who counselled a rigorous curtailment of desire so as to steel the self against disturbance, and guard against self-inflicted pain. Properly speaking, the aim of the Epicurean sage was *ataraxia*, the freedom from anxiety, the minimization of pain.

La Mettrie focused, by contrast, on the other half of the proposition. If pleasure, quite simply, was an affair of the organs – a matter of the senses, the sensation of matter – we should seek it any way we can. Without hesitation, La Mettrie embraced openly the prospect that had so haunted John Locke: 'It is thus very clear that with respect to happiness, good and evil are in themselves indifferent. The one who receives more satisfaction from doing evil will be happier than whoever receives less from doing good. Happiness is individual and particular, and may be found in the absence of virtue and even in crime.' Slightly later in the *The Anti-Seneca* La Mettrie is even more explicit: 'If not content to outdo yourself in the great art of sensual pleasures, and if debauchery and dissolution are not to your taste, perhaps filth and infamy will be more to your liking. Wallow in slime like a pig, and you will be happy in their fashion' (quoted in Mauzi 1979: 251).

La Mettrie had a taste for provocation, and some of this was precisely that – inflammatory words intended to shock and arouse. Yet he also expressed in no uncertain terms the logic of the calculus of pleasure taken to its extreme. If reason concluded that the soul was a fiction, that human beings were machines, why not run them in any way we desired? To deny ourselves the pleasures that clearly moved us – for the sake of virtue, or honour, or some better life to come – was prejudice that could no longer be sustained. *All* impediments to our subjective experience of happiness must be removed. Without flinching, La Mettrie pointed clearly in the direction that this would lead: 'The world', he observed, 'will never be happy until it is atheist' (La Mettrie 1747: 58).

ATHEISM: *ECCE HOMO*

'Atheism' had long existed as a term of abuse in European culture, employed by theologians and religious polemicists of many stripes in the sixteenth and seventeenth centuries to impugn the orthodoxy of their opponents. But, despite the widespread use of the term, the recorded instances of actual atheism – the professed denial of the existence God – were comparatively few. An offence punishable by death, atheism prior to the eighteenth century was a creed that even those who harboured it were reluctant to commit to print. During the course of the eighteenth century, however, controversial authors grew increasingly bold in sharing their views, none more so than Paul-Henri Thiry, Baron d'Holbach.

Born in Edesheim, in the Rhenish Palatinate, in 1723, Holbach studied law at the University of Leyden in the 1740s, and settled in Paris directly thereafter, employing an ample inheritance to finance his two great passions: philosophy and intellectual discussion. From mid-century until his death in 1789, he hosted a series of regular dinners, gradually forming an established salon, at which he gathered many of the leading minds of the French Enlightenment, including Diderot, Saint-Lambert, Chastellux, Suard and Naigeon, the Abbés Raynal and Morellet, among others. At the same time, he pursued a prolific career as an anonymous author of radical materialist and atheist tracts. As we now know, a number of these works, including Holbach's magnum opus, the *Système de la nature* (1770), figured among the leading 'best-sellers' of illegal books sold in the eighteenth century (Darnton 1995: 63–6).

As the title would indicate, *The System of Nature* describes nature as a system, a complex, interlocking unity of cause and effect, matter and motion. 'The Universe, this vast assemblage of all that exists, presents us with matter and movement alone,' Holbach explains in the work's opening chapter, 'an immense and uninterrupted chain of cause and effects' (Holbach 1999: vol. 2, 172). Taken on its own, this statement is not terribly surprising, save for the fact that Holbach proceeded to treat motion as a primary quality of matter itself, inherent in the nature of things. In doing so, he abolished in one blow the need to explain motion's origin by recourse to a prime mover or first cause – to a god, that is – who set nature's system on its way, and who continued to control its course. For Holbach, 'motion is a manner, which matter derives from its own proper existence', a truth that applied to *everything* in the universe. Sharing La Mettrie's materialism, Holbach refused to leave any space at all for spirit or soul.

It followed, Holbach believed, that if all was matter in motion, then all could be explained in terms of the basic laws of attraction and repulsion that governed the physical universe. There was, as a consequence, 'neither chance nor fortune in nature', a truth that applied as much to feeling and thought as it did to the mechanics of objects (Holbach 1999: vol. 2, 206). Taking Locke's sensationalism to an extreme, Holbach explained laughter, anger, intellection and love in the same way that he explained the growth of plants, a raging battle or a violent storm. The interactions of matter in its multiform combinations – its impressions, sensations, causes and effects – were governed by iron laws.

Nor was anything else needed to explain them. The idea of God was not only a chimera – dreamed up by ignorant men in all cultures to assuage the fear of forces they could not explain – but an enormous obstacle to our well-being. 'False systems of superstition had produced a vast chain of evils on earth,' teaching men and women to hate their bodies and their minds, to spurn pleasure and the gratification of desire, to deny themselves and their comforts for the sake of the great lie of a world to come (Holbach 1999: vol. 2, 300). In every one of his works, with great vehemence and rhetorical fury, Holbach pressed the need to free ourselves from this terrible tyranny, to throw off the yoke of God.

And what did he envisage in its place? Happiness, earthly happiness, was the reward, so long denied by religion, that would now burst forth. Released from repression, guilt and false belief, pleasure could finally flow free. Like so many thinkers of his age, Holbach measured happiness exclusively in pleasure's terms.

Much of this is reminiscent of La Mettrie. Yet in Holbach's mind there was an important difference between his own work and that of the man he described as a 'frenzied lunatic' (quoted in Taylor 1989: 334). Diderot, a frequent guest at Holbach's table and likewise an atheist and materialist, was similarly dismissive, writing off La Mettrie as 'dissolute, impudent, a flatterer, and buffoon' (quoted in Mauzi 1979: 249). One suspects, however, that they protest too much, and that their protest is revealing. For, although Holbach shared, in virtually every way, La Mettrie's assumptions – that there is no God, that all is matter, that man is a pleasure-seeking machine – he attempted to avoid the radical egotism of La Mettrie's conclusions with reference to noble words. 'Nature', flanked by 'virtue', 'reason', and 'truth', Holbach explains repeatedly, will reveal to all right-thinking minds that happiness lies in more than personal gratification, in more than the subjective fulfilment of individual desire. 'Man cannot be happy without virtue,' Holbach insists, where virtue is defined as our willingness to 'communicate happiness' to others (Holbach 1999: vol. 2, 358). It is in our self-interest, it seems, to serve the interests of those around us. By making our fellows happy, so we render ourselves.

This is a laudable sentiment, one that is at the heart of not only Holbach's and Diderot's thought, but of a much wider current of eighteenth-century utilitarianism, in which the greatest happiness of the greatest number is considered the primary standard of virtue. This notwithstanding, it is also true, as modern commentators have pointed out, that the conclusions of Holbach and company do not follow easily from their premise (Taylor 1989: 329–37). For, if human beings are indeed the pleasure-seeking machines that they are portrayed to be – prompted by nature to maximize their own enjoyment at every turn – then why they should work to maximize the pleasure of their fellows is by no means clear. Were self-interest and social interest really so closely linked? Were happiness and virtue so clearly one? This was certainly a widespread assumption of the age, but it drew its force from the received stock of the ancients and centuries of Christian reinforcement. Whether it could stand on its own terms, in a context far removed from the ancient *polis* and by men who increasingly questioned the promise of eternal reward, was by no means clear. La Mettrie had already summoned Locke's spectre. And in the next century others would be inclined to see in a godless universe not the smiling face of nature but a cold and impersonal place where all might be permitted.

Such observations point to the way in which the system of Holbach rested on a fundamental contradiction. Positing, on the one hand, an amoral world that ran smoothly on its own, he invested nature, on the other hand, with moral power when this world failed to run as he believed it should. Nowhere is this more apparent than in the final paragraphs of *The System of Nature*, in which Holbach addresses nature as God:

> Oh Nature! Sovereign of all beings. And you, her adorable daughters, Virtue, Reason, and Truth. Be forever our only divinities; it is to you that are due the homage and incense of the earth. Show us, then, Oh Nature, what man should do to obtain the happiness that you desire for him.
>
> (Holbach 1999: vol. 2, 642–3)

'Men are unhappy only because they are ignorant,' Holbach remarks in another work, of 1772, entitled *Le Bon-Sens* (*Common Sense*). But what he accepted as simple wisdom – that in clearing away the darkness of religion happiness would be revealed in nature's light – was hardly common sense. It was an article of faith.

END WITHOUT END

It is testimony to the complexity of Enlightenment thought – to its internal debates, disagreements and tensions – that the trajectory I have followed here – from deism to atheism along the road of happiness – was by no means the sole enlightened path.

No less an enlightened figure than Voltaire continually paid deference to the contingency and uncertainty of human experience, refusing to discount entirely the 'fatality of evil' (Baczko 1997). Similarly, Immanuel Kant, the celebrated author of the celebrated essay 'What is Enlightenment?', mocked the facile association of happiness with reason and virtue throughout his oeuvre, even denying that happiness was the goal of human life.

Such qualifications remind us that the assumption of the rigid unity of Enlightenment belief is as tired as the hackneyed fallacy that the enlightened were all optimistically naive. Yet, having said as much, it is also true that a good many men and women of the time *did* follow the steps marked out in this chapter, coming to see happiness in nature where previous centuries had seen salvation in God. Convinced of the natural harmony of the universe, and of humankind's ability to control it, they put forth a world in which happiness was part of the order of things; in which fortune and fate were under our control; in which the will of God (if this existed at all) was largely irrelevant to earthly concerns. Human beings *could* be happy, they believed; they *should* be happy. And if they were not, then something was wrong – with their institutions, their beliefs, their bodies, their minds. We have travelled in many different directions since the Age of Enlightenment. But in this respect, at least, we continue, for better or for worse, to walk in its way.

REFERENCES

Annas, Julia (1993) *The Morality of Happiness*, New York: Oxford University Press.

Aristotle, *Nichomachean Ethics*.

Augustine, *City of God*.

Baczko, Branislaw (1997) *Job, mon ami: promesses du bonheur et fatalité du mal*, Paris: Gallimard.

Chaucer, Geoffrey (1387–1400) 'The Monk's Tale', in *The Canterbury Tales*, ed. Sinan Kökbugur, http://www.librarius.com/cantales.htm (© Librarius).

D'Alembert, Jean Le Rond (1751) *Preliminary Discourse to the Encyclopaedia of Diderot*, trans. and intro. by Richard N. Schwab (1995) Chicago and London: University of Chicago Press.

Darnton, Robert (1995) *The Forbidden Best-sellers of Pre-Revolutionary France*, New York: W. W. Norton & Co.

Holbach, Paul-Henri Thiry d' (1999) *Oeuvres philosophiques*, ed. Jean-Pierre Jackson, 3 vols, Paris: Editions Alive.

Hunter, Michael and Wootton, David (eds) (1992) *Atheism from the Reformation to the Enlightenment*, Oxford: Clarendon Press.

Israel, Jonathan I. (2001) *Radical Enlightenment: Philosophy and the Making of Modernity, 1650–1750*, New York: Oxford University Press.

Kors, Alan Charles (1996) *Atheism in France, 1650–1729*, Princeton: Princeton University Press.

—— (1976) *D'Holbach's Coterie: An Enlightenment in Paris*, Princeton: Princeton University Press.

La Mettrie, Julien Offray de (1747) *Man a Machine*, trans. Richard A. Watson and Maya Rybalka (1994) Indianapolis: Hackett.

—— (1750) *Anti-Seneca or the Sovereign Good*, ed. and trans. Ann Thomson in *Machine Man and Other Writings* (1996) Cambridge: Cambridge University Press.

Locke, John (1689) *An Essay Concerning Human Understanding*, ed. Peter H. Nidditch (1991) Oxford: Clarendon Press.

Mauzi, Robert (1979) *L'Idée du bonheur dans la littérature et la pensée françaises au XVIIIe siècle*; 2nd edn (1994) Paris: Editions Albin Michel.

McCready, Stuart (ed.) (2001) *The Discovery of Happiness*, London: MQ Publications.

McMahon, Darrin M. (forthcoming) *Happiness: A History*, New York: Grove Atlantic Press.

Nussbaum, Martha C. (1996) *The Fragility of Goodness: Luck and Ethics in Greek Tragedy and Philosophy*, Cambridge: Cambridge University Press.

Rostvig, Maren-Sofie (1962) *The Happy Man: Studies in the Metamorphoses of a Classical Ideal*, New York: Humanities Press.

Taylor, Charles (1989) *Sources of the Self: The Making of Modern Identity*, Cambridge, Mass.: Harvard University Press.

Trinkaus, Charles (1940) *Adversity's Noblemen: The Italian Humanists on Happiness*, New York: Columbia University Press.

Yolton, John W. (1991) *Locke and French Materialism*, Oxford: Clarendon Press.

CHAPTER ELEVEN

PROGRESS AND OPTIMISM

———•◆•———

Clare Jackson

'Never, never was Britain so glorious,' declared the Welsh nonconformist minister Richard Price in a sermon preached in the London parish of Newington Green on 29 November 1759. Deeming George II's British subjects to be 'unspeakably happier' than any other people in the world, Price exhorted his congregation 'to push things to that point of perfection which we have brought so nearly within our reach' (Price 1759: 12, 19–20). Entitled 'Britain's Happiness, and the Proper Improvement of It', Price's sermon captured the spirit of insatiable optimism that pervaded the political culture of Georgian Britain and Enlightenment Europe. In a public address at the Sorbonne nearly a decade earlier, on 11 December 1750, a young theology student, Anne-Robert-Jacques Turgot, had rejoiced that '[t]he time has come' for Europe to escape 'the darkness which covered thee!' Exhorting his contemporaries to '[o]pen your eyes and see!', Turgot had predicted that the glorious achievements of Louis XV's France would 'extend over the whole world' as mankind would 'continually become better and happier!' (Turgot 1750: 57, 59). Exuding confidence, Turgot's vision encapsulated an optimism that eighteenth-century Europe represented the best of all possible worlds, securely reinforced by a trust in the idea of progress that ensured the future melioration of the human condition. In similar vein, Richard Price acclaimed the aspirations of the American revolutionaries in the 1780s, observing that '[s]uch are the nature of things that progress must continue', so 'mankind may at last arrive at degrees of improvement which we cannot even now suspect to be possible' (Price 1784: 118). As revolutionary fervour extended to Continental Europe, 'the proposition that the human race has always been progressively improving' was held by Immanuel Kant to be no complacent platitude, but rather 'tenable within the most strictly theoretical context' (Kant 1798: 185).

This chapter first revisits the Enlightenment's vaunted affirmations and aspirations regarding the future happiness of mankind. It begins by illustrating how late seventeenth-century literary and philosophical controversies concerning the relative superiorities of ancient and modern cultures inspired eighteenth-century champions of progress. Recognition of the accumulated wisdom inherited from previous generations was wedded to an assurance that new intellectual discoveries constantly confirmed the perpetual expansion of knowledge. Meanwhile, increasing interest in sensationalist psychology and the evolution of linguistic communication were held to endow individuals with the creative capacity to secure a better future. Hence, as another contributor to this volume, Larry Stewart, has previously argued, '[i]mprovement became not so much an ideology as an epistemological conclusion' (Stewart 1992: xxxiii). Second, the chapter turns to consider how belief in secular progress challenged traditional concerns about spiritual salvation and divine judgement by placing an increased premium on the potential for individuals to enlarge their temporal happiness. At the same time, however, clerics such as Joseph Butler, Bishop of Durham, also invoked theories of progress to predict parallel improvements in theological understanding as knowledge of divine revelation became increasingly sophisticated. More broadly, Enlightenment concepts of optimism contributed to early eighteenth-century debates about theodicy and the need to accommodate the apparent existence of evil in God's creation, while Newtonian natural philosophy provided attractive analogical foundations for adherents of the 'design argument' to defend religious belief on the grounds that a complex universe necessarily indicated the prior existence of a divine creator. Third, since the recognition of human progress entailed qualitative comparisons with earlier eras of human existence, the chapter proceeds to examine the influence of progressivism on Enlightenment conceptions of history and historical teleology. In particular, it shows how the construction of stadial, or 'conjectural', forms of history enabled the progress of different countries to be traced from primitive states of barbaric 'rudeness' to modern conditions of civilized refinement. The chapter then concludes by considering a range of critical challenges to optimistic affirmations of inevitable progress, together with an indication of the various ways in which the scope and character of future progress was envisaged.

EIGHTEENTH-CENTURY VISIONS OF PROGRESS

Enlightenment orthodoxy regarding mankind's future betterment was essentially innovative and involved an implicit rejection of the predominantly cyclical interpretations of history that had been articulated by Renaissance, medieval and classical authorities. The term 'optimism' was itself an eighteenth-century neologism, devised by Gottfried Wilhelm Leibniz in his *Theodicy* (1710) to explain how the 'optimum' human condition emerged in terms comparable to objective notions of maximum and minimum circumstances. Early historiographical attention was directed towards Enlightenment interest in progress and optimism in J. B. Bury's *The Idea of Progress* (1920), wherein progress was defined as 'a theory which involves a synthesis of the past and a prophecy of the future' (Bury 1920: 5). Subsequent generations of commentators have concurred in describing the zenith of popularity enjoyed by concepts of progress and optimism in the eighteenth century. For Roy Porter, for example, 'central to enlightened modernizing were the glittering prospects of progress . . . [p]rogress proved the ultimate Enlightenment gospel' (Porter 2000: 14–15, 445).

In the modern era, religious portends of future millennia co-exist alongside secular optimism for progressive historical change. Teleological histories, such as Francis

Fukuyama's *The End of History and the Last Man* (1992), for instance, posited a perceived progress of mankind manifested in the universal political aspiration to embrace liberal democracy. Yet historiographical endorsement of progressivism is by no means uncontested. Throughout the twentieth century, disillusionment with doctrines claiming to promote human betterment bred a nervous scepticism about both the inevitability of human progress and the desirability of invoking past improvements as a means of predicting future happiness. Bitter experience indicated that locating predetermined paths of history could instead serve to supply manipulative ideologues with ostensible pretexts for exploiting ideas of alleged human perfectibility to promote partisan purposes. As early as the mid-1930s, Carl Becker thus challenged the attractiveness of the idea of 'progress' by pointing out the intellectual irony of rejecting older religious claims of infallibility while simultaneously continuing to 'seek, in the half-wrecked doctrine of progress, securities that only infallibility can provide'. Far from representing an evident ambition, Becker deemed the idea of progress to be 'heavily loaded with moral and teleological overtones' and redolent with subjective ambiguity (Becker 1936: 10, 1).

Enlightenment conceptions of progress were, however, far from monolithic, and often generated a multiplicity of competing evaluations. Viewing William Hogarth's engraving of *A Harlot's Progress* (1732) alongside that of *A Rake's Progress* (1735), for example, provided eighteenth-century spectators with visual warning that progress was not the exclusive preserve of the virtuous. The concluding chapter of Adam Ferguson's *An Essay on the History of Civil Society* (1767) examined 'the Progress and Termination of Despotism', thus endowing misgovernment with the same capacity for predetermined change, or 'progress', as enlightened rule. Perhaps the most searing vision of human regress to be penned during the eighteenth century was Jean Jacques Rousseau's *Discourse on the Origin and Foundations of Inequality among Men* (1754). Deliberately seeking to subvert conventional certitudes concerning mankind's inevitable advancement, Rousseau instead argued that 'all subsequent progress has been so many steps in appearance towards the perfection of the individual, and in effect towards the decrepitude of the species' (Rousseau 1754: 167).

THE ANCIENTS AND THE MODERNS

Self-consciously conceived as an arresting polemic for an essay competition sponsored by the provincial academy of Dijon, Rousseau's account of human regress juxtaposed the relative physical and moral superiorities of a primitive and 'noble' savage alongside those of a supposedly refined and reasoning European. In doing so, Rousseau's *Discourse* drew resonantly on earlier intellectual debates that had originated in France concerning the competing cultural supremacy of classical antiquity over modern civilization. Works such as Charles Perrault's *Parallèle des anciens et des modernes* (1688–96) and Bernard Fontenelle's *Digression sur les anciens et les modernes* (1688) championed modernity and defended the pre-eminence of contemporary culture on the grounds of the cumulative wisdom conferred through mankind's collective memory. Insisting that the issue could be resolved by simply asking 'whether the Trees which formerly grew in our Fields were larger than these of the present Time',

Figure 11.1 *Richard Price*, Thomas Holloway engraved after a portrait by Benjamin West. By permission of Dr D. O. Thomas.

Fontenelle had argued that since modern man was physically no different from his illustrious classical progenitors, his competitive advantage must derive from the additional knowledge inherited from previous generations. As Fontenelle perceived, excessive admiration for ancient authorities such as Aristotle merely conspired to ensure that 'Philosophy has not only made no advancement, but was sunk into the

Depths of a pedantick Jargon, and unintelligible Ideas; from when it has cost the greatest pains imaginable to set her free' (Fontenelle 1688: 179, 210). The quarrel extended to late seventeenth-century England, where its acrimonious character attracted the satirical interest of Jonathan Swift. In Swift's vivid imagination, 'the Books in St James's Library, looking upon themselves as parties principally concerned, took up the controversie, and came to a decisive battel', enigmatically adding that 'we cannot learn to which side the Victory fell' (Swift 1697: 'The Bookseller to the Reader').

Although largely retrospective in its comparisons of the achievements of previous generations with those of modern successors, such rivalry between champions of 'the ancients and moderns' provided important inspiration for eighteenth-century theorists of progress. Since post-Renaissance culture remained deeply imbued with admiration for classical models and mores, Enlightenment eulogists avoided directly denigrating the successes of earlier generations. Modern culture could, nevertheless, still be acclaimed as superior by virtue of the quantitative accumulation of knowledge and the process by which one generation transmitted the fruits of its practical experiences and learned reflections to the next. Progress was thus assumed to be inevitable, for although individuals could claim no greater physical strength or intellectual capacity than their illustrious ancestors, the reservoir of inherited wisdom would always increase without limit. Further analogies were also drawn between the collective experiences of an individual over a lifetime with those of mankind in general. As the French revolutionary fugitive the Marquis de Condorcet insisted in 1793, for example, progress was historically 'subject to the same general laws that can be observed in the development of the faculties of the individual', representing 'indeed no more than the sum of that development realized in a large number of individuals joined together in society' (Condorcet 1793: 210–11).

Hence Enlightenment accounts of human progress invoked the unique way in which individuals were endowed not only with a collective memory, but also with an instinctive readiness to use prior experience as a means of informing future expectations. In this context, language represented a particularly vital repository for progress, since it enabled the communication of knowledge from one generation to another and from one geographical environment to another. In his address to the Sorbonne in December 1750, for instance, Turgot celebrated how 'arbitrary signs of speech and writing' both preserved and explained discoveries, rendering 'all the individual stores of knowledge a common treasure-house which one generation transmits to another' (Turgot 1750: 41). Reflecting a particularly keen Enlightenment interest in linguistic origins and development, eighteenth-century observers thus perceived a reciprocity between linguistic evolution and the historical progress of society. Linguistic advance occurred when new ideas demanded new modes of expression, as witnessed by the term 'optimism', coined to describe the Leibnizian belief that the created world was the 'best of all possible worlds'. Furthermore, it was also assumed that social and cultural improvement could be promoted by careful linguistic regulation and refinement. The publication of Samuel Johnson's *Dictionary of the English Language* in 1755 represented one colossal lexicographical attempt to direct semantic attention to the ways in which classical linguistic constructions had been subjected to vernacular modifications across a range of philosophical, professional and educational contexts. For, as Johnson conceived, although entire

Figure 11.2 *Marquis de Condorcet*, from *Corréspondence inédite de Condorcet et de Turgot* (1883) Paris. By permission of the National Library of Australia.

transformations of expression were rare, languages nevertheless evolved in ways 'which, though slow in their operation, and invisible in their progress, are perhaps much superiour [*sic*] to human resistance, as the revolutions of the sky, or intumescence of the tide' (Johnson 1755: 'Preface', sig. C2r).

Enlightenment interest in linguistic evolution as a reflection of human progress was also stimulated by investigations of the natural ways in which individuals received sensory impressions, reflected critically on their content and communicated the products of such reasoning to one another. For, just as languages were deemed to be susceptible of continued development, expansion and refinement, so too were men and women themselves. Hence theorists of progress not only emphasized the quantitative accretion of knowledge garnered over time, but also the qualitative transformation of individual intellects as successive generations deployed their rational faculties to best advantage. In the early seventeenth century the former Lord Chancellor of England, Francis Bacon, had proclaimed the limitless potential for empirical observation and inductive ratiocination to promote human ingenuity, insisting in *The New Organon* that 'a new beginning has to be made from the lowest foundations, unless one is content to go round in circles for ever, with meagre, almost negligible progress' (Bacon 1620: 39). As theories of progress acquired widespread popularity during the eighteenth century, the Baconian concept of the advancement of learning thus evolved into a much broader vision, encompassing the improvement of civilization. Publicizing the *Encyclopédie* projected by Denis Diderot, Jean Le Rond D'Alembert publicly honoured the 'immortal' Bacon in 1751, regarding him as 'the greatest, the most universal, and the most eloquent of philosophers' who 'joined the most sublime images with the most rigorous precision'. Drawing attention to the important role of dictionaries and encyclopaedias in disseminating knowledge, D'Alembert hoped that Diderot's *Encyclopédie* would 'expound the true principles of things and note their relationships' and thus 'contribute to the certitude and progress of human knowledge' (D'Alembert 1751: 74, 128). Published between 1751 and 1765, the *Encyclopédie* eventually extended to twenty-eight volumes.

Scientific and technical innovation further kindled the imaginations of Enlightenment prophets of progress. In 1687 Isaac Newton's *Philosophiae Naturalis Principia Mathematica* had invoked the concept of gravitational force to explain complex relationships subsisting between temporal and celestial bodies. Numerous admirers quickly endorsed and popularized Newton's contributions to subjects as diverse as dynamics, mechanics, optics, astronomy, alchemy, chemistry, history and theology. Following Newton's death in 1727, Voltaire observed that the natural philosopher had been 'buried like a king who had done well by his subjects', perceptively attributing Newton's overwhelming reputation to his posthumous elevation as 'the Hercules of the fable, to whom the ignorant attributed all the deeds of the other heroes' (Voltaire 1733: 69, 71). Experimentation became increasingly popular as inventions such as the microscope and the telescope transformed appreciation of hitherto unknown living organisms and prompted the English poet Alexander Pope to wonder in his *Essay on Man* (1733–4):

Above, how high progressive life may go!
Around, how wide! How deep extend below!

Vast chain of being, which from God began,
Natures æthereal, human, angel, man,
Beast, bird, fish, insect! What no eye can see.
(Pope 1733–4: I.235–9)

Numerous other eighteenth-century advances, including chronometers to determine longitude at sea and seismic instruments to detect earthquakes on land, immeasurably enhanced human knowledge of the earthly environment. Even the hold of the earth's gravity was dramatically surpassed when the hot-air balloon was invented by Etienne and Joseph Montgolfier in 1783 and the first cross-Channel balloon flight between France and England was accomplished two years later. As the idea of human flight became a practical possibility for the first time, the Parisian author Louis-Sébastian Mercier witnessed a balloon ascent over the Tuileries Gardens in 1783, beholding 'a moment which can never be repeated, the most astounding achievement the science of physics has yet given to the world' (quoted in Simpson 1933: 314). Balloon ascents aside, transport infrastructure rapidly developed throughout Europe, while buildings, landscapes and gardens were subjected to sustained 'improvement' and artistic taste and manners were similarly 'refined'. The expansion of large-scale printing generated the production of learned journals and reviews across the eighteenth-century republic of letters, ensuring the speedy dissemination of ideas and images to urban coffee houses, Parisian salons, Masonic lodges, debating clubs, provincial academies and scientific societies. Having himself conducted experiments that led to the invention of the lightning-rod, in 1783 Benjamin Franklin accounted himself 'almost sorry I was born so soon, since I cannot have the happiness of knowing what will be known 100 years hence' (Smyth 1905–7: IX.74–5).

HUMAN PERFECTIBILITY AND
THE THEODICY DEBATE

Belief in human progress thus embraced free intellectual enquiry and the revision of entrenched orthodoxies. It was stimulated by prolonged periods of relative stability, economic prosperity and a retreat from confessional warfare and pervasive theological disputation. A faith in human perfectibility accompanied increasing human dominion over the natural environment as, for example, the sensationalist psychological theories of John Locke inspired confidence in human capabilities by emphasizing the natural tendency of men and women to act in ways that promoted pleasure and avoided pain. As Locke had observed in *An Essay Concerning Human Understanding*, if it were to be 'asked, what 'tis moves desire? I answer, happiness and that alone' (Locke 1690: 258). Denying the existence of innate ideas, Locke had encouraged his readers to believe that individuals could pursue an active role in shaping their future destiny. Elsewhere, in *Some Thoughts Concerning Education*, he had insisted that 'of all the Men we meet with, Nine Parts of Ten are what they are, Good or Evil, useful or not, by their Education'. Locke's description of children 'only as white Paper, or Wax, to be moulded and fashioned as one pleases' indicated to an Enlightenment audience that the natural advantages of individuals were considerably less important than the need to devise appropriate forms of moral and pedagogical instruction to promote perfectibility and progress (Locke 1693: 114, 325).

As well as trusting that perfectible humans possessed both the acquired knowledge and critical capacity to secure an optimistic outcome to their affairs, Enlightenment theorists of progress also needed to rely on the permanence of objective moral values. From this perspective, Locke's attack on innatism entailed a decisive repudiation of the constrictions imposed by original sin. Dominance over the physical world was alone insufficient to ensure progress without confronting supernatural constraints. In 1697, the French Huguenot refugee Pierre Bayle had published his *Dictionnaire historique et critique*, in which the existence of both good and evil were discussed in terms of a dualistic struggle from which evil possibly triumphed. Such arguments challenged Christian teaching that the divine creation of an imperfect universe was deliberate, since God had endowed individuals with free wills and the ability to choose between virtuous and vicious actions. Such a creation of an imperfect universe was held as preferable to the alternative idea of creating a perfect, but prescriptive, world wherein free will was denied. In the early eighteenth century, however, attempts were made to eradicate the concept of evil as far as possible, by regarding apparent evil as a form of corrupted perfection that was reversible through positive human remedy. Leibniz's theodicy was thus framed on the optimistic belief that 'this universe must be indeed better than every other possible universe' in accommodating the least amount of intrinsic evil (Leibniz 1710: 378). Vindicating the wisdom of a benevolent deity, Leibniz envisaged happiness as 'a perpetual progress to new pleasures and new perfections', rather than unmitigated pleasure that rendered nothing else desirable (Leibniz 1714: 424). Pessimistic accounts of good and evil locked in incessant competition were thus discounted. Alexander Pope's *Essay on Man* defended the Leibnizian principle that the universe had been devised by an omnipotent deity who permitted the existence of evil only in order to facilitate greater good. Echoing Leibniz's claim that the world represented the best of all possible universes, Pope bid his readers to accept:

> All partial Evil, [as] universal Good:
> And, spite of Pride, in erring Reason's spite,
> One truth is clear, Whatever Is, is Right.
> (Pope 1733–4: I.292–4)

Enlightenment *a priori* theories of optimism thus remained largely dependent on such beliefs in a benign deity. Newtonian natural philosophy had claimed Providential sanction in promoting the extension of human dominion over the physical world. Natural theology was held to reinforce revelation, for, as the Edinburgh mathematician Colin Maclaurin confirmed, 'a manifest contrivance immediately suggests a contriver' (Maclaurin 1748: 381). Moreover, the Newtonian universe was regular and uniform, unlike previous theories of divine Providence that had emphasized the unfathomable, unpredictable and arbitrary character of God's omnipotence and vengeance. Hence individuals could be encouraged to direct their energies more profitably towards securing optimistic outcomes in their worldly affairs, as opposed to remaining impotent and fearful pawns oppressed by the vagaries of divine salvation. In this way, even largely secular theories of progress continued to bear a religious imprimatur as eighteenth-century prophecies of temporal fulfilment gradually replaced older Christian eschatologies.

Fascinated by the far-reaching implications of Newtonian cosmology, the early eighteenth-century Professor of Moral Philosophy at the University of Glasgow, Francis Hutcheson, perceived a parallel moral universe where divine benevolence operated in an analogous manner to gravitation in the physical world. In his *Inquiry into the Original of our Ideas of Beauty and Virtue*, Hutcheson declared 'that Action is best, which accomplishes the greatest Happiness for the greatest Numbers; and that worst, which, in like manner, occasions Misery' (Hutcheson 1725: 164). Reformulated in arithmetical terms, this argument later became known as the 'felicific calculus'. Rejecting Hobbesian convictions regarding human self-interest and egoism, Hutcheson defended sociability and sentiment, attributed evil to ignorance and deemed progress to have been achieved when such ignorance was dispelled. Emphasizing the impressionable character of human nature, Hutcheson's moral Newtonianism thus adopted a reformatory theory of punishment by deeming it 'poor policy merely to punish crimes when they are committed'. Instead, he advocated the need 'to contrive such previous education, instruction, and discipline, as shall prevent vice, restrain these passions, and correct these confused notions of great happiness in vicious courses' (Hutcheson 1755: vol. 2, 310).

The psychological impact of seeking to understand progress was also considered by Hutcheson's erstwhile student at Glasgow, Adam Smith. Endorsing arguments for the importance of sympathy in individual motivation articulated by his colleague David Hume, Smith examined the role of sympathy in impelling individuals to better their material circumstances by emulating their social superiors. Instead of fearing divine vengeance, Smith held the spirit of avarice responsible for ensuring that rich and poor alike were 'led by an invisible hand' to promote general prosperity, claiming that it was 'this deception which rouses and keeps in continual motion to industry of mankind' (Smith 1759: 214, 215). Smith's passing rhetorical image of an 'invisible hand' echoed older theological ideas of the 'invisible hand of Providence' to the secular sphere and emphasized the notion of irresistible temporal forces, independent of divine intervention or miracles. Echoing Leibniz's belief that happiness did not consist in satiated pleasure but in the anticipation of future delights, Smith's political economy endorsed the human propulsion towards prosperity, concluding in *The Wealth of Nations* that '[t]he progressive state is in reality the cheerful and hearty state to all the different orders of the society', since '[t]he stationary is dull; the declining melancholy' (Smith 1776: 184). Despite eschewing altruism, Smith's account nevertheless placed a greater premium on human sociability than the more cynical claims of those such as Bernard Mandeville that sociability should more accurately be regarded as an artificial regulation of instinctive human selfishness. Propounding the maxim that 'private vices' necessarily yielded 'public benefits', Mandeville's *The Fable of the Bees* (1729) had acknowledged progress as an inevitable feature of civil society, but had emphasized the role of human conflict and competition in its promotion.

THE HISTORY AND POLITICAL ECONOMY
OF PROGRESS

Increasing interest in ideas of causal relations and their unintended consequences influenced Enlightenment conceptions of historical narrative and teleology. Addressing the Sorbonne in December 1750, for example, Turgot had insisted that 'all the ages are bound up with one another by a succession of causes and effects which link the present state of the world with all those that have preceded it' (Turgot 1750: 41). In eighteenth-century Scotland, particular energy was directed towards the construction of stadial, or 'conjectural', histories that revealed chain-like mechanisms governing the historic progress of civil societies from primitive barbarism to civilized sophistication. As adumbrated by David Hume, Adam Smith, Adam Ferguson, John Millar and William Robertson, among others, modern civil society was held to have emerged in response to four paradigmatic stages of economic development. The first phase was that of hunting and fishing, which subsequently yielded to pastoralism, before being replaced by agriculture, and eventually concluding with commerce. Assuming a basic constancy in human nature over time, this progress removed the need for any supernatural involvement or unexplained progression from one stage to the next. As the Scottish Historiographer-Royal William Robertson confidently asserted in *The History of America*, since 'in every part of the earth the progress of man hath been nearly the same . . . we can trace him in his career from the rude simplicity of savage life, until he attains the industry, the arts, and the elegance of polished society' (Robertson 1777: vol. 2, 31). Transition from one economic mode of subsistence to another was, however, accompanied by changing sets of ideas and institutions governing political and legal arrangements, as well as social manners and mores. Conjectural history thus became 'a theory of progress of the utmost power' that 'emphasised the cultural chasm which separated peoples who lived in different situations' (Phillipson 1997: 59). Furthermore, the division of labour, the decline of feudalism, the increase of public debt, the establishment of professional armies and the spread of international trade collectively emphasized the distinctiveness of modern commercial society. Nostalgic aspirations to recreate the virtuous achievements of classical republicanism could be comfortably eschewed.

As the researches of Robertson and other conjectural historians revealed, newly discovered societies provided essential standards of comparison by which the laws of historical progress could be measured and understood. In his *Essay Concerning Human Understanding*, Locke had reinforced the epistemological argument against innatism by drawing attention to the rich diversity of customs and beliefs to be found throughout the world, as reported by explorers, colonial adventurers and overseas merchants. Locke's further suggestion in his *Two Treatises of Government* (1690) that 'in the beginning, all the World was America' proved particularly suggestive for those eighteenth-century observers keen to argue that such rustic and exotic societies were similar to those from which contemporary European civilisation had evolved (Locke 1690: 301). Remarking that '[i]n America, man appears under the rudest form in which we can conceive him to subsist', Robertson thus emphasized the didactic importance of historical enquiry over its antiquarian attractions in enabling

Enlightenment observers to 'contemplate man in all those various situations wherein he has been placed' (Robertson 1777: vol. 2, 51, 50).

In addition to the burgeoning amount of anthropological literature about remote regions of the world, elements of imaginative reconstruction were also required to trace the conjured course of human progress, as suggested by the term 'theoretical or conjectural history' later bestowed on such endeavours by Adam Smith's first biographer, Dugald Stewart. For Stewart, it was indeed 'of more importance to ascertain the progress that is most simple, than the progress that is most agreeable to fact' (Stewart 1794: 296). The unforeseen and unintended character of past progress thus warranted optimism regarding the likelihood of similarly accidental good fortune in the future. As another practitioner, Adam Ferguson, observed in his *Essay on the History of Civil Society*, changes in the human condition were achieved 'with equal blindness to the future' as 'nations stumble upon establishments, which are indeed the results of human action, but not the execution of any human design' (Ferguson 1767: 119). Yet, while the vaunted objectivity of stadial histories provided apparently secure grounds for optimistic faith in human progress, Ferguson remained sensitive to the potential for advanced societies to regress through complacency, arrogance and misgovernment. Moreover, he insisted that temporal progress would never attain perfection, later acknowledging in his *Principles of Moral and Political Science* that, although humans were 'susceptible of infinite advancement', the path of perfectibility remained asymptotic since '[w]hat is created can never equal its creator' (Ferguson 1792: vol. 1, 183–4). This conviction was echoed by the English radical William Godwin in his *Enquiry Concerning Political Justice*, published the following year. Godwin agreed that perfectibility did not signify the capacity for humans to be perfected, but instead 'stands in express opposition to it', for 'if we could arrive at perfection, there would be an end to our improvement' (Godwin 1793: 59).

Comparisons between primitive savagery and contemporary civilization also extended to prose fiction, where Daniel Defoe's *The Life and Adventures of Robinson Crusoe* (1719) proved an eighteenth-century best-seller, spawning numerous sequels and imitative *robinsonades*. After being shipwrecked, Crusoe was able to experience life in a state of primitive nature, before using his superior technical knowledge to reinvent a form of modern civilization without the encumbrance of inherited institutions. For somewhat different polemical purposes, Jean Jacques Rousseau also sought to divorce what was natural to human existence from what had been artificially acquired through societal living by imagining 'a state which no longer exists, which perhaps never did exist, [and] which probably never will exist' (Rousseau 1755: 125). As seen earlier, Rousseau rejected contemporary convictions regarding the superiority of modern civilization and traced an aetiology of corruption to argue that primitive savages were endowed with greater integrity and nobility than their deceitful and dishonest successors.

Aside from such speculative scenarios, optimistic Enlightenment beliefs that 'whatever is, is right' were also rendered increasingly fragile by specific historical events, including the destruction unleashed by the Lisbon earthquake that killed 30,000 people and devastated the Portuguese capital on All Saint's Day, 1 November 1755. In his *Poem on the Lisbon Disaster* (1755), Voltaire specifically reflected on the maxim that 'whatever is, is right'. For him, it was simply untenable delusion for individuals to adopt a pious resignation when confronted by such suffering, electing to believe that the disaster and distress would somehow enable an unfathomable greater good that had been sanctioned by divine Providence. Voltaire's distaste for 'facile optimism' and comfortable complacency regarding 'the best of all possible worlds' further provoked the composition of his satirical novel, entitled *Candide, or Optimism* (1759). In this tale, Leibniz was depicted in disguised caricature as Dr Pangloss, a teacher of 'metaphysico-theologico-cosmolonigology', whose resolute confidence that he inhabited 'the best of all possible worlds' belied the series of catastrophic misfortunes that befell him and provoked the eponymous Candide to muse that '[i]f this is the best of all possible worlds, what on earth are the others like?' (Voltaire 1759: 2, 13)

Enlightenment endorsements of progress were thus by no means universal or unambiguous. Voltaire's disillusionment following the Lisbon earthquake confirmed, for example, David Hume's scepticism regarding teleological arguments intended to demonstrate God's benevolence through appreciation of His complex creation. In Hume's posthumously published *Dialogues Concerning Natural Religion*, the character 'Philo' insists that analogical modes of reasoning depended on individuals being 'antecedently convinced of a supreme intelligence, benevolent and powerful'. Deprived of such prior knowledge, however, 'there can be no grounds for such an inference, while there are so many ills in the universe', assuming that such injustices could have been averted by an omnipotent creator (Hume 1779: 106, 113). Hume's hesitation stemmed from his emphasis on the primacy of human experience and his rejection of metaphysical foundations for religious or moral beliefs. Embracing a form of mitigated scepticism instead, he had denied absolute proof in both the physical and moral sciences, urging restrictions to be placed on the bounds of human reason. In a letter to Turgot in 1768, however, Hume acclaimed his French correspondent as 'one of those who entertain the agreeable and laudable, if not too sanguine hope, that human society is capable of perpetual Progress towards Perfection'. Acknowledging that Turgot's optimism served as 'an Incitement to every Virtue and laudable Pursuit', Hume himself remained more equivocal (Greig 1932: vol. 2, 180–1). Studying 'the populousness of ancient nations' in an essay first published in 1752, he had concluded that he could deduce no overall pattern of human progress, indicating that 'it must still be uncertain' whether the world was 'currently advancing to its point of perfection, or declining from it' (Hume 1767: 378).

Interested in understanding the political economy of progress, Hume's investigations into 'the populousness of ancient nations' indicated ways in which discussions about mankind's improvement often also extended to debates about domestic demographic rates, as well as the anthropological customs of exotic and distant societies. Population growth traditionally provided an objective index of wider progress and prosperity. As Rousseau insisted in his *Considerations on the Government of Poland* (written in 1772 but published posthumously, ten years later), since the 'infallible effect of a free and just Government is population . . . the more you perfect your Government, the more you increase your people without even thinking about it' (Rousseau 1782: 229). The absence of reliable quantitative demographic statistics, however, fuelled a persistent fear that the population of eighteenth-century Europe was in a state of terminal decline. In his *Persian Letters*, for example, Charles Secondat,

Baron de Montesquieu, had observed the 'startling thing is that the world is becoming less populous, and, if this continues, in ten centuries, it will be nothing more than a desert' (Montesquieu 1721: 204).

Somewhat ironically, however, just as the production of dependable statistics seemed likely to defy such pessimism about demographic decline, the alternative spectre of excessive population expansion was mooted as a potential restriction on future human progress. Arguments articulated in the 1750s by a Scots clergyman, Robert Wallace, and later developed in the 1790s by his English clerical counterpart, Thomas Robert Malthus, drew attention to the reproductive capacity of humans to achieve a geometric increase in population that could not be sustained by corresponding increases in food production. It was difficult to regard this demographic aspect of the natural order as altruistic. As Malthus argued in the first edition of *An Essay on the Principles of Population as it Affects the Future Improvement of Society*, 'if the premisses are just, the argument is conclusive against the perfectibility of the mass of mankind' (Malthus 1798: 17). Articulated in order to curb the rationalistic optimism of William Godwin and the Marquis de Condorcet, Malthus's bleak predictions were, however, revised, as subsequent editions of the *Essay* incorporated a more melioristic account of the potential for moral restraint to provide 'preventive' checks against future overpopulation.

VISIONS OF FUTURE PROGRESS

Conflicting predictions of demographic expansion and decline reflected the wider potential for tensions to subsist within eighteenth-century accounts of progress and optimism. As Turgot's pluralistic conception of '*les progrès*' suggested, progress was often divided into subsidiary progressions of uneven and inter-related political, moral, religious and scientific advancements. While recognizing that 'the human mind everywhere contains the potential for the same progress', Turgot himself emphasized the historical and geographical specificity of different civil societies and 'the infinite variety of these circumstances' that determined 'the inequality in the progress of nations' (Turgot 1750: 43). As a keen mathematician, however, Turgot anticipated the construction of a calculus of probability that could foretell future human experiences. For, as his biographer, the Marquis de Condorcet, later confirmed, whatever 'happens at any particular moment is the result of what has happened at all previous moments, and itself has an influence on what will happen in the future' (Condorcet 1793: 211). Accurate diagnosis of past and present events was thus held to facilitate the prognosis of future occurrences. In this way, progress and posterity became inextricably associated with each other as compressed interpretations of the past informed present conceptions that were themselves used to prefigure the future. As Leibniz had once evocatively observed, 'the present is big with the future, the future might be read in the past, the distant is expressed in the near' (Leibniz 1714: 419).

Enlightenment attempts to envision the scope and character of future progress found rich expression in imaginative literature. Indeed, Leibniz's maxim that 'the present is big with the future' was placed prominently on the title page of one of the eighteenth century's most widely read fictional works, Louis-Sébastien Mercier's *L'An 2440*. First published in 1771, the tale of *L'An 2440* was recounted by an unnamed narrator who fell asleep after discussing the shortcomings of contemporary Parisian life with an English acquaintance and subsequently awoke to find himself an old man, still living in Paris, but in the year 2440. One of the first time-travellers in prose fiction, Mercier's narrator found the architecture and sanitation of twenty-fifth-century Paris vastly improved and observed its citizens to be the embodiment of civic virtue, ruled by a constitutional monarch and happily subscribing to a deistic civil religion. As the narrator's guide explained, '[s]overeigns have, at last, been prevailed on to listen to the voice of philosophy', having 'opened their eyes to those duties which the safety and tranquillity of the people exacted from them'. By contrast, 'in your enlightened century (as it is called), your magistrates dared, in their haughty stile, to dictate a set of dogmatic decrees, in the same manner as your theologians dictated in matters of religion, treating the law as if it were divested of reason' while demanding unquestioning obedience from subjects (Mercier 1771: 113–14, 189). Furthermore, by 2440, an agreed arrangement securing perpetual peace among nations had also removed the need for standing armies and aggressive overseas colonialism had been abandoned. In the domestic sphere, poverty and crime had been eliminated and taxes replaced by voluntary contributions. Although the subtitle of Mercier's work, '*Rêve s'il en fut jamais*' ('*A dream if ever there was one*'), confirmed its self-consciously fantastical nature, *L'An 2440* nevertheless served to offer an enthusiastic paean of progress in the future. While fictional accounts of idealized societies were generally located either in exotic geographical environments or in past 'golden ages', Mercier's Utopia achieved important verisimilitude by retaining a familiar Parisian setting, but describing the city at a precise future date. Although *L'An 2440* was banned immediately in France for its implicit criticisms of existing *ancien régime* institutions and was also condemned as blasphemous in Spain, the work went through eleven editions between 1771 and 1799 and was translated into English, Dutch, Italian and German.

To conclude, as official disapproval of *L'An 2440* indicated, Mercier's predictions of future progress involved criticism of the present in much the same way as eighteenth-century affirmations of progress invariably entailed unfavourable comparisons with earlier eras. For all the Enlightenment's attachment to rationalism, its fascination with progress required a subjective depiction or distortion of the past, since present improvements depended on a contrast with previous degradations. Hence eighteenth-century optimism tended to coexist alongside a more nervous self-criticism and a concern to understand the laws of progress sufficiently well to perceive and avert potential obstacles. As revolutionary zeal extended from the American colonies to Continental Europe in the 1780s and 1790s, the synoptic view of indefinite human progress in the future initially appeared to receive dramatic endorsement, before such experiences as the French Terror rendered such confidence increasingly fragile and contingent. Nineteenth-century defenders of human progress were thus obliged to confront the difficulty of defining ultimate aspirations of intrinsic and absolute moral worth that would enable an empirically verifiable 'proof' of progress propelling human society to be discovered.

ACKNOWLEDGEMENTS

The author would like to thank Martin Fitzpatrick and Mark Goldie for their comments on an earlier draft of this chapter.

REFERENCES

Bacon, Francis (1620) *The New Organon*, ed. Lisa Jardine and Michael Silverthorne (2000) Cambridge: Cambridge University Press.

Becker, Carl L. (1936) *Progress and Power*, Stanford: Stanford University Press.

Bury, J. B. (1920) *The Idea of Progress: An Inquiry into its Origin and Growth*, ed. C. A. Beard (1932) New York: Macmillan.

Condorcet, Marquis de (1793) 'Sketch for a Historical Picture of the Progress of the Human Mind', in Keith Michael Baker (ed.) (1976) *Condorcet. Selected Writings*, Indianapolis: Bobbs-Merrill.

D'Alembert, Jean Le Rond (1751) *Preliminary Discourse to the Encyclopedia of Diderot*, ed. Richard N. Schwab (1995) Chicago: University of Chicago Press.

Ferguson, Adam (1767) *An Essay on the History of Civil Society*, ed. Fania Oz-Salzberger (1995) Cambridge: Cambridge University Press.

—— (1792) *Principles of Moral and Political Science; Being Chiefly a Retrospect of Lectures Delivered in the College of Edinburgh*, Edinburgh.

Fontenelle, Bernard le Bovier de (1688) 'A Discourse Concerning the Antients and the Moderns', appendix to *Conversations with a Lady on the Plurality of Worlds*, trans. J. Glanvill (1719) London.

Fukuyama, Francis (1992) *The End of History and the Last Man*, London: Hamish Hamilton.

Godwin, William (1793) *Enquiry Concerning Political Justice*, abridged and ed. from the 3rd edn (1798) K. Codell Carter (1971) Oxford: Clarendon Press.

Greig, J. Y. T. (ed.) (1932) *The Letters of David Hume*, 2 vols, Oxford: Clarendon Press.

Hume, David (1767) 'On the Populousness of Ancient Nations', in Eugene F. Miller (ed.) (1985) *Essays Moral, Political and Literary*, Indianapolis: Liberty Classics.

—— (1779) 'Dialogues Concerning Natural Religion', in J. C. A. Gaskin (ed.) (1993) *David Hume: Principal Writings on Religion, Including Dialogues Concerning Natural Religion and The Natural History of Religion*, Oxford: Oxford University Press.

[Hutcheson, Francis] (1725) *An Inquiry into the Original of our Ideas of Beauty and Virtue; In Two Treatises*, London.

Hutcheson, Francis (1755) *A System of Moral Philosophy*, 2 vols, London.

Johnson, Samuel (1755) *A Dictionary of the English Language: In which the Words are Deduced from their Originals, and Illustrated in their Different Significations by Examples from the Best Writers &c.*, 2 vols, London.

Kant, Immanuel (1798) 'A Renewed Attempt to Answer the Question: "Is the Human Race Continually Improving?"', in H. S. Reiss (ed.) (1991) *Kant: Political Writings*, Cambridge: Cambridge University Press.

Leibniz, Gottfried Wilhelm (1710) *Theodicy: Essays on the Goodness of God, the Freedom of Man and the Origin of Evil*, ed. Austin Farrer (1951) London: Routledge & Kegan Paul.

—— (1714) 'Principles of Nature and of Grace', in Robert Latta (ed.) (1925) *The Monadology and Other Philosophical Writings*, Oxford: Oxford University Press.

Locke, John (1690) *An Essay Concerning Human Understanding*, ed. Peter H. Nidditch (1979) Oxford: Clarendon Press.

—— (1690) *Two Treatises of Government*, ed. Peter Laslett (1988) Cambridge: Cambridge University Press.

—— (1693) 'Some Thoughts Concerning Education', in James L. Axtell (ed.) (1968) *The Educational Writings of John Locke*, London: Cambridge University Press.

Maclaurin, Colin (1748) *An Account of Isaac Newton's Philosophical Discoveries*, London.

Malthus, Thomas Robert (1798) *An Essay on the Principles of Population as it Affects the Future Improvement of Society*, London.

Mercier, Louis-Sébastien (1771) *Astræa's Return; or, the Halcyon Days of France in the Year 2440; A Dream*, trans. Harriet Augusta Freeman (1797) London.

Montesquieu, Charles Secondat, Baron de (1721) *Persian Letters*, ed. C. J. Betts (1973) Harmondsworth: Penguin.

Phillipson, Nicholas (1997), 'Providence and Progress: An Introduction to the Historical Thought of William Robertson', in Stewart J. Brown (ed.) *William Robertson and the Expansion of Empire*, Cambridge: Cambridge University Press.

Pope, Alexander (1733–4) *An Essay on Man*, ed. Maynard Mack (1982) London: Methuen.

Porter, Roy (2000) *Enlightenment: Britain and the Creation of the Modern World*, London: Allen Lane.

Price, Richard (1759) 'Britain's Happiness, and the Proper Improvement of It', in D. O. Thomas (ed.) (1991) *Richard Price: Political Writings*, Cambridge: Cambridge University Press.

—— (1784) 'Observations on the Importance of the American Revolution and the Means of Making it a Benefit to the World', in Thomas (ed.) *op. cit.*

Robertson, William (1777) *The History of America*, 3 vols, 6th edn (1792) London.

Rousseau, Jean Jacques (1754) 'Discourse on the Origin and the Foundations of Inequality among Men', ed. and trans. Victor Gourevitch in (1997) *The Discourses and Other Early Political Writings*, Cambridge: Cambridge University Press.

—— (posth. 1782) 'Considerations on the Government of Poland and on its Projected Reformation', ed. and trans. Victor Gourevitch in (1997) *The Social Contract and Other Later Political Writings*, Cambridge: Cambridge University Press.

Simpson, Helen (ed.) (1933) *The Waiting City: Paris 1782–1799, Being an Abridgement of Louis-Sébastian Mercier's 'Le Tableau de Paris'*, London: G. G. Harrap & Co.

Smith, Adam (1759) *The Theory of Moral Sentiments*, ed. Knud Haakonssen (2002) Cambridge: Cambridge University Press.

—— (1776) *The Wealth of Nations: Books I–III*, ed. Andrew Skinner (1974) Harmondsworth: Penguin.

Smyth, Albert Henry (ed.) (1905–7) *The Writings of Benjamin Franklin*, 10 vols, New York: Macmillan.

Stewart, Dugald (1794) 'Account of the Life and Writings of Adam Smith, LL.D.', in W. P. Wightman, J. C. Bruce and I. S. Ross (eds) (1980) *Adam Smith: Essays on Philosophical Subjects*, Oxford: Clarendon Press.

Stewart, Larry (1992) *The Rise of Public Science: Rhetoric, Technology, and Natural Philosophy in Newtonian Britain, 1660–1750*, Cambridge: Cambridge University Press.

Swift, Jonathan (1697) *A Full and True Account of the Battel Fought Last Friday, Between the Antient and the Modern Books in St James's Library*, London.

Turgot, Anne-Robert-Jacques (1750) 'A Philosophical Review of the Successive Advances of the Human Mind', in Ronald L. Meek (ed.) (1973) *Turgot on Progress, Sociology and Economics*, Cambridge: Cambridge University Press.

Voltaire (1733) *Letters on England*, ed. Leonard Tancock (1980) Harmondsworth: Penguin.

—— (1759) 'Candide, or Optimism', in David Wootton (ed.) (2000) *Candide and Related Texts*, Indianapolis: Hackett.

CHAPTER TWELVE

THE SCIENCE OF MAN

———◆•◆———

Christa Knellwolf

The 'science of man' is a prominent achievement of the High Enlightenment. Of course, the wish to understand the nature of human existence did not suddenly emerge in the eighteenth century. From the seventeenth century, ideas and procedures from scientific enquiries had been borrowed for the study of human nature (Jones 1989: 1). What was new was the framework in which familiar questions were asked. The 'science of man' developed as a forum for exploring questions of the foremost political and cultural consequence, as they occurred in natural theology, studies of society, culture and human nature. The term 'science' did not yet have its twenty-first-century sense, but was still more or less equivalent with the Latin *scientia*, so that the 'science of man' can essentially be paraphrased as *knowledge* of man. However, the term's allusive reference to scientific practices, which were gradually gaining serious credentials, indicates its aspiration to make use of the most topical knowledge for the comprehensive study of all questions pertaining to human existence. This chapter describes the stated and implicit objectives of the period's endeavour to grasp human nature, paying special attention to the entanglements between the nascent human sciences and contemporary polite culture.

The science of man was the precursor of a number of academic disciplines familiar today under such labels as the philosophy of mind, cognitive psychology, anthropology, ethnology and sociology, disciplines which assumed their modern forms during the nineteenth century. In the eighteenth century, the science of man concentrated on the study of human nature, engaging with the mechanics of understanding as much as with debates on morality, politics, luxury, propriety and manners. Its debates and discussions aroused a keen interest among the cultural elite and indeed turned into a major concern among the members of the 'republic of letters' (Goodman 1996).

The significance of the study of human nature was enhanced during the early modern period when it was couched in the empirical terms of the new science. Bacon's scientific programme, expressed by his inclusive 'classification of knowledge', laid the foundation for systematic examination of all human questions (Kusukawa 1996: 69). His intellectual inventory served to persuade his audience of the immense future potential of the knowledge, if compiled and ordered properly. The implicit claim that it possessed almost unlimited power for reducing controversial subject matter to simple problems – with simple solutions – inspired those contemporaries exploring geographically remote areas, or trying to cut through the Gordian knot of religious schisms and political factions. Appeals to the powers of reason and rationality pervaded the period, but reasoned judgement was its ideal and by no means its standard practice.

The seventeenth century developed an increasingly mechanistic understanding of physical processes, suggesting analogies for the interpretation of emotions and other mental and bodily processes, as well as social 'mechanisms'. For instance, William Harvey's discovery that the blood circulates in a well-organized system made it possible to imagine that all components of human nature operated under equally well-organized principles. Moreover, the idea that it should be possible to investigate human existence with the methodological accuracy of science, and to pin down its rules and regularities, is already present in the work of Malebranche, Pufendorf and Grotius, but it was only articulated as a coherent project, called the science of man, in the context of the Scottish Enlightenment. It was a key term in David Hume's philosophical study, *A Treatise of Human Nature* (1739–40), in which he offers a radical critique of morality, politics, social practices and religious beliefs.

One of the fundamental assumptions of Enlightenment philosophy was that human nature is uniform and unites humankind both as objects of study by the sciences, and subjects capable of enlightenment (Garrett 2003). The sense of shared humanity informed ambitious attempts to discover and describe its qualities. This chapter describes how and why Enlightenment thinkers classified the individual elements of human nature and tried to make sense of them in the light of political arguments, social arrangements and religious conventions.

ENTHUSIASM AND THE ROLE OF RELIGION

Seventeenth-century Europe was ravaged by moral and religious conflicts, notably the Thirty Years War (1618–48) on the Continent and the English Civil Wars of the 1640s. Since those conflicts concerned in part political and religious liberty, and since civil strife was bound up with different views of human nature and destiny, a well-defined philosophy of government would ideally include a theoretical analysis of human nature. Indeed, the divisive conflicts of the time led Thomas Hobbes to formulate a deeply pessimistic analysis of human nature. At the same time he emphasized the need for a systematic account of it and announced in the introduction to *Leviathan* that '[h]e that is to govern a whole nation, must read in himself, not this, or that particular man; but mankind' (Hobbes 1651: 8). His idea of an innately depraved human nature was entirely familiar to his contemporaries, albeit expressed by them in traditional Christian theological terms, which he sought to replace with a secular vocabulary drawn from mechanistic philosophy. Such a powerfully pessimistic rational analysis of human nature challenged the optimism of Enlightenment thinkers, who had to refute not merely theological notions of man's sinfulness but rational notions of his inadequacy. Indeed, the conflicts at the heart of eighteenth-century theories about human nature were between optimists and pessimists.

A related question was whether culture and society had improved or degenerated since ancient times.

The discussion of highly controversial views ranged from the elegant and allusive wit of Shaftesbury to the explicitly confrontational style of Bernard Mandeville. Shaftesbury assumed that a good-natured and conciliatory manner of handling conflict is more important than being in the right. His *Characteristics of Men, Manners, Opinions, Times* (1708) is to a degree a textual parallel to the coffee-house conversations celebrated by Addison and Steele in the *Spectator*. He argues that if religious believers presupposed the goodness of God, they also had the right, or indeed duty, to explore the nature of the divine being (Shaftesbury 1708: 25). Shaftesbury recommends candid self-enquiry as the best recipe for eradicating enthusiasm and the concomitant abuses of religion. Those who know themselves will never be duped, or, as he puts it himself: 'For to judge the spirits whether they are of God, we must antecedently judge our own spirit, whether it be of reason and sound sense; whether it be fit to judge at all, by being sedate, cool, and impartial, free of every biasing passion, every giddy vapour, or melancholy fume' (Shaftesbury 1708: 39). The secularizing developments of the period tend to be overstated in recent scholarship. The biblical allegory played a major role in the understanding of human nature. Even those who adhered to a latitudinarian religion believed that reason and revelation were alternative approaches to the same truth.

PRIVATE VICES, PUBLIC BENEFITS

Bernard Mandeville asked why his age flourished in spite of the evident failings of man: hypocrisy, double standards and deceit. Sharply separating the characteristics of individuals from the social groups in which they conduct their lives, Mandeville outlined the view that the economies of commercial societies are self-generating systems. Because of the complex links within society, Mandeville cautions against well-meaning interventions: disruption of one part would inevitably, and probably as an unintended consequence, cause disruptions in others. It was therefore prudent to preserve the existing unequal distribution of wealth in society which meant that the prerogatives of the rich were to be left undisturbed.

Mandeville's controversial assessment of society began with a poem in doggerel verse entitled 'The Grumbling Hive, or Knaves Turn't Honest' (1705). In response to his period's outcry against his inhumane perception of human nature, he added extensive explanatory sections and republished the work under the title of 'The Fable of the Bees' (1714; substantially revised in 1723). In a further supplement to 'The Fable of the Bees', entitled 'An Enquiry into the Origin of Moral Virtue', Mandeville complains that '[o]ne of the greatest Reasons why so few People understand themselves, is, that most Writers are always teaching Men what they should be, and hardly ever trouble their heads with telling them what they really are' (Mandeville 1714; 1723: 77).

In 'An Essay on Charity and Charity-Schools', Mandeville delves into the motives behind his period's sentimental morality. He argues that 'in a Free Nation where Slaves are not allow'd of, the surest wealth consists of a multitude of Laborious Poor

. . . To make the Society Happy and People Easy under the meanest Circumstances, it is requisite that great numbers of them should be Ignorant as well as Poor' (1714; 1723: 294). Mandeville's argument for brutal self-interest and his profound suspicion of altruism reveals a moralist strain in his thought which leads him down rather dark alleys: a flourishing economy needs 'Sharpers, Parasites, Pimps, Players' (1714; 1723: 64). Petty criminals, along with those who rob the state and abuse their power, he insists, enhance the overall wealth of their nation.

Mandeville's view that private vices made public benefits found a loose analogy in Alexander Pope's *An Essay on Man*, in which he suggested that 'Self love and Social be the same' (1733–4: III.215). His system was both natural and providentially ordained, and yet, as with Mandeville, it is the harmony of the whole which is important to him. The poem is addressed to Henry St John, Viscount Bolingbroke, expressing the gist of his philosophy in verse and intermingling Bolingbroke's philosophy with home-spun ideas and observations. The poem gives rein to the imagination to conjure up sensory experiences of what it feels like to be human. Pope's *Essay* was successful precisely because it reconciled mechanical philosophy with unwavering belief in the goodness of God. This framework allowed him to disseminate the view that a 'ruling passion' (1733–4: II.138), rather than moral principles, was the primary rationale behind human actions. This idea was developed by David Hume, although from other sources.

THE PSYCHOLOGY OF UNDERSTANDING:
DAVID HUME

A number of thinkers in France and Britain before David Hume (1711–76) had attempted to analyse and explain the mechanisms of the mind. Prominent among them was John Locke, who was initially concerned to demonstrate that human beings were not born with innate ideas of morality or truth. In his *Essay Concerning Human Understanding* (1690), he describes the mind of the newborn child as a blank sheet of paper on which sensory impressions can be inscribed. From these, the faculty of reason can construct complex ideas which constitute human identity. Only by means of the exercise of reason can the potential of humanity be achieved. Hume, deriving inspiration from other sources, believed that Locke underestimated other elements in the formation of human identity. In his *A Treatise of Human Nature* (1739–40) he reinstates an ancient view that man is not simply a reasoning animal, and that reason itself cannot be a motive to action. Rather, our actions are motivated by our passions, and the most basic animal motivation consists in the effort to avoid pain or sustain pleasure. Reasoning only has the capacity of analysing and guiding our passions. Moreover, human beings must be understood as essentially social animals, learning in the first place from those about them: knowledge is not something that an individual can acquire by himself. It is always anchored in the particular detail of an interpreted context, and since contexts are always changing, what we regard as knowledge is itself always open to revision. On such foundations Hume strove to lay bare the pernicious effects of ignorance and superstition on people's lives, not least on their religious beliefs and practices, and his posthumously

Figure 12.1 *David Hume*, James Tassie, paste medallion (n.d.). By courtesy of the National Portrait Gallery, London.

published *Dialogues Concerning Natural Religion* was only the last of his many assaults on religion.

Roy Porter describes the relevance of scientific discoveries for arguments about human nature as follows:

> Systematic doubt, as advocated by Descartes, experimentation, reliance upon first-hand experience, rather than second-hand authority, and confidence in the regular order of Nature – these procedures would reveal the laws of man's existence as a conscious being in society, much as they had demonstrated how gravity, as Newton proved, governed the motions of the planets in the solar system.
>
> (Porter 2001: 15)

By introducing the experimental method of reasoning into moral subjects, Hume believed that conclusions of immense practical benefit to society could be drawn and implemented. His radical analysis of beliefs, attitudes and social practices was therefore modelled on his grasp of the new conception of science. He held that unless the enquirers themselves understood the nature of their own capacities, such as the tendency to remember inaccurately, or merely imagine what they wished to be so, they would not understand the nature of their knowledge claims about themselves and the external world:

> Even *Mathematics*, *Natural Philosophy*, and *Natural Religion*, are in some measure dependent on the science of MAN, since they lie under the cognizance of men, and are judged by their powers and faculties. 'Tis impossible to tell what changes and improvements we might make in these sciences were we thoroughly acquainted with the extent and force of human understanding, and cou'd explain the nature of the ideas we employ, and of the operations we perform in our reasoning.
>
> (Hume 1739–40: xix)

On many issues Hume argued that we lacked evidence for our claims. For example, he held that identity can be characterized in terms of our capacities for remembering experiences. Moreover, if experiences are regarded as separate events, our apparent ability to make sense of at least some of them needs careful analysis. The central notions here are those of causal inference and causal connection. Hume holds that our ability – absolutely necessary as it is for our bare survival – to explain the past, understand the present and predict the future depends upon assumptions that patterns of events recur, and that we can make reliable inferences from present experiences to anything not currently within our experience, whether past or future. Such a view, however, means that there can be no certainties about the future, that our understandings are always open to potential revision, and that there are always likely to be matters of relevance about which we remain ignorant.

GENDER, LUXURY AND THE HISTORY OF SOCIETY

A notable side-effect of the increasing wealth of eighteenth-century Europe was that women acquired greater visibility and appeared to have gained more independence. At the same time there were renewed fears, familiar from earlier historical periods, about the licentiousness associated with luxury and the supposedly effeminating effects of sensual indulgences. Irrespective of whether women were merely looked upon as highly visible adornments of society and culture, or whether there was some recognition of their intrinsic claim to equality, gender relations were increasingly discussed. Indeed, in many systematic assessments of foreign cultures, the respective position and esteem accorded to women became an index for determining their respective place on the scale of civilization. Hume described the idea as 'the free intercourse between the sexes, on which the politeness of a nation will commonly much depend' (Hume 1994: 91).

A great deal of effort was spent on attributing a hierarchical ranking to the non-European peoples encountered in the course of the eighteenth century's journeys of exploration. Accounts of the primitive idylls of Tahiti and other Polynesian societies put European culture and civilization on trial and seemed to challenge their very foundations. The question of what held societies together achieved unprecedented urgency. To a degree, the characteristics of the four-stages theory with which writers of the period commonly evaluated societal progress differed mainly in the emphasis placed upon variously structured gender relations. When Adam Smith defined the four stages of the hunter, pastoralism, agriculture, and commerce, he used them to discuss the nature of increasingly more sophisticated conceptions of property and jurisdiction (Smith 1978: 13–23). Subsequent writers, however, argued that property inadequately characterized the differences between the stages, and that the vital element of a society must be control over the means of reproducing itself. This explains why women – or, to be more precise, women's sexuality – became the focus of attention.

In John Millar's *Origin of the Distinction of Ranks* (1771), kinship structures, and the resulting nature and value of social interactions, are dependent on a particular society's treatment of its women. The first step from a 'rude' state towards civilization is seen to be accompanied by curtailment of women's sexual liberties. He comments that '[i]t will be thought, perhaps, a mortifying picture . . . when we contemplate the barbarous treatment of the female sex in early times, and the rude state of those passions which may be considered as the origin of society' (Millar 1771: 44). In associating the development of societies with women's liberties, he writes:

> in the ages of rudeness and barbarism . . . women enjoy the most unbounded liberty, because it is thought of no consequence what use they shall make of it. [In refined and polished nations,] they are entitled to the same freedom, upon account of those agreeable qualities they possess, and the rank and dignity which they hold as members of society.
>
> (Millar 1771: 101)

Millar goes to great lengths to explain that the different stages were accompanied by varying degrees of sexual passion. The demise of the chivalrous spirit, which had been developed in order to protect the boundaries of an agricultural nation, he claims, was accompanied by less violent attraction between the sexes. The present commercial age can permit free social intercourse between the sexes because the cultivation of honour, reputation and dignity guarantees that the boundaries will not be violated. Or, as such feminist critics as Mary Hays and Mary Wollstonecraft were to argue, the age's restricted views on the appropriate behaviour of men and women had been internalized as standards of propriety and decorum (see Chapter 37 of this volume).

Countless writers of the period expressed anxiety about the damaging consequences of luxury. Millar, for instance, thinks, that it will detract from women's performance of 'the duties of their station' and from their being 'the ornament of private life' (Millar 1771: 90). While he celebrated commerce as a harbinger of politeness and easy interactions between the sexes, he was also concerned about its insidious involvement in social exchanges. Since they were worried about the consequences of such excesses, most members of the Scottish Enlightenment preached against luxury. They maintained that as long as commerce is restricted to an exchange of conveniences suitable for the lifestyle of prosperous but sober Scottish burghers and, for instance, involves the exchange of simple goods, such as British woollen cloth for French wine, it was a healthy boost to the economy. However, when it extended to the importation of luxury goods, such as silk, brocade, perfume, ivory, spices, tea and chocolate, it was feared that the source of prosperity had been poisoned.

It was often assumed that the civilizing influence of commerce on the 'free intercourse between the sexes' permitted a certain amount of sensory gratification. While playful gallantry featured as licit compensation for the sexual act that, in the savage stage, was assumed to take place without delay, polite banter also had the titillating effect of keeping sexual interest alive. So, once commerce tilted over into the irrational consumption of luxury, it was feared that subtle balances within commercial society might collapse into the chaos of savagery. The precise contexts and interests of many writers who discussed such matters must not be ignored, since they range from legal and economic concerns in urban or rural France to religious and political priorities in a rapidly changing Calvinist Scotland.

Hume rejected many orthodoxies of his time, including that which simplistically rejected everything associated with indulgence and luxury. In his essay 'Of Luxury', he argued that '[n]o gratification, however sensual, can of itself be esteemed vicious. A gratification is only vicious, when it engrosses all a man's expence, and leaves no ability for such acts of duty and generosity as are required by his situation and fortune' (Hume 1994: 113). He did not think that mankind in general, or individuals in particular, were likely to change very much. It would therefore be both realistic and prudent to accept that since it is impossible to uproot all vices, the ills attendant upon luxury, such as sexual promiscuity and indolence, were still preferable to the drunken gluttony of an uncivilized society.

THE NATURAL HISTORY OF MAN

The individual volumes of Buffon's monumental work *Histoire naturelle* were published between 1749 and 1788 (the year of his death); and the work was republished in various editions during his lifetime. The section on 'the natural history of man' (Buffon 1749–88: 205–86) was inspired by the materialist principles of immediate predecessors such as La Mettrie. Buffon accordingly describes the newly born human body as 'this delicate and hardly existing machine' (Buffon 1749–88: 209). However, he takes great pains to argue that no inferences can be drawn from physiological analogies between man and animals, insisting that the reasoning capacity of man accounts for a radical difference. Buffon mentions the following uniquely human capacities as evidence that there is an essential qualitative difference between mankind and animals: man is uniquely able to dominate other species as well as other human beings; man is uniquely able to express his reasonings; and man's reflective ability enables him to refine technological designs so that, unlike the beaver, he is not forced to reconstruct the same type of habitation for all eternity. Mankind can change and improve indefinitely. Man is the historical animal, capable of bringing about and interpreting change.

Natural historical investigations of human nature and existence sometimes arrived at lofty interpretations of man's place among the species, although the close relationship between humans and animals moved into the centre of debate. Comparisons between man and the great apes began to pose serious problems, generating fierce controversies and satirical refutations, such as the satirical image illustrating Restif de la Bretonne's 'Lettre d'un singe' (Restif 1781: vol. 3, 19). It attributes the features of Denis Diderot to a monkey, but, far from ridiculing him, uses the comic likeness to make social criticism worthy of the freethinking *philosophe* himself. Restif's scribbling monkey refers to the deathbed speech of the blind philosopher Saunderson, who, in Diderot's 'Letter on the Blind' (1749) proposes the idea of evolution by arguing that existing life-forms result from continual change and development (Crocker and Coltman 1966: 19–24). Restif's work is reminiscent of Diderot's 'Supplement to Bougainville's *Voyage*' (1773–4), where he had roundly condemned the arrogance of European explorers towards the inhabitants of the newly discovered parts of the world, insisting that the natives had the same intelligence and the same rights as Europeans.

Arguments that the great apes possessed at least a certain amount of reason – and cultivation – fundamentally challenged eighteenth-century views about the unique role of man. La Mettrie, Kames and Monboddo, in different ways, reflected upon similarities between man and other animals to argue for a continuum, rather than a strict division, between them. If such studies challenged a sense of human superiority, they also fuelled racist claims when Buffon's arguments about varieties and species were used to subdivide mankind into different species. Buffon, like Montesquieu, argued that there 'was originally only one species, who, after multiplying and spreading over the whole surface of the earth, had undergone various changes in response to differences in climate, food, mode of living, epidemic diseases, and the mixture of dissimilar individuals' (Buffon 1749–88: 286). Nineteenth-century observers then used craniometric measurements to interpret the observed differences according to racist standards, concluding that male, white Westerners were the most perfect human examples.

CIVILIZATION, PROGRESS AND THE ROLE OF HISTORY

While the science of man sought to define the constants of human nature, it also encountered numerous obstacles to the achievement of this task. The main problem was to determine which were natural propensities and which were social and cultural influences. Moreover, the audiences to whom the works were addressed were not typically composed of specialists. It is no coincidence that many of the key thinkers of this peculiarly eighteenth-century science gained reputations as historians before they were recognized for their analytical work on the individual and national character. Even though Hume wrote his *History of England* (1754–62) after his *Treatise of Human Nature* (1739–40), his public fame as a historian long preceded wide

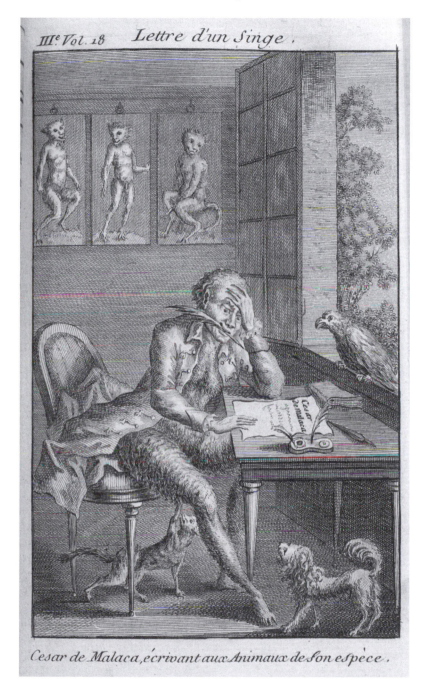

Figure 12.2 *Lettre d'un singe, aux êtres de son espèce* [*Letter of a monkey to others of his own species*], from Restif de la Bretonne (1781) *La Découverte australe par un Homme-volant, ou Le Dédale français, nouvelle très philosophique*, vol. 3, Leipsick, p. 19. By permission of the National Library of Australia.

recognition of his philosophical work. Only in the later twentieth century was the emphasis reversed.

Nor did Montesquieu start his career as a political philosopher. His early life was distinguished by the publication of his fictional *Persian Letters* (1721), in which the manners and conventions of contemporary Europe were described as they might strike visitors from Persia. The imaginary framework for the analysis could not disguise its aim of underlining the contextual nature of existing rules and laws. He published a full systematic study in *The Spirit of Laws* (1748). A sense of progress and development provided the rationale for Montesquieu's comparative evaluation of the relationship between laws and different forms of government. He first argues that different political structures have inspired different experiences of being human. Distinguishing three types of government, he maintains that life in a republic generates (political) virtue since all its members know that they are equally subject to the law and are, therefore, equally interested in observing it. Montesquieu identifies honour as the defining quality of monarchies, on the grounds that monarchies encourage individuals to distinguish themselves in the eyes of their kings. Finally, he claims that tyrannical governments rule by fear.

Montesquieu sought to identify the causes behind the different experiences of subjects of different governments, and a striking aspect of *The Spirit of Laws* lies in his attempt to balance empirical facts about political systems and psychological observations. To account for the variety of social systems observed by travellers in remote parts of the globe, he resurrected an earlier French idea that climate is a differentiating criterion. He argued that tropical climes offered their natural bounty without requiring hard work and thus encouraged indolence, while the harsh conditions of the north required strenuous efforts for mere survival. He located the climate conducive to the ideal blend between industry and the cultivation of arts and crafts in Western Europe.

Montesquieu's correspondent Hume agreed that laws and conventions were conditioned by contextual factors but denied that climate was a significant feature. On the contrary, '[i]f we run over the whole globe, or revolve all the annals of history, we shall discover every where signs of a sympathy or contagion of manners, none of the influence of air or climate'. He underlined his emphasis on the social determinants with the facetious observation: 'I believe no one attributes the difference of manners in Wapping and St James's, to a difference of air or climate' (Hume 1994: 83).

It had long been recognized that cultural context greatly influenced human character, and increasingly the idea was canvassed, in Britain as in France, that the natural core itself was not constant, suggesting that the capacity for change was an essential part of human nature. Adam Ferguson, echoing several of the *philosophes*, formulates this as follows:

> If we admit that man is susceptible of improvement, and has a principle of progression, and a desire for perfection, it appears improper to say, that he has quitted the state of his nature . . . or that he finds a station for which he was not intended, while, like other animals, he only follows the disposition, and employs the powers that nature has given.
>
> (Ferguson 1767: 13)

By insisting that there is nothing that is *not* natural, Ferguson denied that culture and civilization remove man from his natural condition, irrespective of whether this is taken to be a state of innocence or a state of crude moral and psychological imperfection. Civilization, on these premises, cannot be interpreted as an achievement of Western supremacy, but simply amounts to a natural drive shared by all members of the human species.

As Rousseau had famously observed in his 'Discourse on the Origin and Foundation of Inequality among Men' (1755), civilization is the source and motor of inequality, which is to say that the less sophisticated a society is, the more equal are its members. When he claimed that the original difference lay in the irretrievable historical past (Rousseau 1997: 127), he implicitly argued not only for the equality of all cultures and societies, but also for the idea of change. For later thinkers the cross-overs between natural history and human history became increasingly important. Johann Gottfried Herder (1744–1803) was an immensely influential voice who drew attention to the role of national, personal and historical context in forming human nature. His philosophy of history (1784–91) was seminal in efforts to refute the idea that human nature was a stable and graspable entity. For the most part, later studies of the topic took historical development for granted and focused their interests on explaining the dependence of human nature on historically contingent factors.

REFERENCES

Buffon, George Louis Le Clerc, Count of (1749–88) *A Natural History, General and Particular*, trans. William Smellie (1866) London: printed for T. Kelly.

Crocker, Lester G. and Coltman, Derek (1966) *Diderot's Selected Writings*, London: Macmillan.

Descartes, René (1637) 'Discourse on Method', in Richard S. Westfall and Victor E. Thoren (eds) (1968) *Steps in the Scientific Tradition: Readings in the History of Science*, New York: Wiley.

Diderot, Denis (1773–4) 'Supplement to Bougainville's "Voyage"', in *Rameau's Nephew and Other Works*, trans. Jacques Barzun and Ralph H. Bowen (1956) Garden City, NY: Doubleday.

Ferguson, Adam (1767) *An Essay on the History of Civil Society*, facs. edn (1969) Edinburgh: Westmead.

Garrett, Aaron (2003) 'Human Nature', in Knud Haakonssen (ed.) *Cambridge History of Eighteenth-century Philosophy*, Cambridge: Cambridge University Press.

Goodman, Dena (1996) *The Republic of Letters: A Cultural History of the French Enlightenment*, Ithaca: Cornell University Press.

Herder, Johann Gottfried (1784–91) *Ideen zur Philosophie der Geschichte der Menschheit; Outlines of a Philosophy of the History of Man*, trans. T. O. Churchill (1800) New York: Bergman.

Hobbes, Thomas (1651) *Leviathan*, ed. J. C. A. Gaskin (1996) Oxford: Oxford University Press.

Hume, David (1739–40) *A Treatise of Human Nature*, ed. L. A. Selby-Bigge (1951) Oxford: Clarendon Press.

—— (1754–62) *The History of England, from the Invasion of Julius Caesar to the Revolution in 1688*, 6 vols, ed. T. Gaspey (1852–4) New York: Harper & Brothers.

—— (1779) *Dialogues Concerning Natural Religion*, ed. Martin Bell (1990) London: Penguin.

—— (1994) *Political Essays*, ed. Knud Haakonssen, Cambridge: Cambridge University Press.

Jones, Peter, (ed.) (1989) *The 'Science of Man' in the Scottish Enlightenment: Hume, Reid and their Contemporaries*, Edinburgh: Edinbugh University Press.

Kames, Henry Home, Lord (1774) *Sketches of the History of Man*, 2 vols, Edinburgh: W. Creech.

Kusukawa, Saschiko (1996) 'Bacon's Classification of Knowledge', in Markku Peltonen (ed.) *The Cambridge Companion to Bacon*, Cambridge: Cambridge University Press.

Locke, John (1690) *An Essay Concerning Human Understanding*, ed. John W. Yolton (1961) London: Dent.

Mandeville, Bernard (1714; 1723) *The Fable of the Bees*, ed. Phillip Harth (1989) Harmondsworth: Penguin.

Millar, John (1771) *The Origin of the Distinction of Ranks*, ed. John Valdimir Price (1990) Bristol: Thoemmes.

Monboddo, James Burnet, Lord (1773–92) *Of the Origin and Progress of Language*, 6 vols; repr. (1963) Menston: Scolar Press.

Montesquieu, Charles de Secondat, Baron (1721) *Lettres Persanes; Persian Letters*, trans. C. J. Betts (1973) Harmondsworth: Penguin.

—— (1748) *De L'Esprit des lois; The Spirit of Laws*, trans. and ed. Anne M. Cohler, Basia Carolyn Miller and Harold Samuel Stone (1989) Cambridge: Cambridge University Press.

Pope, Alexander (1733–4) 'An Essay on Man', in Pat Rogers (ed.) (1993) *Alexander Pope*, Oxford: Oxford University Press.

Porter, Roy (2001) *The Enlightenment*, Basingstoke: Palgrave.

Restif de la Bretonne (1781) 'Lettre d'un singe, aux êtres de son espèce', *La Découverte australe par un Homme-volant, ou le Dédale français, nouvelle très philosophique*, vol. 3, Leipsick: s.n.

Rousseau, Jean Jacques (1997) *The Discourses and Other Early Political Writings*, ed. and trans. Victor Gourevitch, Cambridge: Cambridge University Press.

Shaftesbury, Anthony Ashley Cooper, Earl (1708) *Characteristics of Men, Manners, Opinions, Times*, ed. John M. Robertson (1964) Indianapolis: Bobbs-Merrill.

Smith, Adam (1978) *Lectures on Jurisprudence*, ed. R. L. Meek, D. D. Raphael and P. G. Stein, Oxford: Clarendon Press.

CHAPTER THIRTEEN

HISTORICAL WRITING IN THE ENLIGHTENMENT WORLD

Johnson Kent Wright

There are good reasons why the Enlightenment's contribution to modern historical writing has long proved difficult to characterize. Early in the nineteenth century, German scholars such as Niebuhr and Leopold von Ranke set rigorous procedures for the training of professional historians and profoundly influenced the teaching of the discipline in the universities. No doubt the Enlightenment helped to pave the way for these developments; indeed, most of the basic component parts that went into the Rankean view of historiography were pioneered in the eighteenth century. Nonetheless, judgements about the nature of Enlightenment historiography tend to be various and equivocal. At one end of a spectrum of opinion there are many who regard the Enlightenment as fundamentally 'unhistorical' in outlook, its historical writing superficial and amateurish at best; or, at worst, all too willing to subordinate historical truth to political and ideological purposes. At the other end, a smaller number of commentators insist that it was not Ranke but the 'philosophical historians' of the Enlightenment – Voltaire, Hume, Gibbon – who were the true founders of modern historical science. Amid wide disagreement, however, there is one feature of eighteenth-century historical writing whose salience no one doubts – its close connection with 'philosophy'. The phrase 'philosophical history' was itself an eighteenth-century coinage typically circulated as a matter of proud self-description: Gibbon, for example, widely seen as the greatest of all Enlightenment historians, aspired to no higher title than that of 'philosophic historian'. Both Voltaire and David Hume were historians and philosophers, a combination that has been very rare since then. Yet one of the major gains of recent scholarship has been to demonstrate the sheer variety of historical writing and thought in the eighteenth century.

CONTINUITY AND INNOVATION: ANTIQUARIANISM, POLITICAL HISTORY AND NATURAL LAW

Two traditional forms of early modern European historiography continued to flourish in the eighteenth century. Both were altered in crucial ways, however, by an engagement with Enlightenment 'philosophy'. One was the primarily religious tradition of 'antiquarian' or 'erudite' history which focused on the recovery and preservation of the entire range of primary records of the past – philological, documentary, archaeological, numismatic, and so forth. The volume of such work increased vastly in the eighteenth century, under the monastic patronage it had traditionally enjoyed, as well as newer sponsorship of the kind offered by royal academies and learned societies. On the eve of the Enlightenment, however, antiquarianism had undergone a kind of trial by fire – the onslaught of a fiercely sceptical 'Pyrrhonism', which sought to cast doubt on the very possibility of accurate knowledge of the past. One masterpiece was the equally controversial and influential *Historical and Critical Dictionary* (1697) of Pierre Bayle. Yet the sceptical attack on antiquarianism was not merely destructive; it left a permanently critical awareness of the 'subjective' character of all of the sources for the writing of history. Thus, although Hume and Gibbon remained amateur historians in crucial respects, they already practised something very close to the *Quellenkritik*, or source-criticism, of Niebhur and Ranke.

No less persistent and vital than antiquarianism was another characteristic form of early modern writing, the narrative historiography of political states. This tradition, revived during the Renaissance, remained neo-classical in form, taking Thucydides, Livy and Tacitus as its models, and focusing its story-telling on the rise and fall of forms of government, still often conceived of in terms of cyclical rotation. Adapted for the histories of modern monarchies, neo-classical history of this kind remained a staple of eighteenth-century historical literature, often taking on considerable political importance in specific contexts – the long debate over the history of the Bourbon monarchy in France is a vivid case in point (Wright 1997: 23–35).

By this time, however, a dramatic transformation was occurring in the writing of narrative history: a shift of attention away from forms of government in the narrow sense towards the larger social 'structures' in which they were embedded. At the same time, conceptions of cyclical historical change were replaced by more linear notions of development. Some have suggested that a debate beginning in the sixteenth century about the relative superiority of the modern over the ancient world, known as the 'Battle between the Ancients and the Moderns', eroded the notion of cyclical change. An aspect of the growing confidence in the present was historical writing which sought to show how, over the course of time, a nation had been favoured by God. The superiority of Louis XIV's France over its predecessors and rivals was recounted in the supreme example of such providential history, Bishop Bossuet's *Histoire universelle*. A less obvious source for such changes, but one which has been noted by recent scholarship, can be found in the modern natural law school of the seventeenth century. A key figure here was the German jurist Samuel Pufendorf (1632–94), who, following Grotius and Hobbes, developed the most influential of all seventeenth-century accounts of the transition from the 'state of nature' to 'civilized society'. Pufendorf's decisive innovation was to present this transition as stadial, the stages involved being defined in terms of specific property regimes. What resulted was an early version of a theory of historical and economic evolution later made famous as the 'four-stages' theory (Hont 1987).

Two unusual works influenced by natural law theory made contributions to stadial theory. The first was of long-term importance; the second of immediate significance. The former was *The New Science*, by the Neapolitan jurist and philosopher Giambattista Vico (1668–1744), who developed a highly idiosyncratic theory of stadial social evolution out of a critical confrontation with contemporary natural lawyers. Almost entirely ignored by his contemporaries, Vico was immediately claimed as one of the precursors of 'historicism' when his work was rediscovered early in the nineteenth century. The other major work was Montesquieu's *On the Spirit of the Laws*, published in 1748. His book proceeded from analysis of the three possible forms of political government – republican, monarchical and despotic – to a theory of a general 'spirit of the laws' for each state, compounded out of multiple causal factors, including climate and geography. The entire construction was tacitly governed by a theory of global historical development. Montesquieu consigned 'despotism' to what he considered to be the historically stationary empires of the East, but claimed that the West had generated a unique transition from the virtuous republics of the classical world to the large, commercially oriented monarchies of modern Europe. Amid hints that the reasons were to be found in the nature of feudal society, Montesquieu highlighted what proved to be the central problem for the 'philosophical history' of the Enlightenment – that of explaining the apparently unique dynamism of European civilization.

THE FOUR-STAGES THEORY

It was the achievement of Montesquieu's successors to address the problem by means of sweeping reconstructions of large-scale historical change in terms of progressive stages of social development. The Scottish philosopher Dugald Stewart named this kind of literature 'conjectural history'. Contemporaries and later historians have sometimes objected to this term on the grounds that it falsely implies the substitution of mere 'speculation' for empirical evidence when, in reality, 'conjectural history' was made possible by unprecedented amounts of data about the historical development of societies. In any case, the most famous stadial theory of this kind has retrospectively come to be known as the four-stages theory. Influenced by Pufendorf's natural jurisprudence, the first major statements of the theory came in the 1750s, appearing more or less simultaneously in scattered writings by Turgot, Quesnay, Helvétius and Goujet in France, and Dalrymple and Kames in Scotland. It then received its classic presentation in the great masterpieces of the Scottish Enlightenment – Adam Ferguson's *An Essay on the History of Civil Society* (1767), John Millar's *The Origin of the Distinction of Ranks* (1771) and Adam Smith's *An Inquiry into the Nature and Causes of the Wealth of Nations* (1776). For all the obvious differences between these works, they shared two basic concerns about the shape of history. The first was that 'In every enquiry concerning the operations of men when united together in society, the first object of attention should be their mode of subsistence. Accordingly as that varies, their laws and policy must be different' (Robertson 1777: vol. 1, 324). Second, it was held that these 'modes of subsistence' normally evolved from a hunter–gatherer society, to pastoral, agricultural and commercial successors, in the standard version of the theory; or, in a more stylized vocabulary, from 'savagery' to 'barbarism' to 'civilization', the last coming in two forms, agricultural and commercial. If the basic direction of historical change was thus 'progressive', none of the historians of the 'four stages' presented this evolution as either universal or inevitable – and their judgements on its social and moral results were famously various. Smith, of the three authors cited above, was the most sanguine about the prospects for modern 'commercial' civilization, but *The Wealth of Nations*, notoriously, expresses every kind of anxiety about the difficulty of creating and maintaining the commercial prosperity on which modern European states depended, as well as about the effects of the 'division of labour' itself on human well-being. Smith's compatriot Ferguson feared the corrosive effects on political community of 'commercial' society. His notion of 'unintended consequences' in history resembled that of Smith: 'Like the winds, that come we know not whence, and blow withersoever they list, the forms of society are derived from an obscure and distant origin . . . and nations stumble upon establishments, which are indeed the result of human action, but not the execution of any human design' (Ferguson 1767: 119).

The second half of the eighteenth century abounded in abstract reconstructions of the whole of human history in stadial terms, some far more 'conjectural' than the relatively restrained writings of Ferguson, Millar and Smith. One of the earliest and most influential reconstructions was Jean Jacques Rousseau's *Discourse on the Origins and Foundations of Inequality among Men* (1755). For him, a stadial theory could be one of regress as well as progress. Rousseau described a three-part evolution away from the 'state of nature': a first 'revolution' established the institutions of the family and private property; a second, driven by technological innovation in metallurgy and agriculture, created a massively unequal division of labour and its spoils; and a third led to the invention of the political state – which then evolved from democracy, to aristocracy and finally to the 'despotism' that characterized all contemporary states. This was the most pessimistic eighteenth-century vision of the past. But France also produced what is by all accounts the most optimistic, Condorcet's *Sketch for a Historical Picture of the Progress of the Human Mind*. This work, left unfinished at its author's death in 1794, posited no fewer than ten stages of historical development: three corresponded roughly to the eras of 'savagery', 'barbarism', and 'civilization' familiar from the four-states theory; the next six traced historical development from ancient Greece to modern Europe. The tenth stage was inaugurated by the French Revolution itself, which promised an end to history in the fulfilment of three conditions: 'the abolition of inequality between nations, the progress of equality within each nation, and the true perfection of mankind' (Condorcet 1976: 158).

PHILOSOPHICAL HISTORIANS: VOLTAIRE, HUME AND GIBBON

Three major proponents of 'philosophical history', Voltaire (1694–1778), Hume (1711–76) and Gibbon (1737–94), were responsible for popularizing narrative history. An important aspect of their philosophical history was their critical approach to their own sources. Another, examined in the best recent study of the histories, is that their works, along with those of other philosophical historians, shared a common structure, and deployed a distinctive narrative form for explaining key episodes or problems (see O'Brien 1997).

Voltaire was a generation older than his fellow philosophical historians, and his first major work in the field, a *History of Charles II* (1731), was an exercise within a conventional neo-classical genre, a 'morality tale' involving the rise and fall of a single exalted figure – in this case, the amazing career and uncanny death of the Swedish King. It was during the long composition of his second work that Voltaire began to move in a philosophical direction. He began writing *The Age of Louis XIV* as early as 1734, but by the time he had published a full version in 1751 and then a revised one two years later, he had fallen under the influence of Montesquieu. The result was a new kind of history, which ranged over the political, social and cultural elements of an age. The 'philosophical' biases of the enterprise were unconcealed: Voltaire portrayed the reign of the Sun King as the last of four great ages in which 'enlightened' monarchs had presided over decisive advances in the arts and sciences: the ages of Pericles, Augustus, the Medici and finally Louis XIV. This focus on cultural achievement was sharpened in Voltaire's masterpiece, the *Essay on the Manners and the Spirit of Nations*, published in 1754. Beginning with brief profiles of Chinese, Indian, Persian and Arabic civilization, the *Essay* recounts the gradual emancipation of a common European intellectual and artistic culture from 'barbarism and religion'. There was no doubt about Voltaire's polemical purposes, and his revisions of the *Essay* over the next fifteen years reveal a gradual subordination of his historical aims to the campaign against religious 'fanaticism' that dominated his later career. If 'the satirist steadily gets the better of the historian' in the *Essay on Manners*, as O'Brien (1997: 52) puts it, no other work did more to restore the fortunes of history as a form of popular literature in the eighteenth century.

Where Voltaire's 'narrative of Enlightenment' expressed a partisan attachment to French absolutism, whose virtues were then projected on to the history of Europe as a whole, the work of the second great philosophical historian was focused entirely on the political history of the major European nation to have overthrown absolutism. David Hume began composing his history after the publication of his more purely philosophical and political works. *The History of England* was written in reverse-chronological order: two volumes on the Stuarts were published in 1754, two on the Tudors in 1759, and two on medieval Britain in 1762. Hume's proudest claim for his *History* was his success in having risen above partisanship, which was a feature of contemporary political culture. He begins in his volumes on the seventeenth century by rejecting a central tradition in English historical writing which in different ways traced English liberties to a distinctive 'ancient constitution'. On the contrary, as he moves backward in time, his approach becomes ever more comparative, so that in his writing on medieval England he portrays the 'feudal system' in England as a variation on a more general Continental pattern. Indeed, his *History of England* was the first great attempt to trace in a dispassionate way the emergence of a distinctive national identity. This was exemplified in his willingness to acknowledge the importance of religion in the emergence of English liberties. Although he was no friend of religious enthusiasm, he conceded that 'So absolute was the authority of the crown, that the precious spark of liberty had been kindled, and was preserved,

EDWARD GIBBON Esq: born the 8th May 1737.

Figure 13.1 *Edward Gibbon*, John Hall after Joshua Reynolds, published 1780. By courtesy of the National Portrait Gallery, London.

by the puritans alone; and it was to this sect, whose principles appear so frivolous and habits so ridiculous, that the English owe the whole freedom of their constitution' (Hume 1754–62: vol. 4, 145–6).

The last and greatest of the philosophical historians, Edward Gibbon, was perfectly positioned to take advantage of the innovations of his predecessors. An Englishman with a thoroughly French intellectual formation, Gibbon also possessed a more extensive command of his source material – everything that ancient sources and modern erudition could offer – than any of his peers. This perhaps owed something to his eventual choice of topics, which, at first glance, looks more conventional than those of Voltaire or Hume, whose common focus was the emergence of modern European civilization out of the decay of feudalism. Interest in decline was not new; Renaissance historians such as Machiavelli and Guicciardini, whose concept of time was cyclical, were preoccupied with the causes of decay and the means of preventing it. Montesquieu had published in 1734 a little book, *Considerations on the Causes of the Greatness and Decline of the Roman Empire*, which, although inferior to Gibbon's later work in its treatment of sources, foreshadows his interest in studying decline. Indeed, despite his famous lines about the happiness and prosperity of the Roman Empire at its peak, Gibbon was far more interested in its decline, which was explained in the first volume (1776) by a combination of social and political decay, and the ideological corruption represented by the advent of Christianity, the latter described in tones so acidic as to earn Gibbon the reputation of being second only to Voltaire as a scourge of religion. However, Gibbon's decision to study the end of the ancient world by no means represented a turning away from the problem of the origins of the modern, and five more volumes of *The Decline and Fall* were to follow, extending its story across another thousand years of history. The second and third volumes (1781) described the shift of Roman power to the East in the last years of the Empire, and the barbarian capture of the West; and the final three (1788) contrasted the slowly declining Empire in the East with the gradual emergence of a new civilization in Europe out of the collapse of the Empire in the West.

It is unsurprising that the later volumes of *The Decline and Fall of the Roman Empire* should have attracted so much attention from recent scholars of the Enlightenment. O'Brien (1997) highlights the originality of Gibbon's cultural explanation for the origins of European civilization, involving a distinction between the mere 'imitations' of Roman cultural forms in the Greek East and the more creative 'emulation' of them in the Latin and Germanic West. For J. G. A. Pocock, Gibbon, viewed in his contemporary context, is the greatest synthesizer among Enlightenment historians (Pocock 1999).

BEYOND EUROPE: OLD WORLDS AND NEW

Voltaire, Hume and Gibbon were not the only great philosophical historians of the epoch. Hume's compatriot William Robertson moved from a national narrative of his *History of Scotland* (1759), to an enormously influential study of the emergence of the early modern state system, in *The History of the Reign of Charles V* (1769), before undertaking what was to be a vast narrative account of the European conquest and settlement of the Americas. Only a portion of the work was published, *History of America* (1777), which employed a version of the four-stages theory to explain the results of the Iberian conquest of South America in the sixteenth century. Robertson's foray into the history of European colonial expansion was itself influenced by a remarkable philosophical history, the *Philosophical and Political History of the Two Indies*, published in1770, and revised 1774 and 1780. Conceived by Abbé Guillaume-Thomas Raynal (1713–96), the work turns out to be a collective enterprise, rather in the manner of the great *Encyclopaedia* of Diderot and D'Alembert. Indeed, Diderot himself seems to have written up to a third of the pages of the *History of the Two Indies*. Beyond that, Raynal wove together an extraordinary array of sources, reliable and otherwise, drawn from around the world. The result was an astonishing pot-pourri which aimed at nothing less than a comprehensive narrative account of the European colonization of Africa, the Americas and Asia, from the fifteenth to the eighteenth century. Though the driving force of 'commerce' was central to their story, Raynal's and Diderot's analytic tools were derived not from four-stages theory, but from Montesquieu and Voltaire – an oscillation between 'feudalism' and 'despotism' forming the basic pattern for historical change around much of the globe. Europe, however, had managed to escape from both, and, although Diderot's contribution to the *History* was profoundly critical of European colonialism and imperialism, he and Raynal believed in the possibility that the whole of mankind could be emancipated from 'feudalism' and 'despotism'.

PHILOSOPHY OF HISTORY IN THE GERMAN ENLIGHTENMENT

German historical thought in the eighteenth century developed out of a close engagement with that of its western European counterparts, and claims about its uniqueness should not be exaggerated. This is exemplified by the work of the most distinguished philosopher of history of the German Enlightenment, Johann Gottfried Herder (1744–1803). His early statement, 'Yet Another Philosophy of History for the Cultivation of Humanity' (1774), was a response to an essay competition sponsored by the Prussian Academy of Sciences. In answering the question, 'Which were the happiest people in history?', Herder attacked the abstract universalism of contemporary philosophers of history: Voltaire's tale of advancing 'Enlightenment'; Montesquieu's taxonomy of forms of government; and Ferguson's stages of social development. Herder answered the question by insisting on the significance of historical difference: 'each nation has its centre of happiness within itself, just as every sphere has its own centre of gravity' (Herder 1774: 186). It is often forgotten that Herder soon retreated from this early statement of 'historicist' theory with its apparent moral and epistemological relativism. Although his last major contribution to historiography, *Ideas for a Philosophy of the History of Mankind* (1784– 91), repeated his earlier claims on behalf of cultural particularity, they were now embedded within a much more abstract theory of history. Individuals and individual nations each expressed a common humanity, founded on the traits and dispositions of a single human nature, whose development towards the fullest expressions of its potentialities unfolds through a succession of progressive stages. The result is thoroughly predictable narrative, ranging from the ancient Hebrews to contemporary Europe, every bit as 'linear' and 'progressive' as Condorcet's *Sketch for a Historical Picture of the Progress of the Human Mind*.

Paradoxically, one of the harsher critical reviews of Herder's *Ideas for a Philosophy of the History of Mankind* came from his own teacher and mentor, Immanuel Kant – the one German thinker whose Enlightenment credentials are rarely doubted. Fresh from the epistemological revolution of his *Critique of Pure Reason*, Kant here taxed Herder with excessive reliance on a facile conception of human nature, grounded in a now discredited sensationalist psychology. Herder's presumption of a benign 'natural' harmony between the individual and society was plainly false: 'all that nature reveals to us is that it abandons individuals to total destruction and preserves only the species' (Kant 1991: 209). The notion of a fundamental natural antagonism had been the starting point of Kant's own major contribution to the philosophy of history 'Idea for a Universal History with Cosmopolitan Purpose', published a year earlier in 1784. Using a concept inherited from Pufendorf's natural jurisprudence, Kant here spoke of the 'unsocial sociability' of mankind, emphasizing the tension between competition and co-operation that was discernible in every stage of historical progress, 'from barbarism to culture'. Nonetheless, Kant believed that history was destined to progress, via creative antagonism, towards increasing harmony within, and between, nations, and an end state in which happiness and moral perfection were one.

CONCLUSION

No brief survey can do justice to the sheer variety of historical thought and writing produced in the eighteenth century. On the one hand, by the end of the seventeenth century, a number of long-standing assumptions about the form and content of historical writing had come under intense critical scrutiny; at the same time, the temporal and spatial horizons of the European imagination had been permanently transformed by three centuries of sea-borne exploration. On the other hand the discipline of history had not yet narrowed, as it would do under the influence of Ranke, when it came to focus on national political history. Yet variety should not be exaggerated. For all the important differences between Ferguson and Smith, Rousseau and Condorcet, Herder and Kant, there is at least a family resemblance among the great 'conjectural historians' of the Enlightenment. They all focused on the 'stages' that seemed to underlie the historical development of Europe. Moreover, the topics chosen by their 'philosophical' counterparts seem to have converged on significant moments of European development. In the work of both the 'conjectural' and the 'philosophical' historians, it is easy enough to glimpse instances of history being pressed into the 'service' of one kind of 'philosophical' purpose or another: Voltaire's or Gibbon's anticlericalism, or Diderot's anticolonialism; Smith's defence of economic modernity, or Ferguson's critique of it; Herder's advocacy of cultural particularism, or Kant's promotion of rationalism. At the same time, in the light of the continuing appeal, both lay and scholarly, of the conjectural and the philosophical historians of the eighteenth century, it is worth keeping in mind that the Enlightenment was also a period in which philosophy did incomparable service to the study of history in its own right.

REFERENCES

Condorcet, Marquis de (1976) *Selected Writings*, ed. Keith Michael Baker, Indianapolis: Bobbs-Merrill.

Ferguson, Adam (1767) *An Essay on the History of Civil Society*, ed. Fania Oz-Salzburger (1995) Cambridge: Cambridge University Press.

Gibbon, Edward (1776–1788) *The History of the Decline and Fall of the Roman Empire*, 6 vols, ed. David Womersley (1994) London and New York: Penguin.

Herder, Johann Gottfried (1774) 'Yet Another Philosophy of History for the Enlightenment of Mankind', in F. M. Barnard (ed.) (1969) *J. G. Herder on Social and Political Culture*, Cambridge: Cambridge University Press.

Hont, Istvan (1987) 'The Language of Sociability and Commerce: Samuel Pufendorf and the Theoretical Foundations of the "Four-Stages" Theory', in Anthony Pagden (ed.) *The Languages of Political Theory in Early-Modern Europe*, Cambridge: Cambridge University Press.

Hume, David (1754–62) *The History of England*, 6 vols, ed. William B. Todd (1983) Indianapolis: Liberty Press.

Kant, Immanuel (1991) *Political Writings*, trans. H. B. Nisbet, Cambridge: Cambridge University Press.

Montesquieu, Charles de Secondat, Baron (1748) *The Spirit of the Laws*, ed. Anne M. Cohler, Basia Carolyn Miller and Harold Samuel Stone (1989) Cambridge: Cambridge University Press.

O'Brien, Karen (1997) *Narratives of Enlightenment: Cosmopolitan History from Voltaire to Gibbon*, Cambridge: Cambridge University Press.

Pocock, J. G. A. (1999) *Barbarism and Religion*, vol. I: *The Enlightenments of Edward Gibbon*; vol. II: *Narratives of Civil Government*, Cambridge: Cambridge University Press.

Robertson, William (1777) *History of America*, 3 vols, London.

Wright, Johnson Kent (1997) *A Classical Republican in the Eighteenth Century: The Political Thought of Mably*, Stanford: Stanford University Press.

CHAPTER FOURTEEN

EDUCATION AND THE REPRODUCTION OF THE ENLIGHTENMENT

Geraint Parry

In his essay *What is Enlightenment?* Kant described his era not as an 'enlightened age' but as an 'age of enlightenment'. His stress was on a continuing process, not on an accomplishment. Human beings had been seeking to free themselves from a condition of mental subjugation and attain a condition of maturity and self-direction. This was, he argued in his lectures on education, not something that came about readily or instinctively (Kant 1803: 5–6). Humans differed from other animals in that they had to undergo a long process of learning before they reached their full development. Hence the importance of education. Enlightenment was therefore itself an educative experience.

The education of its young is an essential aspect of the reproduction of a society and its culture – the incorporation of the new generation into the mores of the old (Bourdieu and Passeron 1990). Alternatively, education is sometimes regarded as remedial: the new generation is called upon to rectify the errors of existing society, offering it a new start. What marks out the Enlightenment period, and permits its description as the Age of Pedagogy, is the widespread confidence that an intellectual foundation had been discovered that enabled a more effective transmission of knowledge to the next generation than had been attainable hitherto. It was this confidence that allowed Helvétius to proclaim that 'education can do all' (Helvétius 1772: II, 332).

THE MIND OF EDUCATION: CREATING
A VIRTUOUS CIRCLE

The source of this confidence lay in the work of John Locke. His *Some Thoughts Concerning Education* (1693) was republished, translated, anthologized, excerpted and cited throughout the eighteenth century (for Locke's educational thought, see Tarcov 1984; Schouls 1992). The importance of *Some Thoughts* lay in the sense that the curriculum and methods were grounded on an appreciation of the human mind and its potentialities for learning. This appreciation was also owed to Locke's path-breaking *Essay Concerning Human Understanding* (1690), in which the account of the human mind was repeatedly illustrated by reference to the capacity of the child to acquire knowledge. Possibly the most widely cited passage from *Some Thoughts* appeared in the opening paragraph: 'I think I may say, that of all the Men we meet with, Nine Parts of Ten are what they are, Good or Evil, useful or not, by their Education. 'Tis that which makes the great difference in Mankind' (Locke 1693: §1).

Locke's basis for this belief lay in his description of the mind in the *Essay* as a *tabula rasa*, a blank sheet, on which experiences of the outside world made impressions that constituted the first ideas from which the mind could actively build more complex ideas. Regular experiences were retained in the mind and habitual ideas were associated together to generate knowledge. This process was gradual and required discipline and observation on the part of the individual, qualities that had themselves to be acquired. The development of such capacities was, for Locke, a moral obligation. God had placed human beings in the world with powers of mind and body that they were under a duty to realize as fully as possible. Unlike brute beasts, humans are not simply driven by desires. They have liberty, which consists in a power to suspend the execution of their desires and thereby allow themselves to stand and consider their course of action (Locke 1690a: II, 21, §8, §52, §67). In particular they are able to weigh the good or evil of their conduct by a norm, which may be civil or natural law. This is what characterizes being a 'person' or moral agent.

The object of education is to inculcate in children the practice of deliberation so that they will grow up to employ their liberty to consider rationally whether to assent to propositions about the physical, intellectual, moral or political worlds. Locke, in making education central to his developed understanding of the person, placed it also at the centre of his metaphysical, moral and political thinking and, through his influence, at the centre of Enlightenment.

The ultimate source of the ideas that are to be shaped and developed by the educated mind are the sensory impression we have of our world. In an important sense, for Locke and most subsequent Enlightenment educationists the whole environment of a man or woman throughout his or her life was an educative force. This led Joseph Priestley to distinguish between 'natural' education gained from ordinary life and 'artificial' education, which consisted in the organized communication of knowledge (Priestley 1780: 2–7). Ideally the natural and artificial should work hand in hand, but often it would be found that the teacher had to counter the effects of false perceptions gained by an unguided assimilation of the child's world. Hence education in the narrower, artificial sense was best begun early so that good habits appear second nature to the child.

Locke's recommendations on physical upbringing were regularly cited in educational literature. Robust health is to be promoted by a plain diet containing the minimum of meat, sugar and salt but allowing fruit in moderation, brown bread and drink only with meals. Children of both sexes are to be encouraged to play in the open air, wear loose clothing and to bathe in cold water. The object is to harden the child, especially the boy, to grow up to be a 'man of business' rather than a 'beau' (Locke 1693: §9).

However, ultimately more significant for subsequent educational thought and practice was his conception of the development of moral, social and political conduct. Locke sought to balance two objectives that have been in tension in all later education. Children should grow up to live an orderly civil life, earning the good opinion of their elders and superiors. Yet, in what was to be the spirit of Enlightenment attitudes, the future adult must also acquire a critical and independent stance towards established beliefs. In intellectual and moral matters they must learn how to give properly reasoned assent to propositions, and in politics they must be in a position to judge when it is right to consent to government.

The answer lay in an education that stimulated curiosity. Learning should begin with the kinds of play which would encourage children to want to learn more. Although early education lay under the discipline of the parents, this should not be severe – beating is frequently counter-productive. As the child matures, discipline should be relaxed and parents and teachers are urged to encourage questions and to respond with reasoned arguments in which the growing child could participate. The stages of this process should correspond to the evolution of the child's mind. Eventually teachers can release the child into the world as an adult moral agent able to think and act responsibly.

The specific world Locke had in mind in *Some Thoughts* was that of the independent English country gentleman – a property-owner whose status carried obligations in local government and magistracy or even Parliament. Locke aligned himself with the moderns in proposing a curriculum designed to equip the future gentleman with the capacities for a useful life. Early in life, through play and experience, children would learn the principles of justice and the meaning of property rights. Latin was useful in law. Political geography, mathematics, geometry, keeping accounts, history (the 'Mistress of Prudence and Civil Knowledge'), the English constitution, the common law, natural law and moral philosophy completed the programme. The end product would be the ideal practitioner of the 'civil government', described in the second of the *Two Treatises of Government* (1690) – one who might be trusted to defend the watchwords of English politics and of many of its Continental admirers: property, liberty and the rule of law.

The mechanism that Locke employed to sustain his education was esteem or reputation. While ultimately virtue lay in following the law of God and nature, the more immediate force shaping conduct was the 'law of opinion and reputation' (Locke 1693: §61; 1690a: II, 28, §§10–12). Humans gain pleasure by winning the good opinion of others, whether in their family, their club or the wider society. A virtuous circle can thus be generated whereby one gains happiness through manners that give others pleasure and earn their praise. At the same time an education in the new spirit was also supposed to train the new generation to be critical of accepted opinion, to, in Kant's later words, 'dare to know'. Locke here implicitly presents a key dilemma of liberal education – how to shape minds without crushing the emergence of the critical spirit.

In British educational thought the key to the science of shaping minds lay in the exploitation of the mechanism of the association of ideas, a notion discussed by Locke but given new impetus by George Turnbull's *Observations upon Liberal Education* (1742), David Fordyce's *Dialogues Concerning Education* (1745) and, in particular, David Hartley's *Observations on Man* of 1749. Hartley offered an explanation of the mental process whereby repeated sensations trigger ideas which can be regularly associated with further ideas. Humans learn to associate certain ideas with pleasure and seek to pursue those sensations that generate it (for Hartley, see Allen 1999;

Passmore 1970). The implications for education, Hartley points out, would be both instructive and alarming. By analysing the process of association, one could recognize and actively promote those steps that led to the formation of associations conducive to religion and morality and root out those that had the reverse effect. Since all humans are identical at birth it would, in principle, be possible to surround them with the same sensations, creating the same associations, and eradicating all differences between them, thus even rendering them equal (Hartley 1749: 52).

Priestley, as scientist as well as educator, seized on Hartley's account of the construction of ideas as offering a new foundation for understanding 'everything that is called political knowledge' (Priestley 1780: 27). The science of education consisted in repeatedly imposing on the minds of children associations between pleasure and civility until decent and respectful behaviour became 'a mechanical habit'. If this might seem to be indoctrinating children with prejudices, Priestley's reply is that all education is precisely a matter of prejudicing children 'in favour of our opinions and practices' (Priestley 1780: 96–7). Catherine Macaulay [Graham] justified adding to the literature on education by the new discoveries concerning the nature of the mind which now permitted tutors to develop in their charges an invariable link between their will and the 'laws of virtue and prudence' (Macaulay [Graham] 1790: i–ii).

In France a parallel development occurred. Again the impetus was the formulation of a radical, sensationalist philosophy, particularly by Condillac. The educational potential of sensationalism was developed by Helvétius in *De L'Esprit* (1758) and *De L'Homme* (1772). Sensations arising from the environment are the only sources of knowledge. There is no innate knowledge. People find that certain sensations are pleasurable and others painful. Education exploits this by shaping the social environment so that, ideally, pupils will discover that their own happiness and self-love, as well as the public interest, are advanced by behaviour that conduces to the pleasure of others and earns their approval. Differences between human beings are the result of education in the widest sense. All are born equal. Genius is the product of education and hard work by teachers and students. For Helvétius, the 'science of education is nothing but the science of exciting emulation' (Helvétius 1772: I, 21–2). The aim is to reproduce an enlightened society as the new generation discovers that interest, wealth and power are the rewards for behaviour that gains the esteem of that society.

THE CHALLENGE OF ROUSSEAU

This confidence in the completion of a virtuous circle was, however, called into question by Jean Jacques Rousseau, that man of the Enlightenment who was at the same time its most powerful critic. In doing so Rousseau came to rival Locke as the major educational theorist of the period (on Rousseau and education, see Jimack 1983; Bantock 1980, 1984; Trachtenberg 1993; Steiner 1994; Parry 2001).

Emile is the story of the education of an average boy, Emile, who represents the children of contemporary society. His tutor is in effect the hero of the book, named Jean Jacques. Emile is to be taught to be a man who can think his own thoughts.

Hence, while he is to be brought up to be a member of society, he cannot be educated merely to fit in with existing society. That would be to repeat the errors of preceding educationists, who, Rousseau alleged, wished the child to earn the esteem of a world pervaded by bad faith. Such children gained advancement by thinking the thoughts of others, becoming dependent upon them and, in effect, selling themselves. It followed that to educate to true autonomy it was necessary to isolate the pupil from society so that he, and Rousseau meant *he*, can be taught by 'nature'. In contrast to the positive, interventionist approach of such Enlightenment educationists as Helvétius, Rousseau presented what he misleadingly termed his 'negative education' (Rousseau 1762a: 93). This consisted in allowing the child to discover the world for himself and at his own pace. Where positive education attempted to hasten the development of rationality and a grasp of moral principles, Rousseau insisted that the child's learning process should be slowed so that his understanding evolved with his natural capacities for reason and emotional response. All that premature education achieved was that the child learned to parrot the opinions of his elders. In particular, and in contrast to Locke and Helvétius, the child's entry into society should be delayed for as long as possible so as to avoid the contamination of artificiality present in even so-called enlightened societies. Before this crucial step he needs to acquire sufficient mental and bodily strength and self-confidence to be able to resist the temptations of the social world and retain such autonomy as is possible when living with others. Early upbringing should expose the boy to the rigours of outdoor life. His understanding of the world should be based on perceiving, handling and working manually with natural objects before any book learning (Rousseau 1762a: 184–5).

The final step in Emile's education occurs when he is about to enter society. Although he is armoured with a sense of self-worth, he has not been exposed to the choices that society offers and that have to be made if one is to be a moral agent. Here the tutor emerges from the shadows and Emile 'chooses' to put himself under his guidance in order to acquire the discipline necessary to the exercise of genuine autonomy (Rousseau 1762a: 325). He learns that civilized men wear masks, seek reputation rather than truth, conciliate rather than uphold principle. They have been educated merely to replicate the compromised values of polite society. The tutorship of Jean Jacques has aimed at the transformation of that society so that it might genuinely realize the enlightened ideals by which it falsely claims to live.

Rousseau startled eighteenth-century educators. Conservatives, such as Vicesimus Knox in Britain or Ernst Brandes in Germany, feared that Rousseau's subversion of established educational authority presaged the subversion of political and social authority (Knox 1781; Brandes 1809). At the other extreme, radicals such as Thomas Day took up Rousseau's educational programme with enthusiasm. More common was the attempt to absorb the more congenial aspects of Rousseau into an eclectic educational system. Thus the liberal German educationist Johann Bernhard Basedow, founder of an influential progressive school at Dessau and author of systematic treatises on teaching and learning, drew on both Locke and Rousseau. Like both, he emphasised the adaptation of teaching to the capacity of the child and the importance of learning by play. But Basedow's games were openly directive and their moral lessons about civil behaviour more explicit. He followed Rousseau in the importance of learning from natural objects but was also prepared to settle for illustrated

Figure 14.1 *Johann Bernhard Basedow*, Daniel Chodowiecki. By permission of the Staatliche Graphische Sammlung, Munich.

Figure 14.2 *Schoolroom at Dessau*, Plate XLVIII of Johann Bernhard Basedow (1770–2) *Elementarwerk* reproduced in James Bowen, *A History of Modern Education*, vol. 3, Methuen 1981. By permission of the National Library of Australia.

representations of them. Yet, in his commitment to introducing the child to social skills as early as possible, Basedow is closer to the Lockean tradition. In this he represents Enlightenment thinking at its most pragmatic, seeking to turn projects of education devised by theorists who often had the most minimal familiarity with children into feasible scholastic arrangements.

The most complete syntheses of Enlightenment positive education and Rousseau's negative or inactive method were offered by Kant and Pestalozzi. *Emile* was one of the works Kant most admired, and his own university lectures on education are concerned with a problem central to Rousseau, and to later liberal education, of whether, in the language of *What is Enlightenment?*, it is possible to guide a person to dare to use understanding without guidance (Kant 1784: 58). Liberation occurs, as in Rousseau, when agents have the capacity to govern themselves by laws they have discovered for themselves. By comparison to Rousseau, however, Kant requires more positive educational intervention and discipline. There must be time for play but it is not to be confused with work. At school the child begins by learning to curb his inattention and sit still because discipline is the essential precondition for the ultimate ability to exercise self-rule. No schooling can make a person moral but it can train pupils, first to follow rules of behaviour and, second, to understand

PESTALOZZI,

Né, le 12 Janvier, 1746.

Figure 14.3 *Heinrich Pestalozzi*, 1746–1836. By permission of the Staatliche Graphische Sammlung, Munich.

such conduct as a duty. Education is therefore precisely the process of enlightenment, of leading the pupil from immaturity. For this reason Kant can assert: 'Education must be compulsory, but it need not be slavish' (Kant 1803: §67).

Perhaps the most direct influence of the various streams of Enlightenment pedagogy on later centuries came through the work of Heinrich Pestalozzi (see Silber 1976). The aim of moral education is the cultivation of autonomous agency. Intellectual education involves a clear understanding of objects and their relationships to one another. The method, as with Locke and Rousseau, is child-centred in being attuned to the child's capacities and experiences. In their homes, on walks and in school, children should start by handling objects, learning about form and number and culminating in a grasp of the interconnectedness of the world. Intertwined with this intellectual development is a growth in moral education as children learn sympathy in the practical exchanges of the home which then, under guidance, extends to the wider world and ultimately leads to a mature and conscious submission to rules of conduct. In this the teacher, in Lockean and still more Rousseauian vein, is the facilitator of self-emancipation. Pestalozzi's school at Yverdon became a place of pilgrimage for progressive educators who took from him what they wanted. Robert Owen, Froebel and Herbart were among the sympathizers. Fichte campaigned for a system of state education for Germany based on Pestalozzian methods which was adopted in Prussian elementary schools until its radical Enlightenment principle of encouraging the new generation to think for itself was found in the 1820s to be incompatible with preservation of the established political order (see Levinger 2000: 191–226).

EDUCATION AND POLITICS

The political potential of the new education had been very readily apparent to theorists in the various polities of Enlightenment Europe. It would, Helvétius suggested, permit the legislator to direct the 'motions of the human puppet' (Helvétius 1772: I, 4). Hitherto, man had not been properly known to governments, and without that knowledge it was unsurprising that they moved in ways contrary to those the legislator wished. In 1763 la Chalotais developed one of the first programmes for national education. The 'children of the state' should be taught by citizens of the state, in secular schools, using state-approved textbooks, rather than be left to the tuition of the established or supranational Churches (Chalotais 1763: 1932). Le Mercier de la Rivière's *De L'Instruction Publique* (1775) argued that governments need to shape opinion by instruction rather than coercion. Children should learn through a civil catechism the qualities that are esteemed honourable by public opinion and the state. Public instruction can render the gallows almost superfluous as a means of maintaining civil order (Le Mercier de la Rivière 1775: 42).

In the German-speaking states the unique blend of traditional patriarchalism, Pietist theology and rationalism that went to make the national version of enlightened absolutism similarly treated education as part of the policing role of the state. Christian Wolff's rationalist political philosophy and the administrative theories of cameralists, such as Justi and Sonnenfels, conceived that the purpose of education was to produce useful subjects. The top-down policies of economic and social recovery demanded educational investment in the skills required for the state to function at its optimum level. If, in addition, subjects could be taught to identify their own good with that of the state, this would provide the regimes with a modern, rationalist form of legitimation (Wolff 1756: 214–66; Justi 1755: I, 348–61; Sonnenfels 1768: I, 117).

In Britain, despite an equal awareness of the political dimension of education, there was distinct hesitation about granting influence over instruction to state agencies. Priestley, for all his enthusiasm for a positive education to 'prejudice' pupils in favour of sound opinions, did not wish to see this power in the hands of a state lest, directly or through the influence of the Church, it threaten religious toleration and civil liberty. Both he and his fellow-radical Catherine Macaulay opposed any yearning for a classical republican public education in civic virtue. Macaulay described the Platonic ideal as attractive to rulers who wished to 'shape man for the use of government and not government for the use of man' (Macaulay [Graham] 1790: 15). For Priestley, such public education ran contrary to the plurality and toleration that should be implicit in Britain's mixed constitution. As one of the protagonists in Fordyce's *Dialogues* had put it, state responsibility for education could imply that 'the Merit of the Teachers be weighed not in the Balance of Justice but in the Scales of an Election' (Fordyce 1745: II, 3).

These reservations concerning state supervision were to have a long influence on British attitudes to educational provision. They were, however, far from implying that education was regarded as non-political. Priestley's own curriculum was designed to prepare pupils for an 'active life', by which he meant positions in which they might 'affect the liberty and property' of their compatriots (Priestley 1780: 194). His students in the dissenting academies were barred by their religion from studying at Oxford, and could not graduate if they studied at Cambridge: consequently they were at a disadvantage in gaining many traditional elite positions. In the view of many teachers in these academies they required a modern education in which the old humanities gave way to courses in the principles of commerce, economic policy, law, modern history and languages and the natural sciences (see McLachlan 1931; Ashley Smith 1954; Simon 1960; Claeys 1999). Not only the students but the country needed a new approach. Britain's economic position, Priestley claimed, was under threat from 'our more intelligent and vigilant neighbours', which could only be remedied by 'more lights' (Priestley 1780: 189). Such illumination not only pre-supposed a new curriculum but also a new mode of learning less reliant on repetition and note-taking and more on enquiry, opening up lessons to questions and discussion and encouraging the writing of student dissertations (Priestley 1780: 211–23). Priestley is extending the Lockean educational project of inculcating habits of critical thinking so that the students will graduate 'able to judge for themselves, and to find what is right, by their own Reason' (Locke 1693: §61). This measured judgement must be applied to politics. Only tyrants, Priestley asserts, fear political knowledge. In free societies private men have much at stake in the decisions of government and cannot be unconcerned spectators (Priestley 1780: 228). Hence Priestley's description of education as a 'branch of civil liberty' (Priestley 1768: 52).

It was, again, Rousseau who questioned whether even the more liberal states measured up to the claims for their civility advanced by Enlightenment theorists. Clearly the 'enlightened absolutisms' fell well short of treating their inhabitants as citizens to be ruled rather than subjects to be governed. But nor did the vaunted liberal model of Britain satisfy the demands of true citizenship. British elections should be viewed as merely occasions when the people elected new masters and renewed their slavery (Rousseau 1762b: 113–16). Genuine citizenship corresponded to genuine moral agency in that citizens were those who lived under a law that they had participated in making in some form of popular rule. In the modern world there were no citizens and, therefore, scarcely any opportunity to learn citizenship.

It followed that Rousseau's account of citizen education had to be very different to the education of the individual in *Emile*. There the pupil was taught to find a space to live as virtuous a life as was feasible within the confines of a corrupt society. Emile aspires to be a whole man, whereas citizens should perceive themselves as merely a fraction of the whole (Rousseau 1762a: 39–40). Citizens, in contrast to Emile, have to be denatured and reconstructed. This task is described in Rousseau's *Discourse on Political Economy*, *Considerations on the Government of Poland* (1782) and *Letter to M. D'Alembert* (1758). It is one of the most important responsibilities of a popular and legitimate government to educate children from early years in the manners, traditions and history of their country. Such education should continue into adult life to reinforce national identity through participation in dancing in festivals or training with the militia to remind citizens that civic virtue involves the dependence of each upon the whole.

The flaw in this evocation of an idealized Spartan citizenship, as Rousseau recognized, was that the world of city-states and small communities that it presupposed no longer existed. The period following the Peace of Westphalia was one of the emerging large-scale sovereign state. Moreover, Enlightenment thinkers had given further impetus to the consciousness of individuality and autonomy that was in fundamental tension with 'ancient liberty'. The contradiction is exemplified in the contrast between the education of Emile and of the citizen, left unreconciled by Rousseau and contained in the legacy Rousseau left to education for citizenship. His goal of a citizenry educated to a total commitment to the state could not but have an appeal to absolutists. At the same time it provided support for those who sought a radical reconstruction of both man and society. If there were to be a reign of virtue, reason and Enlightenment, it might be necessary to start again by taking the blank mind of the child and inscribing upon it the experiences that would lead the new generation to commit itself to the mores of the new order. This would be impossible if education were left in the hands of the unreformed older generation, whether teachers or even parents. The most thoroughgoing exposition was in the 1793 *Plan D'Education Nationale* of Michel Lepeletier, presented to the National Convention by Robespierre. The nation should receive all children 'from the hands of nature' at the age of five, place them in austere state boarding schools and return them to society at eleven (for girls) and twelve (for boys). The result would be a 'new race, strong, hard-working, law-abiding and disciplined, and an impenetrable barrier will have separated it from any impure contact with the prejudices of our out-dated species' (Lepeletier 1793: 371). Such revolutionary plans of civic indoctrination attempt a fusion of the positive education of Helvétius with Rousseau's vision of a reconstructed virtuous citizen (on French revolutionary education, see Palmer 1985; for useful collections of texts, see La Fontainerie 1932; Baczko 2000). Critics of Enlightenment have seen this as the inevitable consequence of what Burke described as its detestable 'project' of 'civic education' (Burke 1790: 130–1). Yet this danger had been recognized by such as writers as Helvétius, Priestley and Macaulay, who wished to harness the new techniques of education while at the same time preventing it falling into the hands of governments who would repress the plurality they saw as essential to the Enlightenment.

EQUALITY AND DIFFERENCE: WOMEN AND EDUCATION

The degree of the plurality of the Enlightenment has, in recent decades, become a contentious issue. The new science of education had been predicated on the assumption of the natural mental equality of human beings and on their educability. However, the implications of these assumptions for the education of women tested the limits of Enlightenment thinking.

Women of the upper and middle classes seldom lacked education, even if what they received is often dismissed as instruction in the 'accomplishments'. At their best, however, such accomplishments could be considerable in literature, history, languages and music. Nevertheless, the opportunities for women even of these ranks to exercise their accomplishments in any public sphere were limited. These restrictions were not new. The new issue raised by Enlightenment philosophy was that Lockean epistemology removed any apparent justification for treating the capacities of women any differently from those of men. Catherine Macaulay, basing her case on the discoveries made in the science of the mind by Locke and Hartley, rejected ideas of sexual difference as irrelevant to intellectual and moral education. The fact that claims for sexual difference worked so powerfully to the advantage of men could not 'willingly be imputed to accident'. Accordingly, 'the Republican Virago' made 'no variation in the fundamental principle of the education of the two sexes' (Macaulay [Graham] 1790: 204, 216). For Macaulay and Mary Wollstonecraft, virtue no more than mind had a sex. It followed that there was no distinct moral education for women. Wollstonecraft's *Vindication of the Rights of Woman* (1792) is less a direct plea for political rights (almost futile since, as she points out, the majority of men lacked them) than for the prior condition of women's rights, namely an education to make women 'rational creatures, and free citizens' and become 'more like moral agents' (Wollstonecraft 1792: 275). The first step would be elementary day schools where boys and girls from all social classes would learn the same subjects together. The more able would continue their education at secondary level, which would constitute a 'school of morality' in which friendship, love and a sense of public duty would be shared by both sexes (Wollstonecraft 1792: 263–5).

In France Riballier proclaimed that he wished to break the chains of women and demanded to know why, when their minds were no different from men's, they were denied the opportunity to devote themselves to science and philosophy (Riballier

1779: 1–7). Among the revolutionaries, Condorcet coupled advocacy of citizenship rights for women with their right to equal education, but his *Report to the National Assembly on Public Instruction* makes only passing reference to female education (Condorcet 1792). Far more explicit was Courdin's *Observations philosophiques sur la réforme de l'éducation publique*, also of 1792, in which women are described as the victims of man-made laws who should have the same right as men to live under laws to which they have consented. France should rise above the century and grant women the right to equal education so that they may assume a civil existence (Courdin 1792: 93–106).

This inference of sexual equality was far from universally drawn, even from mainstream theories of the mind. Humans might be born mentally equal but this was consistent with environmental circumstances affecting in relevant ways a person's intellectual and moral development. In the case of women a combination of social and biological circumstances was cited that legitimated differences of treatment. Talleyrand, in his *Report on Public Instruction* of 1791, admits that at first sight it seems anomalous that half the human race is excluded from all participation in government by the other half and that they are, in effect, treated as foreigners by the law under which they were born and have grown up. Nevertheless, the exclusion of women is for the good of the whole, permitting them to pursue their natural destinies as mothers, away from the distracting tumult of public affairs that would endanger their delicate constitutions. The conservation of society has indicated this natural division of powers. Consequently the education of women should be directed to these responsibilities, not at denaturing their faculties. It is best conducted in the asylum of the paternal home to accustom women to a retired and calm life (Talleyrand 1791: 168–71). This form of argument could appeal even to liberals and radicals, since it did not deny women their intellectual equality but justified differential education on natural and functional grounds.

Nor were women united in sisterhood on the matter. Hannah More's *Strictures on the Modern System of Female Education* (1799) argued, as did liberal feminists, that existing education trivialized women, but drew the very different conclusion that their instruction should be directed to the exercise of a profession, which in the case of 'ladies . . . is that of daughters, wives, mothers and mistresses of families' and should be thoroughly Christian in tone (More 1799: I, 98–9).

Rousseau provided the most influential socio-biological argument for sexual difference in education in Book V of *Emile*, where he recounted the education of Sophie to be Emile's partner. The basis of partnership resides in the complementary character of the sexes. The role of women is to please, support and influence men and the appropriate education according to nature will be the mirror opposite of that for men (Rousseau 1762a: 365). Emile learns to think for himself and escape dependence on others. Sophie has to learn to be dependent on, yet faithfully support, a husband and to direct her natural physical and emotional attributes to that end. These qualities include sensitivity to the feelings of other individuals and a talent for pleasing men. They do not include a talent for the general theorizing required in intellectual and political life (Rousseau 1762a: 377). She is educated at home under the constant supervision of her parents as a preparation for a simple, chaste life in which she, in sharp contrast to Emile, will be constantly subject to the opinions and judgements of men. Her upbringing will be far from that of the Enlightenment bluestockings of the salons which corrupts true femininity – as happens to Sophie herself in the unfinished sequel to *Emile*, when, in an unguarded moment, she is left alone in Parisian society.

Rousseau's theory of sexual difference provided an escape from the apparent consequences of Lockean epistemology for female education. Not only did it appear to chime in with conservative standpoints but an otherwise liberal such as Basedow could cite Rousseau at length in support of distinguishing between the education of the two sexes. The radical Thomas Day embarked upon the tragi-comic enterprise of adopting two orphan girls of twelve and eleven to bring them up in simplicity and domesticity on the model of Sophie. It ended in abject failure. For Catherine Macaulay, however, Rousseau's notion of the complementarity of the sexes adding up to a single complete human was an absurdity exceeding every metaphysical riddle of the scholastics (Macaulay [Graham] 1790: 205). Mary Wollstonecraft argued that Rousseau's view of women was inconsistent with the body of his thought in treating the weaknesses of women as natural instead of, as he recognizes in the case of contemporary men, the product of education and socialization. His portrayal of a specific female excellence is a code for degrading women and reinforces the inequalities and arbitrariness he condemns elsewhere (Wollstonecraft 1792: 156–73).

LEGACIES OF ENLIGHTENMENT EDUCATION

The education of women, and also of the poor (see, for example, Jones 1938; Payne 1976; Chisick 1981; Melton 1988), revealed not merely limitations of practice but represented boundaries to the intellectual horizons of the Enlightenment. That said, it was also a fundamental feature of the Enlightenment that it raised questions about itself and that it bequeathed these questions to succeeding generations. Traditional systems of authority had, at the very least, to seek new forms of rational legitimation, whether it was hereditary government or the subjection of women. Yet this very enterprise, by introducing novelty, opened up issues for debate. In this respect education is a very typical Enlightenment 'project'. For some, education was an element in social discipline and incorporation. For others, it was a means of liberating, but reformative rather than transformative. Radicals perceived it as a tool of moral reconstruction.

Modern critics of liberal education claim that it is 'very much the dutiful child of the Enlightenment and, as such, tends to uncritically accept a set of assumptions deriving from Enlightenment thought' (Usher and Edwards 1994: 24). These assumptions include ideas of critical reason, individual freedom and benevolent progress. Yet all these ideas were subject to debate among Enlightenment educationists – how far critique could be combined with civility; whether discipline was a prerequisite for, or an impediment to, personal autonomy; whether state education promoted civic virtue or threatened civil liberty; how far the education of women would negatively or positively challenge the natural and social order. Education was the chief instrument for the reproduction of an 'Age of Enlightenment'. Nevertheless, it was from within the Enlightenment that questions were raised about the daring hypothesis of Helvétius (1772: I, 3):

If I can demonstrate that man is, in fact, nothing more than the product of his education, I shall doubtless reveal an important truth to the nations. They will learn that they have in their hands the instrument of their greatness and their felicity, and that to be happy and powerful, it is only a matter of perfecting the science of education.

REFERENCES

Allen, Richard C. (1999) *David Hartley on Human Nature*, Albany: State University of New York Press.

Ashley Smith, J. W. (1954) *The Birth of Modern Education: The Contribution of the Dissenting Academies 1660–1800*, London: Independent Press.

Baczko, Bronislaw (ed.) (2000) *Une Education pour la démocratie: Textes et projets de l'époque révolutionnaire*, Geneva: Droz.

Bantock, Geoffrey H. (1980) *Studies in the History of Educational Theory*, vol. I: *Artifice and Nature, 1350–1765*, London: Allen & Unwin.

—— (1984) *Studies in the History of Educational Theory*, vol. II: *The Minds and the Masses, 1760–1980*, London: Allen & Unwin.

Basedow, Johann B. (1771) *Das Methodenbuch für Väter und Mütter der Familien und Völker*, 2nd edn, Leipzig.

—— (1774) *Das Elementarwerk*, Dessau.

Bourdieu, Pierre and Passeron, Jean-Claude (1990) *Reproduction in Education, Society and Culture*, 2nd edn, London: Sage.

Brandes, Ernst (1809) *Ueber das Du und Du zwischen Eltern und Kindern*, Hanover.

Burke, Edmund (1790) *Reflections on the Revolution in France*, ed. J. G. A. Pocock (1987) Indianapolis: Hackett.

Chalotais, L.-R. de C. de la (1763) *Essai d'Education Nationale*, Geneva; trans. in La Fontainerie (ed.) (1932) *op. cit.*

Chisick, Harvey (1981) *The Limits of Reform in the Enlightenment: Attitudes toward the Education of the Lower Classes in Eighteenth-century France*, Princeton: Princeton University Press.

Claeys, Gregory (1999) 'Virtuous Commerce and Free Theology: Political Economy and the Dissenting Academies', *History of Political Thought*, XX: 141–72.

Condorcet, M.-J.-A.-N. Caritat de (1792) 'Rapport et projet de decrét sur l'organisation générale de l'instruction publique', in Baczko (ed.) (2000) *op. cit.*; trans. in La Fontainerie (ed.) (1932) *op. cit.*

Courdin J. (1792) *Observations philosophiques sur la réforme de l'education publique*, Montpellier.

Fordyce, David (1745) *Dialogues Concerning Education*, London.

Hartley, David (1749) *Observations on Man, His Frame, His Duty and His Expectations*, 6th edn, London (1834).

Helvétius, Claude A. (1772) *De L'Homme, de ses facultés intellectuelles et de son education*; repr. (1994 of 1773 edn) Bristol: Thoemmes Press.

Jimack, Peter (1983) *Rousseau, Emile*, London: Grant & Cutler.

Jones, M. G. (1938) *The Charity School Movement: A Study of Eighteenth Century Puritanism in Action*, Cambridge: Cambridge University Press.

Justi, Johann H. G. von (1755) *Staatswirthschaft*, Leipzig.

Kant, Immanuel (1784) 'Beantwortung der Frage: Was ist Aufklärung?', ed. and trans. James Schmidt (1996) as 'An Answer to the Question: What Is Enlightenment?', in *What is Enlightenment? Eighteenth-century Answers and Twentieth-century Questions*, Berkeley: University of California Press.

—— (1803) *Über Pädagogik*, Königsberg, trans. Annette Churton (1899) as *Kant on Education*, London: Kegan Paul.

Knox, Vicesimus (1781) *Liberal Education or, a Practical Treatise on the Methods of Acquiring Useful and Polite Learning*, 3rd edn, London.

La Fontainerie, F. de (ed.) (1932) *French Liberalism and Education in the Eighteenth Century: The Writings of La Chalotais, Turgot, Diderot, and Condorcet on National Education*, New York: McGraw-Hill.

Le Mercier de la Rivière, P. P. F. J. H. (1775) *De L'Instruction Publique*, Stockholm.

Lepeletier, Michel (1793) 'Plan d'Education Nationale', in B. Baczko (ed.) (2000) *op. cit.*

Levinger, M. (2000) *Enlightened Nationalism: The Transformation of Prussian Political Culture, 1806–1848*, Oxford: Oxford University Press.

Locke, John (1690a) *An Essay Concerning Human Understanding*, ed. Peter H. Nidditch (1979) Oxford: Oxford University Press.

—— (1690) *Two Treatises of Government*, ed. Peter Laslett (1960) Cambridge: Cambridge University Press.

—— (1693) *Some Thoughts Concerning Education*, ed. John W. Yolton and Jean S. Yolton (1989) Oxford: Oxford University Press.

—— (1706) *Of the Conduct of the Understanding*, ed. John W. Yolton (1993) Bristol: Thoemmes Press.

Macaulay [Graham], Catherine (1790) *Letters on Education, with Observations on Religious and Metaphysical Subjects*, London.

McLachlan, H. (1931) *English Education under the Test Acts: Being the History of the Non-conformist Academies 1662–1820*, Manchester: Manchester University Press.

Melton, James van H. (1988) *Absolutism and the Eighteenth-century Origins of Compulsory Schooling in Prussia and Austria*, Cambridge: Cambridge University Press.

More, Hannah (1799) *Strictures on the Modern System of Female Education*, London.

Palmer, R. R. (1985) *The Improvement of Humanity: Education and the French Revolution*, Princeton: Princeton University Press.

Parry, Geraint (2001) '*Emile*: Learning to be Men, Women and Citizens', in P. Riley (ed.) *The Cambridge Companion to Rousseau*, Cambridge: Cambridge University Press.

Passmore, John (1970) *The Perfectibility of Man*, London: Duckworth.

Payne, Harry C. (1976) *The Philosophes and the People*, New Haven, Conn.: Yale University Press.

Priestley, Joseph (1768) *An Essay on the First Principles of Government*; 2nd edn (1771) ed. Peter Miller in (1993) *Priestley: Political Writings*, Cambridge: Cambridge University Press.

—— (1780) *Miscellaneous Observations Relating to Education, More Especially, as it Respects the Conduct of the Mind, to which is added, An Essay on a Course of Liberal Education for Civil and Active Life*, Cork.

Riballier (1779) *De L'Education Physique et Morale des Femmes*, Brussels and Paris.

Rousseau, Jean Jacques (1758) 'Lettre à M. D'Alembert', ed. and trans. Allan Bloom in (1968) *Politics and the Arts: Letter to M. D'Alembert on the Theatre*, Ithaca: Cornell University Press.

—— (1762a) *Emile, or On Education*, ed. and trans. Allan Bloom (1991) Harmondsworth: Penguin.

—— (1762b) *The Social Contract and Other Later Political Writings*, ed. and trans. Victor Gourevitch (1997) Cambridge: Cambridge University Press.

—— (posth. 1782) 'Considerations on the Government of Poland', ed. and trans. Victor Gourevitch in (1997) *The Social Contract and Other Later Political Writings*, Cambridge: Cambridge University Press.

Schouls, Peter A. (1992) *Reasoned Freedom: John Locke and Enlightenment*, Ithaca: Cornell University Press.

Silber, Kate (1976) *Pestalozzi: The Man and his Work*, 4th edn, London: Routledge & Kegan Paul.

Simon, Brian (1960) *Studies in the History of Education:1780–1870*, London: Lawrence & Wishart.

Sonnenfels, Joseph von (1768) *Grundsätze der Polizey, Handlung und Finanzwissenschaften*, 2nd edn, Vienna.

Steiner, David M. (1994) *Rethinking Democratic Education*, Baltimore: Johns Hopkins Press.

Talleyrand, C. H.-M. (1791) 'Rapport sur l'instruction publique', in B. Baczko (ed.) (2000) *op. cit.*

Tarcov, Nathan (1984) *Locke's Education for Liberty*, Chicago: University of Chicago Press.

Trachtenberg, Zev (1993) *Making Citizens: Rousseau's Political Theory of Culture*, London: Routledge.

Turnbull, George (1742) *Observations upon Liberal Education*, London.

Usher, Robin and Edwards, Richard (1994) *Postmodernism and Education*, London: Routledge.

Wolff, Christian (1756) *Vernünftige Gedanken von dem Gesellschaftlichen Leben der Menschen und insonderheit dem gemeinen Wesen*, new edn, Halle.

Wollstonecraft, Mary (1792) *A Vindication of the Rights of Woman*, ed. Sylvana Tomaselli (1995) Cambridge: Cambridge University Press.

CHAPTER FIFTEEN

SCIENCE AND THE EIGHTEENTH-CENTURY PUBLIC

Scientific revolutions and the changing format of scientific investigation

———◆◆◆———

Larry Stewart

The idea that the history of science goes through stages of radical intellectual innovation – referred to by the name of scientific revolutions – goes back to a cluster of scholars of the 1940s: Alexandre Koyré, Herbert Butterfield, Rupert and Marie Boas Hall (Porter 1986: 293–5). According to this view, a major scientific revolution was occasioned by the Copernican reinterpretation of the cosmic constellations. Its starting point and rationale were identified in the attempt of science to break away from the traditional modes of analysis dictated by biblical hermeneutics and to claim for scientific enquiry freedom from dogmatic constraints. The resulting method of observation and interpretation was claimed to be disinterested because it was based on experiment.

Experiment and demonstration established a framework for natural philosophical theory and the practice of eighteenth-century Europe and its colonies. This emphasis on method, specifically on the emergent link between experiment, replication and demonstration, helped to complete the revolution set in motion in the age of Galileo. Methodological issues have been overshadowed to a great extent by conflicts with authority and religion. This is hardly surprising since the controversies reached far beyond religion (Porter 2000: ch. 6). There was an increasing demand for publications in the vernacular and a broad range of readers informed themselves on natural philosophy subjects and openly pronounced their views. Public debates, therefore, frequently followed the publication of the *Philosophical Transactions of the Royal Society*. For some, giving public lectures might indeed take precedence over commitments to the Royal Society: John Theophilus Desaguliers, demonstrator to the Royal Society, was rebuked by Newton in 1725 for failing to present sufficient experiments to the Society. His reply was to offer demonstrations of experiments he had already provided to audiences at his public lectures (Stewart 1992: 132–3). While a minor episode, this reflected the attention that was increasingly paid to the latest discoveries in natural philosophy. By mid-century, debates concerning the nature and efficacy of electrical phenomena were especially popular. For example, in 1747 a Mr Booth of Dublin, who had seemingly cured a paralytic arm by applying electricity, enquired of the experimentalist Benjamin Wilson whether he should send his account to the Royal Society for their deliberation or to the widely circulated

Gentleman's Magazine, which, in any case, commonly reported on matters revealed in the *Philosophical Transactions* (Bertucci 2001: 43–68, esp. 54).

Philosophical controversies often explicitly invited a public adjudication. For example, the French–Swedish expedition to Lapland which aimed to settle the shape of the earth depended for its success on the exactness of English instruments, especially the new Graham zenith sector. From the late 1730s, public polemic was quick to follow the advancement of new philosophical principles (Terrall 1992: 218–37 and 2002: 136ff.; Iliffe 1993: 335–75). Indeed, the skill and charm of some writers on natural philosophical issues helped them secure an audience. Louis de Bougainville followed this stylistic tradition when he wrote the celebrated account of his circumnavigation of 1766–9. By describing himself as a '*voyageur & marin; c'est a dire, un menteur, & un imbecille*', he sought to capture his readers (Bougainville 1771: 16–17). When natural philosophical debates entered the public arena, demonstration and replication gained significance as spectacles of public entertainment.

FINDING AN AUDIENCE

Where, then, did philosophical credibility reside? The challenge of demonstration, explored at some risk by Galileo and his disciples, continued to fester throughout the seventeenth and eighteenth centuries. As reports of natural philosophical observation and experimental apparatus proliferated, especially in the numerous scientific societies which had emerged in the second half of the seventeenth century, method inevitably became a subject of concern and contention. Thomas Hobbes levelled his considerable guns at the Royal Society and its experimental creation of natural facts. Remarkably, though, apologists for the Royal Society like Thomas Sprat made much of experimental enquiry as a cure for the evils of dogmatism which had shattered the English political scene during the Civil War. The choice lay between the authoritarian and the publicist. Increasingly, during the Restoration, gentlemanly practitioners of experimental learning brought social status to both the Society and to a method promoted by the likes of Robert Boyle (Shapin 1994: chs 6–7 and 1996: 112). The gentleman's practice and the adjudication of claims of discovery within the Royal Society of London and the Académie des Sciences in Paris simply underscored the problem of the assertion of natural facts. Philosophical assertions seldom went without debate and disagreement. Even those experimental discoveries which we now take for granted, like the vacuum or the refraction of light, were subject to intense controversy. When, for example, such issues were not quite so easily resolved as a gentleman's reputation might demand, then the force of demonstration, observation and ultimately replication became the logical alternative. This was especially the case when philosophers were inclined to claim that one particular experiment – an *experimentum crucis* – might settle an issue.

Method, as well as discovery, became open to dispute. In such a circumstance, the audience inevitably widened. While some readers became aware of the attacks made upon experimentalism by the likes of Hobbes, others increasingly immersed themselves in the experimental process, either as witnesses or as dilettantes seeking to reproduce the results of famous experiments. The fact that Galileo, in his *Dialogues*, and Newton, in his *Opticks*, had chosen to publish in the vernacular clearly suggests an effort to broaden the foundation of debate, to widen the discussion, to till the ground in which philosophical truth might lay down roots. This is not to say that such a strategy was well thought out. Galileo, surely, had been on dangerous ground indeed. Newton, for his part, was deeply ambivalent about pandering to a vulgar audience, a risk that was scarcely possible, given the forbidding and innovative mathematical edifice of his great *Principia*. Even the learned could hardly face that great tome without a guide. And yet, it was also a work which espoused rules for philosophizing that could reveal broad, indeed universal, meaning among all those readers able to comprehend its intense promotion of the business of experimental philosophy. The problems encountered in the public demonstrations of experiment, I submit, were intimately linked to the idea that the ability to interpret and replicate experiments was beyond the solitary philosopher. They initiated a second phase when scientific practice experienced significant changes which depended on the unprecedented emphasis of public observation and adjudication, in tandem with its privileging of experimentation.

THE PROMOTION OF EXPERIMENT

There are numerous examples of the way that Western European philosophers sought to further the cause of experiment. Not the least of these was Newton's own pronouncement in 1713, in the second edition of his *Principia*, with echoes of the Restoration in his head, that 'God does certainly belong to the business of experimental philosophy'. Thus, the older notion that somehow experiment and revelation were at loggerheads was rejected. Nevertheless, Newton's proposition was unlikely easily to convince the champions of orthodoxy in Britain or on the Continent. Furthermore, it was not by any means obvious that even experimental results could be replicated with ease.

One of the most remarkable instances of such a difficulty was in Newton's own claims regarding the refraction of white light into its constituent colours, which he claimed to have discovered in his college rooms in the 1660s. Even by the time he had become President of the Royal Society, Newton's views were not generally accepted. Such a simple piece of apparatus as a glass prism was itself problematic, especially because these were readily available as child's toys, and in varying degrees of quality. This, in itself, may have been part of the reason why some were reluctant to accept Newton's experimental results. A more significant aspect of this second phase of scientific innovation was that various efforts were made to replicate his experiments. To this end, Newton was able to secure the skill of John Theophilus Desaguliers to demonstrate them to visiting philosophers and to diplomats (Schaffer 1989: esp. 95ff). What is important is that replication required an audience.

Enlightenment science emerged in large measure out of the demand for the latest demonstrations and experiments by Newtonian philosophers. This was the arena within which many philosophical disputes came under scrutiny (Clark, Golinski and Schaffer 1999: 23; Melton 2001). Of course, a scientific public was not Newton's invention, nor would he have been terribly happy about it. For Newton, natural

Figure 15.1 Frontispiece engraved by J. Sturt, from Ephraim Chambers (1738) *Cyclopaedia: or, an Universal Dictionary of Arts and Sciences*, 2nd edn, vol. 1, London. This depicts knowledge outside the academy, modelled after Raphael's *School of Athens*. By permission of the National Library of Australia.

philosophy was the preserve of the scholar. Nevertheless, there were emergent forces that Newton could not control. By the end of the seventeenth century London offered a growing number of lectures on chemistry and mathematics to which the inquisitive might subscribe. Some, like those of the mathematician and Newtonian the Reverend John Harris, were given free of charge in a coffee house near the Royal Exchange in London. Although this venture did not survive long, it certainly did not suffer from a lack of interest. Quite the contrary. Soon, there were many competitors who saw mathematics precisely in the way Newton had presented it – as a means of describing the laws of motion governing physical bodies (Stewart 1992: ch. 4). At Gresham College, for example, lectures once intended to improve the mathematical skills of merchants and seamen soon evolved into courses that increasingly included experimental demonstrations.

One of the foremost examples of this transformation can be seen in the career of James Hodgson, who had been an assistant to Newton's rival, the Astronomer Royal, Flamsteed. Hodgson was also a mathematics teacher who taught clients from the Royal Exchange to Westminster. And he had a good eye for the market. As early as 1702, he decided to engage in a partnership with the instrument-maker Francis

Hauksbee, Sr, to give courses of experiments. This was a shrewd venture – for Hauksbee could supply expensive apparatus that otherwise might have depleted Hodgson's purse.

There was a significant element of theatre involved in experimental demonstrations. Indeed, it was especially these dramatic entertainments which served to draw paying subscribers accustomed to formerly free mathematical lectures and, inevitably, they attracted numerous competitors, too. The fees for such courses of lectures were considerable, occasionally more that two guineas, suggesting fairly well-heeled auditors for the most part. But the success of such lectures is also evidence of immense demand. In effect, experimental philosophy generated a new, dramatic form of entertainment. The audience present at such performances was as numerous as the readership of philosophical works published in the vernacular.

Hodgson's career is especially revealing in regard to the emergence of the scientific public sphere, or a public forum of judgement. In 1704 he advertised that his lectures were based on a vast array of apparatus which might have been expected to have been reserved for the exclusive rooms of the Royal Society. He boasted that he would show 'Engines for Raising and Condensing Air with all their Appurtenances, Microscopes of the best Contrivance, Telescopes of a convenient Length, with Micrometers adapted to them, Barometers, Thermometers, and Utensils proper for Hydrostatical Experiments, with such other Instruments as are necessary for the purpose'. Such apparatus, of course, was intended to display the wares that Hauksbee hawked. Even if Newton might look askance at such pandering to the public, Hodgson also adopted experiments intended to demonstrate the principles upon which Newton's *Opticks* were based. Prisms soon became standard equipment, along with all the instruments necessary 'to prove the Weight and Elasticity of the Air, its Pressure or Gravitation of Fluids upon each other: Also the new Doctrine of Lights and Colours, and several other matters relating to the same Subjects' (*Daily Courant*, Thursday, 11 January 1705). By such means Hodgson was able to reach a broad new audience.

A remarkable number of experimental lecturers followed rapidly in the wake of Harris and Hodgson. As far as Britain was concerned, the vast majority of those who attempted to capture such a public were proponents of Newton's natural philosophy, and it did not take long before scholars from Oxford and Cambridge performed in front of large crowds in London. William Whiston, Newton's chosen successor to the Lucasian professorship at Cambridge, took his knowledge of natural philosophy to London when he was expelled for heretical speculations on the doctrine of the Trinity. In 1707, Whiston and Roger Cotes, the mathematician, were presenting a course of twenty-four lectures in experimental philosophy at Cambridge to explicate the Newtonian philosophy – thus following ventures in London. Upon Whiston's expulsion in 1710, he removed to London and his Cambridge experience provided the foundation for lectures which Whiston undertook with the instrument-maker Francis Hauksbee senior in London at least as early as 1712 (Whiston 1749: 135–6; Trinity College Library MS 4.42, Cotes to Smith, 11 December 1703; see also Gascoigne 1989: 150–2).

Robert Boyle had already recognized the obstacle to a broad understanding created by the lack of sufficient mathematical skill. Newton's disciples developed the kind of demonstrations which could produce comprehension of natural principles without the mathematical foundations Newton otherwise insisted as necessary. The response was overwhelming. As early as 1714, Desaguliers was already claiming that he had designed over 300 new experiments and he continued in this vein for the next thirty years. By 1734, when he published the first volume of his *Course of Experimental Philosophy*, he was claiming to be engaged in his 121st course of lectures. Similarly, Whiston continued to lecture on natural philosophy, astronomy and religion until his death in 1752. By then, both men had to contend with many rivals, among them the chemist Peter Shaw, Henry Pemberton, MD, and the anonymous author of *A View of Sir Isaac Newton's Philosophy* (1728). Another was Benjamin Martin, who wrote books on mathematics and natural philosophy which gave him entry into the increasingly competitive world of itinerant lecturers in provincial towns, as well as in London (Stewart 1992: 143–51).

These developments were not exclusively a cosmopolitan affair, although such vast metropoles as London and Paris certainly provided the desired audiences of the experimentalists. Whiston came down from Cambridge and Desaguliers from Oxford with the latest Newtonian experience in their pockets. But it was also notable that the Reverend Stephen Hales, one of the auditors of Giovanni Francesco Vigani, the first Cambridge professor of chemistry, set upon exploring chemical reactions even after Hales, too, had removed from Cambridge in 1709 (in his case to take up duties as Minister of Teddington). Hales's debt to Newton was revealed in his famous *Vegetable Staticks* (1727), a work which would have been unthinkable without the early Cambridge laboratories and which laid much of the foundation for pneumatic chemistry (Thackray 1970: 114–17).

This great work of experimental chemistry was eagerly received. According to John Mickleburgh, the third professor of chemistry, from 1718, the furnaces and utensils at Trinity College had allowed Newton to find 'the first hints and notices of these Phenomena which very hints and notices have since been reduced by the reverend and ingenious Mr Stephen Hales into plain facts and rendered even visible to our eyes by an almost infinite variety of experiments' (Coleby 1952: 171). The experimental programme found some subscribers who could afford to purchase instruments off the shelf in London shops to equip their own laboratories. Public lectures, inspired by Newton's assertion of the critical importance of experimental practice, addressed a vast range of topics. The composition of light and its refraction, capillary action and weights falling in a vacuum, electricity and magnetism, comets and Northern Lights variously became staples in coffee houses, in theatres and on platforms erected to watch eclipses, even at the Hanoverian court. The demonstrations for which many paid handsomely represented the widening scope of public knowledge.

EXPERIMENTAL SPACES

The growth of the scientific public on the Continent was founded partly on the experience of seventeenth-century mechanical lectures, but also relied on Newtonians who moved beyond London. In the early eighteenth century the followers of Descartes or Leibniz who still disputed Newton's doctrine of forces held an especially hopeless position in the face of the overwhelming tide of Newtonian demonstration. Thus, Willem 's Gravesande imported Newton's philosophy into the Netherlands after having attended Desaguliers's lectures in London in 1716. Desaguliers himself extended his reach across the North Sea in 1731 and 1732 with lecture tours of Holland. Similarly in France, in the aftermath of Voltaire's proselytizing *Letters Concerning the English Nation* (1733), lecturers found an audience which appreciated the dramatic elements of their demonstrations.

In the 1750s, the Abbé Nollet adapted his electrical researches to provide public demonstrations, even though he was at odds with the Newtonian Benjamin Franklin over the causes of electricity. The theatrical potential of electricity prompted a number of quite extraordinary displays: boys might be suspended by silk threads to create a static attraction, as was done in London by Stephen Gray and in Paris by Charles Dufay or Nollet; shocks might be dispersed through a line of guards or priests, or even applied to unsuspecting country folk on bridges crossing the Thames (Rifkin 2002: 76ff., 88–90; Bertucci 2001: 44–9; Heilbron 1979: 246–323; Watson 1747–8: 53).

The difficulty with the dramatic was that it was all too readily dismissed as shallow entertainment in the marketplace for magic shows and village strongmen. To have let such a notion stand would have been to defeat the entire purpose of expanding the understanding of physical principles. Public knowledge was the fundamental issue. This conflict, eagerly reported in the *Gentleman's Magazine*, broke open in the 1740s. While Benjamin Martin was to be assailed for providing philosophy for profit, he was frustrated at being taken for a conjuror, an experience he claimed that even the illustrious Dr Desaguliers occasionally had to face. It was the experimentalist and engineer John Smeaton who, in a letter to the electrician Benjamin Wilson, challenged the complaints of pandering to fashion by 'the common Herd of conjuring Philosophers about Town' (British Library, Add. MSS. 30094, fol. 41, Smeaton to Wilson, 24 August 1747). But Smeaton had an important spin on common entertainment, noting that in fact the costs of courses made them a gentlemanly amusement, however much lecturers and auditors might be disparaged. In fact, Smeaton confronted the market place and its meaning, stating, 'I don't take it yt shewing ye wonders of Electricity for Money is much more commendable . . . than ye shewing any other strange sight or curiosity for ye same end, however if L200 could be got by a worth employment in yt way I don't see wheres ye harm as there is no fraud or Dishonesty in it' (British Library, Add. MSs. 30094, fol. 22, 27 September 1746). Trading curiosity for cash might have been unseemly in the gentlemanly quarters of the Royal Society, but Smeaton knew full well that there were those like himself who were forced to live by their wits. The growing audience for things philosophical magnified tensions which had existed in a few gentlemanly and princely scientific societies since their origins.

By the end of the eighteenth century, there were many more scientific societies in existence, many remote from the capital cities of western Europe, among them the Spalding Gentlemen's Society in the English Fens, similar societies in Rouen and Dijon, and the celebrated Lunar Society of Birmingham, and many more in the English Midlands. As philosophy found an audience further afield, it also found deeper resonance in social strata otherwise excluded. For example, the Spitalfields

Mathematical Society in the immigrant and industrial East End of London, which had originated in 1717, was giving lectures by the end of the century to audiences of up to 500 listeners for sixpence a head. This venture explicitly provided 'the public at large an opportunity of increasing their knowledge, on terms so easy, as to be within the reach of every individual, who has a taste to cultivate, or a curiosity to gratify' (*Catalogue of Books* 1804: iii; Royal Astronomical Society 1875: 180–3; Stewart and Weindling 1995). Indeed, the careers of many experimental philosophers of the second half of the eighteenth century suggest that the dissemination of knowledge was one of the most crucial characteristics of this period. That was the view of the Birmingham chemist and industrialist James Keir, who, in 1789, proclaimed in his *Dictionary of Chemistry* that 'The diffusion of knowledge, and a taste for science, over all classes of men, in every nation of Europe, or of European origin seems to be the characteristic feature of the present age' (Turner 1990: 5). Even the mechanics' institutes of the early nineteenth century could trace their origins to the enlightened spread of philosophical curiosity among artisans and craftsmen.

In the eighteenth century the passionate debate over access – social and intellectual – was yet to be resolved, as the works of Jean Jacques Rousseau, patron saint of Jacobins and republicans, would amply demonstrate. But these consequences were not yet acknowledged until chemists like Joseph Priestley began to insist on the democracy of knowledge. In the early eighteenth century, Desaguliers, experimentalist extraordinaire, had lamented those 'full of the Notion of the difference between Theory and Practise' (Desaguliers 1744: vol. 2, 416). He was frustrated by those who resisted the world of work and skill that lay behind the innovations in mechanical construction, as in the early steam engines discussed in his lectures. By 1765, the French mechanic Jacques Vaucanson was at pains to point out that there was a great weakness in the privilege accorded to theory: 'In the one case it is only a matter of explaining as one likes certain known effects; in the other one must produce new effects' (Briggs 1991: 84). To provide pride of place to theory was to induce an unnecessary confusion.

Growing numbers of experiments in the eighteenth century demanded elaborate apparatus, and this itself became a point of contention because of complexity as much as cost. Lecturers sometimes developed careers as instrument-makers. Thus, the Abbé Nollet utilized the newly contrived Leyden jar in his disputes with Benjamin Franklin over the causes of electricity. Like Benjamin Martin, Nollet used his lectures for the sale of apparatus for which there was an increasingly large market (Rifkin 2002: ch. 3; Heilbron 1979: 80, 164–5). Controversy soon arose over the efficiency and accuracy of many instruments, especially those which might be used in laboratory practice or in the field, such as those of the electrical instrument-maker Edward Nairne or of the astronomical instrument-maker George Graham – both used by Maupertuis (Terrall 2002: 102, 105, 136). Moreover, careers were made by those able to contrive apparatus for the delights of electrical or magnetical display – such as that of Gowin Knight, who invented a device for creating artificial magnets. These were much in demand, even at considerable expense (Fara 1996: 41ff.).

Graham in the early part of the century and Nairne at the end were only two of those whose immense skill in instrumental designs reflected the Enlightenment passion for philosophical observation. Not all instruments were either accurate or sophisticated. Of course, skills in experimental and instrumental design were widely sought. Indeed, the Swedish engineer Marten Triewald reported to the Royal Society on his electrical experiments and evidently amassed one of the largest collections of demonstration devices in Europe prior to 1750. Similarly, the engineer John Smeaton was elected to the Royal Society in 1753 specifically on his reputation as a 'maker of Philosophical Instruments', and his skill so impressed Joseph Priestley that he used Smeaton's improved air pump for experiments on specific gravities of air (Heilbron 1979: 80, 292; Royal Society MSS, Certificates, 2, 1751–6, nos. 442 and 7).

A significant international trade in apparatus emerged in the eighteenth century so that no intended experimenter would be limited by a local market. Towards the end of the century many of the leading experimental philosophers and lecturers bought their instruments from the same sources. Hence, the Portuguese instrument-maker, and probable industrial spy, Jean Hyacinthe de Magellan sold instruments from London, sending Gowin Knight's fashionable magnetic apparatus to courts in Spain and Portugal and instruments to his contacts in France and the Netherlands. Similarly, the rancour between Franklin and Nollet encouraged many to buy instruments in an attempt to replicate their experiments. The pace of these researches increased rapidly at the end of the century as a consequence of Italian reports of the voltaic pile and the spread of Galvanism (Fara 1996: 22, 43; Delbourgo 2001: esp. 125; see Pera 1992).

Philosophical conflict, like that between Newton and Leibniz, which had defined the philosophical landscape in the early eighteenth century, or later that between Lavoisier and proponents of phlogiston like Priestley and James Watt, was hardly new. But, following experimental reports in the daily press, it became even more likely that replication would fuel controversy. Disputes arose, for example, between Magellan and his rival Tiberius Cavallo over magnetism and the effectiveness of eudiometers to measure the salubrity of airs. During the 1770s, Magellan was assisting Priestley in the analysis of airs. In 1777 Priestley requested the industrialist Matthew Boulton, in Birmingham, to get some 'air as it is actually breathed by the different manufacturers in this kingdom and hope you will be so obliging as to procure me the proper samples from Birmingham' (Schofield 1966: 161–2). And the celebrated democrat and friend of James Watt, Dr Thomas Beddoes of Bristol, deplored the 'new poisons arising daily in London' (Stansfield 1984: 141, 150). Beddoes went on to be one of the greatest exponents of pneumatic medicine through the application of new airs in the controversial treatment of endemic diseases like consumption. Instrumental simplicity was fundamental here, both in the preparation of these airs and in the manufacture of a portable device that made it possible for ill patients to breathe the gases, and for country surgeons and physicians to prescribe them.

Expensive devices limited participation in philosophical debate while elaborate ones further sowed confusion, privileging instrumental skill while obscuring comprehension. Instrumental improvement and simplification, for example, were behind the success of the Dutch instrument-maker Martinus van Marum (Roberts 1995: esp. 517, 524–5; see also Levere 1999). Simple and affordable instruments enhanced participation, concluded Priestley in 1778. This was critical to the elimination of

Figure 15.2 *Joseph Priestley*, Thomas Holloway after a portrait by W. Artaud (1794). By permission of Martin Fitzpatrick.

the mystery of religious authority and social position (Schaffer 1984: esp. 174; Mason 1991: esp. 156; Fara 1996: 43, 61, 87; Golinksi 1992: 122–3). Priestley, and his associates, such as James Watt, Jr, understood the power of replication to be a force in an emerging scientific culture much wider than that represented by exclusive societies. For them, a social reformation was at stake. Thomas Beddoes once wrote that he was glad of the interest in his chemical lectures at Bristol for he felt that they may be useful in 'preventing some acts of barbarity' that, as the French had demonstrated, demands for social reformation could produce (James Watt Papers, W/9/7, Beddoes to Watt, 21 April [1796?]).

The vogue for experimental philosophy reflected this impatient century, an impatience that surfaced sometimes in the conflicts over who knew truth and sometimes over who had the power to disseminate it. This conflict was, in effect, the legacy of Galileo and his confrontation with authority. Newton looked further because his stunning mathematical achievements made it possible. Even so, it was primarily his disciples' uncompromising commitment to experimental philosophy which secured his renown. As with readers of novels and newspapers, spectators at lectures carried with them new knowledge, including the wish to participate in an intellectual climate which prized observation. The numerous letters sent to the Royal Society and the Académie des Sciences about discoveries and inventions testify to this steadily growing audience for scientific enlightenment.

REFERENCES

Bertucci, Paola (2001) 'The Electrical Body of Knowledge: Medical Electricity and Experimental Philosophy in the Mid-eighteenth Century', in Paola Bertucci and Giuliano Pancaldi (eds) *Electric Bodies: Episodes in the History of Medical Electricity*, Bologna Studies in History of Science, 9, Bologna: CIS, Dipartimento di Filosofia.

Bougainville, Louis de (1771) *Voyage autour du monde, par la Fregate du Roi, La Boudeuse, et la Flute l'Etoile; en 1766, 1767, 1768 & 1769*, Paris: Chez Saillant & Nyon.

Briggs, Robin (1991) 'The Académie Royale des Sciences and the Pursuit of Utility,' *Past and Present*, 131: 38–88.

Catalogue of Books Belonging to the Mathematical Society, Crispin Street, Spitalfields (1804) London: Cicero Press.

Clark, William, Golinski, Jan and Schaffer, Simon (eds) (1999) *The Sciences in Enlightened Europe*, Chicago: University of Chicago Press.

Cohen, H. Floris (1994) *The Scientific Revolution: A Historiographical Inquiry*, Chicago and London: University of Chicago Press.

Coleby, L. J. M. (1952) 'John Mickleburgh: Professor of Chemistry at the University of Cambridge, 1718–56', *Annals of Science* 8: 165–74.

Cunningham, Andrew and Williams, Perry (1993) 'De-centring the "big picture": *The Origins of Modern Science* and the Modern Origins of Science', *British Journal for the History of Science*, 26: 407–32.

Delbourgo, James (2001) 'Electrical Humanitarianism in North America: Dr T. Gale's *Electricity, or Ethereal Fire, Considered* (1802) in Historical Context', in Paola Bertucci and Giuliano Pancaldi (eds) *op. cit.*

Desaguliers, John Theophilus (1744) *A Course of Experimental Philosophy*, 2 vols, London.

Fara, Patricia (1996) *Sympathetic Attractions: Magnetic Practices, Beliefs, and Symbolism in Eighteenth-century England*, Princeton: Princeton University Press.

Finocchiaro, Maurice A. (ed.) (1989) *The Galileo Affair: A Documentary History*, Berkeley and Los Angeles: University of California Press.

Gascoigne, John (1989) *Cambridge in the Age of the Enlightenment: Science, Religion and Politics from the Restoration to the French Revolution*, Cambridge and New York: Cambridge University Press.

Golinski, Jan (1992) *Chemistry and Enlightenment in Britain, 1760–1820*, Cambridge: Cambridge University Press.

Heilbron, J. L. (1979) *Electricity in the 17th and 18th Centuries: A Study in Early Modern Physics*, Berkeley and Los Angeles: University of California Press.

Iliffe, Rob (1993) '"Aplatisseur du monde et de Cassini": Maupertuis, Precision Instrument, and the Shape of the Earth in the 1730s', *History of Science*, 31: 335–75.

Levere, Trevor H. (1999) 'Measuring Gases and Measuring Goodness,' unpublished ms.

Mason, Stephen F. (1991) 'Jean Hyacinthe de Magellan, F. R. S. and the Chemical Revolution of the Eighteenth Century', *Notes and Records of the Royal Society*, 45: 155–64.

—— (2002) 'Galileo's Scientific Discoveries, Cosmological Confrontations, and the Aftermath', *History of Science*, 40: 377–406.

Melton, James Van Horn (2001) *The Rise of the Public in Enlightenment Europe*, Cambridge and New York: Cambridge University Press.

Pera, Marcello (1992) *The Ambiguous Frog: The Galvani–Volta Controversy on Animal Electricity*, trans. Jonathan Mandelbaum, Princeton: Princeton University Press.

Porter, Roy (1986) 'The Scientific Revolution: A Spoke in the Wheel?' in Roy Porter and Mikuláš Teich (eds) *Revolutions in History*, Cambridge and London: Cambridge University Press.

—— (2000) *Enlightenment: Britain and the Creation of the Modern World*, London and New York: Allen Lane.

Rifkin, Jessica (2002) *Science in the Age of Sensibility: The Sentimental Empiricists of the French Enlightenment*, Chicago: University of Chicago Press.

Roberts, Lissa (1995) 'The Death of the Sensuous Chemist: The "New" Chemistry and the Transformation of Sensuous Technology', *Studies in the History and Philosophy of Science*, 26: 503–29.

Royal Astronomical Society (1875) *Monthly Notices*, 35.

Schaffer, Simon (1984) 'Priestley's Questions: An Historiographical Survey,' *History of Science*, 22: 151–83.

—— (1989) 'Glass Works: Newton's Prisms and the Uses of Experiment', in David Gooding, Trevor Pinch and Simon Schaffer (eds) *The Uses of Experiment: Studies in the Natural Sciences*, Cambridge and New York: Cambridge University Press.

—— (1993) 'The Consuming Flame: Electrical Showmen and Tory Mystics in the World of Goods', in John Brewer and Roy Porter (eds) *Consumption and the World of Goods*, London and New York: Routledge.

Schofield, Robert E. (ed.) (1966) *A Scientific Autobiography of Joseph Priestley*, Cambridge, Mass., and London: MIT Press.

Shapin, Steven (1994) *A Social History of Truth: Civility and Science in Seventeenth-century England*, Chicago and London: University of Chicago Press.

—— (1996) *The Scientific Revolution*, Chicago and London: University of Chicago Press.

Smith, George E. (2002) 'The Methodology of the *Principia*', in I. Bernard Cohen and George E. Smith (eds) *The Cambridge Companion to Newton*, Cambridge and New York: Cambridge University Press.

Stansfield, Dorothy A. (1984) *Thomas Beddoes MD 1760–1808: Chemist, Physician, Democrat*, Dordrecht: D. Reidel.

Stewart, Larry (1992) *The Rise of Public Science: Rhetoric, Technology, and Natural Philosophy in Newtonian Britain, 1660–1750*, Cambridge and London: Cambridge University Press.

Stewart, Larry and Paul Weindling (1995) 'Philosophical Threads: Natural Philosophy and Public Experiment among the Weavers of Spitalfields', *British Journal for the History of Science*, 28: 37–62.

Terrall, Mary (1992) 'Representing the Earth's Shape: The Polemics Surrounding Maupertuis's Expedition to Lapland', *Isis*, 83: 218–37.

—— (2002) *The Man who Flattened the Earth: Maupertuis and the Sciences in the Enlightenment*, Chicago: University of Chicago Press.

Thackray, Arnold (1970) *Atoms and Powers: An Essay on Newtonian Matter-Theory and the Development of Chemistry*, Cambridge, Mass.: Harvard University Press.

Turner, Gerard l'Estrange (1990) 'The London Trade in Scientific Instrument Making in the Eighteenth Century', in *Scientific Instruments and Experimental Philosophy, 1550–1850*, Aldershot: Variorum.

Watson, William (1747–8) 'A Collection of Electrical Experiments Communicated to the Royal Society', *Philosophical Transactions of the Royal Society*, 45, January.

Whiston, William (1749) *Memoirs of the Life and Writings of Mr. William Whiston*, London.

PART IV

———◆———

POLITE CULTURE AND THE ARTS

Figure Part IV.1a *Voltaire* and Dresden box.

Figure Part IV.1c *Madame du Châtelet*. By the 1770s Voltaire (1694–1778) had become an iconic figure in Enlightenment culture. This Dresden box (c. 1775), containing miniatures of him and his famous mistress and intellectual companion Madame du Châtelet (1706–49), was an ideal collector's piece. Reproduced by permission of the Trustees of the Wallace Collection, London.

Figure Part IV.1b *Voltaire*.

INTRODUCTION

Peter Jones

At seemingly isolated moments across Western history a reader can be found confessing to private moments of grief or bewilderment, inspiration or despair, when communing with texts of various kinds, sacred or secular. With the astonishing expansion of print culture in the late seventeenth and early eighteenth centuries, countless numbers of new readers learned of these confessions and began more openly to discuss their own responses. In the visual and musical arts, too, a new public emerged, and with it new ways of talking and thinking about the arts themselves. Alongside these much-heralded intellectual and social changes, there developed unanticipated obstacles and misunderstandings. Writers themselves, like painters, sculptors and composers, had always discussed their work and ideas with fellow-practitioners, and occasionally with patrons on whom they typically relied for a living. Those patrons, however, frequently became knowledgeable and discerning critics, albeit motivated by a desire to excel rival collectors in their taste – or wealth. Some works were, of course, 'public' in the most conspicuous senses: vast palaces or churches, ostentatious decorations or lavish gifts, ceremonial music, drama or poetry. And there were public events and ceremonies, associated with the seasons, or markets, or religious festivals, which only recently have been classified as 'cultural'. But when the masses were expected to respond with awe they were not expected to otherwise participate in judgement. In these respects little changed between the Roman games in the Colosseum around AD 20 and the embassy coaches specifically built to impress Pope Clement XI in 1716, with the power and magnificence of the Portuguese King.

However, from the second quarter of the eighteenth century, and at an ever-increasing pace, a new 'public' for the visual and musical arts did emerge: in the newly established public art salons or exhibitions, soon to be supplemented by the first genuinely public museums, in concerts performed by professional musicians with a skill far exceeding that of the amateur audiences, and in the opportunities people gradually acquired to own small-scale decorative or luxury goods. These audiences overlapped with existing literary audiences, but the latter now publicly declared their preferences in journals and other writings. Inspired by French rivals, writers such as Addison overtly addressed essays to 'women', and 'the novel' rapidly achieved great popularity in Britain and on the Continent.

This is part of the background against which we read (Chapters 16 and 17) of 'sensibility' and the self-conscious modes of response that women in particular celebrated. More openly than before, women asked why serious and radical ideas could not be discussed or promoted by and for themselves, and debate expanded to consider communication with and between the ever-growing 'publics' of various kinds. One notion, with ancient origins, was 'politeness', or 'Good Breeding', in George Turnbull's vocabulary: this was a generic means of dealing with difference, and was open to misunderstanding in almost direct proportion to its formalization. The extremes were easily ridiculed, whether in dress or speech, posture or opinion. New modes and venues of sociability and intellectual experimentation weakened the hold of established groups, but also focused attention on the proper sizes and scales of different human practices: what scales of government or justice-keeping best served society; what scales of endeavour best served scientific enquiries or political debate? In society at large, as in the study and laboratory, formerly small-scale tests acquired unexpected complexities when projected on to a wider world. Such findings inevitably generated self-consciousness about context, and about opportunities for comparative study: what might be learned from other nations and cultures; what were our debts to our own past; how, indeed, were such issues to be tackled?

In Part I of this book we saw how self-conscious attention was given to communication. Alongside emphasis on clarity of expression went reflection on the best ways to convey complex or obscure problems: many writers, including Descartes, Berkeley, Hume and Diderot, experimented with the dialogue form, which enabled them to put contrasting views in the mouths of different characters. This literary device harmonized with a rapidly growing interest in the arts of conversation, which had been prompted by Michel Montaigne (1533–92) and taken up by other French writers, such as Pascal (1623–62) and La Bruyère (1645–96) before the creation of the salons and the proliferation of coffee shops and social clubs late in the seventeenth century. The background ideal was Plato's *Symposium*, where the social pleasures of wining and dining eased the flow of argument and exchange. Aristocratic tradition had celebrated the capacity of a ruler to listen to supplicants, and then to issue judgement. The new mode, soon to be labelled 'democratic' and 'republican', required all participants to cultivate the arts of listening and appropriate response. As an ideal it enabled fearless discussion of any idea or belief, but the conditions for implementing the ideal had to be learned, practised and jealously guarded, including the spaces and places in which the practice could thrive. In brief, it was a practice in which the duty to listen preceded the right to speak: it underpinned the promotion of independent thought and speech, toleration of difference, and resistance to censorship, indoctrination and dogma. Authorities of all kinds felt seriously threatened by these developments. Nevertheless, café society and drinking clubs, salons and Masonic gatherings all fostered mutual interest, toleration of difference and awareness of the perils and rewards of effective communication, but, above all, the excitement and necessity of formulating and testing ideas. In his complacent introduction to *Elements of Criticism*, and immediately following his dedication to the King, Lord Kames avers, 'Men now assert their native privilege of thinking for themselves, and disdain to be ranked in any sect, whatever be the science' (1762: 15).

With their increasing wealth, the new middle classes had opportunities for travel, and with it emerged new attitudes to nature and landscape – although it has been estimated that very few Europeans ever travelled more than twenty-five miles from their homes during their lifetime. In any of the economically poor European countries, such as Scotland up to the 1760s, few looked, or could afford to look, upon land as other than an agricultural resource: attempts to beautify it would be a conspicuous demonstration of superfluous wealth. In the richer parts of England and France, however, and in other rich urban centres, attitudes to nature changed dramatically.

One notion above all others comes to prominence in the mid-eighteenth century: 'expression'. This notion, with strong roots in classical antiquity, challenged, and eventually came to replace, 'imitation'. It directed attention to both the emotional character and the effects of a work: an artist was held to express his innermost thoughts and feelings, which spectators could then discern, perhaps by means of a reciprocal mental act, but certainly by interpreting the external manifestations in the works themselves. Rousseau's discussions of music and of Italian opera illustrate the phenomenon, and its roots in literary theory. Practising artists from the end of the seventeenth century onwards expressed dismay that theorists had little or no first-hand practical knowledge or experience of the art form in question; and professional writings in the second half of the eighteenth century by Rameau, Rousseau or Joshua Reynolds did little to stem the growing tide of autonomous critical discussion and theory.

A brief reference to the physical contexts of the time can serve to alert us to our own perspectives and assumptions. In 1759 Edinburgh and Glasgow were the only cities in Scotland with populations of over 20,000, and the stagecoach between them took twelve hours on the first modern roads built in the land. The boat journey to London from Edinburgh could take a month. Jedburgh, a border market town with a population of around 5,000, in 1756 boasted exactly two carpets. Except in the very wealthiest houses, little meat was eaten, few vegetables and no fruit; there were never two courses at a meal. William Robertson (1721–93), the historian, recalled seeing the arrival of potatoes in Edinburgh in 1748. City-dwellers were crammed into decaying medieval buildings up to fifteen storeys in height, with little heat and no sanitation. It was no accident that plans for improvement involved building a New Town, on a new site, the shape of which did not really emerge until after the Napoleonic Wars, sixty years later. This was where the philosophers and medical doctors whose works we study today, such as David Hume and Joseph Black (1728–99), lived. The contrast with the aristocratic salons in Paris could not be more extreme. The very few English travellers to Scotland before the 1770s, themselves usually from urban centres, were appalled by the squalid living conditions they encountered. Modern technologies can distort our own access to the past: the presentation of ancient objects, buildings or settings in apparently pristine condition can seriously mislead us about the contexts in which our ancestors lived. Most places visited by tourists today as centres of cultural significance were perpetual building sites in which everything was in an incomplete state – of collapse or completion. Piranesi's (1720–78) engravings of Rome in the 1750s, and Hubert Robert's (1733–1808) images of Paris ten years later, are reminders of such realities. And if we suspect that the caricatures of William Hogarth (1697–1764) or Thomas Rowlandson (1756–1827) exaggerate social differences, we can be certain that the publicity etchings of newly rebuilt London, Dublin or Bath are as fanciful as they are seductive. The rural towns and villages of Italy, for example, or further east in Europe, had changed little since the fifteenth century.

The social commentary embodied in the work of printmakers such as Hogarth contrasted with the idealizing, and eventually sentimental, landscapes often adorning wealthy homes: nature did not 'look' like that, and never had done. But the moral task of those decorations – as late as the 1740s Hume spoke of paintings as decorative furniture – was to guide the thought of an onlooker to betterment, if not exactly motivate him to take some practical steps himself to change things. Here, indeed, emerged the ineradicable burden of a spectator in every domain: how to reflect and respond without remaining merely passive. It was no accident that almost all the discussion clubs, and musical and art societies from the beginning of the eighteenth century required the attendance, attention and active participation of every member: each member had to prepare a paper, perform or compose on a regular basis and on penalty of expulsion. Such rules could be effective, however, only when the member-ships remained small, and when there was a roughly equal ability among members.

The superior expertise of guild craftsmen – there were a few women also – had always separated them from anyone else who tried their hand at the requisite trade; and all who devoted their lives to a particular skill, whether musician or sculptor, would begin by being an apprentice in some manner. Nevertheless, the accelerating professionalization of activities in the eighteenth century and into the nineteenth had two major consequences: marginalized amateurs developed their own skills and practices in the graphic and performing arts; but, at the same time, opportunities for passivity among spectators also increased.

CHAPTER SIXTEEN

FEMINIZING THE ENLIGHTENMENT
The problem of sensibility

————•◆•————

Jane Rendall

And you, whom I dare not name! One day we shall be united in death and together lament our common woes. Here on earth, despite your passionate love, you never overstepped the bounds of virtue and I cannot think that you will grieve to see me go before you to realms where we may love with impunity and be united for ever.

In the autumn of 1793, in jail and facing the guillotine, Manon Roland, wife to the former Minister of the Interior of the French Republic and a celebrated political hostess, wrote in her 'Last Thoughts' in these terms of the man she had come to love, the young deputy François Buzot (Roland 1820: 254). Her words are almost identical to those Julie spoke to her lover on her deathbed in Jean Jacques Rousseau's novel *La Nouvelle Héloïse* (1761), Manon Roland's favourite work. Roland, with a well-informed and astute political mind, accustomed to the culture of the salon, had consistently championed the improvement of women's education and legal situation, yet also accepted and maintained Rousseau's view of women's inferiority and domestic destiny. Her use of the language of sensibility in her final piece of auto-biographical writing suggests many of its complexities and ambiguities.

Ann Jessie Van Sant has offered a working definition of this difficult term as:

an organic sensitivity dependent on brain and nerves and underlying a) a delicate moral and aesthetic perception; b) acuteness of feeling, both emotional and physical; and c) susceptibility to delicate passional arousal. Though belonging to all, greater degrees of sensibility – often to a point of fragility – are characteristic of women and upper classes. Excessive delicacy or acuteness of feeling produces an impaired or diseased state.

(Van Sant 1993: 1)

Across Europe, though in different degrees, the meanings attributed to sensibility drew upon medical theories of the nervous system and on sensationalist theories of knowledge. Though sensibility was initially associated with bodily experience, it came to be almost interchangeable with the term 'sentiment' (originally derived from the ambiguous French word *sentiment*, covering both thought and feeling). The debate about sensibility signified a growing awareness of refinement and politeness of manners among the men and women of the upper and increasingly the middle classes, and it helped to shape an interior world of sentiment and emotion, to be explored through the rapid expansion of imaginative literature, especially popular fiction. Though linked to the physical receptivity of the senses in its origins, sensibility could also be associated with a broader sense of sympathy with other people and hence with moral and humane values. At the same time, it also offered a way of signifying sexual difference, through women's supposedly greater receptivity to, and identification with, a world of feeling, believed to be appropriate to lives centred on the familial and the domestic.

The vocabulary of sensibility reinforced the idea of women as the weaker sex, but it was not the only language. Notions of equality drawn from seventeenth-century rationalism, from Poullain de la Barre's Cartesian view that 'the mind is of no sex', retained significance throughout the period. Historians of the Enlightenment wrote of the mental and material improvement in women's condition with the progress of European civilization. And in the late eighteenth century criticism of the *ancien régime* could include challenging the hierarchical order of the family, and the rule of husbands and fathers. The language of sensibility could be appropriated by opposing groups, and the emphasis on sexual difference which the language brought could be resisted, as, for example, by Mary Wollstonecraft in Britain and Olympe de Gouges in France.

The concept of 'sensibility' was one which by the mid-eighteenth century was significant across Europe within many different but related fields of knowledge, including physiology, psychology, moral philosophy, history, aesthetics and literature. It could signal a way of understanding human nature and behaviour, operate as a sign of disorder and danger, or provide an instrument for the pursuit of virtue and the improvement of society. Medical science suggested new ways of thinking about the body and its sensations; moral philosophers focused on the interplay of the material and the moral, of sensation, sentiment and the power of reason; novelists offered imaginative representations of the workings of sensibility and the passions.

MEDICAL VIEWS OF SENSIBILITY

Medical ideas were undoubtedly influenced by the philosopher and trained physician John Locke, whose emphasis on a theory of knowledge rested on sensations derived from the external world. But also significant was the view of Sir Isaac Newton's *Opticks* (1704) that those sensations were transmitted through the nerves by vibrations which 'convey into the Brain the impressions made upon all the Organs of Sense' (Barker-Benfield 1992: 5). Early eighteenth-century physiologists were coming to see the body as an organic entity, not as a complex mechanical interaction of material corpuscles, as Hermann van Boerhaave at Leyden had maintained. Leading medical teachers and writers, including Albrecht von Haller at Göttingen, Robert Whytt and William Cullen at Edinburgh, and George Cheyne in London, wrote of the importance of the operations of the nervous system, since it could determine individual degrees of sensibility and receptivity to external impressions. There were differences in their approaches. In mid-century France, the Montpellier physician Henri Fouquet wrote in his article 'Sensibilité' in the *Encyclopédie* of the centrality of sensibility in the overall economy and in the localized responses of the human body (Vila 1998: 49–50). Edinburgh physicians tended to use the notion of 'sympathy' to mean the communication of feeling between different bodily organs, first formulated by Whytt (Lawrence 1979: 27–8). Nevertheless, all came to emphasize that the study of the nervous system bridged the physical workings of the body and the shaping of human personality and character.

The workings of sensibility could vary according to class and gender. George Cheyne wrote that 'the English malady' – melancholy and depression – was produced by the affluence, the over-consumption and over-sensitivity of the wealthy. Women, especially those of the upper and middle classes, were viewed by writers like Cheyne and Fouquet as having a more delicate nervous system, and a greater degree of sensibility than men, qualities which could signal both a greater refinement and politeness, and greater susceptibility to weakness and disorder. By the mid-eighteenth century gendered aspects of sensibility were much more sharply delineated by medical theorists. They increasingly emphasized the fundamental biological differences between women and men and insisted that the differences in their reproductive

Figure 16.1 *The Vapors*, Alexandre Colin, colour lithograph. SmithKline Beecham Corp Fund for the *Ars Medica* Collection (1958); by permission of the Museum of Art, Philadelphia.

systems determined their separate destinies. In France the writers of the *Encyclopédie* drew explicitly on medical theory, defining women in many articles in terms of their reproductive lives. In the article on *Femme*, they suggest the sex-specific nature of attributes: 'If that same delicacy of the organs that renders women's imaginations more lively also renders their minds less capable of attention, one can also say that they perceive more quickly, see as well and look more cursorily' (Steinbrügge 1995: 29). The term 'vapours' was one way of describing those nervous afflictions attributed to an excess of sensibility especially prevalent among wealthy urban women. In France in 1758 Joseph Raulin wrote, 'for at least a century now, vapors have been endemic in large cities; most women who enjoy the comforts of life are vaporous – one might say that they pay for the pleasure of wealth with a succession of languors' (Vila 1998: 235).

If such a degree of sensibility was the product of a mode of living as well as of female nature, men too could suffer for the degeneracy of urban life, perhaps becoming effeminate and losing their masculine characteristics. In Pierre Roussel's *Système physique et moral de la femme* (1775), sexual differences were sharply defined in an essentially sex-specific theory of sensibility, which supposedly established not only basic physical differences in the transmission of sensations, but the behavioural qualities – strength and toughness in men, weakness and sweetness in women – attached to such differences.

PHILOSOPHICAL VIEWS OF SENSIBILITY

Medical and scientific perspectives on sensibility cannot be dissociated from the work of contemporary philosophers across Europe, who also, simultaneously, translated the legacy of John Locke's sensational philosophy into new and secular interpretations of the mental and moral worlds in which individual women and men lived their lives, interpretations which drew upon concepts of what was 'natural'. New analyses of the human mind and emotions emphasized the interaction between environmental forces and the individual self, and the relationship between the senses, feeling and reason.

David Hume's sceptical philosophy argued not only that knowledge rested on experience and custom, rather than abstract reason, but also that human actions were shaped primarily by the sentiments. The implications of what he had to say of the 'artificial' and the 'natural' virtues were different for men and women. So, to Hume, both justice and chastity were artificial virtues, based originally on self-interest but strengthened through sympathy.

Sentiments of shame and modesty had to be socially inculcated among women, since they were likely to give way to temptation (Hume 1739: 620–5). At the same time, Hume also identified the existence of the 'natural virtues', including the love of relations and those close to us, pity, benevolence, meekness and generosity (Hume 1739: 629–31). Both the natural and the artificial virtues were rooted in the sympathy of individuals with the feelings of others. Passions and feelings in both sexes could be destructive to society, yet, when ordered and regulated, provided the basis of the social virtues. Adam Smith elaborated on Hume's concept of sympathy in his *Theory of Moral Sentiments* (1759), in language which occasionally explicitly suggests the gendered nature of such sentiments, as when he wrote:

> Generosity is different from humanity. Those two qualities, which at first sight seem so nearly allied, do not always belong to the same person. Humanity is the virtue of a woman, generosity of a man. The fair sex, who have commonly much more tenderness than ours, have seldom so much generosity.
>
> (Smith 1759: 190)

In a different context, Edmund Burke's *A Philosophical Enquiry into the Origin of Our Ideas of the Sublime and the Beautiful* (1757–9) identified the gendered nature of aesthetic perceptions and sensations, distinguishing the masculine experience of the sublime from perceptions of the beautiful associated with a particular kind of femininity. Beauty for Burke carried with it 'an idea of weakness and imperfection', with which women themselves colluded: 'they learn to lisp, to totter in their walk, to counterfeit weakness, and even sickness' (Burke 1757–9: 110). The very presence of beauty could induce a dangerous relaxation, 'an inward sense of melting and languor' (Burke 1757–9: 149).

Many writers of the Enlightenment, however, believed that gendered sensibilities could be explained not only through physiological and psychological differences, but in the light of the environmental and historical factors which shaped them. Montesquieu wrote in the *Spirit of the Laws* (1749) of the ways in which the physical conditions of societies – climate, geography and size – affected the manners and condition of women and the relations of the sexes; for him, these were also shaped and indeed influenced by the spirit of different types of government of republics, monarchies and despotisms. Jean Jacques Rousseau was to examine, rather, a deterioration in the condition of women. In his early essay *Discourse on the Origins of Inequality* (1755) he traced an imaginary history of the development of humanity from a savage state, first towards the most desirable situation, that of the simple lives of self-sustaining families, with some division of labour in the lives of men and women and the use of language well established within village communities. But as property and production expanded, so corruption and ambition characterized such worlds. It was that early world, which to him embodied a 'natural' way of life and a harmony between personal feeling and everyday life, a life which was for women, simple, rural and domesticated, which all his subsequent works tried to recover. In Scotland John Gregory followed Rousseau in looking backwards to an earlier stage of society, which he found in the ancient Scotland described by James Macpherson, supposedly in the words of the poet Ossian, in which the women embodied a high degree of the right kind of sensibility: 'the women described by Ossian have a character as singular as that of his heroes. They possess the high spirit and dignity of Roman matrons, united to all the softness and delicacy ever painted in modern romance' (Gregory 1788: xi). But there was a possible alternative narrative, one not of primitivism but of progress. John Millar, Glasgow Professor of Civil Law, wrote as a historian in his *Origin of the Distinction of Ranks* of the changing condition of women in terms of 'a natural progress from ignorance to knowledge, and from rude, to civilized manners' (Millar 1771: 176). He argued that among all societies in their very early stages savage women tended to be drudges, labourers, slaves and servants. Not until the emergence of commercial society, with its divisions of labour, its surplus productivity and its sociability, were women's talents, both the useful and the agreeable, properly valued. Only then were women, as the friends and companions of men, able to exercise their full potential for rearing and maintaining children, for employments requiring skill and dexterity, and for the exercise of particular delicacy and sensibility. Wealth and luxury nevertheless also brought with it the danger of the corruption of sexual relations. Many came to share Millar's view that improvements in the condition of women – by which they tended to mean women of the upper and middle ranks, able to display both sensibility and sociability – could act as an index of western European progress in wealth and knowledge. The 1770s was to see across Europe a range of philosophical and historical texts, discussed below, which focused upon the tensions between what was natural, what might be identified with earlier periods in society, and indicators of future progress.

IMAGINATIVE RESPONSES TO SENSIBILITY

Such themes were to be widely found also in imaginative literature. By the middle of the eighteenth century novels of sensibility were already widely circulated. In the French novel sensibility signified mainly an aristocratic form of refinement, which united men and women of quality. It was not necessarily a female characteristic; for example, in Françoise de Graffigny's *Letters from a Peruvian Woman* (1747) both women and men equally exemplify the true qualities of virtue and sensibility. In such novels, and in Samuel Richardson's *Pamela* (1740–1), *Clarissa* (1747–8) and *Sir Charles Grandison* (1753–4), the sentimental man or woman of feeling suffers many traumas when confronting older libertine manners. But an author, such as Richardson, faced difficulties in attributing to their hero the differently gendered characteristics of sensibility and manliness.

From the 1760s to the end of the century, the debate about gender is most actively pursued in the novel. The most significant was undoubtedly Jean Jacques Rousseau's *La Nouvelle Héloïse* (1761), whose full title was translated into English as *Julie, or the New Eloise: Letters of Two Lovers, Inhabitants of a Small Town at the Foot of the Alps*. Seventy-two editions appeared in French and ten in English before 1800. In this love story, related through letters, the heroine Julie was a woman of great moral serious-ness with whom her tutor, Saint-Preux, fell passionately in love. Reciprocating his passion, Julie could not take this relationship lightly, even though her parents disapproved and wished her to marry an old friend of her father, Baron Wolmar. After a passionate affair, she became pregnant. Saint-Preux left her, and Julie resolved to marry Wolmar. She became a model wife and mother on a secluded estate, Clarens, in Switzerland, devoted to the care of her sons and living far from the corruptions of the world. Her husband knew of the affair and believed that by bringing Julie and Saint-Preux together in such a setting, it would be ended. When caught in a storm on Lake Geneva with Saint-Preux, Julie, in saving one of her children from drowning, contracted pneumonia and died. On her deathbed she confessed that she had never ceased to love Saint-Preux.

Rousseau owed a considerable debt to the English novelist Samuel Richardson, and he also drew upon his own relationship with Sophie d'Houdetot in the writing of this work. But the novel went beyond literary models and the representation of experience, for it also offered one answer to the problem posed by Rousseau in the *Discourse on the Origins of Inequality*: namely, the need to recover the 'natural' qualities of an earlier age, through rural seclusion and a reliance on the simple and domestic framework of the household, inspired by the virtuous woman at the centre of the novel. In this book there were no evil characters, only internal conflicts between Julie's unceasing passion for her lover and the fulfilment of a woman who as wife and mother exercised an inspiring domestic power. Though Julie's love, both natural and virtuous, inspired the novel's readers and many imitators, and seemed to suggest that sexual passion could provide a guide to conduct, the book's ending suggested a constant struggle for women and no easy resolution of the dilemmas raised. Julie was able to become a powerful source of moral strength, but only through the sacrifice of her sexual instincts.

The attractions of *La Nouvelle Héloïse*, and of imagining emotional experience, were considerable. In Britain in the 1770s and 1780s just over 40 per cent of all novels were published in the form of letters. Many other writers, both men and women, followed Rousseau's lead. The hero of Goethe's *Sorrows of Young Werther* (1774) was passionately in love with a married woman. The Scottish writer Henry Mackenzie, in his *Man of Feeling* (1771) and *Julia de Roubigné* (1777), also drew upon epistolary conventions in the representation of subjective feeling: Julia, though preserving her chastity, was to die at the hands of her upright, though wrongly jealous, husband.

The popularity of novels of sentiment was accompanied across Europe by the many didactic and educational treatises which, building on existing conventions of advice literature, sought not so much to inspire such sexual passions but to regulate and channel the power of sensibility. These treatises, addressed to one or both sexes, marked out profoundly gendered paths for women and men. The most outstanding example was Rousseau's Emile (1762). This can be read as a radical text about the education of the individual, in which the child Emile was guided on the basis of the development of his natural tendencies, enabling him to keep faith with his natural instincts in a complicated social world. Rousseau stressed the importance of breast-feeding and of the infant's learning from sensation, as well as of the rural education of the young child. But overall his plan was destined for the education of the male citizen of the still Utopian republic of his *Social Contract*. The education of Emile's future wife Sophie was to be conducted on very different principles, for Sophie could not expect to aspire to citizenship. Such a young woman should, according to Rousseau, remain in a state closer to that of an earlier age, much less affected by the development of a commercial society or the power of calculating reason. Sophie still had to be trained to control her desires, not through the exercise of reason but through her modesty, for 'under our senseless conditions the life of a good woman is a perpetual struggle against self' (Rousseau 1762b: 332). Sophie's education was to be planned always in relation to that of Emile, restrained so as to preserve her instinctive moral sensibility, enabling her to recover the familial and domestic virtues of an earlier age, to be preserved in a far more complex society. It was a much more restrictive model than that of Julie, the mother-educator.

The Scottish minister James Fordyce used similar language in his *Sermons to Young Women*: 'Your business chiefly is to read Men, in order to make yourselves agreeable and useful. It is not the argumentative but the sentimental talents, which give you that insight and those openings into the human heart, that lead to your principal ends as Women' (Fordyce 1766: 273). The Scottish physician John Gregory wrote in *A Father's Legacy to His Daughters* of women as 'companions and equals', yet, emphasizing the need for 'propriety of conduct', stressed the importance for young women to be modest: 'When a girl ceases to blush, she has lost the most powerful charm of beauty. That extreme sensibility which it indicates, may be a weakness and incumbrance in our sex, as I have too often felt; but in yours it is particularly engaging' (Gregory 1774: 11). Like Rousseau, Gregory wrote of his wish 'to know what Nature has made you, and to perfect you on her plan' (Gregory 1774: 22). The professional men who published such treatises were here adopting a paternalistic perspective on the importance of a regulated sensibility within a marriage which was no longer arranged by patriarchal authority but viewed as domestic partnership.

Women readers of *La Nouvelle Héloïse* identified intensely with its heroine. One, for instance, Mme Alissan de la Tour, undertook a correspondence with Rousseau over fifteen years, with herself playing Julie, and he Saint-Preux (Trouille 1997: 58). Henriette, a single French woman with a desire for education and intellectual activity, undertook a lengthy correspondence with him in her disappointment at the limitations of the education of Sophie (Trouille 1997: 73–93). Women writers across Europe, though drawing on different literary traditions, rapidly took up and challenged the assumptions that underlay the worlds of Julie, Sophie and Emile. Their responses will be illustrated here through three novels.

Sophie von La Roche, the first female German novelist, drew extensively on Richardson and Rousseau in her highly successful *History of Sophia von Sternheim* (1771). Her heroine, Sophia, beautiful, well educated and full of sensibility, was the target of cruel plans of seduction. While her view of the role of women was conservative, she showed herself to be self-reliant and morally confident, committed to educational and benevolent projects, and ultimately, through her marriage to the English Lord Seymour, able to create a household not unlike that of Rousseau's Clarens.

Mme d'Epinay, who had supported Rousseau financially through the writing of Julie, was a *salonnière*, a close friend of many of the leading French *philosophes*, and an accomplished writer. In her autobiographical novel *Histoire de Madame de Montbrillant*, published long after her death, she challenged Rousseau's sexual politics, yet indicated how greatly she was influenced by him. However, her heroine, Emilie de Montbrillant, like Rousseau's Sophie unhappily married, found fulfilment not in motherhood or religion, but through her lovers and her literary and intellectual life.

Finally, in 1790 the English dissenter Helen Maria Williams published *Julia* (1790), which focused on an intense triangle of relationships, between Frederick Seymour, Charlotte, his future wife and Julia's friend and cousin, and Julia herself. Williams clearly wrote in the spirit of Rousseau and of Goethe, though she was also capable of subtly satirizing the genre, as when she wrote of 'the new novel, the Pangs of Sensibility [.] excessively pretty; but the end's very dismal' (Williams 1790: vol. 2, 49). For her, 'in a mind where the principles of religion and integrity are firmly

Figure 16.2 *Sophie von de La Roche*, frontispiece from *Lettres à Nina, ou Conseils à jeune fille pour former son esprit et son Coeur*, vol. 1 (1799–1804) Leipzig: Chez Henri Graff. By permission of the National Library of Australia.

established, sensibility is not merely the ally of weakness, or the slave of guilt, but serves to give a stronger impulse' (Williams 1790: vol. 1, 178). Frederick Seymour's passion for Julia, spoken but never consummated, ended only in his death, with his deathbed request, like that of Rousseau's Julie, for his lover to be buried alongside him. But Julia, refusing offers of marriage, devoted herself to Charlotte and the

Figure 16.3 *Madame Denis-Joseph la Live d'Epinay*, 1726–83, Jean-Etienne Liotard, *c.* 1759. © the Musée d'Art et d'Histoire, Geneva. Photograph: Bettina Jacot-Descombes.

education of her child, to religious and benevolent projects and 'the society of persons of understanding and merit' (Williams 1790: vol. 2, 244). Julia's moral stance was also in tune with future political aspirations for a more harmonious society, expressed through the poem 'The Bastille: A Vision', inserted in the text on the news of the fall of the Bastille in 1789.

The impact of this literature of sentiment was immense, though it could clearly be turned to different purposes. The Enlightenment offered no single blueprint which could characterize the relations of the sexes. The coincidences of names in the many responses to Rousseau's writings indicate the diversity among approaches to gender relations, which might appropriate elements within *Emile* or *La Nouvelle Héloïse*. They assumed readers' familiarity with those works, but also drew upon alternative ways of writing about women and gender relations.

ARGUMENTS FOR EQUALITY

Older ways of thinking about the relative situation of the sexes retained considerable force during the Enlightenment, a legacy of the *querelle des femmes*. The debate about the relative capacities of men and women was one which looked back to the celebratory biographies of Plutarch's *Bravery of Women* and Boccaccio's *Concerning Famous Women* (*c.* 1360), and it gathered strength during the Renaissance. Seventeenth-century rationalism, which emphasized the separation of mind and body, seemed to make the physical differences between the sexes less significant, providing new ground for the assertion of intellectual equality. The French writer Poullain de la Barre did just that in his influential *The Woman as Good as the Man* (1673). In Britain he was followed by Judith Drake's *Essay in Defence of the Female Sex* (1696), by Mary Astell's *Some Reflections upon Marriage* (1700), and by 'Sophia, a Person of Quality', published in *Woman not Inferior to Man* (1739). Translations and adaptations of Poullain's work were still being published in Britain as late as 1751. The Spanish Jesuit writer Fray Benito Feijóo may have drawn upon Poullain and other French texts for his *Defence, or Vindication of the Women* (1726), which set out to counter misogyny and to prove women's intellectual equality. In 1750, Mlle Archambault's *Dissertation sur la question lequel de l'homme ou de la femme est plus capable de constance?* argued against two anonymous male opponents that the superior intellectual qualities of women compensated for their lesser physical strength. The *Défenses du Beau sexe* (1753) of Dom Philippe-Joseph Caffiaux was clearly indebted to Poullain, and also placed learned women within the history of the progress of human knowledge (Steinbrügge 1995:16–18).

Medical and scientific arguments were by no means homogeneous. The English physician James Drake, in his *Anthropologia Nova; or, A New System of Anatomy* (1707), written with his sister Judith, had emphasized the contribution of both sexes to conception and to heredity, challenging any view of female passivity in the reproductive process. Mme du Châtelet, friend of Voltaire and popularizer of Newton, wrote in the preface to her unpublished translation of Mandeville's *Fable of the Bees* that 'all the researches of anatomy have not yet been able to show the least difference [apart from reproductive organs] between Men and Women' (Cohen 1997: 125–9). Some women were acclaimed for their considerable intellectual achievements. In Britain Elizabeth Carter translated the works of Epictetus, and Elizabeth Montagu's *Essay on the Writings and Genius of Shakespear* [*sic*] (1769) defended the playwright against Voltaire's criticisms. In 1732 Laura Bassi was awarded a doctoral degree in philosophy by the University of Bologna, and, inspired by her, in 1754 Dorothea Leporin Erxleben presented a doctoral degree in medicine to the University of Halle (Offen 2000: 38–42). By the middle of the eighteenth century many writers and intellectuals, women and men, were trying to reconcile sexual difference with intellectual and moral equality.

In the years before the French Revolution such claims were strengthened by the arguments voiced in different countries for social and political reform. In late eighteenth-century Britain sensibility was mobilized in the interests of humanitarian reform, targeting the mistreatment of children and animals and promoting the causes of the poor, the sick and the insane. By the 1780s the campaign against the slave trade consciously employed the language of sensibility and was conducted in novels and poetry as well as in more conventional forms of political protest. Admiration for republican virtue, in part stimulated by the American Revolution, encouraged some to reshape their notions of citizenship in ways which were not gender specific and to promote a form of republican motherhood. The historian Catherine Macaulay, in her *History of England* (1763–83), identified with the seventeenth-century Commonwealth tradition and its challenge to absolute authority in the state. Closely associated with reform circles in Britain, she was sympathetic to the cause of the American colonists. The political radical Ann Jebb, married to a Unitarian, Dr John Jebb, came from the milieu of rational dissent and was active in support of the movements for religious toleration and political reform in Britain.

Similarly, in France the *frondeur* press, associated with political opposition and drawing its inspiration from the seventeenth-century wars of the Fronde, allowed both male and female journalists to comment upon social and political issues for a wider audience, sometimes associated with the politics of the French *parlement*, sometimes with the reforming aims of the *philosophes*. Mme de Beaumer, editor of the *Journal des Dames* from 1761 to 1762, was to campaign not only for recognition of women's intellectual abilities, but also for their employment in all spheres, and for the rights of the poor, social justice and religious toleration. Her less radical successor, Mme de Maisonneuve, forged important links with *philosophe* circles, and printed essays that addressed the need for a new and patriotic system of national education (Gelbart 1987: 95–169). In the late 1780s Louise de Kéralio, from an enlightened and liberal aristocratic background, began to publish, simultaneously, her *Histoire d'Elisabeth, reine d'Angleterre* (1786–9) and a twelve-volume anthology of the best works written in French by women (Hesse 2001: 83–91). In portraying the values of English constitutional monarchy, she intervened in a public debate.

Above all, Enlightenment institutions and print culture provided the context within which women might explore their sometimes deprecatory, sometimes assertive, intellectual claims. Elsewhere in this volume the culture of the salons, the academies, the debating clubs is explored, in which some privileged women participated. In the second half of the eighteenth century an increasing number of women shared in a rapidly expanding print culture across Europe.

DEBATING THE CONDITION OF WOMEN, 1770–1800

By the 1770s some of the more ambitious responses to Rousseau's works attempted to draw together conclusions about the nature of women. Antoine-Léonard Thomas's *Essay on the Character, Manners and Genius of Women in Different Ages* (1771) and William Alexander's *History of Women* (1779) both claimed to address the issues raised by previous writers on the intellectual capacities of women. Drawing on the language of sensibility, they investigated sexual difference historically, in the spirit of a general and enlightened investigation. Thomas found that the biological differences between women and men determined their different intellectual capacities: women had greater powers of imagination and receptivity to sense-impressions, but were less capable of abstract thought. In his *Sur Les Femmes* (1772), Denis Diderot went further, criticizing Thomas for failing to recognize the strength of the relationship between women's sexuality and their capacity for feeling and knowledge.

Alexander drew more extensively on Enlightenment histories to explore the theme of progress in the condition of women. Yet he too constantly asserted the differences between men and women, and the complementary nature of their qualities, sometimes in contradictory ways. In savage states, he wrote, the difference between men and women was far less evident than it was in civilized societies. While he was inclined to attribute this to women's lack of education and different style of life, for 'nature in forming the bodies and the minds of both sexes, has been nearly alike liberal to each' (Alexander 1779: vol. 2, 58), he was also critical, in the spirit of the *querelle des femmes* of the pedantry of 'learned ladies'.

Mme d'Epinay wrote critically of Thomas's work: 'he attributes to nature what is so evidently due to education and social institutions' (Bolufer Peruga and Morant Deusa 1998: 183). And in her educational dialogues *Conversations of Emily* (1773), she drew on her relationship with her granddaughter Emilie to construct a series of dialogues directed against the education given to Sophie. She suggested an ambitious plan of studies which recognized the intellectual equality of women and men and offered a balance of academic, moral and physical education, in the hope of equipping her granddaughter with intellectual and moral autonomy. In France in the mid-1770s a new editor of the *Journal des Dames*, Mme de Montanclos, drew upon Rousseau in writing of the responsibilities, pleasures and fulfilment of motherhood, especially where women taught their sons and daughters themselves, at home. At the same time, she also celebrated Laura Bassi's doctorate at the University of Bologna as an example to be followed by others. Her paper linked its defence of the cause of women to her association with more radical political reform in France (Gelbart 1987: 182–206).

Many similar texts followed. One of the best known, rapidly translated across Europe, was to be the work of Mme de Genlis, later tutor to the family of the Duc d'Orléans. In her popular epistolary text, *Adelaide and Theodore* (1781), Mme de Genlis outlined an ambitious and detailed plan of education for the mother–educator and her daughter, in the context of the education of both son and daughter by their devoted parents in rural seclusion. However, she stressed the equal intellectual capacities of the two sexes, and found Rousseau's representation of feminine coquetry and sensibility designed to preserve an intellectual and moral inferiority which she did not endorse. In Spain, Josefa Amar y Borbón, in essays of 1786 and 1790, defended intellectual education for women, although she acknowledged that women had a supportive role as wives and mothers (Kitts 1995: 155–62, 202–5). In Britain Catherine Macaulay, in *Letters on Education* (1790), defended women's rationality against Rousseau. Denouncing prejudice against learned education for women, she countered the language of sensibility in republican terms: 'for my part, I am sanguine enough to expect to turn out of my hands a careless, modest beauty, grave, manly, noble, full of strength and majesty; and carrying about her an aegis sufficiently powerful to defend her against the sharpest arrow that ever was shot from Cupid's bow' (Macaulay [Graham] 1790: 221).

The French Revolution was to transform the debate about reason and passion, sense and sensibility. Conservatives pointed to events in the course of the Revolution, especially after 1792, as signalling the victory of freely expressed passion and sexuality. Those sympathetic to the Revolution tended to stress the significance of the power of reason in structuring and building a new society, though the influence of Rousseau remained very powerful. In France, Manon Roland, while consciously emulating Rousseau's principles, was also deeply involved in her husband's work as Minister of the Interior. She created a political salon, which became a centre for discussion of ideas about the education of women, the legal reform of marriage, and the improvement in women's condition more generally. The Cercle Social, of which she was a member, founded the first club to admit women, the Confédération des Amis de la Vérité (Kates 1990: 165–70). One leading member of this group, the Marquis de Condorcet, argued unflinchingly for the full extension of full civil and political rights to women, as equally rational and moral beings. Another member, Etta Palm d'Aelders, was one of many women who used the brief intellectual and political freedoms of 1789 to 1792 to write and campaign for education, legal reform and 'equality of rights, without discrimination of sex' (Rendall 1985: 49). Olympe de Gouges, in *Les Droits de la femme* (1791), argued that individual rights could incorporate sexual difference.

Mary Wollstonecraft's early works, the *Vindication of the Rights of Men* (1791) and the *Vindication of the Rights of Woman* (1792), were directed against the conservative Edmund Burke, as well as against Rousseau and his followers. In his *Reflections on the Revolution in France* (1790) Burke's portrayal of Marie Antoinette had evoked the appeal of feminine beauty and sensibility in the defence of the *ancien régime* (Burke 1790: 169–70). The *Vindication of the Rights of Woman*, although it attacked other writers, such as Gregory and Fordyce, may be read as an extended dialogue with Rousseau. Wollstonecraft shared many of his opinions, including his republican politics and his preference for the simple, the frugal and the natural, in education and in domestic life, but fundamentally dissented from his inclination to reject the potential for progress through Enlightenment. Women's lives had, for her, been corrupted by their limited education, and by their encouragement in a sensibility which elevated the romantic, the trivial and the emotional at the expense of reason and moral autonomy. Wollstonecraft defended the powers of enlightened national education and of an expanding and developing knowledge to counter that corruption. And she looked forward to 'a revolution in female manners' which would not only affect the lives of women but contribute to the moral transformation of society (Wollstonecraft 1792: 113).

Ambivalences towards sentiment and sensibility were expressed, as Helen Maria Williams had done, through imaginative literature. The radical British novelist Mary Hays depicted a woman's right to express sexual passion in her *Memoirs of Emma Courtney* (1796). Though in an unconvincing preface she described her heroine as one whose errors were 'the offspring of sensibility'(Hays 1796: 4), the interest of this epistolary novel for readers today lies in its exploration of female subjectivity and desire, linked to a radical politics which looked forward to a different social order. Wollstonecraft, too, in her final unfinished novel, *Maria; or the Wrongs of Woman* (1798), was to represent a heroine suffering from a husband's oppression, caught up in a romantic passion for her lover, a lover whose future and character remained problematic.

In Germany the best-known feminist writer was Theodor Gottlieb von Hippel, whose *On Improving the Status of Women* (1792) advocated political and civil equality, access to the professions and improved education for women. A little more cautiously, a little-known female journalist, Marianne Ehrman, wrote in the periodical she edited, *Amaliens Erholungsstunden* (*Amelia's Hours of Relaxation*), of the need for education to develop in women the spirit of rational self-reliance: 'I want to cry when I see our sex eternally being led like a toddler, completely without culture, merely sensual or infected by some nonsense.' Another journalist, Emilie Berlepsch, wrote directly to counter Rousseau, and denounced the view that women should be educated only to please men, in the name of 'the same, inalienable human rights' they shared with men (Dawson 1986:160–6).

By the second half of the 1790s a conservative reaction was apparent, though it took different forms in different national contexts. In France in October 1793 the deputy André Amar used the language of sensibility to recommend to the Convention that women should no longer participate in public affairs: 'women are disposed by their organization to an over-excitation, which would be deadly in public affairs and . . . interests of state would soon be sacrificed to everything which ardor in passions can generate in the way of error and disorder' (Levy, Applewhite and Johnson 1979: 216). The reaction was long lasting. The works of Rousseau and Pierre Roussel continued to influence legislators, intellectuals and medical men in their views of physiological differences between women and men. In the German states Johann Gottlieb Fichte, in *The Science of Rights* (1796), saw political rights for women as antithetical to the bond of marriage and the very concept of femininity. Immanuel Kant's last work, *Anthropology from a Pragmatic Point of View* (1798), similarly maintained the superiority of the male sex, and the importance of the continuing study of feminine attributes by philosophers like himself (Offen 2000: 71–2).

In Britain conservative and liberal writers united in identifying sensibility and subversion, condemning disorderly passions in the family as in the state. This is one context in which Jane Austen's *Sense and Sensibility* (1811), drafted in the late 1790s, with a plot and a message which mirrored those of many obscure novels, may be understood. But the association of the sexually specific attributes linked to sensibility – delicacy, refinement, compassion, weakness – with the physical and, especially, the reproductive differences between women and men remained an increasingly powerful way of conceiving middle-class gender relations and one with an important legacy to nineteenth-century images of femininity. Concepts of sensibility also contributed to changing versions of masculinity, and especially to views of the middle-class husband and father. At the same time, a sensibility associated with pity, humanity and benevolence could still have some scope within the context of a compassionate philanthropy, exercised by women as well as by men.

However, a respect for rationalist arguments and for continued improvement in women's education by no means disappeared. Maria Edgeworth's *Letters for Literary*

Ladies (1795) dismissed the appeal of the romantic and the sentimental, in the chivalric terms employed by Edmund Burke, and suggested, too, that it was time to discard the terms of the old *querelle des femmes*. There was a utilitarian and a progressive case for women to be educated, both for a future as wives and mothers and for their own sake (Edgeworth 1795: 29–30). In Spain Inés Joyes y Blake added to her translation into Spanish of Samuel Johnson's *Rasselas* (1759; trans. 1798) her *Apología de las mujeres*, in which the language of sensibility is notably absent, but in which she suggests women will find most satisfaction in the broadening of their intellectual horizons, their solidarity with other women and men, and in the achievement of emotional and moral autonomy (Bolufer Peruga and Morant Deusa 1998: 206–7). Constance Pipelet, in France, responded to an atmosphere of misogyny in her *Epître aux femmes* (1797):

> To learning and the arts, the door is open,
> Let us dare go inside. For who could steal
> The right to know them when we their power feel?
> They want to deprive us of quill and brush:
> They scorn us with songs, make wisecracks about us.
> O women! Take up your quill and your brush.
>
> (Fraisse 1994: 42–3)

The Enlightenment debate about sensibility had provided an important focus through which approaches to gender relations and, especially, to the situation of women could be conceptualized, in different degrees in different national contexts. The history of that debate was full of contradictions. Sensibility could be oriented towards the domestic and parental worlds of women and of men, and identified as disruptive of such worlds, too closely linked to unregulated sexual desire and luxury. Though sensibility could serve radical ends, most notably in Rousseau's ideal republic, reformers and feminists of all shades remained ambivalent towards it, seeking to qualify its apparent determinism. The conservative response to the French Revolution saw in Britain denunciation of the supposed association between radical politics and the language of sensibility; but equally apparent across Europe was a widespread emphasis on sexual difference and sexually specific attributes. Though apparently identified with women's educational and moral inferiority, the appeal and growth of the sentimental novel was ultimately to reflect their increasing influence as both writers and readers. Enlightenment versions of sensibility have to be read alongside the extension of broader aspirations of the Enlightenment, including its optimism, its emphasis on the power of knowledge, and its exploration of new social roles.

REFERENCES

Alexander, William (1779) *The History of Women from the Earliest Antiquity to the Present Time* . . ., intro. by Jane Rendall (1995 repr. of 1782 edn) Bristol: Thoemmes Press.
[Anon.] (1739) 'Sophia, a Person of Quality', in *Woman not Inferior to Man*, London: J. Hawkins.

Archambault de Laval, Mlle [Madeleine?] (1750) *Dissertation sur la question, lequel de l'homme ou de la femme est plus capable de constance?* Paris: La Veuve Pissot, J. Bullot.

Astell, Mary (1700) *Some Reflections on Marriage*, London: J. Nutt.

Barker-Benfield, G. J. (1992) *The Culture of Sensibility: Sex and Society in Eighteenth-century Britain*, Chicago and London: University of Chicago Press.

Boccaccio, Giovanni (*c.* 1360) *De Claris mulieribus*; ed. and trans. Guido A. Guarino (1963) as *Concerning Famous Women*, New Brunswick: Rutgers University Press.

Bolufer Peruga, Mónica and Morant Deusa, Isabel (1998) 'On Women's Reason, Education and Love: Women and Men of the Enlightenment in Spain and France', *Gender & History*, 10: 183–216.

Burke, Edmund (1757–9) *A Philosophical Enquiry into the Origin of Our Ideas of the Sublime and Beautiful*, ed. James T. Boulton (1958) London: Routledge & Kegan Paul.

Burke, Edmund (1790) *Reflections on the Revolution in France*, ed. Conor Cruise O'Brien (1968) Harmondsworth: Penguin.

Butler, Marilyn (1975) *Jane Austen and the War of Ideas*, Oxford: Oxford University Press.

Caffiaux, Dom Philippe-Joseph (1753) *Défenses du beau sexe, ou Mémoires historiques, philosophiques et critiques pour servir d'apologie aux femmes*, 4 vols in 2, Amsterdam: aux dépens de la Compagnie.

Cohen, Estelle (1997) '"What the Women at all Times Would Laugh at": Redefining Equality and Difference, *circa* 1660–1760', *Osiris*, 12: 121–42.

Dawson, Ruth P. (1986) '"And This Shield is called Self-reliance": Emerging Feminist Consciousness in the Late Eighteenth Century,' in Ruth-Ellen Boetcher and Mary Jo Maynes (eds) *German Women in the Eighteenth and Nineteenth Centuries: A Literary and Social History*, Bloomington: Indiana University Press

Drake, James (1707) *Anthropologia Nova; or, A New System of Anatomy*, London: Sam. Smith and Benj. Walford.

[Drake, Judith] (1696) *Essay in Defence of the Female Sex*, London: A. Roper and E. Wilkinson.

Edgeworth, Maria (1795) *Letters for Literary Ladies*, ed. Claire Connolly (1993) London: J. M. Dent.

Ehrman, Esther (1986) *Mme du Châtelet: Scientist, Philosopher and Feminist of the Enlightenment*, Leamington Spa: Berg.

Ellis, Markman (1996) *The Politics of Sensibility: Race, Gender and Commerce in the Sentimental Novel*, Cambridge: Cambridge University Press.

Feijóo y Montenegro, Fray Benito Jerónimo (1726) *A Defence, or Vindication of the Women*, trans. John Brett (1778) in *Three Essays or Discourses*, London: T. Beckett.

Fordyce, James (1766) *Sermons to Young Women*, 2 vols, London: A. Millar and T. Cadell.

Fraisse, Geneviève (1994) *Reason's Muse: Sexual Difference and the Birth of Democracy*, trans. Jane Marie Todd, Chicago: University of Chicago Press.

Gelbart, Nina Rattner (1987) *Feminine and Opposition Journalism in Old Regime France: Le Journal des Dames*, Berkeley: University of California Press.

Genlis, Mme de (1781) *Adèle et Théodore*, trans. (1783) as *Adelaide and Theodore*, 3 vols, London: C. Bathurst and T. Cadell.

Goethe, Johann Wolfgang von (1774) *Die leiden des jungen Werthers*; ed. and trans. Michael Hulse (1989) as *The Sorrows of Young Werther*, Harmondsworth: Penguin.

Gouges, Olympe de (1791) *Les Droits de la femme*, trans. in Darline Gay Levy, Harriet Branson Applewhite and Mary Durham Johnson (eds) (1979) *op. cit.*

Graffigny, Françoise de (1747) *Lettres d'une Peruvienne*; ed. Joan DeJean and Nancy K. Miller, trans. David Kornaker (1993) as *Letters from a Peruvian Woman*, New York: Modern Language Association of America.

Gregory, John (1774) *A Father's Legacy to his Daughters*; repr. in *The Young Lady's Pocket Library, or Parental Monitor* (1790) ed. Vivien Jones (1995) Bristol: Thoemmes Press.

—— (1788) *A Comparative View of the State and Faculties of Man with Those of the Animal World*, London: J. Dodsley.

Hays, Mary (1796) *Memoirs of Emma Courtney*, ed. Eleanor Ty (1996) Oxford: Oxford University Press.

Hesse, Carla (2001) *The Other Enlightenment: How French Women Became Modern*, Princeton: Princeton University Press.

Hippel, Theodor Gottlieb von (1792) *Über die bürgerliche Verbesserung der Weiber*; ed. and trans. Timothy F. Sellner (1979) as *On Improving the Status of Women*, Detroit: Wayne State University Press.

Hume, David (1739) *A Treatise of Human Nature*, ed. Ernest C. Mossner (1969) Harmondsworth: Penguin.

Jordanova, Ludmilla (1995) 'Sex and Gender', in Christopher Fox, Roy Porter and Robert Wokler (eds) *Inventing Human Science: Eighteenth-century Domains*, Berkeley: University of California Press.

Kates, Gary (1990) '"The Powers of Husband and Wife Must Be Equal and Separate": The Cercle Social and the Rights of Women, 1790–91', in Harriet B. Applewhite and Darline G. Levy (eds) *Women and Politics in the Age of the Democratic Revolution*, Ann Arbor: University of Michigan.

Kitts, Sally-Ann (1995) *The Debate on the Nature, Role and Influence of Women in Eighteenth-century Spain*, Lewiston, NY: Edwin Mellen Press.

La Roche, Sophie von (1771) *Geschichte des Fräuleins von Sternheim*; trans. James Lynn (1991) as *History of Lady Sophia Sternheim*, London: Pickering & Chatto.

Lawrence, Christopher (1979) 'The Nervous System and Society in the Scottish Enlightenment', in Barry Barnes and Steven Shapin (eds) *Natural Order: Historical Studies of Scientific Culture*, Beverly Hills: Sage.

Levy, Darline Gay, Applewhite, Harriet Branson and Johnson, Mary Durham (eds) (1979) *Women in Revolutionary Paris 1789–1795*, Urbana: University of Illinois Press.

Macaulay [Graham] Catherine (1763–83) *History of England from the Reign of James I to the Brunswick Line*, 8 vols, London: J. Nourse and others.

—— (1790) *Letters on Education, with Observations on Religious and Metaphysical Subjects*, London: C. Dilly.

Mackenzie, Henry (1771) *The Man of Feeling*, ed. Brian Vickers (1967) London: Oxford University Press.

—— (1777) *Julia de Roubigné*, ed. Susan Manning (1999) East Linton: Tuckwell Press.

Millar, John (1771) *The Origin of the Distinction of Ranks*; repr. (1779 edn) in W. C. Lehmann (1960) *John Millar of Glasgow, 1735–1801, His Life and Thought, and His Contributions to Sociological Analysis*, Cambridge: Cambridge University Press.

Montagu, Elizabeth (1769) *Essay on the Writings and Genius of Shakespear* [*sic*], London: J. Dodsley.

Montesquieu, Charles Secondat de (1748) *De L'Esprit des lois*; trans. Thomas Nugent (1750) as *The Spirit of the Laws*; repr. (1949) New York: Hafner.

Mullan, John (1988) *Sentiment and Sociability: The Language of Feeling in the Eighteenth Century*, Oxford: Clarendon Press.

Offen, Karen (2000) *European Feminisms, 1700–1950: A Political History*, Stanford: Stanford University Press.

Plutarch, *Mulierum Virtutes*; trans. and ed. Frank Cole Babbitt (1931) as *Bravery of Women*, vol. 3 of *Plutarch's Moralia*, 15 vols, Cambridge, Mass.: Harvard University Press.

Poullain de la Barre, François (1673) *De L'Egalité des deux sexes; The Woman as Good as the Man; or, The Equality of Both Sexes*, trans. A. L. (1677); repr. ed. Gerald M. Maclean (1988) Detroit: Wayne State University Press.

Rendall, Jane (1985) *The Origins of Modern Feminism: Women in Britain, France and the United States, 1780–1860*, Basingstoke: Macmillan.

Richardson, Samuel (1740–1) *Pamela; or, Virtue Rewarded*, ed. Margaret A. Doody (1980) Harmondsworth: Penguin.

—— (1747–8) *Clarissa; or, the History of a Young Lady*, ed. Angus Ross (1985) Harmondsworth: Penguin.

—— (1753–4) *The History of Sir Charles Grandison*, ed. Jocelyn Harris (1972) London: Oxford University Press.

[Roland, Manon] (1820) *The Memoirs of Madame Roland: A Heroine of the French Revolution*, trans. and ed. Evelyn Shucksburgh (1990) Mount Kisco, NY: Moyer Bell.

Rousseau, Jean Jacques (1755) *Discours sur l'origine et les fondements de l'inegalité parmi les hommes*; trans. and intro. by G. D. H. Cole, rev. and augmented J. H. Brumfitt and John C. Hall (1973) as 'A Discourse on the Origins of Inequality', in *The Social Contract and Discourses*, London: J. M. Dent.

—— (1761) *La Nouvelle Héloïse: Julie, or the New Eloise*, trans. and abridg. Judith H. McDowell (1968) University Park: Pennsylvania State University Press.

—— (1762a) *Du Contrat social*; trans. and intro. by G. D. H. Cole, rev. and augmented J. H. Brumfitt and John C. Hall (1973) in *The Social Contract and Discourses*, London: J. M. Dent.

—— (1762b) *Emile, ou de l'éducation*, trans. Barbara Foxley, intro. by P. D. Jimack (1974) London: J. M. Dent.

Pierre Roussel (1775) *Système physique et moral de la femme*, Paris: Vincent.

Smith, Adam (1759) *The Theory of Moral Sentiments*, ed. D. D. Raphael and A. L. Macfie (1976) Oxford: Oxford University Press.

Steinbrügge, Lieselotte (1995) *The Moral Sex: Woman's Nature in the French Enlightenment*, New York: Oxford University Press.

Thomas, Antoine-Léonard (1772) *Essai sur la caractère, les moeurs, et l'esprit des femmes dans les differens siècles*; trans. and enlarged William Russell (1773) as *Essay on the Character, Manners and Genius of Women in Different Ages*, 2 vols, London: G. Robinson.

Trouille, Mary Seidman (1997) *Sexual Politics in the Enlightenment: Women Writers Read Rousseau*, Albany: State University of New York Press.

Van Sant, Ann J. (1993) *Eighteenth-century Sensibility and the Novel: The Senses in Social Context*, Cambridge: Cambridge University Press.

Vila, Anne C. (1998) *Enlightenment and Pathology: Sensibility in the Literature and Medicine of Eighteenth-century France*, Baltimore: Johns Hopkins University Press.

Williams, Helen Maria (1790) *Julia, a Novel*, 2 vols, ed. Peter Garside (1995) London: Routledge/Thoemmes Press.

Wollstonecraft, Mary (1791) *Vindication of the Rights of Men*, in Janet Todd (ed.) (1994) *Mary Wollstonecraft, Political Writings*, Oxford: Oxford University Press.

—— (1792) *Vindication of the Rights of Woman*, in Janet Todd (ed.) (1994) *Mary Wollstonecraft, Political Writings*, Oxford: Oxford University Press.

CHAPTER SEVENTEEN

POLITE WORLDS OF ENLIGHTENMENT

Margaret C. Jacob

At the time when social boundaries were becoming more fluid and economic success opened the door to the traditional circles of the landed gentry, politeness established itself as an ideal for social interactions and as such dictated certain standards of behaviour. It facilitated encounters with relative strangers but also had the gate-keeping role of excluding as unsuitable those who were not willing to adhere to its formalities. Ineffable, yet supposedly known when experienced, politeness meant finding ways to be civil; it cultivated a tolerantly accepting attitude towards strangers and those who held differences in beliefs and values. It also provided an environment for the consumption of luxury goods, particularly of exotic provenance. In Britain the constant appeal to the ideal of politeness also permitted political parties to vie without the imminent danger of civil war and it allowed rank and status to be negotiated, even diminishing its importance. Politeness was practised in forms of courtesy, subtlety of expression, in smoothing commercial transactions, in negotiating debt and in the giving of gifts. While those who lived in the country were expected to extend generous hospitality to visitors, city life consisted of brief 'polite' visits, generally undertaken by coach with small gifts in tow (Whyman 1999; Langford 1996).

Politeness also made enlightened thought and culture happen in live settings, as well as in books and journals. Critically, the habits of politeness allowed relative strangers to listen to one another and hear what they may not have wanted to hear. In a cultural climate in which international relations were becoming increasingly important, the rules of politeness allowed for cosmopolitanism. When mixing in polite society, tolerance had a fashionable ring and obvious bigotry was derided as uncouth boorishness. There is no indication that any one country in Western Europe, or any one city in the American colonies, had a particular set of polite rules. On the contrary, politeness became an almost international code that facilitated the interactions between people from different social, religious and national backgrounds. This was underscored by the marked concern of the Inquisition in Italy, Spain and Avignon in France about the growing habit of easy mixing, particularly between Christians and Jews. Catholic authorities also associated polite sociability with licence and irreligion.

SALONS AND LIBERTINE SOCIETIES

Many of the numerous social gatherings that sprang up from the early seventeenth century had as their main goal the discussion of the most recent advances in science, philosophy and the arts. In France the urgent need for intellectual exchanges was readily combined with the cultivation of social comforts and salons. Attendance of key figures of contemporary culture at regular meetings (once or twice a week) presided over by aristocratic women, such as, to mention the most influential *salonnières* of the High Enlightenment, Marie-Thérèse Geoffrin, Julie de Lespinasse, Marie Du Deffand and Suzanne Necker, built an immensely influential network of intellectuals and thus provided the infrastructure for what came to be known as the republic of letters. The latter represented an affiliation that went beyond national and historical boundaries, where women were primarily the hostesses and attentive listeners of the arguments presented by male philosophers and artists. This informal republic developed as an important parallel to Enlightenment governments, which, on the whole, invited informed comments, if not open criticism (Goodman 1994). Caution about political topics was imperative since its participants included prominent members of the government.

The meetings of the 'republic of letters', irrespective of whether they took place in the salons of influential women or in an exclusively male circle of *philosophes*, harboured a certain subversive grain; but only to the extent that the cultivation of cutting-edge discussions tends to push against political restraints. In this respect they form a marked contrast to the more subversive libertine coteries consisting mainly of wealthy young men. While drinking circles for the display of male bravado date back into the Middle Ages and beyond, an important origin of the increasingly mobile and open-minded society of the eighteenth century can be identified in the libertine groupings of the later seventeenth. In England, a circle of wealthy young men around John Wilmot, Earl of Rochester, was allowed to lead the lives of rakes or libertines without much restraint. In Avignon, however, the only site north of the Alps where the Inquisition ruled, sociable gatherings late into the night with much drinking and eating were watched upon by Inquisition spies; offenders – except where noblemen – were hauled before the Inquisition courts. During the first decade of the eighteenth century times were hard in Avignon and in France more generally. Louis XIV's aggressive wars to the north, and after 1685 the Revocation of the Edict of Nantes, brought renewed persecution of Protestants amid the reappearance of famine in the countryside. By late in the eighteenth century Avignon also became a long-standing centre of Illuminism, mystical Masonry and apocalyptic prophecy (Garrett 1975).

In this atmosphere of war and rumour of war, some men decided to have a good time. A Bacchic society dedicated to the slogan 'Eat, Drink and Be Merry' took root in a town just outside Avignon. The Inquisition sat up and took notice: 'there is a wretched hamlet in the province of Occitan, and a new country-house near the Rhone apart from this city of Avignon where certain bon-vivants and hooligans have created a Bacchic Society, whose laws are particularly outrageous' (Archives départmentales de Vaucluse 1698–1724: fol. 298, 16 April 1704; Duhamel, Imbert and Font-Réaulx 1954: vol. 2, 218–25). This report went on to assert that the society had invented rituals 'for the ridicule and offence of our Most Holy Faith' and that it had become a debauched and dubious 'new army'. They had elected a *magnus Magister*, bailiffs and commanders. Occasionally this impious fraternity congregated within the walls of Avignon, gathering many members of the first families of the city and surrounding countryside, of noble and non-noble birth. A local Inquisitor told Rome that their membership entailed a certificate, and that imbibers threatened 'our rule and our own safety'. What should we do in these turbulent times? the Inquisitor begged to know. Six years later the society was still going strong, with members now drawn from the clergy as well as the laity, and it was still being watched with 'all care and all caution'. One of the few remaining records of the Bacchic society was a polemical poem bemoaning the famine and turbulence that plagued the town. As Church and state well knew, sociable gatherings of this kind could present dangers. When relative strangers got together they had little else to discuss but public events. Refinement and politeness – the late Roy Porter reminded us – 'was no footling obsession with petty punctilio; it was a desperate remedy meant to heal the chronic social conflict and personal traumas stemming from civil and domestic tyranny and topsy-turvy social values' (Porter 2000: 22).

The Bacchic society was merely a very early example of one form of socializing, almost entirely male, that flourished in many places throughout the century. Men formed clubs to drink and 'hang out', generally also to tell naughty stories and to laugh at their own prowess. While being raucous did not preclude the presence of the polite, it often also mocked polite conventions. A traveller in the American colonies at mid-century could have found in Philadelphia the sedate and eminently respectable American Philosophical Society, whose membership had become a great career honour. Elsewhere were clubs of an opposite stamp: the raucous Tuesday Club in Maryland, the Ugly Club of Annapolis (similar to the Whin-Bush Club back in Edinburgh). Entertainment at the Tuesday Club featured comedy and farce, mock trials, and a general desire to extol the glories of bachelorhood (Micklus 1995). The coexistence of politeness and bawdry was by no means incompatible. Indeed, Enlightenment ideas had always embraced the libertine in print, and the art of fictional pornography was born in the century of light. Being naughty in private life corresponded with what anonymous writers now dared to put into print. By the 1790s, such boisterous and phallic entertainments had given way to serious politics, and in the new American Republic, as well as in Britain and France, men clubbed to discuss democracy's virtues and evils. Yet, in British radical circles the scatological persisted, as did the use of drugs, which is illustrated by the note from Humphrey Davy to Tom Wedgwood: 'I have endeavored but without success to procure for you some of the intoxicating Indian Hemp. The only chance that there is of your procuring it in a short time is by means of Dr Beddoes' (Wedgwood MSS: f. 74, 12 February 1803). Lynn Hunt and Margaret Jacob (2001) argue that libertine clubs flourished in British radical circles in part because young men with Dissenting backgrounds did not go to universities but to austere Dissenting academies where emphasis was given to commerce and science. In the context of challenging political standards, they also wanted to get rid of the shackles of their background's constrictive morality and came therefore to equate political struggles with sexual and moral liberation.

UNIVERSITIES AND SCIENTIFIC SOCIETIES

While hardly in the vanguard of the Enlightenment, universities also practised forms of politeness derived largely from medieval traditions. Perhaps the relative social backwardness of universities reinforced their intellectual conservatism, although being controlled by clergymen everywhere in Europe had a great deal to do with their distrust of the Voltaires of their world. Social hierarchy ruled in eighteenth-century universities, and so too did merry-making and drunkenness (Midgley 1996: ch. 1). Leading British universities – then and now – sequestered their students into the colleges, while on the Continent student societies owned houses and generally enjoyed more freedom. Within every academic setting elaborate rules of polite deference reigned supreme. First and foremost, the universities of Europe were supposed to produce clergymen. Politeness, however, dictated that they should be able to do more socially than simply perform the last rites (if Catholic) or preach a good sermon. The polite arts also allowed for a growing exchange of students at the major European universities. At Leiden, where until mid-century physics and medicine were among the most advanced in the world, foreign as well as Dutch students frequented the classrooms. Yet also by that time the Dutch economy had faltered and eminence in medicine passed to Edinburgh, many of whose fine faculty had been trained at Leiden. One of the exceptions to the general conservatism of the universities lay in German-speaking Halle. (The radical potential of Halle's libertarian Lutheranism is discussed by Ian Hunter in Chapter 34 of this volume.)

Far more than the universities, the advanced science of the day in Europe and America nestled in the philosophical societies and academies, both royal and Dissenting. In the Netherlands a national society was slow to be founded in part because of jealousy from Leiden. The Hollandsche Maatschappij der Wetenschappen (Dutch Academy of Science) took shape in the 1750s in Haarlem (where it still survives) and it became a focal point for advanced work, particularly in electricity.

To illustrate the nature of the new sociability, few examples are better than Spalding, a Lincolnshire town of about 500 families from 1712 to 1755. Here, 374 men joined the town's literary and philosophical society. Its head was also a fellow of the Royal Society of London, illustrating the closely networked character of the philosophical and scientific societies throughout the century (Jacob 1997: 164–9). They were interconnected by correspondence, personnel and a shared body of knowledge. At the same time, they could be deeply aristocratic, as was the case in the famed Académie des Sciences in Paris. Or they could be under royal sponsorship, as was the case, of course, in Paris, but also in Berlin and Moscow. The Haarlem and London societies, like the Dissenting academies for the education of young men, were (and are) private affairs kept alive by dues. But all carried prestige and followed rules of decorum that made conversation easier and they were often indebted to court etiquette.

The scientific academies fostered a climate of collaborative debate in which scientific papers tended to elaborate on existing knowledge, rather than tackle vast issues in their entirety. This approach required social interactions, or clubbing together, and although rivalry between experimenters was common and often vicious, a modicum of politeness prevented fragmentation. Protestant Europe proved exceptionally receptive to Newton's science, leading to some of the earliest fraternizing in the new polite and cosmopolitan mode. Spalding and London were obvious examples, but so too was The Hague. There, one of the earliest groups to disseminate Newton's science set up a secret club which was joined by a young Dutchman, Willem 's Gravesande, one of the most prominent Newtonian scientists after Newton's death in 1727. Its ceremony of admission is described in a letter from St Hyacinthe to Marchand (Marchand MSS 2: 2 March 1713). This little society, where members were Protestants and called one another 'brother', also published a journal in French that disseminated Newtonian science far and wide. The minutes reveal it to have been jovial, even risqué. Likewise, an attendant society with many of the same members left a meeting record of its drinking exploits, causing the handwriting to deteriorate almost by the sentence (Jacob 1981). These two societies included a postmaster in Brussels with literary interests, French Huguenot refugees, a German bookseller, the chaplain to an English aristocratic lady resident in The Hague, and journalists who were busy promoting Newtonian science on the Continent. The interests of the members and their friends branched out into publishing more generally and also to the circulation of clandestine literature, much of it hostile to all religion. Some of the characteristics of the group in The Hague have a decidedly Masonic look, hardly surprising given their close connections with English intellectual life, where Freemasonry was widely prevalent.

In Paris the Académie dragged its feet over accepting Newton's science, and all the leading lights followed the Cartesian model. Advancement in its ranks became exceptionally treacherous, as the young Maupertuis discovered. Yet, throughout the century, its members were by far the most distinguished mathematicians and natural philosophers of the age, beginning with Maupertuis, who turned it towards Newton, followed by D'Alembert, and ending with Laplace, Lavoisier, and Chaptal, the chemist. The form of its gatherings shocked English observers. In Paris, members sat eating at a round table and everyone talked at once. In London, the Royal Society's meeting room resembled a modern lecture hall and members were meant to listen and ask questions. Both, of course, represented forms of politeness. The round table was for equals – that is, almost all were aristocrats or at the very least pensioners of the crown. The lecture hall held men of vastly diverse backgrounds, who had to resort to formality in order to come to terms with the fact that their scientific peers were not necessarily their social peers.

In none of these settings were women expected or allowed to be members. On the other hand, they sometimes observed public lectures and even took courses in science that could be given privately in major American or European towns. One exception to the exclusively male societies surfaced late in the century. Formally established by and for women, this society met from 1785 and finally closed its doors in 1887 (Cohen and Cohen-De Meester 1942: 242–6). Situated in the town of Middelburg on the southern Dutch island of Walcheren in the province of Zeeland, the Natuurkundig Genootschap der Dames (the Lady's Society for Natural Knowledge) challenges our stereotypes of both women and the physical sciences during the eighteenth century, and of the intellectual interests open to some women in the early European republics. Composed of women from the most elite members of society, as well as the wives of clergymen, it attracted perhaps two hundred members and met over roughly a hundred years. Members studied the standard textbooks of the era and bought scientific instruments, which they used both at their meetings and in some cases in their own homes. Their group documents vividly show the integration of science into the fabric of domestic life among the highly literate, a process at work throughout the Western world. The science of Newton could comfortably accommodate any form of tolerant Christianity, but some people wanted more than even the philosophical societies, churches and chapels could provide.

FREEMASONRY

Freemasonry originated as a movement to protect guild secrets. Stonemasons, carpenters, bakers, bell-makers and surgeons had all been protected and supervised by guilds for centuries in many European countries. Medieval and early modern guilds provided social life, benefits, wage protection and quality control over skills and finished goods. Frequently the guild masters acted in concert with town and local officials to maintain order and to ensure the stability of prices and wages, as well as the quality of work. But of the many medieval artisanal crafts, only masons' guilds survived the transition into modern market conditions by becoming something other than a club for workers; by becoming Freemasonry.

In 1717 four old London lodges consolidated, forming the Grand Lodge of London, an umbrella organization to which other British and eventually foreign Masonic lodges would give their affiliation. In seventeenth-century urban Scotland and England, where market conditions and a wage economy were far advanced relative to the rest of Europe, lodges of guild masons began to admit non-masons largely because their dues were needed. The guild system had essentially broken down. If buildings were to be built, capital was needed. What began out of necessity transformed the guild into a private, voluntary society; in the process few of the original stonemasons found a place. The new form of Masonry later became known as 'speculative', as opposed to 'operative' Freemasonry.

Besides conviviality, the new type of Masonic lodges held other cultural attractions for merchants and gentlemen. Master masons were literate and known for their mathematical and architectural skills, particularly in respect to fortifications, military and urban building. The myth and lore associated with the lodges tied the geometrical skills of the masters with traditions of ancient wisdom and learning associated with the biblical Solomon or the legendary Egyptian priest Hermes Trismegistus. Educated non-masons may have been attracted to the lodges because of legends about their antiquity and because, in them, the prosperous found useful men skilled in architecture and engineering. For example, one of the earliest non-masons to be admitted into a lodge of stonemasons in the 1650s was Sir Robert Moray, a Scot, a man of science and a military engineer. He became one of the founders of the Royal Society of London after having been a key player in the English Civil Wars. Moray, like the Oxford antiquarian Elias Ashmole (also admitted to a lodge in the same decade), may have believed that Masonry put him closer to a tradition of ancient wisdom out of which mathematics and the mechanical arts had been nourished. Perhaps, too, such men were drawn by the non-sectarian character

Figure 17.1 Summons to a Masonic meeting, *c.* 1750, Globe Lodge, Fleet Street. By permission of the Guildhall Library, Corporation of London.

I. T. Desaguliers *Legum Doctor, Regiæ Societatis Londinensis Socius, Honoratissimo Duci de Chandos à Sacris. Philosophiæ Naturalis Experimentorum ope Illustrator.*

H Hysing pinx   P Pelham fec. 1725   Sold by John Bowles at the Black Horse in Cornhill

Figure 17.2 *John Theophilus Desaguliers*, Peter Pelham after Hans Hysing, 1725.

of Masonry after the fierce religious divisions of the seventeenth century. By the 1690s many gentlemen had been brought into the lodges. Key players like William Stukeley and John Desaguliers tied the Grand Lodge to the Royal Society, and in the case of Stukeley even to the Spalding Gentlemen's Society. Desaguliers also lectured on experimental philosophy throughout Britain and on the Continent.

The exact historical process by which a guild of workers evolved into a voluntary society of gentlemen with tendencies towards scientific enquiry will probably remain forever lost. While there are Scottish records, the English ones have mostly disappeared. The Scottish historian David Stevenson sees Scotland as the home of modern Freemasonry, which amounts to saying that the Scottish lodges first became social clubs for the genteel. But the Freemasonry of the Enlightenment – the fraternity, ideals and constitution exported to Continental Europe by soldiers and Jacobite Scots – encoded not the local system of Scottish customs and clan governance but the institutions and ideals originating in the English Revolution against royal absolutism. A manuscript from the Royal Society of London (Register Book [C] IX) dated 1659 makes the linkage between the Masonic wisdom and national governance nicely: 'This Craft . . . founded by worthy Kings and Princes and many other worshipfull men' prescribes dedication to the seven liberal arts, particularly geometry. Hermes taught it and he was 'the father of Wisemen [who] found out the two pillars of Stone whereon the Sciences were written and taught them forth, and at the making of the Tower of Babylon there was the craft of masonry found'. The manuscript narration about 'Free Masons' Word and Signs' gives away its contemporary milieu – the revolution, the birth of constitutional government bound by laws or rules – and it speaks in passing about 'parliament' and further admonishes its members: 'You shall . . . truly observe the Charges in the Constitution'.

As the *Oxford English Dictionary* shows, the use of the term *constitution* to mean rules or charges adopted by a body has few, if any, precedents prior to the 1650s. In that revolutionary decade after the execution of Charles I, Parliament created or adopted laws for the new republic. Simultaneously, voluntary societies with constitutions, however loosely structured, came into existence. At one point the 1659 document speaks of a French king as having been 'elected'; at another it speaks of a biblical time when 'the King . . . made a great Councell and parliament was called to know how they might find meanes' to provide for the unemployed. The English Masons saw their history as inextricably bound up, not always happily, with the fate of kings and states. At this same time, and for another century or more, in French (except in Masonic lodges) the word *constitutions* had nothing to do with governance.

Of the many forms of new social behaviour that became integral parts of enlightened culture, Freemasonry has been the most difficult to understand. Secretive, ritualistic, devoted to hierarchy, the eighteenth-century lodges also consistently spoke about civic virtue and merit, and about men meeting as equals. Even while many included an occultic element as well, they emphasized the need for brothers to become philosophers, 'enlightened', *éclairé, verlichte, aufgeklärt*, lofty ideals which surfaced early in the transition from masonic guild to the Society of Freemasons.

Enlightened Masonic practices such as elections, majority rule, orations by elected officials, national governance under a grand lodge and constitutions – all predicated on an ideology of equality and merit – owed their origins to the growth of parliamentary power, to the self-confidence of British urban merchants and landed gentry, and, not least, to a literature of republican idealism. John Toland (b. 1670), a republican Whig activist of the early eighteenth century, can be linked directly to the London lodges and through travel to the scientific group that met in The Hague. The Masonic ideology of rising by merit which justified egalitarian fraternizing among men of property free to choose their governors belongs first and foremost to the English republican tradition. This identity did not prevent the lodges from being hierarchical, and everywhere eager for aristocratic patronage. On the Continent the passion for secrecy inspired new degrees and ceremonies, as well as imitations of Freemasonry, particularly in France, Germany, Sweden and Russia. Such were the Illuminati founded by the canon lawyer Adam Weishaupt in Bavaria in 1776. They were an overtly political group, which most Masonic lodges decidedly were not.

In the 1720s London spawned the earliest lodges of literate gentlemen. The evidence before 1717 shows lodges there by the 1690s, and in 1710 the great architect Sir Christopher Wren was elected Grand Master. Sometime between the 1690s and 1723, when the Grand Lodge of London published its soon to be famous and often translated *Constitutions*, the lodges became ever more fashionable. The use of the plural, rather than the singular 'constitution', in the 1723 document designated it as an amalgam of various constitutions used by individual lodges. As early as the first decade of the century, the Grand Lodge of London was being constituted and governed by its brothers, who embraced a document that specified that men need only believe what they take to be true in their heart. The tone of the *Constitutions* is genuinely secular.

One of the earliest French-language documents of Continental origin reveals a libertine and Masonic group that met under their *constitution* in The Hague in 1710. They called one another 'brother' and had a grand master and a secretary. Unsurprisingly, the club was composed of French Huguenot booksellers, journalists, publishers and probably one or two local men of science. The document, dated 1710, exists in the manuscript remains of John Toland housed at the British Library in London. Many of its signatories were associates of the secretary, Prosper Marchand, a French refugee journalist whose manuscripts, now housed at the University Library in Leiden, are an important source of information about early Continental Free-masonry. Toland had travelled extensively on the Continent and had made contact with men in Marchand's circle. A lodge could appeal to the uprooted, the mercantile and the cosmopolitan: it was of ancient origin, democratic in its ethos, associated with the most advanced form of government to be found in Europe, and capable of being moulded to one's tastes while offering charity and assistance to all brothers. In the first Paris lodges, one member was a 'Negro trumpeter' in the King's guard. The group in The Hague used Masonic terms like 'grand master' while basically devoting themselves to eating and drinking. These are 'the invisible men' of the early Enlightenment for whom sociability was beginning to replace the exclusive dedication to family, church or chapel. Among Marchand's closest friends were men like Jean Rousset de Missy, another refugee who became the leader of Amsterdam Freemasonry and a political agent, first for the House of Orange and then for the Austrians. Among his lifelong passions was a hatred of French absolutism, while in religion, he privately described himself as a 'pantheist'.

The 1723 *Constitutions* said that "'tis now thought more expedient only to oblige [the Freemason] to that religion in which all men agree'. In deference to the deep religious divisions in Britain, Freemasonry endorsed a minimalist creed which could be anything from theism to pantheism and atheism. Unsurprisingly, the lodges in England had a high representation of Whigs and scientists, while in Paris Helvétius was a materialist and in Amsterdam Rousset de Missy was a pantheist (as had been Toland). Montesquieu, also a Freemason, was probably some kind of deist. In both London and Amsterdam, Jewish names can be found in the lodge records. In France there were lodges for both Protestants and Catholics. Rarely, though, do lodge ceremonies, even in Catholic countries, contain overtly Christian language.

When the Catholic Church first condemned lodge membership in 1738, it objected that Freemasonry constituted a new form of religion. It also condemned frequent elections as being republican. For some men, Freemasonry did indeed express beliefs that were new and inculcate practices ultimately at odds with traditional religiosity and monarchical absolutism. The Church's condemnation only made the lodges more attractive to the secular-minded and the progressive. It is hardly surprising that by 1750 membership in a Masonic lodge had come to denote enthusiasm for the new, enlightened ideas, although not necessarily for the materialism and atheism associated with some of the *philosophes*.

Throughout the eighteenth century Freemasonry was – and is now – a supposedly secret society. Yet, paradoxically, the lodges flourished distinctively in the eighteenth century among men – and women – who defined themselves as polite and enlightened, hence open to people of different religions or professions. In any lodge people could be found who had no other reason for being present than their interest in ceremony and the ideals taught by the Masonic creed. In Bordeaux during the 1730s a Captain Patrick Dixon from Dublin fraternized with James Bradshaw, a merchant in the town, and they were joined by a local curate. All would have been familiar with the Masonic *Constitutions* that appeared in 1723 in London. The work proclaimed religious toleration, brothers 'meeting upon the level', and rising in Masonic wisdom because of merit, not blood or birth. Dozens of editions were then published in every European language, and strangers who had little in common save their attraction to sociability in its Masonic form sought initiation. They also sought personal improvement, and eagerly practised democratic principles like voting in elections or giving formal orations before their brothers. They learned polite, disciplined social behaviour and they could be fined for breaches in conduct both inside and away from the lodge.

The self-governance of lay elites outside of confraternities or town councils, and operating on a national scale, was rare in Continental Europe during the eighteenth century. As Masonic lodges spread first to the Dutch Republic and France, then as far east as Prague and Moscow, and as far west as Philadelphia and Cap Français (Haiti), secular-minded, affluent men began to govern themselves. Such governance varied in scope and scale: in colonial settings Masons governed themselves as part of their empires, at home as part of their localities, and through the grand lodges as part of their nations. Lodge membership became a symbol of independence from clerical authority and a sign of political maturity. It also became one means of ensuring cultural cohesion among Europeans in their colonies, an expression of imperial status just like the churches and scientific societies in the empire.

Government ministers, state employees, liberal professionals such as lawyers, doctors and teachers, as well as merchants, flocked to join the lodges. In Sweden the entire court, including the King, joined lodges that were fêted at the royal palace. There, as in Britain and the American colonies, the lodges paraded in public, a sign of their acceptance. In Paris and The Hague British ambassadors played a role in spreading the fraternity. We know about the French connection because in the 1720s the police raided the home of the British ambassador, Lord Waldegrave, in part because a lodge was meeting there. In Berlin by 1750 Frederick the Great was using local lodges to enhance his own cult-like following. In Vienna in the 1780s Joseph II's influence permeated the lodges where Mozart sought out their commissions for musical pieces.

Everywhere they spread, Masonic lodges also denoted relative affluence, drinking and merry-making. Despite their conspicuous consumption, they were also places that sought to instil decorum, at least before dinner. Modifying the behaviour of men helped to internalize discipline and manners. In London, lodges would sometimes take over the theatre for a performance, and there is evidence that brothers behaved better than typical audiences. The habits of listening and silence in theatres and concerts developed only slowly, largely by the second half of the eighteenth century, and as part of a general growth of decorum and interiority. The Masonic lodges contributed to the general refinement of manners. The Enlightenment needs to be seen as a complex process of new ideas as well as new habits: public discussion, polite sociability and private, uncensored reading. All required a new, more commonplace sense of politeness, of discipline and decorum.

In every European country Masonic dues were substantial (although graded by ability to pay), and each lodge came to possess a social *persona* and to give loyalty to a national grand lodge. Some lodges spurned anyone but the noble born; others were entirely for students or doctors. Some lodges admitted lowly merchants and even actors; others banned them. Dues varied according to the means of the brothers. The relationship between the lodge and a brother was partly contractual, based upon dues paid, and partly filial. In the 1780s the French Grand Lodge was dispensing charity to brothers, widows and aged female Freemasons. Their letters tell much about being caught between two worlds: one modern and based upon contract, the other essentially feudal and based upon birth and deference. In the same letter, Freemasons could beg and supplicate while noting that in their youth, or time of prosperity, they had paid their dues, fêted their brothers or sisters and been good citizens in their respective lodges. They were owed assistance, they implied, yet they knew that it had to come from the aristocratic leadership of the Grand Lodge.

Lodge membership could begin to resemble citizenship within a state, a presumed right to participate or even to govern. We can see this forward-looking aspect of lodge membership most clearly in the Austrian case. In the Austrian territories after 1750 lodge membership signalled support for enlightened reform against the traditional privileges of the clergy. Men in the secular professions were drawn into such lodges. By the 1780s the Grand Lodge in Vienna was working with the government, in one instance to suppress lodges in the restless western colony of the southern

Netherlands (today Belgium). The Viennese Grand Lodge authorized only three lodges, closed down all others and drew up lists of appropriate members. In July 1786 it proudly informed Joseph II that 'the General Government of masonry is now in conformity with your edicts'. On this occasion a fraternal organization, commonplace in European civil society, assisted the state in remaking the contours of another colonial society under its jurisdiction.

The masonic instinct for governance fuelled identification with national and state institutions. In 1756, when Dutch Freemasons organized their national system of authority and governance, the Grand Lodge of the Netherlands, they adopted 'the form' of the Estates General of the Republic. Furthermore, they recommended it to German lodges that were having difficulty arriving at a comparable system of national cohesion. An Estates General, the Dutch said (Library of the Grand Lodge, The Hague, Kloss MS 190E47), could work as 'the sovereign tribunal of the Nation'. They meant the Masonic nation. Just like the Estates General where each province retained a high degree of sovereignty, Dutch lodges decentralized their governance and permitted independence. In the 1750s the Grand Master in The Hague, the Baron de Boetzelaer, spoke about the Freemasons holding a 'national assembly at The Hague'. At these assemblies the ceremonies placed brothers standing in rows, the first row symbolizing the 'Staten van Holland', the legislative body of the province of Holland. Behind it stood a row of brothers described as representing the National Grand Master. Finally came the officers of the lodge, visitors and all the other brothers. So arranged, they sang and affirmed their symbolic unity. But were they unifying the nation as well as the lodges? Perhaps unconsciously, they were doing both. By the 1750s nationalism was rising throughout Western Europe.

At the same time, Masonic cosmopolitanism meant that in every major city lodges might have regular visitors from anywhere in the Western world and its colonies, they might correspond likewise throughout the world, and yet simultaneously see the nation as a site where virtue and merit should be rewarded. Enlightenment initiated reforming impulses that were felt in many areas, but its assault on privilege and corruption also suggested to secular elites that new men were needed in government service. More than any other new form of sociability, the lodges became schools of government, places where the reformist impulses could be focused on one's immediate surroundings, potentially on one's immediate province or state.

The Masonic gestures imitative of national government can also be seen in the records of French Freemasonry. In 1738 in Paris the Jacobite refugee the Chevalier Ramsay gave what became a famous oration in which he said that Freemasonry was attempting to create 'an entire spiritual nation'. Copies of the oration turned up in Reims, Dijon and The Hague. In the 1760s a piece of French Masonic jewellery, confiscated from its Jewish engraver by the authorities in Brussels, displayed 'the arms of France illuminating the attributes of freemasonry' (AG Brussels MS 1105 A 124). By the 1770s, the unified French lodges were focused on the institutions of central authority. In their proceedings they seldom mention forms of local power or governance, *parlements* or *intendants*. When the French lodges seek to organize nationally, they are left to invent new forms. In 1774 the new Grand Lodge of Paris chose to establish a national assembly. Representatives came to it from all over the country, and each had one vote. All were expected to pay taxes to the Grand Lodge.

In 1779 an orator in Grenoble lamented that 'in our modern institutions where the form of government is such that the majority of subjects must stay in the place assigned them by nature, how is it possible to contribute to the common good?' (BM: Grenoble, MS Q 50). In the 1770s the French Grand Lodge sought to contribute to the common good by having a public presence in Paris, both to be near the government and to allay suspicions. In addition to a national representative assembly, the Grand Lodge set up charity funds for brothers and sisters fallen on hard times. Seeing oneself as capable of constituting the polity and tending to its needs made Freemasons into a new breed of political men – not necessarily disloyal or even republican – but with a new, and potentially dangerous, confidence about self-governance.

The same impulse to govern surfaced in the women's lodges which spread rapidly on the Continent. The first recorded mixed lodges, known as lodges of adoption, met in Bordeaux in 1746 and in The Hague in 1751, but the French women's lodges of the 1770s and 1780s became the most vibrant and visible in Europe (Jacob 1991: ch. 5). In them, women could identify themselves as enlightened, worship the God of Newtonian science, the Grand Architect, invent rituals and give orations. In one women's ritual the principal figure was the Queen of the Amazons. She ran the ceremonies, despite the 1723 *Constitutions*, which had said that women could not even join lodges (officially they still cannot in Great Britain and America). This Queen initiated both men and women, and her female officers had military titles. The catechism of the lodge called on women to recognize the injustice of men and to throw off the masculine yoke, to dominate in marriage and to claim equal wealth with men. In one ceremony the Queen holds the *Constitutions* and queries the 'Grand Patriarch': 'How do men keep women under them?' She then urges her sisters to cast off the bondage imposed by men, to regard those who will not obey women as tyrants. By the 1780s, the lodges in France had become foci for innovation, particularly in the area of gender relations. To imagine that women were open to the Enlightenment only in the privacy of the home, or in a few select salons in Paris, is to miss the vibrancy of French women's Freemasonry.

Freemasonry could make abstract ideals such as reason, equality and self-governance concrete, even if difficult to attain. By 1750, around 50,000 European and American men had joined lodges; by 1785, there were probably well over 1,500 female Freemasons. The colonial numbers are unknown, but the lodges, like the churches, spread with empire. They expressed the highest ideals articulated during the Age of Enlightenment; they could also be places of exclusion, purposefully remote from peasants, workers, in many places women and, in all places, slaves. Yet in their search for equality and merit, for self-governance, free speech and religious toleration, the lodges looked to the future, towards human rights and egalitarian ideals. For that reason alone they would be hated by the enemies of democracy, both in the eighteenth century and even now early in the twenty-first century in some of the newly emerging Eastern European and Russian democracies.

CONCLUSION

Discussion of the history of societies and – more or less – polite circles reveals the extent to which they participated in, and actively promoted, social change. Politeness, of course, goes much farther than the simple cultivation of civilized manners, a process by which Europe, among other things, hoped to triumph in the discomfiting comparison with the natives of some remote parts of the globe, many of whom were only about to be discovered. On the contrary, politeness embraced a vast range of different circles and coteries by which strong-minded individuals sought to expand the narrow boundaries of religious, moral, social and economic matters. First and foremost, they flocked to such meetings in order to find like-minded soulmates, which explains why many secret or closed groupings established elaborate initiation rites and other practices in order to demonstrate their uniqueness.

Politeness, therefore, was a mark of belonging with which an elite that increasingly defined itself on intellectual grounds emphasized the need to be open to new ideas and new people. This context, finally, explains the close convergence between the principles of politeness and the quest for libertarian principles.

REFERENCES

Archives départmentales de Vaucluse (1698–1724) *Livre des conclusions des consulteurs du St-Office d'Avignon, des lettres patentes des inquisiteurs et de lettres de la congrégation de Rome sur les affaires portées devant le tribunal*, MS 1 G 827.

Burke, Janet M. and Jacob, Margaret C. (1996) 'French Freemasonry, Women and Feminist Scholarship', *Journal of Modern History*, 68, 3: 513–49.

Clark, Peter (2000) *British Clubs and Societies 1580–1800: The Origins of an Associational World*, Oxford: Oxford University Press.

Cohen, E. and Cohen-De Meester, W. A. T. (1942) 'Het Natuurkundig Genootschap der Dames te Middelburg (1785–1887)', *Chemisch Weekblad*, 39, 242–6.

Duhamel, L., Imbert, L. and Font-Réaulx, J. de (1954) *Inventaire-Sommaire des Archives départementales . . . de Vaucluse: Série G*, Avignon: Archives de Vaucluse.

Garrett, Clarke (1975) *Respectable Folly: Millenarians and the French Revolution in France and England*, Baltimore: Johns Hopkins University Press.

Goodman, Dena (1994) *The Republic of Letters: A Cultural History of the French Enlightenment*, Ithaca: Cornell University Press.

Hunt, Lynn and Jacob, Margaret (2001) 'The Affective Revolution in 1790s Britain', *Eighteenth Century Studies*, 34: 491–522.

Jacob, Margaret C. (1981) *The Radical Enlightenment: Pantheists, Freemasons and Republicans*, 2nd edn (2003) London: George Allen & Unwin.

—— (1988) *The Cultural Meaning of the Scientific Revolution*, New York: McGraw-Hill.

—— (1991) *Living the Enlightenment: Freemasonry and Politics in Eighteenth Century Europe*, New York: Oxford University Press.

—— (1997) *Scientific Culture and the Making of the Industrial West*, New York: Oxford University Press.

Langford, Paul (1996) 'Polite Manners from Sir Robert Walpole to Sir Robert Peel', *Proceedings of the British Academy*, 94: 103–25.

Marchand MSS, University Library, Leiden.

Micklus, Robert (ed.) (1995) *The Tuesday Club: A Shorter Edition of 'The History of the Ancient and Honorable Tuesday Club' by Dr. Alexander Hamilton*, Baltimore: Johns Hopkins University Press.

Midgley, Graham (1996) *University Life in Eighteenth-century Oxford*, New York: Yale University Press.

Porter, Roy (2000) *The Creation of the Modern World: The Untold Story of the British Enlightenment*, New York: Norton.

Reinalter, Helmut (ed.) (1983) *Freimaurer und Geheimbünde im 18. Jahrhundert im Mitteleuropa*, Frankfurt: Suhrkamp.

Smith, Douglas (1995) 'Freemasonry and the Public in Eighteenth-century Russia', *Eighteenth Century Studies*, 29: 25–44.

Stevenson, David (1988) *The Origins of Freemasonry: Scotland's Century, 1590–1710*, Cambridge: Cambridge University Press.

Van de Sande, Anton and Rosendaal, Joost (eds) (1995) *'Een stille leerschool van deugd en goede zeden': Vrijmetselarij in Nederland in de 18e en 19e eeuw*, Hilversum: Verloren.

Van Horn Melton, James (2001) *The Rise of the Public in Enlightenment Europe*, Cambridge: Cambridge University Press.

Wedgwood MSS at John Rylands Library, Manchester.

Whyman, Susan E. (1999) *Sociability and Power in Late-Stuart England: The Cultural Worlds of the Verneys 1660–1720*, New York: Oxford University Press.

CHAPTER EIGHTEEN

NATURE AND ART IN ENLIGHTENMENT CULTURE

John Sweetman

INTRODUCTION

Two developments run in parallel in Enlightenment culture. One centralizes thinking on human beings and the rational means to their betterment. The other highlights the variety, often emotional, of individual responses. In both respects 'nature' was the great originating presence: on the one hand, the universal fount of being, against which human life was lived; on the other, the dynamic agent which continuously nourished and troubled it. 'Art' was to take positive clues from this underlying ambivalence of nature. Classicists bound to academies looked to nature for ideal order and permanence, exemplified for artists above all by classical figure sculpture. Independent artists, however, were to look for fresh engagement. The classical past would enjoy continued prestige; but the fresh engagement would have special momentum.

The new initiatives are best seen under four headings. First comes the role of landscape: the unconfined statement of the rural, and the garden as a designed link with nature. Second, there is a search for the origins of man's most physically all-encompassing art – architecture – in nature itself. Third, artists absorb discoveries about plants, animals, the earth, humankind and its past. Fourth, the engagement deepens, after 1750, to sustain new impulses in painting. There is English water-colour. The international practice of open-air sketching in oils, established at least by the seventeenth century, grows. Simultaneously, 'sublime' and 'picturesque' landscapes become widely known through improved travel opportunities and paintings made accessible through the recent phenomenon of public exhibitions.

First, it is worth briefly considering those views of nature linked with art which were inherited from the immediate past. Fundamental was the idea of the natural world as the handiwork of God: full of wonders that, in the theocratic belief of the seventeenth century, made it possible to see that world as a designed work of art. Sir Thomas Browne (1643: 294) had concluded that 'all things are artificial, for nature is the art of God'. This notion of artifice as the final product of divine handiwork, and of its man-made counterpart, was to persist, but was to be undermined by a more secular, and more open-ended, view of human creative possibility.

The terms 'nature' and 'art', still connected by the idea of God's design, were famously conjoined in Pope's *Essay on Man* (1733–4: I.289–92):

All Nature is but Art, unknown to thee;
All Chance, Direction, which thou canst not see;
All Discord, Harmony, not understood;
All partial Evil, universal Good.

The paradox of the first couplet, concerning the limits of human vision, physical and mental – at the end of a hundred-year period in which the telescope and the microscope had been dramatically extending them – could hardly be more pointed. And the second couplet's optimism relates to Pope's belief in God's providence ordering all things. The discoveries of Isaac Newton (1642–1727) also promoted belief in God as designer (*Principia Mathematica*, 1687). Although Newton expressed his views in difficult mathematical equations which only a few cognoscenti could understand, there were many popular prose introductions to his ideas for the lay reader. His demonstration that the same law of gravitation controlled the circling planets and the fall of objects on earth meant that the world of everyday experience could never be viewed in precisely the same way again. Outwardly, aspects of that familiar world might seem arbitrary, even disorderly; but underlying them was a clarifying control that Pope's couplets invited readers to seek out and heed. In his poem *The Seasons* (1726–30, expanded 1744), James Thomson (1700–48) also proclaimed such a message to his international readership: for him, the grand design, despite its prodigality, was that of a 'Master-hand' (Thomson 1744: 'Spring', 559).

Enlightenment thinkers, however, building on more sceptical initiatives, embarked on a search for a demystified, universal religion which might underlie all religions, and be uncovered by reason. One man made his own very personal contribution to the quest for a religion to suit the age – Jean Jacques Rousseau (1712–78). Believing in God as creator, but rejecting church dogma, he evolved a religion of nature itself, felt within the individual conscience as agent of moral sanction. Himself a composer, but not directly concerned with the visual arts, Rousseau was nonetheless a perceptive observer of the natural world as presented to the eye. A stern critic of materialist Enlightenment thinking, he was at greater ease with the Enlightenment experience of looking, testing and interpreting, which also, it is important to remember, lay close to the artist's activity. Newton himself, in his *Opticks* (1704), had specifically prepared the ground for first-hand work on aspects of nature as fundamental to the artist as light and colour. Rousseau's 'internal' religion of nature and specific Enlightenment lines of enquiry into nature's workings were now impressively, if improbably, allied.

The process of scrutinizing the world with fresh eyes, with or without the traditional belief in God as designer, was brought nearer to many artists by debate about the classical doctrine that nature should be 'improved' or 'idealized' in the studio, and by support for individual empirical observation of it in its unidealized state. The notion of perfect nature, with imperfections removed by the artist, was still prized by the academies, and with variations of emphasis by different writers, for example by the Abbé Batteux in his doctrine of *la belle nature* (1746). Against experiment was the view that the only true way to improve nature was to follow the lead of classical art. This ideal of antiquity, and the need to study its productions in preference to unimproved nature, were influentially proclaimed by the Enlightenment scholar Johann Joachim Winckelmann (1717–68). At the Enlightenment's height in the 1780s, Joshua Reynolds (1723–92), President of London's Royal Academy, was also a powerful advocate of history painting based on this teaching: only this, he felt, satisfied the overview of society's needs possessed by men of taste. Yet his annual *Discourses* to Academy students show him repeatedly willing to follow a more empirical line, and many of his own liveliest portraits bear this out. Landscape painting, not part of his normal practice, is seen by him (following tradition) as on a lower plane than history: his only model is Claude Lorrain (1604/5?–82), the classicist who painted what Reynolds calls 'general nature' (Reynolds 1769–90: IV, 69–70). But landscape painters, with their lowlier intentions, he concedes, do well to observe particular effects of nature.

The empirical approach to the natural world clearly required receptiveness and lively reaction, not least on the part of artists. It might well be motivated by emotion, which Hume recognized as a major contributor to human response, as well as by reasoned enquiry. Before landscape entered its modern phase as a subject for art, later in the century, the pivotal figure of the 3rd Earl of Shaftesbury (1671–1713) had made widely read observations about it. In his *Characteristics of Men, Manners, Opinions, Times* (1711), he makes clear his sympathy with the classical doctrine of selecting from and 'perfecting' nature. But in the self-revealing 'rhapsody' *The Moralists* (1709) contained in the work, he famously advocates, 'the horrid graces of the Wilderness'; less of selection, more of spontaneous feeling; less of human control imposed on externals, and more of self-giving to a 'sovereignly good' nature (Shaftesbury 1711: 317). Interest in 'aesthetics', central to the Enlightenment, was to find in nature a key catalyst. It is indeed the overlapping of firm advances in the knowledge of nature with this enhanced pursuit of the inspirational mystery within it that gives much of eighteenth-century culture its very particular character.

NATURE AND LANDSCAPE

In 1700 the classical French garden, with its strong architectural containment of walks and rides preserving the formality of the country house, was in fashion in many parts of Europe; but from about 1730 regard for informality developed, above all, in England. The part near the house, with its divisions for flowers, vegetables and herbs, was gradually to merge with the park beyond, which had traditionally been for game; and the stroller would eventually lose sight of the house and inhabit a world apart, overwhelmingly given up to contemplation of the sights of nature.

Besides Shaftesbury, Joseph Addison (1672–1719), in his *Spectator* essays, wrote influentially about wild nature. While both observed formality in their own garden layouts – Shaftesbury at St Giles', Dorset, about 1710 (Leatherbarrow 1984: 332–8), Addison at Bilton, near Rugby, in 1712 – Pope at Twickenham, about 1720, introduced the kind of serpentine path which William Kent (1684–1748), originally trained as a painter, was to use at Chiswick House for Lord Burlington, soon after 1730. Both Twickenham and the ambitious Chiswick garden, close to London, quickly became famous.

Among the 'Pleasures of the Imagination' Addison had counted landscapes which led the mind 'in the wide fields of nature . . . without confinement' (*Spectator*, 25 June 1712). The enclosure policy in agriculture was to criss-cross England with hedges; but the French sunken ditch, to be known in Britain as the *ha-ha*, made invisible the point at which a garden passed into open country. At Britain's great Whig estates, moreover, well away from court, a concept of political liberty was to be contrasted with French monarchic absolutism, conspicuously at Stowe, Buckinghamshire, designed from 1714 onwards for Sir Richard Temple, later Viscount Cobham. Symbolizing this liberty and incorporating Whig heroes, eye-catching buildings, notably by William Kent in the 1730s (Fig. 18.1), were set in long or cross views. 'Capability' Brown (1715–83), working at Stowe in the 1740s, grouped trees alongside sweeping expanses of grass and lake. In *Ichnographia Rustica* (1718), Stephen Switzer had written that the 'natural gardener' should make his design 'submit to Nature' (Switzer 1718: vol. 3, 5). With Brown, landscape took over the garden, unfolding in an inclusive, nature-based design, albeit one which was 'improved' by his deft but downplayed accentuations.

Stowe's landscape, the result of exceptional spending power and political ambition, achieved a European reputation, through its many visitors and through celebratory poems, guide-books (thirty-one editions between 1740 and 1840) and engraved views. Rousseau certainly knew of it, as he also knew Addison's writings on landscape. From about 1743 the poet William Shenstone's celebrated *ferme ornée*, the Leasowes (Worcestershire), was made to evoke more simply the pastoral world of Virgil. In his 'Unconnected Thoughts on Gardening', he used the new term 'landskip, or picturesque gardening' (Shenstone 1764: II, 125–47).

Gardens in the 'natural' manner spread all over Europe. The French, predisposed to the Versailles-type formal garden, sought informality in the fanciful asymmetries of the Chinese, relayed to them by Jesuit missionaries, but G.-L. Le Rouge's great work *Jardins anglo-chinois à la mode* (1776–88) shows that England too was firmly in mind. In Britain the influential architect William Chambers (1723–96) advocated Chinese effects, the line between artifice and naturalness was steadily broken down by the view of art as itself concealed in nature's own trees, rocks and water, a view which Brown's landscapes confirmed. Though architectural considerations no longer controlled the garden experience, classical and also medieval buildings, often ruined as if relapsing into nature, and previously employed as motifs – to poetic effect – in the paintings of Claude Lorrain, became incidents in 'picturesque' planning. The 'English garden' attracted numerous foreign visitors. Thomas Jefferson, future President of the United States, studied it at first hand in the 1780s. Prince Leopold Friedrich Franz of Anhalt-Dessau paid four visits to England between 1763 and 1791, and laid out his park at Wörlitz, near Magdeburg, along English lines from 1764.

The example of composing landscapes as if they were paintings was prominently upheld by Horace Walpole in his *History of the Modern Taste in Gardening* (1780). 'Claude glasses' which 'composed' views in the English Lake District and other

Figure 18.1 William Kent's Temple of British Worthies, Stowe, Bucks, *c.* 1734, seen across the 'Styx'. Photograph courtesy of Barbara Peacock.

indisputably 'natural' landscapes, became normal equipment for tourists in such places; but the planners of 'picturesque' parks (often amateurs rather than professionals) tended to refer to paintings themselves. In Hubert Robert (1733–1808) the French had a contemporary painter and landscape-designer with a taste for daring bridges and waterfalls. At Ermenonville near Paris from the 1760s, the Marquis de Girardin (who probably visited the Leasowes) had vistas in the styles of Robert and the earlier landscape painters Salvator Rosa and Jacob van Ruisdael. Author of *De La Composition des paysages* (1777), Girardin sums up basic considerations: to reject formality; to associate the garden with nature; and to use the language of contemporary *sensibilité* to evoke reverie. Significantly, he wanted a wilderness based on the description of the Utopian estate in Rousseau's best-selling novel *La Nouvelle Héloïse* (1761). On an island at Ermenonville Girardin's friend, Rousseau himself, was buried in 1778 (Fig. 18.2).

Figure 18.2 Hubert Robert, Tomb for Rousseau on the Isle of Poplars, Ermenonville, 1778, from G.-L. Le Rouge (1780) *Jardins anglo-chinois*, 2nd edn.

La Nouvelle Héloïse traced in letters the love between the married heroine Julie and her former tutor Saint-Preux. In its sub-Alpine setting, Julie's garden at Clarens (described in Part IV, letter xi) is 'natural' insofar as the gardener's hand is not visible, but is nevertheless 'ordered' by Julie: this Utopia would not exist without her contribution and that of her husband Wolmar, who manages the estate and devises an economic system for it and its workers. Against this ideal of closeness to nature regulated by degrees of artifice, Julie's lover Saint-Preux's earlier wanderings in the Alps, seeking solace for his problems, pursue striking sensations of (albeit solitary) freedom, with nature as guide: here is a restoring presence which enables him to breathe and to think more calmly, and 'all base and terrestrial feelings to be left behind' (Rousseau 1761: Part I, letter xxiii, 45). Rousseau's own experiences of scenery round Geneva were reactivated here. 'The countryside is my study,' Rousseau remarked after a botanizing walk beside the lake (Cranston 1983: 343). The Swiss peaks and valleys afforded many such experiences: Rousseau's advocacy, and that of the biologist and poet Albrecht von Haller (*Die Alpen*, 1732), were to contribute powerfully to Switzerland's popularity among tourists and artists.

It was fitting that Rousseau's remains (later removed to the Panthéon in Paris) were at first buried on the Isle of Poplars at Ermenonville. While the garden, as the century progressed, had extended to take in distant horizons, for Rousseau in the 1770s an island had become the ultimate escape. In the seventh of the ten walks that make up his last work, *Rêveries du promeneur solitaire* (published 1782), he compared himself to those who 'discover an uninhabited island . . . I saw myself almost as another Columbus' (Rousseau 1782: 100).

Many, besides Rousseau, were to feel the need to forsake growing cities for respite of mind and body in nature. But artifice and associations of the past were not easily thrown off. The popular Zurich-based poet, etcher and publisher Salomon Gessner (1730–88), with whom Rousseau corresponded, recorded his longing for 'the deepest solitude'. But in his art he reinvents the Virgilian pastoral and Arcadian vision. In his illustrations to a French edition of his internationally famous *Idylls* (1772; original edition 1756), the woodland masses of Dutch seventeenth-century prints frame neo-classical figures in floating draperies. An imaginary sylvan monument to Gessner was illustrated in C. C. L. Hirschfeld's *Theorie der Gartenkunst* (1779–85). His neo-classical evocations of Arcadian country life were taken up after 1800 in the panoramic wallpapers of Zuber of Rixheim. More importantly, Gessner promoted an influential view of Switzerland as a country in which a contemporary Arcadia of virtue and simplicity still existed. His *Brief über die Landschaftsmalerei* (1770; English trans. 1776), celebrating Swiss life flourishing under a bright sky, was esteemed by Constable.

If a genuinely ancient Arcadia seemed irrecoverable, a more comfortable present one might be created, as in the French *hameau*, with its vernacular-style cottage or dairy. In 1780 models in advance of actual buildings were erected in the Petit Trianon grounds at Versailles, so that Marie-Antoinette and her architect could judge their effect. The dairy at Hamels, Hertfordshire (1781), by John Soane (1753–1837), had tree-bark on its columns. The *ferme ornée* and rustic cottage were to spread democratically over the Western world, including America in the work and writings of Andrew Jackson Downing (1815–52). In England the landscape designer Humphry Repton (1752–1818), arguing for the cottage and the defined garden, wrote that 'without . . . art . . . nature is a desert and only fitted to the habitation of wild beasts' (Repton 1816: 220).

The fact that picturesque gardens could offer both escape into the primeval solitudes of nature and the consolations of the familiar provided by art gave vernacular tradition special fascination, as the cult of sentiment extended its influence. More uncompromisingly, however, Enlightenment enquiry into nature was investigating how architecture itself might have originated there.

NATURE AND ARCHITECTURE

From about 1710, the style later to be called rococo (after *rocaille*, 'rockwork') had rendered a wide range of natural forms – shells, corals, icicles – as decorative artifice. After about 1750 the style later known as neo-classicism, coming in on a tide of Enlightenment desire to rebuild and re-energize society, was to reject rococo piecemeal frivolity, and even ornament as such, and seek the origins of architecture itself. By eliminating inessentials, looking within nature and salvaging what was of value, the art would be reformed, indeed purified. Alongside intensified archaeological investigation, there would be re-examination of the most respected architectural traditions of all, those of Rome and, as the country became more accessible, Greece.

For centuries, humankind had developed building skills that had given mastery over natural materials and processes of working them, and classical architecture had evolved a grammar of proportionately fixed relationships. The Roman architect Vitruvius, in his ten-volume work on architecture – the only such treatise to come down from antiquity – had traced this development. But he had not illustrated his statement that architecture developed from a forest hut built from trees, with branches forming gables. Fitness and function, abjuring unnecessary ornament, had been stressed recently by writers on architecture (most notably Cordemoy in 1706). Now, a widely read *Essai sur l'architecture* (1753) by Marc-Antoine Laugier (1713–69), a Jesuit priest, called for architects to return to the example of nature, and be as concerned with basic function, allied with simplicity, as the first builders had been. His second edition (1755) vividly illustrated Vitruvius' forest hut, built on living tree-trunks: here was the origin of the column, the 'true support' and for Laugier the most functional form of all architecture. Wooden uprights, horizontals and gable-ends showed how nature informed art. It behoved eighteenth-century architects to translate their own thinking into stone in terms of the *simple* and the *naturel*. Laugier's contemporary, Jacques-Germain Soufflot (1713–80), made the free-standing classical column the main supporting feature of his church of Ste-Geneviève, Paris (begun 1756, later the Panthéon).

Laugier's *Essai* – influential on Soane – also appreciated function in medieval Gothic. Others were already pursuing the beginnings of this most irresistibly dramatic of styles. Here the tree offered itself not only as load-bearing support but as organic life-force. For centuries a visual correspondence had been observed between forest groves and Gothic naves, but only now, as Enlightenment enquiry brought nature under unprecedentedly close scrutiny, would the correspondence be given positive, if somewhat eccentric, recognition. In 1785 (following the speculations of Bishop Warburton on the 'Gothic' verticals of forest trees in his 1753 edition of Pope's *Essay on Man*), Sir James Hall – geologist, antiquarian and later president of the Royal Society of Edinburgh – was stimulated by the sight of a French vine-yard supported on poles to plant stakes topped by willow rods, which he formed into pointed arches (*Essay on the Origin, History and Principles of Gothic Architecture*, 1813). Hall's experiment provoked doubt, even derision, but the idea behind it – that Gothic essentially proclaimed affinities with natural processes of organic growth and transformation – counted for more. Goethe (1749–1832) had already glimpsed such origins in that 'towering, wide-spreading tree of God', Strasbourg Cathedral (Goethe 1772: 5). The association of Gothic with growth and fecundity – with the powers of nature itself – was to become a persistent inspiration in German thought.

Already, however, very different interpreters of nature were at work. If the 'form-perfecting' aims of classicism prevailed in Soufflot, a work of the visionary architect Etienne-Louis Boullée (1728–99) presented nothing less than a model of the earth itself as at first created. The five-hundred-foot-high spherical cenotaph to Newton that he planned (about 1784, never built) conveyed this immense unity, but, inside, perforations in its surface symbolized an infinity of stars set in space to inspire awe in the darkness in each individual visitor. Other drawings show his ideal, monumental forms, often dramatically placed in landscape: he wanted to set his cathedral either on Mount Valérien, near Suresnes, or on Montmartre.

The architect Claude-Nicolas Ledoux (1736–1806) combined a particularly telling range of 'primitive' effects taken from nature in his work at the royal saltworks at Arc-et-Senans, near Besançon: here, in 1775–9, he designed a director's house and a monumental entrance portico. The latter included Doric columns – the simplest of the orders and nearest to nature – together with a grotto embodying rock-forms and decorative elements in the form of urns from which stone-carved salt appears to spill: an unforgettable underlining of the Age of Enlightenment's need to extract salt from nature to preserve food. *'Toutes les formes'*, Ledoux was to write, *'sont dans la nature'* (Honour 1968: 110; see also Ledoux 1804: xi). He was to design an ideal town, Chaux, on the same site, with buildings that included a gun-foundry with pyramid-shaped furnaces, a spherical cemetery and a cylindrical water inspectors'

Figure 18.3 *House of the Inspectors of the River Loue*, Claude-Nicolas Ledoux, Plate 6 from *L'Architecture considérée sous le rapport de l'art, des moeurs et de la législation*, vol. I (1804). By permission of the British Library.

Figure 18.4 *Ponte Salario*, Giovanni Battista Piranesi, from *Vedute di Roma* (*c.* 1757–61). © the British Museum.

house built over a river (Fig. 18.3). In his book *L'Architecture* (1804), Ledoux presented this reconstruction of a complete social unit as he saw it, set in nature and foreshadowing the garden city.

Ledoux's fervour for ritual initiation proclaimed his Freemasonry sympathies, and, although he never saw Rome, his vision of cyclopean scale and subterranean origins was vividly confirmed by Roman engravings of Giovanni Battista Piranesi (1720–78). Piranesi transfixed the century with imaginatively powerful views of Rome's ancient buildings, once regular, now crumbling, looking like extrusions from the earth in which they stood, invaded by vegetation, yet presenting formidable evidence of survival over time and over later additions (Fig. 18.4). Some Piranesi had shown reconstructed, elementally, block by block, from their foundations (Piranesi 1751/1761).

The idea of placing timelessly Platonic geometrical forms in a natural (albeit idealized) setting had occurred to Goethe when he designed his Altar of Good Fortune, composed of a simple sphere on top of a perfect cube, in his Weimar garden in 1777. Nine years later, primed with Piranesi's views of the city, he arrived in Rome. In his famous landscape-shaped portrait by Tischbein (1787), he sits on a broken obelisk, surveying the ruins of the Campagna. A mysterious drawing of his own (Goethe Nationalmuseum, Weimar) comments on the time-oppressed but still resistant grandeur of both the regular and the ruined that was Piranesi's pre-occupation: the pyramid of Caius Cestius outside Rome stands in a sloping landscape, broken by shadow; a dark horizon runs above a ruined aqueduct.

In the architecture of Thomas Jefferson (1743–1826) in America, the besetting severities of reform in Europe were relaxed. The combination of a 'new' landscape, the bare geometry of the modern French, and the example of Rome and Palladio led him to design buildings that were both personal and practical. At his hill-top villa Monticello, Virginia (1771–1809; Fig. 18.5), Jefferson could follow his taste for 'cubic architecture', as he called it; survey the natural order; and consult the fine arts, as a French visitor, the Marquis de Chastellux, put it, 'to know how he should shelter himself from the weather' (Chastellux 1786: 227). Owner of the vast, rock-formed 'Natural Bridge', which artists were to paint, Jefferson followed nature's promptings in his own creative thinking. The design for the domed library (1822–6) of his final work, the University of Virginia, Charlottesville – based on the Pantheon, Rome – placed the primary forms of cylinder and sphere at its heart. Earlier, for Jefferson's Capitol at Washington (1791), his collaborator, the architect Benjamin Latrobe, had provided sleek corn-cob and tobacco plant capitals (1809) that were unmistakably of the New World.

Figure 18.5 Thomas Jefferson's Monticello, Virginia (begun 1771, remodelled 1793–1809). Photograph courtesy of Robert Lautman/Monticello/Thomas Jefferson Foundation Inc.

NEW ENCOUNTERS IN NATURE AND ART

A characteristic image of the Enlightenment is of societies and corresponding networks of learned men, united by science and connecting such centres as Paris, London, Edinburgh, Rotterdam, Geneva, Berlin and St Petersburg. Nature and art were to be complementary aspects of this study. Both were to receive compendious consideration in the Enlightenment. Buffon's *Histoire naturelle* (1748–1804) classified the whole natural order; Diderot's definition of art in the great *Encyclopédie* (1751–72) took in the technical, 'mechanical' arts, as well as painting and sculpture.

In Britain the Lunar Society of the industrializing Midlands included Erasmus Darwin, physician, natural philosopher and prophet of evolutionary theory. Catching the imaginative possibilities of the moment were the paintings of Joseph Wright of Derby (1734–97). His *Orrery* (1766) portrayed a model of Newton's universe; his equally famous *Experiment on a Bird in the Air-pump* (1768) the natural properties of air. Local geology informs his portraits: the lead-smelting businessman Francis Hurt confronts a lump of galena; the Lunar Society member John Whitehurst draws the rock strata of Matlock. In Wright's Derbyshire landscapes the mystery that remains is brought out in woodland and torrent under moonlight. The flame of local furnaces drew him repeatedly to nature's own furnaces, volcanoes: most prominently Vesuvius in eruption (Fig. 18.6), a view of which was bought by Catherine the Great in 1779.

Figure 18.6 *An Eruption of Vesuvius, Seen from Portici*, Joseph Wright of Derby. Photograph courtesy of the Huntington Library, Art Collections and Botanical Gardens, San Marino, California.

As the scope of enquiry grew wider, countless artists were to record the results. William Hodges (1744–97) drew coastal profiles on Cook's second voyage to the South Seas (1772–5). Johann Reinhold Forster, Cook's naturalist, saw his objective as 'nature in its greatest extent; the Earth, the Sea, the Air, the Organic and Animated Creation, and more particularly that class of Beings to which we ourselves belong' (Forster 1778: Preface, 9). The flora and fauna of Australia and the Americas were now in view. Against this exotic backcloth the very relationship of man himself to the animal world was to be revised.

When in the 1770s the eminent artist and anatomist George Stubbs (1724–1806) painted an Indian blackbuck (Fig. 18.7), the physician William Hunter acquired the picture as an exact representation which could help his wider taxonomic study of antelope and their variants. Omitting a background – and, by conventional standards, leaving the work 'unfinished' – Stubbs nonetheless made his animal fill the space with absolute finality. Internationally famous for his analytical treatise *The Anatomy of the Horse* (1766), Stubbs had painted his rearing horse *Whistlejacket* (1762) also without background – and without rider. Equestrian Western man was no longer dominant, or even present. From 1795, Stubbs worked on *The Comparative Anatomical Exposition of Man, the Tiger and the Common Fowl* (part-published 1804–6). Man, no longer looking down on animals from 'the great chain of being', had now taken his place biologically among them.

Figure 18.7 *A Blackbuck, c.* 1770–80, George Stubbs. Photo courtesy of the Hunterian Art Gallery, University of Glasgow.

The suggested descent of 'natural' man from the orang-utan of Malaya, speculated on by Rousseau (*Discourse on the Origins of Inequality*, 1755), became a firm conviction with James Burnet, Lord Monboddo (*Origin and Progress of Language*, 1773–92). It was much disputed, and the Swiss-born artist J. H. Fuseli (*Remarks on the Writings and Conduct of J. J. Rousseau*, 1767) drew Voltaire riding astride savage man (Voltaire's famous put-down of Rousseau). In 1784, however, Goethe's conclusion that the intermaxillary bone was shared by man and ape made the link closer.

Interests in evolutionary theory, interbreeding and organic transformation of species over time had appreciable implications for artists (see Darwin 1794–6; Lamarck 1802 and 1809). Again Goethe is relevant. The great Linnaeus (1707–78) had classified plants according to the idea of fixity of species; Goethe's botanical work, however, led him to believe in a primal transforming principle, based on the leaf, which was responsible for the variety of plant-forms. This he illustrated in drawings. There is a certain parallel here with his sense of drawing itself as a forward-moving activity which was closer to nature than speech: 'I should like to lose the habit of conversation and, like nature, express myself entirely in drawings', he remarked in a letter to J. D. Falk of 14 June 1809 (quoted in Gage 1980: 73). Goethe would interestingly link nature and art again, among the epigrams of his *Zahme Xenien*: 'Anyone who has knowledge of nature [*Wissenschaft*] and art will never lack religion' (Goethe 1820–1: 367; see also Luke 1964: 280). For him, these two were ready to fill the spiritual void left by the loss of conventional religious belief.

By 1809 Goethe was not alone in this conviction. In the community-conscious spirit of the Enlightenment, especially after 1750, natural history specimens and human artefacts long studied in the cabinets of the wealthy were increasingly made publicly accessible in new museums. They were often shown together. The British Museum (1759) was eventually to receive, in 1816, the Elgin Marbles. Since their first showing in 1807, these ancient Athenian sculptures had been turning London into a place of near-religious pilgrimage for the whole artistic community.

Artists would also benefit from another Enlightenment initiative. As natural scientists set about classifying and cataloguing their wealth of new material, accurate colour standards became a pressing need. Colour had traditionally been downgraded below drawing by art academies and often by philosophers. Locke had proclaimed it only a secondary quality of objects. Newton's separation of the seven constituent colours of white light had improved its credentials, but developing scientific study revealed its value in nature: Moses Harris, an entomologist, dedicated his *Natural System of Colours* (*c.* 1774) to Joshua Reynolds. The colour investigations of Goethe, the painter Runge (1777–1810), the French chemist M.-E. Chevreul (1786–1889) and the pigment-maker George Field (1777–1854) all belong to the ensuing years. In his *Farbenlehre* (1810) Goethe discussed his idea of light modified by darkness or opacity between its source and the perceiving eye, and taking a colour. 'The eye sees no form', he said, 'inasmuch as light, shade and colour together constitute that which to our vision distinguishes object from object' (Goethe 1810: xxxviii–xxxix). J. M. W. Turner (1775–1851), who read Eastlake's translation of Goethe's book (1840), disagreed on a number of points; but Goethe's sense of the role of colour in painting in realizing what he called 'a more perfect world' was to be central to Turner's own approach to landscape, and was formidably expressed by him.

THE PAINTERS OF LANDSCAPE

After 1750 landscape painting was advanced in part by the taste for the larger presences of nature that were experienced as the 'Sublime', discussed by Edmund Burke (*Philosophical Inquiry into the Origin of Our Ideas on the Sublime and the Beautiful*, 1757). This had explored much of the 'dark', ungovernable side of the human mind which enjoyed terror if not directly threatened, and called the pleasure 'sublime'. Aesthetic theory was to emphasize the subjective experience, especially in front of nature. The awe-inspiring qualities of mountains were already being re-evaluated in the wake of Rousseau. Earlier still, William Windham, whose pamphlet on his expedition to a glacier near Chamonix appeared in 1744, had found the prospect 'delicious', though Enlightenment factual enquiry was also a consideration: 'I would recommend . . . portable thermometers and a quadrant to take heights with' (Windham 1744: 98–114). All the merit his expedition of 1741 could pretend to, he said, was to have 'opened the way to others'. The Swiss authority on geology, botany and atmospheric pressures, Horace de Saussure, was to climb Mont Blanc in 1787 and write glowingly of his experiences in *Voyages dans les Alpes* (1779–96). Meanwhile, picturesque tours ensured a market for views (Fig. 18.8). The Swiss artist Caspar Wolf (1735–83), climbing back to his subjects to ensure accuracy, produced 170 oils and watercolours of Alpine subjects for the publisher Wagner. Turner's first sight of the Alps was in 1802; they would remain a lifelong passion.

Developing concern with landscape out of doors did not mean that the studio was in any way abandoned. Encounters with nature in the field by amateurs as well as

Figure 18.8 *The Lauteraar Gletscher*, Charles Melchior Descourtis after Caspar Wolf. Colour etching, *c.* 1785.

professionals were now, however, encouraged by more portable equipment. Water-colour pigments, easily carried to the subject, caught momentary effects of light and dried in minutes. In Britain, especially, the tinted drawing of the past evolved into a full-toned statement about mountain and lake, wind and weather. The momentary and the considered came together brilliantly in the studio watercolours of Thomas Girtin (1775–1802).

The spontaneous open-air oil sketch was also ripe for extended use, even among artists whose respect for tradition was still strong. Pierre-Henri de Valenciennes (1750–1819) recommended such sketches to his pupils, even though his studio paintings were classical compositions in the manner of Nicolas Poussin. With John Constable (1776–1837), the open-air oil study was to be built into his total oeuvre and condition what was done in the studio. Nature's greens were to take over from studio-bred browns, and the throb of daylight be expressed in a profusion of dabs charged with white.

Landscape as a subject for painting was now to be valued for the very factor – plenitude of detail against vastness – that had kept it from more than token recognition in the human-figure-orientated painting academies of Europe. The vastness, noted in sketches on the spot by John Robert Cozens (1752–97) on visits to Switzerland and Italy in the 1770s and 1780s, informed his transparent, bluish-grey watercolours with a strength of feeling which gripped Turner long before he saw these countries for himself. The immensities of the sea also attracted Turner, who sensed here human vulnerability and isolation.

If, however, large-scale landscape or seascape, so varying in mood, could isolate the observer, Erasmus Darwin's botanical work showed how the reverse could be the result from studying nature's detail in close-up. Here were affinities with human life: 'how the plant-world climbs up towards me', wrote Goethe on 9 July 1786 (Goethe 1983: 518, Goethe to Charlotte von Stein). Constable responded similarly to trees. The painter Philipp Otto Runge repeatedly used the child-figure as a link with life-supporting nature: in his *Morning* (1808) botanically real lilies (*Amaryllis formosissima*) in his border enclose a mystic vision of a newborn Christ-baby in a meadow. A post-Enlightenment figure who wrote on colour analysis (*Das Farbenkugel* (*The Sphere of Colour*), 1810), Runge withdrew into his own personal imaginative world to use the colours of the sky, sunset and earth symbolically, as his compatriot the poet Novalis used the 'blue flower' as dream-symbol. For Runge, *Landschafterei*, landscape painting, was in effect a vigorous new plant growing on the grave of classical history painting.

CONCLUSION

How much did artists' contacts with nature owe to Enlightenment culture? Enlarged acquaintance with the natural world undoubtedly provided a stimulus for nature calendars and such books as Jefferson's *Notes on the State of Virginia* (1785) and Gilbert White's *Natural History of Selborne* (1789). For Winckelmann, however, it was still art's business to transform nature through the example of idealized classical sculpture. The *Apollo Belvedere* and the *Antinous* were, he said, 'all that nature, mind and art have been able to achieve'(Winckelmann 1755: para 48; Irwin 1971: 67). Though dedicated to new awareness, the Enlightenment could not forget other conceptions of nature's underlying comprehensiveness: as Winckelmann's defining, sculpture-directed, possessive approach showed. Nature was further translated into the austerities of neo-classicism and the elemental architecture of Ledoux in Paris and Schinkel in Berlin. By contrast, painters, with their more mobile medium, were increasingly to discover nature's limitless variety and power to surprise: Alpine glaciers or the wild setting of Staffa's basalt columns.

A nature possessed by the artist, through the filter of the reasoning mind, was by 1800 to be set against a nature possessing him at the moment of raw encounter. The acute Enlightenment figure Reynolds had recognized those moments when immediate responses counted (Reynolds 1769–90: XIII, 230–1). Turner, devoted Royal Academy student, respected Reynolds, but went far beyond the Academy's walls, facing up to external nature revealing itself as coloured light. Even as Visitor to the Life School, he placed the model against a white sheet to make students see with new eyes. Novelty and precedent were sometimes disconcertingly in balance: Turner's erstwhile admirer Thomas Cole (1801–48), painting the American wilderness, wrote in 1835, 'all nature here is new to art' (Tymn 1980: 131), while feeling oppressed by human 'progress' eroding that wilderness, and constrained to reapply Claude's principles of landscape composition in many works.

For the Enlightenment mind, the ideal landscape had been a prospect, a confident overseeing of a benevolently ordered and economically stabilized distance. In the post-Enlightenment world of industrialization, rural deprivation and urban advance, the countryside looked vulnerable. In the wake of such changes, Enlightenment ideas of the community benefits of both nature and art acquired new validity. By 1800, the reading and viewing public had grown immensely. Improved roads and transport and a stream of travel literature had brought areas of natural beauty within easier reach. The beginnings of public museums and exhibitions across Europe and the eastern states of America were doing the same for art. These Enlightenment developments had now to be taken further. Nature and art were to be twin objectives of nineteenth-century proselytizing. In the third edition (1822) of his Lake District guide, Wordsworth described the region as 'a sort of national property, in which every man has a right and interest who has an eye to perceive and a heart to enjoy'. New York's Central Park, opened at mid-century, was to be joined thirty years later by the great Metropolitan Museum of Art at its edge. Nature and art were brought to the doorstep of the ordinary city-dweller.

In Thuringia, Germany, there was Friedrich Froebel's Kindergarten, opened in 1840 and spreading its influence internationally. In a culture which had seen Goethe's vision of *Bildung*, 'self-formation', and Schiller's highlighting of the child-state, the challenge of education, made topical by Rousseau's *Emile* (1762), was a clear one. In his garden, remotely echoing the eighteenth-century seekers after the origins of human architecture, Froebel gave his children spheres and cylinders, which they could recognize as basic shapes in nature, and use as building-blocks in their future lives.

REFERENCES

Browne, Sir Thomas (1643) *Religio Medici and other Works*, ed. L. C. Martin (1964) Oxford: Oxford University Press.

Chastellux, François Jean, Marquis de (1786) *Voyages . . . dans l'Amérique septentrionale dans les années 1780, 1781 & 1782*, Paris; trans. J. Kent (1787) as *Travels in North America in the Years 1780–1781–1782*; facs. edn (1970) New York: A. M. Kelley.

Cranston, Maurice (1983) *Jean Jacques: The Early Life and Work of Jean Jacques Rousseau, 1712–1754*, London: Allen Lane.

Darwin, Erasmus (1794–6), *Zoonomia; or, the Laws of Organic Life*, 2 vols, London: J. Johnson.

Forster, Johann Reinhold (1778) *Observations Made during a Voyage round the World*, London: G. Robinson; ed. Nicholas Thomas, Harriet Guest and Michael Dettelbach with a linguistics appendix by Karl H. Rensch (1996) Honolulu: University of Hawaii Press.

Gage, J. (ed.) (1980) *Goethe on Art*, London: Scolar Press.

Girardin, R. L. de (1777) *De La Composition des paysages*, Geneva and Paris; trans. D. Matthews (1783) as *An Essay on Landscape*, London.

Goethe, Johann Wolfgang (1772) *Von deutscher Baukunst*, in *Essays on Art and Literature*, ed. John Geary, trans. Ellen von Hardroff and Ernst H. von Hardroff (1986) *Princeton: Princeton University Press.*

—— (1810) Zur Farbenlehre; trans. with notes C. L. Eastlake (1840) as *Goethe's Theory of Colours*, London.

—— (1820–1) *Zahme Xenien*, in (1952) *Goethe: Gedichte und Epen*, ed. E. Trunz, I, Hamburg: Christian Wegner.

—— (1964) *Goethe: Selected Verse*, trans. D. Luke, Harmondsworth: Penguin.

—— (1983) *Goethes Leben von Tag zu Tag*, ed. R. Steiger, II, Zurich and Munich: Artemis.

Honour, Hugh (1968) *Neo-classicism*, Harmondsworth: Penguin.

Irwin, D. (1971) *Winckelmann: Writings on Art*, London: Phaidon Press.

Lamarck, Jean Baptiste Pierre Antoine de Monet de (1802) *Recherches sur l'organisation des corps vivant*, Paris: ed. Jean-Marc Drouin (1986) Paris: Fayard.

—— (1809) *Philosophie zoologique*, 2 vols, Paris; repr. (1960) 2 vols in 1, Weinheim/Bergstr: H. R. Engelmann.

Leatherbarrow, D. (1984) 'Character, Geometry and Perspective: The Third Earl of Shaftesbury's Principles of Garden Design', *Journal of Garden History*, IV: 332–8.

Ledoux, Claude Nicolas (1804) *L'Architecture*, ed. D. Ramée (1847); repr. with trans. of Prospectus and introduction by Anthony Vidler (1984) London: Architectural.

Luke, David (ed. and trans.) (1964) *Goethe: Selected Verses*, Harmondsworth: Penguin.

Piranesi, G. B. (1751/61) *Vedute di Roma*, Rome.

Pope, Alexander (1733–4) *Essay on Man*, ed. M. Mack (1950) London: Methuen.

Repton, H. (1816) *Fragments on the Theory and Practice of Landscape Gardening*; repr. (1982) New York and London: Garland.

Reynolds, Joshua (1769–90) *Discourses on Art*, ed. R. Wark (1959; repr. 1997) New Haven, Conn., and London: Yale University Press.

Rousseau, Jean Jacques (1761) *Julie, ou La Nouvelle Héloïse*, ed. Michel Launay (1967) Paris: Garnier Flammarion.

—— (posth. 1782) *Reveries of the Solitary Walker*, ed. and trans. C. E. Butterworth (1992) Indianapolis: Hackett.

Shaftesbury, A. A. C., 3rd Earl (1711) *Characteristics of Men, Manners, Opinions, Times*, ed. L. Klein (1999) Cambridge: Cambridge University Press.

Shenstone, W. (1764) *Works*, II, London.

Switzer, Stephen (1718) *Ichnographia rustica: or, the Nobleman, Gentleman, and Gardener's Recreation*, 3 vols, London.

Thomson, James (1744) *The Seasons*, ed. J. Sambrook (1981) Oxford: Oxford University Press.

Tymn, Marshall B. (ed.) (1980) *Thomas Cole: The Collected Essays and Prose Sketches*, St Paul: John Colet Press.

Wilton-Ely, J, (1978) *The Mind and Art of Giovanni Battista Piranesi*, London: Thames & Hudson.

Winckelmann (1755) *Gedanken über die Nachahmung der Griechischen Werke in der Malerei und Bildhauerkunst*; trans. J. H. Fuseli (1765) as *Reflections on the Painting and Sculpture of the Greeks*, London.

Windham, William (1744) *An Account of the Glacieres or Ice Alps in Savoy* (1744); repr. in G. R. de Beer (1930) *Early Travellers in the Alps*, London: Sidgwick & Jackson.

CHAPTER NINETEEN

MUSIC AND THE ENLIGHTENMENT

———•—•———

Cynthia Verba

INTRODUCTION

Around the middle of the eighteenth century, some of the leading figures
of the French Enlightenment became engaged in what was to be a prolonged
series of writings and exchanges about music, as they sought to grasp the
essential qualities of this highly elusive art form. It was, moreover, a dialogue of
extraordinary breadth. Music was treated as both an art and a science, making it
almost inevitable that the discussions would deal with some of the most fundamental
issues of the French Enlightenment: the nature of artistic expression, the nature of
scientific enquiry, and the respective roles of reason and experience in art and science.
The debates over these issues were fairly sustained ones, pursued with intensity for
over a decade.

In order to do justice to the richness and depth of the dialogue, this chapter does
not attempt a sweeping overview, but instead focuses on salient musical issues that
vividly convey the kinds of challenge that the *philosophes* had set for themselves in
understanding the nature of music. The depth and richness of the dialogue also
explains the choice of France for the present discussion – the French *philosophes* played
a leading role in recognizing the importance of music as Enlightenment thought
took shape. Their far-sightedness also means that their extraordinary contributions
took place well before the great masterpieces of Haydn, Mozart and Beethoven were
written. We might perhaps say that what the French *philosophes* achieved in launching
a new and enlightened way of thinking about music was soon to be rivalled by
the towering accomplishments of the Viennese classical composers in bringing a new
musical style to full fruition. However, it is only in the realm of musical thought
that we can readily identify the clear and direct presence of the values and spirit of
the Age of Enlightenment. It is a story worth telling.

Many of the discussions of the French *philosophes* centred on the views of the
composer–theorist Jean-Philippe Rameau, who was both a participant in and increasingly a subject of controversy. The *philosophes* were reacting to, or were involved in,
three events which occurred in a short space of time. The first was Rameau's break-
through in harmonic theory with his formulation of a single principle that could
explain the structure and behaviour of a multitude of chords and chord progressions
used in eighteenth-century tonal practice. The far-reaching significance of his theory
is that it reduced a vast number of seemingly distinct and separate chords – as

Figure 19.1 *J. Pil. Rameau* [*Jean-Philippe Rameau c.* 1760]. By permission of the National Library of Australia.

typically presented in the accompaniment manuals of the era – into a coherent system that was based on just three fundamental chords, each with its own unique function. The theory illuminated the very qualities of eighteenth-century tonality that in fact made it a coherent 'system'. (Rameau's first treatise, the *Traité de l'harmonie*, appeared in 1722, but with the continued appearance of new treatises and new formulations, his theories were still a lively subject of debate during the 1750s.)

TRAITÉ
DE
L'HARMONIE
Reduite à ſes Principes naturels,

AVEC DES REGLES
de Compoſition & d'Accompagnement;

DIVISE' EN QUATRE LIVRES.

LIVRE PREMIER.
Du rapport des Raiſons & Proportions Harmoniques.

Figure 19.2 Title-page of J.-P. Rameau (1722) *Traité de L'Harmonie*, Paris. By permission of the Australian National University.

The second event which inspired musical dialogue was the prodigious undertaking of the *Encyclopédie*, with Diderot and D'Alembert as editors, and with Rousseau as principal contributor of articles on music, the first volume of which appeared in 1751. Close on its heels was the third event, which was the eruption of the celebrated musical controversy of 1753, the '*Querelle des Bouffons*', over the relative merits of Italian comic opera, or *opera buffa*, and French tragic opera, the *tragédie lyrique*.

Much of the writing which emanated from these events took the form of a dialogue, as the principal participants – Rameau, Rousseau, Diderot and D'Alembert – addressed their remarks to one another, or to others who entered into the discussion. The continuity of the dialogue was further strengthened by the fact that the principal participants played multiple and overlapping roles. In addition to being active as a music theorist, Rameau was the leading composer of French tragic opera. As such, he was one of the principal defenders of the French in the *Querelle des Bouffons*, arguing chiefly against the *philosophes* who favoured the Italians.

Rousseau's prominence in the *Querelle* was assured through his outspoken criticism of French opera in his *Lettre sur la musique française* (1753). He had also composed a highly successful comic opera, *Le Devin du village*, which premiered at the Paris Opéra on 1 March 1753, at the height of the *Querelle*, and incorporated features of Italian comic opera. (Rousseau's knowledge of Italian opera dated back to 1744, when, as secretary to the French ambassador in Venice, he first acquired a taste for Italian music.) In addition – as mentioned above – he was the author of most of the articles on music in the *Encyclopédie*, and they in turn drew heavily on the theoretical writings of Rameau.

D'Alembert contributed to music theory through his presentation of Rameau's theories in a simplified version, the *Elémens de musique théorique et pratique* (1752). He also played a role as co-editor of the *Encyclopédie*, in which he had primary responsibility for articles on mathematics and related subjects.

Diderot was primarily occupied as chief editor of the *Encyclopédie*, but contributed as well to the *Querelle* by introducing reasoned and conciliatory arguments into the otherwise heated exchanges of the pamphlet war. Also not to be overlooked was Diderot's strong interest in music as science. According to contemporary testimony, he played a direct role in the editing of Rameau's treatise, the *Démonstration du principe de l'harmonie* (1750). Diderot's role in the musical dialogue, however, stands some-what apart from the others. He was less directly involved in the immediate exchanges or quarrels – indeed, his harshest attacks against Rameau, as both opera composer and theorist, came mainly after the heated exchanges had subsided, in *Le Neveu de Rameau*, written in 1761. Through much of the debate Diderot was largely attracted to the dialectical process itself. Each time he adopted a position, he was simul-taneously aware of the complexities and inherent tensions in that position, pulling him onward to a new formulation. His views on music consequently underwent almost constant change, with the important result that he carried many ideas further, and achieved a greater level of synthesis among opposing ideas than had been attained before. It is because of this synthesizing role, especially in dealing with music's aesthetic and scientific components, that Diderot holds a special place in the present discussion.

This chapter also focuses on Rousseau, precisely for his unmatched ability to highlight musical oppositions, often articulating conflicting positions in their most extreme or radical forms, which is very much the case in his criticism of French opera. This tendency, although often provocative, helps to expose in sharpest outline the fundamental issues that were at stake in the musical debates of the time. Another perhaps less well-recognized contribution of Rousseau is that, despite his seeming rejection of the French musical tradition, he offers profound insights into that tra-dition. Since many of these insights tend to be overshadowed by his more provocative views, they will receive considerable attention in this chapter.

THE DEBATE BETWEEN ROUSSEAU AND RAMEAU
ON EXPRESSION IN MUSIC

Most of these insights emerged from Rousseau's debate with Rameau over the principal means of expression in music, as part of the *Querelle des Bouffons*. While my chief concern is the nature of Rousseau's musical thought, rather than his taste in music, I would emphasize here that his musical philosophy had everything to do with actual music and his musical sensibilities. As was made eminently clear during the *Querelle*, Rousseau was an ardent admirer of Italian comic opera, and especially the works of Pergolesi (1710–36), which offered a simple and popular form of entertainment, dealing with ordinary people in everyday situations, singing arias with appealing melodies that epitomized the newly emerging *galant* style. French *tragédie lyrique*, in contrast, reflected the dignity and ornate splendour of the *ancien régime*. It carried the audience into an artificial world of enchantment, or an equally unreal human world filled with noble and legendary characters moved by grandiose passions. The musically austere dramatic scenes were set mainly in the slow-moving and stylized manner of French recitative, interspersed with more lyrical passages, called *petits airs*. Some scholars have pointed out that in pre-revolutionary France, as elsewhere, taste was also influenced by politics: French opera was identified with privilege and authority, while Italian comic opera was considered anti-establishment and egalitarian (Wokler 1978, for a thorough study of this issue).

Let us now review the debate between Rousseau and Rameau, starting with the more familiar disagreement over the role of harmony versus melody as the primary source of musical expression, with Rameau arguing for harmonic supremacy, while Rousseau argues for melody. This in turn is related to more fundamental differences in their respective views on what is natural in music. Rameau's first principle, from which all else follows, is that harmony has its source in nature, in the generation of sound, which also determines music's expressive effects and their universality. Rousseau, on the other hand, is more concerned with human nature, and especially with the role of language in musical expression. This leads to the primacy of the vocal line and melody, and also to the significance of national or cultural differences, rather than universal qualities.

In terms of expressive content, Rameau focuses on music with text – namely, opera – positing that music's goal is the expression of feelings as they are conveyed in a poetic text. The principal harmonic means of fulfilling this expressive function is explained in terms of a complex and sophisticated use of harmonic progressions and modulations in a manner that corresponds to the emotional transitions in a text as a dramatic scene unfolds. It is worth noting that Rameau advanced this view of expression not only in his theoretical writings, but in his operas, as well. His text settings, in arias and recitatives, closely follow the detailed nuances of the text, relying primarily on harmony to do so.

In contrast to Rameau's views on expressive content, Rousseau is not concerned with the rational meaning of words or ideas in a text, but with a more direct form of expression conveyed by the intonations of the human voice itself, as it expresses the underlying feelings in a text. In subsequent writings Rousseau develops the idea more fully that true expression is immediate and direct, through a natural language of the passions, and – when translated into music – through melody. The role of reason is excluded from this process; the degree of expressiveness or feeling depends on the degree of closeness between the melodic line and the natural language of the passions.

The distance between Rousseau and Rameau on musical expression – already considerable in the positions presented in the *Lettre sur la musique française* and Rameau's response in his treatise, *Observations sur notre instinct pour la musique* (1754) – grew even wider as Rousseau developed a theoretical foundation for his views in subsequent writings. As we shall see, a salient feature of these subsequent writings was an increasingly radical rejection of the entire French musical tradition – Rousseau's position became the complete antithesis of Rameau's.

Before these further developments are considered, it is useful first to review the traditional views on expression that Rameau and Rousseau inherited and to some extent shared. Only by understanding their shared heritage and points of agreement can one understand more fully how they drew apart so completely.

IDEAS ON MUSICAL EXPRESSION IN THE FRENCH TRADITION: A COMMON HERITAGE FOR ROUSSEAU AND RAMEAU

One of the most important ideas that the two men inherited was the neo-classical doctrine of art as imitation of nature, and especially the nature of the passions. The doctrine stemmed from Aristotle's *Poetics*, which was revived during the Italian Renaissance, became widespread during the seventeenth century, and remained at the centre of criticism well into the eighteenth century. This revival of the Greek *mimesis*, although subject to many different interpretations, placed an emphasis on the representational side of art – that it must say something, have meaning. Literary theory initially dominated all of the arts, borrowing the techniques and goals of the ancient art of rhetoric. Imitation in music referred to music with text, principally opera. In all of the arts, imitating the passions was to be so powerful that it could move the passions or 'affections' of the audience, producing a purifying or cathartic effect (Sadowsky 1960 and Cowart 1980).

In France, the concept of imitating the passions took on a special meaning under the prevailing influence of Cartesian rationalism during the second half of the seventeenth century and continuing well into the eighteenth. Descartes posited a rational mechanical universe, subject to universal laws that could be known solely through innate reason. This view was paralleled in art through an intellectualized or formal portrayal of the passions, relying on characteristic images and figures of speech. Literature, moreover, continued to dominate all the arts.

The inclusion of music as an imitative or representational art form posed special problems for aestheticians, even when music was defined almost exclusively as opera. There was an awareness that it could never attain the precision of speech – although it too borrowed techniques from rhetoric and relied to some extent on the use of characteristic figures to convey the passions or other non-musical images. At the same time, there was a growing recognition that music had expressive powers of its own – perhaps even more powerful than speech.

The most important step in recognizing the expressive powers of music was taken by the Abbé Dubos in his *Réflexions critiques sur la poésie et la peinture* (1719). Under the influence of Hobbes and, especially, Locke, Dubos assigned a primary role to sensibility as the source of expression in art, and a subordinate role to reason, in both the creation of and response to it. The subordinate role played by thought in all human activities provided Dubos with an excuse for not seeking to give a formal theory of the passions. Moreover, language was no longer the model for all the arts; music acquired a new independent status.

The recognition that music had expressive powers of its own was virtually complete by the time Rousseau and other Enlightenment philosophers were writing about music. They might disagree about the means of expression, and about the relationship between sensibility and reason, but they did not disagree that music can be expressive in its own right, that it is an imitative art.

ROUSSEAU'S FORMULATION OF A THEORY OF MELODY

After the *Querelle des Bouffons* Rousseau's theory of the origin of melody and language went through a number of stages and was presented in several different sources, including the *Essai sur l'origine des langues*, which was published posthumously in 1781 (Duchez 1974; Wokler 1974 and 1978). The theory entails a reconstruction of the parallel histories of language and melody. Starting from a hypothetical common origin in a pre-societal state of nature, Rousseau traces their subsequent historical development in order to explain not only their present condition but also their essential nature. The crux of the theory is that language originated purely for the purpose of expressing feelings or passions, rather than physical needs, as people initially assembled in an ideal state of nature. Expression was direct and spontaneous, through an inarticulate but highly inflected form of vocalization – in Rousseau's terms, a voice shaped by 'accent' – further enlivened through the use of rhythmic patterns, resulting in a vocal line that was essentially singing or melody. Music and language were united.

The Heroic Age of Greece epitomized this perfect union, having a language that was both musical and expressive, shaped by the natural intonations and accents of the passionate voice, rather than precise articulations. This expressive ideal reflected in turn a geographic ideal; the gentle Mediterranean climate of Greece, fertile and rich, required a language only for the expression of the passionate feelings of the heart.

During the course of history, a process of degeneration set in, especially after the invasions from the north during the late Roman Empire. They brought with them a harsh language of need, which replaced the poetic language of feeling. Music and language became separated, and reason and logic gradually prevailed.

In music, these developments led to the birth of harmony. Far from being the natural source of melody or expression (as Rameau claimed), harmony was introduced into music as a supplement or form of compensation for the absence of natural feelings, passions or melody. As such, it was a negative product of culture and society, an artificial convention governed by rules and mathematical calculations. Melody lost its former suppleness and accent. It was now shaped by fixed harmonic intervals, rather than the more continuous and accented vocalizations of natural expression.

The completeness of the victory of convention over spontaneous expression varied from culture to culture, depending on the degree of closeness to the conditions of the ideal state. Warm and fertile southern climes (as in Italy) produced a softer and more musical language, still geared to the expression of feelings. Harsh northern climates (as in France) produced a harsher and more guttural language, which was best suited for arguments and philosophy.

Beyond these general points about musical expression, Rousseau's theoretical reconstruction also has significant implications for his views on opera, which he presented in the *Dictionnaire de musique* (written between 1755 and 1767). As it turns out, the *Dictionnaire* contains the only version of Rousseau's theory of melody that appeared during his lifetime – although in abbreviated form – in a lengthy article entitled 'Opéra'. All the elements of the theory are there: an original ideal state, subsequent decline or decay, and then finally a process of compensation – with opera as the main focus, rather than music in general. (Rousseau's theory of the origin of melody – although closely connected with the musical quarrels – was also an integral part of an overall social philosophy that he had started to develop well before his entry into the musical debate with Rameau. The theme, linking civilized society with decline, was already present in 1750, in Rousseau's *Discours sur les sciences et les arts*.) Progressing through all of these stages in the reconstruction of the history of opera, Rousseau reaches the same conclusions as in the earlier *Lettre sur la musique française*: the Italian language is musical and the French is not, which in turn determines the respective states of opera in the two countries. The case is settled with even greater finality, since it now has theoretical support.

It is important to note that the theory of separation of music and language following the decline of the ideal unity of Greek tragedy is true of all countries, including Italy. The opera of Italy, however, had the potential to compensate for this loss – once again, through the musicality of its language. During the course of the eighteenth century, the Italians in fact found a solution through the creation of a form of opera text, or libretto, that led to a balanced combination of recitatives and arias in the musical setting. The fact that under the proper conditions opera can accommodate the demands of both music and text is an important concession by Rousseau. It leaves an opening for the retention of operatic conventions, although they must be properly understood as part of the theory of loss and compensation.

Above all, Rousseau retains the traditional goal of imitation, which he includes in the article 'Opéra', almost side by side with his dark conclusions about the loss of the Greek ideal of unity. His treatment of the subject in fact surpasses most contemporary statements in clarifying music's expressive powers. He observes that these powers derive from music's greater freedom from pure representation, in comparison to the other arts. Musical imitation can be suggestive; it has the ability to create an impression of silence, solitude, sleep or calm – none of which can be conveyed effectively through direct representation, if at all. He adds that these same suggestive or impressionistic capabilities make music ideally suited for the direct expression of feelings, which is the primary goal of art. In this manner, Rousseau adapts the traditional concept of imitation, making it more amenable to the particular expressive capabilities of music, and recognizing expressive powers in music that surpass the other arts. Rousseau, however, goes considerably further in an anti-rationalist direction than any of his predecessors – reason is now seen as antithetical to expression – making an especially strong challenge to the French tradition.

Because of this odd mixture of the traditional and the new, with serious consideration often given to the former, the *Dictionnaire* is filled with thoughtful critiques, as well as clarifications of the practice of his day. A striking example is in the article 'Récitatif', where Rousseau presents some important distinctions between the respective roles of aria and recitative. Starting with the Rousseauian premise that current opera can never recapture the ideal declamation of the Greeks and therefore must compensate through the artificial conventions of recitative and aria, he explains why recitative is needed: 'It is necessary to divide and separate arias from other texted passages, but it is necessary that the latter be given a musical setting as well . . . Recitative is the means' (Rousseau 1768: 400). Interestingly, after defining recitative as 'a declamation in music, in which the musician must imitate, as much as possible, the inflexions of the voice', he proposes that recitative should rely on harmonic key changes or modulations played in the instrumental accompaniment in order to reflect the changing emotions in the text. Evidently, the close relationship between melody and language does not preclude an important role for harmonic accompaniment, when determined by expressive needs and the nature of the genre. Rousseau describes a special kind of recitative accompaniment in which instrumental passages take on a significant expressive function, whose effect is described in the following evocative language in the article 'Récitatif obligé' : 'The actor . . . transported by a passion that does not permit him to say everything, interrupts himself . . . during which time the orchestra speaks for him' (Rousseau 1768: 48). As we shall see, Diderot also uses an evocative language to describe the effect of harmonic modulations improvised at the harpsichord.

In similar fashion, Rousseau's article 'Air' provides a clearer view of how the music in arias can achieve a true imitation of the passions. Once again, melody is assigned a crucial role – controlling the overall design – but harmony is not excluded from the process: 'The arias of our operas are . . . the canvas or foundation on which imitative musical scenes are painted. Melody is the design, harmony is the colour' (Rousseau 1768: 29).

In each of the above examples, it is worth stressing that the strong presence of lingering traditional elements by no means cancels the radical nature of Rousseau's departures from the accepted views of his day or the seriousness of his rupture with Rameau. It simply confirms that there were significant areas of agreement between them, too, and that these must be recognized if one is to have an accurate measure of their disagreements.

The *Dictionnaire* also includes thorough treatment of music in the scientific realm of music theory. In similar fashion to the articles dealing with aesthetic issues, the scientific entries present the accepted harmonic theories of Rousseau's day – still including Rameau – but always against a philosophical background in which harmony is viewed as an artificial construct and a symptom of decay. Despite the notion of decay, Rousseau engages in a search for viable harmonic theory, and offers insightful comments and criteria for what that should be.

Since harmony as used in music is viewed as an artificial construct, Rousseau's chief concern is to recognize the limitations of music theory as science. He sees much of it as pure conjecture, rather than demonstrated truth, and seeks a clearer definition of the boundaries between the two. But even for Rousseau the boundaries prove elusive. His treatment of theory reveals a constant tension between the desire for universal or scientific laws and his belief that they cannot exist. Once again, these examples are important not only for demonstrating this tension, but for the insights that they offer into the strengths and weaknesses of the music theory of his day.

One of the most telling examples is the article 'Harmonie'. In several passages Rousseau pays tribute to Rameau's principle of the resonating string for providing a more scientific basis for harmonic theory. But before Rousseau goes too far in recognizing the scientific validity of Rameau's theory of harmony, he pulls back to his notion of theory as pure conjecture, offering the following, somewhat contradictory observation: 'I must declare, however, that his system, no matter how ingenious it is, is not at all based on Nature . . . that it was only established on some analogies or convergences that can be overturned tomorrow by an inventive man who finds more natural ones' (Rousseau 1768: 236–7).

Rousseau does not wait for its overturn. He himself provides one of the most compelling critiques of the principle, showing its limitations on the following knowledgeable grounds: 'The resonating string does not give rise exclusively to the perfect chord . . . but to an infinity of other sounds, formed by all the partials of the resonating string, which are not at all included in the perfect chord' (Rousseau 1768: 39). He correctly observes that Rameau's harmonic theory entails a selective use of 'Nature' rather than Nature itself – pleasing consonant sounds are not the only products of the resonating string. Taking another tack, he objects to the use of the principle as the basis for harmony by pointing out that usually we do not hear the resonances, only a simple sound.

The tension between what is conjecture and what is fact is even more pronounced in the article 'Consonance', where Rousseau attaches considerable weight to the resonating string as the generator of consonance: 'In regard to the pleasure that consonances give to the ear . . . we can see the source of this pleasure clearly in their generation.' However, once again Rousseau pulls back and indeed reverses direction, by expressing the following reservations:

But, if one presses the question, and if one demands still further what is the source of the pleasure that the perfect chord gives the ear – while the ear is shocked by the combination of all other sounds – what would we be able to answer to that, except to ask in turn why green rather than gray delights our sight, and why the perfume of the rose enchants while the odour of the poppy displeases. It isn't that the physical scientists [*physiciens*] haven't explained all that – and what don't they explain! But that all these explanations are conjectural, and that one finds little solidity upon close examination.

(Rousseau 1768: 115–16)

Despite this scepticism towards rational or scientific explanations in music theory, Rousseau pays considerable tribute in the *Dictionnaire* to eighteenth-century theorists – singling out Tartini as well as Rameau – and gives extensive and thoughtful coverage to their most important ideas. His praise of Tartini is of particular interest, since it makes explicit his criteria of a good theory: 'Even if it [the theory] does not come from Nature, it is at least, of all those published until now, the one which has the simplest principle and in which all the laws of harmony seem to arise the least arbitrarily' (Rousseau 1768: 475). In this comment, Rousseau reflects the widely accepted view of scientific method as a search for underlying principles that could explain a multitude of phenomena. If we must have harmony – he seems to be saying – then we must have harmonic theory. And in that case, the theory should conform to the above principles. It may never be more than conjecture or hypothesis, but if all goes well, the theory will be able to show how everything is linked.

These examples show clearly that Rousseau was far less extreme in his rejection of harmonic theory than his historical reconstruction would imply. Ultimately, there were two contradictory tendencies within Rousseau's musical thought: a radical rejection of the French tradition; and a serious consideration of that tradition, including adaptation to make it more viable. Given the dialogue context in which these opposing tendencies emerged, as well as the insightful nature of his treatment of the more traditional elements, it is worth emphasizing that Rousseau attained these insights by listening carefully to the views of others – even to his strongest opponents in the debates.

Diderot displayed similar attentiveness, but also very different strategies for dealing with some of the same musical oppositions identified by Rousseau. Whereas Rousseau highlights these oppositions, Diderot goes to great lengths, applying highly original and even experimental strategies, to blend them together, achieving synthesis.

DIDEROT AND SYNTHESIS

No work better illustrates Diderot's inventive strategies for dealing with music's contradictory tendencies than the *Leçons de clavecin et principes d'harmonie, par M. Bemetzrieder* (1771) – his most extensive work on music. In this treatise he achieves a synthesis among seemingly opposing concepts by relying heavily on a well-developed strategy of ambiguity – at times, taking the form of playful deceptiveness. The most well-known ambiguity surrounding the *Leçons* is embodied in the title itself. Diderot scholars have long noted that while his choice of title appears to be assigning unequivocal authorship to Bemetzrieder, which is reinforced in the preface as well, Diderot also includes a number of tell-tale signs that he himself has written this work. (The arguments for including the *Leçons* as part of Diderot's oeuvre are summed up by Jean Varloot in his introduction to the critical edition of the *Leçons*, in the *Oeuvres complètes*.) Aside from the title's misleading information about authorship, it is at least informative in telling the reader to expect a work that presents a combined discussion of both music theory and practice or performance.

The format of the *Leçons* greatly facilitates the presentation of these distinct musical components. It is a dramatization of harpsichord lessons, which uses three 'real' characters, each having a particular musical interest and perspective: the Master, named Bemetzrieder, who was an actual theorist and also the harpsichord teacher of Diderot's daughter Angélique; the Student, Angélique, who was an advanced and gifted student; and the Philosopher, Diderot himself, who frequently attended his daughter's lessons. (The use of 'real' characters is one of the tell-tale signs of Diderot's authorship, since it is a device used in a number of his works.) Through the lesson format and the particular cast of characters, Diderot is able to go well beyond simply combining distinct musical subjects within a single work; he actually succeeds in breaking down the dividing lines between them. Much of this is accomplished through Diderot's portrayal of the Master. He is someone who has a strong tendency to add qualifications to his musical observations, to soften his positions almost as he presents them. In this manner, the Master responds to music's oppositions and ambiguities through ambiguities of his own.

By way of illustration, this discussion will focus on an evocative passage in the *Leçons* which deals with the theoretical and the practical performance sides of music, and which vividly represents the dynamics of synthesis or the process of reconciliation of opposing ideas. It is the passage where the Master gives the Student instructions for improvising at the keyboard, dictating a modulating path that, although initially proceeding in straightforward progressions, ends with a quite daring use of unexpected and unusual harmonic juxtapositions. After dictating these fairly technical aspects of the assignment, the Master turns his attention to the aesthetic effect he desires. In order to arouse the Student to play the improvisation with great feeling, which in turn would arouse the listener, the Master suggests an image that these progressions might evoke if the performer were sufficiently 'enthused'. He conjures up a poetic image of a man caught in a labyrinth who is searching for an exit. He turns in various directions, stops, starts, runs, rests, climbs, only to find that he is at the same spot where he started. He laments his destiny, but abandons himself to it (Diderot 1771: 352–4). At first glance, there seems to be little overlap between the Master's two different descriptions of the improvisation assignment – one, as noted, is a set of technical instructions; the other, a moving poetic image. A closer examination of the passage as a whole, however, reveals that the gap between the two versions is somewhat deceptive. Over and above the fact that the Master inserts fragments of poetic imagery and narrative into the technical version (Thomas 1995: 168), he also reserves a space for thought and reflection, which softens or qualifies his emphasis on pure feeling. Note that he does not allow the Student to touch the keyboard until she has obeyed the following instructions: 'Seat yourself at the harpsichord in a thoughtful mood [*en idée*] and try to follow me by ear'. If we ourselves reflect further and consider the intricate nature of the progressions in the Master's assignment, we know that they cannot be done by relying purely on feeling. Musical improvisation may require spontaneity, but it also requires a profound understanding of the available possibilities before the freer and more creative process can begin. In the *Leçons* the Student has had ample preparation and background: this assignment takes place after the twelfth lesson, as a postlude. It is small wonder, then, that the Master himself injects some qualification, a softening of his own position in regard to the role of pure feeling – small wonder that the Master engages in ambiguity.

The tension in this passage between reflection and feeling parallels a greater tension throughout this work between theory and practice. Elsewhere in the *Leçons* the Master reveals more about his pedagogical method, noting that he has strong reservations about introducing explicit theory and an equally strong desire to safeguard the primacy of concrete experience and feeling. Only during an after-dinner walk – to the Etoile – accompanied by father and pupil does the Master offer his theory of harmony. The father makes the following observation: 'My daughter remarked . . . that in the lessons there were many examples and little theory . . . Bemetz . . . answered that the art of music had its own [principles] to which one more or less conformed, without knowing it' (Diderot 1771: 341). It bears stressing that we conform to music's principles without knowing it, since that is the key to closing the gap between theory and practice, as well as the gap between the reflective and the emotional components of the musical experience. And, once again, it illustrates the role of ambiguity, of a softening of lines, in Diderot's attempt to reconcile conflicting ideas or values.

By way of further context, the *Leçons* was written at a stage in the evolution of Diderot's thought when he shows a growing scepticism towards abstraction and an increasing absorption with concrete experience. In music theory this is manifested in a growing antipathy towards Rameau's rationalist approach. Indeed, an important goal of the *Leçons* is to present an alternative theory, one that explicitly rejects Rameau's use of mathematics and rational laws. The alternative that is proposed by the Master is a more results-oriented pedagogical method for teaching students to accompany and improvise preludes on the harpsichord. In its practical emphasis, it seeks to be accessible to people with little or no training, as well as to more advanced students. (A detailed discussion of the alternative theory is presented in Verba 1993: ch. 6, and further background on the evolution of Diderot's musical thought in ch. 5.)

With these pedagogical insights in mind, the Master's two descriptions of the improvisation assignment acquire fuller meaning. For we see why he places such heavy emphasis on feeling, inserting it into the technical description as well, and why he is so cautious and indirect about the role of reflection – although without banishing its role. If there is a place for theory, he seems to say, it is in the service of better practice, and, ultimately, in the service of art.

The labyrinth passage contains one more unexpected view on musical expression that also requires closer examination. The Master appears to be fully assured that the vivid imagery of the labyrinth can be evoked purely through the use of harmonic progressions played feelingly on the harpsichord, without any apparent role for melody or voice, or the presence of a poetic text. While it is unsurprising to find an emphasis on instrumental harmonic progressions in a work devoted to this subject, the apparently exclusive role assigned here to harmony in musical expression is nevertheless considerably at odds with the strong pro-melody position put forward in Diderot's *Le Neveu de Rameau*, a work dating in part from 1761, but also closely intertwined with the writing of the *Leçons*. More precisely, *Le Neveu* shares the Rousseauian view of musical expression as an immediate and direct vocal cry of passion – essentially a melodic cry. (We have already seen that Rousseau makes a similar recognition of the expressive potential of instrumental harmonic accompaniment, similarly at odds with his views on melody.) Elsewhere in the *Leçons* there is an espousal of a pro-melody position, in this case by Angélique, but it is considerably softened in comparison with the view in *Le Neveu*. She warns against over-interpreting the importance of harmony even as she devotes herself to mastering harmonic progressions on the harpsichord: 'Ah . . . what great folly to pretend along with certain authors that harmony inspires melody. It is genius, taste, sentiment, passion, which inspire melody; it is study that makes a good harmonist' (Diderot 1771: 265–6). There is little doubt that Rameau is the 'certain author' who suffers from this folly. In this remark, melody is closely associated with feeling, which apparently makes it superior to harmony, which is associated only with study.

All of these examples show a pattern of reluctance to allow any position on music, and especially on musical expression, to remain fixed, without the insertion of complicating qualifiers or ambiguities. And while most of these qualifiers stem from the contrasting perspectives of the different personages, the Master often adds qualifiers to his own remarks – he is not one to take an overly simple view. This pattern also illustrates how Diderot gains greater freedom to explore opposing ideas without the inhibiting constraint of a potential charge of self-contradiction. For how can there be such a charge when it is impossible to locate Diderot's views in any single place? (This also illustrates the benefits for Diderot of assigning authorship to Bemetzrieder – or at least pretending to do so.) The pattern of ambiguity in the *Leçons* also liberates the reader, calling for a more independent response to opposing ideas. As a cautionary note, it should be emphasized that Diderot's strategy of deliberate ambiguity should not be seen as an early form of deconstruction or postmodernism. Far from challenging the possibility of writing a text that is meaningful and free of contradiction, he goes to great lengths to head off the potential self-contradictions that might arise through the exposure of opposing positions. The usefulness of ambiguity is that it allows a more nuanced view of music, which, by its very nature, has such elusive qualities.

CONCLUSION

The ease with which Diderot travels back and forth between the realms of music as an expressive art form and as a subject for theory and scientific enquiry – facilitating synthesis – sets him apart, as noted, from the other participants in the musical dialogue. Each contributor, in fact, has a distinctive approach to this duality, which helps to define the very nature of their musical thought.

D'Alembert is the most insistent that the boundary line between art and science be strictly observed. Music theory is to be treated with all the scientific rigour that is possible in a physical science. Aesthetic considerations do not lend themselves to this kind of rigour, and fall outside the realm of theory or science.

Rameau, on the other hand, allows music theory to encompass such a wide range of artistic and broadly philosophical issues that there is little that is beyond its scope. (He invokes for those small exceptions such catch-all concepts as 'Genius', or

'Taste'.) The boundary line between music as art and as science for Rameau is virtually taken off the map; music theory – the provable scientific aspect of music – covers the whole.

Rousseau, the diametrical opposite of Rameau in almost all his views, creates an analogous all-encompassing realm, only for him it is music as art that prevails – a language purely for the direct expression of feelings, a product of culture, rather than a natural science. Here, too, the issue of a boundary line loses most of its meaning, not because of a blending of opposing concepts (as in Diderot), but because of a takeover by sensibility and the concept of music as art.

Looking back on this period from the perspective of our own time, we find many of the same boundary issues still with us today. D'Alembert's insistence on sharp dividing lines and Diderot's resistance to them are both especially pertinent. We are now thoroughly engaged in re-evaluating the compartmentalization that dominates so much of our musical thought. It is small wonder, then, that the Enlightenment figures never brought the issue of music's duality to a satisfactory close. The dialogue was destined to continue.

REFERENCES

Cowart, Georgia (1980) 'The Origins of Modern Musical Criticism: French and Italian Music, 1600–1750', Ph.D. dissertation, Rutgers University; (1981) Ann Arbor: University Microfilms International.

D'Alembert, Jean Le Rond (1751) 'Discours preliminaire des editeurs', in D. Diderot and J. D'Alembert (eds) *Encyclopédie, ou dictionnaire raisonné des sciences, des arts et des métiers*, vol. 1, Paris: Briasson, David l'aîné, Le Breton, Durand.

—— (1752) *Elémens de musique théorique et pratique, suivant les principes de M. Rameau*, Paris: David; facs. edn (1966) New York: Broude; 2nd edn (1762) *Revue, corrigée, & considérablement augmentée*, Lyon: Bruyset.

—— (1756) 'Avertissement des Editeurs', in D. Diderot and J. D'Alembert (eds) *Encyclopédie, ou dictionnaire raisonné des sciences, des arts et des métiers*, vol. 6, Paris: Briasson, David l'aîné, Le Breton, Durand.

—— (1759) 'De La Liberté de la musique', in *Mélanges de littérature, d'histoire, et de philosophie*, vol. 4, Amsterdam: Zacharie Chatelain et Fils.

Diderot, Denis (1748) *Mémoires sur différens sujets de mathématiques*, ed. Jean Mayer (1975), in vol. 2 of (1975–) *Denis Diderot: Oeuvres complètes, édition critique et annotée*, 25 vols, directors: Herbert Dieckmann, Jean Fabre and Jacques Proust; secretary-general: Jean Varloot, Paris: Hermann.

—— (1751) *Lettre sur les sourds et muets*, ed. Jacques Chouillet (1978) in vol. 4 of (1975–) *Oeuvres complètes, op. cit.*

—— (1769; rev. 1773) *Le Paradoxe sur le comédien*, ed. Jules Assézat (1875) vol. 8 of (1875–9) *Oeuvres complètes de Diderot*, 10 vols, ed. Jules Assézat and Maurice Tourneux, Paris: Garnier.

—— (1771) *Leçons de clavecin et principes d'harmonie, par M. Bemetzrieder*, ed. Jean Mayer and Jean Citron, introduction by Jean Varloot (1983) in vol. 19 of (1975–) *Oeuvres complètes, op. cit.*

Duchez, Marie-Elisabeth (1974) '"Principe de la melodie"' et "Origine des langues": un brouillon inédit de Jean-Jacques Rousseau sur l'origine de la melodie', *Revue de musicologie*, 60: 33–86.

Rameau, Jean-Philippe (1722) *Traité de l'harmonie*, Paris: Ballard; facs. edn, ed. R. Erwin Jacobi (1967) vol. 1 of (1967–72) *Jean-Philippe Rameau: Complete Theoretical Writings*, 6 vols, Rome: American Institute of Musicology.

—— (1754) *Observations sur notre instinct pour la musique*, Paris: Prault Fils, Lambert and Duchesne; facs. edn (1968) vol. 3 of (1967–72) *Complete Theoretical Writings, op. cit.*

—— (1755) *Erreurs sur la musique dans l'Encyclopédie*, Paris: Chez Sebastien Jorry; facs. edn (1969) vol. 5 of (1967–72) *Complete Theoretical Writings, op. cit.*

Rousseau, Jean Jacques (1753) *Lettre sur la musique française*, Paris; facs. edn in Denise Launay (ed.) (1973) *La Querelle des Bouffons: texte des pamphlets avec introduction, commentaires et index*, vol. 1, Geneva: Minkoff.

—— (1768) *Dictionnaire de musique*, Paris: Duchesne; facs. edn (1969) Hildesheim: Olms; repr. (1969) New York: Johnson Reprint Corp.

Sadowsky, Rosalie (1960) 'Jean-Baptiste Abbe Dubos: The Influence of Cartesian and Neo-Aristotelian Ideas on Music Theory and Practice', Ph.D. dissertation, Yale University.

Thomas, Downing A. (1995) *Music and the Origins of Language: Theories from the French Enlightenment*, Cambridge: Cambridge University Press.

Verba, Cynthia (1973) 'The Development of Rameau's Thoughts on Modulation and Chromatics', *Journal of the American Musicological Society*, 26/1: 72–91.

—— (1993) *Music and the French Enlightenment*, Oxford: Clarendon Press.

Wokler, Robert (1974) 'Rameau, Rousseau, and the *Essai sur l'origine des langues*', *Studies on Voltaire and the Eighteenth Century*, 117: 179–238.

—— (1978) 'Rousseau on Rameau and Revolution', *Studies in the Eighteenth Century*, 4: 251–83.

CHAPTER TWENTY

ITALIAN OPERAS AND THEIR AUDIENCES

Peter Jones

For at least fifty years, between 1730 and 1780, the dominant musical form throughout Europe was opera. Of course, at that time, few public concert halls had been built, nor had music been composed for performance in them. Possibly 10,000 operas were composed in that period. Dr Charles Burney (1726–1814), during his travels to Italy in 1771, remarked that the greatest living composers in Italy were: Hasse (1699–1783), Jommelli (1714–74), Galuppi (1706–85), Piccinni (1728–1800) and Sacchini (1730–86). Add the names of Anfossi (1727–97), Porpora (1686–1768), Bertoni (1725–1813) and Paisiello (1740–1816), and we have a mere nine composers who wrote more than 500 operas between them. Haydn (1732–1809) directed eighty operas by Anfossi at Esterhazy. Their works were performed in the successive centres of opera – Naples, Rome, Venice, Paris, Dresden, Vienna and Stuttgart. Of course, many composers used the same basic story: more than fifty composers wrote an opera on Metastasio's *L'Olimpiade* and eighty on his *Artaserse*. But no core repertory existed, and the modern convention of a classical canon does not contain them: accordingly, their names are almost unknown to us. Of the vast output, most can be identified today only by means of fragmentary manuscripts, advertisements and private or theatrical archives. In brief, they were loved: and lost.

But, for us, there are lessons to be learned about the contexts of understanding, and about the roles of the arts in society. From the outset, in the 1640s, two types of opera evolved in tandem, corresponding roughly to tragedy and comedy. Historians cannot agree whether *opera buffa*, or comic opera, evolved from comic interludes inserted into serious operas, but the new genre crucially bridged the categories of 'art' and 'entertainment': it was immediately accessible because of its topical allusions, and it enjoyably echoed the practices of improvisational comedy. Human foibles typically caricatured included vanity, cowardice, miserliness, hypocrisy – and plain stupidity. The central features of topicality and improvisation mean that the 'contexts' in which comic operas were written, revised, performed and encountered are so integral to 'the work' that they must be regarded as elements of it, rather than detachable surroundings for it. For example, although a successful work might receive some thirty productions, no two would be identical: new titles might be given to works, major characters renamed, minor characters added or dropped,

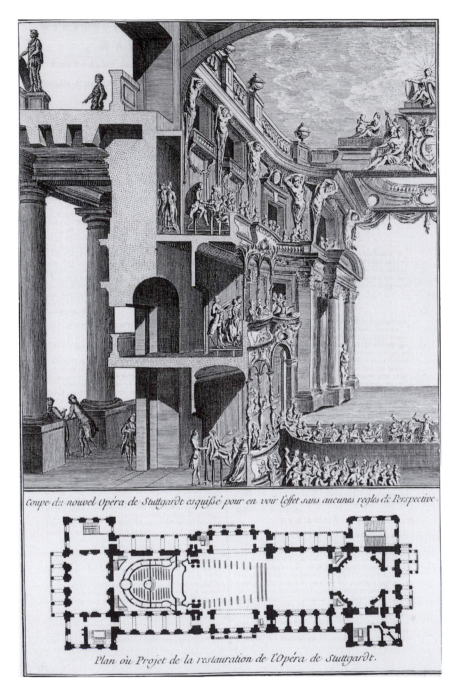

Coupe du nouvel Opéra de Stuttgardt esquissé pour en voir l'effet sans aucunes regles de Perspective.

Plan ou Projet de la restauration de l'Opéra de Stuttgardt.

Figure 20.1 *Salles de spectacles – Opéra de Stuttgardt*, from Denis Diderot and Jean le Rond D'Alembert (1751–80) *Encyclopédie, ou Dictionnaire raisonné des sciences, des arts et des métiers, par une société de gens de lettres*; vol. V of facs. edn (1964) Paris: Cercle du livre précieux. By permission of the National University of Australia.

cut-and-paste procedures regularly adopted, and arias transposed between voices and registers for entirely practical reasons. Commercial necessity might force a work to be pruned by as much as half after an unsuccessful staging, as happened with Gaetano Latilla's (1711–88) *La Finta Cameriera*. From its first performance in 1738 this opera was hugely popular, yet the forty-four arias it contained at its opening were reduced to only fifteen after a Paris production in 1752. Another common practice was to re-use successful tunes, or weld them into composite anthologies (*pasticcios*) for different voices or instruments, sometimes from works by different composers.

Comic opera, as a genre, flourished and evolved quickly because it was unhampered by either theory or tradition. It was typically devised for a local market, runs were usually very short, and novelty was its prime attraction to audiences: even keen opera-goers would see dozens of operas only once or twice, all of them contemporary works. Obviously, experiences of novelty can never be recaptured, and critics and philosophers by the 1750s worried about the significance and reliability of first impressions: in the domains of the performing arts, and of paintings and buildings which, to a degree, were crucially defined by their precise contexts – for example, church ceremonies – most eighteenth-century spectators would encounter such works only *once*. In this respect, published literature was entirely different. But attentive musical audiences were capable of noticing, absorbing and remembering a great deal more during a single hearing than most of us can today – partly because they were still living within a generally oral culture. Moreover – and this is the key – Italian audiences were deeply, if insensibly, grounded in music, as was remarked by countless visitors between 1700 and 1780. Plots were easy to follow and, in any case, performances took place in fully candlelit theatres, and audiences were given not only small books containing the full text – the *libretto* – but, where necessary, translations.

But surely we were all taught that eighteenth-century opera audiences indulged in talking, card-playing, eating, promiscuous philandering and political scheming? Certainly. But traditions not only varied between operatic centres: they also evolved, along with operas themselves. At different times there were silently attentive audiences in northern European courts, noisy Parisian nobles, passionate Neapolitans, and knowledgeable Viennese. Nevertheless, silence in the opera house was not widespread before the 1780s, and thereafter traditions still varied in the display of enthusiasm or disgust.

Seventeenth- and eighteenth-century ballet and opera production evolved in precisely the same way. They all begin as institutional – usually court – events, then become co-operative efforts involving a commercial dimension, and they end as a free market of individual artists. From its courtly beginnings, opera was both socially exclusive and expensive – although comic opera did more to break down such barriers than other genres. Nevertheless, as late as 1770 in Vienna, the cheapest seat was worth a day's wage for a mason. The initial exclusivity itself conditioned the character and attitude of a growing 'public' for the performing and fine arts, as incomes and attendant leisure became available to larger sections of the population.

I mentioned that theoretical comment on comic opera is rare before the 1770s, with only a few dozen texts to contrast to several thousand operas, but from the 1670s onwards we can detect an ever more anxious concern among the newly leisured classes over how to behave towards the arts and how to judge them. Influential French writers proclaimed that 'the public' or 'the people' alone must judge whether a work gives pleasure or is found moving, since it is they who exercise 'taste' and uphold its standards – not the erudite, with their pompous theories. Of course, authors differed widely over who they meant by 'the people', although all agree that, because the public is ignorant, it must, and can only, follow its natural feelings. As early as 1702, the Abbé Raguenet (1660–1722) was deploring the limitations of 'the mere spectator' (Strunk 1950: 471). The chattering classes, who, in their modern dress, emerge during the reign of Louis XIV, foster the attitude of talkers rather than doers. Indeed, precisely because they wished and intended to be socially superior to mere doers, they loudly complain from 1700 onwards that their own *maestri* (tutors) will not tell them what to *say*, or *when* to say it. Professor John Gregory (1724–73), to whom I shall return, writing in Edinburgh in the 1760s, reports the same challenge facing informed writers: 'If they cannot teach people to think and to feel, they teach them what to say, which answers all the purposes of vanity' (Gregory 1765: 168). As late as the 1770s, audiences typically record their approval of individual per-formers, but make no mention of the composers themselves (see Freneuse, in Strunk 1950: 501), and often made no effort to find out. Such socially defended ignorance of first-hand musical knowledge by the French, however, contrasted with deep interest of patrons and their public in the Austro-Hungarian realms. But the rapidly increasing complexity of the works that they enjoyed, along with the phenomenal skills demanded by those works, inevitably widened the gap between audiences as virtual co-performers and audiences as merely passive witnesses. This trend, combined with a transition from *social events* where music was *heard*, to *musical occasions* when *listening* was demanded, further detached music both from everyday life and from the playing capacities of mere listeners. Indeed, in almost all domains, Enlight-enment, in all its diverse national and cultural forms, typically reduced widespread participation, because expertise was now a requirement.

In Britain and France throughout the eighteenth century, the commercialization of leisure was both indulgently welcomed and vociferously deplored. The commercial dimensions were partly defined by the emergence of several new institutions and practices: the beginning of public concerts, the first public museums and galleries, as well as the publication of debate about the nature and importance of taste. But the inherent weaknesses of these new social practices were foreseen by very few. In northern Europe the new public for the arts consisted primarily of non-practitioners, groomed, if at all, only on literature: new modes of attention were required, and audiences, therefore, had to *learn* to listen and *learn* to look. But, to literary audiences, printed commentary about the non-verbal and the performing arts seemed more durable than the works themselves. Kant's friend J. G. Sulzer (1720–79) and Charles Burney, independently, make this very point in the 1770s:

> To the reputation of a Theorist, indeed, longevity is insured by means of books, which become obsolete more slowly than musical compositions. Tradition only whispers, for a short time, the name and abilities of a mere Performer . . . whereas, a theory once committed to paper and established, lives, at least in libraries, as long as the language in which it was written.
>
> (Burney 1776: vol. 1, 705)

The temporal character of wordless music lacked the fixity of painting or literature. Because the new public for painting and music was rightly presumed to lack relevant know-how, verbal comment self-consciously avoided reference to technical aspects of the works themselves, and concentrated on the emotional effects on audiences. Such talk about responses *to* the arts was intended to redirect attention back to the works themselves, but it did the opposite: criticism and theory became autonomous.

Another issue made matters worse. Almost everyone assumed that the arts had meaning because they involved *mimesis*, or representation. But, since meaning was itself assumed to be a property only of languages, either music itself would have to *be* a language – which few then wanted to claim – or music could acquire meaning only when *attached* to a genuine language. The preferred solution was to regard music as enhancing the force of linguistic meaning. Adam Smith (1723–90) was still worrying about the possible meaninglessness of wordless music in the 1780s.

The divorce of art from everyday life by 1800 had spawned a notion of art for art's sake – a view that was fatally seductive for artists and audiences alike, because it encouraged a view that all responses are equally defensible, and that no work need be judged by reference to anything outside it. Belief in the autonomy of art further strengthened separate belief in the autonomy of criticism. But whereas the art work remained the bond between artists, *talking*, or critical comment, became the new bond between non-practitioners. Anchorage within context, however, alone ensures the possibility of communication; works or art could not justifiably be detached from at least the general context of their creation. That was a central insight of practising painters, architects and composers, from at least the 1650s, who accused critics of lacking first-hand understanding, and of substituting theory for practice, where no theory in fact existed. In 1702, the Abbé Raguenet, defending the moderns against the ancients – that is, the Italians against the French – forcibly pointed out that Italian children learned to study and perform music from the outset of their schooling, so that it appeared quite natural and unselfconscious to them as they grew up. In other words, both their interests and judgements as adults were founded on skills taught at an early age, and their experiences were socially embedded.

Such a view is surely true today. Only security in skills enables each of us boldly to experiment, confidently to explore, unashamedly to revise. The insecure – the abbé meant his fellow Frenchmen – constantly sought 'rules', which both constrained experiment and misrepresented past achievement, since 'rules' are only summary devices or aids to practice. Is it not both impressive and depressing that by 1700 several of the most learned French scholars saw that any detachment of judgement upon the exercise of skills from actual possession of those skills would generate both mutual incomprehension and social divisions of indefensible hostility? But indolence is the handmaiden of ignorance. Much further north, in Edinburgh, the musical scene flourished for barely twenty years after the opening of the city's first concert hall in 1762. Standards of playing had risen with the arrival of Continental musicians, and the amateur players of the musical societies had either to improve or withdraw: aristocrats, in music as in other arts, who had typically conflated any notion of practice with merely regular performance, baulked at the relentless demands of independent practice which underlay the new standards of competence. In the sciences, the same thing happened, as enquiry became more specialized, increasingly mathematical and dramatically expensive. Adam Ferguson and Adam Smith, while acknowledging the necessity and advantages of ever more specialized enquiry, feared the social consequences of the division of labour: they did not foresee the consequences of the division of intellectual labour.

Although most eighteenth-century operas are, in a sense, as new to us as they were to those at the time, we encounter them through the forest of subsequent operatic growth, and *listen* to them in entirely different ways. It is commonly said: 'These works do not warrant the attention we give to late Mozart, to Wagner, or to mature Verdi.' But they were not devised for that kind of attention or listening, any more than most Renaissance and baroque altarpieces were intended for the nose-length scrutiny we give them in well-lit modern art museums.

Let us look at some original contexts more closely. Most Italian towns in the mid-eighteenth century had changed little in the preceding hundred years: they continued to house inhabitants within their city walls who, while often poor, were vastly better off than rural labourers. Stendhal (*pseud.* M. H. Beyle, 1783–1842) later even claimed that the enforced idleness of the illiterate helped to foster creative interests (Stendhal 1823: 454). Every theatre, however temporary, was modelled on those designed in Venice for the first popular operas of the 1630s: tiers of boxes were arranged in a horseshoe or oblong shape. The theatre was a substitute for a parliament or a free press, and a form of cultural unity existed between the nine or ten small states, achieved by means of the improvisatory comedy – *commedia dell'arte* – rather than the high-brow and more expensive literary genre of tragic opera – *opera seria* – initially favoured by the upper classes. The key figure was the impresario. He had to know precisely who was influential in his audience, and he invariably required his commissioned works to be completed within a month and to be tailored for specific singers. *In extremis* – serious illness, say – a work would be performed without a part. Single rehearsals were the norm, and sometimes singers learned their parts only hours before opening. First nights were frequently less successful than later performances. The opera world, always on the move, resembled a circus or medieval troupe. Indeed, the Jesuit scholar E. Arteaga (1747–99) in 1785 likened the general interest in opera to that of a sporting crowd at a 'Colosseum of a kind' (Rosselli 1984: 153). (One might note that an enthusiastic audience is still unsettling to many from the sullen Calvinist north, for whom self-righteous silence happily masks both ignorance and disapproval.)

Each theatre box had a dressing room opposite the corridor where servants prepared food: and guests relieved themselves. In spite of constant chatter, audiences did listen to their favourite passages intently, but rather like modern jazz audiences or, better, Indian audiences at a sitar recital, as active participants, responding to selected moments with applause or demands for repetition. Of course, governments were fearful of crowds, and preventive censorship of texts was exercised everywhere. Topical improvisations were always both popular and risky, and people were frequently arrested for an overnight reprimand. Opera orchestras varied in size from about forty to sixty, but the solo singers constituted about half of the total costs. Up to half the audience would attend without paying, as guests, hangers-on or servants, and takings were low. Apart from patronage, the main source of income was from the gambling monopoly held by the theatre itself. Larger theatres, of course, needed to attract larger audiences, and, to the extent that this meant a wider audience, there was a hardening of models and formulae for opera: but these were mainly post-Napoleonic developments.

Here we can turn to the well-known *Letters on Italian Music* of 1739–40, written by the then thirty-year-old Charles de Brosses (1709–77), later president of the *parlement* in Burgundy. Celebrating the fact that *four* operas – by Latilla, Jommelli, Scarlatti (1685–1757) and di Capua (1710–70) – are running simultaneously in Rome, and three are running in Naples, he particularly praises the construction and positioning of the boxes within the theatre, so that no sight lines are blocked: 'Society assembles at the opera . . . The ladies receive for conversazione, so to speak, in their boxes . . . I enter the box as if it were my own house . . . After the first nights, when the silence is respectable . . . it is not stylish to listen except at the best places.' With such constant attendance, 'nobody wants to see again a play, a ballet, a setting, or an actor from the previous season, unless it may be some excellent opera by Vinci (1690–1730) or a very famous singer'. In any case, 'music is not seen a second time and is neither printed nor engraved; consequently people remember only the most famous passages' (Brosses 1739–40: 20–2).

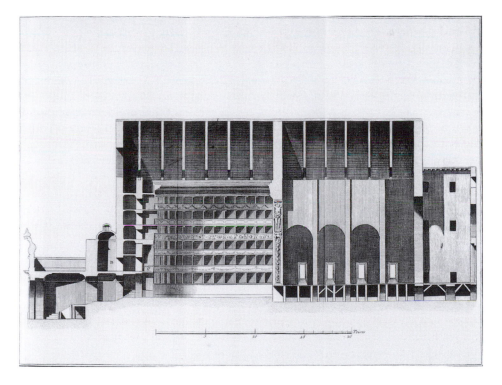

Figure 20.2 *Théatre Royal à Naples*, from Denis Diderot and Jean Le Rond D'Alembert (1751–80) *Encyclopédie, ou Dictionnaire raisonné des sciences, des arts et des métiers, par une société de gens de lettres*; vol. V of facs. edn (1964) Paris: Cercle du livre précieux. By permission of the National University of Australia.

So contemporary observers agreed that the social character of the Italian opera house centred on the life of the box: 'conviviality' defined the experience. Stendhal, by the 1820s, was lamenting its decline and speculated on the proper conditions for 'forming an audience'. He declares that it is necessary to feel perfectly at ease: 'a certain degree of private self-communion is essential to savour the sublimest charms of music' (Stendhal 1823: 428ff.). Burney's delightful brother-in-law Arthur Young (1741–1820) had commented on just such matters in 1789 after hearing a performance in Padua of Cimarosa's *I Due Baroni*. He believed

> that half the charms of a theatre depend on the audience; – one must be in good humour – a certain exhilaration must be springing in the bosom; willingness to enjoy must be expanded into enjoyment by the sympathy of surrounding objects. Pleasure is caught from eyes that sparkle with the expectation of being pleased.

After visiting a new opera house in Lodi, Young has more to say:

> I consider it in a political light, as deserving some attention. Lodi is a little insignificant place, without trade and without manufactures . . . [Y]et there is not a town in France or England, of double the population, that ever exhibited a theatre so built, decorated, filled, and furnished as this of Lodi.
>
> (Young 1794: 250, 240)

Several issues come together at this point. First is the overriding importance of *scale*: a notion sacred to classical and Renaissance thinkers alike, and never to be confused with *size*. Scale introduces the notions of propriety and context – 'what, on reflection, seems appropriate to a place like this?' Even in solemn Edinburgh, Professor John Gregory confesses his admiration for Italian music, but thinks that 'the effects of music depend upon many other circumstances besides its connection with poetry', chief among which is association (Gregory 1765: 160). He observes:

> In Italy we see the natives transported at the opera with all the variety of delight and passion which the composer intended to produce. The same opera in England . . . can raise no passion in the audience, because they do not understand the language in which it is written.
>
> (Gregory 1765: 129)

Gregory deplores the failure of philosophers to cement 'the natural union between philosophy and the fine arts, an union extremely necessary to their improvement'. Instead, all the arts 'have been left in the hands of ignorant artists unassisted by philosophers' (Gregory 1765: 107). He states:

> When Music, Dancing and Poetry, came to be considered as only subservient to pleasure, a higher degree of proficiency in them became necessary, and consequently a more severe application to each. This compleated their separation from one another, and occasioned their falling entirely into the hands of such Men as devoted their whole time to their cultivation.
>
> (Gregory 1765: 121)

Gregory's fascinating remark indicates that when 'music, dancing and poetry' were encountered as constituent parts of much more complex events and processes, attention would not typically, or justifiably, be focused on them as isolable elements. We should remember the various ways in which musical elements contribute to religious or other social ceremonies, along with many other elements, such as food, dress and decoration. When any of these is singled out, however, and becomes the sole focus of attention, audiences inevitably become aware of, and demand, higher standards of performance. Of course, Gregory agrees with everyone else that 'one end of music is to communicate pleasure', 'but the far nobler and more important is to command the passions and move the heart' (Gregory 1765: 115). How would this be done? Did it require, as he thought, that 'music should be subservient to the Poetry' (Gregory 1765: 158)? Sometimes, yes: throughout Europe composers were admired as skilled craftsmen, able to produce on demand, and willing to satisfy both the connoisseur and the amateur. Until at least the 1790s the same kinds of melodies, harmonies and rhythms were used in all kinds of music, because the primary test for eighteenth-century music was its suitability, not its originality.

An emphasis on propriety demands an awareness of context. Composers were as concerned about immediate rhetorical impact as about harmonic experiment: the pragmatic need for entertainment embraced concern for the strengths and weaknesses of particular performers, and the tastes of known audiences: composers composed because they needed to earn money, be of civic use, gain a reputation, secure a job – not primarily because they were inspired. There was little, if any, philosophical speculation. Charles Burney represents the un-Germanic view that theories are unnecessary obstacles, which tend to perpetuate the assumption that music must be subservient to verbal texts. Stendhal has a pertinent observation: 'The German, who lives by theories, treats music as material for erudition' (Stendhal 1823: 175n.]. On the other hand, Burney unhesitatingly admired and championed the superb playing standards achieved in Mannheim, for example, by rigorous conductors and disciplined rehearsals. Such technical excellence, of course, was in his view detachable from any theoretical commitments.

But whatever their views about theory – numerous French and British writers quoted Cicero's view, from *De Oratore* (III, 1.195), that almost everybody is able to judge art without having any theories – all agreed that Italian music was embedded within a rich and diverse culture, having its roots in the life of the Church since the Renaissance. In addition, by the early 1750s, Charles Avison (1709–70) in England, Rousseau (1712–78) and D'Alembert (1717–83) in France, and Count Algarotti (1712–64), travelling in Italy, were declaring that the essence of all music, including comic opera, is expression. The only qualification is D'Alembert's, in 1759: 'in general one can only grasp all the expressive quality of music when it is joined to words or dance', and in the particular case of opera, audiences require dramatic conditions to be satisfied (D'Alembert 1759: 456, 406).

The examples of Sydney Opera House, on the one hand, and several new museums of art, on the other, show that it is still possible to regard such places as social centres, while promoting performances of the highest standard. But if we cannot escape from our modern practices of listening indiscriminately and with equal attention to music of all kinds, cannot ignore two centuries of later tradition, is there any point in recreating Italian operas from an entirely different world? If, by definition, we cannot gain access to the topicality or improvisation of eighteenth-century Italian *opera buffa*, are we not left with the music alone – music that simply lacks the quality of *opera seria*? Should we not concentrate instead on modern equivalents or analogues of the contexts in which those works were created? In fact, no theatre producer can ignore either the context of a work's original conception and creation, or that of his intended audience. Today, we cannot enter the tense political context against which Verdi's operas are so often set, or the volcanic landscape of Beaumarchais's (1732–99) *Le Mariage de Figaro*. Yet, in none of these cases are we restricted to the 'mere music', and all of us have seen great modern productions of such operas. The point concerns not only what the operas are about, but who they are for, and in what context.

Italian opera audiences recognized skill in composition and in execution because they had unselfconsciously absorbed a set of standards in their social upbringing: in the same way that church congregations absorb the standards of choral singing. Today, because of separation and specialization in almost all human practices, such knowledge calls for special study. But skill is a necessary condition of merit in any domain. Artists and performers who lack skill – as so many do, and always have done – neither warrant nor reward sustained attention. So-called 'popular music' is fashionable for an extremely short time: it cannot survive sustained attention. And so-called 'classical music' also has its saturation point, because no human achievement can sustain endless and relentless scrutiny. Happily, some works repay renewed acquaintance after a passage of time. But we can say that when works of art become ever-available consumable objects, they lose not only some of their mystery, but also thereby some of their merit as works of art.

Two central concepts have emerged from reflection upon crowded theatre boxes in small opera houses: those of *scale* and *embeddedness*, or contextual anchorage. Unless and until we identify the appropriate scales of diverse human endeavours and achievements, and reaffirm the essential differences in scale of different practices, we are doomed to assault by a philistine cacophony of meaningless noise. And until we anchor our creative efforts within the rich fabric of our lives, we shall be condemned to self-indulgent gestures pretending to be acts of communication. We shall also be unable to fulfil our duty to honour and cherish our traditions while, at the same time, striving to exceed past triumphs. We cannot fulfil our tasks unless we know what those past achievements are.

REFERENCES

Bianconi, L. and Pestelli G. (1998) *Opera Production and its Resources*, Chicago: University of Chicago Press.

Brosses, Charles de (1739–40) *Letters on Italian Music*, trans. D. S. Schier (1978) n. p.

Burney, C. (1770) *Music Men, and Manners in France and Italy*; repr. (1969) London: Folio Society.

—— (1776–9) *A General History of Music from the Earliest Ages to the Present Period*; repr. (1957) New York: Dover Publications.

Burrows, D. and Dunhill, R. (2002) *Music and Theatre in Handel's World*, Oxford: Oxford University Press.

Cicero, *De Oratore*, Book III, trans. H. Rackham (1942) London: Loeb Classical Library, Heinemann.

D'Alembert, Jean Le Rond (1759) 'De La Liberté de la musique', in *Mélanges de littérature, d'histoire et de philosophie* (1770) Amsterdam.

Fubini, Enrico (1994) *Music and Culture in Eighteenth-century Europe*, Chicago: University of Chicago Press.

Gregory, John (1765) *A Comparative View of the State and Faculties of Man*, new edn (1768) Dublin.

Hunter, Mary (1999) *The Culture of Opera Buffa in Mozart's Vienna: A Poetics of Entertainment*, Princeton and Chichester: Princeton University Press.

Hunter, M. and Webster, J. (1997) *Opera Buffa in Mozart's Vienna*, Cambridge: Cambridge University Press.

Johnson, J. H. (1995) *Listening in Paris: A Cultural History*, Berkeley and London: University of California Press.

Jones, Peter (1993) 'Hume on the Arts and the "Standard of Taste": Texts and Contexts' in D. F. Norton (ed.) *The Cambridge Companion to Hume*, 2nd edn (2007) Cambridge: Cambridge University Press.

Kimball, D. (1991) *Italian Opera*, Cambridge: Cambridge University Press.

King, T. (2001) 'Patronage and Market in the Creation of Opera', *Journal of Cultural Economics*, 25: 21–45.

Lonsdale, R. (1965) *Dr Charles Burney*, Oxford: Oxford University Press.

Pevsner, N. (1976) *A History of Building Types*, Princeton: Princeton University Press.

Rosselli, J. (1984) *The Opera Industry in Italy*, Cambridge: Cambridge University Press.

Stendhal (1823) *Life of Rossini*, trans. R. N. Coe (1970) London: John Calder.

Strohm, R. (1997) *Dramma per Musica: Italian Opera Seria of the Eighteenth Century*, New Haven, Conn. and London: Yale University Press.

Sulzer, J. G. (1776) *Supplément à l'Encyclopédie*, Amsterdam.

Strunk, O. (1950) *Source Readings in Music History*, London: W. W. Norton.

Young, Arthur (1792; 1794) *Travels during the Years, 1787, 1788 & 1789*; repr. (1915) London: Dent.

Zaslaw, N. (ed.) (1989) *The Classical Era*, London: Macmillan.

PART V

MATERIAL AND POPULAR CULTURE

INTRODUCTION

Peter Jones

I n the following chapters some earlier themes are developed, with emphasis on the new publics, their responses and resources.

Yeo (Chapter 21) shows how Bacon's insistence that the basis of enquiry should be factual experience, rather than scholastic texts, and his use of the vernacular tongue instead of the European lingua franca, Latin, had unexpected consequences. Because English was understood by very few outside Britain, translations became a matter or priority if information was to be shared, and these prompted awareness of the philosophical complexities of language, meaning and interpretation. Second, the new audiences for the learned and often serialized volumes adopted new modes of reading, ranging from mere consultation to sequential study. Uniform response became increasingly improbable, a factor enhanced by the diversity of the readership, which soon encompassed women and servants as well as tradesmen and artisans, as Hesse (Chapter 22) shows. Virtual communities of readers were created throughout Europe, united only by a common interest in enquiry, but not by language, religious ideologies or regional traditions. Individually, readers also became aware of the need to order or structure information, since not everything could be recorded, nor all that was selected presented in a random sequence; socially, as we saw in earlier parts of this volume, readers began to congregate in newly formed literary societies, subscription libraries and cafés where like-minded people shared their views. Gradually, authors began to see themselves as commercial agents, owning their texts and rights to them; in these respects the creative community of writers, painters and musicians came closer together.

Historically, those in power had always sought to control dissemination of information; formal constraints such as censorship typically stimulated clandestine counter-measures, including piracy. But the dramatically expanding print cultures of the seventeenth and eighteenth centuries, which canvassed previously unheard-of thoughts and attitudes, inevitably challenged entrenched intolerance and bigotry; and when printed handbills and images, together with songs and banners, were easily available to the least literate parts of society, only draconian measures could eradicate them. In later centuries such measures were perfected.

McNeil (Chapter 23) considers the 'appearance' industry of eighteenth-century urban economies – not the majority of any population at the time, but the richest and most innovative. He identifies many elements in the highly complex phenomena of public behaviour, ranging from the colour, cut and design of clothes, textiles and hairstyles to the design of furniture and the roles of etiquette. It is easy to overlook how relatively abstract notions such as freedom, sensation, individualism, privacy, comfort, warmth can influence how we dress and behave. Clearly the expense of certain materials, such as dyes, bleach, silk or cotton, affect design emphases; but so do views of health, including washing and exercise, also influence the nature of clothing. It is worth recalling that the first known attempt to design comfortable seating for the human frame, by considering anatomy and posture, was not undertaken until the 1760s, in Paris, by André-Jacob Roubo.

Rogers (Chapter 24) stresses that, for the European masses, life was defined by anxiety and ignorance: popular culture, in all its diversity, mirrors this fact, through seasonal festivals, rituals, half-believed myths, witch trials and treatment of miscreants. In the early modern period no established body had resources to guarantee secure policing, and all those in power feared uncontrollable crowds as much as the free flow of information. The loyalty of supporting elites, however, was itself fragile, and subject to independent agendas. Nevertheless, the rapid expansion of large urban societies throughout the eighteenth century accelerated class divides, and popular culture became associated with plebeian interests and practices, officially disdained by those who regarded themselves as upwardly mobile.

Some earlier themes in the book can now be further illustrated.

COSTING VALUES: THEORY AND PRACTICE IN AN EMERGING CONSUMER SOCIETY

Even the tacit and unarticulated values upheld in any community absorb financial and physical resources, and call for both effort and sacrifices: as social priorities change, so the resources needed to support the evolving values also change. And while it can reasonably be assumed that throughout history most peoples have been alert to changes in the meaning and force of key ideas, particularly in matters of taste, the absence of recorded speculation may indicate uncertainty about the causes of such changes, and of appropriate responses to them (see Smith 1759: Part V, ch. 1, §4). It is important to record which evolving ideas and practices cost who what, why, when and where.

In two influential articles published in 1951–2 in the *Journal of the History of Ideas*, Paul Oscar Kristeller analysed the sources of the 'Modern System of the Arts'. He showed how concepts of art, craft and science at the end of the eighteenth century, although rooted in ancient ideas, had evolved from late medieval times in response to increasingly complex contextual influences. All definitions are constrained by their goals and by other contextual beliefs, including views about what might be technically possible or desirable: the rapid technological advances sponsored from the mid-seventeenth century by rich nations such as France, England and the Netherlands hastened the reordering and redefinition of several ancient concepts, such as those denoted in Latin by *ars* and *scientia*.

From the Renaissance on, alterations in the hierarchy of practice, by which certain activities were promoted or demoted, were indicative of the changing relationship between Church and state in which the core concepts were embedded. During the Renaissance, existing conventions allowed mosaic and sculpture to be major forms of art, along with fresco. Nevertheless, some crafts, such as tapestry and silver-smithing, gradually lost their functional roles and became purely decorative, whereas some were always primarily decorative, such as mosaic, stained glass and embroidery; and some always functional, such as furniture or architecture. No one knows or can predict how long it takes for philosophers to articulate formally, under the guise of a definition, the features of an endeavour which have been entirely familiar to practitioners since time immemorial. For example, as D'Alembert observed, all craftsmen learn to adapt to the demands, challenges and constraints of a chosen medium, inherit traditions and styles of work and product, and know about the fickle customers, patrons and audiences they must satisfy in order to survive. While Aristotle recorded most of these features, many later commentators omitted or strongly emphasized some features at the expense of others, in order to promote a particular theory and, where possible, to enlist the endorsement of the practitioners themselves.

From medieval times, guilds aimed to secure legal monopolies on the training and exercise of defined skills, partly to protect local craftsmen from outside intruders, partly to secure job security and thereby social stability, partly to guard against dramatic price fluctuations. Of course, there were considerable variations over time and place, and guilds typically exercised most control in urban centres. Nevertheless, even there, flexibility could be forced on them by patrons powerful enough to ignore their constraints and hence select their own craftsmen. Such preferential treatment raised the status of the chosen few, and encouraged greater interplay between patron and servant. Although many of the craft techniques continued (and are little changed even today) – glass-blowing, mosaics and tapestry-making are clear examples – newly founded academies in the Renaissance promoted the ancient idea that the physical world of manual effort was inferior to the spiritual or intellectual world. This emphasis also exalted textual and verbal dexterity, at the expense of verbally unsophisticated craftsmen who knew very well how to convey traditional skills by demonstration. The humiliation of linguistically inept gardeners or tradesmen became a favoured topic of dramatists and poets from the sixteenth century onwards, and conveniently blended with hostility towards the traditional trade secrecies of masons and others who had no need to explain what could adequately be conveyed by *showing*. At the same time, the notion of an artist as an independent individual gained ground, although, of course, the supposedly anonymous craftsmen of the times were always identifiable by their fellows, by virtue of the quality of their work. There also gradually emerged ideas of individual rights which, somehow or other, were required to harmonize with the collective rights associated with guilds. By the end of the eighteenth century, the proliferation of diverse commercial practices in the rapidly changing economic and political climate meant that reformed guilds were as well able to promote as to inhibit capitalist production.

By the time of Louis XIV, efforts to diminish the influence of the guilds by establishing new academies on the Italian model were already generating unintended and long-lived consequences. First, the rules, practices and structures of the academies quickly replicated the paralysing features of the guilds – thereby distorting and thwarting the new agendas they were devised to implement, especially when struggles for power dominated activity.

Second, the increasing specialization fostered by the academies did intensify enquiry and improve techniques, but at the expense of being understood outside the chosen circle. Moreover, it accelerated the division of labour, and militated against new groupings or mutual help. Sharp divisions between proudly distinct professions – familiar today, for example, between architecture and engineering – have roots in such early Enlightenment practices. Because most of the work sponsored by the French academies was funded by the state, from what today would be a defence budget – such as navigational aids or armament design – participants became increasingly alert to efficient and cost-effective production: it was but a short step to calculate labour costs, and an ever-closer association of time and money.

A third unintended consequence, to which reference has already been made in this book, was the emergence of a new 'public' for the work of the guilds and academies. This public, usually entirely ignorant of the technical problems preoccupying the makers, was nevertheless fascinated by their effects. A nonpractising audience had always been acknowledged by rhetoricians who needed to identify the conditions of effective communication: the new elements in the early Enlightenment period, as our contributors have underlined, were the vastly increased range of information that could be communicated, and the expanding rate of print culture. And the primary concern of the new audience was not the craftsman's concern with *what to do*, but the entirely parasitic indulgence of *what to say*.

Until the seventeenth century most of the activities we today label as the 'sciences' assumed their task to be one of recording observations – with minimal reflection on what those notions might cover, or on the criteria of success. Only towards the end of the Enlightenment period was it widely accepted that there is no perception without interpretation, and that current beliefs always influence present perception. By the 1650s, however, it was readily agreed that existing techniques provide the initial vocabulary for planning what might be attempted, and that collaboration would be essential for any large-scale endeavours. Moreover, for effective international communication, a common symbolism was required which was subject to agreed interpretation. Such factors influenced the publication and popularity of encyclopaedias and dictionaries of the period, discussed throughout this book, but these invaluable volumes themselves masked two fundamental distinctions: the gap between what is done and what is said; and the gap between what is done and what is known. To address both, perceptive writers supplemented their texts with pictorial images, like their less literate predecessors who decorated church walls in fresco or mosaic, and handed down oral traditions from generation to generation. Such images often conveyed multiple messages of different kinds, spanning space and time, process and product, warning and reward, intention and progress. When Diderot, in the early 1750s, disingenuously declared that the intended illustrations to the *Encyclopédie* would uniquely convey multiple messages within a single picture plane, most importantly temporal sequences and causal processes, he knew well that his educated readers would recognize his adherence to a tradition reaching back at least to Roman

times. Religious images, medical illustrations, architectural plans, military formations, navigational aids – to name but a few – all had ancient histories, and many
grappled with the intractable facts that few effects reveal the nature of their causes,
and few products the processes of which they are the result. (Precisely the attraction
of 'philosophical history', popularized by Hume and William Robertson, lay
in replacing mere chronicles of events, all open to debatable descriptions, by efforts
to infer the causes which might explain events.) These images, as all their intended
users knew, required and allowed only a limited range of interpretation: they typically
served as *aides-mémoires*, or as guides to craftsmen who were expected to supplement
them with accepted knowledge and practice. Up to the 1750s most pattern books
of machines, buildings or utensils were of this kind. Where the traditions of interpretation were absent, as in the American colonies, for example, designs were often
interpreted in highly original ways. Drawings confined to elevations, cross-sections
and ground plans gave little indication of internal architectural features, movable
furniture or, more importantly, how certain elements could be built. Spiral staircases
and the internal location of chimney flues were especially challenging (Joseph
Priestley's house in Pennsylvania being but one example).

By mid-century such detail began to appear, precisely because the unknown
viewer, whether patron or local craftsman, could no longer be guaranteed to
understand: representations of what was called 'distribution' of furniture became
fashionable, along with designs of plaster ornament and wall decoration. However,
it was not artisans but their clients and patrons who needed and had access to the
new images accompanying encyclopaedic texts, as D'Alembert clearly stated: for
everyone below the 'middling' classes, in other words for the majority of the
population, printed material was expensive until the end of the eighteenth century.
The publication price of David Hume's *Treatise* in 1738–9 roughly equalled his
servant's annual cash income, over and above her keep. Moreover, although editors
of encyclopaedias intended to convey complex information, their work inevitably
also spawned simplified and trivialized versions, which could raise unrealistic
expectations about change in any less informed or unreflective audiences.

As the size and composition of the non-practising audiences increased through
the eighteenth century, two questions dominated their responses: 'What am I
supposed to know?' 'How am I supposed to behave?' On the one hand, no one could
reasonably expect extensive understanding of increasingly specialized enquiry and
knowledge: by 1728, when he first published his *Cyclopaedia*, Ephraim Chambers
was deploring the fact that people 'of the same profession, no longer understand one
another' (vol. I, xvii). On the other hand, the idea popularized by thinkers such as
Hume – that knowledge is essentially a social phenomenon, learned, practised and
communicated within a peer group – seemed to promise mutual comprehension.
Paradoxically, while many who wrote about scientific matters accepted this latter
aspiration, some commentators on the arts despaired of its possibility, leaning on the
individualistic emphasis, stemming from Bacon, that everyone must undertake their
own enquiries and rely on neither tradition nor authority. Some of the consequences
have been outlined in previous chapters.

By the end of the eighteenth century most self-respecting artists had been socially
coerced into subscription to a theory, and woe betide an ignorant spectator who could

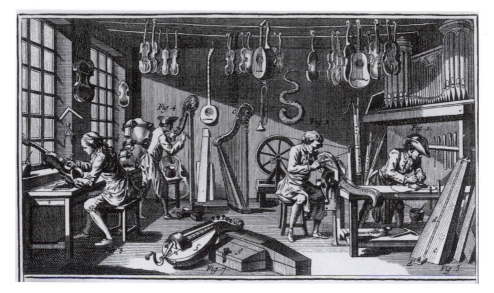

Figure Part V.1 *Lutherie – ouvrages et outils* [musical instrument workshop], from Denis Diderot and Jean le Rond D'Alembert (1751–80) *Encyclopédie, ou Dictionnaire raisonné des sciences, des arts et des métiers, par une société de gens de lettres*; vol. V of facs. edn (1964) Paris: Cercle du livre précieux. By permission of the National University of Australia.

detect no evidence of one: the explicit denials and warnings of earlier artists were blatantly disregarded. Precisely what such theories were supposed to motivate, explain or illuminate invariably remained obscure. But, of course, obscurity was the enviable token of profundity: impenetrable jargon bonded initiates together and signalled exclusivity. Although jargon has been pilloried continuously since antiquity – and the self-deluding nonsense of critics was famously parodied throughout Enlightenment times – it is fatally attractive to those who believe it masks, rather than displays, their manifest intellectual, linguistic and social limitations. And it always betrays hostility to the free exchange of information, the fundamental ideal which reveals the absurdity of pretending that ideas can be personal property. A century earlier, in his 1673 translation of Vitruvius, Claude Perrault had forcefully observed that many people have a 'desire to make the matters of their profession into mysteries that they alone can interpret'. Knowledge of theory, however, was not the key that spectators lacked: the missing ingredient was knowledge of technique and process, and above all context. There is no content without intent; equally, there is no text without context. To know *what* has been done requires provisional answers to a range of questions: who made what, for whom, of what, how, when, why and where? Answers to such questions help us to determine what has been done. By the late 1750s several leading thinkers accepted that works of art are made by conscious beings, using their skills in a chosen medium; these skills are learned and practised within a tradition, and can be modified in the light of experience, needs and context. Further, such works are valued and given significance, but because neither meaning nor value is perceivable by any of the five senses alone, it follows that a measure of interpretation is necessary. Finally, all human practices occur in contexts, which provide the conditions of meaning. It is therefore necessary to have some notion of contexts in which to locate the works under consideration. Contexts are maps, resulting from, and requiring, interpretation, as Chambers, D'Alembert and many others proclaimed. Moreover, as tools of convenience, maps and their symbols are always open to improvement and rejection, and all have histories of success and failure: sometimes, because of radically altered circumstances, entirely new maps will be necessary, in order to arrive at any interpretation at all. While practitioners have traditionally deplored the verbal gyrations of mere commentators, it was rare even in the twentieth century for a distinguished engineer, albeit trained as a philosopher, to acknowledge the practical value of definitions with blurred edges but forcefully warn of the damaging implications of using obsolete concepts: 'the terms Architect, Engineer and Builder are beset with associations from a bygone age . . . and they are inadequate to describe or discuss the contemporary scene' (Arup 1970: 390).

CONSEQUENCES OF CHANGING TECHNOLOGIES

Wealthy patronage, of course, encouraged ever more skilful craftsmanship, but it also promoted more thought about cost efficiency, half-heartedly initiated during Louis XIV's state sponsorship of defence technologies. Jean-Rodolphe Perronet, the most distinguished structural engineer of his time, undertook a time and motion study of pin-making in the 1740s to estimate the economic benefits of a division of labour in their production. The approach threatened to dismantle long-established work practices, upheld by guilds and corporations and integrated into a complex social hierarchy. Nevertheless, with a ritual nod towards Francis Bacon, rather than to earlier thinkers who had canvassed similar ideas, most Enlightenment writers valued practical experience over the abstract speculations of philosophers who typically failed to translate their claims into daily life. How, then, were the skills of the hand and the head to be best harmonized? The question was never fully resolved in the eighteenth century, even when it was explicitly asked.

It was not the new technologies as such, however, which prompted intellectual and social dismay – since technologies have always evolved to meet changing circumstances: rather, it was the scale and rates of change, since little had forearmed anyone either to maximize the potential benefits of change or minimize their potentially harmful consequences. Until the twentieth century almost no one had guaranteed, long-term employment: insecurity defined life in all dimensions. Artisans who were trained in a limited number of defined tasks were especially vulnerable to summary dismissal, against which the traditional guilds and trade corporations were no safeguard. David Hume, albeit writing in Scotland before significant industrial expansion, prominently warned against any long-term social or economic reliance on skills or practices that could not be diversified. Remarkably few who appreciated that the new methods of enquiry were intended to have beneficial utilitarian consequences confessed to alarm over the already detectable negative effects on social practices, traditions or health. Some philosophers, such as Adam Ferguson and Adam

Smith, or widely travelled doctors or farmers, such as Sir John Pringle and Arthur Young, did record their warnings and observations, but wider social concern did not gather pace until after the Napoleonic Wars. For centuries, guilds had grappled with the health hazards of their crafts, resulting from harmful chemicals, gases and poisons or dangerous practices such as grinding stone, glass or metals, but they varied greatly in their efforts to remedy known effects. By the 1760s it was increasingly accepted that the public and private health of workers, as of the privileged classes, depended on multiple physical, chemical and social causes, such as conditions at home and at work, nutritional standards, family background and urban densities. In the late 1740s in Edinburgh, and subsequently in London, Pringle, later president of the Royal Society, was forcefully alerting his colleagues to these facts, and by the end of the century many studies of community health and sanitation were under way.

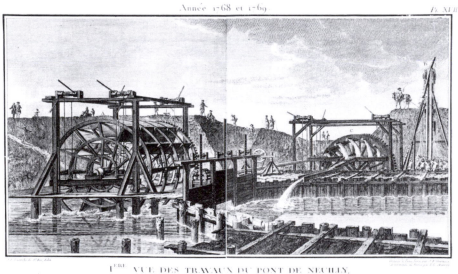

Figure Part V.2 *Preliminary Work on Pont de Neuilly Bridge, 1769–70*, from *Construire des ponts au XVIII siècle: L'Oeuvre de J. R. Perronet*, facs. edn (1970) Paris. From Collectanea Petrus Iohannus, by permission of the owner.

Sir James Steuart expressed surprise that anyone should doubt, albeit on grounds of their social consequences, that machines have always been devised to assist man in his work (Steuart 1767: Book I, xix). Machine design invariably begins from what is known in analogous fields: from the sixteenth century, for example, watchmaking relied upon separate specialized skills, such as gilding and engraving. But when technological improvements emerged either independently, or as a mere side-effect of the specific problems being tackled, their utility was often questioned. In his *Discours préliminaire* of 1751, D'Alembert acknowledged that the eventual benefits of 'scientific' enquiries cannot be predicted, but held that utility is a justifiable pretext for curiosity. Nevertheless Adam Smith ironically remarked that the precision in watches of his day was irrelevant to most people's daily needs (Smith 1759: Part IV, ch. 1, §5; cf. Smith 1776: Book I, ch. xi, section o, § 4). It has been calculated that the loss or gain per day of the most precise clocks fell from ten seconds in a Huygens clock of 1700 to less than half a second in 1800. On the other hand, the celebrated successes of the Harrison family, in devising and refining the reliability of the marine chronometer, had dramatically revolutionized marine navigation by the 1770s by enabling ships to calculate longitude reliably.

There remained, however, a residual theological problem that had been increasingly troublesome ever since Kepler's challenging pronouncements: when discussing men or society, metaphors involving machines were suspect, because they were too easily associated with materialistic or mechanistic philosophies which defined man without reference to the mind or soul. Machines themselves were essentially mindless; and, by association, the activities of those who tended them were also regarded as mindless. Although Malebranche had rendered many of Descartes's troubling mechanistic ideas respectable to fellow-theologians, nothing could persuade believers that La Mettrie's ideas from the 1730s onwards were defensible: his books were banned and burned – and became instantly worthy of attention. Apart from philosophers, however, political or economic theorists who characterized workers as machine-like typically overlooked, if not consciously suppressed, the human condition of those workers, as well as the traditional practices that were being displaced. By the nineteenth century, unnamed craftsmen, who were in that sense anonymous, could become virtually non-human operators, and in that sense non-existent beings.

LUXURY GOODS

Ancient writers, such as the Elder Pliny, frequently commented on the association of wealth with fashion and taste, and the reactions to ostentation that can be reliably predicted. Condemnation of luxury had become a familiar theme for moralists as well as theologians by the end of the seventeenth century, not least in the wake of Caroline and Restoration extravagance in England, and the spectacular displays of Louis XIV in France. In both instances, the wealthy intended to proclaim their unbridgeable distance from the common people, and Louis – like Catherine the Great fifty years later – ensured that the gap between the monarch and the highest nobles was equally unbridgeable. Whoever tried to match his expenditure and display, and attendant domination, was doomed to bankruptcy, if not prior dismissal. Such was the fate of Louis's superintendent of finance, Nicolas Foucquet, whose ambitions in building the magnificent chateau of Vaux-le-Vicomte rivalled (and inspired) the Sun King's for the future chateau of Versailles, and led to his fall, fifteen years in prison, and death in 1680.

Earlier chapters have described various ways in which the emerging sciences shaped eighteenth-century social practice. In France, for example, Voltaire's promotion of Newton's experimental methods encouraged wealthy members of society to signal their interest by conspicuously investing in very expensive scientific instruments –

although nobody could, or dared to, compete with the King. In Britain, too, the wealthy acquired microscopes and barometers for display alongside cabinets of natural specimens and illustrated books. British makers dominated the scene.

The rapidly expanding British economy, and the singular technical expertise of Huguenot immigrants arriving in the late seventeenth century, especially in instrument-making, combined to establish the predominance of British workshops until the 1780s. Several specialists were recruited to France (Daumas 1953: 91 and *passim*). Henry Sully founded a watchmaking industry at Versailles; John Kay, the inventor of the flying-shuttle, settled there; Michael Alcock went over to modernize the manufacture of iron goods; and William Wilkinson helped to found the Le Creusot metallurgical factory. From 1755 onwards the use of flint glass, together with better ways of polishing specula, ensured the supremacy of English optical workshops. For more than thirty years, until the 1780s, the high quality of steel and brass enabled workmen such as John Bell to ensure that English mathematical instruments, including astronomical quadrants, were the best available. In the mid-century, workshops such as those of Dollond dominated the market, and when several makers abandoned the craft traditions in favour of new industrial methods, makers such as Dollond, Ramsden and Adams continued to defeat all commercial opposition. James Bernoulli (1744–1807), the young Swiss mathematician who attended the executors' sale of the instruments of James Short, one of the best makers, found the prices very high (Bryden 1968: 7). Expensive instruments made by Ramsden or Short sold at the equivalent 2002 prices of €50,000–150,000, with 24-inch reflecting telescopes in 1750 priced at €14,000. Nevertheless, by 1770 cheap thermometers were available at the equivalent of €150.

French craftsmen were confined to a small clientele, albeit rich and distinguished. What stifled French development in these areas were still surviving guild restrictions and a moribund economy that was unable to adapt and compete in the emerging markets. The guilds themselves were heavily taxed, and disputes between highly jealous corporations continued until the Revolution. Even in the 1780s, when thermometers had become so commonplace that they were peddled in the streets of Paris by Italian salesmen, makers were not infrequently raided on suspicion of making or adapting instruments to which they had no rights. Since 1608, French kings had lodged some of the most skilful makers of luxury goods in the Louvre, and a few religious communities were also allowed to house artisans within their domains – although from the latter only one cleric, the Benedictine Dom Noel, seems to have been permitted to make instruments sometime in the 1760s.

Because of the difficulty in understanding the meaning and implications of comparative prices and incomes of earlier times, many scholars deplore the use of any figures at all. But some indication, however approximate, seems justifiable to indicate dramatic variations, and the impossibility of whole swaths of society from gaining access to many processes, products and their associated values. Without any figures, historical interpretations too often underestimate the brutal realities of everyday life. A glance at England, Scotland and France must suffice.

In 1759 more than half of the Scottish population of about one million lived in conditions of bare subsistence in the Highlands. An agricultural worker could hope to earn a total of £3 for summer work, plus victuals (in winter he would receive only victuals); a plough cost the farm-owner the same amount. By contrast, a small 24-inch reflecting telescope cost £100, Professor Adam Smith earned about £200 from student fees, the Duke of Argyll paid £500 for a private 'travelling house' (a kind of collapsible caravan), and David Hume earned almost £1,000 from publication rights. (Rough equivalents in 2002 euros would be as follows: agricultural worker €415, 24-inch telescope €14,000, Adam Smith's fees €30,000, Argyll's caravan €61,000, Hume's publication income €130,000.)

In England, as in Scotland, the mere existence of an inventory signals that its owner or inheritor did not belong to the poorest layer of the population, but any comparison between the owner of a small inn, the owner of a large estate, and a wealthy member of the aristocracy reveals gaps which almost no one could expect to bridge. Using 2002 euro equivalents in brackets, we can record that when the comfortably off owner of a small wayside inn in Yorkshire died in 1762, his estate was valued at £22 (€2,400): he owned one cow, a calf, one mare and a few pigs. His furniture included six or seven 'tables', about twenty chairs, and some six or seven beds, some of which folded into cupboards. In 1750 an English country joiner's day wage was 2 shillings, and an apprentice's half that rate (under €2,000 p.a.); they could charge 18 shillings for six chairs, and 25 shillings for large tables (€100, €150). Thomas Chippendale, on the other hand, with clients such as the Dukes of Norfolk, Beaufort and Northumberland, paid his senior workmen 21 shillings a week, and charged the Duke of Atholl at Blair Castle £7 7 shillings for a pair of carved candle-stands – at precisely the time an agricultural worker in Scotland could not expect twice that amount for an annual wage. In 1762–3 William Vile charged the King £24.10s for a mahogany library table and Queen Charlotte £9.18s for a mahogany work table (€3,000, €1,200). Even in 1738 a rich man would readily buy eighteen chairs at 23 shillings each, and £3.5s (€450) for a single pattern chair at Holkham. Pier-glasses were expensive show-pieces. To the cost of the carver's and joiner's work had to be added that of gilding; and finally the glass plate itself, which almost doubled the price. At Woburn Abbey, in 1760, the Duke of Bedford had to add £183.5s for the glass, on top of £229 for the gilded carved frame (€60,000). Before the decade was out Chippendale was charging Sir Lawrence Dundas £130 for ten French carved and gilded arm chairs (€12,000) (Coleridge 1968: *passim*; Gilbert 1991: 15ff.).

In France the relative costs of luxury goods were even higher than in Britain, but because there are no accepted translations between *ancien régime* sums and the present, and considerable fluctuations, broad comparisons in the currency of the day must suffice. The labouring poor between 1730 and 1790 secured an estimated annual income between 100 and 300 livres; a salaried manual or skilled worker could earn up to 1,000 livres; and an office-holder, such as an academic tutor, up to 3,000 livres – the cost of a single mirror. A wealthy doctor might earn 10,000 livres per annum, and some professionals double that amount. On the other hand, bishops and nobles would expect to live on an income of between 40,000 and 100,000 livres; and royal princes could expect much more than that. The Duc de Villeroy had an income of over 370,000 livres, and among the richest men in Paris was the archbishop, with an income estimated at over 1 million livres (Sargentson 1996: xi and *passim*). As in England, successful craftsmen of the highest calibre could become very rich themselves. Jean-Henri Riesener (1734–1806), a master of marquetry and cabinet-maker to Louis XV and XVI was paid 938,000 livres over ten years up to 1784, at a time when a skilled Parisian gilder or cabinet-maker earned no more than 600 livres a year (Chastang 2000: 78). In 1778 the flunkeys and the floor-polishers of the Marquis de Marigny were paid 216 livres, and the concierge 800 livres. Arthur Young, the tireless traveller and commentator, writing just before the Revolution, deplored the 300,000-livre annual income of the abbot of St Germain, and estimated the annual cost of living for a household of four servants, three horses and one carriage, living in a country manor house, at 7,000 livres. He noted that a bottle of Bordeaux cost around 1½ livres.

When the guilds dominated craft practices and traditions, it was accepted that everything they made was intended for use – including items later classified as 'art' and explicitly dissociated from utilitarian intention. But at no time could anyone deny that all furniture is made for use, even multiple use: a bench can be used for sitting or sleeping, as a table or support, as a shelf or worktop. The poor have always survived with a minimum of multiple-use items, sometimes decorated, or uniquely adapted to special needs. By contrast, wealthier classes have always been able to acquire objects for restricted uses, including merely decoration or as a status symbol. But even when objects are made for utilitarian purposes there are indefinitely many design alternatives for form, scale, material, length of life or ease of maintenance.

As the demand for consumer goods increased, particularly in Britain and France, types and forms of furniture, as of clothes, became indicators of social rank and prestige: what formerly satisfied needs could evolve into ornaments. Display furniture, as we have seen, was extremely expensive, but makers were able to experiment with new forms which later filtered down the social scale in cheaper and more modest versions, not least for the more confined spaces they would occupy. Tradesmen and makers were acutely aware that market success depended on responding to clients' decisions, as much as on their own offerings, and those decisions reflected changes in social practices, such as social visiting, dining or music parties, or fashions in dress, such as whooped skirts (which required chair arms to be set back). Design influences typically proceeded from the top downwards, and those in lower social strata had to modify both aspirations and acquisitions in the light of their available resources. Nevertheless, in Paris and London, and many provincial urban centres, there was considerable trade in the second half of the eighteenth century in second-hand dress and furniture. Indeed, as early as 1722 a German visitor to France, Ernst Ludwig Carl, commended the French practice of generating cycles of very costly fashionable goods, which could then be disposed of very cheaply, especially abroad, when competitors produced imitations (Sonenscher 1998: 237–9). He also argued that by separating professions one could cumulatively expand the production of necessities, conveniences and pure luxuries. The downward pyramid of fashion and marketing, strongly 'demand-led', was well understood in the luxury trades and lasted until the Revolution. Movable property was always disposable, and ultimately dispensable.

REFERENCES

Arup, Ove (1970) 'Architects, Engineers and Builders', in *Journal of the Royal Society of Arts*.

Bryden, D. J. (1968) *James Short and His Telescopes*, Edinburgh: Royal Scottish Museum.

Chambers, Ephraim (1728) *Cyclopaedia: or, an Universal Dictionary of Arts and Sciences*, 2nd edn, 2 vols (1738) London.

Chastang, Y. (2000) *Paintings in Wood: French Marquetry Furniture*, London: The Wallace Collection.

Coleridge, A. (1968) *Chippendale Furniture*, London: Faber & Faber.

Daumas, Maurice (1953) *Les Instruments scientifiques aux xvii et xviii siècles*; trans. M. Holbrook (1972) as *Scientific Instruments of the Seventeenth and Eighteenth Centuries and Their Makers*, London: Batsford.

Gilbert, C. (1991) *English Vernacular Furniture 1750–1900*, New Haven, Conn., and London: Yale University Press.

Kristeller, P. O. (1951–2) 'The Modern System of the Arts', *Journal of the History of Ideas*, vols XII, XIII; repr. in *Renaissance Thought II* (1965) New York: Harper Torchbooks.

Sargentson, C. (1996) *Merchants and Luxury Markets*, London: Victoria & Albert Museum.

Sonenscher, M. (1998) 'Fashion's Empire: Trade and Power in Early 18th-Century France', in R. Fox and A. Turner (eds) *Luxury Trades and Consumerism in Ancien Régime Paris*, Aldershot: Ashgate.

Smith, A. (1759) *The Theory of Moral Sentiments*, ed. D. D. Raphael and A. L. Macfie (1976) Oxford: Clarendon Press.

—— (1776) *An Inquiry into the Nature and Causes of the Wealth of Nations*, ed. R. H. Campbell and A. S. Skinner (1976) Oxford: Clarendon Press.

Steuart, Sir J. (1767) *An Inquiry into the Principles of Political Oeconomy*, ed. Andrew S. Skinner (1966) Edinburgh and London: Oliver & Boyd.

CHAPTER TWENTY-ONE

ENCYCLOPAEDISM AND ENLIGHTENMENT

Richard Yeo

Encyclopaedism is often seen as a typical feature of the age of Enlightenment. The label has been used by historians to denote a cluster of activities that includes the passion for systematic classification of knowledge, large-scale collection projects in fields such as history, languages and natural history, and comprehensive coverage of particular disciplines. Thus projects such as Carl Linnaeus's taxonomy of the plant and animal worlds and George-Louis Leclerc, Comte de Buffon's *Histoire naturelle* (1749) have been called encyclopaedic, even though they did not resemble what we, or their contemporaries, would recognize as an encyclopaedia. Nor would eighteenth-century readers have described Louis Moréri's *Grand Dictionnaire historique* (2 vols, 1674) as an encyclopaedia. It clearly belonged to a separate genre, the historical or biographical dictionary, as did Pierre Bayle's *Dictionnaire historique et critique* (2 vols, 1697), which began with the intention of remedying Moréri's errors. Neither of these works attempted a survey of the circle of sciences. Thus, when Denis Diderot and Jean Le Rond D'Alembert began their *Encyclopédie*, they looked to Ephraim Chambers's *Cyclopaedia* (1728), a dictionary of arts and sciences. This work attempted a summary of systematic disciplines (*'scientia'*), such as grammar, theology, logic, music, astronomy, mechanics, optics and other parts of natural philosophy, as well as of subjects that could be brought into scientific order, such as anatomy, medicine, natural history, the practical and mechanical arts and trades – but not biography or history (Yeo 2001).

In this chapter I want to delineate the distinctive features of encyclopaedism in the eighteenth century and its links with Enlightenment. This requires some notice of the fact that the concept of 'encyclopaedia' is a pre-modern one, dating back to Graeco-Roman culture. We owe the word 'encyclopaedia' to Quintilian, who, in the first century AD, offered this Latinized version of the Greek term denoting a circle of study or learning. The concept was extremely influential as an educational ideal in the ancient Western world, and came to inform the notion of the seven liberal arts, or the *trivium* and *quadrivium*, that passed into the medieval university curriculum. Encyclopaedic works reached a high point in the late Middle Ages. The most famous of the medieval works was the *Speculum Maius* (*The Greater Mirror*), completed by the Dominican friar Vincent of Beauvais around 1250. The image of the mirror betrays the assumption, and the confidence, that an encyclopaedia, a collation of textual material, could genuinely reflect the universal structures of the world (McArthur 1986: 67; Blair 1997: ch. 5). The order of subjects was usually informed by some overarching pattern, such as the seven liberal arts, the hierarchy of faculties in the university, or the cosmological chain of being with the Divinity as its apex. Johann Heinrich Alsted's (1588–1638) *Encyclopaedia* (4 vols, 1630) is considered as the last and best of the neo-scholastic encyclopaedias. This incorporated the subjects of the three 'superior' faculties of theology, law and medicine, with the addition of the mechanical arts. Alsted conceived the encyclopaedia as the 'methodological understanding of everything that man must learn in this life' (cited in Kenny 1991: 15). In the spirit of this definition, it was common during the seventeenth century for the term 'encyclopaedia' to refer to the round of subjects an educated person should pursue, rather than to a single work (or several volumes). In his *Glossographia* of 1656, Thomas Blount (1618–79) reflected this position by defining the 'ency-clopedy' as 'that learning which comprehends all Liberal Sciences; an Art that comprehends all others, the perfection of all knowledge' (Blount 1656; see also Yeo 2001: ch. 1). The mathematician and divine Isaac Barrow (1630–77) expressed the ideal at work here when he advised that 'one Part of Learning doth confer Light to another . . . that he will be a lame Scholar, who hath not an insight into many kinds of knowledge, that he can hardly be a good Scholar, who is not a general one' (Barrow 1716: vol. 1, 184).

This ideal was under pressure, however, at least from the early 1600s, when Francis Bacon, in attacking scholastic philosophy, asserted that knowledge was to be found in the world, and not merely in texts. His call for the collection of *new* facts and observations produced an expectation of constant intellectual revision; and responses to such a demand fuelled the struggle between rival claimants for inclusion in the encyclopaedic circle. The controversies between the Ancients and the Moderns, and the sometimes overlapping dispute between the defenders of traditional learning (historical and theological), such as Meric Casaubon, and the advocates of the new scientific philosophy, such as Joseph Glanvill and Thomas Sprat, demonstrate such competition (Hunter 1981: 154–6). Given the rapid expansion of knowledge, it came to be recognized that the encyclopaedic ideal would explode if all subjects were included. Not long after Chambers's work, the *Grosses vollständiges Universal-Lexicon*, begun in 1732 by the Leipzig publisher Johann Zedler, showed how an encyclopaedic work could burst the limits defined by previous examples of the genre. By including biography, history, a *Wörterbuch* of the German language, plus all the arts and sciences, it reached sixty-four folio volumes by 1750 and still needed a four-volume supplement in 1754. Significantly, it defined 'encyclopaedia' in a way that departed from the notion of a circle of studies. Although the preface to the first volume made allusions to the ideal of polymathic knowledge, the entry (published in 1734) on 'encyclopaedia' did not endorse this goal, but defined the concept in abstract terms as the systematic unity of all knowledge, with no reference to any individual effort to embrace this, nor to examples of works that sought to provide a summary of this knowledge (Zedler 1732–50: vol. 8). As I discuss below, Enlightenment encyclo-paedias had to live with this tension at the very heart of encyclopaedism.

Some generalizations may be made about the characteristics of pre-Enlightenment encyclopaedias. First, they belonged to a world of learned elites, based in the Church

Figure 21.1 *A Temple of Learning*, from Gregor Reisch *Margarita philosophica* [*The Philosophical Pearl*]; Basel (1517): Michael Futerius (first published in Freiburg, 1503). The schoolboy is led to the palace of learning in which study of the various subjects, culminating in philosophy and theology, will match the stages of his life. By permission of the National University of Australia.

and the universities; Latin was their *lingua franca*. Their selection of subjects reflected the university curriculum and the hierarchical order of the Christian cosmos. The stability assumed here is evidenced by the reprinting of Vincent of Beauvais's thirteenth-century *Speculum* in Venice in 1590 (Burke 2000: 94). However, this example must be placed alongside developments during the Renaissance that expanded the existing notion of an encyclopaedia by including the *studia humanitatis*, conceived as grammar and rhetoric (already in the *trivium*) plus poetry, history and ethics (Grafton and Jardine 1986). Second, there were assumptions about the relationships between these subjects, often represented in an accompanying illustration – a diagram, chart or tree of knowledge. This classification implied a recommended order of study determined by the logical order of disciplines, and sometimes by matching subjects to particular stages of life, as portrayed in a woodcut (Fig. 21.1) from Gregor Reisch's *Margarita philosophica* (1503), an influential compendium of leading university subjects. Finally, there were also strong expectations that the circle of subjects contained in an encyclopaedia prescribed a circle of learning that could, and should, be undertaken by the educated individual as a foundation for any additional studies required of their position in society. In this respect, stricter compilers distinguished between the liberal studies of the *trivium* and *quadrivium* (the arts curriculum) and the professional studies of theology, law and medicine, although often still including these in their works. Traditional encyclopaedism belonged to a world in which prestigious knowledge was monopolized by Church and university; the emphasis was on guarding and conserving a curriculum. In this sense it does not make an obvious partner for Enlightenment, insofar as that movement shared, or promoted, the values of an open market for knowledge with the aim of reforming society.

This sketch is helpful when seeking to appreciate what happened to the encyclopaedic ideal in the eighteenth century. What, then, was new or different about the encyclopaedias of Enlightenment? I will approach this question in two steps: first, by looking at the scope and audience of these works, their place in the commercial world of booksellers and in the ideal of a republic of letters; second, by discussing the intellectual rationales and reading practices that informed their alphabetical organization. These themes apply (albeit with some differences) to the *Encyclopédie*; but I will focus here on Chambers' *Cyclopaedia*, the work that Diderot acknowledged as his most pertinent model.

EXTENDING THE REPUBLIC OF LETTERS

In his *Enlightenment* (2000), Roy Porter makes the case for Britain as the first enlightened country. The claim is based on the major intellectual advances of Newton and Locke, both idols of declared Anglophiles such as Charles Louis de Secondat Montesquieu, Voltaire, Diderot and D'Alembert. It also rests on the fact that from about the time of the Glorious Revolution (1688) the wish list of Continental reformers had been partly met in England: habeas corpus, the rule of law, a measure of religious toleration, and a comparatively free press (Porter 2000: chs 2–3). This last factor reflected the vibrant printing trade, based in London, and the network of coffee houses affiliated with it. J. H. Plumb's notion of a 'commercialization of leisure' in this period is manifested in the diverse market encouraged by the booksellers, who were both publishers and retailers (McKendrick *et al.* 1982; Porter 2000: ch. 4). Of course, newspapers, magazines and novels were the best-selling commodities and, by comparison, encyclopaedias were weightier and more expensive products. Nevertheless, they are a stunning example of how the trade in knowledge was judged to be worth large capital investment. They also exemplify the assumption that knowledge should circulate freely, that it should be accessible to anyone, irrespective of social rank, who could buy or borrow a copy of such a work. What did these works contain? How were they sold and who bought them?

By the twentieth century most readers mainly consulted encyclopaedias for biographical and historical, rather than for scientific, information. In the 1700s, the reverse was the case: the works that assumed the title of encyclopaedia were the dictionaries of arts and sciences, and these excluded historical and biographical material. As mentioned above, there was a distinct genre – the 'historical' dictionary – that treated these subjects as its special province. Moréri's *Great Historical Dictionary*, as it was called in the first English translation of 1694, comprised a list of names and places, not a treatment of the sciences and arts. In contrast, the dictionaries of arts and sciences did not include history and biography because they sought to record knowledge, not lives (Yeo 1996b: 140–7). Rather, in offering a summary of such technical and scientific subjects, they aspired to encyclopaedic status. Chambers's *Cyclopaedia* was the third, and most successful, of this new genre, inaugurated by Antoine Furetière's (1619–88) *Dictionnaire universel*, published in three volumes at The Hague in 1690, two years after his death. The second was John Harris's (1667–1719) *Lexicon Technicum* of 1704, to which he added a supplementary volume in 1710. In its choice of title, Chambers's work looked back to Alsted's *Encyclopaedia* of 1630; but this continuity must be set against the fact that the eighteenth-century encyclopaedias were written in the vernacular. In this respect they were in tune with the times. Of the 6,000 books held in the Bodleian Library around 1600, only thirty-six were in English; most, of course, were in Latin (Melton 2001: 88). In contrast, by 1700 a Latin encyclopaedia was almost unthinkable as a commercial venture because the expanding demand for books was clearly located in the vernacular. The encyclopaedias of the eighteenth century were practical embodiments of the notion that knowledge should be accessible to a wide public and, as such, their purpose was not just to collate knowledge used by elites, but to facilitate conversation and communication. In short, they show how the notion of a republic of letters was extended during the Enlightenment to include an audience even more diverse than that imagined by Bayle and other Protestant exiles sheltering in Holland after the Revocation of the Edict of Nantes in 1685 (Hazard 1964: ch. 5).

Although not mentioned in D'Alembert's *Preliminary Discourse*, Bayle is often seen as one of the spiritual fathers of the *Encyclopédie* (Schwab 1995: 109). He provided a model for using a dictionary as a vehicle for sceptical and controversial commentary, something taken up by Voltaire in his *Philosophical Dictionary* of 1764. The salient point here, however, is the way in which he also cultivated the ethos of a community of authors and readers, separated by geography and often by religious creed, who shared a common commitment to scholarship and learning. This was the mission of his *Nouvelles de la République des Lettres*, which he edited in Rotterdam from March 1684 to 1687. This journal reviewed books, including those not readily available, and published letters and comments from readers. Both practices gave substance to the ideal of a cosmopolitan fellowship, a republic of letters in which individuals never likely to meet could have their work and ideas discussed by a tribunal of peers (Hazard 1964; Eisenstein 1992). The diplomats and secretaries of Bayle's network were translators, booksellers and information brokers, such as Pierre Coste, Jean le Clerc, Pierre des Maizeaux and Prosper Marchand, who worked as intermediaries between major philosophical figures, such as Bayle himself, John Locke and Gottfried Wilhelm Leibniz (Goldgar 1995). The citizenry of this republic comprised university academics, members of learned institutions such as the Royal Society of London or the Paris Academy, and a diverse range of individuals on the periphery of the scholarly world: clergymen, booksellers, librarians, journalists, printers and proof-readers. These people formed a virtual community held together by a passion for books and ideas, but also by news and gossip about instances of plagiarism, theft and impersonation through which its most lively members tested the unwritten conventions of polite conversation and debate. Although Goldgar (1995) highlights some contrasts between this erudite world and the more politically engaged one of the *philosophes*, I think the place of encyclopaedism in the Enlightenment can be better appreciated if its debt to this legacy is recalled. Two facets may be considered here: the appeal to a universal readership and the notion of intellectual collaboration.

The ideal of a cosmopolitan readership is closely connected with the emergence of the notion of audience as arbiter as well as reader. By Chambers's time, this audience had become 'the public', an entity he addressed in the short-lived periodical *The Literary Magazine: or, the History of the Works of the Learned*, which he co-edited in 1735 and 1736. Its subtitle – almost generic for the period – described the work as 'Containing an Account of the most valuable BOOKS publish'd both at home and abroad, in most of the languages in Europe, and in all Arts and Sciences'. Its preface spoke of a collective set of values:

> We conceive it the duty of a Journalist to give a faithful account of the books which come into his hands . . . When he affects the air and language of a censor or judge, he invades the undoubted right of the *Public*, which is the only foreign judge of the reputation of an author, and the merit of his compositions.
>
> (Chambers 1735–6: Preface)

Chambers thought of this public as cosmopolitan, extending well beyond Latin readers. Like the famous English periodical journals, such as the *Tatler* (1709–11) and the *Spectator* (1711–14), Chambers was addressing the readers of newspapers and magazines, and the denizens of the many London coffee houses in which these publications were exchanged and debated. Similarly, encyclopaedias of this period addressed a larger world beyond the city and country in which they were published. Their imagined audience was not necessarily restricted by the shift from Latin to the vernacular. Certainly, in the case of English works there was the likelihood of a loss of readership in moving to the vernacular, since English was rarely used in northern Europe, where Dutch and German were the dominant vernaculars (Israel 2001:

137–9). But this loss was compensated for by the willingness of booksellers to finance translation of works likely to sell across national and denominational borders. Thus the leading English work, Chambers's *Cyclopaedia*, was twice translated into Italian before Diderot and D'Alembert had begun to transform the French translation of this work into a massively enlarged one of their own.

In the eighteenth century encyclopaedias were imagined as collaborative projects, even when compiled largely by a single person. The editors of the *Encyclopédie* referred, on its title page, to the efforts of the Société de Gens des Lettres who had contributed to this massive work. So powerful was this notion as a source of authority that the first edition of the *Encyclopaedia Britannica* (1768–71), even though largely the result of the labours of William Smellie, attributed its origin to 'a Society of Gentlemen'. The manner in which encyclopaedias were financed and sold also reinforced the notion that they were, in a sense, collaborative. The dictionaries of Harris and Chambers were among the most successful published by subscription, a method pioneered by English booksellers early in the seventeenth century (Wiles 1957; Johns 1998: 450–3). This method allowed the publisher (that is, a bookseller) to test the water and then to proceed without risk: printing only went ahead if sufficient subscriptions were received; if not, the money was returned. The names of subscribers were listed in a prospectus announcing the work and, in turn, seeking additional ones. Such lists were printed at the front of the final publication, thus allowing individuals the chance to be publicly associated with a significant work. But, in addition, subscriptions were an indication of interest from a wide range of social groups and occupations, including not just aristocrats, academics, clergy and gentlemen but lawyers, doctors, surgeons, teachers, merchants, watchmakers, brewers and, of course, printers and booksellers. Subscription represented a form of patronage in which the 'middling sort' of people might participate (Raven 1992).

The related publishing practice was serialization: namely, selling books, especially large works, in weekly or monthly parts. The advantage of serialization was that it spread the cost over a period. In the case of the 1741 edition of the *Cyclopaedia*, serialization meant that one could choose to buy three sheets each week rather than the whole five hundred and twelve half-sheets in one purchase. The former option meant an outlay of sixpence a week rather than four guineas in one transaction. In the case of such large works, there was another advantage: one could begin to read the early parts without waiting for the completion of one or two volumes. This in turn made it possible for authors to ask readers for comments and possibly to act on such feedback in the course of the book's production – a feasible option when works were published over a number of years. In preparing his second edition, Chambers called for contributions from 'Persons of every Rank, Profession, and Degree of Knowledge', asking for comments (Chambers 1738: xxii). Zedler's *Universal Lexicon*, published from 1732, carried a request for comments in its preface to the first volume. Encouraging readers to send in suggestions for corrections and new information, it indicated that the *Lexicon* was a 'joint work' (Zedler 1732–50: vol. 1, 13). This appeal was repeated in the foreword of the *Supplemente*, issued beween 1751 and 1754: apparently, even after sixty-eight volumes, it was not too late for feedback! Thus, when combined, the practices of subscription and serialization made readers of these large works akin to corporate authors: it was their support, at the start, that ensured the appearance of the work; it was their reception of it, as it appeared in parts, that might adjust the content or presentation (Yeo 2001: 46–53).

The conjunction of a widening audience and an ever-increasing number of books created problems identified by various observers – from scholars and philosophers such as Bayle, Locke and Leibniz to the editors of moral weeklies and reviews such as Joseph Addison and Richard Steele. The sheer number of books threatened the notion of close and careful reading; the increasing variety of readers raised concerns about proper taste and judgement. In some ways this echoed similar, earlier concerns about reading of the Bible (Melton 2001: 83–4). Of course, booksellers relished this situation and responded by publishing even more books – small books as guides to larger ones; encyclopaedias condensing large subjects and thus acting as mini-libraries; dictionaries of technical terms in anatomy, chemistry, trade and commerce. Books parading under titles such as 'compendium', 'directory', 'digest', 'epitome', 'glossary', 'handbook', 'itinerary', 'key', 'theatre' and so on claimed to contain a complete education between two covers (Burke 2000: 170–1). This provoked the ire of critics who feared the loss of serious study. One form of attack was directed against the assumption that complex topics could be boiled down to a short vocabulary of key words. Jonathan Swift, in his *Tale of a Tub* (1704), dismissively called this 'Index-learning' (Swift 1704: 145, 147). Later in the century, Thomas James Mathias, the royal librarian, invented the character of Dr Morosophos, a pedant who insists on the importance of 'Method', but in fact depends on alphabetical compilations: 'Chambers Abridg'd! in sooth 'twas all he read,/From fruitful A to unproductive Z' (Mathias 1798: 435). These comments suggest that the format and organization of books, and indeed of encyclopaedias, was a matter of interest and debate.

USING THE ALPHABET

The encyclopaedias of the Enlightenment made the irrevocable switch to alphabetical organization. This broke with the thematic, if not always systematic, arrangement of earlier encyclopaedias. Such a change in format correlates with the changes in language and audience mentioned above. Undoubtedly, one attraction of alphabetical over systematic order was that the former allowed the inclusion of material without any need to confront troublesome issues of classification. Whereas earlier works sought to preserve established knowledge, eighteenth-century encyclopaedias stressed the need to record *new* knowledge, removing error and obscurantism in favour of open-ended enquiry. Consequently, the major publications of the day survived beyond their first editions. In subsequent editions of the same work, new material could then be added, under a convenient letter, without any need to recast the treatment of a complex subject, such as astronomy or medicine. It is tempting to go further, drawing a link between the attacks of the *philosophes* on the authority of the intellectual hierarchies that classification often supported and the manner in which the alphabet scattered subjects without regard to their relative importance.

However, some caution is advisable before casting the alphabet as a destroyer of the older encyclopaedic idea, or, even more sensationally, as a carrier of revolutionary intent. Alphabetical arrangement offered the chance of radical questioning but did not guarantee it. Thus Moréri's alphabetical historical dictionary was conservative, whereas Bayle took advantage of the way the alphabet mixed saints and sinners, pagans and Christians, adding corrosive footnotes with cross-references to other entries (Grafton 1997: 191–4). However, as far as the early eighteenth-century encyclopaedias are concerned, alphabetical order did not necessarily imply a rejection of traditional subject categories or the importance of classification. Rather, the attraction was the simplicity of alphabetical entries over large treatises, a point shared by the various philosophical, chemical and medical lexicons (still often in Latin) common by the end of the seventeenth century. Diderot's comment in the prospectus of 1750 suggests this appeal:

> We believe we have had good reason to follow alphabetical order in this work . . . If we treated each science separately and followed it with a discussion conforming to the order of ideas, rather than that of words, then the form of this work would have been even less convenient for the majority of our readers, who would have been able to find nothing without difficulty.
>
> (quoted in Koepp 1986: 237)

Diderot and D'Alembert called their work a 'reasoned dictionary'. This was a way of registering that its use of the alphabet did not imply a rejection of all systematic classification. Chambers had already confronted this issue over twenty years earlier. In his substantial preface he boasted that his *Cyclopaedia* excelled other works by providing the option of systematic reading: 'Former Lexicographers have not attempted any thing like Structure in their Works; nor seem to have been aware that a Dictionary was in some measure capable of the Advantages of a continued Discourse' (Chambers 1728: vol. 1, Preface, i). How could a dictionary be said to have a coherent structure?

Although his work was alphabetically arranged, Chambers provided a map of the sciences (Fig 21.2). This 'View of Knowledge' shows forty-seven 'Heads' – major subjects of the arts and sciences – numbered simply according to their position on the diagram, from Meteorology to Poetry. In prefacing his dictionary with this map, Chambers was deferring to the traditional practice of displaying the scheme of classification by which earlier (non-alphabetical) encyclopaedias were organized. The diagram also reinforces Chambers's claim that the work had been collated by a proper method, the terms being first collected under an appropriate head before being distributed alphabetically. His use of the word 'Heads' suggests the terminology of the tradition of commonplaces that flourished in the Renaissance. This was mani-fested in the widespread practice, among humanist scholars and students, of keeping a commonplace book that recorded phrases, argument and factual information encountered in the course of reading for later use in speeches and written compo-sitions (Lechner 1956; Moss 1996). Such material was entered under a relevant topic or subject heading and thus recorded in a commonplace book.

We can imagine the *Cyclopaedia* as a large commonplace book (Yeo 2001: chs 4 and 5). The notes attached to each art or science in the diagram give the cognate terms belonging to it, as they might have been listed under one head in a common-place book; but in the text of the work these terms are thrown into alphabetical order.

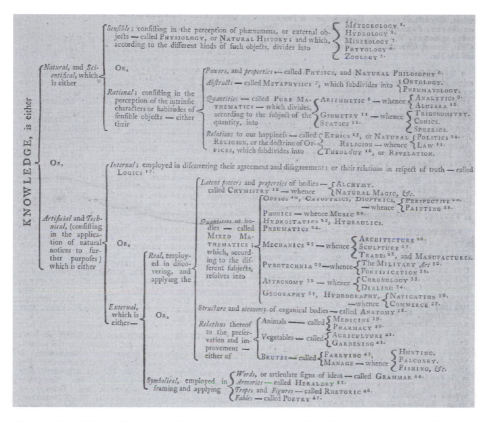

Figure 21.2 *View of Knowledge*, from Ephraim Chambers (1738) *Cyclopaedia: or, an Universal Dictionary of Arts and Sciences*, 2nd edn, vol. 1, London. This shows the arts and sciences that comprise the enyclopaedic circle of learning. This diagram appeared in all editions. From Collectanea Petrus Iohannus, by permission of the owner.

The diagram, and its accompanying forty-seven footnotes listing terms under each subject, allows for the coherence of major subjects, such as various arts and sciences, to be reconstituted by using cross-references among the terms. The diagram also reinforces Chambers's claim that the work had been collated by proper method, the terms being first collected under an appropriate head, as in a private common-place book, before being distributed alphabetically. In his own entry on 'Common-Place Book' he explained the method of assembling material under 'a Multiplicity of Heads', and cited the endorsement of John Locke – 'that great Master of Order', as Chambers called him (Chambers 1728: vol. 1, 'Common-Places'). In 1686 Locke had written an article describing his use of commonplace books and a way to index them; this appeared in the *Bibliothèque universelle et historique*, edited by his friend, the Huguenot journalist Jean le Clerc. Two English translations were published in 1706, two years after Locke's death (Yeo 1996a).

The analogy between an encyclopaedia and a commonplace book enabled Chambers, and later editors and publishers of his work, to imagine two types of reader, each affected in slightly different ways by the growing flood of books. Educated readers and scholars might use the *Cyclopaedia* to prompt their memory for earlier reading, or perhaps to explore topics outside their own field. This 'systematic' reader realized that the alphabetical entries on terms belonged to various recognizable heads, listed in the preface. On the other hand, less scholarly readers could study the work as a single point of reference, accepting the warrant of the author that it was based on reliable abridgement of the major subjects. In fact, it might be argued that the map of knowledge was also crucial to the non-scholar who did not already possess a good sense of the parameters of the various subjects and their cognate terms. For such readers, the *Cyclopaedia* functioned as a ready-made commonplace book to be consulted and studied for almost all their needs.

How does this relate to what Rolf Engelsing has called the *Leserevolution* of the eighteenth century? Studying the reading habits of a section of the German bourgeoisie, he argued that there was a shift during the middle of the century away from the 'intensive', and usually communal, reading of one set of books – such as the Bible, moral and devotional works, and almanacs – that had prevailed since the Reformation. After about 1750 educated readers became more 'extensive' in their habits, quickly reading a greater number of publications, especially novels and periodical journals, but reading each item only once (Engelsing 1974: chs 12 and 13; Chartier 1994: 223–4; Melton 2001: 89–92). The rise of periodical magazines, dictionaries and encyclopaedias seems to support Engelsing's contention about the emergence of more casual and diverse reading practices. Indeed, Jeremy Popkin has suggested that if new 'extensive readers' had to be continually supplied with new texts, periodicals were the ideal answer to their needs, affording ample reading material in manageable bites (Popkin 1991: 204, 208–9). Encyclopaedias, arranged alphabetically, also seem to invite quick consultation and extensive skimming. But this scenario sits uneasily with the emphasis on order and method apparent in Chambers.

Engelsing's thesis has been strongly criticized, largely on the grounds that increasing opportunity for 'extensive' reading did not mean the end of close, 'intensive' reading. Elizabeth Eisenstein has suggested that both practices have long coexisted (Eisenstein 1992: 49; see also Wittmann 1999). In a somewhat different response, Robert Darnton has argued that from the 1760s readers of Jean Jacques Rousseau became emotionally involved in close encounters with his works, especially the epistolary novel *La Nouvelle Héloïse* (1761), probably the leading best-seller of the *ancien régime*. Using the letters of one bourgeois reader, Jean Ranson, a French Protestant, Darnton suggested that his approach to reading was anything but 'extensive'. Indeed, the advice Ranson gave to himself and friends was read less, but read intensely. Darnton points towards the development of what can loosely be called Romantic sensibilities towards texts, especially towards fiction and moral literature, in which 'reader and writer communed across the printed page' (Darnton 1984: 242–5).

My focus in this chapter is on non-fictional works in the first half of the eighteenth century; and, from this perspective, I want to retrieve what might be called the Lockean response. An influential version of this can be found in the didactic writings of Isaac Watts (1674–1748), a dissenting minister and renowned publicist of Locke's work. In his best-selling *Logick* (1725), and its supplement, *The Improvement of the Mind* (1741), he gave practical hints on reading and study, taking his cue from

Locke's stress on methodical study and note-taking. Accordingly, Watts declared against superficial reading, urging both student and scholar not to heap up books without reading them properly, scolding those who went no further than the contents page or the index. Instead he promoted active reading, suggesting that it was even possible to improve the '*Method* of a Book' if it happened to be weak. For example, he said, take notes, make an index of those parts 'which are new to you' and thus 'throw it [the book] into a better Method'. Watts was unambiguous on a key point: 'And remember that one Book read over in this Manner with all this laborious Meditation, will tend more to enrich your Understanding than the skimming over the Surface of twenty Authors' (Watts 1741: 65–7). This may corroborate Engelsing's claim that 'extensive' reading was indeed occurring – sufficiently so for it to be condemned by a pedagogue. Yet it also indicates the high status given to systematic reading of various works, including encyclopaedias, that aimed to convey knowledge of the sciences. Watts recommended that: 'The best Way to learn any Science, is to begin with a regular System, or a short and plain Scheme of that Science, well drawn up into a narrow Compass' (Watts 1741: 316). This combination of accessibility and coherence is what Chambers's *Cyclopaedia* aimed to provide.

John Locke was also Chambers's hero. For the English encyclopaedist, the message of Locke's *An Essay Concerning Human Understanding* (1690) had serious implications. Since knowledge was produced by the mind on the basis of sensory impressions, rather than given through innate ideas, then each individual faced the risk of being lost in a buzz of confusing sensations. Moreover, the objects of perception were not external things, but ideas stimulated by them and also by internal mental reflection. All this meant that knowledge must be carefully garnered: empirical observations, testimony and books all had to be weighed, degrees of probability determined; complex ideas had to be analysed for their relations with other ideas. Locke rejected any presumption to universal knowledge and warned against the premature acceptance of grand syntheses. This message permeated his *Of the Conduct of the Understanding* (1697), which spelled out some of the lessons of the *Essay*:

> God has made the intellectual world harmonious and beautiful without us; but it will never come into our heads all at once; we must bring it home piecemeal, and there set it up by our own industry, or else we shall have nothing but darkness and a chaos within, whatever order and light there be in things without us.
>
> (Locke 1697: III, 272)

One implication drawn from this by Chambers was that the classification of knowledge, as displayed in his own diagram, was to some extent arbitrary and had to be treated with caution (Chambers 1738: vol. 1, ix; Yeo 2001: ch. 5). The problem, however, was that scepticism about such classification could not be pushed too far: general categories, such as those used as heads in commonplace books, were important ways of guiding reading and enquiry.

Another major lesson from the *Essay* concerned the use of language. For Locke, words were only markers for ideas in the mind of the person who speaks them; they were not signs of things in the world. And since words were merely conventional signs, their meaning might well include what Locke calls a 'secret reference', known only to the person who used them (Locke 1690: III.2.§4). Chambers accepted this analysis and offered his *Cyclopaedia* as a Lockean dictionary of the arts and sciences. Lack of care meant that 'great uncertainty' had been introduced into language, thus allowing 'jargon and controversy' to threaten knowledge: 'All the confusion of Babel is brought upon us hereby; and people of the same country, nay the same profession, no longer understand one another' (Chambers 1738: vol. 1, xvii). Of course, this dictionary could not permanently fix the meaning of words: as Samuel Johnson confessed in the preface to his *Dictionary of the English Language* (2 vols, 1755), any attempt to do so was like chasing the sun, since the usage of words shifted, even as the lexicographer was compiling (Green 1996). Yet Chambers insisted that the *Cyclopaedia* did show the range of definitions currently in use, identifying their provenance within certain disciplines and schools. In this way, it might encourage careful use or terms in intellectual exchanges, thus providing the basis for building more general theories and systems.

Locke's admonitions about loose terminology and grand intellectual schemes potentially entailed a damaging criticism of encyclopaedias and their function. After all, in combining alphabetical lists of words (or terms) and maps of knowledge, these works apparently ignored his contention that both general doctrines and elaborate classifications of knowledge were often emasculated by confusion of ideas and careless use of words. Moreover, Locke's emphasis on individuals doing their own thinking threatened the rationale of encyclopaedias as agents for the dissemination of knowledge:

> The floating of other Mens [*sic*] Opinions in our brains makes us not one jot the more knowing, though they happen to be true . . . In the Sciences, every one has so much, as he really knows and comprehends: What he believes only, and takes upon trust, are but shreads; which however well in the whole piece, make no considerable addition to his stock, who gathers them. Such borrowed Wealth, like Fairy-money, though it were Gold in the hand from which he received it, will be but Leaves and Dust when it comes to use.
>
> (Locke 1690: I.4.§23)

Chambers's answer took this form: encyclopaedias play an important role in the establishment of some consensus on the meaning of terms; they offer a coherent account of the sciences as currently understood, and they chart the current status of our knowledge and the relationships between its various parts. All this he took to be in the spirit of Locke.

In the first section of this chapter I situated encyclopaedias within the eighteenth-century republic of letters. Dictionaries of arts and sciences were compiled, published, sold and read by members of this virtual community. Condensing and disseminating science in accessible form, these encyclopaedias supported the values of communication, education and sociability. However, the author of the leading English publication of this kind believed that conversation casually stocked with scientific content could be dangerous. 'The end of learning and study', Chambers advised, in good Lockean style, 'is not the filling of our heads with other men's ideas' (Chambers 1738: vol. 1, xxv). Rather, the advancement of knowledge needed active readers, alert to the capacities of the mind, the subtleties of classification, and the problems of language. Each individual member of the republic of letters had to assume responsibility for what Locke called the conduct of the understanding. Only then would encyclopaedias contribute to Enlightenment.

ACKNOWLEDGEMENT

The research for this chapter was supported by an Australian Research Council Grant.

REFERENCES

Barrow, Isaac (1716) 'Of Industry in our particular Calling, as Scholars', in *The Works of the Learned Isaac Barrow, published by his Grace Dr Tillotson*, 3rd edn, 3 vols in 2, London: J. Round, J. Tonson and W. Taylor.

Becq, Annie (ed.) (1991) *L'Encyclopédisme: Actes du Colloque de Caen*, Paris: Editions aux Amateurs de Livres.

Blair, Ann (1997) *The Theater of Nature: Jean Bodin and Renaissance Science*, Princeton and Chichester: Princeton University Press.

Blount, Thomas (1656) *Glossographia: or a Dictionary, Interpreting all Such Hard Words . . . Now Used in our Refined English Tongue*, London: Thomas Newcomb; facs. repr. (1969) Menston: Scolar Press.

Burke, Peter (2000) *A Social History of Knowledge: From Gutenberg to Diderot*, Cambridge: Polity Press.

Chambers, Ephraim (1728) *Cyclopaedia: or, an Universal Dictionary of Arts and Sciences*, 2 vols, London: J. and J. Knapton, J. Darby, D. Midwinter *et al.*; 2nd edn (1738) London: D. Midwinter, A. Bettesworth, C. Hitch *et al.*

—— (1735–6) *The Literary Magazine: or, the History of the Works of the Learned*, London: T. Cooper.

Chartier, Roger (1994) *The Order of Books: Readers, Authors, and Libraries in Europe between the Fourteenth and Eighteenth Centuries*, trans. L. G. Cochrane, Cambridge: Polity Press.

Darnton, Robert (1984) 'Readers Respond to Rousseau: The Fabrication of Romantic Sensitivity', in *The Great Cat Massacre and Other Episodes in French Cultural History*, Harmondsworth: Allen Lane.

Eisenstein, Elizabeth (1992) *Grub Street Abroad: Aspects of the French Cosmopolitan Press from the Age of Louis XIV to the French Revolution*, Oxford and New York: Clarendon Press.

Engelsing, Rolf (1974) *Der Bürger als Leser: Lesergeschichte in Deutschland 1500–1800*, Stuttgart: J. B. Metzlersche and A. E. Poeschel.

Goldgar, Anne (1995) *Impolite Learning: Conduct and Community in the Republic of Letters, 1680–1750*, New Haven, Conn.: Yale University Press.

Grafton, Anthony (1997) *The Footnote: A Curious History*, London: Faber & Faber.

Grafton, Anthony and Jardine, Lisa (1986) *From Humanism to the Humanities: Education and the Liberal Arts in Fifteenth and Sixteenth Century Europe*, Cambridge, Mass.: Harvard University Press.

Green, Jonathan (1996) *Chasing the Sun: Dictionary-makers and the Dictionaries They Made*, London: Jonathan Cape.

Hazard, P. G (1964) *The European Mind, 1680–1715*, trans. J. L. May, Harmondsworth: Penguin.

Hunter, Michael (1981) *Science and Society in Restoration England*, Cambridge: Cambridge University Press.

Israel, Jonathan (2001) *Radical Enlightenment: Philosophy and the Making of Modernity, 1650–1750*, Oxford: Oxford University Press.

Johns, Adrian (1998) *The Nature of the Book: Print and Knowledge in the Making*, Chicago and London: University of Chicago Press.

Kenny, Neil (1991) *The Palace of Secrets: Beroalde de Verville and Renaissance Conceptions of Knowledge*, Oxford: Clarendon Press.

Koepp, Cynthia J. (1986) 'The Alphabetical Order: Work in Diderot's *Encyclopédie*', in Stephen L. Kaplan and Cynthia J. Koepp (eds) *Work in France: Representations, Meaning, Organization, and Practice*, Ithaca: Cornell University Press.

Lechner, Joan Marie (1962) *Renaissance Concepts of the Commonplaces: An Historical Investigation of the General and Universal Ideas Used in Argumentation and Persuasion with Special Emphasis on the Educational and Literary Tradition of the Sixteenth and Seventeenth Centuries*, New York: Pageant Press.

Locke, John (1690) *An Essay Concerning Human Understanding*, ed. Peter H. Nidditch (1975) Oxford: Clarendon Press.

—— (1697) *Of the Conduct of the Understanding*, in vol. 3 (1823) *The Works of John Locke: A New Edition, Corrected*, 10 vols, London: T. Tegg; repr. (1963) Aalen: Scientia Verlag.

McArthur, Tom (1986) *Worlds of Reference: Lexicography, Learning and Language from the Clay Tablet to the Computer*, Cambridge: Cambridge University Press.

McKendrick, Neil, Brewer, John and Plumb, J. H. (1982) *The Birth of a Consumer Society: The Commercialization of Eighteenth-century England*, Bloomington: Indiana University Press.

Mathias, Thomas James (1798) *The Pursuits of Literature: A Satirical Poem in Four Dialogues*, 8th edn, London: T. Becket.

Melton, James van Horn (2001) *The Rise of the Public in Enlightenment Europe*, Cambridge: Cambridge University Press.

Moss, Ann (1996) *Printed Common-Books and the Structuring of Renaissance Thought*, Oxford: Clarendon Press.

Popkin, Jeremy D. (1991) 'Periodical Publication and the Nature of Knowledge in Eighteenth-century Europe', in D. Kelley and Richard Popkin (eds) *The Shapes of Knowledge from the Renaissance to the Enlightenment*, Dordrecht and Boston: Kluwer Academic.

Porter, Roy (2000) *Enlightenment: Britain and the Creation of the Modern World*, London: Allen Lane.

Raven, James (1992) *Judging New Wealth: Popular Publishing and Responses to Commerce in England, 1750–1800*, Oxford: Clarendon Press.

Schwab, Richard (1995) 'Translator's Introduction', *Preliminary Discourse to the Encyclopedia of Diderot*, Chicago: Chicago University Press.

Swift, Jonathan (1704) *A Tale of a Tub*, 2nd edn, ed. A. C. Guthkelch and D. Nichol Smith (1958) Oxford: Clarendon Press.

Watts, Isaac (1741) *The Improvement of the Mind: or, a Supplement to the Art of Logick*, London: J. Brackstone.

Wiles, R. M. (1957) *Serial Publication in England before 1750*, Cambridge: Cambridge University Press.

Wittmann, Reinhard (1999) 'Was There a Reading Revolution at the End of the Eighteenth Century?', in Guglielmo Cavallo and Roger Chartier (eds) *A History of Reading in the West*, Amherst: University of Massachusetts Press.

Yeo, Richard (1996a) 'Ephraim Chambers's *Cyclopaedia* (1728) and the Tradition of Commonplaces', *Journal of the History of Ideas*, 57: 157–75.

—— (1996b) 'Alphabetical Lives: Scientific Biography in Historical Dictionaries and Encyclopaedias', in Michael Shortland and Richard Yeo (eds) *Telling Lives in Science: Essays on Scientific Biography*, Cambridge: Cambridge University Press.

—— (1998) 'Modèles d'outre-Manche', *Les Cahiers de Science et Vie*, 47: 24–6.

—— (2001) *Encyclopaedic Visions: Scientific Dictionaries and Enlightenment Culture*, Cambridge: Cambridge University Press.

Zedler, Johann Heinrich (1732–50) *Grosses vollständiges Universal-Lexicon aller Wissenschaften und Künste*, 64 vols, Halle and Leipzig: J. H. Zedler.

CHAPTER TWENTY-TWO

PRINT CULTURE IN THE ENLIGHTENMENT

Carla Hesse

No technology better embodied the ideal of 'Enlightenment' than the printing press – a machine of human invention that could make useful ideas manifest in material form and spread them in unprecedented quantities, quickly and accurately, throughout the world. And no image better captures the Enlightenment faith in the power of the printed word than the frontispiece to Prosper Marchand's *Histoire de l'origine et des premiers progrès de l'imprimerie* (*History of the Origins and First Achievements of the Printing Press*), published in The Hague in 1740 to celebrate the tercentenary of the invention of the printing press: the printing press descends from the heavens, spreading light in its path; it is welcomed by the gods of wisdom and dissemination (Minerva and Mercury), who present it to Germany; Germany, in turn, shares its gift with Holland, England, Italy and France (Marchand 1740; Berkvens-Stevelinck 1987).

Prosper Marchand (1678–1756) was a French printer and publisher who became a Protestant and then a freethinker. He fled to the Low Countries in 1709 in the wake of Louis XIV's repression of religious and intellectual dissent. Through the seemingly innocuous form of an elegant and erudite history of the printing press, he subtly conveyed the same message as Voltaire: 'Crush fanaticism!' The weapon of choice in this cosmopolitan battle of light against darkness was the printing press. It made 'useful and delightful' ideas readily available throughout the nations of Europe; it was an engine to dispel ignorance, combat intolerance and thereby improve the condition of humanity.

By the end of the eighteenth century, the French revolutionary Jacques-Pierre Brissot de Warville (1754–93) reflected with the same conviction upon the transformative power of the printed word:

> In order to mobilize an insurrection against absolutist governments, it was necessary to ceaselessly enlighten minds . . . through a newspaper that could spread light in all directions . . . [I] imagined that the project of spreading great political principles in France could be easily achieved if intrepid friends, enlightened by liberty, could unite, communicate their ideas to one another, and compose their works someplace where they could have them printed and circulated throughout the world.
>
> (Hatin 1859–61: 5.22–3)

L'IMPRIMERIE, descendant des Cieux, est accordée par Minerve *et* Mercure *à l'*Allemagne,
qui la présente à la Hollande, *l'*Angleterre, *l'*Italie, *& la* France, *les quatre prémieres*
Nations chés les quelles ce bel Art fut adopté

Figure 22.1 Frontispiece by J. V. Schley from Prosper Marchand (1740) *Histoire de l'origine
et de premiers progrès de l'imprimerie*, La Haye: La veuve Le Vier et Pierre Paupie. By permission
of the Bancroft Library, University of California, Berkeley.

Printing and publishing were thus not only the most important cultural mechanisms for the spread of Enlightenment ideas; printing and publishing were the embodiment of the Enlightenment in action; the medium was the message – spreading light.

In the mid-seventeenth century, when René Descartes's *Discourse on Method* first circulated illicitly in manuscript form, the Churches and states of Europe had an exclusive monopoly on the publication of the printed word. By the end of the eighteenth century, the individual's freedom to print and publish ideas without interference from either Church or state had become the defining feature of an 'Enlightened nation'. The multiple transformations – political, economic and cultural – of the European publishing world in the eighteenth century are thus central to any understanding of how the Enlightenment evolved and ultimately triumphed both as a system of ideas and as a way of life. The rapid expansion of commercial print culture, the struggle to free the printing and publishing worlds from religious censorship and state regulation, and the multiple uses of the printed word as the chosen vehicle for spreading Enlightenment ideas form the key elements of this story.

THE PUBLISHING WORLD BEFORE
THE ENLIGHTENMENT

Christian doctrine held that all knowledge was a gift from God, revealed to the author, His chosen messenger to mankind. The metaphysical doctrine of divine revelation became the basis for the development of commercial printing and publishing in Europe in the sixteenth and seventeenth centuries. Over the course of the early modern period the monarchies and city-states of Europe steadily wrested from the Church the power to determine what God's knowledge was, and who should enjoy the 'privilege' of disseminating it in their territories by means of the printed word. The political interest of the state in censoring what circulated in print was ingeniously wedded to the commercial interests of a select group of printers, publishers and booksellers. Beginning in fifteenth-century Venice, rulers throughout Europe developed elaborate systems of granting exclusive 'privileges' or 'patents' to particular printers, publishers or booksellers (usually members of a royally or municipally chartered guild) to publish a particular work or in a given area of knowledge, such as the law or medicine (Gerulaitis 1976).

Authors were not permitted to publish their works in printed form independently of the powerful guilds. No one but a member of an officially sanctioned printers' and booksellers' guild could own a printing press or sell printed matter, and then only after it had been censored and approved by the issuance of an official 'privilege'. The printers' and booksellers' guild in England, known as the 'Stationers' Company' was chartered by Queen Mary in 1557 and enjoyed a monopoly on the book trade in the entire kingdom (Feather 1994). By the middle of the seventeenth century the French monarchy had organized a national 'Administration of the Book Trade' to co-ordinate censorship of manuscripts, to grant 'privileges' to publish, and to regulate the printers' and publishers' guilds throughout France. No single system of regulation had jurisdiction in the Italian states or in the Holy Roman Empire. But each of the 300-plus German principalities and cities developed its own particular mechanisms of censorship, distributing privileges and establishing guild regulations. All European states thus saw the emergence of very powerful publishing empires founded in these officially sanctioned monopolistic claims upon the literary inheritance of the kingdom. Ancient texts – both biblical and classical – as well as those of living writers were treated as the exclusive and perpetual property of the bookseller who had been granted the 'privilege' to print and publish it. Nothing, in principle, could be printed or published if it did not conform to the religious, moral and political doctrines of the state.

THE RISE OF COMMERCIAL PRINT CULTURE

All this began to change by the beginning of the eighteenth century. The eighteenth century witnessed an explosion in printed materials across Europe. In England 'about 6,000 titles had appeared during the 1620s; that number climbed to almost 21,000 during the 1710s; and to over 56,000 by the 1790s' (Porter 2000: 73). Similar trends are documented throughout Europe (Wittmann 1991; Chartier and Martin 1983). The main cause of this dramatic increase in publishing and printing was rapidly increasing literacy. Even in France, whose literacy rate trailed behind the Protestant nations of the north, literacy increased from 29 to 47 per cent of the population between the 1680s and the 1780s. New types of readers thus emerged on the European landscape: the middle classes, women, and even servants, shopkeepers and artisans. These new readers demanded new kinds of reading matter. The traditional canon of printed books – religious works, classical texts, legal treatises and courtly literature – was rapidly eclipsed by new secular genres aimed at the interests and aspirations of the middle and lower classes. The shift in reading habits was dramatic and definitive. At the end of the seventeenth century religious titles accounted for one-half of the books produced by Parisian printers; by the 1720s religion accounted for only one-third of their output; and by the 1780s the figure had dropped to a mere 10 per cent (Chartier 1991: 71).

The production of sentimental novels, encyclopaedias, self-help manuals, newspapers, pamphlets and broadsides burgeoned everywhere in Europe over the course of the eighteenth century. Whereas in 1747 Johann Georg Sulzer lamented that in Berlin, 'The general public does little reading', by 1798 Immanuel Kant recorded a German literary world transformed: 'This incessant reading has become an almost indispensable and general requisite of life'. Another German remarked in the 1790s that '[p]eople are reading even in places where, twenty years ago, no one ever thought about books; not only the scholar, no, the townsman and craftsman too exercises his mind with subjects for contemplation' (quoted in Ward 1974: 59–60). Sales at the Leipzig book fair show a trend similar to that found in France towards increasing reader interest in secular rather than sacred literature: between 1740 and 1800 religious publications for sale at the book fair declined from 38 to 14 per cent, whereas fictional and philosophical works increased from 10 to 30 per cent (Ward 1974: 59–60).

Not only were there many more readers in the eighteenth century; they were also reading more widely and buying more books than their predecessors. New styles of reading emerged. Pious texts, scholarly and technical works were meant to be reread repeatedly and studied intensively over a lifetime, as they were seen to be the containers of timeless truths. The literature of the Renaissance and neo-classical periods, equally, aspired to eternal ideals of beauty, ones that could never be surpassed. The eighteenth century, however, witnessed a marked shift from what historians call 'intensive' reading practices (the repeated study of a single book, especially the Bible) to 'extensive' reading, an ever-expanding interest in more ephemeral information and pleasures. Collections of immortal poets, to be relished over a lifetime, gave way to a flood of novels, read once and passed on; weighty political treatises received less attention than short pamphlet tracts, legal digests and daily newspapers. The first daily newspapers began appearing in London in the 1710s; by the 1770s there were nine London dailies and fifty provincial weeklies (Porter 2000: 78).

New commercial establishments arose to meet the demands of this new style of reading. Cafés and inns began supplying newspapers to customers, literary societies were formed to create libraries for their members, and reading rooms where subscribers paid a modest annual fee in exchange for the right to read or borrow works that they might not be able to afford opened across Europe. In his *Tableau de Paris* (1782–3) the acute Parisian observer Louis-Sébastien Mercier (1740–1814) documented this new mania for getting one's hands on the latest printed work: '[t]here are works that excite such ferment that the bookseller is obliged to cut the volume in three parts in order to be able to satisfy the pressing demands of many readers; in this case you pay not by the day but by the hour' (quoted in Chartier 1991: 70).

Commercialization of print culture had a significant impact on traditional notions of authorship. The increased demand for printed matter, and especially for modern secular literature (novels, theatrical works and self-help manuals of various sorts), tempted an increasing number of young men (and women) to aspire to become writers. The total number of published writers in France, for example, nearly trebled during the second half of the eighteenth century, from 1,187 in 1757 to 2,819 in 1784 (Darnton 1991: 107–18). And they were writers of a new sort, orientated more towards the commercial potential of their contemporary readership than the attention of a great patron or eternal glory. For the first time, in the eighteenth century, writers like Daniel Defoe and Alexander Pope in England, Denis Diderot and Marie-Jeanne Laboras de Mézières Riccoboni in France, and Gotthold Lessing in Germany, tried to live from the profits of their pens. And, unsurprisingly, they began to demand better remuneration for their products. Older notions that a fixed 'honorarium', or fee, was an appropriate reward for the composition of a manuscript gave way to bolder assertions that the author deserved a share in the profits earned from his creative labour. Rather than selling a manuscript to a publisher, they increasingly sought simply to sell the 'rights' to a single edition. With greater frequency, secular authors began to claim that they were the creators of their own works, rather than the mere transmitters of God's eternal truths. As they came to view themselves as the originators of their work, they also began to claim that their creations were their own property, as susceptible to legal protection and as inheritable or saleable as any other form of property. Thus Daniel Defoe would write in 1710, 'A Book is the Author's

Property, 'tis the Child of his Inventions, the Brat of his Brain, if he sells his property, it then becomes the Right of the Purchaser; if not, 'tis as much his own as his Wife and Children.' Authors thus began to assert that they should no longer be constrained to sell their manuscript in order to see them published (Rose 1993: 34–9). In the face of this burgeoning new world of commercial print culture, the old corporatist publishing system that had been put into place by the new monarchies of the sixteenth and seventeenth centuries began to come apart at the seams.

THE POLITICS OF PUBLISHING IN THE AGE OF ENLIGHTENMENT

The rise in public demand for printed matter led to a dramatic expansion in the practice of literary piracy. Sensing unsatisfied market demand and acutely aware of the artificial inflation in the price of books due to publishers' monopolies, less scrupulous printers and booksellers throughout Europe paid diminishing heed to the claims of guild publishers to exclusive perpetual 'privileges' on the best-selling and most lucrative works. Cheap reprints, produced most frequently across national frontiers or in smaller provincial cities, began to flood local markets. Publishers of pirate editions successfully represented themselves as champions of the 'public interest', against the monopolistic members of the book guilds. Why, they argued, should any particular publisher have an exclusive claim upon a work whose author or heirs were no longer living, or indeed upon many works composed before the invention of printing? Did not the greater good of making good works widely available at lower costs eclipse the selfish interests of individual publishers?

These arguments did not fall upon deaf ears, of either the authorities or the general public. In Germany, in particular, the princes and municipal councils of lesser territories took pride in encouraging printers to produce locally pirated editions of works initially produced and distributed in, and bearing 'privileges' from, the major publishing centres. Piracy made books more cheaply and readily available, and it created employment in their realms. Even in France and England, government officials began to see the potential public benefits, both economic and cultural, to challenging the monopolies of the book guilds.

First in England, and then in France and Germany, too, calls for reform of the regulations of the book trade were coming from all parties involved. Readers wanted cheaper books. Government legislators sought to increase commerce and to encourage cultural literacy in their realms. Foreign and provincial publishers, most notably in Scotland, Switzerland and secondary French cities like Lyon, clamoured against the perpetual monopolies of the London and Paris book guilds on the most lucrative books. Authors, alternatively, wanted their property rights in their compositions recognized as absolute and perpetual. The privileged guild publishers, especially in Hamburg, Leipzig, Frankfurt am Main, London and Paris, also hoped to see their traditional privileges recognized as perpetual property rights which could be defended against pirates in the courts. The loudest calls of all came, unsurprisingly, from Enlightenment thinkers who agitated for an end to pre-publication censorship and freedom of commerce in the publishing and printing world.

The struggle for reform of the publishing world in the eighteenth century was thus twofold: on the one hand, it was a struggle for freedom of commerce and the property rights of authors against corporate monopolies; on the other, it was a struggle to put an end to political and religious censorship. This struggle for enlightened reform of the world of print unfolded in three phases: liberalization; repression; and resistance and reform.

LIBERALIZATION

The continuing presence and acceptance of dissenting Protestant sects in the Low Countries, Switzerland and England led to an end to pre-publication censorship of printed matter in these countries well before the rest of Europe. The earliest agitation for an end to pre-publication and freedom of the press came from England. The cause was taken up as part of the heated struggle for toleration of religious dissent during the English Civil War. In the midst of civil chaos, while government authorities were busy with more urgent political struggles, the poet John Milton was able to publish an eloquent pamphlet, *Areopagitica* (1644), that publicly called 'for the liberty of unlicensed printing' on the ground that freedom of thought and expression were divinely granted by God as natural rights of men, and that governments had no authority to limit them. But it was not just the sanctity of the individual conscience that concerned Milton. He argued, moreover, that censorship harmed the public advancement of reason in general. False ideas can only be discredited if they can be discussed and refuted. And the very fact of discussing competing ideas leads us most rapidly to ascertain which ideas are the best among them. Error is a necessary step on the path to truth, and the sooner errors are made public, the sooner they can be debated and refuted: 'To kill a man', he famously wrote, 'is to kill a reasonable being; but to kill a book is to kill reason itself' (Milton 1644: 6).

Milton's ideas were deeply radical at the time they were written, but they percolated among freethinkers throughout both England and Continental Europe, and they put 'freedom of the press' on the political agenda of the radical Enlightenment throughout the late seventeenth century. Repeated petitions were sent to the House of Commons calling for an end to monopolies on the book trade; one was written by none other than John Locke. In the wake of the 'Glorious Revolution' of 1688, the growing discontent about censorship among religious dissenters converged with the rebellion of the printing and publishing world against the monopoly of the Stationers' Company to bring about the demise of the 'licensing act' which had regulated the world of print in 1695 (Siebert 1965: 261). After 1695, pre-publication censorship ended in England, and restrictions on individual expression in published works were now limited, post-publication, only by laws on sedition and libel.

In 1710 the British Parliament passed a bill that came to be known as the 'Statute of Anne', which definitively separated the question of censorship from that of literary property. The Statute ruled that authors and those who had purchased a manuscript from an author would have an exclusive right to publication of their work for fourteen years, renewable for an additional fourteen. By such means, authors could receive adequate remuneration for their labour. Only after the expiry of the right to publish would their work enter the public domain in which all were free to publish. This meant that all of the monopolies of the Stationers' Company upon classical texts and the great works of the English Renaissance were abolished. These books now became the free province of all publishers. In effect, the Statute, appropriately titled 'A Bill for the Encouragement of Learning and for Securing the Property of Copies of Books to the Rightful Owners Thereof' represented a compromise between advocates of authors' rights and the privileges of the Stationers' Company, on the one hand, and advocates of pirate publishers and 'the public interest', on the other. England thus emerged into the eighteenth century as the liberal model for Enlightenment thinkers in other parts of Europe, seeking to free thought from the 'inquisitions' of state and Church by ending censorship and guild monopolies on the printing and publishing trades.

REPRESSION

As England moved towards a liberal doctrine of freedom of conscience, public expression and commerce in the publishing world, France, the most powerful nation in Europe at the end of the seventeenth century, took a sharp turn in the opposite direction. In the early 1680s Louis XIV returned to the fold of the papacy, and determined to stamp out not only Protestantism by revoking the Edict of Nantes in 1685, but all forms of Catholic diversity (especially Jansenism) and sceptical or materialist philosophy as well. In 1713, under pressure from Louis, Pope Clement XI issued the Bull Unigenitus, which, in its forthright condemnation of Jansenism, was indicative of a new hard line against heresy and freethinking in all of its forms.

In 1699 the French Office of the Book Trade was brought under tighter control by its new head administrator, the Abbé Bignon. A college of censors was organized and the business of policing the printed word expanded rapidly over the course of the eighteenth century. By the 1780s there were more than 160 censors working full time, reviewing books submitted for publication. The number of printers in each French city was fixed (thirty-six in Paris). An army of royal inspectors of the book trade, assisted by local police spies (especially in Paris), was sent forth into the kingdom to inspect every printing shop and every shipment of books from abroad. Their orders were to confiscate and burn any illicit printed matter, to seek out its authors and to send them to be imprisoned in the royal fortress in Paris known as the Bastille. As the century wore on, increasing numbers of writers, booksellers, printers and distributors were imprisoned. In 1690–9 there were only 9 producers or purveyors of print in the Bastille; by the 1730s, there were over 100; and by the 1750s 136 (Darnton and Roche 1989: 3–26).

Between the 1730s and the 1760s most of the key works of the French Enlightenment burst into print, before being summarily banned and burned (Voltaire's *Philosophical Letters* (1734), Montesquieu's *Spirit of the Laws* (1748), Diderot and D'Alembert's *Encyclopédie* (1751), Rousseau's *Discourse on Inequality* (1755) and his *Social Contract* (1762), and Voltaire's *Candide* (1759) and *Philosophical Dictionary* (1764)). Most of the key figures of the French Enlightenment led the lives of quasi-fugitives, suffering repeated imprisonment and exile. Voltaire is a prime example:

in 1717 he was thrown into the Bastille for insulting the Regent; in 1726 he was there again for insulting a nobleman, and subsequently chose to go into exile in England. He did not return to France until 1729. In 1734, after the publication of the *Philosophical Letters*, he took refuge in the chateau of the husband of his friend and mistress, Emilie du Châtelet. Situated at Cirey, it was near the border with Lorraine, at that time an independent province. Voltaire realized its potential and paid to have the chateau restored. Until Emilie's death in 1749, Cirey provided a useful bolt-hole whenever he was under threat. Towards the end of his career, Voltaire finally found safety by purchasing properties near the Swiss–French border, first at Les Dèlices near Geneva and then, on the other side of the border, at Ferney. Shared persecution not only helped to forge the French *philosophes* into a united party to 'crush fanaticism' but also turned them into popular cultural heroes – champions of freedom of conscience against a fanatical and despotic state.

RESISTANCE AND REFORM

Despite this massive attempt to suppress the production and dissemination of Enlightenment thought by both the Catholic Church and the French state, from the 1730s onwards the movement to spread light by means of the printed word gained momentum in France. From the 1720s onwards a vast web of underground printers and publishers grew within France, especially in the provinces, whose mission was to print 'philosophical books' secretly and to sell them 'under the cloak', like other forms of contraband. This business in banned books became so lucrative that many publishers and printers of the royal book guilds could not resist the temptation to become involved in such enterprises under the table. By the late eighteenth century, having a book banned was the best means to ensure its success! However, printing directly under the watchful eye of royal police inspectors was highly risky: it was possible for short works or pamphlets, but prohibitively dangerous for longer books. French writers and publishers thus more frequently contracted with printers across the borders in the major Dutch and Swiss cities, such as The Hague, Neuchâtel and Geneva, for the printing of major books. Most editions of the great French works of the Enlightenment were thus printed outside France, along the borders that became known as the 'Protestant crescent'.

Voltaire's complete works were first printed in Kehl across the Rhine, Rousseau's in Amsterdam and then Geneva. The most famous of the Swiss purveyors of philosophical books for the French market was the Société Typographique de Neuchâtel (the STN), which was commissioned by the wealthy Parisian publisher Charles-Joseph Panckoucke (1736–98) to print the first octavo edition of the entire *Encyclopédie*. This book was printed in 25,000 copies that made their way to largely middle-class subscribers throughout provincial France (Darnton 1979). The illegal books were smuggled into France by ox-cart. Sometimes the smugglers took tortuous back roads to avoid customs officers; sometimes the books were sewn into the multi-layered petticoats of young working girls who crossed the border at Strasbourg to their daily jobs. Most ingeniously, smugglers would use a tactic that they humorously called 'marriage': books were shipped in flat, unbound sheets; the smugglers would carefully intercalate sheets of illicit books between those of the printer's more pious product. The sheets of Voltaire's *Philosophical Letters* would thus be 'married' to a new edition of the *New Testament*, and when the box was inspected, the Voltaire would slip through hidden under one of the Apostles (Darnton 1982 and 1995; Darnton and Roche 1989).

By the middle of the eighteenth century it had become clear to royal officials in France that they were losing the war against illicit literature. Repression only seemed to whet the public appetite for ever-more subversive books. Moreover, provincial printers and publishers repeatedly testified that they were driven by penury to print such books because the Parisian Book Guild had, thanks to the system of royal privileges, a stranglehold on the most lucrative legal books. In 1750 a champion of the moderate Enlightenment, Chrétien-Guillaume Lamoignon de Malesherbes (1721–94) was appointed as the new director of the Royal Office of the Book Trade. Malesherbes attempted reform. He began to issue a variety of tacit permissions for some of the more moderate works of the Enlightenment to be printed and sold, though they were not given the commercial protection or royal endorsement of works bearing an official 'privilege'. Publishers had to take their own risks against pirates, and the risk that some offended reader might gain the King's ear and get the permission revoked (Darnton 1979: 28). This practice, which rapidly became widespread, he hoped, would satisfy appetites for modern ideas without whetting them for spicier fare. Moreover, it would permit provincial printers and publishers to compete for this lucrative unofficial business (Shaw 1966; Wyrwa 1989).

Malesherbes then began the much bigger task of making enquiries throughout the publishing world and royal officialdom in preparation for a major reform of the book trade that would clarify the legal status of royal privileges on books, enhance the power of authors in relation to publishers, and restrict the monopolies of the royal book guilds. The hope was to stem the tide of illegal works and foreign imports, stimulate the French book trade, and redress the imbalance between provincial and Parisian publishers and printers. In 1777 a new Edict on the Book Trade was promulgated. Holding fast to the doctrines of revelation and of the King's prerogative to determine God's knowledge, the crown still maintained that a literary privilege was a form of grace granted by the King, rather than the recognition of a property right. Pre-publication censorship would still be imposed. Nonetheless, for the first time authors were granted their own category of privileges (*privilèges d'auteur*), which were to be perpetual and inheritable in perpetuity. However, once an author sold a manuscript to a publisher, the publisher's claim would be limited to ten years, with the possibility of a single renewal. This meant that all publishers' privileges were to be drastically restricted at the same time as privileges were extended to authors for the first time. The Paris Book Guild, needless to say, was enraged by the new law because it dispossessed them of their monopoly on the literary inheritance of France. The King would now be free to redistribute their privileges to other publishers. They refused to register the new edict in their statutes and the Parisian Book Guild was essentially on strike against the 'Royal Administration of the Book Trade' until the Revolution of 1789 swept the entire legal and institutional infrastructure of French publishing into the dustbin of history.

– Carla Hesse –

THE REVOLUTIONARY LEGACY

The declaration of the freedom of the press

With the *Declaration of the Rights of Man and the Citizen* on 26 August 1789, the new French National Assembly proclaimed the freedom of the press to be a natural and inalienable right (Godechot 1979: 34). But what did 'freedom of the press' mean? Could *anyone* print or publish *anything*? To what extent could authors be held responsible for the consequences of their ideas? What would be the appropriate recourse against slander? And, more troubling still, from the point of view of those who worked in the printing and publishing trades, did the freedom of the press mean the freedom of the presses? Could anyone open a printing shop, go into the publishing business, or launch a newspaper or periodical? The National Assembly answered 'yes'. The Royal Administration of the Book Trade was suppressed in January of 1791 and with the declaration of 'freedom of commerce' all guilds and corporations, including the book guilds, were abolished on 17 March 1791 (National Constituent Assembly 1791: 52–62). Laws on sedition and libel would replace pre-publication censorship.

With the suppression of government-sponsored monopoly on the printed word, scores of guild book publishers went bankrupt. Moreover, the events of 1789 revolutionized the reading public. As aristocratic bibliophiles and religious professionals, the principal clienteles of the old publishing world, fled France, a new reading public emerged, one that demanded 'news' and political commentary, as well as secular enlightened and romantic works. The book publishers and printers of the old regime were soon to be eclipsed by new printers ready to make their fortunes in the revolutionary demand for newspapers, handbills, pamphlets and posters.

The Paris bookseller Antoine-François Momoro (1756–94) was thirty-three years old when the Revolution began. He had arrived in Paris from his native Besançon in 1780. According to Lottin's (1789) reconstruction of Momoro's life, he was admitted as a bookseller by the Paris Book Guild in 1787 but was not successful; his declaration of bankruptcy survives (Archives de Paris ser. D4B6, carton 110, doss. 7811) as well as the papers for his arrest on 19 March 1794 (AN: W, carton 76, plaques 1–2; Momoro 1793). In 1790 his bookshop stocked a mere eleven titles. Momoro was one of the myriad Parisian book dealers with little hope of advancement within the old book guild. But with the declaration of the freedom of the press in August 1789, his career prospects opened up before him. Embracing the revolutionary movement wholeheartedly, he quickly opened a printing shop and boldly declared himself the 'First Printer of National Liberty' (Fig. 22.2). Within a year he had added four presses, ten cases of type and a small foundry for making type characters. In the publishing and printing world Momoro was still small fry, but he was soon to make a big name for himself in ultra-revolutionary politics.

His printing business adjusted to the revolutionary politics of the Parisian Sections, serving first as a propaganda machine for the republican Cordeliers Club, and then, by the winter of 1794, for the ultra-radical Hébertist faction. He built his business entirely around ephemera designed to expose counter-revolutionaries and their perfidious plots. The careers of Sectional politicians and municipal bureaucrats

Figure 22.2 *A{ntoine}-F{rançois} Momoro, First Printer of National Liberty* (1789). By permission of the Musée de la Révolution Française, Vizille.

were made or broken through his neighbourhood terrorist media campaigns. At a moment's notice a flood of handbills and posters could pour forth from his presses, shaping public opinion almost instantaneously. These political tactics, ruthless and demagogic as they were, proved effective. By 1794 he had become president of the Cordeliers Club and served on the directorate of the department of Paris.

Revolutionary print media

Momoro's career, however dramatic, was not untypical. The number of printing and publishing establishments in Paris more than tripled during the revolutionary period, allowing much broader social participation in the production of the printed word, and consequently, in the public exchange of ideas (Hesse 1991). Unsurprisingly, the literary forms created by the freed presses were more democratic as well. Newspapers, pamphlets and handbills were made for (and often by) people who inhabited the world of Momoro rather than for the deputies to the National Assembly, people with little money to spend and little leisure time to read. This is not to suggest that there was no popular literary culture before the French Revolution, but with the declaration of the freedom of the press and the collapse of the literary institutions of the *ancien régime*, the centre of gravity in commercial printing and publishing shifted perceptibly from the elite civilization of the book to the democratic culture of the pamphlet, the broadside and the periodical press. The association of the freedom of the press with both *des presses* (the printing presses) and *la presse* (newspapers) is not a phonetic coincidence or a mere play on words: it is a historical reality (Labrousse and Rétat 1989: 39–47).

On the eve of the French Revolution there were 32 periodicals circulating in Paris, 47 in the provinces and the colonies, and an additional 35 francophone periodicals that appeared in foreign countries. Within the first year following the declaration of the freedom of the press 194 new journals appeared in Paris, 41 in the French provinces and colonies, and 25 more worldwide (Rétat 1988; Labrousse and Rétat 1989; Popkin 1990: 17–34). Along with this explosion in periodicals came a flood of printed matter that was more ephemeral still, pamphlets (over 55,000 during the revolutionary decade) and hundreds of thousands of posters and handbills, whose extent it is impossible for historians to fully recapture.

Print ephemera were not simply an unwitting consequence of revolutionary legislation abolishing censorship and deregulating commerce but the centrepiece of revolutionary cultural policy: to regenerate the political and cultural life of all French citizens through the propagation and exchange of enlightened and liberal ideas. As the great Enlightenment philosopher Jean-Antoine-Nicolas de Caritat, Marquis de Condorcet (1743–94), wrote in 1791:

> The knowledge of printing makes it possible for modern constitutions to reach a perfection that they could not otherwise achieve. In this way a sparsely populated people in a large territory can now be as free as the residents of a small city . . . It is through the printing process alone that the discussion among a great people can truly be one.
>
> (Condorcet 1791: 18; see also Kates 1985)

Democratic deliberation required bringing all of France into dialogue with itself, and the printed newspaper made it possible to achieve this goal.

But neither the newspaper nor the pamphlet reached beyond literate citizens; nor did they reach beyond those who had at least some means to purchase them, to subscribe to a reading society, or to purchase refreshment in a café. A truly universal republic would need to bring *all* citizens into the political conversation. The journalist Jean Baptiste Louvet de Couvray (1760–97) devised a way to extend public discourse to include even the poorest urban reader. His *Sentinelle* was a news broadside that could be posted throughout the neighbourhoods of the city and read aloud, even, to citizens on the street. The mixing of media – image, word and music – could extend the reach of revolutionary print media further still, even to the illiterate and to the young. Broadsides, especially when illustrated, because they can be produced for almost nothing, and 'published' with no greater means than a glue bucket, remain to this day the most universal and most truly democratic mode of spreading the light.

REFERENCES

Berkvens-Stevelinck, Christiane (1987) *Prosper Marchand: la vie et l'oeuvre, 1678–1756*, Leiden and New York: E. J. Brill.

Chartier, Roger (1991) *The Cultural Origins of the French Revolution*, Durham, NC: Duke University Press.

Chartier, Roger and Martin, Henri-Jean (eds) (1983) *Histoire de l'édition française*, vol. 2, Paris: Promodis.

Condorcet, Marquis de (1791) *Des Conventions nationales*, Paris: Imprimerie du Cercle Social.

Darnton, Robert (1979) *The Business of Enlightenment: A Publishing History of the Encyclopédie (1775–1800)*, Cambridge, Mass.: Harvard University Press.

—— (1982) *The Literary Underground of the Old Regime*, Cambridge, Mass.: Harvard University Press.

—— (1991) *Gens de Lettres, gens du livre*, Paris: Jacob.

—— (1995) *The Forbidden Best-sellers of Pre-revolutionary France*, New York: W. W. Norton.

Darnton, Robert and Roche, Daniel (eds) (1989) *Revolution in Print: The Press in France, 1775–1800*, Berkeley: University of California Press.

Feather, John (1994) *Publishing, Piracy and Politics: A Historical Study of Copyright in Britain*, London: Mansell.

Gerulaitis, Leonardas Vytautas (1976) *Printing and Publishing in Fifteenth-century Venice*, Chicago: American Library Association; London: Mansell.

Godechot, Jacques (ed.) (1979) *Les Constitutions de la France depuis 1789*, Paris: Flammarion.

Hatin, Eugène (1859–61) *Histoire politique et littéraire de la presse*, Poulet-Malassis: Paris.

Hesse, Carla (1991) *Publishing and Cultural Politics in Revolutionary Paris, 1789–1810*, Berkeley: University of California Press.

Kates, Gary (1985) *The Cercle Social, the Girondins, and the French Revolution*, Princeton: Princeton University Press.

Labrousse, Claude and Rétat, Pierre (1989) *La Naissance du journal révolutionnaire*, Lyon: PUL.

Lottin, Augustin-Martin (1789) *Catalogue chronologique des libraires et libraire-imprimeurs de Paris, 1470–1789*, Paris.

Marchand, Prosper (1740) *Histoire de l'origine et des premiers progrès de l'imprimerie*, La Haye: La veuve Le Vier et Pierre Paupie.

Mercier, Louis-Sebastien (1782–83) *Tableau de Paris: Nouvelle Edition corrigée et augmentée*, 8 vols, Amsterdam.

Milton, John (1644) *Areopagitica*, John W. Hales (1894) Oxford: Clarendon Press.

Momoro, Antoine François (1793) *Traité élémentaire de l'imprimerie*, Paris: Momoro.

National Constituent Assembly, Committee on Public Contributions (1791) in *Collection générale des décrets rendus par l'Assemblée nationale*, Paris: Baudouin.

Popkin, Jeremy (1990) *Revolutionary News*, Durham, NC: Duke University Press.

Porter, Roy (2000) *The Creation of the Modern World: The Untold Story of the British Enlightenment*, New York: W. W. Norton.

Rétat, Pierre (1988) *Les Journaux de 1789: Bibliographie critique*, Paris: CNRS.

Rose, Mark (1993) *Authors and Owners: The Invention of Copyright*, Cambridge Mass.: Harvard University Press.

Shaw, Edward Pease (1966) *Problems and Policies of Malesherbes as Directeur de la Librairie in France, 1750–1763*, Albany: State University of New York.

Siebert, Fredrick Seaton (1965) *Freedom of the Press in England, 1476–1776*, Urbana: University of Illinois Press.

Ward, Albert (1974) *Book Production, Fiction, and the German Reading Public, 1740–1800*, Oxford: Clarendon Press.

Wittmann, Reinhard (1991) *Geschichte des deutschen Buchhandels: ein Überblick*, Munich: Verlag C. H. Beck.

Wyrwa, Marek (ed.) (1989) *Malesherbes, le pouvoir et les lumières*, Paris: Editions France-Empire.

CHAPTER TWENTY-THREE

THE APPEARANCE OF ENLIGHTENMENT

Refashioning the elites

———◆•◆———

Peter McNeil

INTRODUCTION

In the eighteenth century clothing introduced and worn at court ceased to be the dominant fashion. The strict codification of dress backed by sumptuary laws asserting an unchanging social structure was undone by philosophical, scientific, political and economic change. Rising incomes, the spread of literacy and print culture, the introduction of new cottons and cheaper techniques of production and printing meant that more types and numbers of garments and fabrics entered the wardrobes of the bourgeoisie, as well as artisans, tenant farmers, mechanics and the servant class. Fashion choice accelerated within a market economy, in which choices about commodities became markers of distinction and mobility. Fashion also functioned as a potent symbol for the types of social and economic change which modern capitalism enabled, standing in for values ranging from transformation to deception, which were explored within Enlightenment philosophical tracts and popularizing accounts.

TWO ENLIGHTENMENTS IN DRESS

The relationship of dress to Enlightenment concepts of liberation, sensation and individualism can be tracked within two new clothing styles which may at first seem antithetical but share common features. The first is the taste for luxurious informality (interpreted by some as licentious) which appeared in the more prosperous urban centres of England and France in the first third of the eighteenth century, when an aristocracy of wealth rather than birth was ascendant. Women's dress of the period was innovative and modern, connected to the new taste for exoticism, privacy and family life. All these were evolving in the smaller rooms of Paris town houses and suites of *petits-appartements*, where easy seating and improved fireplace technology during the reign of Louis XV encouraged informality and the search for comfort. The preference for loose, flowing women's gowns and hooped skirts which showed off expensive, large-patterned repeats further blurred old lines of class distinction. Wealthy men's clothing became easier in cut and weight, waistcoats sleeveless, wigs smaller.

Figure 23.1 *L'Art d'ecrire*, from Denis Diderot and Jean le Rond D'Alembert (1751–80) *Encyclopédie, ou Dictionnaire raisonné des sciences, des arts et des métiers, par une société de gens de lettres*; vol. V of facs. edn (1964) Paris: Cercle du livre précieux. By permission of the National University of Australia

Figure 23.2 *Quelle Antiquité*. By permission of the Museé Carnavalet, Paris. Photograph: © Photothèque des musée de la ville de Paris/Cliché: LADET.

The second relationship to Enlightenment ideas in eighteenth-century dress is more easily recognizable as 'modern' – the shift towards the premium for studied informality and comfortable cuts and fabrics which invaded even courtly assemblies in England and France in the decade before the Revolution. This development of more practical clothing for European elites was influenced by English sporting dress, occupational dress and a fantasy of the pastoral peasant life. The pan-European interest in a simplified Grecian classical aesthetic, republican and revolutionary ideas, changing attitudes towards childhood development and gender roles, and new scientific models of the body and hygiene combined to produce major shifts in hair-dressing, deportment and appearance. Clothing was washed and changed more frequently, it was lighter in weight and in palette for both sexes, and the neo-classical use of Graeco-Roman references changed silhouettes, hairstyles and conduct. But the impetus towards informal comfort, sensual pleasure in dressing and individual taste should be recognized as having emerged from within aristocratic and urban merchant *salonnier* society in the first third of the century.

COURT DRESS

However, dress in the presence of the monarchs of Europe remained virtually unchanged from its late seventeenth-century template, a static backdrop to the evolution of fashion outside the court. Indeed, in the eighteenth century court dress was standardized throughout Europe as Bourbon dynastic influence spread and princely courts tried to emulate the architecture and decorative arts and dress at Versailles. The highly specialized nature of French guilds and the centralization in the seventeenth century of the luxury trades, including textiles, had resulted in a pool of expertise at the level of design and manufacture which finally rivalled that of Italy (that this was not true for cotton explains why the fabric was banned in France until the last third of the century). The classical notion of decorum, or *bienséance*, asserting that external marks must be appropriate to social rank, extended from architecture to court dress. Thus spending was neither wasteful nor sinful for a courtier, but an obligation both appropriate and necessary to indicate high status and to sustain the commerce in luxury goods.

Women's dress

Court dress or *grand habit* for women consisted of a heavy open robe with a train, its hoop petticoat (*pannier*) up to six feet wide extending the body outwards, while a whalebone bodice (*corps de robe*) pulled the shoulders back and emphasized the breasts and waist. Later, boned stays became an undergarment, covered with a triangular shaped stomacher. Such clothing, made of woven patterned silk or velvet, could not be washed and was protected by its linings of silk or winter fur, or quilted linings, and by the linen shift (*chemise*) beneath. The emphasis was generally on the two-dimensional nature of the garment as viewed from the front or back. Rigorous movement was impossible; courtiers at Versailles were carried up stairs in sedan chairs. As sitting was a prerogative only of the highest-born at court, the heavy and even painful corsetry of women's clothing which dug into the shoulder (subject of numerous complaints in memoirs) was appropriate to a standing and hierarchical role.

While court dress retained its archaic hoops until these elements were abolished in England in the reign of George IV (the hoops had been merged with the tubular lines of early nineteenth-century or Regency dress, making a very bizarre juxtaposition which probably began to offend on aesthetic grounds), it was continually modified in its details in accordance with contemporary fashion change. From 1730 to 1760 clothing had a more agitated appearance, with multiple layers of lace ruffles (*engageantes*) and other trimmings suggesting rococo movement. *Chiné à la branche* or ikat (warp-printed before weaving to create a smudged effect) and hand-painted Chinese silks had exotic appearances and light colourways which suited new fashions in both clothing and furnishing schemes. The *robe à la française*, or sack-back, an open robe with box-pleated panels falling from the shoulder to form a train, was popular dress for the wealthy women and their upper servants throughout the century and became acceptable at the French court shortly before the Revolution. Shoes covered in equally rich silk had heels which were highly impractical. Louis XIV's court had not required informal dress, apart from riding habits and wrappers for the bedchamber. In the reign of Louis XV closed robes and jackets (*caracos*) with petticoats, quilted for winter, were informal alternatives. An informal dress was one fitted with pleats at the centre back, called the English back or *robe à l'anglaise*. The importance of promenading and moving around parks, gardens and shopping precincts probably accounts for the rise to dominance by the 1780s of this gown; with its fitted back and full, but not dragging, skirts, it was an easier city garment. A similar dress was permitted in the French court in 1787 as a *robe ordinaire de cour* (Delpierre 1997: 94). Other informal dress included dresses with looped-up sections *en polonaise*, popular from the late 1770s. Such skirts kept hems off the ground and made reference to exotic dress from Turkish-influenced central Europe, as well as to a pastoral fantasy of urban and rural working women, who pulled their petticoats out of the mud through attached pockets. Aprons were worn by women of all orders: long, practical ones for workers, and expensive embroidered lawn or lace ones for the rich, which were, of course, solely ornamental. *Fichus*, popular in the late eighteenth century to plump and partly conceal the bosom, also probably derived from the wardrobes of working women. The rise of stagecoach travel also encouraged the spread of masculine tailored and collared jackets and the use of durable woollen broadcloth into the female wardrobe.

Men's dress

Courtier males wore the *habit à la française*, a suit consisting of coat (*justaucorps*) and skirted waistcoat (*veste*), both of which were generally made of brocaded silk or velvet, with knee breeches and silk stockings. The coat, with its tight cut high under the arm, precluded strenuous movement to distinguish deportment from the labouring poor, who wore coarse wool and linen with occupational features including detachable sleeves and leather aprons. Court dress was trimmed or 'laced' with gold or silver braid, or was embroidered, the latter preferred in the last third of the century. Male court dress became progressively lighter over the course of the century, shedding its winged effect. For private leisure and writing throughout the century, a wrapper or banyan was worn and the wig replaced with a turban or cap. The static nature of court dress, which changed its silhouette slightly but not its components, maintained the status quo. Anyone wishing to attend court required such dress, and it could be hired.

English tourists reported having to purchase new clothing for French travel as their garments were not sufficiently rich, or different in cut. According to these travellers' descriptions (although they must never be read literally), men's formal dress was seen less often on the streets of London than Paris: many preferred more sober woollen clothing based on riding and sporting dress. Such dress was worn by some in the House of Lords in the 1780s. After an ultra-fashionable youth in which lavish dress was used to assert a cosmopolitan outlook and Whig confidence, Charles James Fox (1749–1806) adopted a dishevelled appearance, with cropped hair without powder, and wearing the middle-class frock coat and waistcoat in a threadbare state. The democratic colours buff and blue, the identifying colours of George Washington's army, were worn by Fox's female supporters, notably Georgiana, Duchess of Devonshire.

Dress and the body

A courtly persona was about more than the garments. Just as the Enlightenment soldier's figure was produced through rigorous training, famously described by Michel Foucault, the courtly body was registered through an integrated technology of the body dependent upon correct (and corrected) deportment intertwined with the structure and nature of dress and cosmetics, hairstyling and make-up (Foucault 1975: 135). Social historian Georges Vigarello usefully describes the function of court fashion as a barrier which screened the body from the viewer (Vigarello 1985: 83). The faces of both sexes were painted with rouge, and wigs were dressed, pomaded and dusted with powder, including artificial colours, such as green or lilac. Bodies were trained through technologies of dance, horse-riding and, for the men, fencing. The effect of this was to universalize and standardize courtly bodies and faces; the same impetus which saw the adoption of a particular type of French language and etiquette. The ritual of dressing or the *toilette* was elaborate and social, taking several hours in the boudoir, that zone in which mercers and other businesspeople were admitted. Within Europe there were different cosmetic conventions: the French and Germanic tradition was to wear more rouge than the English.

LUXURY AND EMULATION

Throughout the eighteenth century, moralists, playwrights, novelists and other social observers suggested that the spread of luxury and fashion was increasing, that emulation of the habits of social betters had become a universal pastime and fashion 'a spreading contagion, and epidemical foolery of the age' ([Anon.] 1715: 59). The theatres, parks and shopping precincts of eighteenth-century cities, the assembly rooms and wide-paved streets of spa towns such as Bath and Tunbridge Wells, and metropolitan masquerade venues such as the Pantheon, Ranelagh Gardens and Vauxhall Gardens in London and the Colissée in Paris, were new spaces of socially mixed leisure; appropriate dress and payment of a fee permitted entrance. It thus became increasingly difficult to assess the social identity of fashionable figures. There are many surviving accounts of this social behaviour in large towns and the spa resorts, where the gentry and merchant class displayed their clothing and indulged in lavish shopping. Economic historian Lorna Weatherill has argued that under-standings of the consumer revolution have been distorted by focusing on such simplistic notions of emulation. She observes that the English gentry, high in social standing, often spent less and owned fewer material goods than artisans and shop-keepers. She also speculates that middle-class English clothing was relatively more sophisticated than their furnishings and interior decoration (Weatherill 1996: 19–21). Wealthier shopkeepers and artisan–entrepreneurs – particularly those associated with the luxury trades, such as mercers, upholsterers and cabinet-makers – often wore expensive and lavish clothing.

The contemporary objection to the follies of fashion make sense when it is realized that emerging market capitalism was weakening the links between dress and social status. It is significant that French sumptuary laws – regulations whose aim was to limit the use of certain luxurious materials, including cloth of gold and silver for dress, and gilded wood for interior decoration, to the aristocracy and the Church – were not renewed from the reign of Louis XV. These laws had also not been renewed in England after the Glorious Revolution (1688). Nonetheless, luxury in dress continued to preoccupy rulers who were anxious about its financial impact and affect on priorities: George III's 'Windsor' dress for courtiers is similar to Catherine the Great's green uniform dress in that both were based on regimental dress and were attempts to limit expenditure and frivolity.

French inventories specified dress in great detail, and more statistics are available for the contents and value of French wardrobes than for other European countries. Roche has compiled his findings in his magisterial study of French eighteenth-century fashion, a notable source which intertwines the facts and poetics of dress. Although many French nobles spent lavishly on dress, one-quarter of them spent no more than a wealthy shopkeeper. The value of French women's wardrobes, including the serving class, was generally twice that of men's (Roche 1989: 96). The rapid uptake of fashion by workers in the luxury and appearance industries, noted in contemporary sources, is supported by Roche's documentary evidence. It is significant that the French clothing sector owned more books, engravings and mirrors than other trades; all are objects which indicate 'openness' and incite change (Roche 1989: 321–4). Clothing was often gifted to servants or made part of their wages, and some servants dressed elaborately. However, much servant dress continued to mark out this group in terms of shorter, more practical dress lengths, fewer trimmings (which added considerably to the expense of clothes), types of cap and certain anachronisms. Actors and prosti-tutes also had access to clothing which moralists regarded as above their station.

Earle's study of England indicates that apprentices had their wardrobe provided by their masters and that three suits and eight shirts were often expected. Women of the middle orders had an average of three outfits, including silk and silk mixtures. Many men of the middling sort owned one silk suit and silk stockings or a nightgown. The insurance value of an English apprentice's wardrobe in the 1720s ranged from six to fifty pounds. Wardrobes of women of the middling sort averaged forty to fifty pounds. At this time, a labourer spent two pounds per year on his personal dress, while a ducal outfit might cost more than a hundred pounds (Earle 1989: 285, 385). The value of clothing meant it was frequently stolen. The trade in second-hand and stolen clothes meant that poorer members of society had opportunities to transform their appearance. The poorest members of society, however, were buried in their one set of clothes.

Roche argues that the entry of the labouring orders into the 'consumption cycle' is a 'fundamental silent revolution, as important in its way as the spread of literacy' (Roche 1989: 110). Many types of imitation up the clothing scale were possible. A surviving English linen dress from about 1780 in the Kamer Collection (now Metropolitan Museum of Art, New York) is decorated with *appliqué* cut-out floral chintz attached with gold thread and sequins, emulating a much more expensive brocaded fabric. Silks without brocade and metal threads were cheaper, and slightly outdated patterns were sold at discounted prices. The record of fabric and dress purchases of a provincial Englishwoman, Barbara Johnson (1738–1825), functions like a map of her life. Covering the period 1746–1823, it includes about 120 samples, of which 54 are silk, 37 cotton, the others linen and mixtures, all associated with town visits, textile gifts from relatives, and attire for mourning royalty and numerous deaths in the family (Rothstein 1987: 29).

All levels of society recycled cloth and clothing, but this practice was probably more frequent among thrifty people of the middling sort. Thus clothing, along with other material possessions, including ceramics, curtains, mirrors and new furniture types, permitted the spread of the new taste for privacy and comfort. By the end of the century even working women and men could inspect their personal appearance.

COSTUME: COMMUNICATION
AND COMMERCE

The 'appearance industry' (Daniel Roche's term) was a very significant part of all urban economies. In Paris, a city of 600,000 in the late eighteenth century, 40 per cent of all trades, or about 15,000 masters, laboured in the making, selling and maintenance of clothing and wigs (Roche 1989: 279). In London textile workers were the largest group in the economy. After staple food, cloth and clothing were the largest purchases for the middling sort and 'mechanicks'; in England about one-quarter of their income was spent on it (Earle 1989: 272).

CLOTHING TRADES

The status of certain elite workers in the clothing trade shifted in the last third of the century from the old model of patronage and obsequious service to a model of artistic independence and even hauteur learned from practitioners of the fine arts. No longer did customers send a bolt of cloth from the mercer and tell the tailor or mantua-maker what to do with it. Marie-Antoinette's mercer, Rose Bertin – her 'Minister of Fashion' – was derided for her arrogance, and the hairdresser Léonard was a celebrity in pre-revolutionary Paris, and later became part of the émigré community in London. Trimming and headdresses were expensive, carefully crafted and, in the 1780s, even incorporated topical references to current affairs. Whereas England had a long tradition of female mantua-makers, it was only in 1675 that Paris permitted a female guild for the making of women's clothing. Male corset-makers continued to provide the understructure and shape of women's fashion; the female guild provided the embellishment and trimming. The *Description des arts et métiers* (1769) stated that the *maîtresses couturières* lacked the skills and technology found in the male tailor's art. Even the female *marchande de modes*, it was noted, works in the shadow of her husband (Garsault 1769: 54). Perhaps the hostility directed towards Rose Bertin in contemporary accounts was symptomatic of her threatening female power, as well as emblematic of a debased and extravagant queen.

French guilds constantly tested the boundaries. A French tailor announced ready-to-wear suits for export in 1770; smaller items like women's mantles and coats were available in England in 'warehouse' emporia. In her study of eighteenth-century rococo interior decoration, Katie Scott recounts an emblematic legal dispute between Paris wig-makers and hairdressers in the 1760s. The latter argued that their confections were akin to the fine arts, and used terms such as 'composition' and 'colour' in arguing the case. In 1776 they won the right to practise relatively undisturbed by the wig-makers (Scott 1995: 75). The language of academic art practice would be used by late nineteenth-century fashion and interior designers to claim a new social status akin to that of the artist, a process which began with the fashion design of Enlightenment Europe.

DRESS AND DESIGN

Western European design became more stylistically consistent in the course of the eighteenth century. The Huguenot diaspora after the Revocation of the Edict of Nantes (1685) spread technical skill in the silk and silver trades as well as drawing skills and subsequent design sophistication to the British Isles, Holland, Prussia, Switzerland and North America. English production, such as Spitalfields silks based on botanical prints designed by Anna Maria Garthwaite, attempted to compete with silks from Italy and France, as well as providing simple styles at lower prices for the middle class. As Hallett notes of the print trade, French stylistic devices and imagery indicated both social status and refinement, and were extended from the fine arts into all other fields of design in the 1730s (Hallett 1999: 144). From the 1760s, the promotion of the startlingly new 'neo-grec' (neo-classical) design of objects and textiles involved complex circuits of interaction between England, France, Sweden, Russia, Italy and Spain, in which architects, entrepreneurs and patrons circulated designs, models and ideas. The prestige and financial benefit attached to luxury industries such as silk, low-weave tapestry and ceramics drove smaller countries like Sweden to import technical expertise and establish new national workshops. Mrs Elizabeth Montagu noted in a letter to her friend Matthew Boulton, English entrepreneur–designer and manufacturer of Grecian-style ormolu (simulated gold metalwares):

> I take greater pleasure in our victories over the French in our contention of arts than of arms. The achievements of Soho [Birmingham] instead of making widows and orphans make marriage and christening . . . Go on then, sir, to triumph over the French in taste and to embellish your country with useful inventions and elegant productions.
>
> (Smith 1993: 234)

Style, then, was a type of fiscal and emotional warfare and linked to emergent nationalism in Enlightenment Europe.

Ideas about metropolitan fashion spread more rapidly throughout the century as travel became easier, communications improved, and the literate gained access to burgeoning illustrated periodicals. For instance, the ten-day journey from Paris to Lyon of the seventeenth century had been halved by the late eighteenth (Sargenston 1996: 103). The proliferation of detailed engravings permitted the rapid dissemination of fashionable ideals, spreading also the cult of individualism, novelty and self-fashioning. Printed sets of 'modern habits' depicting elegant dress and posture of men and women after French designs by Hubert-François Gravelot and Bernard Picart had circulated in the first four decades of the eighteenth century. Cheaper English ladies' 'pocket books' illustrated existing fashion (not predictions) in the 1760s, but the specialized fashion press first emerged in France in 1768 with the *Journal du Goût* and in England in 1770 with *The Lady's Magazine. Galerie des modes et des costumes français* (1778–87) published seventy portfolios with detailed texts and engravings of breathtakingly variable dress for men and women, naming many suppliers. By the end of the century fifteen fashion journals were printed in England, France, Holland, Germany and Italy, many also showing details of seasonal changes in interior decoration, object and even carriage design. Lyon silk-designers and manufacturers in collaboration with Paris mercers introduced new patterns and modified others slightly each season in order to satisfy the demand for novelty and to reach new sectors of the market, which was stratified between court, Paris, foreign courts, provinces and colonies (Sargentson 1996: 97–109). The production of fashion caricatures in western Europe, particularly the enormous English production from 1760, also taught people how to avoid absurd excess, though the role of caricature should not be reduced to the illustration of moral laxity or limited to the provision of mere amusements. Fashion, after all, involves a relationship between image and reality. Fashionable people saw exaggerated images of themselves on stage, in the print shops and on the streets. They may have emulated them; perhaps seeking to outdo the image. The middle class may have used them to reinforce or signal their fashionable but restrained dress. The upper class may have used them to scorn the pretentious manners of those who sought to dress like them. On the one hand satirical, these images, which poured from English, French, German and Dutch presses in thousands of different versions, also taught people what it was to look 'fashionable'.

FASHION AND NATIONHOOD

Regional and national dress

Eighteenth-century engravings of 'the dress of other nations' indicate the importance of regional differences which were maintained throughout the century, and provided ideas for fancy dress. That the young Austrian princess Marie-Antoinette was stripped at the border on entering France and redressed in French dress indicates that dress and nationhood remained powerful visual and symbolic devices. Despite having modernizing Enlightenment rulers, both Russia and Sweden under Catherine the Great and Gustav III, respectively, developed distinctive national court and even children's dress. Encouraged by the Empress, Gustav III formulated and actively encouraged the adoption of a national dress for his courtiers from 1778. For men, this suit of black trimmed with red or blue with white combined French knee breeches with a Spanish cloak and archaic doublet with shoulder slashing, the features indicating Gustav III's personal interest in masquerade and fancy dress, attempts to link his reign to an earlier tradition, and perhaps a personal vanity, in that the tight-fitting sleeves of French coats would have drawn attention to his shoulder deformity. The corresponding women's court dress incorporated seventeenth-century puffed sleeves and a standing lace collar. Lena Rangström's analysis of this experiment indicates that Gustav III was motivated also by the notion of 'one people, one costume' and the economic advantage of using Swedish-made textiles, although the King himself continued to order luxury versions from Paris (Rangström 1998: 262).

In Russia, Catherine the Great was painted as imperial ruler in both French-style and Slavic-detailed court dress. Even when the overall appearance of Russian aristocratic dress appears Francophile, details of Eastern-derived headdresses and trimmings such as fringe and the extensive use of fur frequently recur in portraiture in order to indicate national identity. In the 1770s Catherine the Great designed a one-piece children's garment which reflected her interest in Rousseauan ideas of unfettered childhood, a theatrical-looking braided design which she hoped might be adopted by other European courts, a Russian mode '*à la Princesse du Nord*'. Regions with Eastern links also preferred stronger, highly keyed colour in textiles – coral-red, violets and yellows dominate Russian court dress as they do the late eighteenth-century Russian palace interiors.

Colour was also highly keyed in Italy, where men's embroidered pictorial waistcoats were executed in wider, more painterly dashes of complementary coloured silks than most English or French work. This use of strong colour was a foil to the extensive wearing of black in Italy, Portugal and Spain, which Aileen Ribeiro attributes to the influence of sixteenth- and seventeenth-century Spanish power, and

Figure 23.3 *Les Jeunes Anglais* (1785), Nicolas Colibert (1750–1806), stipple engraving. By permission of the Collection Peter McNeil, Sydney. Photograph: Vanilla Rita Neto.

Figure 23.4 *Les Jeunes Hollandais* (1785), Nicolas Colibert (1750–1806), stipple engraving. By permission of the Collection Peter McNeil, Sydney. Photograph: Vanilla Rita Neto.

the significance of black as an expensive dye (Ribeiro 1984: 83). Ribeiro argues that sumptuary laws continued to control the appearance of the orders in countries including Prussia, the conservative free towns of Germany, Switzerland and the Italian city-states, but that their power waned in the second half of the century (Ribeiro 1984: 66–88).

That European dress became more homogeneous over the course of the century is indicated in that Gustav III's courtiers were often embarrassed by their imposed national dress when attending foreign courts in the 1780s. As Gustav's favourite male courtier Gustaf Mauritz Armfelt wrote, whenever possible they hurried to 'change into European attire', that is, a French-style suit (Rangström 1998: 263). Whereas Spanish male courtiers wore seventeenth-century dress in the first decade of the eighteenth century, by the last third of the century Madrid fops are depicted wearing French-derived fashion with occasional use of the Spanish cape. Perhaps the impetus to record the dress of peoples, including the first compilation of those of the Russian Empire compiled by ethnographer Johann Gottlieb Georgi and published in St Petersburg 1776–7, was the sense that these were being eroded in modern Europe.

Regional dress and national identity

Fashion caricatures were frequently structured around themes of national difference. Indeed, attitudes towards fashion played a significant role in defining national and regional identity. Although the French court established a model for European courtly society promulgated via conduct books and dancing masters, trenchant criticism of French fashionability was widespread. The first complaint was economic, based upon mercantile theory which resented the flow of national coinage from one country to another in the purchase of goods. Heavy duties were imposed on French textiles throughout the century in order to protect the English silk industry, and many prominent individuals, including Charles James Fox, had their smuggled French and Italian clothing confiscated by customs officers. The second critique of Continental habits was more complex and rhetorical, determined by a developing Protestant nationalism which was anti-Catholic, anti-Jacobite and anti-absolutist, suspicious of external pomp, finery and superstition. Catholic court society was viewed by detractors in Protestant England and the Low Countries as feminized and irrational. John Andrews, who wrote three commentaries on French manners over a twenty-year period, crafted his texts around a set of oppositions which contrasted English vigour, manliness and 'liberty of discourse' with French flattery, vanity and excess. The French, he wrote, are a people obsessed with the triviality of fashion, with 'what dresses were worn on such a day', their minds 'warped from any freedom of exertion'. French men, he argues, wear court dress at inappropriate times, spend too much time with ladies, preside in feminine spaces and indulge in feminine practices such as the *toilette* and the boudoir (Andrews 1770: vol. I, 68, 78–9, 139). This, it was argued, distracted courtiers from their loss of real power at Versailles. Thicknesse wrote in his *Observations on the Customs and Manners of the French Nation*: 'I am apt to think the taking of snuff, the powdering of the hair, and the great attention shewn by all degrees of people in France, to adorn their persons, is a piece of state policy to prevent their employing their intellectual faculties' (Thicknesse 1766: 25).

Historian David Kuchta has argued that post-1688 English aristocrats pre-empted the middle-class and puritanical challenge that their rule was tainted by luxury by promoting a more moderate appearance than their Continental and Catholic counterparts (Kuchta 1996: 54–78). English conduct manuals adopted moderate precepts for masculine behaviour, as outlined in Baldassare Castiglione's *The Courtier* (1528). Ciceronian models were used to chastise both rusticity and foppery. They demanded neat and modest dressing with consideration of social status:

> Be neat without gawdiness, gentile [*sic*] without affectation: In fine, the Taylor must take measure of both your purse and of your quality, as well as of your person: For a sute that fits the character, is more *a la mode*, than that which fits well on the body . . . I have seen some Fops over-shoot extravagance; . . . a man of war might be rigged up with less noise, and some-times at less expense.
>
> ([Anon.] 1704: 39–40)

It was equally damning to adopt a slovenly air: 'this is to sacrifice one vice to another, to attone for vanity with nastiness', the precept advocated by Lord Chesterfield in his *Letters* ([Anon.] 1704: 40). In 1787 the Englishwoman Mary White wrote in her scrapbook next to a carefully pasted engraving of a fashionable headdress: 'disgraceful to English taste' (Donald 1996: 90). Her retort is part of a long English tradition in which French fashion and artifice simultaneously fascinated and repelled. The argument in which rigorous Francophile abstraction and artifice were equated with absolutism and tyranny had also been deployed in the promotion of the informal but carefully designed 'English'-style gardens by Pope, Addison and gentlemen connoisseurs in the immediate post-1688 period.

Attacks on fashion did not come solely from the English. From the 1760s the French *philosophes* focused their attack on the aristocracy as debased by scrutinizing the precious urbanity of courtly mode and manners. They characterized their age as an effeminate one dominated by corrupt female values. In *Emile* (1762) Rousseau linked a theory of gendered education to a critique of contemporary manners: 'In the present confusion between the sexes it is almost a miracle to belong to one's own sex' (Rousseau 1762: 426). When the Englishman John Andrews suggested that Salic law, which barred women from being crowned ruler, encouraged French women to seek revenge by turning the *toilette* into 'the shrine at which all men of genteel rank offer up their daily services', his was a Rousseauan argument (Andrews 1770: 84). The *philosophes* attacked the male courtier type, the *petit-maître* (little master) as indolent, effeminate, dominated by the company of women, lolling in their salons and boudoirs and checking his carefully crafted appearance against theirs. He was the focus of a substantial body of French discourse – philosophical, scientific and aesthetic – which criticized aristocratic indolence and modishness, and warned against an emasculated French manhood and state. Such men, it was claimed by the *philosophes*, deferred to women not only in matters of dress and deportment but in statecraft. Male manners are softening, wrote the satirist L.-A. de Caraccioli, precisely because men wear soft velvet clothing (Caraccioli *c.* 1770: 15). *Petits-maîtres*, figures of languid sartorial excess, masqueraders and artificers had to be excised from the body politic of pre-revolutionary France.

Across the Channel the English counterpart of the French fop was called a 'macaroni', from the 1760s the name given to ultra-fashionable men whose dress was read as an affront to national virtue. The name developed in a theatre context to connote Grand Tour Italy and also suggested the nonsense of much older carnival types and earlier burlesque poetry; empty-headed numbskulls or the blockheads who might be displayed in a popular paid entertainment by George Stevens, 'A Lecture on Heads' (performed in England *c.* 1760). Writers such as Shaftesbury, Locke and Rousseau argued that men were essentially different creatures from women. Why, then, were men wearing cut velvet suits, enormous nosegays, high toupée wigs and heels? Macaronis became figures of fascination and derision, fuelling hundreds of fashion caricature prints, caricature oil painting in Sweden, and even a comedy published in York (1773). Macaroni men wore court dress in spaces where it was not expected, and adopted extremely mannered high hairstyles and Francophile poses. Many of them were young Whigs like Charles James Fox and Sir Joseph Banks, who, in adopting Continental fashions, implied that they were more sophisticated than the courtiers of George III.

Macaronis, like *petits-maîtres*, raised questions in contemporaries' minds about the relationship between dress and gender. The fop was comical and disturbing because he upset the growing belief that men should not be enslaved to fashion. Fops were thus unnatural hybrids, comprising a mingling of male and female attributes, 'unsexed male misses'. Macaroni dress may also have functioned at times as a badge of recognition for an English variant of the same-sex male subcultures which had emerged in urbanized Western Europe by the late seventeenth century (McNeil 1999). These subcultures exploited the same spaces in which fashion was made and disseminated: the Royal Exchange, the piazzas and the modish masquerade venues.

Modern dress

Macaronis and *petits-maîtres* could also be mocked because their dress ceased to look modern in 1760. In the second half of the century the aristocracy promoted the shift towards lighter modes and new classicizing silhouettes. Their Anglophilia played a major role in changing the appearance of European elites and the middle classes. As well as imitating English landscaping and unmounted mahogany furniture, the French and Germans were captivated by the informal sporting and riding dress worn by English men and women. Soft, practical round hats, well-tailored and comfortably cut coats of high-quality woollen broadcloth without heavy stiffened cuffs and flared skirts, chamois-leather men's knee breeches, women's masculine riding coats and military frogged trimmings dominated the French fashion print.

The taste for these fashions, which revealed more of the body's natural outline, and the shift in both academic art and architectural circles and popular taste towards the neo-classical, resulted in new definitions of beauty. A broad-shouldered and slim-waisted type became favoured as the male ideal, with a tall, graceful, small-breasted and high-waisted model for women. Women's hair focused on width rather than height, with artful falling tendrils to suggest natural disarray. From the 1770s fashion adopted more fluid fabrics and even formal dress appeared less stiff. Women's lightweight silks carried window-pane checks, and lace or ribbon meander patterns until the 1760s; thin striped and small sprigged or dotted patterns from 1780 reflecting the taste for the pastoral and a new appreciation of nature. Superfine Indian muslin, which could be woven with spots or stripes, or embroidered, was popularized by Elisabeth Vigée-Lebrun's salon painting (1783) of Queen Marie-Antoinette wearing the *chemise à la reine*, a formerly juvenile summer garment also alluding to classicism and Creole dress. This simple tube-like dress, tied with a sash, was worn by members of the Queen's circle from the mid-1770s in the pastoral setting of the Petit Trianon and the Hameau, the Queen's rustic hamlet. Lavish embroidery continued but was progressively relegated to the borders and hems, creating the optical illusion of greater height. Kashmir shawls, a masculine garment from India, kept women warm and artfully concealed their upper bodies. Male court dress moved its silhouette and cut from a focus on the horizontal, with stiffened wide skirts, to a closer-fitting slim coat with short waistcoats and the side pleats eliminated. High-born and wealthy children, who had been swaddled at birth and dressed in boned bodices in the first half of the century, were permitted flowing sashed dresses and one-piece suits for boys. For full court, Continental children continued to be dressed, wigged and made-up in dress identical to that of adults, whereas the English had not insisted on such exact copies.

WASHING AND WHITENESS

Perhaps the most audacious claim made for the significance of clothing is Roche's suggestion that the Enlightenment was linen (Roche 1989: 151–83). The colour white became a type of guarantee of purity, the role it always played in the Church and at table, people changed their shifts and shirts more, and washing was popularized as no longer sensual but health-giving. In France, piped bathrooms began to appear in plans for mansions in the Louis XV period, whereas they were rarer in the previous century when they had generally been connected with medical activity. People became less cautious about the supposed penetration of water and disease through the pores, and cold water was held to harden the 'fibres' of the modern body. As Vigarello notes, this belief 'discredited the aristocratic code of appearance and manners . . . cleanliness now derived from that which liberated. To be clean was soon to mean removing whatever fixed and constrained the appearance, in favour of whatever freed it' (Vigarello 1985: 130).

Cotton, the new fashionable Indian fibre which could be used to make dresses, nursing bodices and stays was also washable. Berthollet's chlorine bleach was available from 1791 to keep it white. Cotton had been banned in England from 1721 unless it was woven with a linen warp (to make fustian) in order to protect the local textile industry, a restriction that was lifted in 1774. Spinning was mechanized in England in 1770, and dyeing and printing techniques were greatly improved through scientific and entrepreneurial endeavour in France and England, reducing its cost.

In the pre-modern era, colour had served as the principal marker of status, secured by sumptuary laws, and by the prohibitive expense of the dyeing processes, especially for purples, reds, greens and even glossy blacks. By the middle of the eighteenth century, the middle classes could afford to use more coloured materials in their dress and in the decoration of their houses. In England copper-plate printed cotton became available from the mid-1750s, and cheaper roller-printed cottons from the 1780s. In France there was printed monochrome *toile de Jouy* from 1770. Individual garments tended to be worth relatively less and proliferated, indicating a new relationship in the West to the whole world of goods.

HEALTH AND SCIENCE

The supposedly enervating effects of luxury, a much older debate drawn from Graeco-Roman sources, was extended from the 1760s to incorporate new perceptions of health and the body, which affected Enlightenment dress. Doctors and scientists promoted a shift away from fabrics such as silk and velvet, which were unwashable, impervious and therefore unhealthy, towards the greater use of woollen broadcloths and cotton. The new focus on an unencumbered and natural body, free of corsetry, make-up and hair pomade, made the aristocratic courtier type appear debilitated, effete and old-fashioned. Rousseau's moral speculation – 'Everything which cramps and confines nature is in bad taste' – was mapped on to pseudo-scientific experimentation and observation (Rousseau 1762: 330). Doctors denounced paint, powder and clothing for affecting the circulation of blood and the free functioning of the pores of an allegedly declining population. Women's stays and corsets, and even the very cut and silhouette of male court garments, were criticized as enfeebling the populace, threatening the potency of the population. Clairian complained that court dress compressed the male organs and diminished their size (Clairian 1803: 28, 41). Deshais-Gendron's study of the effects of rouge – 'a type of endemic malady' – concluded that it destroyed all natural beauty and produced illnesses ranging from damaged eyesight and headaches to the loss of tooth enamel (Deshais-Gendron 1760: 5, 19). English physician Walter Vaughan merged anxiety about maleness with his experiments on doormice and cloth in *An Essay, Philosophical and Medical Concerning Modern Clothing*: 'Alas! if our venerable ancestors were but raised from the dead to see their posterity disguised so hideously with paint, powder, and several other articles of dress, they might be led to ask – "Where is a Man?"' Like others, he invoked classical ideals to advocate woollen fabrics over silks as 'the most natural, the most wholesome' clothing of the ancients (Vaughan 1792: 91). He proposed that women's cotton and silken stockings caused 'cancer, inflammation, and even abortion' and proposed that stockings be made with toes (Vaughan 1792: 108). Des-Essartz criticized boys' collars, cravats and garters, as well as girls' *paniers*, bonnets, hairdressing and corsetry for hampering the body and perspiration (Des-Essartz 1760: 384–5). By 1785 an endorsement for an elaborate wig in the new journal *Le Cabinet des Modes* was obliged to add that they 'produce no harmful effect on the health' (3e cahier, 15 dec. 1785: 19). In the last two decades of the eighteenth century men even began to wear their own lightly or unpowdered hair in studied disarray. By this date the portraits of J.-L. David, J.-B. Isabey, J.-B. Greuze and the Swede C. Horneman emphasize the natural simplicity and unpowdered texture of men's and women's hair, which hangs in artful but determinedly natural tresses and curls. Another startling contrast with *ancien régime* dress was the adoption of short sleeves in summer for women, boys and girls, well depicted in the art of Louis-Léopold Boilly.

These arguments that court and elaborate dress was emasculating and unhealthy were in turn married to the new pseudo-scientific physiognomy of John Caspar Lavater to produce a picture which rendered the courtier man effeminate and psychologically sick. Lavater's *Essays on Physiognomy* (1789) included 800 comparative engravings, including silhouettes of men's faces from antiquity to the present day. The soft aristocratic face, with hair curled at the side, he described as 'absolutely incompatible with Philosophy and Poetry, with the talents of the Politician, or the heroism of the Soldier' (Lavater 1789: vol. II, 1, 35). His dismissal of aristocratic character and physiognomy extended to their whole demeanour and appearance, so that, for example, he portrayed modern masculinity as forthright and unaffected, characteristically standing bolt upright, wearing a greatcoat and boots, in contrast with the *ancien régime* 'fribble' or trifler, whose clothing and hair were absurd, and whose short, slouched figure was weighed down by the weight of a nosegay (*corsage*). Hardly the figure of a man, as Lavater explains, the 'fribble' has 'a mind incapable of feeling either the great and beautiful, or the simple and natural – a being who . . . will pass his whole life in an eternal childhood' (Lavater 1789: vol. III, 1, 213; see figure 23.2 above). The courtier, then, can appreciate the delights of neither the sublime nor natural simplicity; he is not in touch with the currents of his day. The poses which once had indicated an august and noble persona were now described as conceited and displaying vulgar arrogance.

DRESS AND POLITICS

In post-revolutionary Paris, wearing the dress of the *ancien régime* was also dangerous. This did not mean that fashion was necessarily less mannered; fashion change for the wealthy had sped up so much by the 1780s that the elements of dress became self-referential. Ultra-fashionable men of the late 1780s to the 1790s wore three or four waistcoats simultaneously, sets of buttons were changed every day, several collars overlapped each other, multiple watches and seals jangled from the waist. The *Incroyable* and *Merveilleuse* were Directoire-period types, which included a newly rich class of speculators or *agioteurs*. They replaced knee breeches with tapering trousers, a garment from the wardrobe of sailors and rivermen. Women sported hooped dresses with near-nude muslin and feather-cut hairstyles. Buckled shoes were replaced with boots and even shoe-lacing. Other Parisian groupings used fashion in the post-revolutionary period to emit signals about their political affiliation. Street gangs called the *jeunesse dorée* or *muscadins* retained aspects of court dress as an affront to the authorities and the *sans-culottes*. Bosio, Isabey and Vernet depict them in tight coats with seventeen buttons in memory of the orphan Louis XVII. They wore wigs supposedly made from the hair of guillotine victims, black velvet collars to mourn the decapitated King; *chiné* silk stockings, open shoes and whitened hands, and spoke in affected voices. Consisting of absentee conscripts, deserters, the staff of theatres, luxury shops and banks, they numbered several thousand and congregated around the Palais-Royal, the former site of aristocratic shopping and display. François Gendron theorizes that, until Brumaire, the *jeunesse dorée* were the Committee of General Secretary's private militia and were encouraged surreptitiously (Gendron 1993).

Aristocratic dress, with its trappings of ornament, was feminized practice at odds with masculine democracy. Fashionability and artifice were transferred in the social arena and cultural imagination to the sphere of femininity. Although George Washington wore formal dress with diamond knee-buckles for his second inauguration (1793), Jean-Antoine Houdon sculpted him with a button missing on his coat. A new type of body had emerged. The aristocrat, with a repertoire of courtly gestures learned from the dancing master, had been replaced by the 'natural' body which resisted vain and undeserving gesture. Although a less encumbered, more 'natural' body emerged in the late eighteenth century, it was still a body formed and viewed within social constructs, and the citizens of the era were far from indifferent to fashion. The meanings of Enlightenment dress at the time of the Revolution were less about temporary and contested symbolism adopted at the time – trousers (*sans-culottes*), variously coloured cockades, ribbons, liberty caps (*bonnets rouges/phrygiens*), all subject, as Wrigley has shown, to 'competing, dissonant, interpretative ideas and beliefs', or the promotion of splendid military dress and civil uniforms – than a shift in the relationship between dress and society (Wrigley 2002: 7). Fashion was more of an imperative than ever because it was now the essence of bourgeois liberalism, individualism, self-improvement, urbanism and a market economy.

ACKNOWLEDGEMENTS

In preparation of this chapter I wish to thank the editors; Australian Research Council – Discovery – Projects 2002; University of New South Wales Research Support Programme; University of New South Wales College of Fine Arts Faculty Grant Scheme; Australian National University Humanities Research Centre; National Gallery of Australia Research Library; Dr Ian Henderson, University of Sydney; Mr Martin Kamer, Zug; 'Vanilla' Rita Neto for careful photography, and Mr Roger Leong, Sydney.

REFERENCES

[Anon.] (1704) *A Gentleman Instructed in the Conduct of a Virtuous and Happy Life*, London: E. Evets.

—— (1715) *The Gentleman's Library*, London: W. Mears and J. Browne.

[Andrews, John] (1770) *An Account of the Character and Manners of the French*, London: E. and C. Dilly, J. Robson, J. Walter.

[Caraccioli, Louis-Antoine de] (undated, inscribed '1770') *La Critique des dames et des messieurs à leur toilette*, pamphlet, Bibliothèque Nationale, Paris.

Clairian, L. J. (1803) *Recherches et considérations médicales sur les vêtemens des hommes*, 2nd edn, Paris: A. Aubry.

Delpierre, Madeleine (1997) *Dress in France in the Eighteenth Century*, trans. Caroline Beamish, New Haven, Conn., and London: Yale University Press.

Des-Essartz, M. [Jean-Charles] (1760) *Traité de l'education corporelle des enfans en bas âge, ou Reflexions-pratiques sur les moyens de procurer une meilleure constitution aux citoyens*, Paris: Jean-Thomas Hérissant.

Deshais-Gendron, [Louis-Florent] (1760) *Lettre à Monsieur* ××× *sur plusieurs maladies des yeux, causées par l'usage du rouge et du blanc*, Paris.

Donald, Diana (1996) *The Age of Caricature: Satirical Prints in the Reign of George III*, New Haven, Conn., and London: Yale University Press.

Earle, Peter (1989) *The Making of the English Middle Class*, London: Methuen.

Garsault, M. de (1769) *Description des arts et métiers*, Paris: Saillant & Nyon; Desaint.

Foucault, Michel (1975) *Surveiller et punir: naissance de la prison*, Paris: Gallimard; trans. Alan Sheridan (1977) *Discipline and Punish: The Birth of the Prison*; new edn (1991) Harmondsworth: Penguin.

Gendron, François (1993) *The Gilded Youth of the Thermidor*, Montreal and Kingston: McGill-Queen's University Press.

Hallett, Mark (1999) *The Spectacle of Difference: Graphic Satire in the Age of Hogarth*, New Haven, Conn., and London: Yale University Press.

Kuchta, David (1996) 'The Making of the Self-made Man: Class, Clothing, and English Masculinity, 1688–1832', in Victoria de Grazia and Ellen Furlough (eds) *The Sex of Things: Gender and Consumption in Historical Perspective*, Berkeley, Los Angeles and London: University of California Press.

Lavater, John Caspar (1789) *Essays on Physiognomy*, 5 vols, trans. Henry Hunter, London: John Murray.

McNeil, Peter (1999) '"That Doubtful Gender": Macaroni Dress and Male Sexualities' *Fashion Theory*, 3/4: 411–47.

Rangström, Lena (1998) 'A Dress Reform in the Spirit of its Age', in Magnus Olausson (ed.) *Catherine the Great & Gustav III*, Stockholm: Nationalmuseum.

Ribeiro, Aileen (1984) *Dress in Eighteenth-century Europe 1715–1789*, New York: Holmes & Meier.

Roche, Daniel (1989) *The Culture of Clothing: Dress and Fashion in the 'Ancien Régime'*, trans. Jean Birrell (1994) Cambridge: Cambridge University Press.

Rothstein, Natalie (ed.) (1987) *Barbara Johnson's Album of Fashions and Fabrics*, London: Thames & Hudson.

Rousseau, Jean Jacques (1762) *Emile*, trans. Barbara Foxley (1993) London: J. M. Dent.

Sargentson, Carolyn (1996) *Merchants and Luxury Markets: The Marchands Merciers of Eighteenth-century Paris*, London: Victoria and Albert Museum.

Scott, Katie (1995) *The Rococo Interior: Decoration and Social Spaces in Early Eighteenth-century Paris*, New Haven, Conn., and London: Yale University Press.

Smith, Charles Saumarez (1993) *Eighteenth-century Decoration: Design and the Domestic Interior in England*, London: Weidenfeld & Nicolson.

Thicknesse, Philip (1766) *Observations on the Customs and Manners of the French Nation*, London: Robert Davis, G. Kearsley, N. Young.

Vaughan, Walter (1792) *An Essay Philosophical and Medical Concerning Modern Clothing*, Rochester and London: W. Gillman and the Robinsons.

Vigarello, Georges (1985) *Concepts of Cleanliness: Changing Attitudes in France since the Middle Ages*, trans. Jean Birrell (1988) Cambridge: Cambridge University Press.

Weatherill, Lorna (1996) *Consumer Behaviour & Material Culture in Britain 1660–1760*, 2nd edn, London and New York: Routledge.

Wrigley, Richard (2002) *The Politics of Appearances: Representations of Dress in Revolutionary France*, Oxford and New York: Berg.

CHAPTER TWENTY-FOUR

POPULAR CULTURE

Nicholas Rogers

Tracking popular culture is a little like tracking the 'will o' the wisp', those mysterious lights of churchyards and moors, popularly thought to represent the flaming souls broken out of purgatory. As a devilish delusion, it can lead you down treacherous paths. 'Popular culture' is a loaded concept because there is a lot at stake in how one begins to define 'culture', not simply in history, but in cognate disciplines such as anthropology, sociology and, more recently, literary and cultural studies, with which history has increasingly been associated.

A further problem is that the task of writing a history of popular culture can be approached only obliquely, through elite sources of information or popular genres of ballads and tales gathered by elite collectors and translated into print from oral sources. It is very rare that one can hear an unmediated voice. Part of the challenge of popular history is making sense of sources that are highly mediated, opaque and sometimes transmitted through genres of parody and burlesque betraying condescending attitudes and frequently a sense of anxiety.

THE INVENTION OF POPULAR CULTURE

It is sometimes argued that the discovery of 'popular culture' is coincident with the emergence of folklore as a coherent subject of enquiry, with the disposition of genteel collectors to recover the elements of a quintessentially oral culture that was rapidly disappearing with the onset of industrialization and more modern forms of communication. While it is true that popular culture was reframed by this quest, it now seems clear that the notion of a popular culture had a longer, more complex genealogy. From a European perspective, the fascination with the 'people' or the 'folk' was more accurately a product of the Enlightenment. It was Johann Gottfried Herder who first coined the phrase 'popular culture' (*Kultur des Volkes*), contrasting it with the 'learned culture' (*Kultur der Gelehrten*) of the literati. From the middle of the eighteenth century onwards there was a new curiosity with popular folklore, songs and sayings, generated principally by the literati. Much of this fascination resulted from a reaction to the luxury and 'effeminacy' of elite society, a desire to recover the 'majestic simplicity' of rural folkways. In Britain poets such as Stephen

Duck and Robert Burns gained access to polite circles, ambitious clerics like Thomas Percy collected ballads, and Celtic enthusiasts such as James MacPherson published verses recited by crofters that he misleadingly claimed were derived from Ossian, the Highland Homer. In Germany Herder and the Grimm brothers' national folksongs attempted to recover the true nature of the *Volk* and extolled local festivals as exemplary features of a self-activating populist spirit. The temper of these endeavours was nostalgic and upbeat. They connoted a revolt against refinement, a yearning for the wild and unclassical, a desire for cultural primitivism. The enthusiasm for a popular idiom was also a revolt against the mannered reason of the Enlightenment, and, in some German and Spanish quarters, against the intrusion of French influence in upper-class cultural and intellectual life.

The rediscovery of the 'people' in their rustic simplicity was not always harnessed positively to the quest for national identity. John Aubrey, a fan of political arithmetic and a fellow of the Royal Society, sought to classify the island 'aborigines, or indiginae' as simple adjuncts of soil and topography, men and women of little account in the long-term mission of civilizing England, which was attributed to Anglo-Norman influences. He remarked:

> Old customs and old wives-fables are gross things, but yet ought not to be quite rejected: there may be some truth and usefulness be elicited out of them: besides, 'tis a pleasure to consider the errors that enveloped former ages: as also the present.
>
> (Aubrey 1686–7:132)

Henry Bourne, the curate of All Saints, Newcastle, was broadly of the same opinion. In his *Antiquitates Vulgares* (1725) he condoned those popular customs that were innocent, but condemned those such as Christmas mummery that were conducive to debauchery and frivolity. He also attacked funeral wakes for their 'drunkenness and lewdness', but saw nothing wrong in the praying for dead souls – a relic of pre-Reformation practice – if it encouraged some positive thinking about the afterlife.

Whether these writers cast the people as untainted by affectation and artificiality or compulsively crude and superstitious, a cultural divide separated them. The people had become exotic, a race apart, equivalent in some instances to the colonial 'other'. James Boswell, the son of a Scottish laird, thought his visit to the Hebrides with Dr Johnson to be 'much the same as being with a tribe of Indians', for the villagers 'were as black and wild in their appearance as any American savages whatever' (Boswell 1785: 250).

POPULAR CULTURE: SURVIVAL, RESILIENCE, REJUVENATION

Insecurity and fear were the underlying conditions of popular culture, maintains Robert Muchembled (1985). The 'multiple bonds of solidarity' that people wove to make sense of their lives were inextricably bound up with the politics of survival in what was a harsh and unpredictable world; death could come at any time, although some solace from the travails of existence came from ample harvests and buoyant trade. Muchembled's depiction of popular culture is arguably too fatalistic and introverted. It is certainly too negative as an interpretation of the eighteenth century which experienced population growth, economic expansion and encouraged greater material expectations. But it does make explicable the recourse to magical charms and incantations to handle sickness and disaster, and the complex of superstition and religious belief that informed the important rites of passage of a family and community, whether that meant blessing a marriage or birth, praying for a soul after death, or divining a mild winter and a good harvest. Interwoven into this world was a rich calendar of rituals that were occasions of merriment and communal solidarity, popular devotions and ruling-class or parochial feasts; occasions when the young men of the village or township could exert their masculinity, openly court eligible women, redress perceived grievances within the community, and ape, even criticize, their betters in topsy-turvy rituals of misrule. While there were regional variations to this ritual year, not only between town and countryside but also between pastoral and arable areas, popular culture was characterized by a heavy weight of customary expectations that sought to safeguard a community's survival.

There is sometimes a tendency to see popular culture as 'timeless' and 'unchanging', stretching back to the mists of time. The early interest in folklore promoted this view, as did the claim of some ordinary people that their customs were longstanding, as the phrase went, 'time out of mind'. With this went the assumption that popular culture was relatively autonomous from elite society, bounded by traditions and rituals that were taken for granted and largely self-regulating. In fact, popular culture always stood in dramatic tension to the officialdom of Church and state, which was responsible for the discipline and training of those who were destined to be the drones of society. Even before the Reformation, fear of crime and riot led some urban authorities in England, for example, to ban Christmas mumming and the summer revels in which the famed outlaw Robin Hood served as a symbolic Lord of Misrule. But with the Reformation Protestant reformers sought to eliminate most saints' days from the calendar, ban processions and plays at Whitsun and Corpus Christi, and crack down on maypoles and church ales. Although these festivals had a chequered history in the next hundred years, the Puritans managed for a brief time totally to eliminate the festive calendar in England, Easter and Christmas included, save for the celebration of 5 November, the commemoration of the country's deliverance from a Catholic conspiracy to blow up the Houses of Parliament. A similar purging occurred in other Protestant jurisdictions, while the Catholic Counter-Reformation embarked on its own house-cleaning, curbing the activities of youth abbeys and charivari, prohibiting burlesque revels, and cutting back on the number of obligatory feast days: in France, to 21 by 1666; in Spain, where there was a greater tolerance of traditional festivals, to 31. This campaign against the more self-activating and 'lewder' aspects of popular culture was accompanied in both Protestant and Catholic countries by a systematic repression of witchcraft and a discouragement of any magical beliefs or cures that could conceivably be construed as maleficent. Aiding the state in this quest were wealthy peasants or notables who sought to reassert their control over their own villages and who wished to eradicate marginal elements from their communities, especially single, cantankerous women laying claim to community resources. If the witch-hunting craze signalled the disposition of the state to make a scapegoat of the vulnerable in the interests of national unity or stricter religious observance, as seems to have been the case in the resurgent Catholic states of southern Germany, in many French cities during the religious wars, in the Spanish Netherlands and Scotland, it also signified emergent divisions within village communities about the need for order and discipline.

How did this reforming drive affect popular culture in the eighteenth century? The answer seems to be that this policing drive was incomplete. The early modern state lacked the resources to effect a thorough reformation of manners, even if it was able to use print culture in the battle against carnivalesque custom and superstition. It was always dependent upon the co-operation of local elites to put its reforms into effect. Moreover, religious divisions, regional loyalties, changes in the nature of political regimes, and the importance of local custom to the agricultural cycle and to the communal identity of organized trades mitigated against a comprehensive purge of popular culture. If the pre-Reformation ritual year was indelibly fractured, elements survived or were reworked in different contexts. In Brittany, Sicily and Bavaria mystery plays continued to be staged. In 1779 the Archbishop of Salzburg complained that 'a stranger mixture of religion and profanity' could not be imagined (Burke 1978: 235). In Spain, Venice and Rome Carnival continued apace, even if it sometimes became as much a tourist attraction as a rollicking entertainment for local residents. As many as 30,000 tourists are said to have visited Venice during the Carnival of 1687. And while the Counter-Reformation in France sought to pare down the festive calendar, it had to tolerate the survival or revival of unofficial holidays. In the Yonne department of Burgundy, for example, 109 illegal religious festivals were reported in the 1790s, 45 per cent of which were saints' days, 20 per cent other Catholic holidays and 7 per cent carnivals in the larger towns.

A good example of the difficulty of erasing popular belief from the calendar is the celebration of Halloween, or Hallowmass, as it was sometimes called. In Scotland, where the Protestant regime had a reputation for inquisitorial surveillance, the Scottish Kirk was anxious to erase all trace of pagan rituals from its calendar and to abolish the Catholic practice of praying for souls in purgatory. In eliminating the Catholic practice of souling the Kirk was reasonably successful, but there was a stubborn resistance to eliminating many of the pagan practices that had grown up around the holiday. This was because Halloween was an important time in the agricultural year for the renewing of leases, stock-taking and preparing for the winter ahead. Consequently the Kirk found it virtually impossible to curb the divinatory rites that had grown around the holiday, especially in Gaelic-speaking areas; rites that hoped for a mild winter or a fruitful marriage, warned off evil spirits that might compromise a coupling or blight the crops, and presaged impending deaths in the community. Nor was the Kirk able to repress the youthful masking that marked the holiday, those charivari-like celebrations that sometimes resulted in community sanctions against unpopular neighbours. In England, on the other hand, Halloween was more easily contained because much of the socially directed pranking associated with the festival was transferred to the anniversary of the Gunpowder Plot of 1605 (5 November) a week later. Even so, the traditions of souling, house-to-house festive begging in return for prayers for the dead, continued in some Catholic areas of the countryside, albeit in a more secularized form, principally because it was an important 'dole' for poorer inhabitants as the winter set in. Elsewhere in the country, this dole was simply transferred to another occasion, whether Guy Fawkes Day, St Clement's Day (23 November), St Catherine's Day (25 November), St Andrew's Day (30 November), even St Nicholas's Day (6 December) or St Thomas's Day (21 December) just a few days before Christmas. Which day was chosen would depend on a variety of factors: the local agrarian cycle, the religious legacy of the region, or the patronage of particular saints by industrial trades.

The history of Halloween illustrates the resilience and adaptability of popular custom in a period of state-sanctioned religious change. In effect, it is representative of the larger transformations in popular practice in the eighteenth century. In England, for example, the failure of Puritan rule led to an exuberant revival of some basic public festivities, such as Christmas, Plough Monday, Shrovetide, Easter, May Day and Whitsuntide, although in a somewhat altered form. Christmastide retained its mummings in many parts of the country, although not its institutionalized lords of misrule. Easter and May Day saw the return of hobby-horses and morris dancing, as well as maypoles. In some urban contexts, the May Day festivities were appropriated by select occupational groups, such as milkmaids and chimney-sweeps, while the days following Easter Sunday were devoted to 'lifting' or 'hocking', community-sanctioned rites of sex play which had originated in the fifteenth century, came under threat in the Puritan era, only to be revived in the eighteenth century. Similarly, the Shrovetide revels, which were attacked in the seventeenth century because of their lawless forms of community policing by urban apprentices, revived as an occasion for lent-crocking, that is, soliciting festive doles from householders, as well as for cock-fighting and cock-shying. Plough Monday, another holiday that drew Puritan opprobrium, also retained its place in the calendar because it was an important rite in the resumption of the agricultural year after the Christmas festivities, although its festive doles were now devoted to merrymaking rather than to parish finances. As with the Shrovetide revels, ungenerous neighbours could find themselves in trouble on this holiday, with the ceremonial plough drawing ungainly furrows through their property.

In virtually all of these instances, the religious associations of the festivals had been supplanted by the secular; they had become holidays rather than holy-days. The same was true of the parish feasts or wakes that dotted the calendar in the late spring, or late summer–early autumn. Church-ales, an important aspect of religious sociability in the sixteenth century and the bane of Puritan reformers, had died out in the seventeenth century. In some parts of the south of England parish wakes were also in decline as a result of reformist vigilance. Yet this was not true everywhere. Two-thirds of the parishes of Northamptonshire celebrated a feast of some sort in the early eighteenth century. In 1730, Thomas Hearne recorded a feast day for 132 places in Oxfordshire, while at least 122 places in Devonshire reported one twenty years later. In Essex and East Anglia, where parish wakes had disappeared, moreover, hundreds of country fairs served as occasions for festivity, entertainment and sociability. In these instances many of the carnivalesque traditions that had characterized earlier celebrations were adapted to more commercial venues.

In the light of this evidence it is doubtful whether it is really meaningful to talk of a decline in popular culture or to regard it as purely residual. Both perspectives place popular culture in too passive a light, forgetting the extent to which popular culture was able to adapt, negotiate and appropriate aspects of a more literate, commercial world as well as elude reformist drives to eliminate heresy, superstition and festive revelry from its repertoire. One good example of the resilience and adaptability of popular culture was the charivari, or rough music, the ritual hazing of individuals judged to have broken community norms in some way. Charivari were initially associated with the activities of youth abbeys or *bachelleries* on particular festivals in the year, when designated young men would act as community policemen of moral offenders, especially women who were perceived to have abrogated the prescribed rules of a patriarchal society. Charivaris came under attack in the reforming drives of the early modern era, partly because they presumed to take over responsibilities traditionally associated with the Church, but they were not eliminated. Indeed, they persisted well into the nineteenth century, sometimes even in quite commercial venues such as Horn Fair on the Kentish fringes of London. What is particularly instructive about the charivari in the eighteenth century and beyond is the varied use to which it was put. Shrews, scolds and cuckolds were not the only targets. Charivaris entered the political arena to excoriate politicians, tax-collectors and poor-law officials, and to chastise unpopular employers, some of whom were subjected to 'riding the stang' or 'donkeying' around the market square. Despite the often misogynist timbre of popular culture, it was inflicted upon wife-beaters as well as assertive women. In Billingshurst, Sussex, for example, a group of women rolled up a wife-beater in a blanket and ducked him in the local pond, having 'rung what they call Rough Musick in order to get him out of the house' (*London Evening Post*, 4–6 February 1748). As this incident suggests, the charivari was an adaptable rite of community self-regulation that could be deployed in very different contexts.

This resurgence of popular culture was facilitated by a number of developments. Although a seigneurial or squirearchical presence was very visible in many villages during the seventeenth century, the growth of densely populated early industrial districts where workers retained some control of the labour process meant that many popular customs could be rejuvenated without much supervision from above. Furthermore, the thickening of urban economies, especially in Britain after 1660, accelerated the breakdown of older styles of civic paternalism and the emergence of popular modes of behaviour that expressed the emergent solidarities of the *campagnonnages*, or journeymen associations, most of which were clandestine and all of which were illegal. In France the local authorities found it very difficult to regulate the initiation rites of the *campagnons*, some of which mimicked and appropriated the religious rites of the Catholic Church. New recruits were 'baptized'; in Montpellier they were inducted according to a ceremony known as the *levée du sac*, in which the new arrival washed the hands of the other *compagnons* present and paid for wine and victuals, a ritual that recalled the *lavabo*, the washing of the priest's hands before the Eucharist in the Catholic Mass. When brother journeymen issued an injunction to boycott a master's shop because of unfair labour practices, they sometimes termed it a *damnation*, borrowing directly from the legal language of the Catholic Church.

Figure 24.1 *Hudibras Encounters the Skimmington*, William Hogarth. This is one of Hogarth's illustrations to Samuel Butler's *Hudibras* (1662–78), a satire on Cervantes's *Don Quixote*. Hudibras, seated on a horse in the centre-left of the picture, is about to draw his sword in alarm on encountering a charivari, a skimmington, a rural custom in which a husband and wife are processed tied together on a horse. Intended to bring ridicule on husbands or wives for errant ways, shrewishness, and so on, in this case it is the Amazonian woman (centre-right) who is taunting her husband, sitting with his back to her: 'The warrior whilom overcome;/Arm'd with a spindle and a distaff,/Which as he rode, she made him twist off;/And when he loiter'd, o'er her shoulder/Chastis'd the reformado soldier' (Canto II, part II, 644–8). By courtesy of Nicholas Rogers.

What also accentuated the resurgence of popular culture was the growing cultural divide that separated the ruling classes from the bulk of the population. The popular culture of the sixteenth and early seventeenth centuries had, to a large extent, been a shared culture, one in which the rulers understood and participated in what the anthropologist Robert Redfield rather condescendingly called the 'little tradition'. By the eighteenth century this was less true, even though some local landowners continued to patronize village feasts and sports such as cock-fighting, bull-baiting, boxing and football, just as the Venetian patricians sponsored the famous 'battles of the fists' that occurred over canal bridges. With the urban renaissance, with the disposition of the elite and the wealthier members of the middling sort to adopt the metropolitan mannerisms associated with polite society, popular culture became to all intents and purposes plebeian culture. The cultural divide was probably most manifest in attitudes towards witchcraft and magic, both of which were viewed with scepticism, if not disbelief, by the dominant classes by the early eighteenth century. Witchcraft prosecutions were discouraged, if not banned, by the authorities, yet in more isolated rural areas the belief in witchcraft persisted for decades. In England, a pauper named Ruth Osborne was ducked and drowned by the local inhabitants of Tring in Hertfordshire in 1751 for allegedly bewitching local cattle and their owner. One of the ringleaders, a butcher named Thomas Colley, was hanged for this crime, but this judicial example did not dampen the disposition of some rural folk to 'swim' witches suspected of maleficent acts. Swimmings were reported the next year in Suffolk, in Leicestershire (1760 and 1776), in Cambridgeshire (1769) and Suffolk again (1795).

Magical beliefs were more widespread, even though rising expectations of life, higher standards of living, new medicines, better communications, the spread of literacy and the gradual triumph of mechanical philosophy over animist belief nibbled away at the inclination to deploy supernatural powers to combat illness, scarcity or danger. Amulets were still worn to ward off sickness. Sacramental shillings, rings forged out of a shilling taken from the offertory, were worn as a remedy against fits. People suffering from scrofula, inflammation of the lymph glands, still desired to be touched by the dead hand of a malefactor hanging from the gallows, a macabre but interesting, plebeian reappropriation of the former custom of the 'king's touch'. Cunning men and women could still be found in some villages, ready to interpret dreams, recover lost property, cure common ailments or foretell the future. These conjurers were often thought to be skilled in the rituals of divination, but on particular days of the year, on St Agnes Eve or Halloween, for example, young women believed they could foretell their future husbands and the prospect of marital happiness. Superstitious rites were especially prevalent among occupations involving a high degree of risk, among coal- or tin-miners, for example, or mariners. The belief in spirits, apparitions and even devils was widespread, in spite of attempts to discount its credibility by disparaging believers as irrational, undiscerning simpletons or even hypochondriacs. Augustin Calmet, in examining the vampire scare that had broken out in eastern Europe among the peasants, attributed it to a complex of 'prejudice, fancy, and fear' brought on by a poor diet and climate (Calmet 1759: 289). But the fear of revenants, or tormented souls, certainly influenced the funerary rites of the populace in many places. People routinely strove to ensure that their own relatives were protected and prayed for in the critical period between death and burial when the future of the soul remained uncertain. In Britain there was a strong belief in the metaphysical attributes of the corpse whose spiritual status remained uncertain. There seems to have been an ongoing anxiety, even after the official denunciation of purgatory, as to whether the soul was judged at death or whether it remained with the body until Judgement Day, when body and soul would rise from the grave. Among other things, this set of beliefs prompted the tradition of 'sin-eating', consuming food and drink that had been in contact with the corpse or coffin in order to assume the sins of the dead and smooth the passage of the soul to heaven. Such folkloric beliefs likely had their origin in the intercessory prayers made on behalf of the dead at All Souls, for which the poor had been rewarded with soul cakes and ale.

CUSTOM AND PLEBEIAN CULTURE

Magic and witchcraft were of less concern to the dominant classes in the eighteenth century than they had been earlier. The growth of Newtonian philosophy and the *de facto* tolerance of religious pluralism meant that these plebeian practices were more likely to be regarded as 'vulgar errors' than dangerous ones. Popular belief in the supernatural caused concern only when it encouraged disorder and death, as in the witch-hunt in Hertfordshire, or when it challenged official policy in some way. The riots against the surgeons at London's Tyburn, where crowds resisted turning over the bodies of the condemned for scientific dissection, would fall into this category. Plebeian people greatly resented this practice, which was designed to amplify judicial terror and deter crime by adding a 'peculiar Mark of Infamy' to capital punishment, since the integrity of the body was seen as indispensable to the peace of the soul.

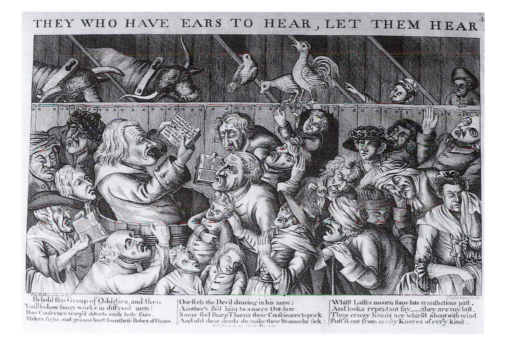

Figure 24.2 *They Who Have Ears to Hear, Let Them Hear*. This cartoon is a parody of communal reading. By courtesy of Nicholas Rogers.

The issues which brought plebeian belief into conflict with the authorities were more likely to be fought out on economic rather than religious terrain. The notion that plebeian habits of leisure were not only profane but tonics to idleness was certainly part of earlier reforming discourse. But it became central to the debate about plebeian habits in the long eighteenth century. Plebeian festivals encouraged idleness and profligacy and dissipated savings. The plebeian preference for 'leisure', particularly the willingness of many artisans to observe Saint Monday, undermined national productivity. Although Adam Smith and the physiocrats believed they could reshape plebeian desires through economic stimuli, induce people to work by the prospect of higher wages and greater consumer power, there was a lingering suspicion that plebeian culture was incorrigibly uneconomic, preferring communal sociability to individual ambition, and idleness to industry.

In the economically advanced areas of Enlightenment Europe the cultural expectations of the plebeian classes were critical to discussions of work discipline. The characteristic work patterns of labouring people were seasonal, spasmodic and, above all, customary. There were traditional ways of doing things that were not easily dislodged, especially in a world where putting-out industries predominated and workers retained considerable control over the labour process. In many trades there was a strong sense of entitlement to waste or surplus products, what were called perquisites. Journeymen tailors believed they were entitled to the remnants of cloth, or 'cabbage'; textile workers to 'fents' and 'thrums'; braziers to 'filings'; shipwrights to 'chips'; so much so that the workers at Deptford refused higher wages rather than part with their time-honoured perk of taking waste wood out of the yard. Riverside porters believed that the spillings of sugar and tobacco from broken barrels were legitimately fair game, although what was considered a perquisite could be considered theft by an employer. Indeed, there was a protracted campaign to criminalize many perquisites over the course of the century and to imprison offenders.

Workers regarded perquisites as part of a package of entitlements of which the actual wage was only one portion. This package could include food provided by the employer, either on a regular basis or on festive occasions, shelter in the case of living-in labourers, tips and used clothing in the case of domestic servants, coal in the case of miners, and truck, or payment in kind, since coin was often in short supply. Workers in incorporated trades, or in industries that were closely regulated by law, were quite prepared to bargain about these benefits and to use the discourse of custom to do so, because it often had the force of law. They would appeal to magistrates or *parlements* about the way in which employers manipulated apprenticeship regulations, abused truck allocations, altered the terms or conditions of piece work, or encouraged outsiders to work under the price. The evidence we have suggests that workers became increasingly assertive about these customary benefits as the eighteenth century progressed. When formal negotiations with employers or authorities failed, workers boycotted unpopular employers and even rioted for their rights by humiliating blacklegs or destroying property. In London in the 1720s silk weavers protesting the importation of Indian calico even stripped dresses from the backs of consumers.

Perhaps the best example of diversity of custom to plebeian culture in the eighteenth century was the food riot. In the seventeenth century peasants and artisans had protested against the abrogation of use rights in the countryside. In France, in particular, they had joined regional rebellions against the imposition of royal taxes. But in the next century the emphasis was upon the rights of subsistence, fair access to grain and bread in particular. Until the 1760s grain markets were heavily regulated to provide some protection or 'subsistence insurance' to the small consumer. As consumers well understood, this was an essential part of the legitimation of the paternalist order. Consequently, if the authorities hesitated or refused to use their powers to maintain a supply of grain, flour or bread at a fair price during periods of dearth, the common people took the law into their own hands, blocking the passage of foodstuffs from their region, hazing unpopular bakers, millers or middlemen, and increasingly fixing the price of food themselves. Popular interventions of this kind occurred in France in 1709, 1725, 1740, 1749, 1768, 1770, 1774, 1775, 1784 and 1785. In 1775, prompted by Turgot's efforts to restore the freedom of trade in grain, they generated a genuine 'flour war' that affected eighty-two market towns as well as routes and waterways leading to Paris. In Britain, too, there was a wave of protest throughout the century, culminating in some widespread rioting in 1756–7, 1766–7, 1772, 1782–3, 1795 and 1800. What distinguished these interventions was a strong sense of social justice for a fair price, a hatred of market manipulators in times of scarcity, and a propensity for swift, direct action that gave crowds a momentary advantage against the relatively slow movement of troops into the riotous areas. Unlike many earlier forms of popular insurgency, these were largely self-activating, autonomous risings, mobilizing local workforces and using the local knowledge of women, in particular, to isolate dealers and farmers who sought to profit from scarcity. As historians have continually stressed, these were not rebellions of the belly but rebellions fired by an insistence on customary entitlements in times of dearth, what E. P. Thompson (1971 and 1991) has described as a 'moral economy', a phrase understood quite differently by eighteenth-century philosophers.

By the end of the eighteenth century, in France and Britain (although not in Spain, Italy and Germany, where the dominance of Church and state was more profound) a revitalized plebeian culture was making its presence felt on important matters of state. On issues of food supply and industrial custom, on work discipline and also on wartime recruitment, where the British had increasing recourse to dispossessed crofters, cotters and landless labourers from Scotland and Ireland to fill its armies and fleets, the popular classes were defining the limits of the possible. Those limits were also to be found in the French countryside, where peasants were becoming increasingly restless about both seigneurial privilege and the fiscal charges of a state geared to war. How these grievances were translated in the sphere of politics, particularly the democratic politics of the last decade of the century, is a question we must now address.

PLEBEIAN CULTURE AND POLITICS

Popular interest in politics was not new to the eighteenth century. During the Reformation and the Wars of Religion it was not easy to avoid political controversy because it intersected with religious practice and belief. During the English Civil Wars it was virtually impossible to ignore politics, not simply because political prints and prophecies abounded with the lapsing of censorship, but because even neutralism – the desire to prevent warring armies from plaguing your region and the hope for some reconciliation between crown and Parliament – was a political stance in itself.

The English Civil Wars expanded the frontiers of political literacy to a point where the state had to continue to marshal the political passions of the populace in a more systematic manner. By the end of the seventeenth century a calendar of political festivals was firmly in place. Holidays celebrating the accession and coronation and birthdays of the ruling monarch and his family, together with the anniversary of the Gunpowder Plot, Queen Elizabeth's accession (17 November), Restoration Day (29 May) and the 'martyrdom' of Charles I (30 January), gave legitimacy to the political order. These were intended to transmit Britain's Protestant and constitutional heritage to the broadest possible audience, and to edify the people about their rights and responsibilities. At the same time they were opportunities for ruling-class liberality and display, assuming many of the former functions of royal progresses and civic processions and providing the plebs with beer, wine and victuals at the celebratory bonfires. Political festivals thus sought to rejuvenate political and social loyalties through the transmission of ideology and munificence.

In practice these festivals were often contentious, raucous events in which monarchs and politicians were openly mocked and local dignitaries shown their ratings with the crowd. Political parody and humour were rife, sharpened by high levels of urban literacy and a robust political press that had penetrated most large provincial towns by the middle of the eighteenth century. Henry Sacheverell's controversial sermon before the Lord Mayor of London on 5 November 1710, in which he debunked the Whigs and maligned the Glorious Revolution, sold 40,000 copies in a few days, ten times as many as Martin Luther's famous *Address to the Christian Nobility* of 1520. Not only that, it has been estimated that this much-pirated tract was read, or read to, 250,000 people; and it brought in its wake, as the Whigs sought to try Sacheverell for his political impudence, riots in London and demonstrations elsewhere.

No other European nation had a political culture of such vitality, sophistication and complexity; one enhanced as the century progressed by a proliferation of clubs, debating societies and associations. The Dutch had a lively press, but its popular politics principally engaged the middling sort, judging from the evidence of the Patriot Revolts of the 1780s. Other European nations had tightly controlled gazettes that usually transmitted only officially endorsed news. What political disaffection surfaced among ordinary people passed largely by word of mouth, as scattered gossip or rumour, enlivened perhaps by seditious placards, anecdotes and tales of criminals as heroes. The celebrated *libelles* that created a pornography of the French court's comings and goings were read largely by officials or professionals, not by the populace. In Paris, where we have a good indication of what servants and journeymen were reading from notarial records, books of piety predominated. But ordinary Parisians, like Londoners, had access to chapbooks, almanacs, parodic booklets on city jokes and slang, prints, broadsheets, bawdy songs and seditious placards. If devotional literature enjoined them to be devout, the print of the street gave them an insatiable curiosity for information and a taste for the marvellous, the scandalous and the profane.

In order to control such profanity and the political incredulity it might generate, the authorities strove to awe the populace into obedience through the judicial terror of the gallows and baroque spectaculars of royal majesty and religious devotion. In Toulouse, where we have a rich account of ceremonial life in the eighteenth century, religious processions drew on the city's own Counter-Reformation heritage to inculcate popular piety and outdoor sociability. While these ceremonies were capable of accommodating craft corporations, they tended to be elitist in tone and effect, attracting only the most devout. In fact, there is evidence that participation in these religious processions waned as the century went on, suggesting that the archaic, timeless quality of the rituals had become too exclusive to accommodate the dynamics of urban life. The more political *Te Deums* honouring the King and his royal victories were potentially more inclusive. Although city dignitaries sponsored bonfires and wine fountains in these celebrations, they were not formally represented in the rituals at the Place-Royale, which were devoted to transmitting a sense of the monarch's power and grandeur. Yet this secular fête, with its games, libations, fireworks and outdoor theatrics, did not translate into any appreciable affection for the King. The crowd that was convoked on these occasions was not integrated into the ceremonial idiom in any meaningful way. If the reordering of public space potentially enlarged the repertoire of public interaction, it was left to the revolutionary order to try to perfect it. Like the *Te Deums*, the revolutionary festivals of the Jacobins used the vista of the open square to construct carefully designed, educative centre-pieces celebrating the virtues of liberty, equality and fraternity. As in the Fête de la Fédération, they also included delegations of the people as integral parts of the event itself.

Charles Pigott, a Shropshire patrician who joined the London Corresponding Society (LCS) and welcomed the French Revolution, greatly admired the new-style festivals choreographed by such artists as Jacques-Louis David. He thought them 'magnificent processions, no longer sullied by the ignoble badges of superstition and fanaticism, but embellished with all the insignia of peace, freedom and equality'. He compared them favourably to the 'royal festivals' of the British, where the people were 'lethargized by dint of BEEF and PORTER' and then invited to shout 'God Save the King' (Piggott 1795: 34–5). Pigott was undoubtedly overreacting to the mobilization of crowds by loyalists in the wake of Louis XVI's execution in 1793, and he certainly underestimated the plebeian scepticism of 'Church and King' celebrations. Yet his anxieties did point to a dilemma that had confronted radicals in their quest for a more inclusive, if not republican, politics: how to transform the profane, raucous crowds of Britain's demotic political order into the democratic citizens of the future; how, in effect, to change the crowd's customary penchant for political mimicry and travesty into something more tangibly progressive.

Pigott's answer, like that of many other Jacobins, was through political edification by example, debate and literacy. As a branch member of the LCS he adopted democratic modes of address and dress that were the hallmark of French citizenship. Recognizing the importance of Tom Paine's homespun but devastatingly iconoclastic critique of Britain's political order, a style of argumentation that appealed pre-eminently to the small masters and artisans of the metropolis and the larger provincial centres, he strove to push the frontiers of political literacy still further by producing radical primers for plebeians outside the political nation; dictionaries in which 'A' stood for 'Adam', the first true *sans-culotte*. These radical endeavours certainly expanded those frontiers at a rapid rate. Cheap runs and extracts made *The Rights of Man* a familiar work in many towns across Britain, including Belfast and Dublin, and translations in Welsh and Gaelic pushed it further into the Celtic periphery. But in England the radical project was compromised by popular loyalism

Figure 24.3 *The Invasion: France*, T. Cook after William Hogarth (March 1756). Reprinted in 1798. This engraving shows the undernourished French soldiers preparing to embark for England. A monk sharpens an executioner's axe, while below him there are symbols of French Catholic intolerance – manacles, a gibbet and a wheel for breaking Protestants – and there is a plan for a monastery at Black Friars. One soldier is cooking frogs over an outside fire. By permission of Martin Fitzpatrick.

and the crackdown on identifiable propagandists, forcing Pigott, among others, into prison and then into exile. In Ireland, the United Irishmen also made great progress in promoting radical ideas, sponsoring schools and book clubs, reworking traditional ballads in a Jacobin idiom, and availing themselves of their strong links to the printing world of Dublin. Yet ultimately the rising sectarianism in Ulster stayed the advance, while the growth of a Catholic-inspired nationalism, Defenderism, stymied the progress of radical Enlightenment ideas in the south. In the end there was great difficulty in reconciling universal radical ideas with the particularism of local popular cultures.

The same dilemma confronted the French in their attempts to expand the geographical horizons of liberty. In Spain there was a huge cultural gulf separating the *luces* from the *pueblo*. Enlightenment enthusiasts, with their Francophilic tastes,

Figure 24.4 *The Invasion: England*, T. Cook after William Hogarth (March 1756). Reprinted in 1799. This shows a corresponding scene on the other side of the Channel. The soldiers and sailors are stout and well nourished – the inn sign advertises 'roast beef every day'. One of the serving maids is measuring a soldier's broad back while a recruiting officer measures the height of a stout but small volunteer who wears high heels in the hope of being accepted. A grenadier paints a graffito of the King of France holding a gibbet. On the table there is a copy of 'Britannia Rules the Waves'. The theme of the intolerant and downtrodden French contrasted with the prosperous freeborn Englishman recurs in Hogarth and in popular representations of the two nations. These prints, issued at the beginning of the Seven Years War, were reissued during the Revolutionary Wars and their themes were still felt to be appropriate after the French had supposedly gained their freedom through revolution. By permission of Martin Fitzpatrick.

deplored the culture of the *pueblo*, whose popular theatre, with its pantomime *tonadillas* and grotesque monsters, flourished alongside the bullfight and the folklore of the rebellious smuggler and bandit. To the enlightened, *pan y toros* (bread and bulls) spelled spiritual imprisonment; while, to the *pueblo*, the Enlightenment meant foreign domination. Unsurprisingly, the *pueblo*, at the prompting of the priests, fought for Church and King in the Spanish monarchy's confrontation with revolutionary France.

A similar sort of alignment can be found in Italy in 1799. In Tuscany there were riots against the French army of occupation and the destruction of liberty trees. In Calabria there were protests against the French and attacks on their local supporters, men who had a reputation for economic as well as political liberalism. In both these cases, as in Spain and the Vendée area of France, the local clergy helped organize the resistance. They interpreted the protests as a defence of their faith against dechristianization, but for most popular resisters their opposition stemmed from a hostility to foreigners and from a fear that French centralization would undermine their customary way of life. As the era of the French Revolution revealed, popular culture did not necessarily translate into political progressivism, however anti-authoritarian it sometimes appeared to be.

REFERENCES

Aubrey, John (1686–7) 'Remaines of Gentilisme and Judaisme', in *Three Prose Works*, ed. John Buchanan-Brown (1972) London: Fontwell Centaur Press.

Beauroy, Jacques *et al.* (eds) (1977) *The Wolf and the Lamb: Popular Culture in France from the Old Regime to the Twentieth Century*, Saratoga: Anma Libri.

Boswell, James (1785) *Journal of a Tour to the Hebrides*, ed. R. W. Chapman (1970) Oxford: Oxford University Press.

Bourne, Henry (1725) *Antiquitates Vulgares, or the Antiquities of the Common People*, Newcastle: J. Wye.

Burke, Peter (1978) *Popular Culture in Early Modern Europe*, London: Temple Smith.

Bushaway, Bob (1982) *By Rite: Custom, Ceremony and Community in England 1700–1880*, London: Junction Books.

Calmet, Augustin (1759) *Dissertations upon the Apparitions of Angels, Daemons, Ghosts, and Concerning the Vampires of Hungary, Bohemia, Moravia and Silesia*, London: M. Cooper.

Chartier, Roger (1991) *The Cultural Origins of the French Revolution*, trans. Lydia G. Cochrane, Durham, NC, and London: Duke University Press.

Farge, Arlette (1992) *Subversive Words: Public Opinion in Eighteenth-century France*, trans. Rosemary Morris (1995) University Park: Pennsylvania State University Press.

Harris, Tim (ed.) (1995) *Popular Culture in England, c. 1500–1850*, New York: St Martin's Press.

Hutton, Ronald (1994) *The Rise and Fall of Merry England*, Oxford: Oxford University Press.

Kaplan, Steven L. (ed.) (1984) *Understanding Popular Culture: Europe from the Middle Ages to the Nineteenth Century*, Berlin, New York and Amsterdam: Mouton.

Malcolmson, R. W. (1981) *Life and Labour in England 1700–1780*, London: Hutchinson.

Muchembled, Robert (1978) *Popular Culture and Elite Culture in France 1400–1750*, trans. Lydia Cochrane (1985) Baton Rouge and London: Louisiana State University Press.

Pellegrin, Nicole (1982) *Les Bachelleries: Organisations et fêtes de la jeunesse dans le Centre-Ouest XVe–XVIIIe siecles*: Poitiers: Mémoires de la Société des Antiquaires de l'Ouest, 4e série, 16.

Pigott, Charles (1795) *A Political Dictionary: Explaining the True Meaning of Words*, London: D. I. Eaton.

Reay, Barry (1998) *Popular Cultures in England 1550–1750*, London and New York: Longman.

Roche, Daniel (1981) *The People of Paris: An Essay in the Popular Culture of the 18th Century*, trans. Marie Evans in association with Gwynne Lewis (1987) Berkeley and Los Angeles: University of California Press.

Rogers, Nicholas (1998) *Crowds, Culture and Politics in Georgian Britain*, Oxford: Clarendon Press.

Schneider, Robert A. (1995) *The Ceremonial City: Toulouse Observed 1738–1780*, Princeton: Princeton University Press.

Sharpe, James (1997) *Instruments of Darkness: Witchcraft in Early Modern England*, Philadelphia: University of Pennsylvania Press.

Sonenscher, Michael (1989) *Work and Wages: Natural Law, Politics and the Eighteenth-century French Trades*, Cambridge: Cambridge University Press.

Thomas, Keith (1973) *Religion and the Decline of Magic*, Harmondsworth: Penguin.

Thompson, E. P. (1971) 'The Moral Economy of the English Crowd in the Eighteenth Century', *Past and Present*, 1: 76–136.

—— (1991) *Customs in Common*, New York: The New Press.

Truant, Cynthia Maria (1994) *The Rites of Labor: Brotherhoods of Compagnonnage in Old and New Regime France*, Ithaca and London: Cornell University Press.

Villaroya, Antoni Arino (1993) *El Calendari Festiu a la Valencia Contemporania (1750–1936)*, Valencia: Edicions Alfons El Magnami.

Whelan, Kevin (1996) *The Tree of Liberty: Radicalism, Catholicism and the Construction of Irish Identity*, Notre Dame, Indiana: University of Notre Dame Press.

Williams, Gwyn A. (1976) *Goya and the Impossible Revolution*, London: Allen Lane.

PART VI

REFORMING THE WORLD

INTRODUCTION

Martin Fitzpatrick

When Diderot travelled to St Petersburg in 1773 to advise Catherine the Great, she enjoyed his attention but spurned his advice. In an apposite metaphor, given her sensual proclivities, she rejected Diderot's suggestion that she could do more for the peasantry: 'You only work with paper, which is supple and even, and places no obstacles in the way of your imagination, whilst I . . . work with human skin, which is irritable and ticklish'. She regarded his ideas as impracticable: 'fine theory but hopeless practice' (Troyat 1977: 213–14; see also De Madariaga 1998: 215–34; Luppol 1972: 62–3).

This sort of attitude towards Enlightenment ideas has had an unfortunate effect. It has led some historians to dismiss their significance. M. S. Anderson, for example, at one time argued that 'Most European rulers . . . could not afford the luxury of close adherence to an ideology, even one so loosely defined as that of the Enlightenment' (Anderson 1961: 121; cf. Anderson 1987: 183–8). Such a view, as Eckhart Hellmuth shows (Chapter 26) is simplistic. In particular, it has carried with it the notion that 'the' Enlightenment existed as an independent intellectual force, and as a reform programme sponsored by the French *philosophes* which swept through Europe. Many at the time did indeed view the Enlightenment as a wind of change challenging hallowed notions in government and society. Since such notions were being challenged, it seemed a valid way of looking at things. Nevertheless, as the chapters in this part show, reforms at this time were influenced by many considerations, not solely by ideas.

The transition from the baroque *ancien régime* world to the modern world was effected in a whole variety of ways. New ways of governing, new ways of ordering the economy and society, and new attitudes towards Church and state emerge at this time, but in a complex way, borne of different social and governmental needs and circumstances. The chapters in this part examine with care and in detail the relationship between the old and the new. They accept that new intellectual forces were motivators and shapers of change. They show that they did not exist in isolation, that there were different goals and objectives in different countries, that there was considerable indebtedness to past ideas, that there were subtle changes in assumptions so that old ideas and attitudes took on new significance and meaning, and finally that, despite the complexity, variety and differences, there was a sense that reformers in different countries were in some ways parts of a collective enterprise, that they shared similar principles even if they might interpret them in different ways, and that they belonged to a common humanity.

Rather than go over the territory of the chapters in this section, it may be helpful to highlight some key aspects of the *ancien régime*. Europe was a patchwork of states and diverse territories, some almost permanently vulnerable to neighbouring powers. The law of nations was essentially that of dynastic law, and even when actions were taken for secular reasons of state, such as Frederick the Great's invasion of Silesia in 1740, Prussian claims were dressed up in terms of dynastic law (Gooch 1947: 5–12; Ritter 1936: 81–2). During the century there were four wars which involved quarrels over succession: the Spanish, Polish, Austrian and Bavarian wars of succession; and the Partitions of Poland (1772, 1793 and 1795) can be traced to a change of dynasty. War can be seen as the most important engine of change. It demonstrated the limitations of *ancien régime* government and society and provided a major motivation for rationalization and the questioning of existing values, including religion. Denominational differences did not cause wars in the eighteenth century; wars usually involved coalitions which crossed confessional lines. Nevertheless, religion helped sustain the national stereotypes that were so important for war propaganda and churches celebrated victories with lavish *Te Deums*. Victories were seen as providential and defeat could lead to serious questioning of the *status quo*. Even Louis XIV reflected in later life that he had loved war too much. Others came to more radical conclusions as to the shortcomings of divine right monarchy and the baroque fusion of Church and state.

One of the features of the old European order was that, as Albert Sorel noted, 'every form of government existed . . . and all were considered equally legitimate' (Sorel 1885: 39). He listed them all:

> Theocracy in the States of the Church, autocracy in Russia, sheer despotism at Constantinople, absolute monarchy in France, Spain, the states of the House of Austria, Prussia, etc.; constitutional monarchy in England; an empire formed from confederated states in Germany; federal republics in the United Provinces and Switzerland; a republic with an elective monarchy in Poland; and in Venice, Genoa, Ragusa and the free cities of Germany all the varieties of republican government that had survived the Middle Ages.
>
> (Sorel 1885: 39–40, fn. 15)

What was true of the international order was also true within states. Although the nature of the social orders and the structure of the estates within each varied considerably, all claimed legitimacy. There were, of course, contested rights and jurisdictions within states, just as there were on the international scene. The common denominator among European states was the pre-eminence of the aristocracy. Aristocratic status could be gained, but it usually took several generations and the typical aristocrat was born into his station. But the aristocrat needed wealth and office if he was to be influential; the more powerful he was, the more privileges he possessed. Theorists of absolutism liked to claim that aristocratic status was dependent upon the will of the sovereign, and, although such claims were often deeply resented, in practice, the status of an aristocrat depended upon his place in the pecking-order at court either in its social or governmental dimension, or both. The wars of the sixteenth and seventeenth centuries had reduced the power of the aristocracy, whose future now lay in service to the state. There were huge variations in wealth and prestige among the aristocracy, but all could claim to be privileged.

Yet this is not to say that the remainder of society was unprivileged (though there were always the underprivileged). *Ancien régime* society was a hierarchical society of privileges; everyone from the highest to the lowest possessed or tried to gain privileges which they would claim were specific to themselves. Privileges were particular to individuals, groups or institutions. They were represented as specific liberties and concrete rights. These would be challenged by universal notions of rights and liberty, which would be seen to be in opposition to privilege. Increasingly, privilege was challenged as socially divisive, economically harmful and morally reprehensible. The Abbé Raynal noted that in all European states 'there are a sort of men who assume from their infancy a pre-eminence independent of their moral character' (Rudé 1972: 96). However, it remained the case that in most states those who had gained wealth did their utmost to gain aristocratic status, usually by the purchase of land and/or an office – the more expensive it was, the more likely it was to be immediately ennobling and prestigious.

One of the main features of the aristocratic lifestyle was that it was leisured and preoccupied with display and conspicuous consumption. Extravagance was a virtue. It was ignoble to be concerned about debt and even more demeaning to take part in trade or manufacturing. But such a lifestyle was increasingly difficult to maintain. In France the wealthy bourgeoisie came to rival the nobility in the size of their household establishments. There were, of course, exceptions to the rule of leisure and display, as some nobles invested in commerce and manufacturing. In Britain there was the greatest social mobility between the landed aristocracy and wealthy merchants and manufacturers. Well-chosen marriages and the purchase of large estates could lead the wealthy to rise up the social scale almost irrespective of the source of their wealth, whether it be from commerce, banking, manufacturing or farming.

Essentially, the values associated with the new lordly lifestyle would be those of the wealthy in a commercial society. Napoleon would later describe the British as a 'nation of shopkeepers'. The phrase was apparently coined by Adam Smith in his *Wealth of Nations* (1776: Book IV, vii, c.63). For him the commercial system was 'the modern system' and 'best understood in our own country and in our own times' (1776: Book IV, Introduction). Yet one should not draw too stark a contrast between Britain and the rest of Europe. Smith accepted that landed wealth was more durable than commercial wealth and that government should reflect that fact. Continental Europe, as well as Britain, enjoyed unprecedented economic growth during the eighteenth century and everyone wanted a share. Economic rationalization and liberalization were features of policies pursued by many countries, even if they did not always come in the obviously enlightened form of the free-trade ideas emanating from the physiocrats in France and Adam Smith in Scotland. Indeed, the continued striving after wealth and power forced all sorts of changes: Enlightenment thought of varying persuasions both shaped new policies and mitigated the effects of the changes occurring.

Reform came not as a result of a single impetus from a united group of enlightened campaigners for reform. There were many different responses to the pressures of the time from enlightened thinkers, and many different contexts in which reform was sought. By the second half of the century, however, the impetus for change was almost irresistible. Discontent with existing forms of government and with social norms was widespread, and there was a sense that the old order was played out. As R. R. Palmer has put it, 'a new feeling for a kind of equality' was abroad (1959: 4). Patriarchal social forms were collapsing, a new sort of individualism was emerging, divine right absolutism had had its day and governments were seen as accountable to the people. But behind an often common rhetoric for change there were different agendas, shaped by history and circumstance and by the adjustment and modification of existing practices and ways of thinking as much as by completely new ideas. As Norman Hampson has argued, the dominant concern of Enlightenment thinkers was amelioration rather than root-and-branch reform; they assumed that 'at best, the future could be a rectified version of the present' (Hampson 1968: 150). Yet the Enlightenment world was one in the process of transformation. What emerged was more secular, more individualistic, more democratic, more egalitarian, more capitalistic, more class based than *ancien régime* Europe. Indeed, the emergence of the modern world helped to define the old order which was passing away.

The chapters in this part examine the way in which individuals and institutions, rulers and ruled dealt with the often painful adjustment required by these changes. All aspects of government and society were under scrutiny; nothing was sacred. Although there was no uniform response, one underlying trend can be detected in the various areas examined: optimism that this world could be made into a better place. This was often an underlying assumption of cautious thinkers and statesmen rather than a clearly articulated doctrine of progress, but there was no longer a pessimistic belief that this world was a vale of tears, that the existing order was the only one possible.

Yet, that being said, as these skilful chapters show, the antithesis between the new and the old was never straightforward, and reform was never simply a matter of following a neatly laid-out ideology of Enlightenment.

REFERENCES

Anderson, M. S. (1961) *Europe in the Eighteenth Century, 1713–1783*, 3rd imp. (1962) London: Longman.

—— (1987) *Europe in the Eighteenth Century, 1713–1783*, 3rd edn, London: Longmans.

De Madariaga, Isabel (1998) *Politics and Culture in Eighteenth-century Russia: Collected Essays*, London and New York: Addison, Wesley Longman.

Gooch, G. P. (1947) *Frederick the Great. The Ruler, The Writer, The Man*, London: Longmans Green & Co; repr. (1962) Hamden, Conn.: Archon Books.

Hampson, Norman (1968) *The Enlightenment*, Harmondsworth: Penguin.

Luppol, Ivan K. (1972) 'The Empress and the *Philosophe*', in Marc Raeff (ed.) *Catherine the Great: A Profile*, London: Macmillan.

Palmer, R. R. (1959) *The Age of the Democratic Revolution. A Political History of Europe and America, 1760–1800: The Challenge*, pbk edn (1969) Princeton: Princeton University Press.

Ritter, Gerhardt (1936) *Friederich der Grosse: Ein historisches Profil*, 3rd edn (1954) Heidelberg: Quelles & Meyer; trans. with introduction by Peter Paret (1968) *Frederick the Great: A Historical Profile*; repr. (1970) Berkeley and Los Angeles: University of California Press.

Rudé, George (1972) *Europe in the Eighteenth Century: Aristocracy and the Bourgeois Challenge*, new edn (1974) London: Sphere Books.

Smith, Adam (1776) *An Inquiry into the Nature and Causes of the Wealth of Nations*, London; ed. with introduction by Edwin Cannan (1904); repr. (1994) New York: Random House.

Sorel, Albert (1885) *L'Europe et la Révolution Française: Les Moeurs et les traditions politiques*, Paris: Plon; ed. and trans. Alfred Cobban and J. W. Hunt (1969) *Europe and the French Revolution: The Political Traditions of the Old Regime*, London and Glasgow: Collins and the Fontana Library.

Troyat, Henri (1977) *Catherine la Grande*, Paris: Flammarion; trans. Emily Read (1979) *Catherine the Great*, new edn (1994) London: Allison & Busby.

CHAPTER TWENTY-FIVE

THE PARTY OF THE *PHILOSOPHES*

David Garrioch

When, in the last year of his life, Voltaire (born François Marie Arouet, 1694–1778) was crowned with a laurel wreath at a performance of his play *Irène* at the Comédie française in Paris, the leading French theatre, his personal triumph was widely seen as that of the group of writers and thinkers known as the *philosophes*. Voltaire himself was a household name. Although many of his works had been banned, he was widely regarded as the foremost literary figure in France, in a period when French literature was read by educated people throughout Europe. He was well known as a campaigner for religious toleration, but he was also seen as the leading figure in a constellation of French intellectuals who since the 1740s had subjected laws, government institutions and a variety of social practices to critical scrutiny. Most notoriously, they had challenged many aspects of conventional religious belief and observance. And they had done so not only in scholarly books and articles, but also through plays, poetry, history books, pamphlets, best-selling novels, eulogies, and prize-winning essays in competitions run by learned societies.

Subsequent generations gave them the credit for the appearance of 'enlightened absolutism' – with persuading monarchs like Frederick II of Prussia (1712–86) and Catherine II of Russia (1729–96) to introduce enlightened reforms. But this is to misunderstand their difficult relationship with those rulers. Others have seen the *philosophes* as undermining the French monarchy and paving the way for the French Revolution. They have been widely seen as the precursors of nineteenth- and twentieth-century liberalism, almost as a political party, or at least a lobby group, pressing heroically for reform and winning against great odds. Some writers have presented them as the vanguard of a capitalist ideology, while others have portrayed them even more grandly as the inventors of 'modernity'. These depictions are anachronistic, interpreting the role of the *philosophes* in the light of what came later. Such accounts also exaggerate the degree of unity and purpose among the *philosophes* and take their rhetoric at face value. Their achievements were enormous, but they need to be understood in the context of their time.

Figure 25.1 *A Party of* 'Philosophes'. This group portrait shows: 1 Voltaire; 2 Le Père Adam; 3 the Abbé Mauri; 4 D'Alembert; 5 Condorcet; 6 Diderot; 7 Laharpe. By permission of the National Library of Australia.

THE EARLY *PHILOSOPHES*

The French word *philosophe* simply means 'philosopher', but in the context of the Enlightenment it is inseparable from the intellectual challenges that characterized the eighteenth century. Among the first and best known of the *philosophes* was the magistrate Charles-Louis Secondat, Baron de Montesquieu (1689–1755), who achieved fame with his *Lettres persanes* of 1721. Presented as a series of letters written by imaginary Persian visitors to France, this highly readable work offered a satirical view of the government, legal system and religion of France. Montesquieu's second major work was *L'Esprit des lois* of 1748, a wide-ranging examination and critique of systems of government and of law. Like the other *philosophes*, he was a champion of religious toleration and criticized the use of torture and the arbitrary use of power.

Voltaire had initially become known as a poet and playwright following the success of his first play in 1718. His first major foray into politics and philosophy was the *Lettres philosophiques* (1734), written after a scandal forced him into exile in England, where he discovered the work of John Locke and was favourably impressed by the English parliamentary system. It was probably this publication that inspired the use of the term *philosophes* to describe those critical of the religion and government of France. The following year the Jesuit *Journal de Trévoux* condemned his book as typical of the writing of 'a *philosophe*', led astray by freethinking English and other Protestant writers.

Figure 25.2 *Voltaire*, engraving after Largillière, from J. C. Collins (1908) *Voltaire, Montesquieu, Rousseau*, London. By permission of the National Library of Australia.

Over the following fifteen years a host of new publications challenged religious and scientific orthodoxies. The *Pensées philosophiques* (1746), the first major work by Denis Diderot (1713–84), was immediately condemned for its anticlericalism and its defence of a natural religion stripped of Christian elements. It was followed in 1747 by *L'Homme machine*, an openly materialist work by Julien Offroy de La Mettrie (1709–51). By 1748 the Assembly of the Clergy was expressing the fear that 'a frightful philosophy has spread like a deadly poison and has dried up the roots of faith' (O'Keefe 1961: 399). In 1749 the Comte de Buffon (Georges-Louis Leclerc, 1707–88) produced the first volume of his huge *Histoire naturelle* (1749–67), in which he questioned the age of the world as it was derived from the Bible. In 1754 the Catholic conservative Elie Catherine Fréron (1718–76) launched his first major attack on *la philosophie* in the newly founded *Année littéraire*, a periodical that was to become a long-running critic of the *philosophes* (Hofman 1988: 156). And by 1760, when the Comédie Française performed the biting satire by Charles Palissot de Montenoy (1730–1814) entitled *Les Philosophes*, which particularly targeted Diderot, Claude-Adrien Helvétius (1715–71) and Jean Jacques Rousseau (1712–78), the term was in current use and everybody recognized those against whom the play was directed. Voltaire happily laid claim to the title, defining a *philosophe* in the 1765 edition of his *Dictionnaire philosophique* as 'a lover of wisdom, that is, of truth'. Hostile writing, like the *Pensées antiphilosophiques* (1751) by the Abbé Allamand, served to reinforce the use of the term to apply to those critical of religious orthodoxy (Masseau 2000: 25–6; McMahon 2001: 6, 205 n.7).

For many people, too, *philosophe* carried a hint of sexual scandal. Diderot first became known as the author of two banned works: the *Pensées philosophiques* and a salacious novel, *Les Bijoux indiscrets* (1748). He was also (wrongly) suspected of having written one of the best-known pornographic books of the century, *Thérèse philosophe* (1748). In both this work and his novel, erotic interludes alternated with philosophical reflection, a formula that the Comte de Mirabeau (Honoré Gabriel Riqueti, 1749–91) and the Marquis de Sade (Donatien Alphonse François, 1740–1814) were also later to adopt (Darnton 1995: 21, 85–114).

FRAGILE UNITY: THE *ENCYCLOPÉDIE*

The work that brought most of the *philosophes* together, that affirmed their identity and cemented their reputation for subversive writing, was the twenty-eight-volume *Encyclopédie*, published between 1751 and 1772. It was originally commissioned by the Paris publisher André-François Le Breton (1708–79) as a four-volume translation of Ephraim Chambers's *Cyclopaedia, or Universal Dictionary of the Arts and Sciences* (1728), with a further volume of plates. In October 1747 the publisher entrusted the project to Diderot and to Jean Le Rond D'Alembert (1717–83). Diderot was still little known, but D'Alembert was building a reputation as a gifted mathematician, was an associate member of the French Academy of Sciences, and was becoming a familiar face in the intellectual salons of Paris (Wilson 1957: 73–82; Kafker 1988: 2–3). Yet Diderot was the dominant figure in transforming the *Encyclopédie* into a much greater work. It was boldly conceived, intended not only to bring together all human knowledge, but to broaden the understanding of 'knowledge' beyond traditional domains like theology, law and medicine, to include manual crafts, the arts and a far greater emphasis on natural science. There were articles on 'the Soul' and 'Natural Law', but also on agriculture, the manufacture of pins, music and clock-making. The eleven volumes of illustrations included diagrams showing everything from the production of hats to the landscaping of gardens.

It was primarily Diderot who brought together a writing team that included many of the major figures of the Enlightenment. By the late 1740s he, D'Alembert and Rousseau were already friends, while Friedrich Melchior Grimm (1723–1807)

Figure 25.3 *Grimm and Diderot*, Louis Carmontelle. By permission of the Collection Baron J. le Vassaeur: Photograph: Lauros-Giraudon.

and Guillaume-Thomas-François Raynal (1713–96) joined their circle around 1750. Soon after so did Jean-François Marmontel (1723–99), André Morellet (1727–1819) and others (Morellet 1821: 67–70). Rousseau was also close to Charles Pinot Duclos (1704–72), who was already well known for his historical writing, and Morellet had been a student at the Sorbonne with Anne-Robert-Jacques Turgot (1727–81). Most of these men frequented the salon of Paul Thiry d'Holbach (1723–89), and all were to contribute to the *Encyclopédie* (Wilson 1957: 119; Kors 1976: 20–32; Cranston 1986: 123). But Diderot drew on many others, too; there were nearly 200 contributors in all.

It was a huge publishing success. By the time the first volume appeared, over 1,400 people had subscribed to the entire work (Wilson 1957: 129). Yet, immediately, it raised a storm, for the *Encyclopédie* was much more than a compilation of knowledge: it had the quite explicit intention of, in Diderot's words, 'changing the general way of thinking' (Diderot and D'Alembert 1751–72: vol. 5, 642 verso). The 'Preliminary Discourse' by D'Alembert argued that philosophy – not theology – was the queen of the sciences and that the senses and reason – rather than revelation – were the sources of true knowledge (Darnton 1984: 191–213). The work was subversive in other ways, too. In his article on 'Political Authority' Diderot wrote that 'the prince holds from his subjects themselves the authority he has over them' (Diderot and D'Alembert 1751–72: vol. 1, 898). In a monarchy based on divine right this was heresy, and in February 1752 the Royal Council revoked the licence authorizing publication. Yet the *Encyclopédie* had powerful defenders, notably Chrétien-Guillaume de Lamoignon de Malesherbes (1721–94), Director of the Book Trade, and as a result the subsequent volumes were able to be published, though now without official approval. The work remained controversial, however, with attacks from the Jesuits and from powerful figures at court, while Voltaire and other major writers defended it.

GROWING DIVISIONS

Despite the controversy, or perhaps in part because of it, the status and influence of the *philosophes* continued to rise. In 1754 D'Alembert became a member of the prestigious French Academy, and Duclos, who had already been elected along with Voltaire in 1746, was named its permanent secretary. The *philosophes* were adopted by fashionable society, although the attacks from their enemies, from religious writers in particular, became more fierce towards the end of the 1750s. In 1757 the political climate changed dramatically. In January of that year, Louis XV was stabbed by Robert-François Damiens, a domestic servant. There was a widespread feeling that the attack on the King was a symptom of declining respect for the monarchy and for religion, and the authorities became increasingly nervous about writing that might undermine the regime. Facing growing official restrictions, and under personal attack from hostile pamphlets, in 1758 D'Alembert decided to abandon the *Encyclopédie*. The same year, Helvétius published his book *De L'Esprit*, which was immediately banned for its apparent claim that humans were no different, in a moral sense, from animals, and that morality was based not on religion but on experiences of pleasure and pain. Though he was not a contributor to the *Encyclopédie*, Helvétius was closely associated with the *philosophes* and ran a salon where many of them met. His work led to a renewed outcry against 'philosophy'. The Attorney General of the *Parlement* of Paris denounced 'a project formed . . . to propagate materialism, to destroy Religion . . . and to nourish the corruption of morals', and in March 1759 a royal decree banned the *Encyclopédie* (Lough 1971: 116–25; Wilson 1957: 333–5).

This did not mark the end of the enterprise. Diderot and the Chevalier Louis de Jaucourt (1704–80) published the remaining volumes of text in 1765, but these events did see the end of the temporary unity the *Encylopédie* had brought among the *philosophes*. After the ban of 1759, Turgot, Marmontel, Morellet, Duclos and Voltaire (for a time) refused to make any more contributions. But even before this, D'Alembert had gravely offended Rousseau by writing unfavourably about Geneva, the latter's birthplace. Rousseau's public reply, the *Lettre à D'Alembert sur les spectacles* (1758), was a resounding attack on both D'Alembert and Diderot. For this reason, but also because of its intellectual arguments, it antagonized almost all of Rousseau's former friends. He argued that religion was a prerequisite for virtue, and developed the idea that the arts were a corrupting force in society, explicitly rejecting the notion dear to almost all the *philosophes* that art and literature were key indicators of 'civilization'. Soon after, the heroine of his enormously popular novel *La Nouvelle Héloïse* (1761) condemned the *philosophes* as 'dangerous reasoners' whose teaching threatened social order and morality (Rousseau 1761: 359). His subsequent novel, *Emile*, and his famous *Social Contract*, both of which appeared in 1762, found a basis for social and moral behaviour in a sentimental natural morality, and moved from pragmatic social and political reform to moral regeneration as the solution to social evils.

The 1760s witnessed the further dissolution of the fragile unity that the great enterprise of the *Encylopédie* had created. Voltaire had detested Rousseau since the latter's denunciation of modern culture as a source of corruption and moral decline in the *Discours sur les sciences et les arts* (1749) (Cranston 1983: 236). In his later work, Rousseau reaffirmed this move away from the rationalism that the other *philosophes* held to be centrally important. At the same time, other writers took that rationalism to extremes that Voltaire and others could not accept. The second major work by Helvétius, *De L'Homme* (1772), was openly materialist, and Voltaire condemned it as 'perhaps the greatest blow yet against philosophy' (Voltaire 1773). The atheism of d'Holbach's *Système de la nature* (1770) was equally unacceptable to many of the other *philosophes*.

While personal and intellectual disagreements were important, growing divisions among the *philosophes* were encouraged by several external political factors. One key change was the disappearance of their most effective opponents, the Jesuits. Caught up in fierce doctrinal and political disputes, the order was banned in France in the early 1760s. Their removal did not destroy religious opposition to the *philosophes*, but did weaken it. With the disappearance of the Jesuits and the victory of their Jansenist opponents, religious politics gradually became less significant and the issues of the day increasingly came to revolve around political and economic reform. Accordingly, the centre of gravity of 'philosophical' writing shifted. There was much debate about economic liberalization in the mid-1760s and again in the 1770s, when the physiocrats, advocating laissez-faire policies and far-reaching tax reform, became extremely influential. These issues divided the *philosophes*, with the encyclopaedists François Quesnay (1694–1774), Turgot and other writers supporting economic liberalism, while Diderot, Ferdinando Galiani (1728–87) and Gabriel Bonnot, Abbé de Mably (1709–85) opposed it. The 1771 reforms of Chancellor René Nicolas Maupeou (1714–92) again divided them: the *parlements* were sacked and replaced in a display of royal power that Voltaire strongly defended but that most of the other *philosophes* saw as a despotic act, even though few of them had much time for the old *parlements* (Echeverria 1985).

ACCEPTANCE AND SUCCESS

Ironically, despite growing divisions, across this period the *philosophes* enjoyed growing acceptance, both as individuals and as a group. As a result of the secularization of both politics and French society, but thanks in some measure to their success in spreading their own ideas, many of the key tenets associated with the early French Enlightenment no longer seemed so radical. Even though the authorities continued to ban 'irreligious' books, the tide was turning. The fulminations of bishops and religious conservatives could not hide the fact that the principle of religious toleration was being accepted by growing numbers of educated people. The rehabilitation of Jean Calas in 1765 showed the degree to which opinion had shifted. Calas, a Protestant, had been executed in 1762 for the murder of his son, who supposedly had been about to convert to Catholicism. Voltaire saw in this execution an example both of religious prejudice and judicial corruption, and led a campaign for the rehabilitation of Calas, and more broadly for religious toleration. He was joined by a broad coalition of writers, who aroused sufficient public indignation to have the condemnation of Calas overturned and compensation paid to his family. This success was followed by another campaign in support of an accused Protestant, Pierre Paul Sirven, who in 1764 had been condemned *in absentia* for the murder of his daughter, in similar circumstances. Again Voltaire led the charge, and in 1769 the charges were dropped.

Thus certain key ideas of the *philosophes* were becoming mainstream among educated people who prided themselves on being 'enlightened'. Another was hostility to slavery, which by the 1780s had become widespread in France. And even the deism of Voltaire, which had seemed so radical and dangerous to many people in the 1740s and 1750s, no longer appeared such a threat after the 1760s. Increasing numbers of educated people began to believe in a less interventionist God, and thousands of French men (and some women) who became Freemasons in the 1770s and 1780s saw nothing objectionable in its blurring of the distinction between Christian and deist: both could speak of 'the Supreme Being', of 'the Creator' and of 'the Architect of the Universe'. Rousseau's *La Nouvelle Héloïse*, perhaps the most popular French novel of the century, used precisely this language.

By the early 1770s, therefore, the climate had totally changed. The *philosophes* now controlled the Académie Française and enjoyed the enormous prestige that it bestowed: the elections of Voltaire and Duclos (1746), Buffon (1753) and D'Alembert (1754) were followed by those of Marmontel in 1763, Etienne Bonnot de Condillac (1714–80) in 1768, Jean-Baptiste Antoine Suard (1733–1817) in 1774 and François Jean, Marquis de Chastellux (1734–88) in 1775. D'Alembert was elected the Academy's permanent secretary in 1772. Reforms urged by many of the *philosophes* were being adopted by key figures in the administration, and in 1774 one of the former encylopaedists, Turgot, was appointed a government minister by Louis XVI. He had already served as the administrator of the Limoges region, where in the 1760s he had introduced a variety of reforms, and he now attempted to implement them on a national scale. Controls on the grain trade were removed and the system of forced labour on the roads was abolished. While he was soon replaced as Finance Minister, and his reforms were mostly undone, his appointment had huge symbolic significance. The *philosophes* were no longer marginal figures, and nor were they purely writers and thinkers. They were having a real impact on government policy and its implementation.

Nor was this confined to France. The Austrian Chancellor Wenzel Anton Kaunitz (1711–94), who had been ambassador to Paris, called himself a *philosophe* and, although a strong Catholic, was hostile to 'superstition'. Like the physiocrats, he felt that agricultural productivity was vital to national prosperity; and, like the future Joseph II (1741–90) and other reformers in Austria, he was influenced by Voltaire's arguments for religious toleration (Szabo 1994: 35, 143, 249). Gustave III of Sweden was also an enthusiast for the writings of the *philosophes* and met a number of them when he visited Paris in 1771. Ten years later he was to abolish torture and introduce a measure of religious toleration in his country. Voltaire and others corresponded with Frederick II of Prussia, who supported religious toleration, abolished torture and many brutal punishments, and introduced educational reforms. Frederick acted as patron to a number of *philosophes*, including Pierre Louis Moreau de Maupertius (1698–1759), whom he appointed president of the Academy of Sciences in Berlin. Catherine II of Russia corresponded with both Voltaire and Diderot. She provided the latter with a pension, and managed to entice him to St Petersburg, though both were disappointed with their encounter. 'Had I placed faith in him,' she later wrote, 'every institution in my empire would have been overturned; legislation, administration, politics, and finances would all have been changed for the purpose of substituting some impracticable theories' (quoted in Cranston 1986: 116). All of these rulers took what they wanted from the *philosophes*: Frederick enjoyed his reputation as an enlightened ruler, was happy to attack the Catholic Church for its persecution of critics, but clamped down on any opposition at home and did not hesitate to wage war on his neighbours when it suited him (Gay 1966–9: vol. 2, 484–5). Gustave III increased press censorship even as he introduced greater religious freedom. It is nonetheless clear that the *philosophes* had a significant impact on these and other rulers, and on enlightened elites in the Italian, German and Scandinavian states. Their ideas, emanating from the foremost cultural capital in Europe, carried the cachet of progress.

Growing acceptance of some of their ideas meant that the meaning of the term *philosophe* changed. Whereas in the 1750s it was widely used to mean someone who was irreligious and radical, it gradually lost those connotations and became almost synonymous with 'enlightened', referring not only to ideas but to polite behaviour. The definition given in the twelfth volume of the *Encyclopédie*, though written much earlier, was one with which, by the 1770s and 1780s, most educated French people could identify: a *philosophe* was a man guided by reason rather than prejudice, a scholar, but also a model of sociable behaviour and virtue, a true gentleman. The Swedish nobleman Gustaf Philip Creutz (1731–85) wrote of Joseph II, who visited Paris in 1769, that he 'travelled as a true *philosophe*', simply and without luxury (Creutz 1766–70: 141, 2 October 1769). In the mid-1780s, Louis-Sébastien Mercier (1740–1814) could write admiringly of 'true *philosophes*', 'agreeable and well-informed men', interested in all the arts and sciences, objective judges of human actions and nature, living simply, decorously and wisely in the midst of folly and vile ambition. For him, they were also patriots, an example to other nations (Mercier 1782–8: vol. 7, 301–8). In short, they were the archetypal enlightened men. Religious conservatives continued to condemn 'philosophy', but to most educated people it no longer seemed a threat. Only during and after the French Revolution would the conservative position regain support.

WHO WERE THE *PHILOSOPHES*?

The changing meaning of the term *philosophe* is not the only obstacle to its definition. The *philosophes* were not a united group, either sociologically or intellectually. There is not even complete agreement among historians about who should be termed a *philosophe* and who should not, for it depends on whether religious ideology, political views, gender, intellectual ability or social connections are taken as the key criteria. While one leading historian of the Enlightenment, Peter Gay, saw the Marquis de Sade as 'a caricature of the Enlightenment', others take him seriously as a *philosophe* (Gay 1966–9: vol. 1, 25). Some historians include Buffon and Raynal, while others do not. There were enlightened women, long excluded by historians, whom many writers today would call *philosophes*. The Marquise du Châtelet (Gabrielle Emilie Le Tonnelier de Breteuil, 1706–49) translated Newton's work into French and produced her own scientific work. Almost any definition of the term would include Madame d'Epinay (Louise Françoise Pétronille Tardieu d'Esclavelles, 1726–83), novelist, reviewer, friend of many of the *philosophes* and frequent contributor to Grimm's *Correspondance littéraire* (Weinreb 1993). Another woman whom many would now also include was Madame de Graffigny (Françoise Paule d'Issembourg du Buisson d'Happoncourt, 1695–1758), author of *Lettres d'une Péruvienne* (1747) and also a friend of Voltaire and of Helvétius. Alongside the key figures conventionally associated with the French Enlightenment were a host of minor writers, many of whom called themselves *philosophes*. Some of them were extremely radical; some made a precarious living from writing pamphlets for whoever would hire them (Darnton 1982; Jacob 1981). Other individuals such as Charles-Georges Le Roy (1723–89) and Suard, were well known in Parisian intellectual circles but wrote no major or lasting works (Kors 1976: 17–19, 24–5).

The writers associated with the *Encyclopédie* are the easiest to define, and the importance of this work encourages some to use it as a way of defining a core group of *philosophes*, even though not all the contributors are known. Yet they, too, were extremely diverse. The very breadth of the project required the inclusion not only of philosophers and scientists, but of men (though it seems no women) who were expert in furniture-making, tanning and other areas of artisan crafts and manufacturing. There were some 140 identifiable contributors in all: nobles like d'Holbach, middle-class intellectuals like Rousseau and Diderot himself, artisans such as the wood-engraver Jean-Baptiste Michel Papillon (1698–1776) and the foreman in Le Breton's printing works, Louis-Claude Brullé (d. 1772). Other contributors were lawyers and army officers, government officials and priests. The Abbé Edme Mallet (1713–55), who contributed over 2,000 articles, was a professor at the University of Paris (Lough 1973: 10, 90–1). There were also Protestants like de Jaucourt and the Calvinist pastor Jean-Edme Romilly (1739–79), who wrote the article on 'religious toleration' (Kafker 1996: xv–xxv).

These individuals certainly shared a belief in the value of the encyclopaedic project. Yet there were other important *philosophes*, such as Maupertuis, Helvétius and La Mettrie, who did not contribute to the *Encyclopédie*. Nor, it seems, did Condillac, though he was friendly with Diderot at the time. Even Montesquieu was not significantly involved: part of only one article came from his pen, and it was published after his death (Kafker 1996: xxii).

Even those whom all would agree must be included as *philosophes* never formed a cohesive or united group. Voltaire was a militant deist, scathing about conventional religion but also attacking materialists and atheists: he described La Mettrie as 'a madman' (Lough 1971: 128). Diderot, d'Holbach and Helvétius were atheists, while Rousseau preached a natural religion with vaguely Christian elements. Condillac retained a conventional Christian faith, and Morellet may have done so, too. The *philosophes* were also socially diverse, drawn from the full range of the educated classes. It is possible to see many of them as outsiders attempting to break into the literary and scientific establishment – most of the men who frequented d'Holbach's house between 1750 and 1770, for example, were under thirty when they first joined the group, and most came from the provinces or from outside France (Roche 1978: 722). Diderot was the son of a provincial maker of surgical instruments, and as a young man often had trouble making ends meet. Marmontel was from an even poorer family. Rousseau felt himself socially excluded from the salons where Buffon and Voltaire rubbed shoulders with 'dukes, ambassadors, *cordons bleus*' (Rousseau 1782: vol. i, 450). Yet Jean-Antoine-Nicolas Caritat, Marquis de Condorcet (1743–94) came from an old noble family, as did Chastellux and Victor Riqueti, Marquis de Mirabeau (1715–89). D'Holbach and Helvétius, both of whom came from recently ennobled families, were enormously wealthy. (The enemies of the *philosophes* were equally diverse, so the intellectual and political division between the two groups was not a social one.)

Many of the *philosophes* were friends, but others were not. Voltaire and Montesquieu, while they were acquainted, do not seem to have liked each other, and Diderot was the only one of the major *philosophes* to attend Montesquieu's funeral. If Morellet is to be believed, Diderot and D'Alembert called Buffon a 'charlatan'. Rousseau fell out with all his former friends. Maupertuis was savagely attacked by Voltaire and Diderot (Wilson 1957: 232; Morellet 1821: 144; Hampson 1968: 224–5).

The generational difference between the writers active in the middle of the century and those who came to prominence after 1760 was also a key division. French politics and society changed dramatically during this time. Religious issues were far less important, economic ones more so. Important elements in the ruling elite had been won over to some of the policies that Voltaire and others had championed, and the surviving older *philosophes* had become establishment figures. Some of the younger generation were far more ready to envisage radical political reform, and they had to make their way in a more crowded intellectual scene. In most respects, therefore, the *philosophes* remained a united group only in the eyes of their enemies, and in those of nineteenth- and twentieth-century liberals who looked back to them for inspiration.

THE IMPACT OF THE *PHILOSOPHES*

What the *philosophes* did have in common was the conviction that the basis of knowledge was observation and human reason, and that it was legitimate to apply this method not only to the natural world but also to the analysis of religion, law, politics and society. This was a direct challenge to religion in an age when most people believed that the source of truth and morality was above all revelation. It was a radical stance in other areas, too, where the antiquity of a practice was universally viewed as the source of its legitimacy. Until the middle of the eighteenth century, almost all writers evoked classical antecedents, religious authorities or custom as the basis for their arguments, even when in reality they were inventing new ones! The *philosophes* asserted boldly that scientific observation and reasoned argument were the sources of truth. Although they drew on principles established by seventeenth-century scientists, the application of these ideas to society, government, religion and history represented a shift in thinking of revolutionary proportions. It led them to widely varying conclusions about human nature, history and metaphysics, although also to some shared convictions about reform.

The widespread adoption of many of their ideas and their own growing reputation encouraged another of the tenets that all of the *philosophes* held dear: the belief that the improvement of humanity was possible, and that enlightened writers had a central role in this process by dispelling ignorance and encouraging the application of reason to every aspect of human endeavour. Theirs was an activist philosophy. This goal was central to the production of the *Encyclopédie*. It underpinned Voltaire's view of history and stimulated the administrative and intellectual work of Turgot. Condorcet, himself politically active during the French Revolution, put the same view strongly in his *Sketch for a Historical Picture of the Progress of the Human Mind* (1794). Despite his own eventual proscription, he saw the French Revolution as proof of the inevitability of progress. Few of the older generation of *philosophes* would have followed him in this, and most of them at some point expressed pessimism at the direction in which humanity was heading. Nevertheless, optimism was implicit in their work, even in that of Rousseau, who most emphatically denied the idea of progress.

Many of the *philosophes* were accomplished propagandists, Voltaire foremost among them. Although their opponents, even in the 1780s, could claim a readership just as large and just as influential, and although some were formidable writers and scholars, most of them are forgotten today (McMahon 2001: 10–11; and 1998). This is testimony not only to the literary and intellectual talents of the *philosophes* but also to their ability to present themselves as the all-conquering heroes of the age and as the harbingers of progress. They very self-consciously and successfully worked to raise the status of men of letters, appropriating and redefining the term *philosophe* and excluding from its growing dignity those who disagreed with them. They used not only logical argument but patronage, innuendo and even plain abuse against their opponents (who, of course, retaliated in kind). They tirelessly proclaimed their own importance, even claiming victories that were not theirs: D'Alembert, for example, portrayed the banning of the Jesuits as primarily their work (D'Alembert 1766: vol. 2, 64). They depicted themselves as victims of persecution, whose love of truth had sustained them and enabled them to defeat their enemies, yet in reality their success owed much to the protection they enjoyed. In 1734 Voltaire avoided arrest thanks to a warning from the Comte d'Argenson (Marc-Pierre de Voyer, 1696–1764) (Cranston 1986: 49). Diderot and other writers were protected by Malesherbes, while the police chief in Paris, Antoine Gabriel de Sartine (1729–1801), turned a blind eye to the continuing work on the *Encyclopédie*. In the late 1750s, key figures at court, while never openly questioning the principles of old-regime society and government, protected the *philosophes* and shared some of their ideas. Etienne François Choiseul (1719–85), a leading minister in Louis XV's government, and the King's mistress Madame de Pompadour (Jeanne Antoinette Poisson, 1721–64) were both correspondents and friends of Voltaire and other Enlightenment figures, and both opposed the clerical hardliners at court who wished to clamp down on the *philosophes*.

The success of the *philosophes* in presenting themselves as staunch opponents of despotism persuaded many of the French revolutionaries to claim them as precursors, though among historians there is much debate both about how far their writings undermined the old regime and influenced events in the 1790s. The language of 'liberty' and of opposition to 'despotism' that they employed was certainly widely used by opponents of the government, and the ideological basis of divine right monarchy was undoubtedly threatened by the *philosophes*. They did much to spread and justify anticlericalism, and many of the revolutionary reforms were clearly inspired by their attempt to construct a rational basis for government and society. Yet most of them would have condemned the democratic aspects of the Revolution. While they wished to improve the lot of working people, they feared the violence and ignorance of the mob. Some believed that it might be possible to educate the people, even women, but none pressed for political or social equality (Payne 1976). All the major philosophers of the mid-eighteenth century would have condemned the republicanism of the Revolution (though Condorcet supported it) and the persecutions of 1793–4.

But there is no denying the enormous influence they had on the eighteenth-century reading public. Although their more theoretical works were little read, they reached a much wider audience through plays, novels and pamphlets, through the *Encyclopédie*, reviews and articles. Another key factor in their success was the Europe-wide networks they constructed, reflecting a cosmopolitan interest that was also one of their hallmarks. These networks were developed through correspondence and by encounters with almost every scientist and intellectual who passed through France. In all these ways the *philosophes* influenced key political actors, both in France and throughout the educated European world, including North America. Government ministers and administrators, magistrates, even some bishops were persuaded by their arguments and supported religious toleration, took action against what they came to see as 'popular superstition', and introduced economic and judicial reforms. As social, political and economic changes created a climate within which the new ideas became acceptable, it was in part through the writing and the activism of the *philosophes* that a wider public gradually came to condemn religious persecution, serfdom, slavery and judicial torture, to reject many widespread religious beliefs (for example, in demons and miracles) in favour of a scientific approach to knowledge, and to support changes in education and reforms in government.

Despite broad agreement on these issues, the *philosophes* had no programme. While some of them, like Voltaire, campaigned vigorously for particular goals, their aim was above all to question, and their technique was to return, as far as possible, to the first principles of scientific method. They did not always do so consistently, and certainly did not escape all the assumptions of their own time. Their achievement, nevertheless, was to challenge received wisdom and to provide a new language with which to discuss matters that were previously either not considered or were debated only in religious terms or in court circles. They pushed the boundaries of what could be written and discussed, and perhaps of what could be thought, stimulating others to consider issues that had not previously been questions for public debate. They had a lasting influence on the intellectual world through the application of scientific method to history, literature and the arts, and more widely through developing key concepts that would be taken up by nineteenth-century liberalism, feminism and utilitarianism.

REFERENCES

Baker, Keith (1975) *Condorcet: From Natural Philosophy to Social Mathematics*, Chicago: University of Chicago Press.

Becker, Carl L. (1932) *The Heavenly City of the Eighteenth-century Philosophers*, New Haven, Conn.: Yale University Press.

Bien, David D. (1960) *The Calas Affair: Persecution, Toleration, and Heresy in Eighteenth-century Toulouse*, Princeton: Princeton University Press.

Chartier, Roger (1990) *The Cultural Origins of the French Revolution*, trans. Lydia G. Cochrane (1991) Durham, NC: Duke University Press.

Condorcet, Jean-Antoine-Nicolas de Caritat, Marquis de (1794) *Sketch for a Historical Picture of the Progress of the Human Mind*, trans. June Barraclough (1955) London: Weidenfeld & Nicolson.

Cranston, Maurice (1983) *Jean-Jacques: The Early Life and Work of Jean-Jacques Rousseau, 1712–1754*, London: Allen Lane.

—— (1986) *Philosophers and Pamphleteers: Political Theorists of the Enlightenment*, Oxford: Oxford University Press.

Creutz, Gustaf Philip (1766–70) *Le Comte de Creutz: Lettres inédites de Paris, 1766–1770*, ed. Marianne Molander (1987) Göteborg and Paris: Acta universitatis gothoburgensis, Jean Touzot.

D'Alembert, Jean Le Rond (1766) *Sur La Destruction des Jésuites en France*, in (1821) *Oeuvres complètes de D'Alembert*, 5 vols; repr. (1967) Geneva: Slatkine Reprints.

Darnton, Robert (1979) *The Business of Enlightenment: A Publishing History of the Encyclopédie, 1775–1800*, Cambridge, Mass.: Belknap Press.

—— (1982) *The Literary Underground of the Old Regime*, Cambridge, Mass.: Harvard University Press.

—— (1984) *The Great Cat Massacre and Other Episodes in French Cultural History*, London: Allen Lane.

—— (1995) *The Forbidden Best-sellers of Pre-revolutionary France*, New York: W. W. Norton.

Diderot, Denis and D'Alembert, Jean Le Rond (eds) (1751–72) *L'Encyclopédie, ou Dictionnaire raisonné des arts et sciences*, Paris: Le Breton.

Echeverria, Durand (1985) *The Maupeou Revolution: A Study in the History of Libertarianism: France 1770–1774*, Baton Rouge: Louisiana State University Press.

Gay, Peter (1966–9) *The Enlightenment: An Interpretation*, 2 vols; repr. (1977) New York: W. W. Norton.

Goodman, Dena (1994) *The Republic of Letters: A Cultural History of the French Enlightenment*, Ithaca and London: Cornell University Press.

Hampson, Norman (1968) *The Enlightenment*, Harmondsworth: Penguin.

Hankins, Thomas L. (1970) *Jean D'Alembert: Science and the Enlightenment*, Oxford: Clarendon Press.

Hofman, Amos (1988) 'The Origins of the Theory of the *Philosophe* Conspiracy', *French History*, 2: 152–72.

Jacob, Margaret C. (1981) *The Radical Enlightenment: Pantheists, Freemasons and Republicans*, London: George Allen & Unwin.

Kafker, Frank A., in collaboration with Serena L. Kafker (1988) *The Encyclopedists as Individuals: A Biographical Dictionary of the Authors of the Encyclopédie*, Oxford: Voltaire Foundation.

Kafker, Frank A. (1996) *The Encyclopedists as a Group: A Collective Biography of the Authors of the Encyclopédie*, Oxford: Voltaire Foundation.

Kors, Alan C. (1976) *D'Holbach's Coterie: An Enlightenment in Paris*, Princeton: Princeton University Press.

Lough, John (1971) *The Encyclopédie*, London: Longman.

—— (1973) *The Contributors to the Encyclopédie*, London: Grant & Cutler.

Masseau, Didier (2000) *Les Ennemis des philosophes: L'Antiphilosophie au temps des Lumières*, Paris: Albin Michel.

McMahon, Darrin M. (1998) 'The Counter-Enlightenment and the Low-life of Literature in Pre-revolutionary France', *Past and Present*, 159: 77–112.

—— (2001) *Enemies of the Enlightenment: The French Counter-Enlightenment and the Making of Modernity*, Oxford: Oxford University Press.

Mercier, Louis-Sébastien (1782–8) *Tableau de Paris*, 12 vols, Amsterdam.

Morellet, André (1821) *Mémoires de l'Abbé Morellet*, ed. Jean-Pierre Guicciardi (2000) Paris: Mercure de France.

Mornet, Daniel (1933) *Les Origines intellectuelles de la Révolution française*, Paris: Armand Colin.

O'Keefe, Cyril B. (1961) 'Conservative Opinion on the Spread of Deism in France, 1730–1750', *Journal of Modern History*, 33: 398–406.

Payne, Harry C. (1976) *The Philosophes and the People*, New Haven, Conn.: Yale University Press.

Pomeau, René (1985–94) *Voltaire en son temps*, 5 vols, Oxford: Voltaire Foundation.

Roche, Daniel (1978) 'Lumières et engagement politique, la coterie d'Holbach dévoilée', *Annales ESC*: 720–8.

Rousseau, Jean Jacques (1761) *La Nouvelle Héloïse*, ed. Henri Coulet and Bernard Guyon in Bernard Gagnebin and Marcel Raymond (eds) (1961) *Oeuvres complètes de Jean-Jacques Rousseau*, vol. 2, Paris: Gallimard.

—— (1782) *Les Confessions*, ed. Bernard Gagnebin (1972) 2 vols, Paris: Librairie générale française.

Shackleton, Robert (1961) *Montesquieu: A Critical Biography*, Oxford: Oxford University Press.

—— (1977) 'When Did the French *Philosophes* Become a Party?', *Bulletin of the John Rylands Library*, 60: 181–99, repr. in Robert Shackleton (1988) *Essays on Montesquieu and on the Enlightenment*, ed. David Gilson and Martin Smith Oxford: Voltaire Foundation.

Szabo, Franz A. J. (1994) *Kaunitz and Enlightened Absolutism, 1753–1780*, Cambridge: Cambridge University Press.

Voltaire, François Marie Arouet de (1773) 'Letter to D'Alembert', 16 June, in (1981–91) *Correspondance générale d'Helvétius*, ed. Alan Dainard, Jean Orsini, Peter Allan and David W. Smith, 3 vols, Toronto and Oxford: Toronto University Press/Voltaire Foundation, vol. 3: 439, letter 702.

Weinreb, Ruth Plaut (1993) *Eagle in a Gauze Cage: Louise d'Epinay, femme de lettres*, New York: AMS Press.

Wilson, Arthur M. (1957) *Diderot: The Testing Years, 1713–1759*, New York: Oxford University Press.

CHAPTER TWENTY-SIX

ENLIGHTENMENT AND GOVERNMENT

Eckhart Hellmuth

ENLIGHTENED ABSOLUTISM

When historians discuss the connection between government and the Enlightenment, they generally do so with reference to the historical concept of enlightened absolutism. This suggests that during the second half of the eighteenth century the business of government in most European states was fundamentally transformed under the impact of enlightened ideas, and that particularly in parts of central Europe an ambitious reform programme was set in motion. It is assumed that the motors driving this modernization programme were the enlightened princes, who, with their bureaucracies, undertook the grand task of reform. Rejecting the divine right of kings, they aimed instead, it is argued, to legitimize their rule on a rational basis, and came to an understanding of self that was dominated by the idea of serving the common good. The main monarchs included were the Prussian King, Frederick the Great; the Habsburg Emperor, Joseph II, along with his brother Leopold II; the Russian Empress, Catherine the Great; the Swedish King Gustav III; and the Spanish King Charles III. To these could be added several minor German rulers, such as Charles Frederick of Baden and Frederick II of Hesse-Cassel, and a number of prominent statesmen who dictated the policies of individual European states.

As a rule, Britain and France are not mentioned in the context of enlightened absolutism, and with good reason. Britain's constitutional system diverged very clearly from the absolutist regimes of the Continent. While George III's lifestyle may have displayed a number of similarities with those of contemporary enlightened monarchs, he could not measure up to his European counterparts when it came to authority, for the British monarchy had been domesticated by Parliament. The French monarchy, too, was a special case. While there was an enlightened milieu which conducted a critical and intensive debate on political, social, legal and religious issues, its influence on matters of state was limited. Attempts at reform took place only sporadically; and, in most cases, they failed. The fact that both Louis XV and Louis XVI held on to the idea of the divine right of kings typifies French conditions. And characteristically, in 1774 – right in the middle of the Age of Enlightenment – Louis XVI had himself anointed at Reims according to the medieval tradition. On the whole, the French monarchy tended towards ossification.

Interest in the phenomenon of 'enlightened absolutism' goes back well into the nineteenth century. The German political economist Wilhelm Roscher, who in 1847 distinguished between three different chronological forms of absolutism (confessional, courtly and enlightened), is often credited with the historical concept. This is correct only to a limited extent. Although Roscher used the term 'enlightened absolutism', the general assumptions that are associated with it come from the Hegel school of the 1830s and 1840s (Blänkner 1993). The question of the genesis of the 'modern state' was of central importance for this school, and it held up the Prussia of Frederick the Great as the European success story of the eighteenth century. For Prussia was a state, it argued, in which autocratic rule was exercised not for its own sake, but in the interests of the general good, and in which an efficient bureaucracy fulfilled its duties with the greatest diligence. On this basis, it suggested, Prussia was able to set out on the path leading to the 'modern state' of the nineteenth century without being embroiled in revolutionary turbulence, like France. This view has left deep traces in the historical research. Such prominent historians as Gustav Schmoller and Otto Hintze were influenced by it, and German historians in particular followed this approach until well into the twentieth century.

When speaking of enlightened absolutism, however, we must also mention another research tradition – the work done in the 1920s and 1930s by the International Commission of Historical Sciences (Scott 1990: 7ff.) – although it spoke of 'enlightened despotism', rather than 'enlightened absolutism'. The work of this commission was of great importance, especially for the Anglo-American and French academic scenes. The central figure in its research was the French historian Michel L'Héritier. Under his influence, the question of what influence the ideas of the French Enlightenment and, in particular, the doctrines of the physiocrats had on the practice of government in the various European countries moved into the foreground.

Present-day research has long left behind such a one-sided view. Historians who study the problem of enlightened absolutism at present assume that there were very different Enlightenment traditions in the various European countries. Thus, the German territories, for instance (on which this chapter will concentrate), were dominated by a moderate, enlightened spirit that clearly diverged from its more critical Western European counterparts. The German case in particular demonstrates that the European Enlightenment contained movements that did not oppose the political and social *status quo*, but aimed primarily to improve the existing system (Ingrao 2002). In this case there is no question of a fundamental contradiction between Enlightenment and absolutism, as the older research in particular often suggests.

Another favourite cliché has also been demolished: namely, that the era of enlightened absolutism represented a radical new beginning. It has become apparent that reform attempts were made in various European countries even before the late eighteenth century, and that we are dealing more with a continuum than with an abrupt change in politics. The policies of enlightened rulers did not represent a radical new beginning in every case; often they built on the reforming attempts of their predecessors. Thus, in Prussia, for example, there was an element of continuity between the rule of Frederick William I and that of Frederick the Great. And the case of Maria Theresa and Joseph II was similar.

All these nuances, however, have not silenced criticism of enlightened absolutism as a historical concept. While few historians now would claim, as M. S. Anderson did in 1961, that the phenomenon of enlightened absolutism was mainly a figment of historians' imaginations, doubts have remained. Probably the most telling criticism has come from Günter Birtsch (1987). He starts from the fact that the term 'enlightened absolutism' is frequently extremely vague. Birtsch himself defines three criteria which, in his view, must be fulfilled before we can even use this term: the ruler must not have recourse to the divine right of kings, rather, rule must be legitimized on a rational basis; the ruler must take part in the enlightened discourse; and there must be empirical evidence that certain enlightened ideas have inspired the ruler and his bureaucracies, and that they have been translated into practical policies. If we take these three criteria as a yardstick and use it to evaluate, for example, the leading representatives of enlightened absolutism in the Holy Roman Empire, the results are highly diffuse. For instance, where legitimation of rule is concerned, by no means all of the rulers described as 'enlightened' had rejected the notion of the divine right of kings. Both Joseph II and Charles Frederick of Baden retained it, although in a weakened form. And only in exceptional cases did late eighteenth-century rulers seriously engage with the philosophical movements of the Age of Enlightenment. Above all, however, it is difficult to establish an unambiguous connection between enlightened philosophy and practical politics. On the basis of these findings, Birtsch came to the conclusion that it makes little sense to continue to use the term 'enlightened absolutism'. Instead, he proposed the term 'reform absolutism', for it is undisputed that a number of rulers committed themselves to a policy of reform, although its shape and intensity varied.

FREDERICK THE GREAT

Regardless, however, of whether historians speak of reform absolutism or enlightened absolutism, none of them can avoid a figure central to the eighteenth century: Frederick the Great (Schieder 1983). Frederick the Great found a unique way of redefining the role of the ruler in a way appropriate to the Age of Enlightenment. This was largely to do with the fact that he had genuinely intellectual interests, and was well versed in contemporary philosophy. In his youth, he amassed a considerable library of 3,000 volumes, including the works of Descartes, Bayle, Locke and Voltaire. In addition, he was familiar with the works of Christian Wolff, the most important German philosopher of the middle of the eighteenth century. Frederick the Great's fame as a political philosopher was based mainly on two works: his *Antimachiavell* of 1739–40 and his *Essai sur les formes de gouvernement et sur les devoirs des souverains* of 1777. In *Antimachiavell*, Frederick argued that monarchy was the best of all forms of state, presupposing, of course, that the monarch fulfilled his duties. This meant, among other things, that his objective was the rule of morality, that he defended humanity and that he felt obliged to uphold the law. In his *Essai sur les formes de gouvernement*, Frederick's concern was to provide a natural-law legitimization for monarchical rule. In this argument, monarchy was based on a contract between authority and subjects. Under the terms of this contract, the subjects had unconditionally and irrevocably ceded sovereignty to the ruler; in return, the monarch guaranteed external security, upheld peace and the law at home, and promoted general welfare. This argument followed the conventions of natural law, and was to be found in many contemporary works on that topic. It was unusual, however, for such ideas to be expressed by a ruling monarch, who thereby decisively rejected the divine right of kings. And there is something else remarkable about this text: in it, Frederick the Great describes the king as 'le premier serviteur d l'état'.

Figure 26.1 *Frederick the Great Inspecting his Troops*, Daniel Chodowiecki (n.d.). By permission of the Staatliche Graphische Sammlung, Munich.

For Frederick the Great to call the monarch the first servant of the state was by no means mere rhetoric. His lifestyle reflected this idea, for among the features of his autocratic rule was an intense concern with the business of governing which was occasionally obsessive. The fact that he almost always wore uniform was not only an expression of his special closeness to the military; it also expressed the idea of service to the state. The Prussian monarch had an immense workload, which was made even more onerous because he did not trust his administration and insisted on taking on many tasks himself. Each day he subjected himself to a routine which demanded a high degree of personal commitment. From early morning he read reports which his ministers sent him. At the same time he dictated *Ordres*, which had the force of laws. It has been estimated that throughout his reign on average twelve such documents were drawn up daily. Thus the total number of *Ordres* issued by Frederick the Great during his period of rule would have been well over 100,000. In addition, the monarch undertook regular tours of inspection in order to gain an overview of conditions in the various parts of the country. His government had an almost ascetic character, and it is indicative that during the second half of his reign court life almost ceased altogether. And it must also be mentioned that at times of military conflict, Frederick the Great personally went to the front with his troops and shared their suffering and deprivations. When he returned to his capital, Berlin, in 1763 after the end of the Seven Years War, he was a man marked by war.

THE PRUSSIAN EXAMPLE

In many respects Frederick the Great was unique, but there were numerous contemporaneous monarchs and territorial rulers who took their tasks very seriously. Often they acquired a remarkable degree of expertise in the fields of domestic and foreign policy. And a new ethos spread among them, one shaped by diligence, a sense of responsibility and concern for the welfare of their subjects. This new ethos corresponded to a trend towards personal rule; that is, rulers kept their administrative apparatuses at a distance, and governed with the help of their *Kabinetts* (Dipper 1991: 223ff.). In their cabinets, rulers surrounded themselves with a small number of close confidants who were tied to them by bonds of utter loyalty. Known as cabinet secretaries, these men often rose from the ranks of subaltern officials and could exert a great deal of influence on the business of state, but their primary task was to assist in dealing with the bureaucratic routine. Occasionally individual ministers acted as personal advisers to the ruler. Monarchs and territorial rulers cultivated this form of personal rule because they felt it was the only way in which they could cope quickly and competently with the business of governing. Whether this was always the case is another story. It largely depended on whether individual rulers had the necessary degree of self-discipline and the requisite intellectual potential. Moreover, there was an inherent inconsistency in this form of personal rule. Rulers tried to withdraw from direct contact with their bureaucracies in order to maintain the maximum room for manoeuvre. But at a time when the state's activities were expanding, rulers were dependent on the expert knowledge of their officials. This resulted in a lively correspondence between the ruler's cabinet and the various sections of the state apparatus. The business of governing was impossible without the active assistance of the bureaucracies.

Compared with the state apparatuses with which we are familiar today, these bureaucracies were tiny (Capra 1996: 251f.). Around the middle of the eighteenth century, even a powerful state such as Prussia probably had no more than 3,000 civil servants, including subaltern officials, and a much smaller figure is likely (Johnson 1975: 15ff.). Some of the higher officials were drawn from the aristocracy, but a considerable proportion came from middle-class backgrounds. What united them was professionalism. Anyone who studies the portraits of these officials sees the faces of a new social type: the 'bureaucratic virtuoso' (Schmoller 1870: 172). Eschewing all baroque bombast, dressed simply, sometimes wearing uniform, these people lived totally for their office. At the end of the eighteenth century, Prussian trainee officials were taught that the official had to sacrifice

> all his days and hours, his intellectual and physical strength, his comforts and his pleasures, his relaxation and even his nightly rest [to his professional duties] whenever the general happiness requires . . . He knows no greater pleasure than the awareness of having done his duty . . . Every other duty ceases to be a duty for him . . . as soon as a holier one calls, that of promoting the best interests of the state.
>
> (Lamprecht 1783: 6–8)

Certainly not all civil servants could live up to such lofty aims, but there are numerous examples to demonstrate that the principle of unceasing professional work for the general good was largely accepted as the norm within bureaucracies at the end of the eighteenth century.

This new type of official was essentially the product of a new qualification structure. At the beginning of the eighteenth century, amateurs had still been able to enter the bureaucracy, but this changed during the second half of the century. The standardization of criteria for entering the administration in the form of examinations meant that aspiring officials had to have studied at a university, where their course of studies was unique. It involved not only administrative techniques and law, but also philosophy. Wolff and his school were mainly responsible for shaping the study of philosophy in this context (Hellmuth 1985). A contemporary account of the university studies of one of the leading officials of Frederick's bureaucracy casts light on how an aspiring government official was trained in the specifically Wolffian philosophical spirit:

> In 1763 at Easter . . . [he] went to Halle to devote himself to the study of law. In the first years philosophy had been his main subject of study. At that time, Wolff's philosophy still ruled supreme at German universities. Its lucid order, its strict coherence, and a comprehensiveness of terminology made this philosophy, despite all its shortcomings, a wonderful introduction to the subject.
>
> (Ancillon 1816: 36–7)

An established component of this philosophical instruction was *philosophia practica*, which comprised natural law, ethics and politics. Natural law was studied not only by aspirant legal officials, but also by future *cameral* officials and clergymen. Thus the characteristic feature of the course of study pursued by servants of the state is that, in addition to the specialist knowledge relevant to their specific professional field, they acquired a wider system of general knowledge in the form of *philosophia practica*.

The reform spurt that many states put on during the second half of the eighteenth century was not only the result of a new enlightened *Zeitgeist*; it was also the outcome of rivalry between states. Thus the Habsburg monarchy's reform efforts essentially grew out of its defeat in the Silesian Wars by Prussia, the parvenu among the European powers. And the outcome of the Seven Years War made it doubly clear to

Maria Theresa and her advisers that the machinery of the Habsburg monarchy needed a thorough overhaul. That war, or the need to remove the consequences of it, was undoubtedly one factor driving the reform process in many territories. The large and middling states tried to prepare themselves for possible conflicts with other states. This sort of inter-state rivalry also required the ability to learn from one's rivals. The classic example is the partial adoption of the Prussian military system by the Habsburg monarchy.

REFORM POLICY

The reform policy developed by enlightened states during the second half of the eighteenth century embraced almost all areas of life. Although policies varied from state to state, a few general trends may be distinguished. Reform efforts were often concentrated on making administrations more efficient and coherent. This involved strengthening the role of the central power, establishing clearly structured hierarchies, improving the expertise of officials, and restricting the power of the Estates. These administrative reforms were frequently accompanied by legal reforms. These included, among other things, standardizing the law, both civil and criminal. There were also proposals to make the criminal justice system more humane, most clearly expressed in the abolition of torture, the reduction of draconian punishments and the removal of ancient crimes such as witchcraft and sorcery from the statute books. At the same time, there was a greater tolerance towards religions which had previously been discriminated against. Thus it became easier for Protestants to live under a Catholic ruler, and vice versa. In a few individual cases, the first steps were even taken towards the emancipation of the Jews. Another focus for reform work in the enlightened states was education policy, whose primary aim was to convey an elementary knowledge of reading, writing and arithmetic to a wider circle. For the Catholic states, church reform was a separate problem. This involved securing the primacy of the state against the Church, eliminating forms of popular piety, gaining the clergy's commitment to parish welfare work and ministry, and abolishing the contemplative religious orders. Finally, mention should be made of a number of other measures designed to: stimulate trade and commerce; improve agriculture; abolish serfdom; increase investment in infrastructure (including road- and canal-building); implement welfare reforms, such as the establishment of hospitals; and sometimes also relax censorship.

SUCCESS OR FAILURE?

There is no doubt that many states made energetic attempts at reform during the second half of the eighteenth century, but how successful were they? In looking for an answer, we are confronted with two different narratives. The first is a story of success; the other of failure, chaos and disaster. Although these two stories sometimes overlap in historiographical practice, they will be presented separately here for the sake of clarity.

Those historians who see these reforms as a success point above all to the example of the smaller territories (Ingrao 1990). They start from the position that structural conditions in these states were particularly suitable for the implementation of reform. Several arguments are generally put forward to substantiate this thesis. The smaller territories, it is said, were able to concentrate on domestic policy because they were not involved in the great conflicts of the time; their state budgets were not strained by a bloated military apparatus; their small bureaucracies simplified decision-making procedures; and, finally, they did not have the regional and thus constitutional diversity which complicated the policy of reform in larger territories, such as Prussia and Austria. It is further argued that this reform policy had a number of positive consequences for the populations of these states. These included rising living standards and levels of education, improvements in agrarian technology, the blossoming of trade and commerce, the defusion of tension between the confessions, and the rapid administration of justice.

However, historians ascribe effective reform policy not only to the smaller states. The same applies to the Habsburg monarchy and Prussia. To a large extent, we find the same arguments to which historians refer when pointing to the positive impact of reforms in the smaller states. Beyond this, Prussia is also seen as a state which, in respect of its administration and justice systems, set standards for the eighteenth century (Behrens 1985). And, in the case of the Habsburg monarchy, attention is drawn to the economic dynamism which it developed towards the end of the century (Ingrao 1994: 212ff.). The growing industrial sector, the expansion of the food supply for the people and increasing urbanization are taken as indications that the policy of reform was successful.

Next to such a positive view one can place an interpretation of reform policy which emphasizes its limitations and its partially chaotic character. Historians have regularly pointed to the miserable failure of Joseph II's policy of radical reform. It is becoming increasingly clear that it was not only the opposition of the traditional powers and the complexity of the Josephinian reform programme that led to disaster, but that the excessive demands placed on the state apparatus also contributed crucially to the failure (Stauber 2001). Agencies working at local level, which were regularly inundated by streams of edicts, were able to put the ruler's will into practice only to a limited extent. There could be no question of a targeted and controlled implementation of the Josephinian policy of reform. Much was nothing but waste-paper, largely because the state apparatus was not properly balanced. Too many civil servants were occupied with the paper rituals of the Leviathan; too few worked on pushing ahead practical reform policy (Dickson 1995).

And for Frederick's Prussia, too, which in the past was often celebrated as a stronghold of Enlightenment and progress, one can draw up a scenario which raises doubts concerning the efficiency and reforming ability of the bureaucratic–absolutist states of the eighteenth century. In any case, a number of factors undermine the image of the perfectly functioning Prussian machinery of state. In the period following the Seven Years War in particular, the weaknesses of the over-centralized system of government became clear. Directives from Potsdam were increasingly ignored, or only partially followed; at the same time, officials hesitated to assume responsibility themselves (Scott 2000: 197ff.). Moreover, under the rule of Frederick the Great,

Figure 26.2 *Joseph II, Holy Roman Emperor*, engraving by J. G. Janota (1775). By permission of the Staatliche Graphische Sammlung, Munich.

the Prussian bureaucracy was subjected to a process of constant reorganization, which suggests a certain lack of direction in Prussia's internal administration. A number of projects which the monarch set in motion with the assistance of his administration were obviously non-starters. The state seems to have achieved only limited control over fundamental problems such as taxes and duties. Prussia's highly praised education policy was largely a sham, created on paper by the bureaucracy; it had little to do with people's real lives (Neugebauer 1985). It is becoming increasingly clear that sections of the urban and rural population were able to avoid intervention by the authorities. There was obviously a large gap between the claims of absolutist regimes and the situation on the ground.

Even in the smaller territories, reform efforts do not seem to have had as much success as is sometimes assumed (Zimmermann 1996). Here, too, the reforming–regimenting will of the authorities frequently failed in the face of traditional ways of life. This applied in particular to attempts to eliminate specific forms of popular piety. Wherever the process of reform is examined more closely, shortcomings and frictions appear. Often there was simply a lack of people, money and information (Lindemann 1997). And studies of the smaller territories in particular have shown that historians should not take the edicts which eighteenth-century authorities produced in such large numbers at face value. At most, they signalled what the state intended to do; they did not show what was achieved. Some historians have gone so far as to see these edicts primarily as symbolic acts. The issuing of edicts, it is argued, was 'an important area in which the state displayed itself' (Schlumbohm 1997: 661).

The question now, of course, is: which of the two stories concerning the reform policy of enlightened regimes is correct? Although there can be no doubt that reform policy had some success, on the whole the sceptical view is more persuasive. The enlightened regimes of the eighteenth century had an inherent structural flaw: they were unable to distinguish between the important and the unimportant. As their policies were based on the assumption that the authorities should, in principle, regulate *all* spheres of life, they often simply could not cope, and the activity that ensued frequently missed its target. The denser the network of regulations, the further actual conditions were left behind. A sobering conclusion has recently been drawn:

> By the eighteenth century society had reached a degree of complexity which was beyond the capacity of autocratic rulers to deal with. Many, especially large territories remained dilettantes, and their interventions often did more harm than good. Thus, despite the numerous decrees which it produced, the eighteenth-century state apparatus was concerned mainly with itself.
>
> (Dipper 1999: 207)

ENLIGHTENED GOVERNMENT?

Does all this mean that the question of the connection between government and Enlightenment is irrelevant? By no means. Although the state in the period of Enlightenment had considerable shortcomings and its reform policies frequently failed, this did not mean that it gave up the attempt to bring as many fields of activity into its orbit as possible, and to submit them to the continuous efforts of the authorities. The consequence of this was that knowledge about politics, society, economics and law increased exponentially. It could even be argued that the frequent failure of practical politics gave the process of reflection an extra boost, and generated new knowledge about the state.

The eighteenth-century universities played a key role in this, especially those, such as Halle or Göttingen, which were strongholds of the Enlightenment. At these universities a wide spectrum of subjects, known collectively as the 'science of government', became established (Bödeker 1985). They included natural law, economics, the specifically German academic disciplines of *Kameralwissenschaft* and *Polizeiwissenschaft*, and politics. Added to this was *Universitätsstatistik* (university statistics), which, despite its name, had nothing to do with political arithmetic. The Göttingen professor Gottfried Achenwall defined it as the 'theory of the political constitution of individual states described in terms of their separate parts' (Streidl 2003: 130). The 'parts' which were considered worth describing included territory and population, constitution and administration, military and finances. Thus an intimate knowledge of internal conditions in contemporary states was required. Natural law also had another, very different function. As the main component of the complex of subjects studied as the science of government, it was intended to convey fundamental insights into politics, society and law. This included the definition of the aims and purpose of the state as they arose out of human nature. The other subjects which comprised the science of government, *Kameralwissenschaft* and *Polizeiwissenschaft* (economics and politics) were then required to describe the ways and means by which these aims and purposes could be achieved. Often the contours of these subjects were woolly, but they were unified by a single leitmotif: namely, that the purpose of science was to be useful to the state.

But it was not only the academic milieu that produced knowledge about the state. This process also occurred within the bureaucracy itself, for a large number of officials took an active part in the public debate on issues to do with the polity which began from 1750 and grew rapidly in the last quarter of the eighteenth century. For academically trained, philosophically schooled administrative officials, this debate was an intellectual challenge, especially as academic and literary activity conferred a great deal of prestige and was the yardstick of social success. A contemporary manual for the training of civil servants states that 'for every servant of the state, the need to free his intellect is paramount . . . A truly philosophical intellect . . . is beneficial to the whole administration, indeed, absolutely essential . . . if it is to fulfil its purpose' (Voss 1799: 326, 327). The real lives of many civil servants did, indeed, reflect this programmatic claim. They did not concentrate solely on the sphere of their professional activities; rather, the debate about issues concerning the polity formed a central part of the way in which they chose to live their lives.

In many cases, such ambitions were not merely passive, but led to active partici-pation in the contemporary discourse. Thus, in addition to their professional duties, officials dedicated themselves to publicly interpreting the world by writing journal articles, academic works, tracts, treatises and larger studies in the tradition of academic philosophy. If one examines the German-language writings of the late eighteenth century, it becomes clear that the majority of authors were servants of the state. Myriad officials, or would-be officials, thought and argued about what the world should be like. The simple fact that hundreds of sometimes rudimentary state apparatuses coexisted within the borders of the Holy Roman Empire conferred its own dynamic upon this process by which members of the state administrations generated knowledge.

All this points to a highly interesting state of affairs. Those who debated public affairs were frequently part of the system which they made into the subject of public debate. It therefore makes little sense to assume an antagonistic relationship between the public sphere and the state. In other words, in the central European territories of the later eighteenth century, the anti-governmental public sphere which played such a significant part in Jürgen Habermas's (1989) concept of the 'structural transformation of the public sphere' was present only to a limited extent. The press and the various associations of the Enlightenment period – that is, those institutions which in Habermas's notion represent the critical catalyst, not bound to the state – were dominated by the same people who occupied the government offices of the late eighteenth century. We are therefore dealing with a closed system.

From this perspective, the journalism of the second half of the eighteenth century, which expanded dramatically (Hellmuth and Piereth 2002), no longer looks exclusively like a sounding board for the ambitions of an emergent bourgeois public sphere. Instead it can be seen as a unique warehouse of novel ideas concerning the state. Anyone leafing through late eighteenth-century publications comes across a remarkable catalogue of proposals for improvement and reform concepts. Sensible proposals were often mixed up with the bizarre. The spectrum of subjects ranged from instructions for how best to catch lost dogs to proposals for the establishment of mortuaries, and topics which, in our eyes, are typical of the age: plans to reform the education system; proposals to make the criminal justice system more humane; suggestions for the improvement of industry and agriculture; public health measures and so on. The explosion in the print media clearly increased and accelerated the circulation of knowledge relevant to the administration. A key role in this was played by specialist journals in law, medicine, education, the natural sciences, economics, architecture and military science, whose readers were primarily drawn from the 'experts' in the state apparatus. This was also, to a large extent, true of general literature. Thus the so-called historical–political journals inundated their readers with a flood of information about government campaigns, industry and commerce, and military enterprises. Often statistics formed essential components of these articles. They included figures relating to state budgets, the military potential of the European powers, birth and death rates, and import and export statistics.

This information, which circulated in public, was in many respects merely the tip of the iceberg, for the mass of data which enlightened regimes generated was intended for the internal use of their bureaucracies. With undiminished enthusiasm, the servants of the state set about capturing the world in figures and measurements, in texts and tables. Their controlling glance fell on all manner of things: the condition of the roads, waterways and bridges; how fields, woods and meadows were managed; the technological expertise of people in trade and commerce; the quality of food; the educational level of subjects; the numbers of idlers, beggars and vagabonds; precautions against fire and flood; the dissemination of superstition and sorcery. The list of subjects which were addressed could be extended at will. While this looks like aimless curiosity, it was not. Enlightened regimes assumed that precise information about the living conditions of their inhabitants was a prerequisite for the competent administration of a territory (Holenstein 2003). Consequently, it was believed that there was a connection between density of data and good government.

Contemporary political theory provided a more profound justification for all these activities generating new knowledge about the most diverse areas of life. The concept of the interventionist state was energetically developed within the framework of the science of government during the Enlightenment. Natural law played a key role, especially natural law of Wolffian provenance (Klippel 1999). It was axiomatic within this natural-law tradition that mankind could develop its potential for civilization and culture only when organized in a state. In other words, individuals could not perfect themselves; a contribution by the state was required. Consequently, the argument operated with a wide definition of the purpose of the state community. Stated objectives such as the 'general happiness' (*allgemeine Glückseligkeit*), the common good, or *bonum commune*, became the hallmark of an understanding of the state which, at heart, placed great trust in the comprehensive powers of the government. These objectives gave rise to demands which were tailored to the authoritarian state: the duty of subjects was to serve the common good; the claims of the state were to take priority over those of the individual; and state activity was to expand to bring as many tasks as possible within its orbit. And the principle of political participation was rejected, while absolute monarchy was affirmed. This constitutional form alone, which uniquely concentrated political power in one decision-making centre, seemed to guarantee rapid, purposeful and expert activity on the part of the state authorities. In addition, absolute monarchy stood for the values of social peace, personal security and the integrity of property.

This sort of political theory clearly had strongly affirmative features. At the same time, however, it was part of a new culture of knowledge, within which the people had been promoted to the central object of the art of government. And the same applies to the elaborate statistical initiatives and the countless suggestions for reform found in the journalism of the late eighteenth century. Often, this culture of knowledge had little or nothing to do with real life. But, within it, a blueprint was developed for what was to be done in the future. Not the least among its achievements was that it allowed the principle of state intervention to become a cultural given. The age of Enlightenment was not necessarily the great age of reform, but it did create a remarkable store of ideas upon which future generations could draw.

ACKNOWLEDGEMENT

I am grateful to Angela Davies for translating this chapter.

REFERENCES

Ancillon, F. (1816) 'Denkschrift auf Ernst Ferdinand Klein', in *Abhandlungen der königlichen Akademie der Wissenschaften in Berlin, aus den Jahren 1812–13*: 33–50.
Anderson, M. S. (1961) *Europe in the Eighteenth Century 1713–1783*, London: Longman.

Behrens, C. B. A. (1985) *Society, Government and the Enlightenment: The Experiences of Eighteenth-century France and Prussia*, London: Thames & Hudson.

Birtsch, G. (1987) 'Der Idealtyp des aufgeklärten Herrschers: Friedrich der Große, Karl Friedrich von Baden und Joseph II. im Vergleich', *Aufklärung*, 2: 9–47.

Blänkner, R. (1993) 'Der Absolutismus war ein Glück, der doch nicht zu den Absolutisten gehört', *Historische Zeitschrift*, 256: 31–66.

Bödeker, H. J. (1985) 'Das staatswissenschaftliche Fächersystem im 18. Jahrhundert', in R. Vierhaus (ed.) *Wissenschaften im Zeitalter der Aufklärung*, Göttingen: Vandenhoeck & Ruprecht.

Capra C. (1996) 'Der Beamte', in M. Vovelle (ed.) *Der Mensch der Aufklärung*, Frankfurt: Campus.

Dickson, P. G. M. (1995) 'Monarchy and Bureaucracy in Late Eighteenth Century Austria', *English Historical Review*, 110: 322–67.

Dipper, C. (1991) *Deutsche Geschichte 1648–1789*, Frankfurt: Suhrkamp.

—— (1999) 'Government and Administration: Everyday Politics in the Holy Roman Empire', in J. Brewer and E. Hellmuth (eds) *Rethinking Leviathan: The Eighteenth-century State in Britain and Germany*, Oxford: Oxford University Press.

Habermas, J. (1989) *The Structural Transformation of the Public Sphere: An Inquiry into a Category of Bourgeois Society*, Cambridge, Mass.: Harvard University Press.

Hellmuth, E. (1985) *Naturrechtsphilosophie und bürokratischer Werthorizont: Studien zur preußischen Geistes- und Sozialgeschichte des 18. Jahrhunderts*, Göttingen: Vandenhoeck & Ruprecht.

Hellmuth, E. and Piereth, W. (2002) 'Germany 1760–1815', in H. Barker and S. Burrows (eds) *Press, Politics and the Public Sphere in Europe and North America 1760–1820*, Cambridge: Cambridge University Press.

Holenstein, A. (2003) *'Gute Policey' und lokale Gesellschaft im Staat des Ancien Régime: Das Fallbeispiel der Markgrafschaft Baden(-Durlach)*, 2 vols, Epfendorf/Neckar: Bibliotheca academica.

Ingrao, C. (1990) 'The Smaller German States', in H. M. Scott (ed.) *Enlightened Absolutism: Reform and Reformers in Later Eighteenth Century Europe*, London: Macmillan.

—— (1994) *The Habsburg Monarchy 1618–1815*, Cambridge: Cambridge University Press.

—— (2002) 'A Pre-revolutionary *Sonderweg*', *German History*, 20: 279–86.

Johnson, H. C. (1975) *Frederick the Great and his Officials*, New Haven, Conn.: Yale University Press.

Klippel, D. (1999) 'Reasonable Aims of Civil Concerns of the State in German Political Theory in the Eighteenth and Early Nineteenth Centuries', in J. Brewer and E. Hellmuth (eds) *op. cit.*

Lamprecht G. F. (1783) *Ueber das Studium der Kameralwissenschaften*, Halle.

Lindemann, M. (1997) *Health and Healing in Eighteenth-century Germany*, Baltimore: Johns Hopkins University Press.

Neugebauer, W. (1985) *Absolutistischer Staat und Schulwirklichkeit in Brandenburg-Preußen*, Berlin: de Gruyter.

Schieder, T. (1983) *Friedrich der Grosse: Ein Königtum der Widersprüche*, Berlin: Ullstein.

Schlumbohm, J. (1997) 'Gesetze, die nicht durchgesetzt werden – ein Strukturmerkmal des frühneuzeitlichen Staates?', *Geschichte und Gesellschaft*, 23: 647–63.

Schmoller, G. (1870) 'Der preußische Beamtenstand unter Friedrich Wilhelm I', *Preußische Jahrbücher*, 26: 148–72.

Scott, H. M. (1990) 'The Problem of Enlightened Absolutism', in H. M. Scott (ed.) *Enlightened Absolutism: Reform and Reformers in Later Eighteenth Century Europe*, London: Macmillan.

—— (2000) '1763–1786: The Second Reign of Frederick the Great?', in P. G. Dwyer (ed.) *The Rise of Prussia 1700–1830*, London: Longman.

Stauber, R. (2001) *Der Zentralstaat an seinen Grenzen: Administrative Integration, Herrschaftswechsel und politische Kultur im südlichen Alpenraum*, Göttingen: Vandenhoeck & Ruprecht.

Streidl, Paul (2003) *Naturrecht, Staatswissenschaft und Politisierung bei Gottfried Achenwall (1719–1772)*, München: Utz, Herbert, Berlag GmbH.

Voss, Ch. D. (1799) *Versuch über die Erziehung für den Staat als Bedürfnis unserer Zeit, zur Beförderung des Bürgerwohls und der Regenten-Sicherheit*, Halle.

Zimmermann, C. (1996) 'Grenzen des Veränderbaren im Absolutismus: Staat und Dorfgemeinde in der Markgrafschaft Baden', *Aufklärung*, 9: 25–45.

CHAPTER TWENTY-SEVEN

ENLIGHTENMENT, REPUBLICANISM AND RADICALISM

Mark Philp

Several paradoxes are raised by the discussion of republicanism and radicalism in the Enlightenment period. Radicalism was not a self-conscious category of political action and agency – and, in that sense, what we think of as radicalism is not a phenomenon of the eighteenth century. While republicanism was occasionally embraced explicitly, particularly at the end of the eighteenth century, the academic case for eighteenth-century republicanism revolves around a model of government, a set of assumptions about the role of civic virtue and institutional balance, and a rhetoric of liberty and the common good, which, although drawn on by many, was not usually self-consciously conceived of as republicanism – those who self-consciously espoused it tended to do so as 'commonwealthmen' (Robbins 1959). Moreover, while Enlightenment was a category of action and mobilization in some European states, especially but not exclusively France, it was not in England. Enlightenment, republicanism and radicalism are, then, each problematic terms of art with respect to the eighteenth century. Yet each is also pertinent: there was a widely shared sense of the potential for rational progress and the casting off of 'man's . . . self-incurred immaturity' (Kant 1784: 54). And if England was less self-conscious about its Enlightenment, as Porter (1981: 33) argues, 'English' and 'enlightened' were treated almost as synonyms in many parts of Europe, and England stood as a model for other states which more self-consciously pursued Enlightenment values.

Similarly, classical republicanism influenced, albeit in different ways, the language of debate in each of France, Britain and America – and in each case, texts travelled across national boundaries (following in the wake of the classics) and permeated local traditions to give the appearance of a common transatlantic language of republican virtue. And, while radicalism had yet to appear in the lexicon of those seeking reform and political change, this was the century which issued in radical (because progressive and emancipatory) American and French revolutions, and in which the roots of British radicalism can be traced. For all three terms, then, despite the paradoxes, there is a case for recognizing them as central to intellectual agendas and political aspirations in Britain, France and America in the eighteenth century. Indeed, the case has been extended – by both radicals and reactionaries during and after the French Revolution – to see the reform movement in Britain, and the French and American revolutions, as the culmination of republicanism and Enlightenment.

Price's *Discourse on the Love of our Country* (1789) ends with a heady concoction of revolution and Enlightenment, which set the tone for the counter-Enlightenment criticisms of the next thirty years:

> After sharing in the benefits of one Revolution, I have been spared to be a witness to two other Revolutions, both glorious. – And now, methinks, I see the ardour for liberty catching and spreading: a general amendment beginning in human affairs; the dominion of kings changed for the dominion of laws, and the dominion of priests giving way to the dominion of reason and conscience.
>
> (Price 1789: 50–1)

It is not difficult to see why Burke chooses Price as his target, nor difficult to understand how the Abbé Barruel could link Enlightenment to revolution in a dramatic conspiracy theory which attributed every excess of the French Revolution to the prophets of reason (Barruel 1798). In the wake of the revolutionary Terror, the values of reason, progress and liberty, and the hopes for reform that they spawned, seemed irredeemably compromised. But that narrative demands resistance. It runs intellectual and political history together as if the thought were the deed, and fails to notice either the dislocation between 'languages' of Enlightenment and republicanism and their own complex characters. Indeed, towards the end of the century the language of republicanism became increasingly fractured, increasingly blended with other political (and religious) languages, and increasingly rhetorical in character. In the heat of revolution these fragments, together with other traditions, were dramatically reworked to link the radical and revolutionary agendas of Britain, American and France in demands for republican democracy. But this demand, articulated most powerfully by Thomas Paine, is the expression of new popular forces that neither Enlightenment thinking nor classical republicanism would have endorsed.

TWO REPUBLICAN TRADITIONS

Two forms of republicanism can be distinguished in eighteenth-century political thought and practice: a popular, non-technical idiom and a more specialized language of, and framework for, political analysis. In ordinary parlance a republic is a form of government without a monarch: one in which the supreme power rests in the people and their elected representatives or officers. To be accused of republicanism is to be accused of being straightforwardly anti-monarchical in sentiment: a common charge in the literature of the 'Association for the Preservation of Liberty and Property against Republicans and Levellers' of the 1790s. Anti-monarchical republicanism does exist on the borders of political controversy throughout the eighteenth century, finding occasional expression in people's less guarded moments, as in Edward Swift's outburst – 'Damn the King and Queen, they ought to be put to death the same as the King and Queen of France were . . . I would as soon shoot the King as a mad dog' (Emsley 1981: 157). But popular anti-monarchical sentiment was not widespread among ordinary members of the British public, and, where it appeared,

Figure 27.1 *The Hopes of Party, prior to July 14*, engraving by James Gillray (19 July 1791). In the early years of the French Revolution, reformers in Britain celebrated the anniversary of the fall of the Bastille, 14 July 1789, but they were increasingly tainted by accusations of revolutionary republicanism. In this caricature George III is about to meet his end at the hands of an executioner, the masked Charles James Fox, aided by fellow-members of the Whig Party, while the Revd Joseph Priestley is offering the King spurious consolation. Queen Charlotte and Prime Minister William Pitt hang from nearby lanterns. Published on 19 July, it is unclear whether Gillray had already heard that Priestley's house, library and laboratory had been destroyed by rioters in Birmingham, but he still continued to portray him as a republican and regicide. By permission of the Guildhall Library, Corporation of London.

alongside reference back to the Civil War, the thrust was often rhetorical rather than substantive in character, so it remains obscure whether those who struck the pose fully intended, or were willing, to practise what they preached. Ireland, towards the end of the century, provides one exception, since emerging nationalist feeling became inevitably anti-monarchical – to reject English rule was seen as necessitating the rejection of the crown. Surprisingly, the same cannot be said of America, where resistance to Britain was conceived of, until very late in the day, as resistance to the British Parliament and the lack of representation. As a result, America slipped into a republican order, without altogether intending it, and among the revolutionists there remained monarchical sympathizers (such as Hamilton) and the democratic influences of the revolution seemed to some to be all too quickly usurped by the emergence of a quasi-aristocracy.

Scholars referring to eighteenth-century republicanism are not, for the most part, referring to anti-monarchical ideas, so much as to an understanding of the nature of politics that drew heavily on ancient and classical sources, and whose influence was revivified and concentrated by the writings of Machiavelli and Harrington. Classical sources have much to say about monarchy and about the proper order of politics, and Roman and Greek literature – Homer, Herodotus, Thuycidides, Polybius, Livy, Tacitus, Plutarch, Juvenal and Cicero – the immortal Tully – provided a substantial part of the staple of upper-class education throughout Europe and the Americas. Many will have known the history of the fall of the Roman Republic as intimately as the history of their own state (if not more so), and this shared literary inheritance profoundly influenced the way people conceived of politics and their place in it. Rome remained the most potent symbol of ancient forms of rule, but Sparta retained the allegiance of many, not least Rousseau, even if Voltaire, Mably and Chastellux denounced it as little better than a monastery (Rawson 1969: 256–7). But this literature on its own does not produce republicanism – nor should republicanism be deduced from the willingness to cite Cicero. Classical sources informed the terms in which people discussed politics, influenced the assumptions they made about human nature and provided a culture of common reference. Writers drew from this culture a cluster of judgements, theoretical models and intellectual reflexes that informed political analysis and helped frame their debates in a relatively systematic and self-conscious way.

As Pocock has demonstrated, there is something like a consistent train of republican writing, inspired by Machiavelli, Harrington and Sidney (Pocock 1973: 80–147; 1975), which informed traditions of Country Party opposition in Britain in the first half of the eighteenth century and subsequently migrated to North America, where it made a major contribution to the development of revolutionary opposition to British rule (Bailyn 1967; Wood 1969 and 1991). This 'language' of republicanism proposed a Polybian model of mixed government; it emphasized the importance of civic virtue and feared the corrupting impact of luxury and political faction. However, it was republicanism without, for the most part, being expressly anti-monarchical, because it largely accepted the principle of mixed government and saw the relevant contrast as one between limited and unlimited governments, rather than between monarchies and republics. (It was also connected to a distinction between small and large states, with republicanism being seen as inapplicable in the latter.) Limited government required mixed government, involving the combined rule of king, nobility and commons. For many, this was not just an acceptable form but the best form of government. The key factor in distinguishing good monarchies from tyrannies or despotisms was whether the king claimed to be above the law (see, for example, Milton 1658: 129–30). Republican government (indeed, the label 'republican' was rarely appealed to – 'good government' could substitute) was a government of laws directed towards the common good of the people; despotism was arbitrary government, with the capricious will of a ruler subordinating the political realm to his or her personal interests.

THE CLASSICAL REPUBLIC

The classical source for the ideal of a mixed government of the one, the few and the many, sustaining a balance of class forces which could steer the state away from domination by any particular class, was Polybius' opening comments to book VI of his *Rise of the Roman Empire* and Machiavelli's restatement of the doctrine in his *Discourses* (1531: I, 2). Nonetheless, kingly rule remained a point of tension because one major threat to the state was the tendency of power to corrupt, so that more danger was to be feared from the usurpation of power by the monarch than was ever likely to stem from the tumults of the people (Machiavelli 1531: I.58; Harrington 1656: 30–5). Counterbalancing this was the wide acceptance of the view that classical republics were feasible only in very small city-states, so that limited monarchical rule became the ideal viable form for the moderately sized British and French states (see, for example, Whatmore 2000: 23–31, 77–82, 95–8).

The end of republican rule is the common good:

> The good of the people is the ultimate and true end of government. Governors are, therefore, appointed for this end, and the civil constitution which appoints them, and invests them with their power, is determined to do so by that law of nature and reason . . . Now, the greatest good of a people is their liberty . . . Liberty is to the collective body, what health is to every individual body; without liberty no happiness can be enjoyed by society.
>
> (Bolingbroke 1738: 244)

The appeal to the common good (and to liberty as a central feature of it) in republicanism takes differing forms and has given rise to conflicting interpretations. Some commentators have stressed the influence of the Aristotelian view that man is a political animal to whom the *polis* offers a distinctive form of liberty or self-realization. Recent commentators, however, have suggested that the common good should not be understood as a life of political participation but in terms of the security and liberties which are achieved when a stable republic is formed (Skinner 1998; Pettit 1997). The disagreement, while relevant to modern debates in political philosophy, is of less significance for understanding Enlightenment thought. Liberty was widely understood as a type of independence, but this independence was both necessary for and nourished by involvement in the political world; and while liberty, in a narrower sense of freedom from interference, could be valued independently of political participation, in Britain the reflex reference to the liberties of the free-born Englishman came increasingly to generate further demands for representation and participation not just to 'protect' but actively to 'restore' those liberties. Bolingbroke's encomium might be interpreted either way, and many other authors merged both types of argument.

On both interpretations, political participation, civic virtue and people's involvement in political life tended to play major parts in ensuring the existence of a stable and flourishing regime – although there were disagreements over the extent to which laws could substitute for civic virtues. Good laws in some combination with civic virtue were required to subordinate the pursuit of private interests to the common good and to avoid the corruption of the regime and its decay into inter-necine struggle in which self-serving interests and the unbridled indulgence of the passions predominated. The Polybian model assumed that all states decline, but that it was possible to delay the inevitable fall of the state by understanding the interplay between material, political and cultural forces and by acting in politics on the basis of this understanding. In England, at least, in the early part of the eighteenth century, this analysis focused increasingly on the threatened equilibrium between the three orders, crown, Lords and Commons – the one, the few and the many – as in *Cato's Letters* of Trenchard and Gordon, which attacked the dominance of Walpole and his 'court' faction and went on to provide a central text for reformers in England and America for much of the rest of the century. But, while some of those using these arguments, such as James Burgh, are notably republican, others, such as Richard Price and Joseph Priestley, blended republican elements with a very wide range of other influences. Prominent among these was the natural-rights tradition, strength-ened by Locke's *Second Treatise*, a major contributory discourse to demands for political reform and the restriction of the sphere of legitimate government action. Similarly, demands for a separation of Church and state, or alternatively for a state-sponsored civil religion, embodied resistance to the confessional state and also informed sympathy for elements of a secular republican politics.

REPUBLICAN TENSIONS

The republican tradition falls short of being a creed or dogma, offering instead a nascent form of political sociology that was open to successive refinement and adaptation in the light of changing historical experiences. This was partly because the tradition itself was already fissured. Wootton (1986: 70–2) has suggested three tensions in the model which new generations of political theorists probed and expanded. The first concerns the degree to which the account of mixed government as competing power blocks draws on or displaces the demand for civic virtue as the core to the collective consciousness of the state. Machiavelli is unclear (like Polybius before him) as to whether the balancing of these forces should be understood as creating remedial resources that could respond to tyrannical tendencies in one or other part of the government, so that civic virtue remains central to people's motives; or whether we should see good government as the unintended outcome of the continuous pressures and forces exerted by the pursuit of their interests by different elements of the polity. As the eighteenth century progresses, in Britain at least, it is fair to say that the tendency is to accept a greater role for interests. Moreover, it is clearly this account which becomes ascendant in America in *Federalist Paper* 10.

The second fissure is in the divergence between self-interest and civic virtue: the modern proposal that republican rule should be understood in terms of the protection of individual liberty and security clearly takes the view that there is little disparity. Yet the classical texts and examples inspired a powerful strain of patriotism and heroic self-sacrifice in discussions of the political realm. The tension between the two models was also implicitly a tension between the private and the public, the former interpreting politics as simply an instrument for protecting people's interests, and the latter finding in it a shared life of virtue. But the contrast also gives rise to further contrasts – universalism against particularism, and an enlightened cosmopolitanism against an emerging nationalism. And, while elements of republicanism, such as its validation of liberty and its sense of the good life, have universalist components, its emphasis on civic virtue and patriotism pulls in a quite other direction.

The final tension concerns the role of the people, especially in contrast to the aristocracy. Classical republicanism offered a vision of the world in which nobility was linked to noble self-sacrifice and, while the people could be crucial in counter-balancing usurpation by kings, they are not widely viewed as a secure repository for republican virtues. The tendency was to trust the people to look after their interests in a less destructive way than would kings, but to place a good deal more reliance on an elite of the good, as the critical mediating body. Increasing confidence in the rule of law diminished the emphasis on the elite, although this raised the more basic question of the wisdom and probity of those who formulate and pass the laws. The *Federalist Papers* (1788) show an elite at work designing and implementing a set of institutions that will dispense subsequent generations from the need for the kinds of virtues their founders possessed! Nor were they alone: constitutional design becomes a widespread hobby towards the end of the century, with the United Provinces, Poland and Corsica providing practical material for theoretical speculation, as in Rousseau's proposals on Poland and Corsica. These various tensions opened up the tradition to innovations and substantial departures from the original model.

One of the most transforming of eighteenth-century innovations, linked to the issue of interests, was writers' increasing willingness to commend commerce and the accumulation of wealth as symptoms of civic health and strength, rather than of corrupt self-seeking (although the financing of the public debt remained a source of anxiety). This acceptance, in a tradition in which they had hitherto been condemned as inevitably corrupting (they were systematically distrusted within the classical world as activities of the household rather than of the polity), issued in a new ideal of the commercial republic, celebrated by Montesquieu in a gloss on England in *L'Esprit des Lois* (1748) and subsequently by Ferguson (with reservations), Hume, Smith and others in the Scottish Enlightenment. A further change was a growing emphasis in the British context on the importance of the liberty of the press and freedom of speech, on broadening popular participation in elections, and on particular institutional and constitutional safeguards against usurpation – including petitioning, the use of juries and so on. These innovations both reflected and further contributed to the growing tolerance for the pursuit of individual interests and the willingness to interpret the common good of the commonwealth in terms of the protection of individual liberty and security that were themselves understood in terms of common-law traditions and customary liberties. But writers varied, and different national contexts certainly influenced such matters. Rousseau's *Discourse on the Origin of Inequality* (1755) is an eloquent attack on commerce, the accumulation of wealth, and the rise of inequality and its fateful consequence for government, while, from the previous century, Harrington's sense of the importance of landed property retained a powerful appeal in America, being hymned in Price's *Observations on the Importance of the American Revolution* (1785: 144–5), and enduring in the Jeffersonian tradition well into the nineteenth century.

Two further developments helped transform eighteenth-century republicanism. The first was a gradual move from historical pessimism. For the ancient world, the polis was a fragile achievement, beset by forces within and without, capable of a brief flourishing before decaying into corruption and tyranny, but which in that brief moment could offer a form of life that uniquely realized man's nature as a political animal. The classical world had no real sense of progress and a predilection to assume that the most glorious states lay in the past. Between the beginning of the eighteenth century and its end, optimism about the nature of historical change became first possible, then commonplace. A corollary was a change in the way that people understood the character of political reform. Classical republicanism understood reform in terms of the re-establishment of an order: 'In order that a religious institution or a state should long survive it is essential that it should frequently be restored to its original principles' (Machiavelli 1531: III, 1). Integral to the idea of progress is a view of change as potentially innovative, based on an improved understanding of the workings of the world derived from philosophical speculation and scientific study, and no longer hide-bound by the examples of the past. The very possibility of progress entailed that it might be possible substantially to improve the way in which states were ruled. This development is clearly linked to 'Enlightenment rationalism', and it is closely linked to the *querrelle* that persisted throughout the Enlightenment, between the ancients and the moderns. In moving away from a position in which the classical world epitomized the summit of human achievement, the eighteenth century gradually opened up a new canvas for experimentation and a new set of vistas for human achievement, but in doing so they further transformed their republican inheritance.

A major example of this shift from old forms to new was the celebration of representative government as an innovation in the art of government, which freed direct democracy from its inconveniences and subsequently increased the demand for more democratic forms of representation (for example, *Federalist Paper* 10). An associated development concerned the extent of the franchise. Harrington and his successors saw landed property as a prerequisite for a stable citizenry, and, although he did not restrict citizenship to those with land, eighteenth-century theories of representation began by limiting suffrage to those with immovable property in the state. The pressure to extend the suffrage came in part from republican, Commonwealthman or 'Old Whig' views that the problem for British politics was to diminish the potential for arbitrary executive power by increasing the independence of the legislature. That independence was threatened by the Septennial Act (1716), the declining proportion of those entitled to vote, the falling numbers of free boroughs, and the existence of substantial new urban and manufacturing areas without representation. During the American and French revolutions the issues of popular representation and democratic participation moved to the centre of British political writing and controversy. From the beginning of the American Revolution arguments for manhood suffrage developed in Britain (either unattached to property or using the ownership of one's own labour as a sufficient form of property (Price 1778: 24,

80)) and became an important component of radical politics in Britain in the 1790s, and thereafter of the popular radicalism of the early nineteenth century. Manhood suffrage was a minority preference throughout the 1790s, but from then the widening of the suffrage is firmly on the political agenda of those seeking political reform. However, where, earlier in the century, claims were linked to a sense that reform would redress the balance with the crown, by the end of the century a mélange of claims about the original form of the Anglo-Saxon constitution, the natural rights of man, expedience, utility and so on were used to support reformers' claims.

In these shifts in the commitments of 'republicanism' the claim is not that every writer influenced by the republican paradigm followed the trend but that the broad lines of debate increasingly did. In this process, the more classically inspired language of republicanism evident in the early eighteenth century became mixed promiscuously with other strands of political and philosophical thought – Lockean natural-law theory, Scottish political economy, moral epistemology, civic jurisprudence, dissenting models of church government, early forms of utilitarianism and so on. These multiple strands were woven into an increasingly broad consensus in the second half of the century – one that took the institutions, traditions and constitution of the British state as largely given and shared an expansive, undogmatic and not always terribly coherent language in which to debate their differences. But a further consequence was that the language of republicanism, rather than providing an integrated and sophisticated explanatory and normative paradigm for politics, became increasingly thinned and accommodated to a wide range of potentially divergent political and philosophical positions whose coexistence and interweaving resulted in a latitudinarianism in British politics comparable to that in its establishment's theology.

This is true for Britain, and it also partly plausible as a way of understanding the American case, in which a similar range of arguments cohabit, until pressed into more dogmatic form in the Revolutionary War. In France, while individual thinkers work with aspects of the tradition, notably Montesquieu and Rousseau, the influence of the Machiavellian and Harringtonian inheritance is less extensive, and owes a good deal to Montesquieu's stay in Britain in the 1730s. But it is less a part of the culture and practice of politics in France, which remained more hierarchical and exclusive in character. Whereas the participatory institutions of American townships and state governments, and those of the British Parliament, provided arenas for the practice of virtue, civic-mindedness and some version of citizenship, the French court did not, and the *Parlements* struggled in vain for a more substantial role. When the monarchy collapsed, and the country faced foreign invasion, classical images of civic glory and incorruptible virtue produced a zealous extremism and some of the century's most bizarre political events. As Whatmore (2000) shows, it is only in the aftermath of the Terror that a more liberal republicanism begins to find a voice.

A further indication of the increasingly diffuse character of republican language is that it sits uncomfortably alongside more traditional Enlightenment claims for the power of reason. The weakness of reason and rationality, the strength of men's passions and their overweening ambition drive them to form states, and then overreach themselves and risk all. The balance of powers and mixed government are presented, for the most part, as lucky accidents: chanced on rather than designed. Civic virtue is required to mould human nature, not express it. The republic is an achievement precisely because it cannot be willed by those who have not been steeped in its *moeurs* and disciplined to appreciate its order. Rousseau epitomizes the republican commonplace that republics cannot rationally be willed in a state of nature:

> For a young people to be able to relish sound principles of political theory and follow the fundamental principles of statecraft, the effect would have to become the cause; the social spirit, which should be created by these institutions, would have to preside over their very foundation; and men would have to be before the law what they should become by means of law.
>
> (Rousseau 1762: 196)

A fundamental incompatibility is implied between social-contract arguments and the commitments of the republican tradition, yet the traditions often interleave without embarrassment (whether at the hands of Algernon Sidney or Rousseau himself).

It is the very malleability of republicanism that makes it increasingly difficult to think of it as a language that constrains or shapes the way that political writers interpret the world. If not at the beginning of the century, then certainly by its end, republicanism had become fractured and was increasingly modified by or absorbed into other traditions, so that it has little or no structure to support the surviving inflections and rhetorical flourishes. In losing its coherence and form, its materials become susceptible to dramatic reworking in a way that redefines republicanism and momentarily links the radical and revolutionary agendas of Britain, France and America. At the end of the century radical republicanism has a brief effervescence that identifies it unequivocally with demands for populist democratic political participation. Thomas Paine (1737–1809) best represents that iconoclastic moment.

RADICAL REPUBLICANISM AND THE DEMOCRATIC REVOLUTION

When Paine embraced the term 'republic' from the early 1780s he defined it in apparently traditional terms:

> What is called a *republic*, is not any *particular form* of government. It is wholly characteristical of the purport, matter, or object for which government ought to be instituted, and on which it is to be employed, RES-PUBLICA, the public affairs, or the public good . . . It is a word of a good original, referring to what ought to be the character and business of government; and in this sense it is naturally opposed to the word *monarchy*, which has a base original signification. It means arbitrary power in an individual person.
>
> (Paine 1792: 230)

Figure 27.2 *Thomas Paine*, William Sharpe after George Romney. © the British Museum.

What is striking about Paine's republicanism is that he was not looking for a mobilized republic, mass political virtue, and an active and engaged citizenry. Indeed, he betrays an almost complete lack of interest in politics as a distinctive and creative domain of agency. By the time of his *Rights of Man, Part Two* (1792), he had become still more expressly libertarian – seeking to cut government and taxation, and to enable every individual to take his or her place within a commercial society by providing them with support for those in distress and an initial capital for each with which to begin adult life. The demand for simplicity in government was not driven by a sense of the simplicity of republican *moeurs* and the potential for civic virtue among the citizenry. It is a demand for the removal of the institutions of monarchy and aristocracy – portrayed as corrupt, leechlike political excrescences on the social body. It is the court, the king and his ministers, with their webs of patronage, sinecures and pensions, which subvert representative institutions. Without these elements, society is, as he says, in almost every aspect capable of self-regulation:

> the more perfect civilisation is, the less occasion it has for government, because the more does it regulate its own concerns and govern itself . . . All the great laws of society are laws of nature. Those of trade and commerce, whether with respect to the intercourse of individuals, or of nations, are laws of mutual and reciprocal interest. They are followed and obeyed because it is in the interest of the parties so to do.
>
> (Paine 1792: 216)

It is society that Paine represents as the basis for a consensual order, linked by commerce and mutual interest, with a very minimal degree of political intervention. The scope of politics is extremely narrow: representatives pass laws that the people periodically confirm or rescind, but society should be allowed largely to get on with its business without interference. Paine also rejected the core Polybian model of mixed government as an illusion: monarchy is 'the Popery of government' and the hereditary aristocracy 'an insult and imposition on posterity' (1776: 15).

After the success of the American Revolution had confirmed his belief in the new democratic order, Paine brought his heady and iconoclastic brew back to Europe. It informed his *Rights of Man* (1791), his reply to Burke's *Reflections*, and broadened the 'debate on the French Revolution' by the radicalism of his views, the vehemence of his defence, and his ability to command an extremely wide popular audience through sales in the hundreds of thousands. The British reform movement was not Painite in doctrine, but his pamphlet was the most circulated and widely known, and his audience clearly felt the power of his willingness to think the unthinkable, and say the hitherto unsayable, especially with respect to the institutions of monarchy and aristocracy, the illusion of the British constitution, and the true liberties of the free-born Englishman: 'what is this metaphor called a crown, or rather what is a monarchy . . . ? Doth the goldsmith that makes the crown, make the virtue also?' (1791: 175); 'the idea of hereditary legislators is as inconsistent as that of hereditary judges, or hereditary juries, and as absurd as an hereditary mathematician, or an hereditary wise man; and as ridiculous as an hereditary poet-laureat' (1791: 134). Above all, Paine offered his readers a very democratic reading of the impact of Enlightenment on the practice of government in the Western world: 'what we now see in the world, from the Revolutions of America and France, are a renovation of the natural order of things, a system of principles as universal as truth and the existence of man, and combining moral with political happiness and national prosperity' (1791:194).

Rights of Man: Part the Second (1792) was more radical still. Instead of focusing on events in France, it presented America as the embodiment of 'a revolution in the principles and practice of government' (Paine 1792: 220). It offered an example of a society, freed from government, united by the bonds of society, and constructing its institutions by constitutional convention, or acts of popular sovereignty. In taking America as the exemplar Paine epitomizes the view that, where Europe had only fomulated theories of Enlightenment, America achieved the full, practical realization of its principles (see Commager 1977). It was coupled with a set of proposals for the distribution of the tax revenues saved by the avoidance of war, which in many respects anticipates the welfare states of the early twentieth century. Paine's radicalism took a decidedly more practical turn in France in July 1791, following Louis XVI's flight to Varennes, when he produced a republican manifesto with Brissot and Condorcet. In two years Paine introduced a reading of republicanism, and of the American and French revolutions as the expressions of the sovereign rights of their people, which rode rough-shod over the latitudinarian consensus which marked much English political debate.

The broad outline of Paine's work is not dramatically original. He combined Lockean natural-rights traditions with Enlightenment optimism, and a confidence in the sufficiency of society, with an intense (and intensely entertaining) anti-monarchical and anti-aristocratic fervour. What makes Paine's work distinctively important is its profound influence on popular radicalism. Its reach was so extensive that, even though its universalist, natural-rights language was resisted in favour of local traditions and customary claims, its implicit message was taken to heart. That message was that the people had the right to judge, the right to discuss politics, the right to hold their governments accountable, and the right to change their form of government, and that this right was inalienably theirs as men. Paine was hardly the only author to write in this way, but it was his fortune (and misfortune, since it nearly cost him his life on the guillotine) to act as the most prominent link between three radical movements: those for American independence, for the reform of the British Parliament, and for the eradication of the *ancien régime* in France. He linked them in practice and in theory, for the British especially but also partly for Americans. His reading of the events was initially more classically Old Whig (of which there remain signs in his *Common Sense* of 1776 and *Crisis Letters* of 1776–83). But it became progressively more radical, more confident about the progress of reason, more conventionist and contractualist in character, and more universalist in its commitment to natural rights and their inalienability. And its 'silences' on the equality of women and slavery could be easily rectified by the logical extension of the core doctrine. His principles was designed for the masses and coincided with their stepping on to the political stage. They were progressive, rejecting the past as outdated; they were fundamentally egalitarian, having no time for hierarchy or birth; and they accorded Paine's readers the inalienable right of judging their institutions and reforming them if they saw fit.

Subsequent generations of radicals often used a constitutional rhetoric in the demands they made of Parliament, but their organization and principles of participation were egalitarian, democratic and profoundly influenced by Paine. In the space of twenty years, popular radicalism comes of age in the three countries. The disastrous turn of the French Revolution, following the collapse of the centre of political power and the gathering of armies on its borders, did not change that fact, but it did fundamentally realign the structure of the political agenda. Throughout the eighteenth century, the apparently ineradicable assumption was that the power of the crown was the major threat to liberty and the established order. In the wake of the Revolution, liberals and conservatives – as they became for the first time – sought to preserve the state (and liberty and security) from the capricious irrationality of a mobilized populace.

Radicalism, liberalism and conservatism were outcomes for Britain of the French Revolution. They draw on a common inheritance of eighteenth-century political language, but do so in ways that replace that broad pragmatic consensus with terrain that is sharply ideologically divided. The conservative/liberal divide over the respective weight to be given to order and the state, as against the liberties and constitutional rights of the people, is in stark contrast to a popular radicalism inclined towards egalitarianism, democratic rights and the sovereignty of the people.

Britain was not alone. In America the *Federalist Papers* argued for the fragmentation of the popular will in a system designed to ensure the cross-cutting play of interests. In France Benjamin Constant's *The Liberty of the Ancients Compared with that of the Moderns* (1819) depicted the republic at arms as a historical fantasy to be replaced by a limited republic, in which the private concerns of individuals could be protected against extremism. In nineteenth-century Britain John Stuart Mill looked for ways to moderate the impact of public opinion and the masses on the political elite whom the Enlightenment had made possible, and who had rightly challenged the ascendancy of those whose claim to rank and power depended on birth rather than ability and talent. Substantial reform is resisted decade after decade, and it takes nearly a century for Britain to have much claim to be a democracy.

By the early nineteenth century the language of classical republicanism that had marked the political debates of the previous century largely disappears. Yet its eclipse also attests to its success. Monarchical forms may have persisted, but the real republican legacy was the widespread delegitimation of arbitrary government. For a time at least, liberal constitutionalism was established as the basic model for modern states – constraining both the ruler and the sovereign people. But that model was always contested, precisely because it excluded the more populist, democratic and egalitarian elements of the political spectrum, and it had to struggle in the second half of the century to contain the growing class conflict within liberal-constitutionalist constraints. Towards the end of the nineteenth century, in some parts of Europe, we find more positivist, elitist and often authoritarian political theories emerging that turn back to appeal to elements of the classical tradition, and which adopt the rhetoric of the common good. But they do so while displacing the classical emphasis on liberty and intensifying its demands on the patriotism of its supporters through a nationalist rhetoric. This new radical right offers a republicanism without Enlightenment or liberty. It is a disquieting resurgence for a tradition defined by its repudiation of tyranny.

REFERENCES

Bailyn, Bernard (1967) *The Ideological Origins of the American Revolution*, Cambridge, Mass.: Belknap Press.

Barruel, Augustin, Abbé de (1798) *Mémoirs pour servir à l'histoire du jacobinisme*, London.

Bolingbroke, Henry St John (1738) *The Idea of a Patriot King*, ed. David Armitage in (1997) *Political Writings*, Cambridge: Cambridge University Press.

Commager, Henry Steele (1977) *The Empire of Reason: How Europe Imagined and America Realized the Enlightenment*, New York: Doubleday.

Emsley, Clive (1981) 'An Aspect of Pitt's "Terror": Prosecutions for Sedition during the 1790s', *Social History*, 6, 2: 155–84.

Harrington, James (1656) *The Commonwealth of Oceana and a System of Politics*, ed. J. G. A. Pocock (1992) Cambridge: Cambridge University Press.

Kant, Immanuel (1784) *Beantwortung der Frage: 'Was ist Aufklärung?'; An Answer to the Question: 'What is Enlightenment?'*, in Hans Reiss (ed.) (1970) *Kant's Political Writings*, Cambridge: Cambridge University Press.

Machiavelli, Niccolò (1531) *Il Discorsi*, ed. Bernard Crick, trans. Leslie J. Walker with revisions by Brian Richardson (1970) *The Discourses*, Harmondsworth: Penguin Press.

Madison, James, Hamilton, Alexander and Jay, John (1788) *The Federalist Papers*, 2 vols, New York: J. and M. Lean; ed. Isaac Kramnick (1987) Harmondsworth: Penguin.

Milton, John (1658) *Angli Pro Populo Anglicano Defensio*, ed. Martin Dzelzainis, trans. Claire Gruzelier (1991) as *A Defence of the People of England*, Cambridge: Cambridge University Press.

Paine, Thomas (1776) *Common Sense*; (1791) *Rights of Man*; (1792) *Rights of Man: Part the Second*, all ed. Mark Philp in (1995) *Thomas Paine, Rights of Man, Common Sense and Other Political Writings*, Oxford: Oxford University Press.

Pettit, Philip (1997) *Republicanism: A Theory of Freedom and Government*, Oxford: Clarendon Press.

Pocock, J. G. A. (1973) *Politics, Language and Time: Essays on Political Thought and History*, New York: Atheneum.

—— (1975) *The Machiavellian Moment: Florentine Political Thought and the Atlantic Republican Tradition*, Princeton: Princeton University Press.

Porter, Roy, 'The Enlightenment in England', in Roy Porter and Mikuláš Teich (eds) (1981) *The Enlightenment in National Context*, Cambridge: Cambridge University Press.

Price, Richard (1778) *Two Tracts*; (1785) *Observations on the Importance of the American Revolution*; (1789) *A Discourse on the Love of our Country*, all ed. D. O. Thomas in (1991) *Price: Political Writings*, Cambridge: Cambridge University Press.

Rawson E. (1969) *The Spartan Tradition in European Thought*, Oxford: Clarendon Press.

Robbins, Caroline (1959) *The Eighteenth-century Commonwealthman*, Cambridge, Mass.: Harvard University Press.

Rousseau, Jean Jacques (1762) *Du Contrat Social*, trans. and introduction by G. D. H. Cole, rev. and augmented J. H. Brumfit and John C. Hall in (1973) *The Social Contract and the Discourses*, London: J. M. Dent & Son.

Skinner, Quentin (1998) *Liberty before Liberalism*, Cambridge: Cambridge University Press.

Whatmore, Richard (2000) *Republicanism and the French Revolution: An Intellectual History of Jean-Baptiste Say's Political Economy*, Oxford: Oxford University Press.

Wood, Gordon (1969) *The Creation of the American Republic 1777–1783*, New York: W. W. Norton.

—— (1991) *The Radicalism of the American Revolution*, New York: Vintage Press.

Wootton, David (1986) *Divine Right and Democracy: An Anthology of Political Writing in Stuart England*, London: Penguin Books.

CHAPTER TWENTY-EIGHT

THE NEW ECONOMICS OF THE ENLIGHTENMENT

Kathryn Sutherland

THE OLD ECONOMICS

From the middle of the eighteenth century, a set of trading principles and practices, dominant in Europe over the previous two hundred years, now known as mercantilism, was challenged by a variety of Enlightenment thinkers. The key features of mercantilism were monopoly of the home and colonial markets, restraint in the import of foreign goods, and a belief in the durability of reserves of precious metals or bullion. But its fundamental concern was the relationship between a nation's wealth and strength and its balance of trade. Under attack from liberalizing thinkers from the late seventeenth century onwards, mercantilism's leading exponents were such Englishmen as Sir Thomas Mun, a director of the East India Company, and Gerard de Malynes, a merchant and government official. By the mid-eighteenth century, mercantilist explanations of national wealth appeared primitive and inflexible in relation to an increasingly complicated economic expansion. In Scotland David Hume challenged as false the mercantilist equation of wealth and money, while in France a group of thinkers known as physiocrats (see below), led by François Quesnay, a surgeon by profession, directly opposed the mercantilists by arguing that agriculture is a primary source of wealth and proposing reforms of taxation and the currency, and the institution of free trade. Despite the acknowledged persuasiveness of the new economic thinking, in the wars it waged with France to maintain its trading monopolies with its North American, Caribbean and Indian colonies, British foreign policy remained effectively mercantilist for much of the eighteenth century. Navigation Acts dating back to the previous century enforced trading monopolies in sugar, tobacco and cotton-wool, while other goods had to be carried in British or plantation vessels owned and largely manned by British subjects.

Colonies were at the heart of European political and economic thinking in the eighteenth century. According to mercantilist theories, they were to be seen as valuable sources of raw materials, as a means of adding to the mother country's stock of bullion, as markets for surplus home products, and as dumping-grounds for excess population. The exclusive benefits of trade with colonies ensured a healthy and controlled circulation of wealth and a strong nation. As Montesquieu argued in *De L'Esprit des lois* (1748),

The colonies they [the European nations] have formed are under a kind of dependence, of which there are but very few instances in all the colonies of the ancients . . . The design of these colonies is, to trade on more advantageous conditions than could otherwise be done with the neighbouring people, with whom all advantages are reciprocal. It has been established that the metropolis, or mother country, alone shall trade in the colonies, and that from very good reason; because the design of the settlement was the extension of commerce, not the foundation of a city or of a new empire.

(Montesquieu 1748: XXI, xxi, 10–11)

In thinking about the use and value of money, the debate between the old and new economics centred on whether money could be considered as an end in itself (a stock of gold, for example) or merely as a commercial facilitator. For John Locke, a mercantilist sympathizer, money is 'some lasting thing that Men might keep without spoiling, and that by mutual consent Men would take in exchange for the truly useful, but perishable Supports of Life' (Locke 1690: 318–19). Sir William Petty, another mercantilist, made important contributions to monetary theory, arguing in *Political Arithmetick* for a hierarchy of productivity in terms of the perishability of goods. Food is the most perishable, followed in ascending order by clothes, furniture, houses, the working of mines and fisheries, and eventually the most productive employment (in terms of durability) is that which brings '*Gold* and *Silver* into the Country: Because these things are not only not perishable, but are esteemed for Wealth at all times, and everywhere' (Petty 1690: I, 269). It was an argument to which David Hume would later rejoin that 'If we consider any one kingdom by itself, it is evident, that the greater or less plenty of money is of no consequence.' As an anti-mercantilist, Hume was convinced of the unimportance of money as such, arguing instead that a nation's real riches lie in its raw materials, its people and their skills, all of which money merely measures as value: 'Money is not, properly speaking, one of the subjects of commerce; but only the instrument which men have agreed upon to facilitate the exchange of one commodity for another.' Its properties being substitutive rather than essential, '[Money] is none of the wheels of trade: it is the oil which renders the motion of the wheels more smooth and easy' (Hume 1741–2: 289).

The mercantilist explanation of wealth typically rested on notions of what we now describe as national self-sufficiency, cultural independence, the inelasticity of total demand, and the subversive threat of foreign merchandise. Committed in policy and practice to a nationally defensive economic strategy, mercantilism proposed to harmonize the private and public pursuit of wealth through a strong state presence in the market place and in the minds of its citizens. Accordingly, it was an article of mercantilist faith that the subordination of ranks within a closed economy served national security, as it was a prime mercantilist fear that the self-interested pursuit of free trade might unsettle the providentially fixed establishment of rich and poor. Mercantilists feared the levelling effect which they believed would follow the expansion of a consumer market. Indeed, what divides them from free traders are the political implications of commercial activity, not their view of man as everywhere impelled by the desire for gain, an aspect of human nature which they equally acknowledged.

When John Brown criticized 'our exorbitant Trade and Wealth', and distinguished the ruling 'Character of the Manner of our Times' as 'a *vain*, *luxurious*, and *selfish* EFFEMINACY' (Brown 1757: 29), he signalled the cultural danger inherent in the economic switch from mercantilism to free trade as the primitive fear it releases for the defeat of virtuous, or manly, restraint. According to mercantilist thinking, free trade jeopardizes the regulated universe of fixed resources, replacing it with an unfixed and potentially limitless generation of commodities. Such deregulation portends a destruction of national security by the potential for an imbalance of trade; it accelerates the growth of credit, with all the risks that entails; it approves and requires the mobility of property and an ever more complex system of exchange; and in releasing consumerism from social constraint, it even threatens the erosion of hierarchies, of rank and distinction, which the patriotic and patrician asceticism of mercantilism worked to uphold. Worst of all, it threatens to redefine relations between the sexes.

Not coincidentally, an unprecedented rise in the fashion for satires against women accompanied the early arguments for the deregulation of the economy and the advocacy of growth through consumption beginning to appear from the late seventeenth century. Against such liberalizing economists as Henry Martyn, John Houghton, Dudley North and Nicholas Barbon can be set Bernard Mandeville's provocative dissociation of virtue and the economy, *The Fable of the Bees* (1714), and the perverse role he assigns there to women in promoting this happy disjunction. Mandeville's cynical championship (in Remark *T*, added to the *Fable* in 1723) of female consumer-power as the linchpin of the healthy economy is explained by his identification of luxury (not restraint) with the national interest and his topsy-turvy defence of vice as the beneficial foundation of trade and full employment. Hence, '[T]he variety of Work that is perform'd, and the number of Hands employ'd to gratify the Fickleness and Luxury of Women is prodigious', and will be fully acknowledged as such by 'the experienc'd [male] Reader'. He,

> as soon as he shall have laid these Things together, and, from what he has observ'd in the common Affairs of Life, reason'd upon them consequentially without prejudice . . . will be oblig'd to own, that a considerable Portion of what the Prosperity of *London* and Trade in general, and consequently the Honour, Strength, Safety, and all the worldly Interest of the Nation consist in, depends entirely on the Deceit and vile Stratagems of Women.

Against such powerful incentives to trade, 'Frugality and all the Virtues together, if [women] were possess'd of them in the most eminent Degree, could not possibly be a thousandth Part so serviceable, to make an Opulent, powerful, and what we call a flourishing Kingdom, than their most hateful Qualities' (Mandeville 1723: 236–38). On female 'Deceit and Stratagems' 'depend' the 'Honour' and 'Strength' (traditional mercantilist male virtues) which maintain the nation's power.

Arguing in his turn for the economic necessity of some attempt at equilibrium in Britain's foreign trade and for the importance of government vigilance, Mandeville nevertheless diverges sharply from the extreme mercantilist condemnation of luxury as economically and morally enervating. For him, morality and economics are separate. People are naturally attracted to luxury, and foreign imports stimulate the domestic economy.

COMPETING SCHOOLS OF ECONOMICS

Three major schools of thought shaped economic discourse in the eighteenth century – mercantilism, physiocracy and Scottish political economy. Where mercantilism placed the emphasis on trade and commerce as indicators of national wealth, physiocracy (literally, 'the government of nature') directly opposed this, arguing that agriculture provides the only real return on investment and directs much of the general theorizing about society towards the rational planning of agricultural production. Its central tenet – that all wealth comes from the fruits of nature (not from towns and commerce, as in mercantilism) – encourages economists to develop ideas of how best to harness nature in order to improve living standards and relieve the suffering of the poor. These ideas included freedom of production and trade and a single tax on all, including the privileged, based on agricultural revenue. Physiocracy's chief proponents were the French thinkers Quesnay and Victor de Riqueti, Marquis de Mirabeau, and the modernizing Anne-Robert-Jacques Turgot, whose reforms are sometimes seen as ushering in French revolutionary ideas.

In arguing that both commercial and agricultural systems were vital to a nation's prosperity, the third, Scottish model presented itself as an advancement on mercantilism and physiocracy, but only by virtue of its assimilation of some of the best ideas of both. For example, the major concern of the Scottish philosophers David Hume, Lord Kames, William Robertson, Adam Smith, Adam Ferguson and John Millar, who shaped the new economic discourse, is to render all difference, beyond the simplest observations of biology and human psychology, explicable in terms of the economics of subsistence, of how people gain their livelihoods in different societies and times. Not only, they argue, will laws and institutions reflect a society's modes of production at any given time, but human personality and sexuality will be generated by the same economic means. This immensely influential idea is embedded deep in physiocratic thinking as Mirabeau and Quesnay outline it in their *Philosophie rurale* (1763).

Generally speaking, from the mid-eighteenth century, political economists regularly describe society's progress in terms of a model of subdivided labour, production and consumption. The wealth of nations, they suggest, is a complex network of private interests commensurate with the drives of its members at all levels of society, humble and elevated, to self-improvement through the acquisition of goods. Economic description, moreover, becomes at this time the origin of all social descriptions. Eighteenth-century economists extrapolate from theories of human nature universal laws to explain the observed 'facts' of contemporary conduct and to render 'natural' the widening division between domestic production and the public workplace. Whether defined as private or public, identity for male and female is now seen to be determined in the market and through the internalization and enactment of market forces.

In Britain such anti-mercantilists and balance-of-payments critics as North and Barbon start the economic argument from psychology which Adam Smith, John

Millar and other Scottish thinkers will perfect. As Barbon explains it, 'There are Two General Wants that Mankind is born with; the Wants of the Body, and the Wants of the Mind; To supply these two Necessities, all things under the Sun become useful, and therefore have a Value.' While the 'Wants of the Body', those 'things necessary to support Life', are few, the 'Wants of the Mind' or 'all such things that can satisfie Desire' chiefly promote trade. He continues by sketching a thesis which, in its late eighteenth-century form, will provide a psychologically plausible explanation of human appetite as the foundation of a free-market society:

> The Wants of the Mind are infinite, Man naturally Aspires, and as his Mind is elevated, his Senses grow more refined, and more capable of Delight; his Desires are inlarged, and his Wants increase with his Wishes, which is for every thing that is rare, can gratifie his Senses, adorn his Body, and promote the Ease, Pleasure, and Pomp of Life.
>
> (Barbon 1690: 13–15)

Like Hume fifty years later, Barbon argues for the vital stimulus that social emulation and the acquisition of perishable goods give to the national economy. North shares Barbon's confidence in the power of appetite to regulate the operations of the market – 'the growth of Wealth in the Nation . . . never thrives better, than when Riches are tost from hand to hand' (North 1691: 15) – and draws his examples from the same glittering and fragile world of luxury items. Coaches and lace, Indian chintz and muslin, these are what eighteenth-century men and women desire and what the new economic arguments legitimate in terms of a theory of nationally profitable consumption. '[I]t is an Invention to Dress a Man, as if he Lived in a perpetual Spring; he never sees the Autumn of his Cloaths,' declares Barbon (1690: 65). Adam Smith observes that, as a result of commercialization, 'the accommodation of a European prince does not always so much exceed that of an industrious and frugal peasant as the accommodation of the latter exceeds that of many an African king, the absolute master of the lives and liberties of ten thousand naked savages' (Smith 1776: I, 24).

When Joyce Appleby states, in a classic article, that '[t]he acceptance of the idea of universal economic rationality was the key step in the triumph of modern liberalism' (Appleby 1976: 514), she recognizes what historians of other disciplines have defined as the naturalizing drives behind any liberal consensus. The economic rationality of the eighteenth century, which finds its full and late celebration in Adam Smith's *Inquiry into the Nature and Causes of the Wealth of Nations* (1776), triumphed by virtue of a total programme of explanation, in terms of history, moral philosophy and sexuality, which anticipated and rendered natural Smith's eventual economic analysis. In the new Enlightenment thinking economic explanation becomes the foundation for all human behaviour.

Central to this 'scientific' explanation of human progress is the so-called 'four-stages theory', which dominated French and Scottish debate in the second half of the eighteenth century. In its generally deployed Scottish form, the stadial explanation posits four types of economic organization through which societies will, in the course of nature, progress in fixed order: the hunting, pastoral, agricultural and commercial economies. In its French, physiocratic interpretation, society falls into three organizational types with, unsurprisingly, the commercial model harnessed to the agricultural, rather than developing beyond it. Though, as a theory of causation the stadial subsistence theory becomes more complex, incorporating at the primary level more variables as society enters its modern phase, always uppermost is the shaping initiative of the economy in prompting identity. As, for example, in the 'general truth' stated by the Scottish historian William Robertson, that '[i]n every inquiry concerning the operations of men when united together in society, the first object of attention should be their mode of subsistence. According as that varies, their laws and policy must be different' (Robertson 1777: I, 324).

The determining power of economic activity within history extends even to those aspects of behaviour which we might consider timeless or essentially private. For example, Adam Smith argues that primitive societies are unacquainted with sexual jealousy, which is a function of advancing manners and prosperity (Smith 1766: 439). Similarly, Lord Kames pronounces that '[w]here luxury is unknown, and where people have no wants but what are suggested by uncorrupted nature; men and women live together with great freedom, and with great innocence'. And he deduces from this that '[j]ealousy accordingly is a symptom of increasing esteem for the female sex . . . It begins to have a real foundation, when inequality of rank and of riches takes place' (Kames 1779: vol. 1, 327–8). Accordingly, societies in their earliest stages are characterized by so-called 'masculine' qualities (physical strength, martial prowess, the 'virtues' of conquest, dominion and self-denial); 'progress', on the contrary, is marked by the gradual ascendancy of 'feminine' qualities (the accumulation of property, the privileging of leisure and comforts, the attendant increase of sexual desire and humanity). The power of the late eighteenth-century stadial theory, as outlined by Scottish thinkers, ensured that economic factors became key elements in any explanation of the social activities of men and women.

ECONOMICS FOR A CONSUMER SOCIETY

Before the systematic Scottish analyses of Smith and Millar, Hume had cut through the familiar early eighteenth-century condemnation of luxury to voice his enthusiasm for advanced commercial societies and the diffused benefits of a self-regulating consumer economy. In 'Of Refinement in the Arts' he sets out to prove that 'ages of refinement are both the happiest and most virtuous', because '[t]he more these refined arts advance, the more sociable men become' (Hume 1741–2: 276–8). Sociability is the cardinal characteristic of a refined or commercially progressive society. After Hume, Kames, Millar, Robertson and Smith all take sociability as the barometer of economic progress.

In several essays Hume addresses the anxieties of mercantilists to preserve an ideal hierarchic polity of citizens trained in martial, masculine virtues. Luxury, like extensive foreign trade, he claims, can be shown to contribute conveniently to the enlargement of individual happiness *and* to the strengthening of the state. Happiness itself, he insists, lies in the accumulation of a variety of manufactures and commodities, prompted by the envy and profitable emulation of the productivity of others across the social divides. In the pursuit of 'the pleasures of luxury' and 'the profits of commerce', the individual, regardless of rank, becomes less indolent and more energetic. Debated throughout the eighteenth century were the competing moral and economic advantages of extended luxury and lower-class poverty. After Hume, Smith defines economic prosperity in terms of 'the great multiplication of the productions of all the different arts . . . which occasions . . . that universal opulence which extends itself to the lowest ranks of the people' (Smith 1776: I, 22).

Paradoxically, too, the conditions of international peace which trade both requires and advances are also those which render the state more powerful for times of war: the profitable manufactures of peace serving to enlarge the public revenue from taxes without hardship to anyone. Progressive commercialization, Hume argues, is only one aspect of a simultaneous infusion of energy through all areas of society, which, under the influence of the 'spirit of the age', fosters new refinements in philosophy, politics, astronomy and poetry. 'Thus', he writes, '*industry, knowledge*, and *humanity*, are linked together, by an indissoluble chain, and are found, from experience as well as reason, to be peculiar to the more polished, and, what are commonly denominated, the more luxurious ages' (Hume 1741–2: 334–6, 268–70, 277–8).

Industry, knowledge and humanity, the three 'indissoluble' elements in Hume's advanced commercial model, are all purchased by labour because '[e]very thing in the world is purchased by labour', Hume declares in 'Of Commerce' (Hume 1741–2: 267). The most refined products of leisure are, in fact, among the deferred products of industry at the most inferior levels of manufacture: poetry is supported by shipbuilding. Hence Hume's only apparently inconsequential statement that '[w]e cannot reasonably expect, that a piece of woollen cloth will be wrought to perfection in a nation which is ignorant of astronomy, or where ethics are neglected' (Hume 1741–2: 277–8).

According to Hume, the expanding commercial interests of eighteenth-century Britain entailed a more thorough regrouping of the divisions in society than ever before, and in particular a widening of the influence of a middle ground of citizen-consumers. The hierarchical model of aggression, acquisition and defence which characterizes societies in the agricultural stage will, at the commercial stage, be modified, he argues, by those multilateral networks which promote and consolidate the interdependent pursuit of mutual benefits in accordance with which manufactures and commerce thrive. Through commerce, a rigid feudal model of discrete and warring authorities is transformed into an enveloping system of institutions, incorporating some new freedoms and the levelling of old hierarchies. Hume concentrates on a newly empowered social division, the 'middling rank' of gentry, tradesmen and merchants, who represent 'the best and firmest basis of public liberty' (Hume 1741–2: 284). They form the heterogeneous group who will be considered by social historians to represent the general interests and condition of British society for the next two hundred years.

SEXUAL COMMERCE AND THE NEW ECONOMICS

The Scottish thinkers are particularly preoccupied with the changing position of women through the ages. For them, the role of women provides insight into the structures of different societies. Because women reveal their social status through their absorption of, and responses to, trends in man's social interactions, the 'commerce of the sexes' in an age of manufacture will acquire new features. The danger, as John Millar interprets it in *The Origin of the Distinction of Ranks* (1771; revised 1779), lies in the loss of correspondence between manufactures and 'propriety'. Yet a well-regulated sexual economy, characterized by the virtuous domestic restraint of the female, is the true measure of national prosperity – what Millar terms 'the real improvements arising from wealth and opulence' (Millar 1779: 123–4).

As Hume outlines, the control of commercial activity by consumer demand would appear to relate directly to women's assumption of a more public presence in society. But the shift from mercantilist to liberal thinking, with its new confidence in markets, signals the overthrow of all restraint, moral and material, and in so doing reverses the relative status of the sexes. The terms of the argument suggest that this shift is a step sideways in the progressive economic history of civilization. Hence, man's capacity for self-realization through his rights of possession becomes an increasingly insecure foundation for authority as society approaches the fourth, commercial, stage.

In the Scottish Enlightenment debate in particular, woman is made to represent a demanding conjunction: on the one hand, domestic prudence and control; on the other, an expanded international consumer-power indicative of national advancement. Hence, the most detailed economic arguments provide the discursive context for considerations of the history of the female sex. At the same time and justified by the increasingly complex exchange between the sexes which is observed to distinguish society in a commercial age, sexuality is now first explained as the cultural representation of sex and is seen to include a set of characteristics which are social. By placing the economy and sexuality in a historical context, it became possible to conceive of society as a set of male and female features which themselves evolved, and were worthy of analysis. As Millar argues, escalating production and new freedoms in sexual behaviour are aspects of an opulent *laissez-faire* economy. In particular, the prosperity of the open market presented women with irreconcilable standards of domestic good by which the monitoring of social appetite was in direct competition with the injunction to consume.

At the same time, cultural and economic theorizing ignored women's active engagement in labour outside the home. Women's employment in workshops and factories, in textile industries and down mines was a vital contribution to the early industrialization of Britain in the eighteenth century. Employed in increasing numbers in the manufacture of mass-consumer goods, women were not only domestic purchasers, but were grossly exploited as wage-earners. As the century drew to a close, their employment came to depend on the low status of their labour and their lack of rights as a workforce. From medieval times, urban women were admitted to a wide range of trades, as blacksmiths, plumbers, carters, booksellers and petty retailers, regardless of any contrary notions of sexual appropriateness. But as cheap labour came to play a crucial part in the industrializing process the status of their contribution was systematically eroded. At one end of the scale, the small independent trades (a traditional resource for businesswomen) were squeezed out in favour of extensively capitalized workshops capable of employing a large labour force; at the other, male journeymen fought for the unionization (and exclusive masculinization) of their crafts. This, too, meant narrower opportunities for women to serve apprenticeships and earn skilled wages. Their labour became a means to drive down the rates for a job and to bypass orthodox training customs; hence, they were as readily laid off as engaged by employers. By the 1790s a generation of polemical women writers, like Priscilla Wakefield, in her *Reflections on the Present Condition of the Female Sex, with Suggestions for its Improvement* (1798), were complaining about such unfair practices, noting the role of male economic thinkers in suppressing their grievances.

ADAM SMITH AND THE WEALTH OF NATIONS

The comprehensiveness of Adam Smith's vision of a self-regulating market appears to confirm him as the chief technician of the new economics of the Enlightenment. In fact, *An Inquiry into the Nature and Causes of the Wealth of Nations*, his historically based theory of commercial capitalism, shares much with the stylized history writing of other Scottish Enlightenment thinkers, especially with Hume and Millar, Smith's pupil at Glasgow University. In providing a history on a grand scale, Smith identifies precisely how economics is the motor for those cultural transformations which occupy his contemporaries in the emergent Enlightenment disciplines of anthropology, psychology and sociology.

Figure 28.1 *Adam Smith*, James Tassie, paste medallion (1787). From Collectanea Petrus Iohannus, by permission of the owner.

In his *Wealth of Nations* Smith discusses economic activity alongside the social institutions which provide its context and the human traits which define its character. In the first of the five books which constitute the work, Smith argues that the key to both national and individual prosperity is a division of labour, which entails specialization in almost all complex activities. Landlords, workers and capitalists seek to secure rent, wages and profit from manufacture and trade. It is this tripartite division of the socio-economic structure and, in particular, emphasis on its crucial third component, capitalism and its profits, which distinguish the *Wealth of Nations* as a major new contribution to economic thinking. After discussion of accumulation in the second book, Smith turns to the relations between town and country in what, in Scotland and much of Europe, was still an agrarian economy. Like his mentor Hume, he sees a steady growth towards commerce and manufacture, displacing exclusively rural economies. In the fourth book Smith criticizes the twin aspects of mercantilism – war and empire – and shows their harmful effect on British domestic and foreign policy. The American Revolution (1775–83), which finally broke during the latter stages of the writing of *Wealth of Nations*, appears in context like a vindication of its anti-mercantilist stance. Smith offers only qualified support to the physiocrat's belief in the superiority of agricultural production. In the final book he examines legitimate forms of government expenditure, revenue raising and public debt, and even explores the possibility of some services funding themselves.

Smith was not the first to suggest that division of labour might be essential for economic growth. Anticipations of the view appear in Petty, Locke and Mandeville, and the famous example of pin-manufacture was already well known before being dramatically publicized by Diderot in the *Encylopédie*. But Smith extends the idea to 'every art', asserting that in a commercial economy even philosophy itself will subdivide and 'the quantity of science [will be] considerably increased' (1776: Book 1, ch. 1, §10). But while specialization enhances commercial progress and mutual reliance in a workforce, it reduces individual self-sufficiency. Nevertheless, a diversified economy is kept healthy because of the self-interest underpinning the co-operative practice of exchange: 'every man . . . lives by exchanging, or becomes in some measure a merchant' (1776: Book 1, ch. 4, §1).

The psychological foundations of Smith's moral philosophy are always behind his arguments about economic behaviour and account for some of the more unexpected remarks in Wealth of Nations. For example, he argues, in apparent opposition to Mandeville, that a desire to save rather than to spend fuels economic growth, because frugality secures social approval, and that enhances self-esteem. His point is also that savings, by increasing the stock of capital available, set in motion a greater quantity of productive labour than direct spending, although both contribute to a consumer economy (1776: Book 2, ch. 3, §§14–42).

Smith's larger contention is that the complex of desires which drive human behaviour and regulate the economy in all its aspects is directly subject to neither reason nor morality. Mutual dependence fuels economic growth but its basis is self-interest in the context of a psychological compulsion to exchange. As he commented in his earlier *Lectures on Jurisprudence*: 'that principle in the mind which prompts to truck, barter, and exchange, tho' it is the great foundation of arts, commerce, and the division of labour, yet it is not marked with any thing amiable' (Smith 1766:

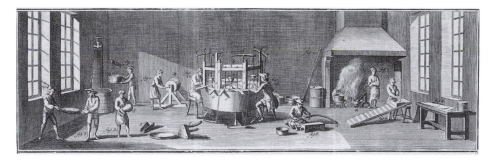

Figure 28.2 *Epinglier*, from Denis Diderot and Jean Le Rond D'Alembert (1751–80) *Encyclopédie, ou Dictionnaire raisonné des sciences, des arts et des métiers, par une société de gens de lettres*; vol. V of facs. edn (1964) Paris: Cercle du livre précieux. This illustrates the final stages of pin manufacture. By permission of the National University of Australia.

527). Material progress, it is implied, is attended by no corresponding moral advance; and its economic description entails no necessary ethical judgement. In the new economics effects rather than motives are what matter. As the science of an advanced commercial society, the new economics became increasingly distinguished, in the course of the nineteenth century, from moral debates about what wealth is good for. But it is worth noting that, for Smith, an indirect ethics, or simply a cohesive optimism, is still at work and observable by the economist.

Tucked away in the final chapter of the third book, for example, is Smith's important explanation of the non-providential birth of modern commercial society itself. The unintended by-product of a shift in consumption by the feudal landowners who exchanged their control of land for manufactured goods, the commercial revolution was secured when land itself fell into the hands of merchants, as anxious to become country gentlemen as landowners were to buy their manufactured luxuries. Hence it is that the improvement of the countryside, as much as the 'gradual descent' of the landowners' fortunes, is the consequence of commerce. Smith writes, '[a] revolution of the greatest importance to the publick happiness, was in this manner brought about by two different orders of people, who had not the least intention to serve the publick' (1776: Book 3, ch. 4, §17). Such apparent negligence of motive is itself a function of the social ethic of natural liberty which characterizes free-market economics. According to Smith, the free market left to itself will naturally produce, for example, the balance of supply and demand on which its successful operation depends. Nevertheless, Smith's widespread use of the term 'nature' is not morally neutral; he frequently uses it to describe ideal states of affairs.

Only in the final book does free-market thinking find a check and Smith modify his famous declaration that 'I have never known much good done by those who affected to trade for the publick good' (1776: Book 4, ch. 2, §9). Now he attempts to delineate the duties that fall to the state in a society of natural liberty, a subject which continues to be the unsolvable paradox at the heart of free-trade economics. What is the role of the state where the private sector is free to generate its own self-regulating policies? For example, in outlining the potentially deleterious effects on the human intellect of the division of labour – imaginative and moral poverty, even social delinquency – Smith suggests that the state should shoulder some responsibility and compensate its members through programmes of basic education (1776: Book 5, ch. 1, pt 3, article 2, §61 and article 3, §1; and *ibid.*, §§12–13). Unlike some late twentieth-century advocates of the free market, Smith does not imagine the stateless society. Nor could he do more than glimpse the problems awaiting an industrializing society. Smithian free-market philosophies have been adapted to far-reaching ends in the intervening centuries, yet he could not anticipate multinational interests, the dangerous consumption of non-renewable natural resources or the problems of overpopulation and post-industrial societies. For all that his thinking was progressive, his experiences as an eighteenth-century citizen were of pre-industrial, small-scale technologies, and of regional, or at the very most national, interests.

REFERENCES

Appleby, Joyce (1976) 'Ideology and Theory: The Tension between Political and Economic Liberalism in Seventeenth-century England', *American Historical Review*, 81: 509.

B. N. [Barbon, Nicholas] (1690) *A Discourse of Trade*, London.

[Brown, John] (1757) *An Estimate of the Manners and Principles of the Times*, London.

Hume, David (1741–2) *Essays Moral, Political, and Literary*; repr. (1963) London: Oxford University Press.

[Kames, Lord Henry Home] (1779) *Sketches of the History of Man*, 3rd edn, 2 vols, Dublin.

Locke, John (1690) *Two Treatises of Government*, ed. Peter Laslett (1960) London: Cambridge University Press.

de Malynes, Gerard (1622) *The Maintenance of Free Trade, According to the Three Essential Parts of Traffique*, London.

Mandeville, Bernard (1723) *The Fable of the Bees*, ed. Phillip Harth (1970) Harmondsworth: Penguin Books.

Millar, John (1779) *The Origin of the Distinction of Ranks; or, An Inquiry into the Circumstances which Give Rise to Influence and Authority in the Different Members of Society*; rev. 3rd edn (1781) London.

Mirabeau, Marquis de and Quesnay, François (1763) *Philosophie rurale*, Paris.

Montesquieu, Charles Louis de Secondat, Baron de (1748) *De L'Esprit des lois*, ed. F. Neumann, trans. Thomas Nugent (1949) New York: Hafner Press.

Mun, Thomas (1664) *England's Treasure by Forraign Trade; or, the Ballance of our Forraign Trade is the Rule of our Treasure*, London.

[North, Sir Dudley] (1691) *Discourses upon Trade*, London.

Petty, William (1690) *The Economic Writings of Sir William Petty*, ed. C. H. Hull (1899) 2 vols, Cambridge: Cambridge University Press.

Pocock, J. G. A. (1985) 'The Mobility of Property and the Rise of Eighteenth-century Sociology', in *idem*, *Virtue, Commerce, and History*, Cambridge: Cambridge University Press.

Robertson, William (1777) *History of America*, 2 vols, London.

Smith, Adam (1766) *Lectures on Jurisprudence*, ed. R. L. Meek, D. D. Raphael and P. G. Stein in (1978) *Glasgow Edition of the Works and Correspondence of Adam Smith*, vol. 5, Oxford: Clarendon Press.

——— (1776) *An Inquiry into the Nature and Causes of the Wealth of Nations*, ed. R. H. Campbell, A. S. Skinner and W. B. Todd in (1976) *Glasgow Edition of the Works and Correspondence of Adam Smith*, vol. 2, Oxford: Clarendon Press.

Turgot, Anne-Robert-Jacques (1766) *Reflexions sur la formation et la distribution des richesses*, Paris.

Wakefield, Priscilla (1798) *Reflections on the Present Condition of the Female Sex, with Suggestions for its Improvement*, London.

CHAPTER TWENTY-NINE

MAKING A BETTER WORLD

Enlightenment and philanthropy

⎯⎯•◆•⎯⎯

David Garrioch

In 1780 a small group of men in Paris founded 'an association of several persons who, inspired by benevolence, work to assist, through uniting their fortune and their understanding [*lumières*], suffering and indigent virtue' (*Calendrier philantropique* [*sic*] 1789: 31). The new body was called the Société Philanthropique, and within a very few years it could claim as members a brilliant cross-section of Paris high society: by early 1789 it had 744 subscribers, half of them nobles, including members of the most powerful families in the kingdom and no fewer than seven serving or past government ministers, bishops and dukes. Other members were clergymen, financiers, lawyers and office-holders of all kinds (Duprat 1993: 65–75). By the late 1780s they were directly assisting some 1,500 poor people in Paris, as well as providing funds to other charitable bodies. Within France the Société provided a model for a host of similarly named societies in provincial towns, a profusion of philanthropic associations that provoked the Parisian commentator Louis-Sébastien Mercier (1740–1814) to exclaim that 'No previous century has seen benevolence and charity distribute their largesse more liberally, or with greater constancy and compassion' (Mercier 1782–8: vol. 2, 902).

Mercier's statement was typical of Enlightenment self-congratulation. Yet in certain respects he was right to distinguish the philanthropic endeavours of his age from those of previous centuries. This chapter outlines the main features of Enlightenment philanthropy, and suggests that it was, if not entirely new, certainly qualitatively different from what had gone before. It was not a heroic step on the onward march of human progress, as the Enlightenment itself imagined, nor primarily a new form of social control, but a product of debates and changing social and political practices closely linked to changes in the European world-view and to the emergence of new national, racial, class and gender identities.

FEATURES OF ENLIGHTENMENT PHILANTHROPY

The Société Philanthropique was in many respects the archetypal philanthropic organization of the late Enlightenment. Although there had long been many charitable bodies in Paris – hospitals, monasteries, charity schools, religious confraternities

and mutual-aid societies – it was unlike any of them. First, it was independent of the Church and of government, a new kind of association that was simultaneously public and private. In this respect it resembled other, earlier Enlightenment institutions, like Thomas Coram's Foundling Hospital and many other charities founded in London from 1720 onwards, like several hospitals established in Paris in the 1770s and 1780s, the Irish houses of industry of the 1770s, the Freemasons' orphanage opened in Stockholm in 1753, and many similar institutions across Europe (Innes 1999: 236; Roche 1987a: 197; Dickson 1988: 155–6; Johansson 1984: 98). Like them, it depended on a mixture of private foundation and public subscription. The Société Philanthropique, like a number of other 'societies' that sprang up in the late eighteenth and early nineteenth centuries, departed from these earlier foundations in its focus on charitable *activity*, rather than on a particular institution. It differed even more markedly from earlier forms of charity, and was, in fact, suspicious of most established poor-relief institutions (Andrew 1989: 44–134; Innes 1998: 37–40).

A second distinguishing feature of the Société was its secular character. There was no mention in its publications of spiritual aims, its emphasis being rather on the importance of its work for the suffering poor and above all for society as a whole. It departed, therefore, from the dominant Christian tradition in which the act of giving was as important as the gift. In that tradition charity was encouraged as a duty to God and as a gesture which would help redeem the giver (Roche 1987a: 186–7; Andrew 1989: 3, 12–15). Most mid- to late eighteenth-century thinkers, by contrast – including many within the Churches – thought of giving as a duty to humankind. They recognized that the benefactor would enjoy the gratitude of the poor and the admiration of their fellow-citizens, but made little or no mention of spiritual rewards, now or in the afterlife. This is not to say that religious motives – a Christian spirit of charity – were unimportant. Within Catholic and Protestant Europe alike, clerics and believers played a significant role in most benevolent associations (*Calendrier philantropique* 1789; Andrew 1989: 7–43; Innes 1998: 33–7). In northern Germany the Pietists, a reform movement within the Lutheran Church, pushed for the same sorts of changes to poor relief as many writers of the Enlightenment, while the Dutch Protestant Maatschappij tot Nut van 't'algemeen (Society for the General Good) of 1784 has been described as a 'social church' (Decker 1998: 135). Nor did Enlightenment philanthropists see themselves as abandoning Christian belief. 'Charity', wrote Mercier, once again an eloquent spokesman for educated Parisians, 'has a sublime depth that "benevolence" lacks; it is the love of the created being as the work of the Creator' (Mercier 1782–8: vol. 2, 902). The 'paganism' even of the French Enlightenment has been greatly exaggerated.

Nevertheless, most philanthropic thought of the period was secular in that, if it invoked religious duty at all, it stressed serving God by serving humanity and set physical needs above spiritual ones. These were not new arguments, but they had not been the dominant ones. In the eighteenth century, though, they were put strongly by influential reformers within the Churches. Thus the theologian Ludovico Muratori (1672–1750), often identified as a key figure within the so-called 'Catholic Enlightenment', argued that the needs of the living should take priority over concern for the souls of the dead, and that Christian charity should be directed towards

Figure 29.1 *Captn Thomas Coram*, William Nutter (1796), after William Hogarth. After years of perseverance, in 1739 Captain Thomas Coram succeeded in obtaining the charter for the London Foundling Hospital, which was opened two years later. By permission of the National Library of Australia.

assisting the poor rather than to memorial Masses (Pullan 1996: 78). Mainstream Christian charity of the early modern period had accepted that 'the poor you shall have always with you'. From the middle years of the eighteenth century, by contrast, Enlightenment philanthropy increasingly rejected the view that the presence of the poor was simply part of God's plan, designed to recall the affluent to holiness. Rather, it saw poverty as a social ill that could be cured by determined and appropriate action (Duprat 1993: xvii; Andrew 1989: 13–22; Norberg 1985: 91, 164; Jones 1982: 1–2).

To achieve this, a two-pronged approach was necessary. First, philanthropy needed to go beyond immediate assistance and find ways of helping people to escape permanently from the affliction of poverty. This was the intention underlying the reformed poor-relief programmes in late eighteenth-century Hamburg, Bremen and other northern German cities, in Bohemia, and in a number of other places, where instead of being given alms or food to tide them through a crisis, the 'genuine poor' were given work and trained in skills that might in future provide them with a living (Bernard 1994: 242, 244). The same general principle led to growing support, towards the end of the century, for dispensing aid to people in their homes, recognizing the importance of the family as both an economic unit and a moral influence. Keeping families afloat in this way, it was hoped, would prevent their members from falling into crime and permanent poverty; though the same logic could be used to justify the removal of delinquents who might lead the others astray, or, as in the case of the London Philanthropic Society, founded in 1788, the separation of children from their parents in order to give them a properly moral and vocational education (Cavallo 1998: 109; Andrew 1989: 135, 156–62, 183–4). The idea of helping people to remain independent through hard work also inspired a number of ambitious pension schemes that drew on the new statistical science to calculate average longevity and the regular investment necessary to provide a modest ease to workers in their old age (Cunningham and Innes 1998: 6–7; Piarron de Chamousset 1770; Faiguet de Villeneuve 1763; Price 1771).

Enlightened philanthropic concern therefore went well beyond conventional poor relief, and this too distinguished it from older forms of charity. The poor and the disadvantaged were to be taught to help themselves, freed from the ignorance, superstition and hopelessness that drove them to crime or left them in poverty. The educational programmes of the Dutch Society for the General Good, the creation of public libraries across Europe and North America, the provision of medical care, and the founding of institutions like that of the Abbé de l'Epée (1712–89) – a school to teach the deaf and dumb to communicate by signing – were all inspired by such ambitions (Dekker 1998: 135; Duprat 1993: 19–22; Mortier 1979: 178–81). Through such schemes, as a 'Citizen of Philadalphia' put it in 1787, 'the stock of human happiness shall be raised to the utmost height, to which the nature of man is capable of attaining' (Lloyd and Burgoyne 1998: 212).

BEYOND MODEL INSTITUTIONS:
REFORMING SOCIETY

Yet, to achieve this noble goal, creating model institutions and programmes was not enough. Enlightenment thinkers stressed repeatedly that the greatest impediments to human improvement were outworn institutions and bad laws that perpetuated ignorance, superstition, poverty and inequality, and hence crime, prostitution and unnecessary suffering. Growing numbers of writers attacked the giving of alms (both private and institutional), the existing Poor Laws, the hospitals, the prisons, the workhouses and other long-standing forms of poor relief. Hospital and prison mortality rates were extremely high. And all of these institutions, they said, failed to tackle the underlying causes of human misery, and often made matters worse, perpetuating poverty by discouraging the poor and the indolent from being industrious and making provision for the morrow (Payne 1976: 48–54; Norberg 1985: 259). In mounting such an argument, they were again building on older ideas. It had long been commonplace, even among proponents of Christian giving, to condemn indiscriminate charity. 'They indeed who prefer an Idle and vagabond Life of Beggary before honest labour, ought not to be encouraged in it by Relief, but abandoned to the Wretchedness which they chuse', preached Archbishop Secker in the first half of the century, and most educated people agreed (Andrew 1989: 19). Many, indeed, suggested that the idle poor should be forced to work, an idea which underlay the reform of poor relief in the Habsburg Empire in 1704, the creation of workhouses in England, Scotland and Ireland early in the century, and of similar institutions in Holland, the German states, Austria and later in France (Dickson 1988: 150–1; Bernard 1994: 241; Innes 1999: 239–52). But by the second half of the century, while some were still prepared to argue for harsh workhouses, more people came to feel that such institutions failed in what should be their central aim: to reform the poor and the delinquent.

A second fatal flaw of existing institutions, many critics suggested, was that, although they consumed excessively large sums of money, they did not help the genuinely deserving: those who were too proud to accept charity or who were thrust aside by able-bodied beggars. Workhouses did nothing to assist poor widows burdened with children, elderly men with infirmities or orphans (Innes 1999: 260, 275–6; Adams 1990: chs 6, 9). The solution was to restrict poor relief to such groups. And this was indeed the principle followed by most of the privately funded hospitals of the later eighteenth century and by the Société Philanthropique, which assisted only workers aged eighty or more, pregnant women, widows and widowers with young children, families with nine children or more, and injured workers with at least three children. It dispatched inspectors to 'comfort' the poor, but also to check that these conditions were met (*Calendrier philantropique* 1789: 36–9).

But longer-term solutions, reformers increasingly insisted, required much more far-reaching measures. Placing poverty and poor relief in a larger economic frame-work, they took up the argument that indiscriminate charity perpetuated poverty by giving the poor too great an assurance of assistance, but stressed the damage this caused not only to the poor themselves but also to national prosperity. If there were no incentive to work, they suggested, the supply of labour was reduced, and so was productivity. At the same time, funds devoted to poor relief consumed resources that should be used to create new wealth. These ideas were disseminated by groups of economists – in the German-speaking world by those known as 'cameralists', notably Johann von Justi (1720–71); and in France by the physiocrats, particularly François Quesnay (1694–1774) and Anne-Robert-Jacques Turgot (1727–81). They broadly agreed that poverty was the product of a malfunctioning economic system and that the solution was to fix the economy first, but there were fundamental disagreements between these groups over the role of the state and the relative importance of agriculture and manufacturing. The cameralists saw state-sponsored reform as the answer, urging governments to take over poor relief, particularly from the religious orders, and to encourage manufacturing (Lindemann 1990: 74–8, 100–2). The political economists and physiocrats, on the other hand, placed their faith in the market. For them, the solution was to remove 'artificial' obstacles to its operation and to the movement of labour. They condemned the proliferation of customs barriers and tolls and attacked the guilds, which controlled the labour market in almost all European towns, as obstacles to commerce (Bernard 1994: 241–2; Herr 1958: 50–7). In Catholic areas they called for reductions in the number of monasteries and convents, which they saw as a drain on resources and whose celibacy they condemned as an impediment to population growth and hence prosperity. The removal of such anachronisms, they argued, would enable everyone to find work, leaving only the sick and the disabled, the old and the very young in need of assistance (Innes 1999: 252–5; Adams 1990: 33–5, 123–6; Norberg 1985: 261–5).

Governments, even absolute monarchies, were not immune to the new philosophy, nor to demand for reform from an increasingly vocal, educated public that included many of their own bureaucrats and policy-makers. Here, too, nevertheless, there was no sudden break with the past. New philanthropic thinking blended with concern about social order and with an older kind of paternalism to mobilize governments and local elites in harmonious co-operation. The *ateliers de charité* established throughout France in the early 1770s to provide work for the unemployed enjoyed both government support and large contributions from local landowners, merchants and clergy that were actively solicited by the authorities (Olejniczak 1990–1). Meanwhile, with similar motives, Joseph II (1741–90) institutionalized across the vast Habsburg domains the Armeninstitut that had been set up in Bohemia by the philanthropic nobleman Johan Buquoi, in reaction against the old system run by the religious orders. Both church and state poor-relief funds were diverted to the new institutions, which depended on the co-operation of local elites and particularly of the parish clergy (Bernard 1994: 243–6; Lis and Soly 1979: 212–13). A similar blend of monarchical paternalism and enlightened philanthropy motivated the Paris police in the 1770s and 1780s: like the *philosophes*, they saw poverty as a result of social evils, though, like them, the police stopped short of condemning economic inequality. Responsible for maintaining order in the city, in the service of the monarchy but increasingly of an abstract 'public', they tried to create institutions that would reduce what a later century would term 'poverty traps'. They used revenue from gaming licences to establish a spinning workshop for poor women and a Mont-de-Piété – a state pawnbroker that lent small sums at modest rates of interest. They also founded a wet-nursing agency for poor families who could not afford to have the new mother's income reduced by the demands of an infant. The wet-nursing agency was also designed to reduce both abandonments of babies and the mortality rate among the newborn, a humanitarian gesture but one that drew equally on the populationist arguments of the political economists, who condemned the loss to the fatherland of so many potentially productive citizens (Garrioch 1992: 47–9).

NATION, STATE AND PHILANTHROPY

The conviction that both social stability and national prosperity depended on solving the problem of poverty was one reason why administrators and 'enlightened' monarchs increasingly harnessed the resources of the state to the reform programme. And, indeed, the physiocrats and cameralists placed growing stress on the importance of philanthropy to the well-being of the state and the nation. Philanthropy gradually became an element of good citizenship, and philanthropic reform proposals were published under titles such as *Vues d'un citoyen* (*Views of a Citizen*) and *Idées d'un citoyen* (*Ideas of a Citizen*). Nicolas Baudeau (1730–92), in 1765, called almsgiving (of the right kind) 'patriotic', while by the 1780s the Société Philanthropique insisted that assisting one's fellows was 'the first duty of the citizen'. The Dutch Society for the General Good saw its work as a means of reinforcing national unity, while in the city-state of Hamburg the key forum for the dissemination of enlightened ideas, and the major sponsor of poor-relief projects, was named the 'Patriotic Society'. Like other such bodies, it appealed to a sense of civic responsibility in order to raise funds. Populationist and economic arguments, the needs of war as well as humanitarian concerns, underlay the creation of the London Foundling Hospital in 1739. They continued to inspire philanthropists, like the 140 Parisians who in 1783 subscribed to a celebration in honour of a mother of nineteen who had just adopted a twentieth child (Duprat 1993: xxx, 55, 68; Adams 1990: 47–8; Dekker 1998: 135; Lindemann 1990: ch. 4; Andrew 1989: 54–9). The adoption of philanthropic ideals was directly linked to the development of national consciousness.

The new economic thinking and new ideas about national character provided a foundation for international action in defence of what would now be called 'human rights': reformers did not see any opposition between international and national considerations. Samuel Johnson (1709–84), John Wesley (1703–91), Adam Smith (1723–90) and others attacked the slave trade in the 1760s and 1770s, while in France there was a swelling critique from the *philosophes* and the physiocrats. In 1787 the Society for Effecting the Abolition of the Slave Trade was launched in London and by the late 1780s mass petitions were circulating throughout Britain. The arguments were of two sorts. The political economists stressed the economic ineffi-ciency of slavery: poor treatment and the absence of any incentive to work, wrote Pierre Samuel Dupont de Nemours (1739–1817), made slaves very poor workers. 'Liberty and property are the foundations of plenty and of good farming', insisted Pierre Poivre. Therefore, 'slavery has been as contrary to [European] interests as well as to natural law and to honour' (Poivre 1768: 94; Duchet 1971: 154–70). But it was the argument about honour that assumed greater significance after the American War of Independence. This was especially the case in Britain, where the anti-slavery

Figure 29.2 *View of the Foundling Hospital*, J. P. Boitard (1753). By permission of the Guildhall Library, Corporation of London.

movement had been widely condemned as contrary to the national interest, whereas after the war it became a defining symbol of British freedom and virtue. So, for some, did the reform of prisons and lunatic asylums, which they argued would set their nation above all others (Colley 1992: 352–4; Andrew 1989: 50).

In a similar way, when English and French travellers and intellectuals criticized serfdom in Poland and Russia, they contrasted the poverty of those 'backward' countries with the prosperity of their own free yeomen and peasant farmers: 'How can [the Russian serfs] possess that spirit and elevation of sentiment which distinguish the natives of a free state?' asked William Richardson. If Russia was to prosper, suggested Joseph Marshall in 1772, 'liberty must be diffused, all slavery of the lower ranks broken through, and every man allowed to become a farmer that pleases'. Madame Geoffrin (1699–1777), the Paris *salonnière*, was more prosaic: 'Everything that I have seen', she wrote to the *philosophe* Jean-Baptiste Le Rond D'Alembert (1717–83) from Warsaw, 'makes me thank God to be born French' (all quoted in Wolff 1994: 82, 85, 255). Such comparisons reinforced emerging national identities framed by notions of civilization, freedom and prosperity. Even within Western Europe, similar comparisons were made: the English believed that they looked after their poor better than Catholic France, and that this reflected their superior religion and better government, and underlay (and justified) their greater prosperity (Wolff 1994: 81–8, 360–1; Lough 1987: 49; Andrew 1989: 11; Colley 1992: 368–9).

Nevertheless, there was a self-consciously international element in eighteenth-century philanthropic thought and action that was part and parcel of Enlightenment universalism. Again, it built on one tradition of Christian charity, in which donors often felt themselves to have a primary responsibility to the poor of their own area: this was how they interpreted the biblical injunction to 'love thy neighbour'. Most early modern forms of charitable giving were inclusive, reinforcing bonds between the affluent and the poor, who were recognized as having reciprocal obligations and rights by virtue of belonging to a single community (Cavallo 1998: 113–14). By the late eighteenth century, however, mutual obligations within the local community were being complemented and even replaced by a broader sense of responsibility. Here again, enlightened thought was not entirely new, because there was a powerful theological argument that stressed the greater selflessness of giving to strangers from whom no return could be expected (Andrew 1989: 3). But, as local horizons gradually broadened into national ones, and the emphasis shifted from the donor to the recipient, educated Europeans felt a growing responsibility for people beyond their own community.

This was related to the expansion of European trade and colonial possessions and with the growing rapidity of communications, which made educated Europeans of all ranks increasingly aware of other parts of the world. Thomas Haskell has pointed out that trade, particularly international trade, relied on mutual trust and created threads of interdependence: no merchant could function alone. In this way, he suggests, the development of market capitalism extended people's 'sense of causal involvement in other lives' beyond their own local community, and hence created feelings of personal responsibility for the sufferings of others (Haskell 1985: 559). It has also been suggested that the new career structures of middle-class men, particularly in trade and state service, encouraged them to reflect on their own place within a much wider territorial and social world (Hagemann 2000: 184). There was thus an important link, this work suggests, between the way individuals saw their own place in the world, and the way they interpreted their relationship to other people, even those they did not know.

Yet there was also an important and continuing religious dimension to these new ways of seeing the world: the reduction of anti-pagan propaganda that accompanied the end of wars against Islam and the slackening hold of the Churches on individual conscience both facilitated the spread of a broader sense of responsibility for human suffering. From an enlightened Catholic perspective, Manon Phlipon (1754–93), perhaps inspired as much by her reading of Jean Jacques Rousseau (1712–78) as of the Bible, worried about the souls of the heathen: 'I reflected on the extent of the world,' she wrote, '[on] the succession of the centuries, the march of empires . . . I found small-minded, ridiculous, appalling, the idea of a creator who condemns these innumerable individuals to eternal torment' (Phlipon 1905: vol. 1, 91). This new sense of common humanity was a key factor in the growth of anti-slavery organizations, and it contributed to the universalist discourse we associate with the Enlightenment.

RACE, CLASS AND GENDER IDENTITIES

Such humanitarian action, however, remained Janus-faced. It tended to stereotype the recipients of enlightened philanthropy, to make them, in the imagination of the donors, into ideal types without any agency or individual identity: poor but virtuous widows, worthy old men, noble savages. Such people were not threatening, and could thus be sentimentalized, becoming objects of compassion (Colley 1992: 355). The accompanying types against which they were contrasted – the sturdy beggars and vagabonds, the barbarous serfs of Eastern Europe, the savage American Indians, or the Hawaiians who murdered James Cook (1728–79) – were equally stereotypical. Both were part of the construction of a new self-image among educated Europeans, one based on culture, science and, increasingly, race. They began mentally to reconstruct both history and geography, imagining a chronological scale of civilization in which Western European countries were at the top and 'native' cultures at the bottom (Wolff 1994: 13, 19; Outram 1995: 75). The development of a humanitarian philanthropy thus went hand in hand with a growing conviction of the superiority of 'European' (in reality Western European) culture and civilization.

In the same way, philanthropy was part of emerging class identities among the European elites. The broadening of a sense of responsibility from the local poor to suffering humanity as a whole was a new form of 'boundary marking', cutting off the elites from the poor who surrounded them. It was part of a broader process by which the cultured, civilized elite distinguished itself from the vulgar masses. This was a function of Enlightenment sociability generally: the academies, the various literary and musical societies, the salons, the Freemasons were all socially exclusive yet relatively egalitarian in their internal proceedings. The same was true of the Société Philanthropique, which proclaimed 'a perfect equality between all its members, whatever their rank and condition' (Duprat 1993: 69). Yet it included only people of education and standing. As in other enlightened institutions, membership was almost certainly by invitation or nomination only. Precisely the same distinction applied when philanthropists founded public libraries, like that created by Abraham Redwood at Newport, Rhode Island, 'having nothing in View but the Good of Mankind'. In practice, such institutions were restricted, like Enlightenment itself, to the respectable (Raven 1996). The Freemasons, too, self-proclaimed philanthropists, loved to distance themselves from those they termed 'the profane' or 'the vulgar'. While in a technical sense this meant non-Masons, most lodges grouped people whose manners, wealth and education enabled them to mix easily. Where state and religious ceremonies of the baroque period publicly translated fine gradations of rank into visible distinctions, the key institutions of the Enlightenment drew a bold line between those on the inside and those on the outside. It was a very deliberate mechanism of exclusion, accentuated in the case of Freemasonry by the cultivation of secrecy surrounding ceremonies and accoutrements, while the membership of the lodges was widely known. In this case there was also a gender dimension, since women were usually excluded, but Freemasonry typified the same broad distinction between the educated and the unenlightened that underlay Enlightenment philanthropy (La Volpa 1992: 90–7). The sense of belonging to a wide, cultured public, defined by its enlightenment and in opposition to an 'other' composed of the vulgar, was a crucial factor in the formation of class consciousness.

Philanthropy was thus a crucial part of new collective identities that were developing in the eighteenth century. It was equally crucial to the definition of gender roles. Certain male philanthropists became heroes, as highly regarded as any victorious general or admiral, primarily for scientific discoveries and public foundations. Edward Jenner (1749–1823) was widely cited as a philanthropist for his work on smallpox; Antoine Augustin Parmentier (1737–1813) for his promotion of potato cultivation. Benjamin Franklin (1706–90) earned the title of 'friend of humanity' for inventing the lightning-rod. The Duc de La Rochefoucauld-Liancourt (1747– 1827) became widely known as a friend of the people for his establishment of a school farm to provide agricultural training to the sons of soldiers in his regiment, his promotion of vaccination, education, prison reform and savings schemes. It did not matter that his 'manufacture de bienfaisance', in which poor women were given jobs producing cloth, returned him a good profit. The same was true of Voltaire's agrarian reforms at Ferney (Duprat 1993: 3–4, 24–6).

The female models that abounded in the philanthropic anecdotes which became a regular rubric in many periodicals in the 1770s and 1780s were somewhat different. Although some men received praise for their sensibility, on the whole women were portrayed as naturally more compassionate than men, because they were more swayed by their emotions. Even a 'public' woman, such as the actress in the Paris Opéra Mlle Guimard, was moved by her 'natural' womanly instincts to become an almsgiver after she witnessed the extent of poverty in the suburbs of the city (Duprat 1993: 52–6). This was very much the literary image of the day: 'the misfortunes of humanity find her receptive,' wrote Louis-Sébastien Mercier of an ideal bride, 'and she could not hear them recounted without feeling almost indisposed' (Mercier 1782–8: vol. 1, 84). Male role-models were overwhelmingly philanthropic, in the new enlightened sense of actively changing the world, whereas those for women were more often charitable. Women's action focused on areas that were stereotypically female: women philanthropists were primarily mother figures – nurses and educators – moved above all by the woes of poor women and children. In accordance with this stereotype, the Parisian Société de Charité Maternelle, founded in 1788 by Madame Fougeret and assisted by funds from the male Société Philanthropique, aimed (according to its statement of principles) 'to recall to nature hapless mothers, degraded by poverty, who abandon their infants'. But, more broadly, 'its project is to restore the morals of the people' by strengthening family ties, an objective that soon attracted large numbers of supporters: court ladies and the wives of administrators, scientists, financiers and lawyers (Woolf 1991: 100–3; Duprat 1993: 91). Philanthropic images thus reinforced the increasingly influential image of women being designed by nature to fulfil a moralizing and familial role. Many women found this an inspiring role, and in some places used the new philanthropic approaches to move into areas of public life formerly closed to them (Innes 1998: 39; Pope 1977).

So there was indeed a set of ideas and practices that we can describe as 'Enlightenment philanthropy', one that was both qualitatively different from what had gone before, and inseparable from the intellectual and social movements that we describe as 'the Enlightenment'. In fact, philanthropy was central to the Enlightenment's definition of itself. Those two key elements of behaviour that were such central characteristics of the enlightened individual, sensibility and sociability, were both inextricably linked with philanthropy. Although it was feasible to be esteemed as a 'man of feeling' or a 'woman of feeling' without engaging in any charitable activity, philanthropy nevertheless became, for many people, the practical dimension of sensibility, the external sign of a sensitive soul (Sauder 1997). It was equally inseparable from 'sociability', which earlier in the century had meant simply the human tendency to live in society, but was redefined by the *Encyclopédie* in the 1760s as 'being well-disposed towards other men', 'the disposition which pushes us to do all that is within our power to help others' (Larrère 1997).

Admittedly, there was much in Enlightenment philanthropy that drew on earlier ideas and practices. Yet it differed from the older tradition of Christian charity in a number of important ways. It was far more secular, stressing change in the here and now rather than the spiritual elevation of either the giver or the recipient. And because it saw the key causes of human suffering residing in the faulty organization of human affairs, it saw the solution as nothing less than a wholesale reform of society, both through the creation of model institutions (very often removed from church control) and through the reform of existing foundations and laws.

EXPLANATIONS FOR THE GROWTH OF PHILANTHROPY

How, then, can we account for the appearance of this Enlightenment philanthropy, and at this particular moment? I have stressed the factors that were transforming – slowly and unevenly – the collective and individual identities of Europeans and European Americans. The growth of national states, accompanied by a new relationship between the state and the individual – particularly the educated, male individual – was one important factor. Another was the onset of class and racial consciousness and the set of demographic and economic changes that this accompanied. Along with all of these things went new gender identities, whose sources are similarly broad and much debated. Secularization was another central factor, rooted in the growth of toleration, European expansion, the new scientific knowledge, and the declining role of the Churches.

I have not presented Enlightenment philanthropy as a response to the growth in the numbers of the poor and the strain they placed on existing charitable institutions, even though there seems no doubt that increasing numbers of people in eighteenth-century Europe were being driven into poverty (Hufton 1974: 15–25; Roche 1987b: 86–91; Bernard 1994: 238–40; Lis and Soly 1979: 130–88; Jones 1982: ch. 2). Yet there was no direct connection with the new philanthropic thinking. First, the rising prices of necessities and the stagnation of wages were almost universal, yet the new ideas about poverty and how to deal with it varied in their timing and spread in ways that were not consistent with the incidence of poverty. The perception that the old system was not working was certainly important, but it was shaped more by where people lived and the nature of their contact with the poor than by the real incidence of poverty. Variations in official policy could have dramatic effects, since measures that increased the numbers or visibility of beggars in the cities were likely to have a significant impact on educated opinion. In the early 1770s, for example, the Parisian authorities decided to admit to the hospital system only those who had been born in the city. This excluded around 70 per cent of the population, many of whom therefore resorted to begging (Roche 1987a: 204). Thus the emergence and spread of enlightened philanthropy had more to do with changes in the shape and thinking of the educated elites – in their religious attitudes and in their perceptions of and relationship with the poor – than with the numbers or needs of the poor. Furthermore, there is some evidence that the new attitudes towards poor relief themselves contributed to the problem of poverty, at least for certain categories of the poor. In Paris, Grenoble and Montpellier, certainly, the old poor-relief system was less resourced by the early 1790s than it had been at mid-century, in part because of a dramatic drop in charitable donations and a trend towards new types of giving (Roche 1987a: 193–7; Norberg 1985: 171, 244; Jones 1982: 86–94).

Another approach to Enlightenment philanthropy is to present it as a new form of social control, designed less to relieve suffering than to oblige the labouring poor to internalize the work discipline and self-image required by the military and economic demands of European states, or by new methods of production for growing consumer markets, or by a patriarchal order under threat from new ideologies (Foucault 1977; Donzelot 1977; Lindemann 1990: 101; Finzsch 1996: 5–11). There is little doubt that social and political change diminished the effectiveness of certain forms of discipline, and produced new ones. It is also true that Enlightenment philanthropy adopted new ways of thinking that both reflected and created new identities, new awareness of the self and of the body that in some cases facilitated such types of control.

Yet social-control arguments can be overly reductionist, and certainly tend to underestimate the humanitarian commitment of most reformers. They also overlook the contested nature and the radical potential of much philanthropic thought: many reformers were very critical of rich and powerful groups in society. The anti-slavery movement is a good example, for it was directly at odds with the powerful mercantile interests that dominated many of the Atlantic ports. Much depends, too, on which part of Europe (or America) is the focus of study. Those who stress the development of mercantile and industrial capitalism often downplay the fact that outside England and the Low Countries many leading proponents of reform were less interested in providing a docile industrial workforce than in promoting higher agricultural productivity and rural population growth, often through a semi-seigneurial system that gave a key role to noble landowners. Similarly, those who stress state control – particularly historians of central Europe – perhaps forget that some philanthropic organizations presented a challenge to the state, not only through their implicit or explicit criticism of existing institutions, but through the very nature of their action. The Association de Bienfaisance Judiciaire, formed in Paris in 1787 and attracting 200 subscribers in its first year, aimed to provide legal aid to the poor, but, with critiques of arbitrary arrest and imprisonment one of the issues of the day, also to compensate those who had been unjustly detained. The Unitarians, who included such influential philanthropists as Joseph Priestley (1733–1804) and Richard Price (1723–91), were very critical of state poor relief, which, in their view, was corrupt and unfair (Duprat 1993: 82–8; Ditchfield 1998: 195–203).

While the focus in this chapter has been on the common elements in Enlightenment philanthropy, it is important to note the diversity of approaches and to acknowledge the vivacity of some of the debates among the reformers themselves. There were also very significant changes in thinking across the eighteenth century.

Where similar ideas and practices were adopted across Europe and America, England, Scotland and the Low Countries on the whole moved to new approaches earlier than other places. But there was no single pattern, a point stressed in much of the recent literature on poor relief, in particular, which has been concerned to distinguish national differences and to differentiate between Catholic and Protestant forms (Woolf 1986: 31–5).

Until recently, much writing about philanthropy told a familiar story of progress, tracing the steady growth of humanitarianism and often linking it with a 'civilizing process' that distinguished modernity from the benighted past. This was the Enlightenment's view of itself. Over the last generation, however, attitudes have become more negative, stressing the 'totalitarian' implications of the 'Enlightenment project', and focusing more on the 'dark side of the Enlightenment'. Neither of these depictions is the complete picture: light and shade, after all, are defined in relation to each other. Nor should we forget that between theory and practice there may be a vast gulf. Some philanthropists did not, we may suspect, always bear true charity in their hearts, while the most ardent ideologues did not always observe their own strictures. There were those who, with Samuel Johnson, stated firmly that giving alms was simply encouraging idleness, yet who often emptied their pockets to the beggars who surrounded them (Bremner 1994: 59, 86).

ACKNOWLEDGEMENTS

I would like to thank Stephen Lay for invaluable research assistance. All translations are my own.

REFERENCES

Adams, Thomas McStay (1990) *Bureaucrats and Beggars: French Social Policy in the Age of the Enlightenment*, New York and Oxford: Oxford University Press.

Andrew, Donna T. (1989) *Philanthropy and Police: London Charity in the Eighteenth Century*, Princeton: Princeton University Press.

Bernard, Paul P. (1994) 'Poverty and Poor Relief in the Eighteenth Century', in Charles W. Ingrao (ed.) *State and Society in Early Modern Austria*, West Lafayette: Purdue University Press.

Bremner, Robert H. (1994) *Giving: Charity and Philanthropy in History*, New Brunswick and London: Transaction Publishers.

Calendrier philantropique [*sic*] (1789) Paris.

Cavallo, Sandra (1998) 'Charity as Boundary Making: Social Stratification, Gender and the Family in the Italian States (Seventeenth–Nineteenth Centuries)', in Cunningham and Innes (eds) *op. cit.*

Colley, Linda (1992) *Britons: Forging the Nation, 1707–1837*, New Haven, Conn., and London: Yale University Press.

Cunningham, Hugh and Innes, Joanna (eds) (1998) *Charity, Philanthropy and Reform from the 1690s to 1850*, Basingstoke and London: Macmillan.

Davidoff, Leonore and Hall, Catherine (1987) *Family Fortunes: Men and Women of the English Middle Classes, 1780–1850*, London: Hutchinson.

Dekker, Jeroen J. H. (1998) 'Transforming the Nation and the Child: Philanthropy in the Netherlands, Belgium, France and England, *c.* 1780–*c.* 1850', in Cunningham and Innes (eds) *op. cit.*

Delon, Michel (ed.) (1997) *Dictionnaire européen des lumières*, Paris: Presses universitaires de France.

Dickson, David (1988) 'In Search of the Old Irish Poor Law', in Rosalind Mitchison and Peter Roebuck (eds) *Economy and Society in Scotland and Ireland, 1500–1939*, Edinburgh: John Donald.

Ditchfield, G. M. (1998) 'English Rational Dissent and Philanthropy, *c.* 1760–*c.* 1810', in Cunningham and Innes (eds) *op. cit.*

Donzelot, Jacques (1977) *The Policing of Families*, trans. Robert Hurley (1979) New York: Pantheon Books.

Duchet, Michèle (1971) *Anthropologie et histoire au siècle des Lumières*, new edn, postface by Claude Blanckaert (1995) Paris: Albin Michel.

Duprat, Catherine (1993) *'Pour l'amour de l'humanité': Le temps des philanthropes: La philanthropie parisienne des lumières à la monarchie de juillet*, vol. 1, Paris: Editions du CTHS.

Faiguet de Villeneuve, J. (1763) *L'Econome politique: Projet pour enrichir et pour perfectionner l'espèce humaine*, [London].

Finzsch, Norbert (1996) 'Elias, Foucault, Oestreich', in Norbert Finzsch and Robert Jütte (eds) *Institutions of Confinement: Hospitals, Asylums, and Prisons in Western Europe and North America, 1500–1950*, Cambridge: Cambridge University Press.

Foucault, Michel (1975) *Discipline and Punish: The Birth of the Prison*, trans. Alan Sheridan (1977) London: Allen Lane.

Garrioch, David (1992) 'The Police of Paris as Enlightened Social Reformers', *Eighteenth-century Life*, 16: 43–59.

Hagemann, Karen (2000) 'Gender Order in Prussia', in Ida Blom, Karen Hagemann and Catherine Hall (eds) *Gendered Nations: Nationalisms and Gender Order in the Nineteenth Century*, Oxford: Berg.

Haskell, Thomas L. (1985) 'Capitalism and the Origins of the Humanitarian Sensibility', *American Historical Review*, 90: 399–61, 547–66.

Herr, Richard (1958) *The Eighteenth-century Revolution in Spain*, Princeton: Princeton University Press.

Hufton, Olwen (1974) *The Poor of Eighteenth-century France*, Oxford: Clarendon Press.

Innes, Joanna (1998) 'State, Church and Voluntarism in European Welfare, 1690–1850', in Cunningham and Innes (eds) *op. cit.*

—— (1999) 'The State and the Poor: Eighteenth-century England in European Perspective', in John Brewer and Eckhart Hellmuth (eds) *Rethinking Leviathan: The Eighteenth-century State in Britain and Germany*, Oxford: Oxford University Press/German Historical Institute.

Johansson, Ulla (1984) *Fattiga och tiggare i Stockholms stad och län under 1700-talet*, Stockholm: Kommittén för Stockholmsforskning.

Jones, Colin (1982) *Charity and Bienfaisance: The Treatment of the Poor in the Montpellier Region, 1740–1815*, Cambridge: Cambridge University Press.

Larrère, Catherine (1997) 'Sociabilité', in Delon (ed.) *op. cit.*

La Volpa, Anthony (1992) 'Conceiving a Public: Ideas and Society in Eighteenth-century Europe', *Journal of Modern History*, 64: 79–116.

Lindemann, Mary (1990) *Patriots and Paupers: Hamburg, 1712–1830*, New York and Oxford: Oxford University Press.

Lis, Catharina and Soly, Hugo (1979) *Poverty and Capitalism in Pre-industrial Europe*, Hassocks: Harvester.

Lloyd, Katherine and Burgoyne, Cindy (1998) 'The Evolution of a Transatlantic Debate on Penal Reform, 1780–1830', in Cunningham and Innes (eds) *op. cit.*

Lough, John (1987) *France on the Eve of Revolution: British Travellers' Observations, 1763–1788*, London: Croom Helm.

Mercier, Louis-Sébastien (1782–8) *Tableau de Paris*, ed. Jean-Claude Bonnet, 2 vols (1994) Paris: Mercure de France.

Mortier, Roland (1979) 'Diderot et l'assistance publique, ou la source et les variations de l'article "Hôpital" de l'*Encyclopédie*', in J. Bingham and V. W. Topazio (eds) *Enlightenment Studies in Honour of Lester G. Crocker*, Oxford: Voltaire Foundation.

Norberg, Kathryn (1985) *Rich and Poor in Grenoble, 1660–1814*, Berkeley: University of California Press.

Olejniczak, William (1990–1) 'Working the Body of the Poor: The *Ateliers de charité* in Late Eighteenth-Century France', *Journal of Social History*, 24: 87–107.

Outram, Dorinda (1995) *The Enlightenment*, Cambridge: Cambridge University Press.

Payne, Harry (1976) *The Philosophes and the People*, New Haven, Conn.: Yale University Press.

Phlipon, Manon [Madame Roland] (1905) *Mémoires de Madame Roland*, ed. Claude Perroud, 2 vols, Paris: Plon.

Piarron de Chamousset, Claude-Humbert (1770) *Mémoire sur l'établissement de compagnies, qui assureront en maladie les secours*, n.p.: Chez d'Houry.

Poivre, Pierre (1768) *Voyages d'un philosophe, ou Observations sur les moeurs et les arts des peuples de l'Afrique, de l'Asi et de l'Amérique*, Yverdon.

Pope, Barbara Corrado (1977) 'Angels in the Devil's Workshop: Leisured and Charitable Women in Nineteenth-century England and France', in Renate Bridenthal and Claudia Koonz (eds) *Becoming Visible: Women in European History*, Boston: Houghton Mifflin.

Price, Richard (1771) *Observation on Reversionary Payments; on Schemes for Providing Annuities for Widows and for Persons in Old Age*, London: T. Cadell.

Pullan, Brian (1996) 'Charity and Poor Relief in Early Modern Italy', in Martin Daunton (ed.) *Charity, Self-interest and Welfare in the English Past*, London: UCL Press.

Raven, James (1996) 'The Representation of Philanthropy and Reading in the Eighteenth-century Library', *Libraries and Culture*, 31: 492–510.

Roche, Daniel (1987a) 'A Pauper Capital: Some Reflections on the Parisian Poor in the 17th and 18th centuries', *French History*, 1: 182–209.

—— (1987b) *The People of Paris: An Essay in Popular Culture in the 18th Century*, trans. Marie Evans, Leamington Spa: Berg.

Sauder, Gerhard (1997) 'Sensibilité', in Delon (ed.) *op. cit.*

Wolff, Larry (1994) *Inventing Eastern Europe: The Map of Civilization on the Mind of the Enlightenment*, Stanford: Stanford University Press.

Woolf, Stuart (1986) *The Poor in Western Europe in the Eighteenth and Nineteenth Centuries*, London: Methuen.

—— (1991) 'The Société de Charité Maternelle, 1788–1815', in Jonathan Barry and Colin Jones (eds) *Medicine and Charity before the Welfare State*, London: Routledge.

CHAPTER THIRTY

LAW AND ENLIGHTENMENT

———◆•◆———

Randall McGowen

The complex history of law in eighteenth-century Europe has a great deal to tell us about the paradoxical character of the Enlightenment itself. In one sense the promise of the law lay before the advocates of the Enlightenment as an ideal. Indebted as they were to the philosophers, jurists and scientists of the preceding century, they looked upon the discovery of laws as the highest activity of the human mind. Social progress seemed attainable if one could discover the true shape of human nature and use this knowledge to fashion legal codes. The law might then shelter individuals from the cruel effects of superstition and arbitrary power. A rationalized judicial system might reduce the costs and aggravations that flowed from multiple courts with overlapping jurisdictions, governed by dated and contradictory rules. In addition, reformed legal codes promised to make the state more efficient as it sought to advance social progress. Yet there was a tension among these various objectives. On the one hand, the law was seen as a contrivance, a device for the better regulation of society and the promotion of the ends of the state. Justice could be understood as the servant of government; it facilitated the operation of authority. Its deepest concerns were efficiency and obedience. On the other hand, some talked of the more sacred mission of the rule of law; it was to guarantee the rights of the individual and restrain the heavy hand of government. It offered a bulwark behind which liberty blossomed. Some of the most stirring prose of the period was written in support of the law as the weapon of justice against tyranny. No doubt these conflicting versions of the task of the law seldom found clear expression. Philosophers and legal scholars focused on the common concerns that united both perspectives, particularly the desire to weaken the dead hand of the past. Simplicity, fairness and predictability were principles that won universal admiration. The contest between efficiency and freedom, between the needs of the individual and the state, lay in the future.

Much more frequent were the complaints directed at the failings of the existing legal order. If the law was a frequent target for reform, it was because it loomed as an intractable obstacle to the triumph of a reasonable and humane social order. The law represented a massive institution, a set of ingrained habits and parochial interests that frustrated change at every turn. It was particularistic, encumbered with irrational customs and privileges. The operation of justice, particularly as painted by the *philosophes*, presented a portrait of absurdity, delay, venality and folly. The existing law was an embarrassment that frequently excited outrage. Pamphleteers offered biting satires on judicial authorities who perpetrated abuses. Still, the dilemma for the proponents of the Enlightenment was that legal tangles and particularism represented more than mere loss. For, in practice, these elements afforded protection for those who defended liberties against the threats arising from expanding royal absolutism. In England the defence of the common law helped to secure the triumph of limited monarchy, while in France the *parlements* mounted the most successful challenges to the sweeping claims made for royal power. The law could inspire dramatically different sentiments, depending on the specific circumstances when it came up for discussion.

The law was much more than a topic for debate. It was an old and prestigious institution, consisting of courts and officials, as well as a large and varied body of practitioners. The relationship between the ideal and the practical in the operation of justice was often dynamic and distant. Lawyers possessed both prestige and power, as individuals and as an occupational group. They had a vested interest in supporting an established order that afforded them status and a comfortable livelihood. For much of the century, lawyers were more active in defending traditional forms and arrangements, rather than agitating for reform. Still, the legal community was composed of educated men, and they were not untouched by Enlightenment publications, ideas and fashions. Enlightenment themes and rhetoric infiltrated legal circles. A few legally trained individuals embraced the movement with greater enthusiasm. By the end of the century the community was undergoing rapid transformation, brought on in part by a sudden increase in the number of practitioners. In the rough and tumble of professional life, some lawyers were more ready to put themselves forward as spokesmen for popular causes and as aspiring politicians. The occupation itself came to look less like a guild and more like a profession. These changes would have considerable consequences for how lawyers regarded the law.

The story of law and the Enlightenment, then, is not one of uniform development, let alone a tale of steady progress. The level of interest that it excited varied considerably over time. Attempts at legal reform can be traced back at least to the humanists of the sixteenth century. The publication of several celebrated works in the middle decades of the eighteenth century contributed new enthusiasm to the cause. Later still the task of legal codification came to preoccupy monarchs and legislators. Utility and reason promised new ways of judging existing practice and rules, and offered new models for how to compose codes of law. Still, it is easy to exaggerate how much changed. Despite all of the attention the law received from authors and officials, the results were ambiguous at best. Until the last years of the century, or perhaps the first decades of the next, concrete measures were limited or ineffective. Nonetheless, the effect of Enlightenment thought upon jurisprudential thinking would be immense.

THE PRACTICE OF THE LAW

The law was a powerful ideal. The ceremonies practised in courts, the rituals observed there, were meant to inspire reverence. The authorities intoned the familiar biblical injunctions about the origin of law in God's decrees, and spoke of the necessity of obedience as an antidote to human sin. The repeated public spectacles of terrible punishments served to reinforce this message. Rulers relied upon the frequent return to these solemn events to overawe the lower orders. The practical experience of going to law, however, often undercut these trappings of justice. The courts constituted a dense institutional network, with often conflicting jurisdictions. Courts existed in endless variety – church courts, manorial courts, merchant courts, courts of admiralty, royal courts. The law was learned in pieces, and different rules applied in different places. Roman law competed with customary law, while royal or parliamentary legislation created special regulations or exceptions. England might possess a single system of law, but this did not prevent it from being characterized by great complexity and frequent contradiction. In France, and even more in German lands, there were multiple jurisdictions. Legal treatises might try to lend coherence to this ramshackle judicial structure, but with little to show for the effort. The confusion gave hope to all classes that they might secure a favourable ruling, and, upon occasion, even the poor found a resource in these legal thickets. More often, though, the law produced expense, delay and frustration.

Lawyers were an inescapable element of early modern society. Throughout Europe, amid a confusing tangle of jurisdictions and competing legal traditions, practitioners of the law enjoyed similar wealth and status. They were easily recognized. The degree of their influence varied considerably from place to place, but they played a vital role in the life of communities everywhere, not only in the capital cities, but in provincial towns as well. Collectively lawyers acted as a closed corporation that carefully regulated entry, remuneration and the distribution of positions. They jealously guarded the privileges they enjoyed. While the law served as an important avenue to high positions in the state, the work of most lawyers involved such humdrum tasks as drafting legal instruments, representing the parties to disputes, or assisting in the collection of debts. As a group they inspired both envy and respect. They were the frequent butt of coarse jokes and bitter diatribes. An author in the English literary journal the *Monthly Review* complained in 1759 (vol. 21: 302) that 'the profession of the Law, which, next to religion, is of the highest importance to the peace and happiness of society, has, from the avarice and incapacity of its professors, incurred the reproach of being sordid and illiberal'. Prints and cartoons portrayed lawyers as vultures keen to clean the bones of their clients. Lawyers, Jonathan Swift remarked in 1726, formed 'a society of men . . . bred up from their youth in the art of proving by words multiplied for the purpose, that white is black, and black is white, according as they are paid' (cited in Lemming 2000: 18–19). Such gibes formed the staple of plays and popular jingles alike. They were the price to be paid for the success enjoyed by the legal profession.

The law offered an attractive career. When Johann Jakob Moser (1701–85), a German constitutional lawyer, contemplated in his youth a choice of careers, he saw three options: theology, medicine and the law. While he recognized that each choice

Figure 30.1 *The Bench*, William Hogarth. The main characters depicted here are Chief Justice Willes (with the pince-nez), who was both learned and a rake, and Henry, Earl Bathurst, later Lord Chancellor, who has nodded off. He reappears in profile above as part of a point which Hogarth is making about caricature, to show that it thrives through comic exaggeration rather than wild distortion of features. By permission of Martin Fitzpatrick.

promised comfort and prestige, it was not surprising that he followed his father in becoming a civil servant and jurist. The law promised a steady income and respectability. Still, there were few guarantees of success, especially if one lacked a family connection. The legal order constituted a finely graded hierarchy: it stretched from the drudges who scraped by on the tedious legal paperwork that formed so much of the routine of legal work to the heights composed of judges and the advisers to princes. The gulf between those whose clients were from the nobility and those who met the legal needs of modest farmers and shopkeepers was equally wide. The legal hierarchy took account of birth and wealth; more distantly, it recognized ability. The law enabled a fortunate and skilled few to rise high. Instances of dramatic social mobility were infrequent, but in a society where it was rare, the law appeared to be an avenue for the ambitious and clever to achieve advancement. More typically, the career was passed on carefully from one generation to the next, by members of clans who used their influence to advance their own. Occasionally a wealthy merchant might secure a legal education for a promising son. There were always some members of the order ready to complain that people from the less respectable classes were invading the bar, thus detracting from its honour. As the number of lawyers increased rapidly by the end of the century, the concern with overcrowding escalated. The competition for honour and income intensified as well.

Legal education varied widely from one region to another. In Germany the vigorous universities contributed to the rise of a sophisticated study of the law. Scottish universities likewise acquired a high reputation for the quality of the education they offered. In Italy ancient institutions continued to sustain a vibrant intellectual life, at least in places like Tuscany and Naples. In many other countries, however, the training amounted to little more than an apprenticeship in the rudiments of law. The Inns of Court in England offered more shadow than substance. Attorneys in France learned on the job, but barristers were supposed to possess a university education. By 1710 the barristers of Paris were required to attend legal seminars in order to complete their training. The provinces soon followed the lead of the capital. In England such a requirement met with little success. In both countries there were frequent complaints about the woeful state of legal education. These laments, however, may indicate rising standards rather than declining skills. Legal works – some prosaic summaries of cases and legislation, others reflecting a higher level of scholarship – poured from the printing presses. Lawyers contributed to the rising tide of pamphlet literature that surrounded every controversy; they joined literary and debating societies. If the quality of intellectual life in legal circles was not distinguished, lawyers nonetheless contributed an important audience for the reception of Enlightenment ideas.

LAWYERS AND POLITICAL STRUGGLE

Across much of Europe the bar enjoyed a large measure of self-regulation. This independence had political as well as legal consequences, and was fiercely defended. In England the relative autonomy of the law was the result of a long constitutional struggle. In France it owed more to the fact that legal authorities purchased office and so held it as a kind of property. In every state legal practitioners possessed a sense of themselves as belonging to a tight-knit group. They felt they had much to protect, and, since the law was a central aspect of government in the period, there were frequent occasions for conflict with other powerful groups, like the Church, the nobility or, especially, the prince. Indeed, some of the most spirited opposition to the expansion of executive authority in the eighteenth century arose not from those who sponsored Enlightenment notions, but from the proud and defensive legal fraternity. For much of the century, lawyers belonged to a conservative culture, bound by traditional ideas and rituals, jealous of any effort to infringe upon specific privileges. Only in its closing decades did the corporate character of the legal community begin to give way to more ambitious individualists who joined in popular struggles that opposed authority along new lines, some of them revolutionary.

The French case is instructive. By the early eighteenth century, the highest sovereign courts, the *parlements*, and especially the court in Paris, had become the chief opponents of royal power. Quiescent under Louis XIV, the magistrates of the *parlements* under the Regency sought to reclaim their right to question royal legislation. Religious tensions sharpened the rivalry. Jansenism, a movement among Catholics that desired moral reform and complained of the influence of the Jesuits, found influential supporters among the magistrates. In 1730–1, in the midst of a religious confrontation, Cardinal Fleury, the King's chief minister, attempted to control access to the order and to punish political misconduct. Lawyers rallied to the defence of the magistrates. They resisted what they saw as an attempt to infringe their rights. Ultimately the barristers went on strike, refusing to use the courts. The result was a suspension of their operation, to the great inconvenience of the rest of society. Outraged royal officials threatened to abolish a body which they accused of acting like a 'little republic'. The lawyers, in turn, complained of a royal assault upon the principles of justice. In the end, the crown was forced to back down. This episode foreshadowed conflicts of the mid-century which culminated in the momentous Maupeou reforms of 1771–4, when the Chancellor sought to break the power of the legal order and to defeat the independence of the *parlements*. In this struggle the lawyers issued an unusually large number of pamphlets, adeptly exploiting print to put their case before the public and to press more radical constitutional claims. On this occasion, however, the legal foes of the crown were less successful in preserving their interests. Only the death of Louis XV saved them from a major defeat. The upshot of the conflict surprised all sides: while the lawyers collectively lost ground, individual practitioners achieved a new prominence as champions of what they called a 'public interest'.

By mid-century, struggles around the law in France took on a new dimension with the rise of *cause célèbre*. Ostensibly no more than typical criminal cases, these episodes gave rise to sensational trials that found in the sordid details of particular crimes elements that spoke to the concerns of a wider audience. Voltaire's intervention in the Calas affair inaugurated the genre. In 1761 the son of a Huguenot family named Calas was found hanged. The family was slow to report the incident, perhaps from a desire to suppress evidence of his suicide, since the act was treated as a crime that deprived one of a decent burial. Rumour soon reported that the son, who was said to have been on the verge of conversion to Catholicism, had been murdered to prevent the change of faith. Despite his protestations of innocence, the judges found the father guilty, and he was broken upon the wheel. Voltaire seized upon the episode as a revelation of the religious bigotry and injustice that infected the operation of the law in France. Aided by two prominent lawyers, he presented compelling evidence that the father had been the victim of a cruel abuse of power. The wide publicity afforded to the case produced a public outcry. The Royal Council overturned the verdict of the Toulouse court that had condemned the father. Voltaire's use of the printing press to advance the cause of legal reform proved only the first of a succession of such cases that altered the perception of justice in France. Pamphlets and trial briefs that blasted corruption and intrigue sold in large numbers and became part of a political process that brought on a crisis of authority by 1788. When the climax arrived, lawyers comprised the largest group in the Estates-General, and they did much to shape the demands for reform.

The role of lawyers in the campaigns that surrounded the activities of the London radical John Wilkes, a politician who challenged the government during the early years of George III's reign, offers further evidence of this trend. Wilkes began his career by publishing a rabidly anti-ministerial paper called the *North Briton*. When the government arrested him for libel in 1763, under a general warrant, Wilkes successfully appealed to the courts, where a judge announced that these orders to arrest unnamed persons were illegal. Wilkes and his followers subsequently made frequent use of the courts to stage their dramatic appeals to the liberties of Englishmen against what they called the arbitrary actions of the government. Trials became set pieces in which the drama of brave citizens defending themselves against the cruel and wicked agents of the crown became vastly popular public performances. In addition to using the law to protect their activities, these London-based radicals made reform of the law a central concern. Lawyers were prominent in the creation of the Society of the Supporters of the Bill of Rights. News of these struggles found a receptive audience in the American colonies, where lawyers were busy articulating their grievances against an administration that they felt was violating the spirit and letter of the law that governed all Englishmen, both at home and abroad. Upon the successful conclusion of their revolution, American lawyers would help to compose a constitution based upon the lessons they had learned in these contests.

THE NATURAL LAW INHERITANCE

The most powerful intellectual movement acting upon legal circles in the eighteenth century was associated with the study of natural law. Strongest in Germany, this rich and varied tradition was an international movement influencing scholars in many lands. The seventeenth century had produced a dramatic break with earlier natural-law thought. The Dutch jurist Grotius (1583–1645) portrayed the relationship between human and natural law in a new light, carefully distinguishing both from divine law. In an age marked by the violence of deep religious conflict, he sought to show why law was binding, even in the absence of any accepted universal authority. Grotius argued that the principles of law were clear and self-evident if one used reason to investigate the human situation. Humanity, he suggested, was marked by the desire to live together and to enjoy our property in security. From this discovery, he derived rules which he believed were universal, not bound by differences of time or place. Right reason demanded that we live in peace with our neighbours and fulfil our obligations willingly. One could use logic to deduce a complete and self-sufficient system of law. Any particular human code was imperfect, constantly in need of being measured against the perfection of natural law. The challenge for jurists was to avoid being distracted by the particular differences that marked different nations. They should approach the confusing tangle of existing law guided by the light of reason.

While a host of eminent scholars followed the lines laid down by Grotius, sharply different versions of natural law emerged in the following two centuries. The debate was most intense, once again, in Germany. The philosopher Leibniz (1646–1716) and the jurist Christian Wolff (1679–1754) remained committed to the idea that God's law formed the basis for natural law. They were confident that human and divine reason overlapped, and that human nature could be improved by being brought into closer conformity with the eternal order. Samuel Pufendorf (1632–94) and Christian Thomasius (1655–1728), on the other hand, argued strongly for the complete separation of religion from law. For them, law was a product of state action; it had no divine sanction. Given humanity's passionate nature, will as much as reason played a role in the creation of the law. The goal of the law, then, was not perfection, but simply security and social peace. Lord Stair (1619–95), the leading Scottish jurist of the seventeenth century, followed a subtly different path. While he hoped that human law would conform to reason, he made more room for authority as a source of law, saying that in this respect law did not follow mathematics. He also attempted to show how Scottish law, even in its particularity, possessed a unity whose principles could be appealed to in reaching judicial decisions. Still, for Stair, the central challenge of legal work remained the same as it did for all who shared the natural-law perspective, to look for unity and reasonableness in all aspects of the law. This orientation gave impetus and direction to those who sought legal reform. Where there was diversity, obscurity or contradiction, the task of the jurist was to apply reason in the belief that greater clarity was possible. Advocates of legal codification drew confidence from such a claim. When Austria inaugurated a period of legal change, the crown required universities to offer courses in natural law, even if the books were written by Protestants.

Natural-law theories, however, were far from establishing undisputed supremacy, even in Germany. The imperial jurist Moser conducted a stout defence of existing practice against what he saw as the simplifying rationality and dangerous statism of the rival tradition. He was no friend of the kind of legal reforms that flowed from the Prussian court. Most of the books he published consisted of collections of laws and judicial decisions, organized by topic, with no attempt to define a wider system or logic. His great achievement was a huge compendium of German public law. He made little effort to solve the large philosophical questions that so troubled his opponents. He was equally uninterested in tracking down the earliest expression of a legal principle of the first appearance of a law. The task of jurisprudence, he believed, was to find the appropriate laws that applied to particular cases. The clear statement of contemporary usage should be enough to resolve legal disputes. He was confident that a society's best hope for stability lay in a reliance upon the pragmatic skills of the practising jurist. Moser was not an original scholar, but his great publishing enterprise reminds us of the diversity of views that characterized legal circles during the Enlightenment.

MONTESQUIEU AND BECCARIA

Occasionally the publication of a book creates a sensation that marks a pivotal trans-formation in the way a society approaches a subject. Within the space of two decades at mid-century, two such works appeared. The first was written by Montesquieu (1689–1755), an aristocrat who inherited from an uncle an important judicial position in Bordeaux. A man with a strong sense of his class and position, he took great pride in the management of his own estate. Yet he was also attracted by the salons of Paris, and was well versed in the currents of the early Enlightenment. The result was a distinctive style, wide-ranging and eclectic, critical and yet moderate. *The Spirit of the Laws*, published in 1748, was an instant best-seller, quickly translated into many languages, going through twenty-two editions in its first eighteen months. It was a peculiar work to claim such an influence, large, multifaceted, often indirect, nuanced in many of the judgements it offered on the institutions of his own day. It made room for a variety of positions without sponsoring any one exclusively. Elegantly written, the book was the antithesis of the typical weighty legal tome.

At the outset, Montesquieu adopted a position that appeared indistinguishable from that of natural-law thinkers. 'Law in general', he wrote, 'is human reason insofar as it governs all the peoples of the earth' (Montesquieu 1748: 8). Yet the entire thrust of his work was to demonstrate that reason was relative to a host of different circumstances, some natural, such as climate or geography, and some historical, such as customs, forms of government or economic institutions. These differences made it impossible to pass simple judgements on the multitude of different systems of law. Laws, therefore, must not only answer to reason, but must take account of the circumstances of a people. 'Laws', he argued, 'should be so appropriate to the people for whom they are made that it is very unlikely that the laws of one nation can suit another' (Montesquieu 1748: 8). These different relations formed 'the spirit of the laws'. His book was full of examples of the variety of human institutions and beliefs. He deftly surveyed an immense amount of material, some of it historical, much of it collected by European travellers. He was as likely to offer an example from China as from ancient Rome. His approach to these different cultural expressions was secular and objective; his relativism served to rob existing institutions of any special claim upon the feelings of his readers.

Despite the potentially corrosive effect of his approach, for Montesquieu the study of the law required caution and tact. He believed that laws should coincide with reason; he was ready to condemn slavery and too severe punishments as in conflict with basic human rights, but he was reluctant to attempt to alter legal institutions too quickly or radically. He doubted that such 'revolutions' could succeed. Still, he believed, there was much room for improvement. He adopted positions that embodied conventional Enlightenment ambitions for justice. Laws, he wrote, should be simple: 'The laws should not be subtle; they are made for people of middling understanding.' A legal code that was cluttered with obscure or conflicting principles was a snare to catch the unwary. 'Useless laws', he observed, 'weaken necessary laws' (Montesquieu 1748: 614–16). Equally, laws that were overly harsh made a people cruel, so wise legislators made penalties mild. Montesquieu believed in a government limited by law, and in the existence of intermediary institutions, like the *parlements* in France, that mitigated the operation of a ruling power. In sum, he presented a portrait of the law as evolving. Indeed, no system for him was static; change was inevitable in social organization. In this process social conditions shaped the law, and the law, in turn, helped to mould a people and their society. Herein lay the great significance of his book: it shifted thinking about the law, encouraging readers to look at it more critically and creatively. Legal systems were no longer endowed with a sacred character. While Montesquieu approached the law with care, others took his conclusions in a more radical direction, confident of their ability to produce a dramatic reformation of both law and society.

One area that attracted Montesquieu's particular attention was the criminal law. 'The citizen's liberty', he wrote, 'depends principally on the goodness of the criminal laws' (Montesquieu 1748: 188). He was not exceptional in this belief. Dissatisfaction with existing penalties and punishments was widespread by the early eighteenth century. Many states had moved away from the use of torture in criminal investigations, and there is evidence of a decline in the numbers being executed in a number of countries. These measures had sources other than the narrow movement of ideas. They drew upon wider cultural changes, above all the spread of new canons of conduct. The new sensibility owed much to the popularity of such publications as the English journals the *Tatler* and the *Spectator*. These periodicals helped to enshrine principles of reason, order and restraint as guides to social behaviour. Montesquieu had argued that the laws should be consonant with the feelings of an age, and the sentiments of his age were moving against such things as the public infliction of pain. These occasions came to seem more threatening, both at a social and a psychic level. The criminal law, once a means for enlisting a divine sanction in support of human laws, now seemed a measure of a society's moral level and a test of the character of its government.

Many of these attitudes were slowly gaining ground by mid-century, but the movement gained momentum with the publication of a widely acclaimed, thin volume written by an Italian aristocrat, Beccaria, in 1764. *On Crimes and Punishments* quickly became a publishing sensation, much to the surprise of its young author. Milan in the 1760s was home to a particularly vigorous society of men interested in the law. Beccaria had been inspired by the ideas he encountered in these circles. He acknowledged his debt to Montesquieu, even as his book testified to the differences between the two men. Montesquieu approached his topics in a roundabout fashion, while Beccaria was direct, strident and logical. The latter had none of the former's hesitation about proposing change: Beccaria's volume set forth a clear and simple programme of reform. His confidence was symptomatic of the shift in mood and opinion that marked the second half of the century. His task was not to explain how the law had come to be. Rather, he censored what he found and demanded a new beginning.

Beccaria challenged a legal system that was particularistic and reflective of a deeply hierarchical society. He proposed to replace it with a code grounded in a particular understanding of human psychological laws. Superstition, ignorance and laziness were the enemies he sought to combat, the sources of the mischievous measures that littered the criminal code. 'There are very few', he wrote in self-justification, 'who have scrutinized and fought against the savagery and the disorderliness of the procedures of criminal justice, a part of legislation which is so prominent and so neglected in almost the whole of Europe' (Beccaria 1764: 8). He promised relief alike to individuals suffering unjustly under severe penalties, and to societies afflicted with high levels of crime and disorder. He appealed to reason as to a geometric proof, even as the strident tone of his indignation suggested that less scientific ideals lay behind many of his proposals. In particular, he wanted to leave no room for uncertainty in the operation of justice, since such uncertainty was productive of crime and misery. The evil crept in when judges acted from passion rather than reason. 'The judge', he asserted, 'should construct a perfect syllogism about every criminal case' (Beccaria

1764: 14). Similarly, the legislator should behave 'like the skilled architect' as he constructed the criminal code (Beccaria 1764: 9). The result of this calculus appeared felicitous. He had great confidence that if the law offered a precise description of offences and their associated punishments, and if this relationship was in harmony with reason and feeling, there would be little crime. Above all, certainty was the key: 'The certainty of even a mild punishment', he argued, 'will make a bigger impression than the fear of a more awful one which is united to a hope of not being punished at all' (Beccaria 1764: 63). Guided by a proper understanding of the principles of human psychology, the legislator, Beccaria believed, was in a position to secure both better order and greater humanity.

THE MOVEMENT FOR CODIFICATION

Justice, in early modern Europe, was central to the ruler's relationship to his subjects. Few denied that, in theory at least, the monarch possessed extraordinary powers when it came to exercising his legal capacity. Yet the situation everywhere was more complex. Rulers were often checked by competing jurisdictions. Bohemia alone possessed nearly 400 courts of various sorts. Each had its own regulations, its own practitioners and clients. Classes and regions protected their rights; they appealed to custom as a sanction against change. The attempt to impose greater uniformity often seemed more trouble than it was worth. Yet by the eighteenth century an increasing number of rulers undertook the effort to bring their legal systems under tighter control. In Austria, following humiliating defeat in war, Maria Theresa appointed a commission to investigate imposing greater order on the law. To some extent, Enlightenment ideas may have contributed to the programme; they may have broadened the vision of what was possible or offered new justifications for the measures. But codification had much more to do with consolidation than with reform. The dominant motive remained the desire to expand the scope and efficiency of royal power. By midcentury, it was clear that a powerful movement was sweeping through Europe.

The character of this movement, however, remained ambiguous. In Prussia it was the conservative Frederick William I who inaugurated change and appointed the man who would be its chief architect, Samuel von Cocceji (1679–1755). The King, in his rough and ill-tempered fashion, sought codification for reasons of administrative efficiency rather than out of a spirit of enlightened idealism. He wanted to speed up justice, reduce its cost, and bring judges to account, especially by curtailing corruption. He spoke in his political testament of the duty he felt to ensure that justice was 'fair and quick'. The effort was renewed by Frederick II. He ordered Cocceji to construct a code 'based purely on reason and on the constitution of the territory' (Robinson 2000: 258). The Chancellor attracted to him men who would play an important role as legal reformers throughout the rest of the century. He reduced the number of courts, and sought to improve judicial salaries so as to raise the social standing and quality of judges. The outcome of these measures was the creation of a highly professional legal body with a more sharply defined sense of the mission of the law. This effort continued after Cocceji's death and would culminate, in 1794, in the drafting of the Prussian General Law Code, which embodied the ambition to create a single structure of law for the kingdom. Although the code went a long way towards standardizing legal practice, it stopped short of imposing full equality before the law. At the same time the rule of law that it created remained under the direct command of the King.

This movement did not succeed everywhere. Much depended on the balance of forces in any particular territory. Naples, despite being home to a vigorous intellectual culture, saw little reform in the face of the entrenched opposition of the nobility and the Church. While Joseph II made some headway in Austria in limiting manorial courts, he was less successful in altering the civil law. In England the chief obstacle was the self-satisfaction derived from a sense of the superiority of its distinctive legal inheritance. Yet even here voices were raised expressing sentiments at one with the currents flowing from the Continent. William Blackstone (1723–80) wrote the single most important legal work in English of the century: his four-volume *Commentaries on the Laws of England* (1765–9) was a stout defence of the genius of the common law. Nonetheless, he shared many ambitions that marked the Enlightenment project. He deliberately avoided obscurity and technical language, in the hope of educating a wider public. He also sought to reform legal education. He appealed approvingly to the work of Montesquieu and Beccaria. Indeed, the latter figured largely in his attack on the English criminal law, which, he wrote, 'should be founded upon principles that are permanent, uniform, and universal; and always conformable to the dictates of truth and justice, the feelings of humanity, and the indelible rights of mankind' (Blackstone 1765–9: vol. IV, 3). In an interesting twist, however, Blackstone argued that the problem arose from the haphazard way in which Parliament passed legislation creating new capital offences. In this, politicians departed from the wisdom of the common law, that tradition which, when properly understood, could be seen as the truest expression of reason. In essence, Blackstone suggested, appealing to Enlightenment rhetoric, codification in England was unnecessary and dangerous, more likely to create confusion and error, in contrast to the prudent path of relying on common-law principles.

It fell to another Englishman, Jeremy Bentham (1748–1832), to challenge Blackstone's effort to bend Enlightenment principles to a defence of the common law. In the process he articulated a justification and ambition for codification that knit together at least some of the major themes that arose over the century. Bentham employed biting sarcasm to dismiss the claims of natural law. It was no more than a fiction, he said, an appeal to private prejudice posing as universal reason. Law, he argued, arose from commands expressed in legislation; nothing else counted as law. Here, the legal positivism that was lurking in the background of one strand of natural-law thought burst to the fore. The problem with codification thus far, Bentham contended, was that it had proceeded with an inadequate understanding of human psychology. Pain and pleasure were the true springs of all human behaviour. All legislative activity should be judged, using this calculus, on the basis of its utility in increasing the sum of human happiness. Legal codes should be rewritten in the light of these simple scientific principles. He offered his services to several newly independent nations to undertake this task. Bentham himself devoted years to the goals of achieving a proper categorization of acts, and to developing a new language of law that would be unencumbered with imprecise terms. There was no aspect of life that escaped the reach of Bentham's ambition. Social regulation would achieve a new level of efficiency and harmony, like a well-oiled machine. Jurisprudence would give way before the science of the legislator.

Bentham's project was nowhere realized. Famously, he could not complete his own books. Yet he shows how far the eighteenth century had travelled in its understanding of the law. The fact of ever-increasing levels of legislation altered how people regarded the law. While much of their normal business remained largely unchanged, lawyers themselves assumed a larger role in the political processes that created the law. Law was no longer simply what one endured, but something that one made. Its legitimacy or illegitimacy depended increasingly on how people saw the validity of this making of the law.

REFERENCES

Beccaria, Cesare, Marchese de (1764) *Dei delitti e delle pene*, in *idem*, *On Crimes and Punishments and Other Writings*, ed. Richard Bellamy, trans. Richard Davies with Virginia Cox and Richard Bellamy (1995) Cambridge: Cambridge University Press.

Bell, David (1994) *Lawyers and Citizens*, Oxford: Oxford University Press.

Blackstone, William (1765–9) *Commentaries on the Laws of England*, 4 vols; facs. of 1st edn (1979) Chicago: University of Chicago Press.

Brewer, John and Styles, John (eds) (1980) *An Ungovernable People: The English and Their Law in the Seventeenth and Eighteenth Centuries*, New Brunswick: Rutgers University Press.

Hull, Isabel (1996) *Sexuality, State, and Civil Society in Germany, 1700–1815*, Ithaca: Cornell University Press.

Hunter, Ian (2001) *Rival Enlightenments*, Cambridge: Cambridge University Press.

Kelly, J. M. (1992) *A Short History of Western Legal Theory*, Oxford: Clarendon Press.

Lemmings, David (2000) *Professors of the Law*, Oxford: Oxford University Press.

Lieberman, David (1989) *The Province of Legislation Determined*, Cambridge: Cambridge University Press.

Maza, Sarah (1993) *Private Lives and Public Affairs*, Berkeley: University of California Press.

Montesquieu, Charles Louis de Secondat (1748) *De L'Esprit des lois*; ed. and trans. Anne M. Cohler, Basia Carolyn Miller and Harold Stone (1989) as *The Spirit of the Laws*, Cambridge: Cambridge University Press.

Robinson, O. F. *et al.* (2000) *European Legal History: Sources and Institutions*, 3rd edn, London: Butterworths.

Scott, H. M. (ed.) (1990) *Enlightened Absolutism*, Ann Arbor: University of Michigan Press.

Walker, Mack (1981) *Johann Jakob Moser*, Chapel Hill: University of North Carolina Press.

PART VII

---·◆·---

TRANSFORMATION AND EXPLORATIONS

INTRODUCTION

---•❖•---

Iain McCalman

On 1 January 1785 *The Times* urged its readers to see a new Covent Garden pantomime called *Omai, or a trip around the world*:

> To the rational mind what can be more entertaining than to contemplate prospects of countries in their natural colours and tints – to bring into living action, the customs and manners of distant nations! To see exact representations of their buildings, marine vessels, arms, manufactures, sacrifices and dresses.

Other newspaper accounts extended this praise by calling the show 'a living history' and a 'school for the history of man' (McCalman 2001: 11, 12–13).

Nothing better illustrates how pervasively the enquiring spirit of the Enlightenment had infiltrated British society than that such a traditionally light and popular theatrical genre should be recommended in these didactic terms. Audiences were encouraged to expect not only the usual satire, farce and *commedia dell'arte* fun of the pantomime, but also something much more serious and salutary. The chief set designer, Philippe Jacques de Loutherbourg had worked to reproduce realistic landscapes and social settings by painstakingly copying engravings and paintings from Cook voyage artists William Hodges and John Webber. The latter was also hired to advise on and paint several of the South Sea scenes. De Loutherbourg even purchased a variety of Polynesian artefacts to lend authentic detail to the designs of his pantomime costumes. Attending *Omai* was thus a further opportunity for Britons, young and old, to experience the unrolling of what Edmund Burke had in 1777 called 'the Great Map of Mankind', a map that Captain Cook and other explorers were at that very time charting on the other side of the globe. No subject, Burke had gone on to say, was so fruitful for revealing the character and behaviour of man and society in the past and present (Sambrook 1986: 168).

Theatrical performances supplemented the printed voyage accounts, engravings, paintings, satires, poems, decorative arts, scientific treatises and museum displays which transmitted the fruits of enlightened explorations to the peoples of Europe. For relatively modest outlays, men, women and children could sample morsels of the new empirical disciplines of history, geography and ethnography in a wide range of forms. Thanks, especially, to the burgeoning of popular print, they could join a vogue for philosophical travel which had by the end of the century transformed the character and purpose of the traditional aristocratic Grand Tour. For men like the amateur naturalist Sir Joseph Banks, the acquisition of social manners and sexual experience had been supplanted by eagerness to contemplate the fascinating operation of the laws of nature that seemed to generate marked cultural differences among peoples according to time and place, yet at the same time to reveal the common universality of humankind.

Covent Garden manager Thomas Harris's choice of a pantomime, based on the life story of Mai, the celebrated Polynesian visitor from Tahiti who spent 1774–6 in Britain, also aptly illustrates the central theme canvassed in this part of the book. Indigenous visitors had found their way to Europe since the sixteenth century, usually as traders, diplomatic envoys, or objects of curiosity. During the eighteenth century, however, North American Indians, Inuit Eskimo peoples, Polynesians and Aboriginal Australians were increasingly treated as fertile sources of speculation about global history and society. All three of the essayists in this part of the book analyse the interweaving of empirically based Enlightenment knowledges with both old and new theories of human morality, social development and cultural difference. Whether drawing on the Bougainville *supplements* of Frenchmen Philibert Commerson and Denis Diderot or adapting much older foundational British literary texts, such as Milton's *Paradise Lost* and the King James Bible, eighteenth-century Europeans generated an unprecedented body of empirical and Utopian theories about peoples and places outside their own civilizations.

As both Jonathan Lamb (Chapter 31) and Dorinda Outram (Chapter 33) here attest, the Pacific had, by the second half of the eighteenth century, supplanted the Americas as the primary site of European exploration, intellectual enquiry and geopolitical ambition. Not surprisingly, *Omai* had been shortly preceded in London by a rival Drury Lane pantomime based on the most influential literary Utopia of the century, Daniel Defoe's *Robinson Crusoe* (1719). In this work, which Outram sees as emblematic of the relationship between Enlightenment Europe and the rest of the world, the shipwrecked Crusoe is brought to ponder his own morality and culture through his confrontation with the markedly different values of the native cannibal 'Man Friday'. Following the South Sea voyages of Samuel Wallis (1767), Louis Antoine de Bougainville (1768) and James Cook (1769), the island of Tahiti, rather than Defoe's model of San Fernandez, became the dominant literary Utopia. To numerous readers of both French and British voyage accounts, it became resonant of guiltless Polynesian eroticism, unfettered social harmony and natural tropical abundance. For perhaps the first time, voyages of exploration were being undertaken primarily for the purpose of accumulating knowledge about man and the natural world. Here it was Captain James Cook – navigator, mathematician and astronomer – who stood as the emblem of the age.

But, as Outram argues, the fleeting cross-cultural encounters and exchanges effected by Pacific voyagers often carried a potential for mutual misunderstandings across the barriers of language and culture. In the aftermath of these encounters, indigenous societies were inevitably disrupted or altered by their exposure to Western legacies, such as iron implements, firearms, missionaries and sexually transmitted diseases. Moreover, even when more reflective Europeans were led by these experiences to question the benefits of colonialism, prevalent Enlightenment beliefs in the unity of man and the progressive movement of history proved incompatible with any real understanding of indigenous cultural dynamism. Cook's belief that the nomadism of Aboriginal Australians made the continent a virtual *terra nullius* was to have devastating consequences when colonization eventually followed. Lamb and Outram remind us that the scholarly trappings of Enlightenment empiricism could coexist with, or even cloak, much older literary fantasies of paradises lost and gained, just as they could disguise darker European motivations of conquest, commerce and imperialism. Despite its ethnographic realism, the pantomime *Omai* typically sports a plethora of magical wonders, mythic impositions from classical Greece, skewed European social analogies, titillating hints of sexual exoticism, and nostalgic evocations of the noble savage. Portentously, it concludes with a hymn of praise to future British colonial acquisitions in the South Seas, symbolized by the marriage of Omai the Polynesian prince to Princess Londina of Britain. In the after-piece of the play, entitled 'The Apotheosis of Captain Cook', a giant transparency also depicts the self-made Yorkshire navigator being carried heavenwards by a host of genial cherubs, signifying his literal transformation into a deified idol of the Enlightenment.

Roy Porter (1999: 419) has suggested that Enlightenment explorations included redrawings of the 'topographies of the soul' as well as the traditional cultural maps of heaven and hell. A theist himself, Cook's popular apotheosis nevertheless hints at the persistence in the eighteenth century of Christian contributions to the theories of the natural world. Comte de Volney attacked biblical literalism in his influential travel dystopia *The Ruins or Revolutions of Empire*, which linked Christian theology to pagan astronomical myths, but the idea of nature as a progressive and self-regulating work of divine design was still commonplace among Enlightenment thinkers. Jon Mee (Chapter 32) cautions that the late eighteenth-century proliferation of secular and exotic Utopias can lead us to overlook a widespread continued deployment of biblically based models of material progress and historical change. Such scriptural structures of thought, Mee argues, could encompass both older-style apocalyptic prophecies (millenarianism) as well as more scholarly predictions that assimilated many of the approaches of Enlightenment *philosophes*. Learned divines such as Joseph Priestley and James Bicheno studied the scriptures in a meticulously rational and empirical spirit in order to make prophetic and foreign-policy predictions. New mental 'sciences' such as mesmerism could also be interpreted within materialist and natural-philosophical frameworks, a phenomenon that historian Clarke Garrett has called the 'mystical enlightenment'.

Just as Enlightenment explorations of the South Seas strove to reconcile the tensions between cultural differences and human unity, so too did Enlightenment theosophers work to reconcile the workings of human reason and divine spirituality. Behind both enterprises stood a deep-seated and common Enlightenment urge to extend order, balance and human progress.

REFERENCES

McCalman, Iain (2001) 'Spectacles of Knowledge: Omai as Ethnographic Travelogue', in *Cook and Omai: The Cult of the South Seas*, exhibition catalogue, Canberra: National Library of Australia.

Porter, Roy (1999) 'Afterword', in David N. Livingstone and Charles W. J. Withers (eds) *Geography and Enlightenment*, Chicago and London: University of Chicago Press.

Sambrook, James (1986) *The Eighteenth Century: The Intellectual and Cultural Context of English Literature, 1700–1789*, London and New York: Longman.

CHAPTER THIRTY-ONE

FANTASIES OF PARADISE

———— ◆ ————

Jonathan Lamb

From almost the beginning of the Christian era it was believed by some influential thinkers (St Augustine among them) that the Garden of Eden had survived the Deluge and that a terrestrial paradise still existed somewhere beyond the limits of the known world (Delumeau 1995: 17). By the late Middle Ages this belief had crystallized into a conception of paradise quite different from the popular image of a walled garden, or *hortus conclusus*, where trees and shrubs were laid out in orderly patterns. The terrestrial paradise was not artificial but wild, and like the original garden in Genesis 1.19 it was thick with vegetation (the home of 'every herb which is upon the face of the earth, and every tree'). On the medieval 'T and O' maps, this paradise was located at the verge or just beyond the verge of the world, but was indicated always at the easternmost point of the map. When Columbus sailed west, beyond the horizon of the known world, in order to arrive at the extreme edge of the Orient and forge a treaty with Prester John on behalf of Ferdinand and Isabella, it was inevitable that he would encounter this desideratum of geography. He duly reported from the New World that he found 'great indications of the earthly paradise' (Scafi 1999: 68). He was followed by other navigators – da Zuarza, Vespucci, Vasconcelos – who made the same report. They described the same wild and overgrown place that had competed with the walled garden as the model of Eden. In Haiti Columbus saw numberless trees so high that they seemed to touch the sky. Vespucci described a land 'covered with countless tall trees' interspersed with 'fields of of thick grass' (Delumeau 1995: 110–11). A visitor to Brazil saw 'the thickest forests' and another to North Carolina declared that there 'the earth bringeth forth all things in abundance as in the first creation' (Prest 1981: 33).

Under the influence of these narratives of discovery and exploration, poets and dramatists were inclined to show paradise as a dense thicket of trees and plants, such as the clustered orange trees in Marvell's *Bermudas* or the self-activating vines of *The Garden*. In his poem 'Of Plants' Abraham Cowley imagines a parliament of American trees all talking from 'the rougher Paths of obscure Woods,/All gloom aloft, beneath o'ergrown with Shrubs,/Where Phoebus, once thy Guide, can dart no Ray' (Cowley 1881: 2.6.243). In *The Tempest* considerable attention is paid to trees and surplus timber in the form of firewood; and, of course, in Milton's epic, paradise is represented as a 'woodie Theatre', so closely planted that only the fiend can make a way through terrain whose 'hairie sides/With thicket overgrown, grotesque and wilde,/Access deni'd' (*Paradise Lost*: 4.136).

When Magellan made his way into the South Seas in 1520, the achievements of his colleagues in the New World shaped his expectations. In the Spice Islands he found what he called the promised land of Palaon, where the trees shed animated leaves, and where the bird of paradise flew on iridescent plumes only when the wind blew – or, in Ramusio's account, a creature so pure it touched the earth only when it died (Pigafetta 1874: 109, 119, 143, 205). Nearly a century later Pedro Fernandez de Quiros went with Alvaro Mendana to fetch the Queen of Sheba from Solomon's isles and in the course of the voyage found the New Jerusalem in Vanuatu, a place beyond imagining, rich and fruitful, where, when the sun rose over the crowns of the trees and shot its beams through the branches, the sight (accompanied by the sound of delightful birdsong) caused his company to weep for joy (de Quiros 1904: 1.261). The sight of abundant vegetation was a constant in reports of terrestrial paradise in the next century, when the Pacific became the object of intense French and English attention. Richard Walter, the historian of Anson's circumnavigation, described Juan Fernandez in terms that clearly recall Milton and, via Milton, the first scenes of the New World by Columbus and his epigones, for Anson set up his tent on a lawn 'screened by a tall wood of myrtle sweeping round it, in the form of a theatre' (Walter 1776: 120). It recalls vividly the woodie Theatre of Milton's epic, whose irriguous valley exhibits crisped brooks flowing under pendant shades (*Paradise Lost* 4.247). The scene is commemorated in Piercy Brett's engraving, although he omits the two crystal brooks that border it. This natural amphitheatre will be seen again on different islands. Bougainville said that Tahiti, a new Cythera, stood 'elevated like an amphitheatre' with its highest summits heavily wooded (Bougainville 1772: 217). At Dusky Bay Anders Sparrman saw a circuit of green, 'a sense covering of thickets and trees, foliage and pine needles, in such profusion that not the smallest patch was left for further adornment by green grass and plants' (Sparrman 1783: 43). On Mauritius Jacques-Henri Bernardin St Pierre saw 'a verdant amphitheatre' (Bernardin St Pierre 1819: 46), and at the Marquesas Herman Melville beheld the same phenomenon, 'the appearance of a vast natural amphitheatre' (Melville 1846: 34).

When it came to peopling these woods with Adams and Eves, it seemed to present as little difficulty for voyagers in the South Seas as for the more liberal observers of the indigenes of the New World. Tahitian men and women went naked without shame, Cook wrote, and ate the bread that grew abundantly on the trees without having to season it with the sweat of their brows (Cook 1970: 20, 18). Louis de Bougainville described a scene of guiltless erotic pleasures that he associated with Cythera, the island of Venus, and which his companion Philibert Commerson compared to the enjoyments of Utopians. William Hodges feasted the spectator's eye with the voluptuous possibilities of Tahiti in his picture of tattooed maidens bathing, *Oaitepeha Bay* (1776). The landscape, its creatures and its people entered the popular imagination via fiction and satire. Defoe reinvented the thicket of wild trees as the living palisado of Crusoe's fort, an idea, he noted in his *History of the Pyrates*, that had already been put to use by the buccaneer communities on Madagascar (Defoe 1972a: 60; 1972b: 76). Bernardin St Pierre makes his wooded

Figure 31.1 *A View of the Commodore's Tent at the Island of Juan Fernandez*, from George Anson (1776) *A Voyage Round the World in the Years MDCCXL, I, III, IV*, London: W. Bowyer. By permission of the University Library, Princeton.

paradise the setting for the pure but doomed passion of Paul and Virginia. In Rousseau's *La Nouvelle Héloïse* (1761) Julie and St Preux consider their own ill-fated love affair in the context of a wild garden that reminds him of his voyage with Anson, and the landfalls of Juan Fernandez and Tinian. Swift borrowed Magellan's bird of paradise to make a metaphor of the human fancy, which can soar for a while to ideas 'of what is most Perfect, finished and exalted', but is destined to fall in the end 'like a dead Bird of Paradise, to the Ground' (Swift 1964: 101–2). Robert Paltock in his *The Life and Adventures of Peter Wilkins* (1751) and the anonymous author of *The Adventures of Hildebrand Bowman* (1778) both transfer the paradisal feathers of the bird to women, composing erotic fantasies of winged odalisques on desert islands and describing the exquisite sensual pleasure they afford.

But there is always something to spoil the completeness of the picture, whether it be real or fictional, and whether it comprise people in a landscape or the foliage alone. For Cook and Bougainville, it was the rapid introduction of venereal disease into the islands of Tahiti, as if they had themselves functioned as Satan by entering Eden only to destroy it. In this sense their divided mood of wonder and of loss was faithful to their literary original, for when he arrives at paradise Milton's Satan views a delightful scene without delight, 'sight hateful, sight tormenting!' (4.285, 505). In New Zealand Sparrman was charmed by the landscape but repelled by the taste for cannibalism among the Maori. The Forsters in Dusky Bay at first admired the

Figure 31.2 Frontispiece of Jacques-Henri Bernardin St Pierre (1797) *Paul et Virginie*, London: Baylis. By permission of the National Library of Australia.

lush vegetation, but when it came to building a camp and searching for botanical specimens, they complained of the resistance of the woods to penetration, and the fatigue of making their way through 'the prodigious intricacy of various climbers, briars, shrubs, and ferns . . . [in] this spot, where immense numbers of plants left to themselves lived and decayed by turns, in one confused inanimated heap' (Forster 1777: 1.127, 177). Paul's Virginia is destined to drown in sight of the shore of the paradise she is trying to regain. Julie may re-encounter St Preux amid the unconstrained foliage of paradise, but not as a free agent. When he viewed the desolation of Mauritius, Pierre Poivre reflected on the blind greed of colonists: 'Reckless and ignorant men, thinking of nothing but themselves, have ravaged the island, destroying the trees to make a fortune . . . leaving nothing for their successors but arid lands' (quoted in Grove 1995: 202). Commerson agreed, and thought the outlook grim, for 'a society of men once corrupted cannot be regenerated' (1772: 243). As for the bird of paradise, when he first saw its unearthly colours, Alfred Russel Wallace thought some sights should be reserved to nature alone, knowing that as soon as such a rarity fell under human observation, it was unlikely to last long.

In order to see how the encounter with paradise develops into its next stage, it is necessary to specify a little more closely these disappointments. The manner in which they were consciously processed by the voyagers, and in which their descriptions and judgements were largely received, bespoke an objective assessment of an experience that had been expected to be, or had partially been experienced as, fantastic. Paradise and Utopia had a lodgement only in the public's imagination. When it found that the terrestrial paradise had been located, and that its distinctive sights and smells had, no matter how briefly, been deliciously present to the senses of some fortunate voyager who associated this pleasure with either Eden or Utopia, it required a new effort of imagination. The narrators and journalists tried to provoke this extra effort by means of a conjunction of the quotidian and the marvellous, the incidents of daily maritime life suddenly illuminated by the glimpse of a wonderful other world. Aesthetically, it was the rapid and unaccountable sequence leading from privation (on the voyage) to delight (at the landfall) and then to loss (of the paradise relished only for a moment, then relinquished). The tendency of such narratives of alternating and intense feelings for a place generally regarded as fictional is not towards some consensus about its reality. Columbus and Raleigh experienced the hostility of their audiences towards the eyewitness of paradisal wonders. Even a reporter as sober as Cook, or as socially pre-eminent as Banks, had trouble convincing the readership of the decency and truth of what they told. The isolation of the autoptic first person in the New Worlds of America and the South Seas was owing to the persistence of the public's belief that fantasy is absolutely distinct from the real world, unless it can be proved otherwise by gold, a metal whose power to realize fantasies was well understood. There was no gold in the South Seas, so the voyaging ego with tales of paradise islands laid claim to a truth that tradition, time and distance conspired to make improbable, and was destined seldom or never to be believed. William Wales thought it was either because the quotidian details were too petty to engage any interest or that the paradisal interlude was too marvellous to be thought true (Wales in Cook 1961: 839). In any event, the reading public saw little difference between real voyages and invented ones. Thus Lemuel Gulliver, who cites his cousin Dampier and explores all the dimensions of this predicament, comically confounds the ordinary and the wonderful in the second book of his travels, when he says of the kitchen equipment in the palace at Lorbrulgrud, 'But if I should describe the kitchen-grate, the prodigious pots and kettles, the joints of meat turning on the spits, with many other particulars, perhaps I should be hardly believed; at least, a severe critic would be apt to think I enlarged a little, as travellers are often suspected to do' (Swift 1904: 131). When in his version of Utopia he talks to talking horses of how horses are treated in Europe, and points out to his disbelieving host how a narrative of the present scene would be greeted with the same incredulity back home, he is uncomfortably aware that neither among horses nor humans can he win an audience. It is generally the case therefore that when a traveller steps ashore in paradise, he anticipates this state of affairs by placing the audience in abeyance. This is performed with a gesture emphasizing not so much the truth of what is told as its uniqueness, either by quoting or alluding to poetry (Richard Walter's use of Milton at Juan Fernandez, or William Wales's use of Thomson's *The Seasons* at Dusky Bay, for example) or by saying outright that an eyewitness alone could confirm the truth of what he saw. Thus Joseph Banks, writing of the exquisite island of Savu in the Timor Sea, does both at once when he declares of its beauty: 'It requires a poetical imagination to describe and a mind not unacquainted with such sights to conceive [it]' (Banks 1962: 2.159).

PARADISE SEEN THROUGH THE LENS OF SCIENCE

In anthropological terms this union of the best and the worst in the vicinity of paradise was proposed and handled as the contrast between noble and ignoble savages. But it was a contrast based on a fundamental resemblance between them, for both the inhabitants of Eden and their benighted antitypes are identified as wanting what Europeans possess; and it was a contrast that developed out of the reporter's inability directly to say what he saw. The utter unfamiliarity of noble and ignoble savages lies in the endless negative differences they exhibit when compared with the metropolis, and this unmodified strangeness of their appearance operates as another alienating symptom of uniqueness. In the New World it was observed only how the people went without things, for good or ill. Montaigne's Brazilians were triumphantly destitute of letters, numbers, contracts, property and clothes. Rather less triumphantly, Vespucci's Caribbeans went without eyebrows, shame, marriage, horses and mules. In the Pacific the Tahitians gloriously lacked shame, labour and clothes, but the Aborigines and the Tierra del Fuegans competed for the most shameful position on the ladder of privations in wanting almost everything Europeans possessed, including the faculty of curiosity. Dampier said the inhabitants of New Holland had 'no Houses, and skin Garments, Sheep, Poultry, Fruits of the Earth, Ostrich-Eggs . . . no Instruments to catch great Fish . . . there is neither Herb, Root, Pulse nor any sort of Grain for them to eat . . . nor any Bird or Beast that they can catch . . . Neither did they seem to admire anything we had' (Dampier 1729: 1.464–8). A scene of such particularized privation is imagined rather than disclosed, for not one thing in the description is actually there, a technique of representation kindred to the negative stress in the names and descriptions of More's *Utopia*, which was borrowed in part from the rhetoric of nothing used by Vespucci in his account of the Caribbean. Faced with similar lists of things that are lacking, travellers such as Pedro Fernandez de Quiros, Lemuel Gulliver and Herman Melville react quite differently from Dampier, and in their enthusiasm for the innocence and novelty of the place specify quite obsessively the corruptions that are not to be found there. Margaret Hodgen (1964) locates the origin of anthropology in these inventories of missing things; and certainly the rival systems of monogenesis and polygenesis, on which nineteenth-century theories of evolution and race were to be raised, spring from them, too.

According to the sponsors of polygenesis, such as Lord Kames, it was understood that humanity had developed in distinct races and that the Polynesians and Melanesians, for instance, represented different lines of descent with different capacities for improvement, and were in fact different species (Young 1995: 1–28). In the system of monogenesis, favoured by Johann Reinhold Forster, among others, the human race was undivided, but various factors such as climate caused variable degrees of degeneration. If the Tierra del Fuegans were the lowest form of humanity in the South Seas, then the Tahitians were the most finished, and the Maori lay somewhere between. In the nineteenth century Alfred Wallace proposed his famous line that divided the paradisal side of the Malay and Indonesian archipelogos from the primitive and less attractive species on the other side. However, any attempt to tabulate the differences between various populations on the islands of the South Seas was prone to the contradiction at the heart of all types of degenerationist thinking, which is the impossibility of locating a model of steady-state perfection uninfluenced by environment, climate or history. The condition from which islanders are supposed to have degenerated always bears an uncanny resemblance to the condition to which progress aspires; as if time were at once the agent of both corruption and amelioration. That is why the Yahoos are instanced both as primordially imperfect and as degenerate Europeans. In examining this confused line of thought from Magellan to Wallace, James Boon (1985) has concluded that the appearance of scientific accuracy in reports from hitherto undiscovered places really disguises (intentionally or not) the original deep ambivalence of the eyewitnesses.

The parallel between anthropological and botanical witnessing is not quite symmetrical. Objectively the botanist is presented with an array of species so vast that he gains a sense of the multifariousness of paradise. At the same time such riches are an embarrassment for they strain or demolish the systems of categorization by which they might be rendered intelligible. This state of affairs can produce one of two outcomes, Eurocentric or Edenocentric. Before they reached New Zealand the Forsters were complaining that they had seen no new species; but after the experience of the thickets of Dusky Bay George called the 'rude unimproved state of nature' there not paradise but 'its original chaotic state'. Leaving the scene of their operations, he said, 'It is obvious that the shoots of the surrounding weeds will shortly stifle every salutary and useful plant', marking a division between weed and plant that denies primitive vegetation any excellence until it has been modified – in this case, by being chopped down (Forster 1777: 1.127, 180).

But it is precisely this chopping down that Pierre Poivre and Philibert

Commerson deplore as a sign of the corruption introduced by the European presence. Commerson carries this intuition further into a denial of the epistemological value of the Linnaean system of taxonomy, which he says is limited to such an exiguous number of examples, and is so ignorant of the paradisal abundance disclosed by the islands of the Pacific, that it is driven to thin and deplete it in order to understand it. '*Quelle presomption,*' he exclaimed, '*de prononcer sur le nombre & la qualite des plantes que peut produire la nature, malgre toutes les decouvertes qui restent a faire*' (Commerson 1772: 257). He pitied, he said, '*ces sombre speculateurs de cabinet qui passent leur vie a forger de vains systemes, & dont tous les efforts n'aboutissent qu'a faire des chateaux de cartes . . . Tous leurs caracteres classiques, generiques, &c sont precaires . . . tous les lignes de demarcation qu'ils ont tracee s'evanouissent*' (Commerson 1772: 256). Systems of categorization performed the same vanishing trick when Wallace and Darwin beheld the wealth of existing species and also came to understand the metamorphic power of nature to produce variations and novelties. Wallace concluded, 'Many causes, no doubt, have operated of which we must ever remain in ignorance, and we may, therefore, expect to find many details very difficult of explanation' (Wallace 1895: 4). When Erasmus Darwin introduces this endless diversity to the British nation in *The Botanic Garden*, he calls himself a second Ovid because it intends to exhibit so many stunning transformations (Darwin 1789: vi). As for his grandson, Charles, when he heard the noise of this transformation in the high valleys of the Andes – the rattle of stones being endlessly rolled down to the sea where their pounded fragments end as mud – he called to mind that 'whole races of animals have passed away from the face of the earth, and that during this whole period, night and day, these stones have gone rattling onwards in their course,' and he asked, 'can any mountains, any continent, withstand such waste?' (Darwin 1888: 317).

SCORBUTIC FANTASIES

An intuition as vast as Commerson's, Wallace's or the Darwins' cannot subsist independently of a mood either of excitement, astonishment or humility. If nature presents the eyewitness with a task beyond the grasp of enumeration or abstraction, then it is bound to provoke those emotions the eighteenth century associated with the sublime and which Burke named delight; that is, a modification of pain. To some extent, all visitors to paradise were aware of this mixture, since their most exquisite moments of delight were bordered by discomforts of which the most vivid belonged to scurvy, the plague of these seas. Before they arrived at the promised land, Magellan's crew were sick and exhibiting the loathsome symptoms of this disease: namely, gums so overgrown with extra tissue that they could not eat (Pigafetta 1874: 65). No sooner had de Quiros located his New Jerusalem than his crew were laid low from a combination of scurvy and poison fish. Conventionally, the mariner in the first stages of scorbutic decline longs for land with a yearning that goes beyond all reason and self-control. Walter describes the scenes of voluptuous delight that took place on Juan Fernandez – when the stricken sailors of the *Centurion* were able to drink fresh water and eat fresh fruit – as a fantastic entry into Eden from the subjective side as well as from the objective point of view of his audience: 'It is scarce credible with what eagerness and transport we viewed the shore' (Walter 1776: 111). With minds so labile from disease and the strange susceptibility to sensation typical of scurvy, named by Banks and Thomas Trotter as 'scorbutic nostalgia' (Banks 1962: 2.145; Trotter 1792: 44), it was ultimately impossible to draw any line between the privative nature of paradisal uniqueness and the privations which accompanied and invaded the perception of them. Bougainville wonders to what extent the beauty of the Tahitian Venus that arose upon the deck of his ship was owing to her intrinsic qualities, and to what extent it was sharpened by the appetites of men who had seen no women for months. George Forster describes the joy felt by the crew of the *Resolution* as they entered Dusky Bay, only to add, 'such are the general ideas of travellers and voyagers long exhausted by distresses; and with such warmth of imagination they have viewed the rude cliffs of Juan Fernandez, and the impenetrable forests of Tinian' (Forster 1777: 1.125). Suffering mildly from scurvy before he tasted fresh fruit and vegetables at Savu, Joseph Banks at first talked of the island's attractions as beyond the grasp of any but a poetical imagination. Later he withdrew from his enthusiasm and gave a sober and critical account of the quality of the fruit he consumed, but with enough candour to add, 'Bad as the character is that I have given of these fruits, I eat as many as any one, and at the time thought as well and spoke as well of them as the best friends they had' (Banks 1962: 2.211).

The vagaries of nostalgia, scorbutic and otherwise, in which the pains of yearning and the pleasures of satisfaction blend into an intense perception of paradise, only to fade into a less enthusiastic estimate, have been well represented in the fictions of the South Seas, from Crusoe's fierce swings of mood as he tries to accommodate in a single formulation the advantages and disadvantages of his situation, to the uneven register of Tommo's feelings in *Typee*, as he tries to adjust erotic pleasure to his fear of cannibalism. More recently the sinister tales told by William Golding and Marianne Wiggins of children exposed to the state of nature on remote islands are offered as correctives to the simpler vision of the South Seas shared by R. M. Ballantyne and Pierre Loti. The most remarkable instances of this ambivalence are given by Robert Louis Stevenson, not in a fiction but in his first impressions of those coral atolls that are most expressive of what we recognize now as a South Seas paradise. He manages in one sentence to combine Erasmus Darwin's sense of Ovidian metamorphosis with Charles Darwin's sense of evolution as waste: 'It adds a last touch of horror to the thought of this precious annular gangway in the sea, that even what there is of it is not of honest rock, but organic, part alive, part putrescent' (Stevenson 1900: 159).

UTOPIAS

How was this ambivalence to be organized, since it wasn't sure of its own nature, its object or its duration? The most general answer lies in the transition from paradise to Utopia, where the singular qualities and sensations of Eden are formalized as a highly organized society operating in a contrived landscape and a definite architectural space. That these Utopias are in fact projections of a highly egoistic experience, and not solutions to existing social and political problems, is evident in the emphasis that is laid upon pleasure in them, particularly in More's *Utopia*, where Raphael Hythloday is surprised to find that an economy of pleasure lies behind all the institutions of Utopia and her colonies. Every Utopia is preoccupied with the distribution and foci of pleasurable sensations, sometimes with disgust, too, and thus demonstrates its close links with the original sensational singularity of paradise. That is why Commerson sees no contradiction in calling his experience of Tahiti Utopian. Even in the notoriously frugal fourth book of *Gulliver's Travels* (1726), it is not reason but pleasure that makes the final distinction between a Houyhnhnm and a Yahoo: each is a thinking machine mounted on an animal body, the difference being that the horse-body pleases Gulliver more than he can say, and the other revolts him.

In the eighteenth century there are three treatments of this problem, all bearing the title *Supplement*. The first is the Abbé Coyer's fantasy, *Supplement to Lord Anson's Voyage round the World* (1752), in which he imagines how Juan Fernandez might have seemed had its natural delights furnished a social equivalent. The second is Commerson's reflections upon his own botanical enthusiasm, *Supplement au voyage de M. de Bougainville* (1772), in which he tries to explore amphitheatrical vegetation as a stage for Utopian as well as paradisal experiences. The third and most famous is Diderot's *Supplement au voyage de Bougainville* (1771), in which he explores the connections between the metropolis and the Tahitian paradise. Diderot's is certainly the most accomplished, for he allies the intuition of nature's metamorphic power – 'a sky that doesn't remain fixed for an instant . . . caverns poised on the edge of collapse . . . a cliff crumbling into dust . . . a tree shedding its bark, beneath a quivering stone' (Diderot 1992: 51) – with an elastic treatment of the Pacific both as a reality and as 'an ocean of fantasy'. In brief, he proposes that the discovery of a terrestrial paradise is not necessary because the Church Fathers proposed it, or because Columbus sailed to the most extreme point of the east, but because the restraints of civilization require a corresponding fantasy of erotic liberation. Bougainville, he suggests, has not discovered an alternative to Paris; rather, he has located its imaginative core.

Rather along the same lines, Coyer has Anson discover at the centre of his island a place called Frivoland, where everything is pure artifice, made for delight and not for use. Horses are too frail to bear a rider; birdsong is so exquisite it is inaudible. He intends this gimcrack Utopia to express in cabinet form the wonders that Richard Walter adduced from nature alone, as if to suggest (like George Forster and Joseph Banks) that such astonishment depends upon the strains of the voyage, the overextension of the nerves and the contraction of the stomach, and that there is nothing really natural or perfect in the amazing discovery of a distant paradise.

For his part, Commerson believes that the natural abundance of islands in the South Seas and the Indian Ocean causes '*une forte preuve de la bonte, de la douceur & de l'humanite*' to be found there, which is neither artificial nor dependent upon social structures as they currently exist in Europe (Commerson 1772: 262). The pleasures, specifically of the erotic kind, enjoyed by the Tahitians, who recognize no other god than love, causes them to taste delights '*de sorte que le bon Utopien jouit sans cesse*'. Hence his decision to give Tahiti the same name – Utopia – that More gave his ideal republic

(Taillemite 1977: 2.501). As Erasmus Darwin put it: 'Thus where pleased VENUS, in the southern main,/Sheds all her smiles on Otaheite's plain,/Wide o'er the isle her silken net she draws,/And the Loves laugh at all, but Nature's laws' (1789: 165). There are enough hints of Rousseau in Commerson's account of Tahiti to cause him to hesitate before equating even an ideal social structure with a state of nature. The reasons why he doesn't are: first, that he reads More's fiction very acutely as a story about the production of pleasure rather than as a theory of perpetual and ahistorical social reproduction; and second, that he has a plan to create by botanical means the same conditions for pleasure on Mauritius that he found on Tahiti. Commerson's *supplement* is, as it were, Diderot's in reverse, and a total contradiction of Coyer's. It is a project designed to show that Eden is not a fantasy or an artifice: it can be found, lost and restored, and play a real part in the lives of people everywhere.

BOTANIC GARDENS

I don't want to linger on the erotic side of this experiment, although it is clear from the tangled relations between Poivre, Bernardin St Pierre and Commerson, particularly with regard to their partners, that some sort of utopian sexual experiment was partly under way on Mauritius by the 1770s. What is more intriguing is the accompanying development of the botanic garden at Pamplemousse by Poivre and later Bernardin St Pierre, and the large-scale plans they formulated for the environmental recovery of the island (see Grove 1995; Spary 2000). More clearly than any other botanists, they understood the connection between the terrestrial paradise and the botanic garden. Certainly it had been widely agreed earlier that botanic gardens along the lines of those at Chelsea, Oxford, Paris, Montpellier and Padua were effectual paradises to the extent they embraced (or aimed to embrace) all known species of plant and tree. But it was only a specialized area of horticultural aesthetics explored by gardeners such as John Evelyn and later Horace Walpole that accommodated the dense plantation of what became known as the Elysium garden to certain sensations of pleasure, and in the process united the descriptions of the woodie Theatre of paradise to the construction of a garden and the arrangement of its plants. For this they did not depend on close attention to the voyages in the South Seas – Walpole relied on a close reading of Milton, and Evelyn upon an equally close reading of Spenser's *The Faerie Queene* – but the effect was to make a botanic space fit for what had been discovered as paradise: a garden utopia. As there is no utopian conception of paradise in *Paradise Lost*, it is to Evelyn and Spenser we are indebted for an idea of how the botanic garden comprises this utopian dimension of Eden, and how Poivre and his associates were combining a scientific horticultural project with a plan to make a publicly available utopianized paradise.

Briefly, this relationship can be observed in the structural similarities between the arrangement of the beds, or *pulvilli*, of a botanic garden, as described in Spenser's Garden of Adonis, and the social arrangements of people in More's *Utopia*. Spenser describes how the germs of all living things are nurtured by the genius of the garden:

Infinite shapes of creatures there are bred,
And uncouth formes, which none yet ever knew,
And every sort is in a sundry bed
Set by it selfe, and ranckt in comely rew;
Some fit for reasonable soules t'indew,
Some made for beasts, some made for birds to weare,
And all the fruitfull spawn of fishes hew.
In endlesse rancks along enranged were,
That seemed the Ocean could containe them there.

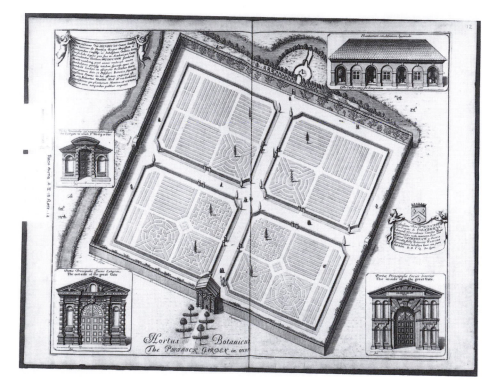

Figure 31.3 *Hortus Botanicus: The Physick Garden in Oxon*, from David Loggan (1675) *Oxonia Illustrata*. By permission of the Bodleian Library, University of Oxford.

The garden's enemy is Time, who scythes down these young plants as they come to maturity. If it were not for Time, 'All that in this delightfull Gardin growes,/Should happie be, and have immortal blis' (Spenser 1596: 3.6.35, 39). The garden suffers from the same mortality as Adonis himself, killed by a boar-wound; and just as Adonis must be restored to life by Venus' love, so the forms of the garden are restored by a systole and diastole of colonization and return; for each plant is sent out into the world, where it gradually decays until it is placed once again in its original bed, where it grows fresh, as if it 'had never seene/Fleshly corruption, nor mortall paine' (3.6.33). The same bed-formation, the same planting in the world at large, followed by return and restoration, are observable in More's *Utopia*. In the Styward's building thirty households eat their meals, fifteen on one side, fifteen on the other. The diners are arranged in fours, four young people, and four old ones, alternately (More 1516: 82). When necessary, these families are broken up so that colonies can be established on the mainland, but should the Utopian population decrease for any reason, the colonists are called home, and once again settled within the *pulvilli*-like family beds, where they are recreated by food, conversation and music.

Evelyn's own plan for a paradise garden in his *Elysium Brittanicum*, comprises beds of various plants laid out like a botanic garden, and culminating as it were in an Eden, a stepped pyramidal structure thickly planted with trees on all four sides and rising to a height of seventy-two feet. Thus his garden comprehends the circuit of birth, decay and renewal that Spenser outlines for plants, and More for people.

By turning the whole of Mauritius in effect into a vast botanic garden, Poivre, Bernardin St Pierre and Commerson were able to plan for the sort of restoration that brings Adonis back to life and preserves Utopia as an immortal commonwealth of pleasure. Although they had suggested that the process of colonial corruption was irreversible, they were acting on the opposite assumption, and if *Paul et Virginie* is in some respects a dramatization of their programme, you can see that it is not in the colony but the metropolis that corruption develops; and if only the plant can be brought back to its acclimatized bed and the company of the huge variety of trees Mauritius boasts, the opportunity for real felicity is restored. Fully acclimatized plants such as Paul and Virginia – creolized innocents, in effect – are troubled only by the exotic malice of a decadent civilization and a dangerous sea. That is all that stands between them and the consummation of their love, and between the innumerable species of the island and a regained paradise. Although Richard Grove has called this plan an idealization and a delusion (1995: 201) it was more substantial than the other dreams of paradise in the Pacific which fled, along with the fancied Great Southern Continent, and left not a rack behind.

REFERENCES

Banks, Joseph (1962) *Endeavour Journal of Joseph Banks*, 2 vols, ed. J. C. Beaglehole, Sydney: Public Library of New South Wales and Angus & Robertson.

Bernardin St Pierre, Jacques-Henri (1819) *Paul and Virginia*, trans. Helen Maria Williams, London: John Sharpe.

Boon, James (1985) 'Anthropology and Degeneration: Birds, Words, and Orangutans', in J. Edward Chamberlin and Sander L. Gilman (eds) *The Dark Side of Progress*, New York: Columbia University Press.

Bougainville, Louis de (1772) *A Voyage around the World*, trans. Johann Reinhold Forster, London: J. Nourse and T. Davies.

Commerson, Philibert (1772) 'Lettre de M. de Commerson', in *Supplement au voyage de M. de Bougainville, ou Journal d'un voyage autour du monde fait par MM. Banks et Solander*, Paris: Saillant.

Cook, James (1961) *The Voyage of the Resolution and Adventure 1772–75*, ed. J. C. Beaglehole, Cambridge: Cambridge University Press for the Hakluyt Society.

—— (1970) *Captain Cook in the South Seas: Two Letters to Captain John Walker*, Sydney: Library of New South Wales.

Cowley, Abraham (1881) 'Of Plants', in *idem, The Complete Works*, 2 vols, ed. Alexander Grosart, Edinburgh: Constable.

Dampier, William (1729) *A Collection of Voyages*, 4 vols, London: J. & J. Knapton.

Darwin, Charles (1888) *A Naturalist's Voyage: Journal of Researches into Natural History and Geology*, London: John Murray.

Darwin, Erasmus (1789) *The Loves of the Plants* [Part 2 of *The Botanic Garden*], Lichfield: J. Jackson.

Defoe, Daniel (1972a) *A General History of the Pyrates*, ed. Manuel Schonhorn, London: J. M. Dent.

—— (1972b) *The Life and Strange Surprizing Adventures of Robinson Crusoe*, ed. J. Donald Crowley, Oxford: Oxford University Press.

Delumeau, Jean (1995) *History of Paradise*, New York: Continuum.

Diderot, Denis (1992) *Supplement to the Voyage of Bougainville*, in *idem, Political Writings*, ed. John Hope Mason and Robert Wokler, Cambridge: Cambridge University Press.

Forster, George (1777) *A Voyage round the World in the Sloop Resolution, 1772–75*, 2 vols, London: G. Robinson.

Grove, Richard (1995) *Green Imperialism: Colonial Expansion, Tropical Island Edens and the Origins of Environmentalism, 1600–1860*, Cambridge: Cambridge University Press.

Hodgen, Margaret T. (1964) *Early Anthropology in the Sixteenth and Seventeenth Centuries*, Philadelphia: University of Pennsylvania Press.

Melville, Herman (1846) *Typee: A Peep at Polynesian Life during a Four Month's Residence in a Valley of the Marquesas*, afterword by Harrison Hayford (1964) New York: New American Library.

More, Thomas (1516) *Utopia*, trans. with an introduction by Paul Turner (1965) Harmondsworth: Penguin.

Pigafetta, Antonio (1874) *The First Voyage round the World*, ed. H. E. Stanley, London: Hakluyt Society.

Prest, John (1981) *The Garden of Eden: The Botanic Garden and the Re-creation of Paradise*, New Haven, Conn., and London: Yale University Press.

Quiros, Pedro Fernandez de (1904) *The Voyages of Pedro Fernandez de Quiros*, ed. Sir Clements Markham, London: Hakluyt Society.

Scafi, Alessandro (1999) 'Mapping Eden: Cartographies of the Earthly Paradise', in Denis Cosgrove (ed.) *Mappings*, London: Reaktion.

Sparrman, Anders (1783) *A Voyage around the World with Captain James Cook in HMS Resolution*, trans. Avril Mackenzie-Grieve and Huldine V. Beamish, introduction by Owen Rutter (1944), London: Golden Cockerel Press.

Spary, E. C. (2000) *Utopia's Garden: French Natural History from Old Regime to Revolution*, Chicago: Chicago University Press.

Spenser, Edmund (1596) *The Faerie Queene: Disposed into Twelue Bookes, Fashioning XII: Morall Vertues*, London: William Ponsonbie.

Stevenson, Robert Louis (1900) *In the South Seas*, London: Chatto & Windus.

Swift, Jonathan (1904) *Travels into Several Remote Nations of the World by Lemuel Gulliver*, Oxford: Oxford University Press.

—— (1964) *A Tale of a Tub and Other Satires*, London: Dent.

Taillemite, Etienne (1977) *Bougainville et ses compagnons*, 2 vols, Paris: Imprimerie Nationale.

Trotter, Thomas (1792) *Observations on the Scurvy*, London, T. Longman.

Wallace, Alfred Russel (1895) *Natural Selection and Tropical Nature*, London: Macmillan.

Walter, Richard (1776) *A Voyage round the World by George Anson 1740–44*, London: W. Bowyer.

Young, Robert J. C. (1995) *Colonial Desire: Hybridity in Theory, Culture and Race*, London: Routledge.

CHAPTER THIRTY-TWO

MILLENARIAN VISIONS AND UTOPIAN SPECULATIONS

Jon Mee

The intellectuals of the Enlightenment in Europe were almost uniformly opposed to the 'priestcraft' that seemed to render Christianity a religion of sacred mysteries kept hidden from the light of reason. Yet there remained large sections of the population who continued to value spiritual experience, whatever their doubts about religious institutions. The disenchantment of the universe was one aspect of the Enlightenment that was far from popular, but the movement had its own wing that continued to be interested in prophetic, occult and other spiritual matters. This mystical Enlightenment, as it has been called, regarded these areas as a legitimate source of interest for 'scientific' enquiries into the powers of the mind and nature. For many others, religious structures of feeling, often building upon long traditions of interpreting the Book of Revelation in terms of a struggle against the Antichrist of temporal authority, also offered more immediate ways of conceiving political and social change than Enlightenment ideas of scientific enquiry and rational debate. Those traditions that thought of human freedom and progress in terms of preparing for the Second Coming promised in biblical prophecy are known as millenarianism. The possibility of a Millennium wherein the world would be reformed into an ideal society had permeated deep within the thought patterns of Christian Europe over many centuries; its presence persists even in the most secular of the Utopian projections that were essential to the eighteenth century's interest in progress. The modern origin of Utopianism as a genre describing the perfect state of society is usually traced back to Thomas More's *Utopia* (1516), but it was deeply ingrained with biblical tradition as well as classical ideas of the Golden Age and specific texts, such as Plato's *Republic*.

AN AGE OF VISIONARIES

The eighteenth century's propensities towards Utopianism and millenarianism can hardly be overestimated. Isaac Newton himself had been obsessed with calculating the timing of the Second Coming. Ideas of Enlightenment were usually predicated on the possibility of progressive change, and sometimes even on the prospect of human perfectibility. With the American and French revolutions a great boost was given to speculations about the renewal of society. From early on in its English usage 'Utopian' had a pejorative sense identified with extravagant or impractical ideas of reform in political and other spheres. A similarly charged term was 'enthusiasm', which Samuel Johnson's *Dictionary of the English Language* (1755), quoting Locke, defines as follows: '*Enthusiasm* is founded neither on reason nor divine revelation, but rises from the conceits of a warmed or overwhelming brain'. Utopianism and enthusiasm were frequently criticized as the twin consequences of a stubborn refusal to accept reality at face value.

After the French Revolution any scheme aimed at 'improvement' or 'innovation' was likely to be dismissed as imprudent Utopianism, especially by thinkers such as Edmund Burke, but others insisted on the possibility of realizing their speculations on progress and even perfection in the world around them as the ultimate aim of Enlightenment. These speculators were not always purely secular in their thinking, as we shall see. Although Enlightenment philosophers often defined themselves against the spectres of popular religious enthusiasm and superstition, their speculations also coincided with an evangelical revival across Europe and North America. Leaders of the latter, such as John Wesley, were relatively tolerant of 'extraordinary calls' and immediate conversion experiences among their followers, but equally they were nervous of placing 'experiential religion' beyond the bounds of contemporary ideas of polite and reasonable behaviour. Many of those involved in the mystical Enlightenment also struggled to keep their interest in such things as mesmerism,

Figure 32.1 *Smelling out a Rat*, James Gillray, 1790. Here, Edmund Burke disturbs the Revd Richard Price as he plots revolution. © the British Museum.

Freemasonry and Swedenborgianism within the pale of what could be described as rational or scientific enquiry. Within popular culture, however, many were still eager to think in terms of the Second Coming and looked to public and political events as Signs of the Times, but the same reflex was also present in the political thinking of Rational Dissenters, such as Richard Price and Joseph Priestley. If their millenarianism was cast in a language of scholarly research and enlightened enquiry, it could also take on a prophetic tone of its own at times of political crisis, such as the 1790s. Even the most atheistic thinkers, such as William Godwin, owed a great deal to a religious education when it came to thinking about the possibilities of human development. Thomas Holcroft, for instance, greeted the publication of Thomas Paine's *Rights of Man* in decidedly millenarian terms when he wrote to Godwin in 1791: 'Hey for the New Jerusalem! The millennium! And peace and eternal beatitude be unto the soul of Thomas Paine' (Kegan Paul 1876: vol. 1, 69). For conservatives, such as Edmund Burke, both religious millenarianism and political Utopianism were equally guilty of 'enthusiasm' when they disregarded contemporary social arrangements and the weight of tradition and custom in their promotion of innovation. After 1789 the role of dissenters such as Price and Priestley in the British reform movement only confirmed Burke's sense of the synergy between religious and secular visionaries of all kinds. For Burke, where it placed too much faith in human reason, the Enlightenment itself was nothing better than a dangerous enthusiasm.

SIGNS OF THE TIMES

A readiness to see God's hand at work in both everyday affairs and more catastrophic disasters, such as the Lisbon earthquake of 1755, was a familiar feature of eighteenth-century popular culture across Europe. Certainly catastrophic events, both natural and political, were often widely regarded as a fulfilment of biblical prophecy and a sign of Christ's imminent return. Prophetic tracts offering commentaries on such events were 'a staple of English popular literature' (Garrett 1975: 169). If the presses on the Continent were less busy, due to various religious and political restrictions, this way of viewing the world seems to have been no less prevalent among the common people there.

Modern scholars often make a distinction between popular millenarianism, on the one hand, and scholarly millennialism on the other. Ernest Tuveson, for instance, identified the former with those who believed in the imminent physical return of Christ (Tuveson 1968: 33–4). The latter he associated with ideas of the evolutionary triumph of Christian principles that would eventually be cemented in a Utopian Millennium. Tuveson identified millennialism with a moderation and gradualness that found expression, for instance, in the progressive thinking of Dissenters such as Price and Priestley. In their hands the Second Coming was transformed into something like a metaphor for human progress:

> The human powers will, in fact, be enlarged; nature, including both its materials, and its laws, will be more at our command; men will make their situation in this world abundantly more easy and comfortable; they will

probably prolong their existence in it, and will grow daily more happy, each in himself, and more able (and, I believe, more disposed) to communicate happiness to others. Thus whatever was the beginning of this world, the end will be glorious and paradisaical, beyond what our imaginations can now conceive. Extravagant as some may suppose these views to be, I think I could show them to be fairly suggested by the true theory of human nature, and to arise from the natural cause of human affairs.

(Priestley 1771: 4–5)

Much the same view of progress is more fully secularized in the thinking of someone like the former Dissenter William Godwin. Tuveson identified millenarianism with the more populist stress on sudden and violent transformations and the continuing possibility of the immediate interference of the divine in the temporal world. E. P. Thompson's influential conception of a 'chiliasm of despair' (1963: 411) points to the way the latter tradition could feed into a passive acceptance of the status quo and a displacement of the desire for progress on to supernatural agencies and a distant hereafter. Certainly the anticlerical strains of Enlightenment thinking often represented popular millenarianism as a form of false consciousness, but J. F. C. Harrison (1979: 5) has rightly warned of using distinctions between millennial and millenarian thinking too rigidly. Although elite commentators were apt to take popular millenarianism as a symptom of the sort of popular ignorance and priestly superstition that Enlightenment progress was meant to overcome, such beliefs were often tied to platforms of social protest by those excluded from the benefits of education and leisure. Nor were Tuveson's millennialists necessarily without fervour of their own. In the crisis years following the French Revolution there existed in both Britain and France 'a public eager to read prophetic utterances of all kinds' (Garrett 1975: 169–70). (Throughout this chapter the term 'millenarian' is used to describe this constituency in the broadest sense.)

In France from the seventeenth century various messianic individuals associated with Jansenist groups such as the Convulsionaries had appeared. They looked to the restoration of all things with the coming of 'Elias', often preaching reform of a corrupted Church and even presenting France as the progenitor of a universal spiritual regeneration. Early responses to the Revolution often saw in it the possibility of the regeneration of both the Catholic Church and the French state. Although these hopes dimmed once the secularist drive of the Revolution became clear with the Civil Constitution of the Clergy in 1790, small groups associated with the likes of Suzette Labrousse and Catherine Théot kept open the idea of the Revolution as the fulfilment of millenarian prophecy. Both Labrousse and Théot displayed behaviour typical of the 'holy women' who have appeared throughout the history of Christian Europe. By 1789 both had already been promoting ideas of spiritual regeneration and calling for the reform of the Church for two decades. Labrousse had pursued a solitary life of piety and good works in Périgord from the late 1760s. Between 1790 and 1792 her writings were promoted in Paris by pro-revolutionary priests through organs such as the *Journal Prophetique*, which claimed that the fall of monarchy had been predicted in Isaiah, but these publications were never distributed as widely as the works of Richard Brothers and Joanna Southcott

Engraved by Ridley from a Drawing by Lawrence in the Possession of Dr Batty.

William Godwin Esqr

Pub by Verner & Hood. Poultry. 31. Jany 1805.

Figure 32.2 *William Godwin*, engraved by W. Ridley (1805) from a drawing by Sir Thomas Lawrence.

in Britain. Eventually Labrousse set off in 1792 on a pilgrimage to Rome in order to convince the Pope to accept the revolutionary regime. Little was made of her pilgrimage in France, but she was imprisoned by the Church until freed by the invading French army in 1798.

That other groups in France continued to promulgate similar ideas is suggested by information that came to light after the arrest in Paris of Catherine Théot in 1794.

Théot, like Labrousse (some of whose followers she inherited), had also been practising as a holy woman before the Revolution. She never achieved the public role of Labrousse, or of Southcott in Britain, but her attacks on priestcraft had already earned her incarceration in the Bastille for a few weeks in 1779. Although she claimed never to comment on worldly affairs, her teachings seem to have offered her followers a way of understanding the Revolution as part of the divine plan that prepared the way for the Second Coming of Christ.

These currents of popular religion on the Continent and in Britain were augmented by more intellectual manifestations of millenarianism that fed off the remarkable resurgence of interest in mysticism in late eighteenth-century Europe, but its followers less often rejected science than responded to mesmerism and other such movements as taking forward the advances of the Enlightenment into new spheres. The best known of these groups of the mystical Enlightenment seem to have been centred in the papal territory of Avignon in the 1780s. Avignon even attracted pilgrims in the form of the English artisans William Bryan and John Wright, who were to become followers of Richard Brothers, although many of those involved in the mystical Enlightenment, such as the Polish Count Grabianka, were from much more elevated social circles. What united the different members of these loose groups seems to have been a conviction of imminent spiritual and moral regeneration. Many of those involved in the Masonic rituals of the Avignon society seem to have participated in the patriotic rites of the new republic (Garrett 1975: 117); others were dispersed as threats to the purpose of the Revolution. But the phenomenon of Masonic millenarianism lent credence to the paranoid claims of the Abbé Barruel and John Robison, writing in the immediate aftermath of the Revolution to explain its origins, that they were the centre of an international conspiracy of illuminati that had consciously engineered the events of 1789.

Although fears of an international network of mystical conspirators gained some currency in Britain after 1789, millenarianism had long been associated there with the dangerous religious zeal of the masses. Unlike in France, a vigorous print culture fuelled an alternative public sphere of religious dissent and popular enthusiasm throughout the eighteenth century in Britain. The fear of popular millenarianism among the elite was based on memories of what had happened during the English Civil War, when groups such as the Fifth Monarchy Men had made the biblical prophecies of the Second Coming their authority for rising against the state to proclaim the rule of King Jesus. Over a century later Robert Southey's *Letters from England* (1809) could still claim that the ruling classes had much more to fear from the religious enthusiasm of the masses than from political radicalism. Southey had been in London during the 1790s when the most spectacular example of popular millenarianism in eighteenth-century Britain had manifested itself around the person of Richard Brothers. The popularity of Brothers and his prophecies shocked a periodical press that desperately wanted to believe in its own narratives of Enlightenment progress as proof of British superiority. Conservative commentators, it is true, sometimes found the emergence of latter-day prophets welcome proof of the unstable and untrustworthy nature of the masses. More liberal opinion – whether supportive of the French Revolution or not – was more often simply shocked to see such a public refutation of its faith in the progress of Enlightenment. Typical of the latter is the

Analytical Review's somewhat bewildered account of the widespread interest in Brothers:

> Facts sometimes occur, which, though not miraculous, almost as much astonish the philosopher, as if he saw a miracle. Such a fact is the recent attention, which at the close of the 18th century, and in the metropolis of one of the most enlightened nations of Europe, has been paid by people of all ranks to a mad prophet.
>
> (*Analytical Review*, 21 (1795): 318)

The extent to which Brothers engaged public attention in 1795 can be gauged by the fact that even the *Analytical Review*, however reluctantly, was forced for a few months in the middle of that year to devote a special section to reviewing prophecies.

The outline of the Brothers story itself is now quite well known. He was a former naval lieutenant who had been discharged on half pay at the end of the American War of Independence. In 1790 he had refused on religious grounds to swear the oath of loyalty to the King required for him to draw his pay. The result was a period in a workhouse, followed by a brief stay in Newgate. When he was released in 1792, Brothers began writing prophetic letters to the government claiming that God had revealed to him that the French Revolution was the fulfilment of biblical prophecy and should not be challenged by force of British arms. His prophecies became the centre of a very public controversy when he published *A Revealed Knowledge of the Prophecies and Times* (1794–5), a text that quickly went through several editions. The Brothers controversy witnessed an outpouring of enthusiasm not seen for many decades. Anthologies filled with visionary material, such as George Riebau's *God's Awful Warning* (1795) and Garnet Terry's *Prophetical Extracts* (1794–5), quickly appeared to meet the demand for millenarian visions, much of it reprinting what we might call the canon of seventeenth-century enthusiasm. Bastions of politeness, such as the *Gentleman's Magazine* (65 (1795): 218), regarded such material as feeding the irrationality of 'the bulk of the people, whose minds in these days do not need disquiet'. The government finally listened and arrested Brothers on suspicion of treasonable practices. He was subsequently interrogated by the Privy Council and then confined to a madhouse until Pitt's death in 1806. The government may not have believed that Brothers himself was a radical, but they were wary of the influence of his prophecies on the mood of the people.

There is no doubt that a more scholarly tradition of millenarianism also played an important part in the radical response to the French Revolution in Britain. The scientist and dissenting minister Joseph Priestley can be counted among the number of those Rational Dissenters who applied biblical eschatology to contemporary political events. Samuel Taylor Coleridge, who came under the sway of the Rational Dissenter William Frend while at Cambridge in the early 1790s, was deeply affected by this eschatological view of history. Price and Priestley both related their millenarianism to a discourse of Enlightenment reason. The violence of their language in the pulpit may sometimes have suggested otherwise, but they did not claim the unmediated access to truth associated with popular religious enthusiasm. Both usually validated their prophetic view of history through careful historical and textual scholarship.

Radicals and reformers more generally – whether religious or otherwise – reiterated that they were not seeking to unleash a torrent of popular enthusiasm. Indeed, they often defined themselves as the true heirs of a process of Enlightenment of which enthusiasm usually appeared as the explicit antithesis. From their point of view, vulgar enthusiasm was the product of ignorance, but an ignorance that could be ameliorated by greater cultural and political participation. It was not an irremediable condition of the people. The popular radical movement associated from 1792 with the Corresponding Societies, seeking to ameliorate ignorance by a more vigorous dissemination of knowledge across classes, constantly stressed its commitment to 'reform not riot', distancing itself from the passions of the crowd, but there were those who seemed to pay scant regard to the question of regulation and even some who continued to proclaim that political change was directly ordained by God. Their eager expectations of an imminent political Millennium intensified fears even inside the radical movement about the unstable nature of popular enthusiasm. Brothers and those associated with him were widely regarded as the crazy products of popular enthusiasm: a kind of miraculous throwback to an age of irrationality in religion.

Burke sometimes regarded Enlightenment faith in the candle of reason as simply a transmutation of the seventeenth-century Puritan faith in the inner light, but the distinction was not easily collapsed. Priestley looked to the fulfilment of the events prophesied by the Bible as proof of the truth of the scriptures. The *Evangelical Magazine* still wanted to distinguish between those whose 'hope that a glorious period is at hand' had 'led to study' and those 'not content with so sober and commendable inquiry, have been bold enough to boast of a prophetic spirit' (*Evangelical Magazine*, 4 (1796): 303). Men and women such as Brothers, who boasted of their own ignorance as proof of their inspiration, were readily consigned to the former category by the enlightened organs of the periodical press. What was more of a matter for dispute was whether the millenarianism of Rational Dissenters of Priestley's ilk deserved the same disapprobation. In the *Analytical Review* the Dissenters James Bicheno and J. L. Towers were both praised for the sober nature of their scholarly arguments in favour of a millenarian reading of contemporary political affairs.

The *Gentleman's Magazine* was less inclined than the *Analytical Review* to accept such distinctions. Its judgement on Bicheno, for instance, was pithy: 'He has studied the prophetic parts of Scripture till he has bewildered himself' (*Gentleman's Magazine*, 55 (1795): 759). Bicheno believed that the Reformation 'originated from Christians assuming the right of searching the Scriptures, and of judging for themselves, as to the mind of Christ taught in them' (Bicheno 1798: 14–15). Searching for signs of the times in the eighteenth century was consonant for Bicheno with Enlightenment principles of free enquiry inherited from the Reformation.

EDMUND BURKE AND REVOLUTIONARY ENTHUSIASM

Horace Walpole regarded the spectacle of 'enthusiasm without religion' (Walpole 1937–83: vol. 34, 182) as the great novelty of the French Revolution, ignoring the fact that from at least Swift onwards the word had always attached itself to schemes of innovation or improvement, however 'rational' or scientific their rhetoric. By the end of the decade the *Anti-Jacobin*, 34 (1798: 268) could take as proven what to Horace Walpole seemed a strange and almost unbelievable idea: 'the French Revolution has proved that Enthusiasm does not belong only to Religion: that there may exist as much zeal in blaspheming GOD as in praising him'. The second of Burke's *Two Letters on a Regicide Peace* (1796) reads almost as if it were a direct rejoinder to Walpole's perception of the novelty of the Revolution on this point:

> They who have made but superficial studies in the Natural History of the human mind, have been taught to look on religious opinions as the only cause of enthusiastick zeal, and sectarian propagation. But there is no doctrine whatever, on which men can warm, which is not capable of the very same effect. The social nature of man impels him to propagate his kind. The passions give zeal and vehemence. The whole man moves under the discipline of his opinions.
>
> (Burke 1796b: 278)

There are two key assumptions at work in Burke's definition of enthusiasm. The ability of opinions to turn into indiscriminate zeal is acknowledged as part of secular as well as religious discourse, and, second, this ability is defined by its need to propagate itself. Burke crystallized a definition of enthusiasm as the inclination of the mind to privilege its own productions over the world, or, more specifically, 'any attempt to establish the reasoning mind's ascendancy over the contexts in which it reasoned' (Pocock 1989: 26). From this perspective, radicals like Godwin and Holcroft, who demanded absolute freedom in the quest for truth, were as guilty of enthusiasm as the wildest Methodist. Revolutionary *transparence* that claimed to know and represent immediately the will of the people was a latter-day enthusiasm to someone such as Burke.

'Enthusiasm' was often seen as the prerequisite of political liberty in the Whig tradition from which Burke came; it was even conceived as an important engine of progress. At the beginning of the eighteenth century the Earl of Shaftesbury had seen in enthusiasm the desire to transcend the world of mere getting and spending. Popular religious enthusiasm was the diseased form of an innate human propensity. All heroic endeavour depended on a degree of enthusiasm from this point of view. Against Burke's attack on enthusiasm, James Mackintosh launched the defence that 'all improvements in human life have been *deviations* from experience' (Mackintosh 1791: 111). Utopian speculation was effectively being defended by Mackintosh as a store-house of human possibility. Burke had asserted his own 'love' for 'a manly, moral, regulated liberty' (Burke 1790: 57) against unrestricted enthusiasm of radical projectors. He put forward a Humean view of the dangers of innovations proceeding in an unregulated fashion on the basis of the wishful thinking of philosophers.

Regulation, morality and manliness were touchstones of Whig political tradition and Burke seized on another when he suggested that English liberty differed both from the excesses of France and from the enthusiasm of English Dissenters such as Richard Price in its concern with conforming to the manners of the world-as-it-is. Politeness meant adapting oneself to 'circumstances' for Burke, as it did for the tradition of British moralists, including Hume and Adam Smith. Circumstances determine for Burke whether any scheme of improvement will be 'beneficial or noxious to mankind' (Burke 1790: 58). The enemy of a flourishing society was 'a systematick unsociability' (Burke 1796b: 257) in which the obsessions of the zealot threatened to dominate all aspects of life. But Burke also supplemented the familiar Whig discourse of manners with a respect for tradition embodied above all else in the compact of Church and state. Without tradition one is open to the delirium of individual consciousness that might mistake the literary genre of Utopianism for a practical political programme. The Bill of Rights was not framed 'by warm and inexperienced enthusiasts' (Burke 1790: 67) for Burke; rather, it was the product of a Humean weighing of the practical demands of government against the zeal for liberty with an additional reverence for precedent. Tradition was also embodied in the external forms of the constitution and the Church, neither of which ought lightly to be tampered with by reformers. Burke identifies disestablishment as a highly dangerous element in the revolutionary agenda, both in Britain and in France, precisely because it aims at the destruction of the most important of these constraining powers. He presents Price as a man who believes that anyone who cannot find a form of public worship that suits them should 'set up a separate worship for themselves' (Price 1790: 18). Rational Dissent is 'remarkable in its zeal for any opinion' (Burke 1790: 63). 'Candour' made into a principle of *transparence* for Burke always ends up as mere Utopian enthusiasm.

Compared to the weighty presence of tradition embodied in the external institutions of the Church and state, enthusiasm represents a 'dreadful energy' (Burke 1796b: 289), one which Burke sees as a defining trait of men of letters. Living by the productions of their brains, Burke believed such men were necessarily committed to believe in what Pocock calls 'the freedom of discourse to create the world unilaterally' (1989: 20). They are by their very nature enthusiasts in that they locate cultural value in the power their own ideas can extend over circumstance:

> These philosophers are fanaticks; independent of any interest, which if its operated would make them much more tractable, they are carried with such an headlong rage towards every desperate trial, that they would sacrifice the whole human race to the slightest of their experiments.
>
> (Burke 1796a: 176)

For Burke, Rousseau becomes the chief representative of Utopian speculators. Only fleetingly mentioned in *Reflections*, Burke later developed the image of Rousseau as the high priest of revolutionary *transparence*. Gregory Dart has recently emphasized the difference between Rousseau and the more sceptical tradition of French Enlightenment thought in this respect. Certainly, within Britain, as Dart shows, Rousseau was originally perceived as a writer who consulted his own heart above all other authorities. Early reviews had stressed the 'enthusiasm' of *Emile* and often represented Rousseau as a brave (Protestant) defender of religious freedom of conscience (Dart 1999: 13). Rousseau, to Burke, is a man who believes his own prophetic visions of mankind, abandoning received wisdom to 'the infinite void of the conjectural world', and disseminating a 'restless, agitating, activity' (1796b: 188, 224). Practical human sociability contrasted, for Burke, with Rousseau's Utopian benevolence is predicated on the importance of local and above all domestic attachments: 'The little platoon we belong to in society, is the first principle (the germ as it were) of public affections' (1790: 97–8). Victims of enthusiasm abjure such a mediated view of human sociability, in favour of a vision of universal benevolence that believes it possible to love the whole without progressing through the links of more local human affections.

Many of those in the radical movement and beyond who disagreed with Burke's reading of the Revolution regarded his representation of the spirit of enquiry as itself nothing more than an overemotional form of enthusiasm. Burke's zeal for monarchy was clouding his judgement about what they regarded as a specifically political phenomenon with determinate socio-economic causes. But some of these critics of Burke, including Mary Wollstonecraft, like Mackintosh, believed some version of utopian speculation necessary to the idea of progress (see Chapter 11 of this volume). For them, Burke had failed to see the deep differences between the world in 1790 and the world of the Fifth Monarchy Men when it came to the relationship between speculation and political praxis. These differences became an important theme in radical writing of the 1790s. John Thelwall, for instance, turned to it several times in proclaiming the universality of the virtues of the Enlightenment. He believed that the people were now capable of regulating their aspirations for themselves without the external authorities of Church and state. Their desire for liberty could now be trusted to find its own limits, because the Enlightenment had produced a newly educated popular political constituency. Yet Thelwall and others within the radical movement never entirely exorcized their own fear that the Burkean scenario might be true in a number of ways. At times they seemed to fear that the spirit of enthusiasm in the people had not and even could not be regulated by a process of general Enlightenment, and, worst of all, that their own writings and speeches might actually be provoking this infection in the body politic. For all reform-minded writers in the period there remained a pressing need to demonstrate that their visions of progress and change were not simply the effusions of the enthusiasts or the fantasies of Utopian fictions.

UTOPIAN LITERATURE

Enlightenment ideas of progress were not couched only in terms of a biblical millenarian. There was a flourishing literary tradition of Utopian writing that offered elaborated accounts of the future state of mankind. Leaving aside earlier influences, such as Plato and More, the eighteenth-century literary genre of Utopia was particularly influenced by two key prototypes: Daniel Defoe's *Robinson Crusoe* (1719) and Jonathan Swift's satirical *Gulliver's Travels* (1726). The latter seems to have provided a model for several dystopian satires on ideas of primitive virtue, including Edmund Burke's *Vindication of Natural Society* (1756) and Samuel Johnson's *Rasselas* (1759), although sometimes judgements about whether specific works were meant to be satirical attacks on ideas of progress or really Utopian were and are often difficult to make. The account of the rational society of the Houhnyhmns in the fourth book of Swift's novel was read by at least one commentator, for instance, as a classical republican Utopia. Alternatively some readers understood Burke's pamphlet as a straightforward satire on the artificiality of modern manners that really espoused a primitivist agenda.

The eighteenth century was undoubtedly an age that 'swarmed with projectors, adventurers, moralists and improvers of all sorts' (Claeys 1994: vii). Although modern readers might see a clear difference between the more worldly constitutional innovations of the American and French republics and unworldly Utopian and millenarian fantasies, such distinctions were much less clear to contemporaries, even to those less hostile to reform than Burke was to become. Manifesting the sceptical aspects of the period, Swift's *Gulliver's Travels* had to jostle for space with the plethora of texts that looked either back towards a naturally harmonious state of society or forward towards human perfectibility. Godwin even claimed the fourth book of Swift's novel as an inspiration for his *Political Justice* (1793) and its vision of human perfectibility. In fictional form, Godwin's ideas were propounded in Thomas Northmore's *Memoirs of Planetes, or a Sketch of the Laws and Manners of Makar* (1795). Makar is a primitive republic on a Pacific island (a favourite setting for such Utopian fiction after Cook's voyages) where civil and religious freedom reigns. Such narratives as Cook's journals or accounts of the mutiny on the *Bounty* produced fictional Utopias in their image, and also encouraged model commonwealths for the development of new colonies, such as Carl Wadstrom's *Essay on Colonization* (1784) and Granville Sharp's *A Short Sketch of Temporary Regulations . . . for the Intended Settlement Near Sierra Leone* (1786). If the constitution of the United States itself could be regarded as one practical outcome of the eighteenth century's Utopian speculations, North America continued to be a site for European Utopian experiments even after the War of Independence. Plans for a pantisocratic community developed by the poets Samuel Taylor Coleridge and Robert Southey in the 1790s were part of this strain of Enlightenment speculation on ideal societies.

By no means all of these Utopian plans and experiments looked backwards for their models, however. The increasing importance of science and technology played its part in influencing ideas about progress and perfectibility, such as the ideas on the prolongation of human life in Godwin's *Political Justice* as well as the more dystopian reflections of his daughter Mary Shelley's novel *Frankenstein* (1817). The growing popularity of ideas of progress and related thinking about stages of human social development had an important influence on Utopian writing. Influential statements of these ideas are found in the writing of *philosophes* such as Condorcet, as well as most of the thinkers involved in the Scottish Enlightenment, but they often supplemented rather than simply displaced older Christian ideas in relation to the Millennium. Although Priestley's *Observations on the Increase of Infidelity* (1797) contained an attack on the atheism of Volney's *Les Ruines*, for instance, the latter's vision of humanity liberated from the chains of priestcraft could find itself circulated in contexts that were far from hostile to the Christian millenarian tradition. Thomas Spence was quite happy to mix Volney with the biblical 'Jubilee'. The Presbyterian minister Morgan John Rhys translated the popular vision of the 'New Age' in Volney's fifteenth chapter into Welsh. Volney's faith in a religion of nature whereby God revealed Himself in His works and humanity gradually progressed towards a society governed by reason was easily accommodated from this perspective into the Christian idea of progress towards the Millennium. Many eighteenth-century Utopias represented humanity as progressing towards a 'New Age' that would be more egalitarian and even based on goods held in common. Indeed, the term 'Utopian' was sometimes simply contrasted not just with practical politics but specifically to 'the system of private property' (Reid 1990: 284). Some of the period's Utopias indeed recommended forms of social ownership. In Thomas Spence's version of Crusoe's island, *Supplement to the History of Robinson Crusoe* (1782), Europeans have married into the indigenous population and set up a version of his agrarian programme where land is taken over for the nation and managed through parishes. Spence's thinking was eclectic in the extreme, as we have seen, but his agrarian programme owed a great deal to James Harrington's seventeenth-century Utopia *Oceana* (1656). Propounded by Spence and his followers into the nineteenth century, these ideas merged with the development of what came to be explicitly described as 'socialism'.

By no means all Utopias of this period were hostile to property ownership, however. Thomas Paine did not care 'how affluent some may be, provided none be miserable in consequence' (1797: 10). Nor did William Hodgson's Painite *Common-wealth of Reason* (1795) put forward any plan based on community ownership of property, although it offered a vision of a society based on deep-seated constitutional and social reforms. Their political opponents were not often interested in acknowledging the distinctions between Spencean ideas of social ownership and the more liberal Utopias of men such as Paine and Hodgson, however. Burke and his followers were likely to denounce all radical reformers as dangerous enthusiasts. Utopian thinking was frowned upon where it seemed to undermine tried and trusted distinctions between practical politics and philosophical speculation.

There remains one other account of the fate of Enlightenment Utopianism and millenarianism to be considered. Romanticism is often represented as a retreat from the political programmes of the Enlightenment that attempted to translate Utopianism into political practice in the American and French revolutions. An influential restatement of this narrative by M. H. Abrams represents the process in terms of the transformation of one kind of prophetic ardour into another: 'faith in an apocalypse by revolution . . . gave way to faith in apocalypse by imagination or cognition' (Abrams 1971: 334). Abrams made much of Schiller's idea that 'in the realm of Aesthetic Semblance, we find that ideal of equality fulfilled which the Enthusiast would fain see realized in substance' (quoted in Abrams 1971: 352). Faced with the defeat of their political ambitions in the French Revolution, according to this narrative, poets such as William Wordsworth and Samuel Taylor Coleridge turned to an apocalypse of the imagination that would bring about a paradise within. Whether the realm of the imagination explored so fully in Romanticism ought to be regarded as an alternative to the possibility of translating millenarian aspirations into this world remains a moot point, however.

William Blake continued to echo Thomas Holcroft's faith in the palpability of the New Jerusalem well into the nineteenth century. If the abstruse and mystical writing of late prophecies such as *Jerusalem* seem a long way from the practical politics of the 1790s, the insistence that Utopia could be built on England's green and pleasant land kept alive the possibility that the Millennium could be achieved in reality. Certainly for someone such as Percy Bysshe Shelley, the power of the imagination remained defined in terms of 'going out of our own nature' in a way that remained intimately tied in with political possibilities in this world (Shelley 1821: 282).

Utopian and millenarian strains in Enlightenment thinking, therefore, made their way into the nineteenth century in a multiplicity of forms. They could produce ways of thinking that were essentially nostalgic and even escapist. Sometimes they looked to a transcendental realm for their fulfilment, whether explicitly religious or otherwise. But they continued to feed into political agendas and continued to be preoccupied with the attempt to improve the human condition.

REFERENCES

Abrams, M. H. (1971) *Natural Supernaturalism: Tradition and Revolution in Romantic Literature*, repr. 1973, New York and London: W. W. Norton.

Bicheno, James (1798) *A Glance at the History of Christianity, and of English Nonconformity*, London: Joseph Johnson *et al*.

Burke, Edmund (1790) *Reflections on the Revolution in France*, ed. L. G. Mitchell (1991) in vol. VIII of *The Writings and Speeches of Edmund Burke*, 9 vols, general ed. Paul Langford, Oxford: Oxford University Press.

—— (1796a) *Letter to a Noble Lord*, ed. R. B. McDowell (1991) in vol. IX of *The Writings and Speeches of Edmund Burke, op. cit.*

—— (1796b) *Two Letters Addressed to a Member of the Present Parliament, on the Proposals for Peace with the Regicide Directory of France*, ed. R. B. McDowell (1991) in vol. IX of *The Writings and Speeches of Edmund Burke, op. cit.*

Claeys, Gregory (1994) 'Introduction', in *idem* (ed.) *Utopias of the British Enlightenment*, Cambridge: Cambridge University Press.

Dart, Gregory (1999) *Rousseau, Robespierre and English Romanticism*, Cambridge: Cambridge University Press.

Garrett, Clarke (1975) *Respectable Folly: Millenarians and the French Revolution in France and England*, Baltimore: Johns Hopkins University Press.

Harrison, J. F. C. (1979) *The Second Coming: Popular Millenarianism 1780–1850*, London and Henley: Routledge & Kegan Paul.

Kegan Paul, C. (1876) *William Godwin: His Friends and Contemporaries*, 2 vols, London: H. King.

Mackintosh, James (1791) *Vindiciae Gallicae: A Defence of the French Revolution and its English Admirers against the Accusations of the Right Hon. Edmund Burke*, London: G. G. J. and J. Robinson.

Paine, Thomas, *Agrarian Justice* (1797) Paris and London: Adlard & Ballard.

Pocock, J. G. A. (1989) 'Edmund Burke and the Redefinition of Enthusiasm: The Context as Counter Revolution', in vol. III of François Furet and Mona Ozouf (eds) *The French Revolution and the Creation of Modern Political Culture 1789–1848*, 4 vols, Oxford and New York: Pergamon Press.

Price, Richard (1790) *A Discourse on the Love of Our Country, Delivered on Nov. 4 1789, at the Meeting House in the Old Jewry, to the Society for Commemorating the Revolution in Great Britain*, London: T. Cadell.

Priestley, Joseph (1771) *An Essay on the First Principles of Government; and on the Nature of Political, Civil, and Religious Liberty*, 2nd edn London: J. Johnson.

Reid, Thomas (1990) *Practical Ethics*, ed. Knud Haakonssen, Princeton: Princeton University Press.

Shelley, Percy Bysshe (1821) 'A Defence of Poetry', in David Lee Clark (ed.) *Shelley's Prose* (1954); repr. 1988, London: Fourth Estate.

Thompson, E. P. (1963) *The Making of the English Working Class*; repr. 1968, Harmondsworth: Penguin.

Tuveson, Ernest Lee (1968) *Redeemer Nation: The Idea of America's Millennial Role*, Chicago: Chicago University Press.

Walpole, Horace (1937–83) *The Yale Edition of Horace Walpole's Correspondence*, ed. W. S. Lewis, 48 vols, New Haven, Conn.: Yale University Press.

CHAPTER THIRTY-THREE

CROSS-CULTURAL ENCOUNTERS IN THE ENLIGHTENMENT

Dorinda Outram

INTRODUCTION

Over the last decade, the traditional idea of the Enlightenment as confined to European nations and their colonies has given way to a new perception of Enlightenment as a world drama of cross-cultural contact, a drama with enormous consequences for both European and indigenous peoples. For the latter, contact with Europeans often changed their social, economic and intellectual order. For the Europeans, such encounters often triggered anxieties about the nature of European society, and about the meaning of their identity as 'civilized'. At the same time, encounters with other cultures supplied data to important debates on the nature of human variety and difference, on their relation to environment, and on the possibility of a common human history. These concerns are still with us in the form of debates over multiculturalism. Should European values be the universal standard, or should there be a plurality of value systems and meanings? If so, how is this variety to be integrated into the process of globalization? These were questions set in motion by Enlightenment cross-cultural encounters (Joppke and Lukes 1999).

APPROACHES

What is a cross-cultural encounter? 'Culture' is not an easy word to define, and even anthropologists have pointed out its problematic nature (Kroeber 1952). Another source of difficulty is the fact that such terms are not used by Enlightenment writers. In talking about 'cross-cultural encounters' we are thus facing the charge of anachronism. As Raymond Williams pointed out in his classic *Culture and Society* (1958: xvi), it was only in the nineteenth century that in English 'culture' came to mean 'culture as such, a thing in itself . . . a whole way of life, material and intellectual and spiritual'. Previously, before the late eighteenth century, 'culture' meant 'the tending of natural growth', and then, by analogy, 'the process of human training'. The *Oxford English Dictionary* tells us that the term 'cross-cultural encounter' itself came into use among professional anthropologists only as late as the 1950s. It was, of course, a concept unknown to any of the indigenous peoples who met Europeans in the eighteenth century.

Enlightenment peoples assumed themselves to be the norm. For them, the opposite of 'our culture' was not 'their culture' but 'barbarism'. They were also unlikely to see 'cultures' as organically unified or traditionally continuous. So, if the phrase 'cross-cultural encounter' is an anachronism to this period, what are we concerned with in this chapter? What is in contact? Not entire cultures, surely, but particular representatives of cultures in particular situations and places. Explorers like Bougainville (1729–1814), La Pérouse (1741–88), Bering (1681–1741), Cook (1728–79), Anson (1697–1762), Vancouver (1758–98) and Bligh (1754–1817) did not embody the whole culture which lay behind them, any more than the indigenous peoples who met them represented the whole of theirs. In fact, contacts between Europeans and non-Europeans were often highly structured, focused on particular questions, and saw each side interpreting the other in accordance with existing religious beliefs and cultural norms. Neither side thought it was making a 'cross-cultural contact' (Lamb, Smith and Thomas 2000: xv–xxv).

BACKGROUNDS

As well as avoiding anachronism, we have to set the new contacts of the Enlightenment period in the context of the many pre-existing contacts with non-European peoples. In the sixteenth century the establishment of the Spanish Empire in Mexico, Cuba, Peru and what is now southern California, Texas and Florida, and of the Portuguese Empire in Brazil, had led to sustained contact with conquered indigenous peoples. Almost all of them had been devastated by epidemic disease introduced by the invaders, as well as by the collapse of their governments, societies and cultures. In the East Indies a Dutch trading empire established in the seventeenth century was still working to absorb the lucrative commerce in spices controlled by local rajahs. In Labrador and Hudson's Bay a long-standing fur trade with Inuit people continued in this period, and was extended by missionary contact from the 1790s. In North America French colonies in what is now Canada and English colonies that stretched down the eastern seaboard, guarded by chains of forts in the Ohio and Mississippi valleys, initiated sustained contact with American Indian tribes in the early seventeenth century (Axtell 2001). Missionary activity in all European colonies was a form of long-standing contact. Another was the import since the sixteenth century into the Spanish Empire, and from the seventeenth into British colonies, of African slaves. In the Caribbean their labour replaced that of the exterminated original peoples.

This chapter, however, will concentrate on those contacts specific to the Enlightenment. Many happened as the result of the organization and spread of the practice of exploration. Land exploration produced new contacts with the peoples of the vast area of Siberia. The exploration there began as a result of the efforts of the Russian monarchy to find out the full extent of its territories and their resources. In 1804, in an attempt to establish a transcontinental route by river, Meriwether Lewis (1774–1809) and William Clark (1770–1838) travelled from St Louis to the Pacific, meeting as yet unknown American Indian peoples. Maritime exploration concentrated on the Pacific. Little was known of Russia's Pacific coast, nor was it known whether a land bridge existed between what is now Alaska and Russia. In 1728 the Danish sailor and explorer Vitus Bering discovered the existence of the channel between the two continents which bear his name. In 1741, he set out on his last, disastrous voyage across the North Pacific, taking with him, however, the young German naturalist Georg Wilhelm Steller (1709–46), who was the first to record contacts between Russians and the peoples of the Aleutian Islands (Steller 1988).

If Bering's efforts helped to fill in the outline of the North Pacific, the rest of the ocean was explored for the first time in a number of British and French expeditions. In 1768–71 James Cook, sailing with a single ship, the *Endeavour*, was the first European to see, map and claim the east coast of what is now Australia. In 1791 Vancouver, building on Cook's work and contact with Indian peoples around Nootka Sound in the North Pacific, extended the survey of the North Pacific coast of North America. All this gave a huge impetus to trade in the Pacific, which had scarcely seen three or four European ships a year until the 1790s. Now flotillas of American and European ships traded in an integrated system between London or Salem and the Pacific. They carried Chinese tea, whale oil, sea-otter furs from Nootka and tropical wood from the Marquesas (Dening 1980). All this exploration and trade by Europeans was accompanied, inevitably, by repeated contact with indigenous peoples.

Behind exploration often lay geopolitical, as well as trading, imperatives. There were massive shifts in the balance of power among the European states after the end of the Seven Years War in 1763. Britain replaced France as the major European power on the Indian subcontinent, and began to extend and stabilize her trading empire there. As scholars such as Christopher Bayly (1997) have pointed out, this led to an enlarged and sustained contact with Indian society very different from the fleeting contacts between European ships and Pacific islanders that were occurring at the same time. After 1763 Britain also replaced France in what is now Canada, and in the territories of the Ohio valley, and thus became the dominant power in North America. Britain became for the first time a global power, sustaining primarily maritime links between her different possessions, and between them and London.

Yet geopolitics does not provide the only framework for cross-cultural encounters. Unlike the discoveries by Columbus and his contemporaries, European contacts in the Pacific did not result directly or immediately in settlement or in the exploitation of the indigenous peoples. Cook claimed the eastern coast of Australia for the first time in 1771, yet it was not until 1789 that the first European settlement was established at Sydney Cove. The motives of exploration could be broader than those of geopolitical advantage and have a chronology – in Cook's case the predicted course of the planet Venus – dictated by other time-scales than those of statesmen. The German states sent out few expeditions, yet much significant thinking about man and society arising from encounters with the Pacific peoples comes from German thinkers, including Cook's companions on his second voyage, Johann Reinhold Forster (1729–98) and his son Georg (1754–94) (Hoare 1982; Thomas *et al.* 1996) and Johann Gottfried Herder (1744–1803) at the end of the century.

The eighteenth-century voyages of exploration were the first to be centrally concerned with the gathering of information about man and the natural world. It is important to realize that information about man was often gathered as part of enquiry into natural history. Earlier circumnavigations, like that of the freebooter William

Dampier (1652–1715), had resulted in the first contact with Australian Aboriginal peoples (Lamb 2001: 111, 214, 277), and the mapping of some of the coast of western Australia. But these had been the accidental by-products of voyages whose objectives were loot and plunder. The next century saw voyages organized, often on an international basis, in the pursuit of scientific objectives. La Condamine's (1701–74) exploration of the Amazon and its peoples originated in his participation in an international effort to make observations that would determine the true shape of the earth. James Cook sailed on his first voyage as part of an international effort to observe the transit of Venus between the sun and the earth. This is not to deny that Cook was also given instructions by the Admiralty on all his voyages, to claim for George III all new lands he encountered, but, for Cook and his contemporaries, deliberate gathering of knowledge about new cultures was high among their objectives. Exploration in this period was becoming an information-gathering activity.

HOW ENCOUNTERS HAPPENED

Johann Reinhold Forster wrote in his Essay 'Cook der Entdecker' ('Cook the Discoverer'):

> Let us look, however, at the most important object of our researches, at our own species; at just how many races, with whose very name we were formerly unacquainted, have been described down to their smallest characteristics, through the memorable efforts of this great man! Their physical diversity, their temperament, their customs, their modes of life and dress, their form of government, their religion, their ideas of science and works of art, in short everything was collected by Cook for his contemporaries and for posterity with fidelity and with tireless diligence. No one knew the value of a fleeting moment better.
>
> (quoted in Frost 1976: 798)

Forster's observation reveals how central the study of man became to exploration at this time. It also shows that the explorers' observations were not made randomly. Nor do they try to take in an entire 'culture'. Explorers wanted, rather, to know specific details about technology, religion, gender roles, language, whether the indigenous people have more or less complex and hierarchical systems of government and religion, whether they are nomadic or practise settled agriculture, use money, understand bargaining and markets.

Forster's comments also tell us that the use Cook and others like him made of the 'fleeting moment' was a matter of some importance. Sometimes these moments were 'fleeting' indeed. This means that accounts of encounters cannot be read as complete accounts of the indigenous societies concerned. There was always much that was unseen, unknowable and unspeakable in these encounters. Violence and fear of it often prevented them happening at all. Joseph Banks (1743–1820), future president of the Royal Society, who travelled with Cook on his first voyage, gives us the following account of the ship passing the low islands of Marokau and Rarahere on

6 April 1769. Signals from the islanders were ambiguous, and 'Our situation made it very improper to try them further – we wanted nothing, the island was too trifling to be an object worth taking possession of; had we therefore out of mere curiosity hoisted out a boat, and the natives by attacking us obliged us to destroy some of them, the only reason we could give for it would be the desire of satisfying a useless curiosity.' The ship sailed on. Curiosity could not always be indulged (quoted in Beaglehole 1962: vol. I, 247).

Even in situations presenting no obvious threat, entering into contact was often difficult. Here, for example, is Georg Forster's account of Cook making contact with a Maori in Dusky Bay, New Zealand.

> Captain Cook went to the head of the boat, called to him in a friendly manner, and threw him his own and some other handkerchiefs, which he would not pick up. The Captain, then taking some sheets of white paper in his hand, landed on the rock unarmed, and held the paper out to the native. The man now trembled very visibly, and having exhibited strong marks of fear in his countenance, took the paper; upon which Captain Cook coming up to him, took hold of his hand, and embraced him, touching the man's nose with his own, which is their mode of salutation. His apprehension was by this dissipated, and he called to . . . two women, who came and joined him, while several of us landed to keep the Captain company. A short conversation ensued, of which little was understood on both sides, for want of a complete knowledge of their language.
>
> (Forster 1777: vol. I, 137–8)

In the absence of a common spoken language, Cook makes contact by using small objects to make bridges between himself and the Maori. Objects are very important in contact situations. Physical contact then follows. Cook crosses the boundary between his own culture and that of the Maoris by adopting the Maoris' own gesture of rubbing noses for a literal face-to-face encounter. At the same time, he makes the physical transition between the boat and shore. He moves out of his world and into that of the islanders. In this island world of the Pacific the defining place of contact is a beach. Cook was to die on Kealakekua beach, Hawaii, in February 1779. The ever-present fear that, in the absence of a common language, and in ignorance of the meaning of physical gestures in each culture, even a peaceful encounter like this could easily turn into violence is shown by Cook's companions 'keeping him company'. For the Maoris, it was also clearly a situation of extreme fear and uncertainty.

There are many common features in encounters. Thirty years before Cook, in 1741, the German naturalist Georg Steller, sailing in the North Pacific with Bering, found himself in contact with inhabitants of the Aleutian Islands. Again, there was no common language. Again, exchange of objects played a large part in establishing friendly contact. An Aleut fashioned a falcon out of a stick and two real falcon wings, and flung it into the sea separating the vessels. Possibly intended as a magic gesture, the Russians interpreted it as a signal of welcome, and began to initiate the ritual of exchange:

Then, for our part, we bound two Chinese tobacco pipes and Chinese glass beads to a small piece of board, and threw it in exchange to them. He picked it up, looked at it a bit, and handed it over to his companion . . . Then he became somewhat braver, came still closer to us, yet with the greatest caution, bound a whole falcon to another stick, and presented it to our Koriak interpreter, to receive from us a piece of Chinese silk and a mirror.

At a later encounter, Steller traded for some Aleut hats, made out of feathers, 'with a rusty iron kettle, five sewing needles, and a thread' (Steller 1988: 99). The exchange of objects, which initially occurs in these encounters at the symbolic level, can shade into relationships of trade.

In spite of the many common features in the accounts of contact between Europeans and indigenous peoples, there were also significant differences. Situations of sustained contact were very different from those of 'fleeting moments'. One such situation of sustained contact was that between Indians and Englishmen in India. This occurred as a direct result of the geopolitical struggles that left Britain as the dominant European power in the Indian states after 1763. While trading relations had existed since the sixteenth century, it was not until after 1763 that the East India Company began dramatically to enlarge its governmental functions. It became crucial for the Company to set up courts incorporating local legal systems. This project could not have been carried through without the co-operation of Indian legal experts with their English opposite numbers, such as the judge and Sanskrit scholar Sir William Jones (1746–94). Company officials and Indians alike had to make great efforts to learn the other's language and legal concepts. The Indians were not passive informants, and over many years each 'culture' became involved in a process, dependent to some degree on trust, of negotiation and explanation with the other. This negotiation both depended upon and fortified institutional bases for knowledge (Lawson 1993: 114; Bayly 1997; Raj 2001).

The Indian situation contrasts with that of the majority of Pacific contacts. Here, the relationship between Europeans and islanders lacked institutional stabilization, and the periods of contact were not long enough to establish trust. Whereas India had been known in Europe since classical times, and had been part of Roman trade exchanges, European ships in the eighteenth-century Pacific were alone in a largely unknown island world. Trust was lacking, and this meant that theft was a sensitive issue. In the Pacific metalworking was unknown before European contact. Technological inequalities, absent to the same degree in India, meant that, for the islanders, metal objects were worth stealing because of their power and extraordinary rarity. For Europeans, the issue was one of replaceability. At home, nails, instruments and ships' boats could be easily replaced. In the Pacific, this was difficult or impossible, and their loss could endanger the voyage, or many individual lives. Cook's taking of hostages after the theft of a boat on Hawaii was crucial to the events leading up to his death. It also demonstrates the way in which an island, rather than a mainland, situation, technological imbalance and lack of stable negotiating patterns could give contact a fatal outcome.

Contacts varied considerably. Much depended on whether indigenous peoples had written language at the time of contact, whether the contact was institutionalized, whether it took place on an island or mainland, whether there were notable differences between the technologies of either side, and whether there were sexual relations, marriages or formal friendships between the two sides – as there were on Tahiti, but not on Nootka. There were differences even between North and South Pacific. Cook's contacts with Nootka Indians on Vancouver Island, while brief, were still substantial enough to develop a measure of trust around the controlled market that developed with Europeans in sea-otter pelts. The Indians won the respect of the sailors because of their bargaining skills, and the market gave stable rules to encounters. It may also have made a difference that Cook and his men seemed unable to idealize the Nootka as they had the Tahitians. Nootka Sound was not the tropical paradise of Tahiti. When idealization was largely absent, so was the inevitable subsequent disappointment (Fisher 1979).

GATHERING KNOWLEDGE IN TRANSITION

How could information be gathered in encounters such as these? The 'fleeting moment' could be just that: Steller had about a quarter of an hour to make observations on his first encounter with the Aleuts. Brevity of contact was a particular problem of encounters made in the Pacific islands. Contact was often inhibited by fears of violence, or the demands of the voyage outweighing those for observation of new peoples. European vessels could not linger indefinitely for the ship's naturalist or artist to observe and draw. Sailing ships had to be in place to encounter winds and currents at the right times of the year. Otherwise, months or even years could be added to a voyage. Even land expeditions, such as those made by Lewis and Clark, and Alexander von Humboldt (1769–1859) in what is now Mexico and the Amazon basin in 1799–1804, could not stay indefinitely in one place. Wishing to gather more information, mindful of distant geographical objectives, fearful of outstaying their welcome, or, alternatively, of losing expedition members to the allure of the apparently greater freedoms of Pacific or American Indian life, they too kept moving.

Contemporary discussions in Europe about experience and observation helped to determine whether the knowledge gained in transition by contact with unknown peoples would be regarded as legitimate. Cook was well aware of evidence problems. He confessed to James Boswell (1740–95) in April 1776

> that he and his companions who visited the South Sea Islands could not be certain of any information they got, or supposed they got, except as to objects falling under the observation of the senses, and anything which they learnt about religion, government, or traditions might be quite erroneous.
>
> (quoted in Frost 1976: 798)

Cook spoke in the middle of Enlightenment debates about the reliability of different forms of knowledge. The reliability of eyewitnesses (like explorers), and knowledge gained from direct sensory impressions of images and events (like seeing an Aleutian kayak), was challenged by thinkers such as Hume (1711–76) and Condillac (1714–80). The explorer's claim to knowledge rested on his reliability as an eyewitness, albeit subject to the pressures of the fleeting moment (Outram 1999). But problems remained because, by definition, the explorer was reporting on things previously unknown to his European audience, which thus could not use any standard of probability to measure the veracity of the things reported. The practice of exploration raised basic questions about the relationship between seeing and knowing.

In this situation, as in other contexts, it was the personal authority of the explorer that resolved uncertainty. Cook provides us with an account of his struggle to gain true information, which is meant to illustrate his heroic self-dedication. In New Zealand, during his second voyage, he encountered on a beach a Maori with a partially eaten human head.

> The sight of the head . . . struck me with horror, and filled my mind with indignation against these cannibals. Curiosity, however, got the better of my indignation, especially when I considered that it would avail but little, and being desirous of becoming an eye-witness of a fact which many doubted, I ordered a piece of the flesh to be broiled and brought to the quarter-deck, where one of these cannibals ate it with surprising avidity. This had such an effect on some of our people as to make them sick. That the New Zealanders are cannibals can no longer be doubted.
>
> (Beaglehole 1968: vol. II, 294)

Cook here was producing exactly the facts 'falling under the observation of the senses' that gave greatest grounds for belief, especially when attested by a national hero such as he. That the 'facts' had been obtained at the price of the suppression of his own feelings made them more credible because more 'objective'. What gave them moral authority, however, was Cook's heroic victory over his own feelings in the cause of knowledge.

Cook discussed with Boswell not only the reliability of certain forms of information but also the transfer of knowledge between cultures. It was a vital, practical issue for Europeans sailing in unknown waters thousands of miles from the nearest European settlement, and in constant need of accurate navigational information. Cook was able to stay long enough on Tahiti for some reciprocal language learning to begin, which allowed him on his departure to take along the priest Tupia, who lent his navigational knowledge to the voyage until his death in Batavia. Such people, intermediaries between the cultures and languages (just like the American Indian woman Sacajawea who accompanied the Lewis and Clark expedition) were vital to the continuation of contact between cultures. In the Pacific islands the European castaways and beachcombers found themselves in similar roles (Dening 1974).

In less prolonged contacts, visual representations allowed information to be transmitted. The French explorer La Pérouse found himself in unknown waters off the coast of Kamchatka in 1786. He urgently needed to know whether sailing down a narrow channel would bring him to open ocean or whether it would prove a dead end, force him to beat his way back, and lose valuable time and provisions. After several days on the beach communicating with indigenous people by signs, the exchange of small gifts, and drawings on the sand, he was able to obtain the desired information. He also saw with astonishment that by the end of this intense interchange the inhabitants left off drawing in the sand, learned the use of pencil and paper, and were able to draw the relationship of their island to the mainland in a form comprehensible to the French sailors (Bravo 1999; Dunmore 1994–5).

This was also an important problem for Enlightenment thinkers. If it was possible to transmit knowledge between seemingly incommensurable cultures, then it was likely that human beings from different cultures were more like each other than unlike, and could well share a similar rationality. Such thinkers also experienced the tug between needing to account for the fact that there was difference between cultures and the need that came out of the global spread of contact, to construct a universal human subject for the new 'world-history'. The question of the commensurability of cultures was also important for those who were involved in the construction of a 'science of man', able to integrate knowledge of the physical constitution of man with a law-based, scientific explanation for the diversity of races and cultures (Fox *et al.* 1995; see also Chapter 12, this volume).

Contact, information-gathering and possession-taking always lay in uneasy relationship to one another. How Europeans assessed the indigenous peoples at their first encounter was often also how they would justify taking possession of their territory. In the seventeenth century justification for the dispossession of North American Indians had been based on (mistaken) descriptions of them as nomadic hunters who had no settled form of government or habitation (Chaplin 2001). The same occurred after James Cook's fleeting contacts with Australian Aborigines. As Allan Frost (1981) has shown, both Banks and Cook perceived the Aborigines as nomadic, without agriculture, clothing, industry, trade or material culture beyond the very simplest, without political and social hierarchies, or property in land. These (inaccurate) perceptions enabled the land to be seen as a *terra nullius*, as having no true owners. They allowed Cook to apply the instructions in his commission from the Admiralty that he should 'with the consent of the natives . . . take possession of convenient situations in the southern continent in the name of the King of Great Britain' (Beaglehole 1968: vol. I, cclxxxiii). Such ideas were not unchallenged. James Burney (1750–1821), who sailed with Cook on the second and third voyages, strongly attacked the right of European nations to take possession of inhabited territories in this way, as had Jonathan Swift (1667–1745) in his famous *Gulliver's Travels* (Burney 1803: vol. 4, 1–3; Swift 1726: 343). Here we find a typical Enlightenment dilemma. The questioning of the effects of the European presence on indigenous peoples was increasing; but few were radical enough to recommend, in an age of mercantile profit, either the reduction of global markets or the abolition of slavery; or, in an age of intensified geopolitical competition in Europe, the end of 'taking possession' of territories inhabited by indigenous peoples, however admirable or appealing. Cook's admiration for what he saw as the Stoical and austere lifestyle of the Aborigines did nothing to impede his acts of possession (Williams 1981).

EFFECTS OF CONTACT WITH INDIGENOUS
PEOPLES

It is difficult to gain an impression of how Europeans appeared to indigenous peoples. Most indigenous societies, encountered for the first time in the eighteenth century, were without written language at the time of encounter. Their verbal narratives about the Europeans are now accessible to us only in the much later versions narrated today, or in written versions produced by Europeans, often missionaries unlikely to be sympathetic to the culture which produced them. Indigenous reports are, in any case, as full of presuppositions about the Europeans as were the Europeans' about them. If the Europeans could see the indigenous as classical heroes, so did the indigenous peoples see the Europeans as members of their own pantheon. It was probably because Cook's ship was perceived as the abode of a god that he was welcomed with extraordinary displays of hospitality on Tahiti. It was because of a very different ritual situation on Hawaii, as Marshall Sahlins (1985, 1995) has argued, that James Cook was murdered. Cook's actions unwittingly corresponded to those expected of the god Lono. He arrived at the right time in the ritual year, circled the island, mapping it, in the correct ritual direction of the god, and departed the island at the right time in the calendar, having participated in ceremonies dedicated to the god. Forced to return unexpectedly for repairs to the ship, Cook found the originally enthusiastic welcome of the islanders replaced by hostility or indifference. The scene was set for the events leading up to his murder.

The effects of European contact, even the quite fleeting contacts that took place in the Pacific, were often very profound. The explorers' ships introduced metal-working and firearms into an area which previously had neither. On Tahiti, struggle for control of iron objects was won initially by the women, who traded sex for them at the price of abandoning the taboo system of restrictions that had previously organized island symbolic life (Dening 1992). In the major island groups, already in semi-permanent conflict between different lineages, this more advanced technology enabled the decisive victories impossible with older-style weaponry, and changed island society from a highly fissiparous system to one of increasingly united government. These effects were particularly dramatic in the Hawaiian group of islands. One lineage, that of King Kamehameha (d. 1819), gained undisputed control for the first time. Kamehameha used relics of Cook's visits, as well as parts of his body, for veneration and to legitimate his seizure of power. Around this, he created a new ruling class on the islands, which had chosen to leave traditional ways of life and embrace Christianity and the island's role in the world trading system in which the Pacific was ever more deeply embedded from the 1790s (Kirch and Sahlins 1992).

THE EUROPEAN RECEPTION

No century before the eighteenth had ever witnessed the publication of so many accounts of newly discovered places and cultures. Accounts of voyages by James Cook and Count Louis de Bougainville (1729–1814) were rapidly translated, and sold out in a few days (de Bougainville 1772). Stage plays with 'Tahitian' settings played to packed houses in London. For the first time, naval expeditions of discovery carried professional artists, whose images of unknown plants, animals, places and peoples could be cheaply reproduced by means of engraving. As Bernard Smith (1985) has demonstrated, these images gave a new and highly charged aesthetic dimension to exploration and encounters with new peoples (see also Outram 1995). Without them, it is impossible to understand the impact of cross-cultural encounters on Enlightenment Europe. The printed accounts and the images became an important part of the European repertoire of ideas, images, hopes and feelings. All this flow of information and image was eagerly taken up by a reading public defining itself as enlightened precisely by virtue of its encounter with the printed word, the theatrical performance and the visual representations given wide currency by engraving. It was this expansion of print culture that allowed cross-cultural encounters on the edges of the known world to become the imaginative property of ordinary Europeans who never ventured far from home.

The deluge of visual representations and written accounts of contact meant that explorers' tales also became easier to believe, especially as images were backed up by artefacts from remote peoples which began to make their way into European museums and collections. The Göttingen University Museum acquired the Forsters' collection of Pacific artefacts at the same time as it took possession of Baron von Asch's (1729–1807) collection of artefacts from Siberia (Hauser-Schäublin and Krüger 1998; Buchholz 1961). Living representatives of newly contacted cultures came back with returning explorers. James Cook's fellow-captain Tobias Furneaux (1735–81) brought back Omai from Tahiti in 1774; Bougainville had already brought back Aortourou from the same island in 1768. Finally, the credibility of explorers' accounts increased, because, very differently from those of the seventeenth century, most had objectives which were at least partly scientific. They were not, like Walter Raleigh's (1552–1618) voyages of discovery in the sixteenth century, or Dampier's in the seventeenth, closely tied to commercial projects of whose value the explorer needed to convince his potential investors by, if necessary, fabricating an elaborate exotic background.

There was another reason for the impact of the encounter stories. The eighteenth century saw the golden age of travelling for information by 'philosophical travellers' (Canizares-Esguerra 2001; Bödeker 1986). Kings and bureaucrats, scholars and economists, young men finishing their education, all travelled in Europe in varying degrees as if encountering exotic worlds. Behind many of them stood a new idea of travel as a necessary part of self-development and education. A truly educated person was one who had encountered and gathered information about the world himself, rather than just absorbing second-hand knowledge at home. Travel was a practice that demonstrated eligibility for membership in the new elite of Enlightenment Europe, based on knowledge and experience rather than birth. This is the elite that was going to seize power in France after 1789, and become increasingly dominant in the German states. All these reasons explain why explorers became cultural heroes even outside their own nations. They had travelled the world, and had, in an age of mask and masquerade, seen it face to face. They explain too the kudos gathered by those who, like Joseph Banks, travelled with explorers. Printed accounts of

Figure 33.1 *Dancer*, Philippe Jacques de Loutherbourg after John Webber. Costume design for the pantomime *Omai*, produced by William Shield. By permission of the National Library of Australia.

Figure 33.2 *Omai*, James Caldwell, from James Cook (1777) *Voyage towards the South Pole*, London. By permission of the National Library of Australia.

exploration voyages were acceptable substitutes for the direct experience of the world that marked the new elite.

Explorers' accounts of Pacific islands in particular became not only credible but also important to Europeans for other reasons. This was a time when the need for change was keenly felt in many European states. Anti-slavery agitation also led to an increasing consciousness of the contradiction between the growing prosperity of much of Europe and the evils of plantation slavery in the Caribbean that underpinned it. This heightened consciousness made Europeans more prone to see Pacific islands as Utopian places where man could live at peace, without economic problems or intrusive government, without competition, and without sexual repression; as places where men could live a natural life far removed from the corruption of European society (Frost 1976: 806). When known only through explorers' accounts, the islands became a focus for European hopes and desires. By the 1790s, contemporaries citing the integration of the Pacific into world trade argued that it should no longer be armies and navies which changed the balance of power between competing power blocs but merchant fleets creating a web of trading networks which held the world together (Lemontey 1789). There seemed to be a hope for a new basis of commerce, one based not on the misery of indigenous peoples or enslaved Africans, as had happened in the Americas, but on free workers (Smith 1979). However, in spite of their idealization of island life, Europeans also saw them as powerful places which could seduce Europeans into 'going native', becoming something different and other. These fears were realized in the men who tried to desert from Cook's crew on Tahiti, or the *Bounty* mutineers who tried to establish themselves on the same island, and then set up a small commonwealth on distant Pitcairn (Dening 1992).

THE CREATION OF A UNIFIED WORLD

Contact between cultures in this period took place on a global scale, and for many reasons. European settlement spread in North America and geopolitical imperatives led governments to explore and, ultimately, try to establish bases in areas of the world like the Pacific, previously largely immune from European influence. Exploration fed global flows of information. Institutions began to have global reach. Armies, navies and trading companies such as the British East India Company, or its Dutch equivalent, were involved in several different regions of the globe, and introduced standardized practices of information-gathering. This meant that debates on man were now conducted on the basis of information drawn from all over the world. Such knowledge was also the basis of the integration of the Pacific into the world economic system. Both the growth of institutions with global reach and a growing world trade system meant encounters between Europeans and indigenous peoples began to build a global system.

Missionary endeavour was highly important in this formation of a global experience of encounter. Missionary activity outside Europe had, of course, begun at the inception of white settlement in the Americas, and had been extended into China and Japan by the sixteenth century (Spence 1985). The Enlightenment saw, however, the emergence of a new missionary Church that could only have taken the form it did during an age of accelerating global contact. The Moravian Church, a radical offshoot of Lutheranism, had first appeared in the sixteenth century, but it was reconfigured by its leader Count Zinzendorf (1700–60) as a world missionary Church in the early eighteenth century. Based at the small village of Herrnhut in Saxony, its membership remained tiny, yet missions were established at the Cape of Good Hope, in Jamaica among the slaves, in Labrador and Greenland among the Inuit, in Pennsylvania and Delaware among the Indians, in Siberia and in the Russian Arctic at Archangel; even in London (Sensbach 1998).

Such a Church wholly devoted to the world mission field could never have been conceived of before this age of global cross-cultural contact. Zinzendorf repeatedly used the image that his Church was the 'salt of the earth', to be scattered by God anywhere it could be of most use. Moravianism deviated notably from Lutheranism in its Christocentric theology, and its emotionalism. Cutting through generations of complex theology, Enlightenment Moravians insisted that the assurance of salvation was a childlike surrender to Christ through and in the heart. This was an experience potentially reachable by all men, not just Europeans. This was a Church organized to be able to carry out a worldwide task. The humble social status of most of those sent out as Moravian missionaries must also make the Church figure in the history of the poor man's experience of global culture contact. It should not be forgotten that the growth of worldwide institutions meant that the social origins of those involved in contact experiences became more diverse: East India Company soldiers and clerks, French, Russian, Spanish and English sailors, Moravian missionaries who had begun life typically in skilled trades, settlers on the American frontiers; these were all examples of those who were outside the social elites yet contributed to the experience of contact.

CONCLUSION

Can we write a single history of contact between Europeans and others in this period? Or are contacts between different cultures simply so diverse that such a history is impossible? It should be clear that there were important differences between contacts. Nonetheless, contacts did increase and accelerate during this time. Because of them, the sense of the world as a single system of exchanges, history and trade also increased. The history of eighteenth-century Europe is a part of the history of the globalization process, in which cross-cultural contact is a vital factor, and which made possible a single human history for the first time. Understanding Enlightenment thought and activity means moving away from national histories and away from a focus on print culture. Underlining the importance of cultural contacts means abandoning the view of Europe as the centre of the world. If this is the point at which the world becomes a system, then this is the point at which distinctions between centre and periphery become less useful. This is the challenge: to write Enlightenment history in a way that sees the world as a unity containing many differences.

REFERENCES

Axtell, J. (2001) *Natives and Newcomers: The Cultural Origins of North America*, New York and Oxford: Oxford University Press.

Bayly, C. A. (1997) *Information and Empire: Intelligence Gathering and Social Communication in India, 1780–1870*, Cambridge: Cambridge University Press.

Beaglehole, J. C. (ed.) (1962) *The* Endeavour *Journal of Joseph Banks 1768–1771*, 2 vols, Sydney: Angus & Robertson.

—— (ed.) (1968) *The Journals of Captain James Cook on His Voyages of Discovery*, 2 vols, Cambridge: Cambridge University Press for the Hakluyt Society.

Bödeker, H. E. (1986) 'Reisen: Bedeutung und Funktion für die Deutsche Aufklärungsgesellschaft', in W. Griep and H.-J. Jager (eds) *Reisen im 18 Jahrhundert: Neue Untersuchungen*, Heidelburg: Carl Winter.

—— (1999) 'Aufklärische ethnologische Praxis: Johann Reinhold Forster und Georg Forster', in H. E. Bödeker, P. H. Reill und J. Schlumbohm (eds) *Wissenschaft als kulturelle Praxis, 1750–1900*, Göttingen: Vandenhoek & Ruprecht.

Bougainville, Louis de (1772) *Voyage autour du Monde*, 2 vols, Paris: Saillant et Nyon; trans. Johann Reinhold Forster (1772) London: J. Nourse and T. Davies.

Bravo, M. (1999) 'Ethnographic Navigation and the Geographical Gift', in D. N. Livingstone and C. W. Withers (eds) *Geography and Enlightenment*, Chicago: Chicago University Press.

Buchholz, A. (1961) *Die Göttinger Russlandsammlungen Georgs von Asch: Ein Museum der russischen Wissenschaftsgeschichte des 18 Jahrhunderts*, Giessen: Universitätsverlag.

Burney, J. (1803) *A Chronological History of the Discoveries in the South Seas or Pacific Ocean*, 5 vols, London: Hansard.

Canizares-Esguerra, J. (2001) *How to Write the History of the New World: Historiographies, Epistemologies and Identities in the Eighteenth-century Atlantic World*, Stanford: Stanford University Press.

Chaplin, J. (2001) *Subject Matter: Technology, the Body and Science on the Anglo-American Frontier, 1500–1676*, Cambridge, Mass., and London: Harvard University Press.

Dening, G. (1974) *The Marquesan Journal of Edward Robarts, 1797–1824*, Canberra: Australian National University Press.

—— (1980) *Islands and Beaches: Discourse on a Silent Land: Marquesas 1774–1880*, Honolulu: University of Hawaii Press.

—— (1992) *Mr Bligh's Bad Language: Passion, Power and Theatre on the Bounty*, Cambridge: Cambridge University Press.

Dunmore, J. (1994–5) *The Journal of Jean-François de Galaup de la Perouse, 1785–1788*, 2 vols, London: Hakluyt Society.

Fisher, R. (1979) 'Cook and the Nootka', in R. Fisher and H. Johnston (eds) *Captain James Cook and His Times*, London: Croom Helm.

Forster. G. (1777) *A Voyage Around the World in His Britannic Majesty's Sloop* Resolution *Commanded by James Cook, during the Years 1772,3,4, and 5*, 2 vols, London: B. White.

Frost, A. (1976) 'The Pacific Ocean: The Eighteenth Century's "New World"', *Studies in Voltaire and the Eighteenth Century*, 22: 779–822.

—— (1981) 'New South Wales as *Terra Nullius*: The British Denial of Aboriginal Land Rights', *Historical Studies*, 19: 513–23.

Fox, C., Porter, R. and Wokler, R. (1995) *Inventing Human Science: Eighteenth-century Domains*, Berkeley, Los Angeles and London: University of California Press.

Hauser-Schäublin, B. and Krüger, G. (1998) *James Cook: Gifts and Treasures from the South Seas/Gaben und Schätze aus der Sudsee: The Cook/Forster Collection, Göttingen: Die Göttinger Sammlung Cook/Forster*, Munich and New York: Prestel.

Hoare, M. E. (1982) *The* Resolution *Journal of Johann Reinhold Forster*, 4 vols, London: Hakluyt Society.

Joppke, C. and Lukes, S. (eds) (1999) *Multicultural Questions*, Oxford: Oxford University Press.

Kirch, P. V. and Sahlins, M. (1992) *Anahulu: The Anthropology of History in the Kingdom of Hawaii*, Chicago: Chicago University Press.

Kroeber, A. L. (1952) *The Nature of Culture*, Chicago: Chicago University Press.

Lamb, J. (2001) *Preserving the Self in the South Seas, 1680–1840*, Chicago: Chicago University Press.

Lamb, J., Smith, V. and Thomas, N. (2000) *Exploration and Exchange: A South Seas Anthology: 1680–1900*, Chicago: University of Chicago Press.

Lawson, P. (1993) *The East India Company*, London and New York: Longman.

Lemontey, P. (1789) *Eloge de Captain James Cook*, Paris: Didot.

Outram, D. (1995) *The Enlightenment*, Cambridge: Cambridge University Press.

—— (1999) 'On Being Perseus: New Knowledge, Dislocation and Enlightenment Exploration', in D. N. Livingstone and C. W. Withers (eds) *Geography and Enlightenment*, Chicago: Chicago University Press.

Raj, K. (2001) 'Refashioning Civilities, Engineering Trust: William Jones, Indian Intermediaries and the Production of Reliable Legal Knowledge in late Eighteenth-century Bengal', *Studies in History*, 17: 23–47.

Sahlins, M. (1985) *Islands of History*, Chicago: Chicago University Press.

—— (1995) *How Natives 'Think': About Captain Cook for Example*, Chicago: Chicago University Press.

Sensbach, J. F. (1998) *A Separate Canaan: The Making of an Afro-Moravian World in North Carolina, 1763–1840*, Chapel Hill: University of North Carolina Press.

Smith, B. (1979) 'Cook's Posthumous Reputation', in R. Fisher and H. Johnston (eds) *op. cit.*

Smith, B. (1985) *European Vision and the South Pacific*, New Haven, Conn., and London: Yale University Press.

Spence, J. D. (1985) *The Memory Palace of Matteo Ricci*, London and Boston: Faber & Faber.

Steller, G. W. (1988) *Journal of a Voyage with Bering*, trans. Margritt A. Engel and O. W. Frost, Stanford: Stanford University Press.

Swift, Jonathan (1726) *Gulliver's Travels into Several Remote Nations of the World*, ed. M. Foot (1967) London: Penguin.

Thomas, N., Guest, G. and Dettelbach, M. (eds) (1996) *Johann Reinhold Forster: Observations Made during a Voyage round the World*, Honolulu: University of Hawaii Press.

Williams, G. (1981) '"Far More Happier than We Europeans": Reactions to the Australian Aborigines on Cook's Voyage', *Historical Studies*, 19: 499–512.

Williams, R. (1958) *Culture and Society*, London: Chatto & Windus.

PART VIII

———◆———

THE ENLIGHTENMENT
AND ITS CRITICS

Then and now

INTRODUCTION

———◆◆◆———

Christa Knellwolf

After the 1970s, some influential thinkers espoused postmodernism as their critical approach to meaning and representation. Much of their effort was spent on indicting what they took to be the Enlightenment. Describing this as the period when the bulk of Western critical thought was formulated, they have held the Enlightenment accountable for the damaging consequences of striving for universally valid definitions of all aspects of physical and moral existence. Enlightened quests for systematic order and prescribed ways of inferring the general from the particular were seen as having threatened minorities and suppressed heterodox definitions of human nature and behaviour. However, as many of our contributors have argued, Enlightenment was not confined to the ruling elite but, instead, inspired people from all walks of life to question the foundations of received wisdom about their lives as political subjects and individuals. As such, it fostered libertarian dreams while enlightened absolutism wielded firm control over the common people. Moreover, criticism of the undesirable and even dangerous consequences of Enlightenment was launched almost simultaneously with the earliest advancement of eighteenth-century ideals of improvement and progress.

This volume of essays has sought to portray the period as a tapestry of harmonious as well as conflicting social, cultural and intellectual interests and developments. Knowledge of science, technology and the arts was growing so rapidly that it threatened to drown contemporary minds in a deluge of disorganized information. The period's noted production of dictionaries, encyclopaedias and scientific taxonomies represents an attempt to control this flood of facts and ideas. When confronted with an abundance of questions and issues about mind and world, contemporary philosophers found it increasingly difficult to orient themselves. This is why Coleridge, for instance, defined conscious existence as a struggle to experience one's self in relation to an ungraspable universe, writing, 'grant me a nature having two contrary forces, the one of which tends to expand infinitely, while the other strives to apprehend or *find* itself in this infinity, and I will cause the world of intelligences with the whole system of their representations to rise up before you' (Coleridge 1817: vol. I, 297).

The first chapter in this section argues against the assumption that Enlightenment necessarily led to secularization and an increasingly mechanistic explanation of world and experience. Concentrating on the seething atmosphere of early Enlightenment Halle, Ian Hunter shows that the separation between civil and religious authority provoked fierce controversies over the meanings of private and public, individual and society, civil government and religion. Memories of bitter religious controversies were still fresh in the late seventeenth century when the Hohenzollern dynasty founded its new university. It therefore made every attempt to ensure that it should become an exemplary place for the dissemination of progressive thought. The university's rationale was the education of the future ruling elite, which is why the law faculty became its intellectual core. Secularizing the civil sphere appeared to guarantee the peaceful coexistence of different religious factions, but the task of separating private and public domains shook the very foundations of the existing world order. In practical terms, the process of secularizing the civil sphere could not but infringe on areas that had hitherto been the prerogative of theology.

Other contemporaries found quite different reasons for resisting movements towards Enlightenment. Two such critical positions are next represented in this part: Jean Jacques Rousseau's view that cultural sophistication crippled the hearts and souls of its adherents and Edmund Burke's warning of the political dangers of its subversive ideas. Rousseau began as a member of the circle of the *philosophes* but soon became one of the most savage critics of their commitment to progress and improvement. In what came to be called his *First Discourse* (1751), he argued that the arts and sciences, far from refining the character of individuals and societies, actually numbed their sensibilities and led to a general decay of morality and mutual respect. While living in an isolated environment, Rousseau also gained his immortal reputation as a writer of novels: his fictional visions of moralistic future societies reached the hearts of the masses and encouraged them to follow the principles most dramatically proclaimed during the French Revolution.

Burke, by contrast, decried the French Revolution as the dangerous consequence of misguided Enlightenment beliefs. The preservation of traditional values, he argued, was more important than the education of the masses, who would be liable as a result to slight time-honoured customs and conventions and, when aroused by irresponsible political leaders, to trample peace and order into a state of complete anarchy. Enlightenment, for Burke, had therefore to be handled with extreme care. His insight into the role of power in the promulgation of knowledge led him to adopt conservative positions and to imply that Enlightenment should be restricted to those who had committed themselves to the values of their culture and society.

While the eighteenth century brought advantages for the majority of women, Enlightenment thinkers did not specifically espouse gender equality, leading both contemporary and later critics to criticize the movement for disregarding the interests of one-half of the population. True, the educational endeavours of the period improved female literacy and heightened the general visibility of women, but an increasing separation between public and private tended to generate negative consequences for middle-class women who found it more difficult to participate in public issues. (The division of labour between working-class women and men was never a bone of contention and women worked as mill hands from the earliest days of the Industrial Revolution.) Throughout the period, intellectual women attacked this double standard and many sought to align themselves with the politics of the Tories, rather than attempting to explore the theoretical potential of Whiggish contractual-based political theories. Radical feminists like Mary Wollstonecraft associated themselves with the egalitarian principles of the French Revolution, only to be derided and ostracized when it turned into a bloodbath.

While the eighteenth century had claimed that reason became the instrument of progress, science and technology, a range of critics clearly recognized that Enlightenment had its dark side. Even when Enlightenment encouraged emancipatory objectives, it could not, these critics claimed, prevent unanticipated abuses of its principles of equity and social justice. A major problem – for example – concerned reason's failure to comprehend its own limits. During the 1940s, Theodor Adorno (1903–69) and Max Horkheimer (1895–1973), therefore, pronounced the defeat of what came to be known as the 'project' of the Enlightenment. Howard Williams's chapter assesses the principles of Enlightenment critique in the context of its historical emergence, arguing that it should be treated as an unresolved and evolving debate.

From its earliest days, postmodernism defined itself in opposition to the Enlightenment, imagined as a period of homogeneous philosophical principles and controlled by a male, white, Western elite. Meaning and representation came to be understood as the vehicles of power and control, and the existence of the disinterested critique was rejected. In the 1960s Michel Foucault (1926–84), Roland Barthes (1915–81), Louis Althusser (1918–90) and others were at the hub of a new intellectual movement that rigorously questioned the racial, sexual and class privileges of the Western elite founded on philosophical aspirations of many eighteenth-century writers. Twentieth-century critical debate chiefly prided itself on showing that there was no such thing as an objective reality; only representations existed, according to their theory. However, in his *Three Dialogues between Hylas and Philonous* (1713) George Berkeley had long ago argued that we can know only our own notions and cannot gain access to the true qualities of either spiritual or material entities. Berkeley's contemporaries attempted to refute these claims as passionately as many twentieth-century philosophers and historians have disputed the basic premises of postmodernism. James Boswell famously recorded Samuel Johnson's passionate response to Berkeley's claims: 'never shall I forget the alacrity with which Johnson answered, striking his foot with mighty force against a large stone, till he rebounded from it, "I refute it *thus*"' (1798: 321–2). Johnson's 'stout exemplification of the *first truths*' has been much quoted in attempts to discredit 'the linguistic turn' (the mainstay of poststructuralist–postmodern philosophy) and challenges the adequacy of a philosophy of language that reduces reality and history to linguistic representation.

The conflict between Johnson and Berkeley has been echoed in modern times by the vigorous debate between Jürgen Habermas (1929–), one of the major advocates of Enlightenment reason, and the postmodern philosopher Jean-François Lyotard (1924–98). Sharing Johnson's desire to validate physical experience, if not his philosophical outlook, feminist and queer critics like Judith Butler (1956–) have formulated a series of theories which see gender and sexuality as 'inscribed' on the body, which is to say that they contend that gender and sexuality should be interpreted as integral elements of embodied existence (Butler 1993). The transformation of people into discursive abstractions is seen to foster the tacit suppression of their individual and cultural uniqueness. This is why contemporary postcolonial and feminist scholars equally insist that defining knowledge as a universally valid and abstract entity entails being complicit with imperialist oppression. Instead, they define knowledge as 'situated': that is to say, a product of concrete historical circumstances and practices.

The ills of colonialism and imperialism are sometimes also represented as painful legacies of the eighteenth century. The European legal code, for instance, provided a basis for the establishment of colonial dominion in the Caribbean, even though Parisian customary law required many adjustments when applied to a state whose economic rationale was founded on slavery. So emphasis on 'local knowledge' (Ghachem 2001: 17–19) allowed for the administration of a blatantly exploitative system in particular colonial environments. Such examples shed critical light on the eighteenth century's propensity for accommodating exploitative practices into a legal code founded on principles of equity and universality.

Criticism of postcolonial ideas emphasizes the need to tell the history of resistance and to offer detailed accounts of the strategies by which subjugated peoples asserted themselves in the face of imperial and colonial power. Even while long traditions of silencing and brain-washing made it difficult for oppressed, subaltern communities to express their identities and rights, the post-colonial critique provides a framework for giving voice and visibility to those 'others' who have been marginalized and excluded by the Western traditions (Guha and Spivak 1988; Barker, Hulme and Iversen 1994; Ashcroft, Griffiths and Tiffin 1998). By arguing that representations are the most effective tools of power, postcolonial theory replaces the fiction of a simple version of universal meaning with a plurality of heterogeneous discourses (Bhabha 1990; Said 1983). After two hundred – and in some cases four hundred – years of colonial intervention, the ideas, attitudes and identities of the colonizers have shaped and hybridized the colonized peoples, and, more recently, subsumed them into the interests of global capitalism (Young 2001). Some of our own period's worst problems and social ills, such as poverty, pollution, fundamentalist rejections of capitalist *laissez-faire*, and even terrorist attacks on its ideological strongholds, have been traced back to the philosophy and politics of the eighteenth century. At the same time the Enlightenment period also ascribed unprecedented importance to the role of critique: of society, culture, aesthetics, politics, morality, religion. Its most positive and important legacy, therefore, is to encourage modern intellectuals to keep this critique alive and to make every effort to provide space and hearing for those who were originally excluded from sharing in the debates on reason and rationality.

REFERENCES

Ashcroft, Bill, Griffiths, Gareth and Tiffin, Helen (1998) *The Empire Writes Back: Theory and Practice in Post-colonial Literature*, London: Routledge.

Barker, Francis, Hulme, Peter and Iversen, Margaret (eds) (1994) *Colonial Discourse/Postcolonial Theory*, Manchester: Manchester University Press.

Berkeley, George (1713) *Three Dialogues between Hylas and Philonous*, ed. Jonathan Dancy (1998) Oxford and New York: Oxford University Press.

Bhaba, Homi K. (ed.) (1990) *Nation and Narration*, London: Routledge.

Boswell, James (1798) *Dr. Johnson's Table-talk: Containing Aphorisms on Literature, Life, and Manners*, London: C. Dilly.

Butler, Judith P. (1993) *Bodies that Matter: On the Discursive Limits of 'Sex'*, New York: Routledge.

Coleridge, S. T. (1817) *Biographia Literaria or Biographical Sketches of My Literary Life and Opinions*, ed. James Engell and W. Jackson Bate (1983) 2 vols, Princeton: Princeton University Press.

Ghachem, Malick W. (2001) 'Montesquieu in the Caribbean: The Colonial Enlightenment between *Code Noir and Code Civil*', in *Postmodernism and the Enlightenment: New Perspectives in Eighteenth-century French Intellectual History*, London: Routledge.

Guha, Ranjit and Spivak, Gayatri Chakravorty (eds) (1988) *Selected Subaltern Studies*, New York: Oxford University Press.

Said, Edward (1983) *The World, the Text, and the Critic*, Cambridge, Mass.: Harvard University Press.

Young, Robert J. (2001) *Postcolonialism: An Historical Introduction*, London: Blackwell.

CHAPTER THIRTY-FOUR

MULTIPLE ENLIGHTENMENTS

Rival *Aufklärer* at the University of Halle, 1690–1730

Ian Hunter

INTRODUCTION

Recently the Enlightenment has been subject to both good and bad press. The good press is typified by those who speak of an unfinished Enlightenment project (Honneth *et al*. 1992). On the one hand, this project is envisaged as a synthesis of reason and democracy, derived from Kant's moral philosophy, in a public sphere based on unhindered communication. Its bad press focuses on the negative consequences of exaggerating individual reason, such as sexual repression, and the failure to pursue aesthetic, sexual, or communal goals as ends in themselves (Böhme and Böhme 1996). This image of a generalized philosophical Enlightenment that one might endorse or lament is now under pressure from two sources. First, there has been a move to pluralize the Enlightenment. This pluralization began gently enough with the observation of divergent national Enlightenments (Porter and Teich 1981), but has since progressed to recovery of a multiplicity of Enlightenments – religious and secular, metaphysical and civil, radical and conservative (Pocock 1989; Hunter 2001; Israel 2001). Such a pluralization puts in doubt not just the periodization of an age of reason, but also the historical existence of a single Enlightenment that one might love or love to hate. Second, and more recently, there has been a move to detach notions of Enlightenment from a universalizing philosophical history and to ground them in the political, religious and cultural circumstances of particular Enlightenment cultures. J. G. A. Pocock's (1999) reconstruction of a conservative English Enlightenment – grounded in the 'Anglican' defence of civility and civil authority rather than an unleashed philosophical rationality – offers a striking example. This too has had a pluralizing effect, drawing attention away from the drama of a monolithic Enlightenment, and focusing instead on the historical circumstances and agendas of cultures, groups and networks which regarded themselves as enlightened and sometimes sought to bestow this condition on others.

This chapter makes a small contribution to the pluralization of Enlightenments by discussing a particular example: the conflict between three rival Enlightenment movements at the University of Halle in Brandenburg at the beginning of the eighteenth century. This three-cornered conflict took place between an anti-scholastic civil philosophy championed by Christian Thomasius (1655–1728); the anti-scholastic theological Enlightenment advanced by the Halle Pietists under the leadership of August Hermann Francke (1663–1727); and the neo-scholastic Leibnizian metaphysics entrenched in the Philosophy Faculty by Christian Wolff (1679–1754). The Halle conflicts illuminate the issue of multiple Enlightenments in part because each of the three movements represented a blueprint for the enlightenment of the individual and of society more generally, albeit envisaged in quite different terms. For a long time historians claimed that these conflicts had been reconciled and transcended with the emergence of a true *Aufklärung* (Enlightenment), ushered in by Immanuel Kant (Stuke 1972; Schmidt-Biggemann 1988; Schneiders 1992). This chapter moves in the reverse direction. Suspending belief in a final Kantian *Aufklärung*, it seeks to recover the conflicting Enlightenments in their unreconciled circumstances. The objective is thus not to uncover a set of reciprocal shortcomings that would be transcended by Kantian philosophy; rather, it is to clarify the historical context in which these rival Enlightenment cultures emerged, the terrain on which they clashed, and the significance this might have for our under-standing of a German *Aufklärung*, in the first place, and our notions of a European Enlightenment more generally. The chapter concludes with a postscript that applies the perspective of multiple Enlightenments to a more recent attempt to recover a unified European-wide Enlightenment, Jonathan Israel's account of a Spinozist radical Enlightenment (Israel 2001).

THE SETTING

The foundation of the University of Halle between 1691 and 1694 formed part of a series of state-building measures undertaken by the Hohenzollern dynasty, to be crowned in 1701 with the merging of two electoral principalities into the monarchy of Brandenburg-Prussia under King Friedrich I (1688–1713). In considering these developments we need to focus on the tight intermeshing of religious and political factors. As electoral princes of Brandenburg, the Hohenzollerns had inherited a Lutheran population and landed nobility. With the conversion of the ruling house to a moderate form of Calvinism at the beginning of the seventeenth century, the twin factors of confessionalization and state-building began their volatile and unpredictable interaction. Dissatisfied with the 'conservative' Lutheran disposition of the Brandenburg Reformation in 1618 the Hohenzollerns and their Calvinist advisers announced a 'Second Reformation' designed to rid themselves of all 'left-over papal dung' (Nischan 1994). This included all signs of 'real presence' in the Eucharist; the crucifixes, stained-glass windows and altar cloths from the churches; and the various saints' days, processions and rituals associated with a quasi-magical popular religion. The fact that this second Reformation ended in stalemate and compromise was in part due to the stubborn resistance and crowd violence with which the popular classes met this attempt to purify their familiar forms of worship – an interesting inversion of the English case, where puritan iconoclasm was largely popular and resistance largely elite. But the lack of success was due more to the resistance of the landed nobility. Treating the Lutheran religion as one of their rights as an imperial estate, the Junkers were determined to resist the Hohenzollern attempt to incorporate them within a princely territorial state, particularly a Calvinist one. In the event, it was only the exigencies of the Thirty Years War that forced the Lutheran nobility to relinquish their attachment to the Catholic Emperor and align themselves with their Calvinist ruling house, which had always conducted its foreign policy in terms of the need to forge an alliance of Protestant territorial states against the Empire and the Catholic Church.

Although these struggles continued after the Thirty Years War, the terrain on which they took place had altered fundamentally. In recognizing the territorial princes as independent signatories, the French-brokered Treaties of Westphalia (1648) gave international legal recognition to a post-imperial system of territorial states. At the same time, by declaring the legitimacy of the three main religions (Lutheranism, Catholicism and Calvinism), no matter what the religion of the ruling house, the treaties signalled a certain secularization or desacralization of politics, initially by mandating limited forms of religious toleration (Dickmann 1959: 456–65; Heckel 1984). Although its full development still lay in the future, here we can recognize the emerging reciprocal relation between a certain 'autonomizing' of the state – that is, the attempt to make the state independent of the religious or moral communities it must govern – and a certain 'liberalizing' of a private sphere (religion, family, commerce), now declared to lie outside the state's exclusive concern with security. While no less committed to the incorporation of the imperial estates into the emerging territorial state, the Hohenzollern court was now convinced that this could be best achieved not through the enforcement of a state religion, but by declaring that the state as such had no religion. For this declaration to become a reality, however, the state required political, juristic and religious officials who themselves conceived of politics as largely independent of religion, or at least as independent of Lutheran orthodoxy, which continued to function as a bulwark for the estates.

This broadly was the set of circumstances in which the University of Halle was conceived, in order to provide the state with a source of political and religious officials independent of such neighbouring universities as Leipzig and Wittenberg, which remained bastions of Lutheran orthodoxy (Hammerstein 1978). It also helps to explain why it was Law rather than Theology that became the pre-eminent faculty, and why the Berlin court maintained a constant oversight of the university, not hesitating to intervene directly in its organization and management, which the court regarded as integral to those of the fledgling state (Hammerstein 1989). Finally, we can observe that the court's sensitivity to the destabilizing power of religion had been heightened by Louis XIV's 1685 Revocation of the Edict of Nantes, which had previously granted limited toleration to French Protestants. The consequent influx of Huguenot religious refugees into Berlin put the court on the alert against papism abroad and crypto-Catholicism at home.

JURISTS, PIETISTS, RATIONALISTS

Emerging in these circumstances, the new university offered academics extraordinary intellectual latitude in relation to Lutheran orthodoxy, yet inside an institution that was strictly controlled by a monarchical court bent on using it to provide the state with a deconfessionalized ruling elite. In occupying their respective faculties, the three intellectual movements – juristic civil philosophy, German Pietism and metaphysical rationalism – thus found themselves in an institution that permitted intellectual experimentation yet was highly sensitive to religious and political conflict.

The leading figure of the first of these movements – juristic civil philosophy – was Christian Thomasius. Appointed to the Law Faculty as one of the foundation professors in 1694, Thomasius was already famous (or notorious) as a result of his battles with the Lutheran scholastics at the neigbouring Saxon University of Leipzig, which had ended with his banning by the Saxon court and flight to Brandenburg in 1691 (Lieberwirth 1953; Grunert 1997). Thomasius was the most important follower of the political philosopher and natural jurist Samuel Pufendorf (1632–94) who, nearing the end of his life, was historian and political adviser to the Hohenzollern court. Understanding that it would have to govern permanently divided religious communities, Pufendorf had developed an influential intellectual architecture for the post-Westphalian territorial state (Seidler 2002). He did so by conceiving sovereignty in largely Hobbesian terms: as the deployment of an unchallengeable, unified and secular political authority over a territory and population, yet an authority restricted to the single end of preserving social peace, to the exclusion of all higher religious and moral ends (Behme 2002). Pufendorf's civil philosophy thus provided a powerful articulation of the dual strategy – the desacralizing of politics and the privatizing of religion – around which Hohenzollern domestic and foreign policy seemed to rotate (Doring 1993b).

In the context of Halle's Law Faculty, Thomasius conceived his role in terms of providing the boys with a formation that would allow them to separate their civil office as future jurists of a desacralized state from their religious vocation as Christians seeking salvation (Hunter 2001: 209–17). It was just this capacity to separate the execution of civil office from the pursuit of moral regeneration – outward civil conduct from inner religious purity – that Thomasius and his followers regarded as enlightened. The goal of this civil Enlightenment was the creation of a deconfessionalized tolerant civil sphere within the envelope of security provided by a secularized sovereign state. In constructing the curriculum and pedagogy designed to achieve this end, Thomasius's great enemy was Lutheran scholasticism. For, in Thomasius's eyes, as a result of its metaphysical mixing of philosophy and theology, Lutheran scholasticism not only gave birth to an intolerant credal religion, but was incapable of separating civil and religious authority (Hunter 2000). The Lutheran Church thus continued to claim its share of civil sovereignty by invoking civil sanctions against heretics and by supporting witchcraft trials.

The second movement, German Pietism, had begun as a conventicle religion – small groups seeking spiritual renewal in house meetings – dedicated to the reform of Lutheranism from within (Brecht 1993b). Inspired by the spiritualistic theology

Figure 34.1 *Samuel Pufendorf*, from *De officio hominis & civis juxta Legem naturalem libri duo*, 2nd edn, (1737) London. By permission of the National Library of Australia.

Figure 34.2 Frontispiece of Christian Thomasius (1688) *Introductio ad philosophiam aulicam: Enleitung zur Hofphilosophie*. By permission of Herzog August Bibliothek Wolfenbüttel. Photograph: Australian National University.

of Gottfried Arnold and initially under the direction of Philipp Spener, Pietism was brought to Halle in the 1690s by August Herman Francke, who would transform the town into the movement's headquarters (Brecht 1993a). Theologically, Francke's Pietism was an anti-ritualistic, intensely inward spiritualist religion. It was hostile to both the metaphysical formulations of Lutheran orthodoxy – which it regarded as a philosophical corruption of simple Christian faith – and to orthodoxy's claimed monopoly of the sacramental means of grace. These were hostilities it shared with the Thomasian civil philosophers, whose religious agenda was broadly Pietistic. Halle Pietism, however, was grounded in a theology and pedagogy of conversion. Understood as spiritual rebirth, this led to a rigorist division between the saved and the unsaved: the children of God who had been spiritually transformed through a profound inner experience of grace, and the children of the world who remained trapped in fleshly pursuits and desires. Francke characterized this shattering influx of grace as *Erleuchtung*, enlightenment as sudden divine illumination.

Unlike Spener's Pietism, whose turning from the world led to quietism, Francke turned from the world only in order to return to it, now arrayed in purity and viewing society as an object of spiritual enlightenment and reform. Drawing on the political support of influential Pietists at the Berlin court, and the financial support of Pietist nobility, Francke and his collaborators transformed Halle in an extraordinary burst of institution-building (Hinrichs 1971: 1–125). Beginning in 1695 with a school for the poor, Francke soon added a *Bürgerschule* for the children of tradesmen and a Latin grammar school for those destined for the university, and then, in 1698, a huge orphanage, supported economically by a printers' workshop, publishing house and pharmacy. All of the educational institutions were organized around a scheme of conversion and spiritual rebirth and, at the higher end, in the university's Theology Faculty, by interpretations enabling the reborn to discern the kernel of spiritual truth inside the scriptural husks of the Bible (Bühler and Madonna 1993). Like Thomasius's, Francke's pedagogy was thus self-consciously dedicated to the formation of a particular kind of elite, whose role in the first instance would be to effect a Pietistic reform of the Lutheran clergy. Unlike Thomasius's juristic elite, however, Francke's 'earthly saints' would not be imbued with a capacity to separate civil life from the imperatives of spiritual renewal, treating any such separation as inimical to the promotion of a godly society in which their own salvation was invested.

The third rival for the hearts and minds of the Halle students was a fully fledged metaphysical philosophy, whose rise can be dated to Christian Wolff's appointment to the Philosophy Faculty in 1706. The basic elements of Wolff's philosophy were derived from Leibniz's, although, unlike his polymathic mentor, Wolff created a complete scholastic system, beginning with textbooks in logic and metaphysics, then in ethics, politics, philosophical theology, and natural law and several supporting sciences. Despite its extraordinary scope, the core of Wolff's philosophy was contained in a rationalistic metaphysics whose immediate precursor was Leibniz's, but some of whose central elements could be traced back to the scholastic metaphysics of Aquinas and, especially, of Scotus (Honnefelder 1990). According to this metaphysics, the spatio-temporal world is to be understood as the form in which a purely intelligible world appears to a being who happens to have man's sensory apparatus. The intelligible world consists of pure forms or concepts which determine what kinds of

Figure 34.3 *August Hermann Francke* (1663–1727). By permission of the Staatliche Graphische Sammlung, Munich.

thing are possible in actuality. Wolff called these forms *possibilia*, and defined them as being immune to self-contradiction.

Now the abstract and rationalistic character of this philosophy might seem to make it an unlikely participant in the culture wars that were about to break out at Halle. It needs to be kept in mind, however, that the privileged form of rationality – the reason capable of grasping the pure concepts lying behind empirical appearances – is the rationality of the divine mind. Identified with a being whose pure spirituality allows it to create the forms of things through continuous creative intellection, the divine mind serves both a moral and a metaphysical purpose. It belongs to a culture of intellectual self-purification dedicated to transcending merely empirical knowledge and activating the pure intellect that allows man to participate in God's intellection of the pure forms of things (Hunter 2001: 52–8, 98–102). This, of course, is a heady incentive to dangle before teenage boys in search of a moral career. This pure and purifying insight into the rational forms of things, prior to their embodiment in material things and their unfolding as merely historical events, was what Wolff called *Aufklärung* (Schneiders 1986; Schmidt-Biggemann 1994). Kant's modified account, with its emphasis on subjectivity and universal abstract reason, becomes the dominant version of the German Enlightenment (Schmidt 1996). Modern historians have adopted it to look back on rationalism's civil and religious rivals from the vantage point of the triumph of reason and the emergence of *Aufklärung* (Stuke 1972). Far from representing a simple defence of reason against its civil and religious rivals, however, Wolffian philosophy was an aggressive and expansionist intellectual culture. It viewed recovery of transcendent concepts as the key to reconciling reason and faith and, on this basis, claimed the right to show how the whole of society should be reformed in accordance with the dictates of a rationalist perfectionism (Link 1986). Whatever else it was, then, Wolffian metaphysical philosophy was also an educational project, seeking to form a specific kind of enlightened elite, in competition with those being groomed by the civil philosophers and the Pietists.

Given the deep differences in their intellectual foundations, their rival conceptions of Enlightenment, the conflicting ways in which they conceived the relation between civil, religious and moral authority, and their struggle to capture and configure a powerful new academic institution, we should not be surprised at the ferocity of the battles that soon broke out between Halle's three Enlightenment cultures. Nor should we be surprised at the immediacy of the Hohenzollern court's reactions, given the watchful eye it was keeping on its new university.

THOMASIUS AND THE PIETISTS

Beginning in 1699, the conflict between Thomasius and the Pietists was the first to break out. The flashpoint was Thomasius's doctrine of decorum, which he taught to the law students as part of their intellectual and ethical formation. It was central to Thomasius's desacralizing programme that almost the whole of civil life should consist of *adiaphora* – things indifferent with regard to salvation (Thomasius 1705). This was to allow as much of life as possible to be placed beyond religious control, thence to be treated either as a matter of personal ethics or, if social peace was at stake, as a matter for law and political decision. Thomasius argued that citizens should not attempt to govern their civil intercourse in accordance with religious imperatives and the pursuit of salvation, which led only to intolerance, persecution and conflict. They should instead govern their civil conduct through the rules of decorum (Barnard 1989). Modelled on the lifestyle and manners of the *gens du court*, these were rules for the conduct of a 'decent public life', having no bearing on man's inner moral condition, but useful in facilitating civil relations between religious groups who not too long ago had been engaged in confessional strife. Throwing down the gauntlet to the Pietists, Thomasius argued that their highly disciplined pedagogy of conversion, rebirth and spiritual enlightenment was entirely unsuited to life in an emergent deconfessionalized society. It led, he claimed, to an ascetic inwardness, giving rise to spiritual pride, and robbing young men and women of the affable manners needed to get on with fellow-citizens with whom they might be in radical religious disagreement (Hinrichs 1971: 354–62).

There was thus a certain justice to the Pietists' initial complaint against Thomasius – that his teaching of decorum infringed on the domain of religion, which they claimed as the exclusive preserve of the Theology Faculty. For, in dividing the governance of civil conduct between decorum and law, Thomasius was effectively excluding the question of salvation – hence the institutions of religion – from the civil domain altogether. This formed part of the larger civil-philosophical strategy for pacifying salvationist communities, by confining their lust for salvation to a private sphere, within a state whose sole aim was security. For the Pietists, however, dedicated as they were to a process of social reform based on spiritual enlightenment, such a divorce of public civil conduct from inner moral condition made no sense at all. Hence they regarded Thomasius's decorum doctrine as hypocritical and worldly, while he regarded their pursuit of a society based on a general spiritual rebirth as prone to fanaticism and incapable of forming citizens suited to a tolerant pluralistic civil society (Hinrichs 1971: 369–87). In the event, owing to their friends at court and the success of their institution-building, the Pietist theologians managed to silence Thomasius – temporarily at least – securing in 1702 an order from the Berlin Oberkuratorium that he cease lecturing on decorum, on pain of dismissal.

Thomasius's programme of juridical deconfessionalization and the Pietists' programme of spiritual awakening and reform may both be regarded as responses to the political and religious circumstances of post-Westphalian Germany, sharing some common features, yet divided by deep moral and intellectual differences. On the one hand, the two movements shared a common hostility to Lutheran scholasticism in general and to *Schulmetaphysik* in particular. Both Thomasius and the Pietists adhered to a voluntarist theology – that is, to the teaching that God rules man and the universe through his inscrutable will rather than through scrutable rational laws. Further, both groups gave expression to this voluntarism via the doctrine of man's incapacity for theo-rational insight and intellectual self-governance. This was the doctrine through which both Thomasians and the Pietists expressed their radical opposition to the central doctrine of university metaphysics: namely, that God created the a priori forms of things, and humans might perfect themselves by sharing in His process of contemplation.

On the other hand, the two cultures put the voluntarist doctrine of human incapacity to very different uses. For the Pietists, this doctrine formed part of a practice of religious self-scrutiny and self-transformation. This was a practice for cultivating faith in divine grace – as opposed to the self-sufficiency of human reason – and was intended to culminate in the transforming experience of spiritual rebirth and the emergence of a 'new man' (Brecht 1993b). Thomasius, however, embedded the doctrine of human incapacity in an Epicurean anthropology – a view of humans as mutually predatory creatures of their passions – which was linked to a Hobbesian or Pufendorfian conception of the state as the only means to security (Kimmich 1997). Hence, while he too criticized the orthodox theologians and metaphysicians for claiming access to God's intellection of the forms, Thomasius's attack had quite different religious and political objectives. If man was a creature of his passions and incapable of theo-rational insight, then his public conduct would have to be governed either by civil manners or else coercively, in accordance with a politics whose end was restricted to the end of social peace, by a state indifferent to transcendent truth. This, according to Pufendorf and Thomasius, was what it would take to exclude the pursuit of salvation from the institutions of civil governance, paving the way to an enlightened and tolerant civil society. The dispute that broke out between Thomasius and the Pietists over the question of decorum may thus be regarded as indicative of a clash between two related but opposed intellectual cultures, each proposing to create an enlightened society through the manner in which it formed an intellectual elite, but in profoundly different ways.

THOMASIANS AND WOLFFIANS

The second outbreak of hostilities at Halle, between Thomasian civil philosophy and Wolffian metaphysics, needs to be seen against the backdrop of civil philosophy's uncompromising hostility towards university metaphysics. Reminiscent of Hobbes's invective against metaphysics in chapter 46 of the *Leviathan*, and anticipating the attacks of Gibbon and Hume, Thomasius rebuked metaphysics for allowing Platonic and Aristotelian philosophy to corrupt 'simple active Christianity', and for allowing theologians to practise 'priestcraft' by claiming access to esoteric doctrines held to be necessary for salvation (Thomasius 1707). While Thomasius was primarily concerned with scholastic metaphysics, whose mixing of theology and civil philosophy he held to be complicit with the mixing of religious and civil authority in the confessional state, he was also deeply opposed to rationalist metaphysics on similar grounds. In claiming privileged insight into an intelligible world, and on this basis to explicate such matters as sin and moral regeneration, the rationalist metaphysicians followed their theological precursors in mixing civil philosophy and theology. In doing so they also corrupted simple faith and threatened the civil domain with a new kind of priestcraft.

The stand-off between civil philosophy and metaphysical rationalism thus pre-dated Wolff's appointment to the Halle Philosophy Faculty in 1706, and the ensuing conflict was neither the first nor the last between these two intellectual cultures. Wolff would claim that he had delayed lecturing on metaphysics owing to the hostility of the Thomasians. Nonetheless, the metaphysical character of his programme was made quite clear with the publication of his *German Logic* in 1713. For this logic was explicitly metaphysical, treating logical analysis as a means of recovering the intelligible relations that determined the a priori possibility of things. The Thomasians, however, regarded logic simply as a means of formalizing the conceptual relations used by men in civil communication, which was the theme of a logic by Nicholas Gundling, published in the same year as Wolff's (Arndt 1989). Gundling had taken over the editorship of the Halle house journal – the *Hallische Neue Bibliothek* – in 1712, and it is noteworthy that the 1713 issue, while it contained no mention of Wolff's logic, published a lengthy review of Gundling's. In addition to praising Gundling's logic this review attacked syllogistic logic – which was central to Wolff's – treating it as a pedantic drill, symptomatic of a hated scholasticism, and useless for discovering anything significant or interesting. Wolff was not without his defenders, however; for in the same year an anonymous pamphlet appeared whose central argument was that Gundling's openness to scepticism – presumably scepticism regarding the metaphysical essences – paved the way to atheism. This pamphlet, it transpired, had been written by Johann Schneider, professor of logic and metaphysics in Wolff's faculty.

We catch a glimpse of the intellectual issues that might have come to a head here in the eponymous book *Gundlingiana* that appeared in 1715 (Arndt 1989: 282–6). In this work Gundling included a mock-dialogue, in which the 'spirit of finesse' personified by Montaigne and the 'geometric spirit' represented by Archimedes go proxy for Thomasian civil philosophy and Wolffian metaphysics. Gundling's Wolffian Archimedes says that happiness is to be found in continuous contemplation and withdrawal from the entire world of the senses; while his Thomasian Montaigne responds that he possesses a body as well as a soul, and lives in the world of the senses rather than the intelligible world. Gundling's Montaigne is, of course, a thinly disguised personification of Thomasius's decorum doctrine, permitting Gundling to mock the Wolffian mathematics and metaphysics personified by Archimedes for failing to produce the wise and affable deportment required for life in civil society.

In other words, the same aspect of Thomasius's decorum doctrine that triggered his conflict with the Pietists – that is, his insistence that men could learn the manners needed for civil enlightenment without undergoing a profound inner spiritual or intellectual enlightenment – also led to friction with the Wolffians, and for analogous reasons. For the Wolffians also taught that civil conduct had to be based on a deep inner transformation. This was not the Pietists' spiritual rebirth, but the metaphysicians' recovery of the a priori laws of reason and nature. In teaching that the increasing perfection of man and society depended on men contemplating and conforming themselves to these rational laws, Wolffian metaphysics was also inimical to the division of transcendent truth and civil governance that lay at the heart of civil philosophy. The fact that this dispute never really came to a head at Halle, however, meant that the quasi-religious dimension of Wolff's metaphysical rationalism would be revealed in another context, through his frontal collision with the Pietists.

THE PIETISTS *CONTRA* WOLFF

Halle's Pietist theology professors had begun to take an actively hostile interest in Wolff's teaching with the publication of his seminal *German Metaphysics* in 1719. Open conflict broke out in 1721, with the publication of the first of what would grow to more than 126 *Streitschriften*, pamphlets, some of them running to 500 pages or more (Hinrichs 1971: 388–421). Despite the proliferation and prolixity of this controversial literature, we can identify some of the central matters of contention by concentrating on the works of Wolff's two main opponents – Joachim Lange, Pietism's leading controversialist, and Franz Budde(us), a more reflective writer who would later become identified with the so-called 'theological Enlightenment' (Bianco 1989; Sparn 1989).

Drawing deeply on Lutheran theological voluntarism and spiritualism, Lange and Budde unerringly targeted the rationalist and intellectualist dimensions of Wolff's metaphysics, drawing out their deleterious consequences for religious life as understood by the Pietists. First, Lange and Budde attacked the 'fatalistic' consequences of Wolff's rationalism. If God created the world through non-contradictory intellection of the conceptual *possibilia*, and was therefore Himself bound by the laws of reason and nature, then, Lange argued, God's freedom and providence were diminished, for He would lack the capacity for direct intervention in the metaphysical order of things (Hinrichs 1971: 409–10). Budde argued in similar terms regarding the consequences of Wolff's Leibnizian doctrine of the pre-established harmony of the body and soul. If the discrete series of physical and spiritual events had been pre-coordinated, prior to the existence of the temporal world, then God would lack the freedom and power required for providential governance of the cosmos, and men would lack the freedom of will necessary for the attribution of moral responsibility (Budde 1724: 810, 76–82, 123–33).

Second, the Pietists attacked the 'Pelagian' consequences of Wolff's intellectualism and perfectionism. According to Wolff, the goodness of an action depends on whether it leads to a more perfect world, and this depends in turn on man's knowledge of the laws of reason and nature governing the world. Men possessing this knowledge could govern their conduct simply by deducing whether a proposed course of action increased this overall harmony or perfection of the best of all possible worlds. No special religious revelation is required for this knowledge, which means that even such non-Christian peoples as the Chinese could achieve an acceptable ethics, as indeed Wolff had argued. Budde was quick to seize on the 'godless' implications of this doctrine, arguing that it corrupted scholarly youth by teaching them that they might achieve moral renewal through their own unaided human reason, independent of Christ's mediation and God's grace (Budde 1724: 10–15, 136–55, 177–86). In answering the Pietists, Wolff challenged the orthodoxy of their spiritualist theology; pointed out that his metaphysics had found widespread acceptance among the religious, even among the Jesuits; and insisted that such doctrines as the pre-established harmony of the body and soul were only philosophical theories, having no direct religious consequences. Nonetheless, for the time being, the Pietists remained ascendant, using their contacts at court to secure Wolff's exiling by royal decree in November 1723 (Hinrichs 1971: 417–18).

Considering the vehemence of the original conflict, and the bitterness engendered by Wolff's exiling, it might seem surprising to observe that Wolffian metaphysics and Pietist theology would undergo a gradual process of negotiation and reconciliation during the mid-to-late eighteenth century. We have already noted the gulf between the intellectual underpinnings of the two cultures – between a rationalist metaphysics dedicated to modelling man in the image of a theo-rational intelligence, and a voluntarist theology dedicated to faith, conversion and spiritual rebirth. Yet we have also noted some points of overlap between Wolffianism and Pietism. In contrast to Thomasian civil philosophy, both of these intellectual cultures were dedicated to a unified conception of religious and civil governance, grounded in a single transcendent truth, even if they initially construed this truth in very different terms. Moreover, both cultures used a personal perfectionism grounded in inner enlightenment as the model for millennial doctrines of progress towards a perfect society; that is, a polity based on true reason or true religion in which mankind as a whole would be perfected. More generally, we have observed that the theo-rational character of Wolffianism permitted it to inherit the two central functions of university metaphysics: the harmonization of faith and reason; and the tethering of the positive sciences to the metaphysical core of a Christian academic culture. In proclaiming the virtues of his metaphysics in these two regards, Wolff was in fact laying claim to the mantle of Protestant scholasticism, presenting his doctrines as the only ones capable of stemming the tide of empiricism, materialism, atheism and Spinozism. These claims were not lost on some Pietists, particularly those like F. A. Schulz who had been taught by Wolff, and who saw Wolffianism as providing Pietism with a new metaphysical basis. This helps to explain the fact that even while the dispute was raging in the early 1720s, some moderate Pietists at the Berlin court were urging Lange to adopt a more conciliatory attitude towards Wolff.

We do not have space to discuss the mutual transformation of Wolffian metaphysical philosophy and Pietist theology that began in the 1740s and continued to the end of the century. We can note, however, that philosophers and theologians at the University of Königsberg took a leading role in this process of reconciliation, and that the process itself gave birth to the Neology movement, perhaps the most important current of German Protestant theology of the later eighteenth century (Erdmann 1876; Aner 1929; Malter 1975). The Königsberg philosophers and theologians were looking for a way to reconcile a metaphysical doctrine of rational self-governance with a revealed theology of salvation understood as spiritual rebirth. Such a reconciliation might be effected, they argued, by means of textual interpretations that treat revealed doctrine as an historical scaffolding for human reason, progressively falling away as reason undergoes historical maturation or enlightenment (Bohatec 1938: 429–76). The reconciliation of Wolffianism and Pietism would also require harmonizing a rationalist ('Pelagian') conception of man's capacity for intellectual self-sanctification with an 'Augustinian' conception of sin and the need for divine grace. This might be achieved via a philosophical theology which treats the access to 'pure' reason as itself a kind of grace delivering enlightenment as a total revolution of character, or birth of a 'new man'.

Let us close this observation by remarking that, together with the Neology movement, Kant's moral and religious philosophy provided a prime source of these reconciliatory figures of thought. In doing so it paved the way for a distinctively modern kind of intellectualist spirituality. This appeared in the form of a metaphysical culture dedicated to rationalist self-sanctification and social perfectionism that would eventually be known simply as the *Aufklärung*. In short, the intellectual comportment still widely identified with the *Aufklärung* – in which philosophy extends the claims of reason to all areas of life while simultaneously defeating scientism through the recovery of the a priori conditions of experience – may be regarded as the triumphant alliance of two powerful academic cultures: 'rational' Protestantism and German metaphysical rationalism.

POSTSCRIPT: THE RADICAL ENLIGHTENMENT AT HALLE

This triumph was, however, neither uncontested nor complete. Thomasian civil philosophy remained important in the law schools of Protestant Germany throughout the eighteenth century (Lestition 1989). Moreover, more radical Enlightenment cultures associated with Socinian and Spinozist thought made their way through often clandestine intellectual networks, surfacing in unexpected places and surprising ways. In fact, Jonathan Israel has recently argued that Spinozism deserves the mantle of harbinger of a European Enlightenment, bearing the seeds of reason that would eventually flourish in modern secular democratic states (Israel 2001). Israel's claims, though, run the risk of simply transferring the garland of Enlightenment from Kant to Spinoza and, despite his erudition, suffer from a lack of historical contextualization. I will conclude by offering a brief contextualization of Israel's radical Enlightenment, at the point where it crossed paths and swords with the three Enlightenment cultures we have been discussing.

The radical Enlightenment surfaced in Brandenburg in 1692, with the publication of an anonymous work entitled *Concordia rationis et fidei* (*The Harmony of Reason and Faith*). The author was Friedrich Wilhelm Stosch (1648–1704), son of a former Calvinist pastor to the Berlin court, and himself until recently a privy secretary to the court. The *Concordia* was not untypical of a certain genre of clandestine rationalism that was dedicated to reconciling faith and reason (religion and philosophy) under the aegis of a secularized metaphysical theology. Drawing somewhat haphazardly on Socinian, Hobbesian, Spinozist and deist sources, the *Concordia* denies Christ's divinity, rejects the reality of miracles and of hell, and affirms that biblical stories should be read allegorically, as an attempt by primitive peoples to understand a God who is, in effect, pantheistically (or metaphysically) identified with the cosmos (Stosch 1692: 35–6, 98–118). This set of doctrines provided Stosch with a platform to attack the clergy for foisting a superstitious Christianity on the people in order to keep them in thrall and aggrandize themselves. On being drawn to the attention of the authorities by the Lutheran theologians, the book was confiscated and its well-connected author detained pending the judgement of a special commission of inquiry set up by the Elector Friedrich III. The members of this commission were Paul von Fuchs, the Minister for Religious Affairs; Benjamin Ursinus, Calvinist Pastor to the Court; Daniel Jablonski, Court Preacher; Ezechial

Spanheim, a leading intellectual in the Berlin Huguenot colony; and, most significantly for us, Philip Spener, the theological founder of Pietism, and Samuel Pufendorf, the great political philosopher. Pufendorf was now Court Historian but, as mentioned, had earlier elaborated a European-wide civil philosophy dedicated to the secularization of the state and the privatization of religion. In the event, sitting in 1693–4, the commission confirmed the suppression of the book as harmful to the religious peace, but recommended no further punishment against Stosch, who was quietly returned to his former rank and entitlements.

How should we understand the Stosch affair? As far as Jonathan Israel is concerned, the issues are clear cut and all point in the direction of the progressive emergence of a rational, secular and ultimately democratic future. Flying in the face of the commission's express concern with Stosch's theological heterodoxy, Israel insists that 'Stosch's radicalism is essentially philosophical and non-local' (Israel 2001: 641). This is because Israel's Stosch is a disciple of Spinoza who was in turn the intellectual architect of a radical Enlightenment through which secular philosophical reason sought to overturn all authority – religious and political – right across Europe. Israel's account is thus a return to the notion of a single, philosophically based Enlightenment, now located in a radical underground, and hence even more implacably opposed to and by the forces of 'authority, religion and tradition', which is the light in which Israel views the Stosch commission of inquiry (Israel 2001: 643–5).

Drawing on Detlef Döring's fine reconstruction, we can offer several reasons for questioning Israel's account of the Stosch episode and, with it, his larger invocation of a general Enlightenment grounded in a radical rationalist philosophy (Döring 1995). In the first place, it makes little sense to see the affair in terms of the progressive force of the Enlightenment encountering the reactionary obstacles of authority and religion. Two members of the commission, Spener and Pufendorf, were themselves self-conscious representatives of particular kinds of Enlightenment: the anti-orthodox theological Enlightenment of the Pietists, and the anti-scholastic civil Enlightenment of the political jurists. Moreover, von Fuchs, the Court's Minister of Religious Affairs, was himself connected to Socinian circles and almost certainly shared some of Stosch's views regarding the non-divinity of Christ. This was no simple case, then, of an Enlightenment martyr confronting obscurantist reactionaries; rather, Stosch's somewhat derivative philosophical theology was judged by some of Berlin's leading political and theological intellectuals.

It is quite anachronistic to view this as a case of a champion of secular philo-sophical reason confronting those intent on defending religion against its progressive unmasking. A strong case can be made that Stosch's doctrines were not unambig-uously secular and philosophical. Not only did he draw on Socinian conceptions of Christ the moral teacher, but his Spinozist conception of nature as a single metaphysical substance itself has a powerful theological dimension. After all, this doctrine is based in the notion of God as a metaphysical being who unfolds His attributes in the intellectual and material registers simultaneously. In using this doctrine as the basis of his rationalist reconstruction of Christianity, Stosch was thus not so much moving from theology to philosophy or faith to reason but rather elaborating a theological philosophy – a theosophy – designed to fulfil many of the same functions as religion; that is, provide a single, ultimate, true world-view and way of life. Recalling that many of Stosch's central themes were common property for both Calvinist and Lutheran 'rationalists', and considering that they would later surface in the Neology movement, there is much to be said for Emanuel Hirsch's long-standing judgement that the *Concordia* belongs to the history of modern Protestant theology (Hirsch 1949: vol. IV, 305). In fact Stosch, like many other clandestine rationalists, may be regarded as a relay point for a quasi-religious philosophical movement, dedicated to transcending 'mundane' political and religious cultures through access to an esoteric true Enlightenment (Koselleck 1988).

Finally, if Stosch was not as secular as he appears to Israel, then, with the exception of Ursinus, the members of the commission were not simply defenders of religion in some straightforward sense. We have already sketched the fragile political and religious settlement achieved by the Hohenzollern state, which entailed maintaining religious peace between Lutherans, Catholics and Calvinists in keeping with reason of state and the provisions of the Westphalia treaties. We have also seen that this settlement was maintained by policies dedicated to separating the civil and religious spheres, and to removing the religious causes of civil conflict by insisting that the Churches restrict themselves to man's spiritual rather than his civil happiness. Pufendorf, Spener and von Fuchs were all parties to this partitioning of the civil and religious spheres, albeit for different reasons. We must also observe that all three regarded the separation of reason and faith, philosophy and theology as one of the keys to this partitioning of the spheres. Pufendorf in particular argued that the mixing of secular and religious knowledge in rationalist explications of Christianity was a hindrance to the separation of civil and religious authority; because such explications only tempted rationalists to think that they had found a new metaphysical foundation for civil government (Döring 1993a). Pufendorf's politics thus required that civil authority be severed from all metaphysical justifications – that it be grounded instead in the single goal of social peace – precisely in order to avoid conflict between those committed to rival metaphysical doctrines.

Seen in this light, then, the publication of Stosch's idiosyncratic theosophy not only jeopardized the Berlin court's delicate management of a fragile religious peace, it also signified the appearance of yet another cultlike rationalist pseudo-religion – consequences equally unwelcome to the commissioners. Their ambivalent response – suppressing the work while quietly rehabilitating the author – should thus not be seen as anti-Enlightenment, but as an attempt to preserve one kind of Enlightenment against the threats posed by another.

REFERENCES

Aner, K. (1929) *Die Theologie der Lessingzeit*, Halle: Niemeyer.

Arndt, H. W. (1989) 'Erste Angriffe der Thomasianer auf Wolff', in W. Schneiders (ed.) *Christian Thomasius 1655–1728: Interpretationen zu Werk und Wirkung, mit einer Bibliographie der neueren Thomasius-Literatur*, Hamburg: Felix Meiner.

Barnard, F. M. (1989) 'Rightful Decorum and Rational Accountability: A Forgotten Theory of Civil Life', in W. Schneiders (ed.) *op. cit.*

Behme, T. (2002) 'Pufendorf's Doctrine of Sovereignty and its Natural Law Foundations', in I. Hunter and D. Saunders (eds) *Natural Law and Civil Sovereignty: Moral Right and State Authority in Early Modern Political Thought*, Basingstoke: Palgrave.

Bianco, B. (1989) 'Freiheit gegen Fatalismus: Zu Joachim Langes Kritik an Wolff', in N. Hinske (ed.) *Zentren der Aufklärung I. Halle: Aufklärung und Pietismus*, Heidelberg: Lambert Schneider.

Bohatec, J. (1938) *Die Religionsphilosophie Kants in der 'Religion innerhalb der Grenzen der bloßen Vernunft': Mit besonderer Berücksichtigung ihrer theologisch-dogmatischen Quellen*, Hamburg: Hoffmann & Campe.

Böhme, H. and Böhme, G. (1996) 'The Battle of Reason with the Imagination', in J. Schmidt (ed.) *What is Enlightenment? Eighteenth-century Answers and Twentieth-Century Questions*, Berkeley: University of California Press.

Brecht, M. (1993a) 'August Hermann Francke und der Hallische Pietmus', in M. Brecht (ed.) *op. cit.*

—— (1993b) 'Philipp Jakob Spener, sein Programm und dessen Auswirkungen', in M. Brecht (ed.) *op. cit.*

M. Brecht (ed.) *Geschichte des Pietismus. Bd. 1: Der Pietismus vom siebzehnten bis zum frühen achtzehnten Jahrhundert*, Göttingen: Vandenhoeck & Ruprecht.

Budde, J. F. (1724) *Bescheidener Beweis, daß das Buddeische Bedencken noch fest stehe, wieder Hrn. Christian Wolffens Nöthige Zugabe aufgesetzet*, Jena: Meyerischen Buchladen.

Bühler, A. and Madonna, L. C. (1993) 'Von Thomasius bis Semler: Entwicklungslinien der Hermeneutic in Halle', *Aufklärung*, 8: 49–70.

Dickmann, F. (1959) *Der Westfälische Frieden*, Münster: Aschendorff.

Döring, D. (1993a) 'Leibniz als Verfasser der "Epistola ad amicum super exercitationes posthumas Samuelis Puffendorfii de consensu et dissensu protestantium", *Zeitschrift für Kirchengeschichte*, 104: 176–97.

—— (1993b) 'Säkularisierung und Moraltheologie bei Samuel von Pufendorf', *Zeitschrift für Theologie und Kirche*, 90: 156–74.

—— (1995) *FrühAufklärung und obrigkeitliche Zensur in Brandenburg: Friedrich Wilhelm Stosch und das Verfahren gegen sein Buch 'Concordia rationis et fidei'*, Berlin: Duncker & Humblot.

Erdmann, B. (1876) *Martin Knutzen und seine Zeit: Ein Beitrag zur der Wolfischen Schule und insbesondere zur Entwicklungsgeschichte Kant's*, Leipzig: Verlag Leopold Voss.

Grunert, F. (1997) 'Zur aufgeklärten Kritik am theokratischen Absolutismus: Der Streit zwischen Hector Gottfried Masius und Christian Thomasius über Ursprung und Begründung der summa potestas', in F. Vollhardt (ed.) *Christian Thomasius*, Tübingen: Niemeyer.

Hammerstein, N. (1978) 'Die Universitätsgründungen im Zeichen der Aufklärung', in P. Baumgart and N. Hammerstein (eds) *Beiträge zu Problemen deutscher Universitätsgründungen der frühen Neuzeit*, Nendeln: KTO Press.

—— (1989) 'Jurisprudenz und Historie in Halle', in N. Hinske (ed.) *op. cit.*

Heckel, M. (1984) 'Das Säkularisierungsproblem in der Entwicklung des deutschen Staatskirchenrechts', in G. Dilcher and I. Staff (eds) *Christentum und modernes Recht: Beiträge zum Problem der Säkularisation*, Frankfurt am Main: Suhrkamp.

Hinrichs, C. (1971) *Preußentum und Pietismus: Der Pietismus in Brandenberg-Preußen als religiös-soziale Reformbewegung*, Göttingen: Vandenhoeck & Ruprecht.

Hirsch, E. (1949) *Geschichte der neuern evangelischen Theologie im Zusammenhang mit den allgemeinen Bewegungen europäischen Denkens*, Gütersloh: Mohn.

Honnefelder, L. (1990) *Scientia transcendens: Die formale Betimmung der Seiendheit und Realität in der Metaphysik des Mittelalters und der Neuzeit (Duns Scotus–Suárez–Wolff–Kant–Peirce)*, Hamburg: Felix Meiner.

Honneth, A., *et al.* (eds) (1992) *Philosophical Interventions in the Unfinished Project of Enlightenment*, Cambridge, Mass.: MIT Press.

Hunter, I. (2000) 'Christian Thomasius and the Desacralization of Philosophy', *Journal of the History of Ideas*, 61: 1–16.

—— (2001) *Rival Enlightenments: Civil and Metaphysical Philosophy in Early Modern Germany*, Cambridge: Cambridge University Press.

Israel, J. I. (2001) *Radical Enlightenment: Philosophy and the Making of Modernity 1650–1750*, Oxford: Oxford University Press.

Kimmich, D. (1997) 'Lob der "ruhigen Belusting": Zu Thomasius' kritischer Epikur-Rezeption', in F. Vollhardt (ed.) *op. cit.*

Koselleck, R. (1988) *Critique and Crisis: Enlightenment and the Pathogenesis of Modern Society*, Oxford: Berg.

Lestition, S. (1989) 'The Teaching and Practice of Jurisprudence in 18th Century East Prussia: Königsberg's First Chancellor, R. F. von Sahme (1682–1753)', *Ius Commune*, 16: 27–80.

Lieberwirth, R. (1953) 'Christian Thomasius' Leipziger Streitigkeiten', *Wissenschaftliche Zeitschrift der Martin-Luther-Universität Halle-Wittenberg (Gesellschafts- und sprachwissenschaftliche Reihe)*, 3: 155–9.

Link, C. (1986) 'Die Staatstheorie Christian Wolffs', in W. Schneiders (ed.) *Christian Wolff 1679–1754: Interpretationen zu seiner Philosophie und deren Wirkung, mit einer Bibliographie der Wolff-Literatur*, Hamburg: Felix Meiner.

Malter, R. (1975) 'Zeitgenössische Reaktionen auf Kants Religionsphilosophie: Eine Skizze zur Wirkungsgeschichte des Kantischen und reformatorischen Denkens', in A. J. Bucher, H. Drüe and T. M. Seebohm (eds) *Bewußt Sein*, Bonn: Herbert Grundmann.

Nischan, B. (1994) *Prince, People, and Confession: The Second Reformation in Brandenburg*, Philadelphia: University of Pennsylvania Press.

Pocock, J. G. A. (1989) 'Conservative Enlightenment and Democratic Revolutions: The American and French Cases in British Perspective', *Government and Opposition*, 24: 81–105.

—— (1999) 'Enlightenment and Counter-Enlightenment, Revolution and Counter-Revolution: A Eurosceptical Enquiry', *History of Political Thought*, 20: 125–39.

Porter, R. and Teich, M. (eds) (1981) *The Enlightenment in National Context*, Cambridge: Cambridge University Press.

Schmidt, J. (ed.) (1996) *What is Enlightenment? Eighteenth-century Answers and Twentieth-century Questions*, Berkeley: University of California Press.

Schmidt-Biggemann, W. (1988) *Theodizee und Tatsachen: Das philosophische Profil der deutschen Aufklärung*, Frankfurt am Main: Suhrkamp.

—— (1994) 'Aufklärung durch Metaphysik: Zur Rolle der Theodizee in der Aufklärung', in W. Malsch and W. Koepke (eds) (1994) *Herder Jahrbuch/Herder Yearbook*, Stuttgart: J. B. Metzler.

Schneiders, W. (1986) 'Deus est philosophus absolute summus: Uber Christian Wolffs Philosophie und Philosophiebegriff', in *idem* (ed.) *Christian Wolff, op. cit.*

—— (1992) 'Aufklärungsphilosphien', in S. Jüttner and J. Schlobach (eds) *Europäische Aufklärung(en): Einheit und nationale Vielfalt*, Hamburg: Felix Meiner.

Seidler, M. J. (2002) 'Pufendorf and the Politics of Recognition', in I. Hunter and D. Saunders (eds) *op. cit.*

Sparn, W. (1989) 'Auf dem Wege zur theologischen Aufklärung in Halle: Von Johann Franz Budde zu Siegmund Jakob Baumgarten', in N. Hinske (ed.) *op. cit.*

Stosch, F. W. (1692) *Concordia rationis et fidei*, ed. W. Schröder (1992) Stuttgart: Frommann-Holzboog.

Stuke, H. (1972) 'Aufklärung', in O. Brunner, W. Conze and R. Koselleck (eds) *Geschichtliche Grundbegriffe: Historisches Lexikon zur politisch-sozialen Sprache in Deutschland*, vol. I, Stuttgart: Klett-Cotta.

Thomasius, C. (1705) *Vom Recht evangelischer Fürsten in Mitteldingen oder Kirchenzeremonien* [De jure principis circa adiaphora, 1695], vol. 1, Halle: Renger.

—— (1707) 'Von der Historie des Rechts der Natur bis auf Grotium' [Foreword to the first German edition of Grotius's *Law of War and Peace*], in W. Schätzel (ed.) (1950) *De Jure Belli ac Pacis (Drei Bücher vom Recht des Krieges und des Friedens)*, Tübingen: J. C. B. Mohr.

CHAPTER THIRTY-FIVE

ROUSSEAU

Enlightened critic of the Enlightenment?

————◆◆◆————

Tom Furniss

ean Jacques Rousseau (1712–78) is sometimes seen as a central player in the
Enlightenment and sometimes as an anti-Enlightenment figure who paved
the way for Romanticism. His paradoxical relationship to the Enlightenment
can best be observed in his highly influential *Discours sur l'origine et les fondements de
l'inégalité parmi les hommes* (1755), in which he articulates a powerful critique of what
he calls 'the fatal enlightenment of Civil man'. In seeming to endorse primitivism,
he provoked Voltaire (1694–1778) into writing a sarcastic letter to him in which he
says that: 'One acquires the desire to walk on all fours when one reads your work'
(Rousseau 1755: 48; Voltaire 1755). A modern commentator, however, describes the
Discourse on the Origins of Inequality as 'Rousseau's most distinctly *scientific* work, the
one closest to the mainstream of Enlightenment thinking' (Cranston 1984: 46–7).
In the *Second Discourse*, as Cranston points out, 'Rousseau outlined a theory of the
evolution of the human race which prefigured the discoveries of Darwin; he
revolutionized the study of anthropology and linguistics, and he made a seminal
contribution to political and social thought' (Cranston 1984: 29). It is possible, then,
to see Rousseau as both a key voice in the dialogue that was the Enlightenment and
as a figure who entered into one of the most searching critical dialogues with the
Enlightenment.

In order to contrast Rousseau's sometimes contradictory views with those of
some of the leading thinkers of the time, I shall begin by outlining the assumptions
of the editors of the *Encyclopédie*, Denis Diderot (1713–84) and Jean Le Rond
D'Alembert (1717–83), with whom Rousseau initially collaborated. I shall then
focus on Rousseau's *First Discourse* – the *Discours sur les sciences et les arts* (published in
January 1751) – and on his polemical contributions to the critical controversy that
the *First Discourse* provoked in the following three years. I shall suggest that these
writings allowed Rousseau to develop a critique of Enlightenment thinking and that
they help us to understand his own alternative worked out in later major writings
such as *Emile* and *Julie*.

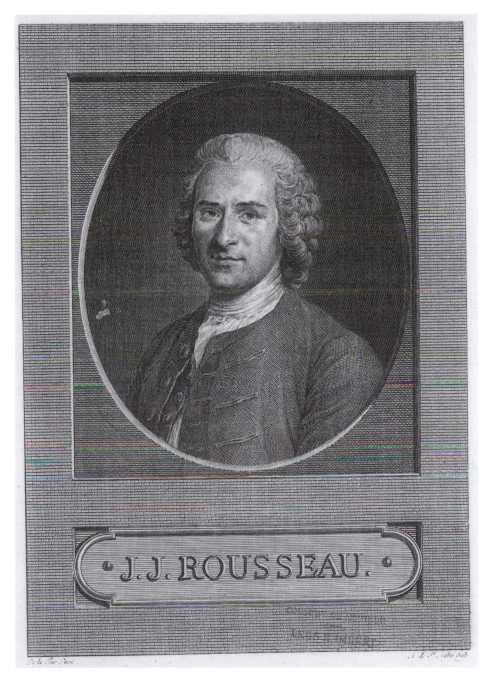

Figure 35.1 *Jean Jacques Rousseau*, A. de St Aubin after Maurice Quentin de la Tour. By permission of the Bibliothèque Nationale de France, Paris.

THE *ENCYCLOPÉDIE*

In the late 1740s and early 1750s Diderot and Rousseau shared 'remarkably similar intellectual interests' and were constant companions (Wokler 1975: 63). Rousseau was, indeed, one of the key contributors to the early volumes of the *Encyclopédie*. In 1749, on Diderot's request, Rousseau wrote numerous important articles on music that were included in the first five volumes of the *Encyclopédie* (see Chapter 19 of this volume; Scott 1998: 198–221). The scope of, and impetus behind, the *Encyclopédie*, which eventually extended to seventeen folio volumes of text published between 1751 and 1765, together with eleven supplementary volumes of plates, can be glimpsed in its full title: *Encyclopédie, ou Dictionnaire raisonné des sciences, des arts et des métiers* (Diderot: 1751–65). In its attempt to be a systematic compendium of all knowledge, the *Encyclopédie* included entries that defined its own aims and assumptions. In his entry on 'Encyclopédie' (1755, vol. 5), for example, Diderot explains that the purpose of an *Encyclopédie* is

> to collect all the knowledge scattered over the face of the earth, to present its general outlines and structure to the men with whom we live, and to transmit this to those who will come after us, so that the work of past centuries may be useful to the following centuries, that our children, by becoming more educated, may at the same time become more virtuous and happier.
>
> (Kramnick 1995: 18)

The *Encyclopédie*, then, was premised on the supposition that knowledge of the sciences, the arts and the crafts was compatible with, and indeed led to, virtue and happiness, and that such knowledge ought to be disseminated as widely as possible to 'the men with whom we live'. The assumption that education would enable future generations to become more virtuous and happier entailed a further assumption about the possibility of human progress and perfectibility – an assumption that Kramnick calls 'a leitmotiv of the Enlightenment' (Kramnick 1995: xiii).

For Diderot, human progress would be promoted through an unflinching rational analysis of the cherished ideas and authorities of the past:

> All things must be examined, debated, investigated without exception and without regard to anyone's feelings . . . We must ride roughshod over all these ancient puerilities, overturn the barriers that reason never erected, give back to the arts and sciences the liberty that is so precious to them . . . We have for quite some time needed a reasoning age when men would no longer seek the rules in classical authors but in nature.
>
> (Kramnick 1995: 18)

The commitment to rational and empirical enquiry is underlined in D'Alembert's 'Discours préliminaire', which prefaced the first volume in 1751 and served as an introduction to the *Encyclopédie* as a whole. In it, D'Alembert celebrates the pioneering achievements of Francis Bacon (1561–1626), René Descartes (1596–1650), Isaac Newton (1642–1727) and John Locke (1632–1704). The Enlightenment that the *Encyclopédie* defined applied scientific rationality and empirical observation to all aspects of human life, and was committed to the idea of human progress through the liberation of the arts and sciences.

ROUSSEAU'S *DISCOURSE ON THE SCIENCES AND ARTS*

In his posthumously published *Confessions* Rousseau represents his decision to write the *Discours sur les sciences et les arts* as a moment of revelation that changed the course of his life. On his way to visit Diderot in prison in the summer of 1749, Rousseau saw the announcement of the Academy of Dijon's prize essay question in the *Mercure de France*: 'Has the Restoration of the Sciences and the Arts Contributed to the Purification of Morals?' He claims that 'At the moment of that reading I saw another universe and I became another man' (Rousseau 1782: 294). Rousseau tells us that Diderot 'exhorted me to give vent to my ideas and to compete for the prize. I did so, and from that instant I was lost. All the rest of my life and misfortunes was the inevitable effect of that instant of aberration' (Rousseau 1782: 295). Rousseau is referring here, in melodramatic fashion, to the fact that the essay he wrote for the competition set him on a course that ran against the grain of the Enlightenment, and provoked, so he believed, the *philosophes* to engage in a relentless conspiracy against him.

The expected answer to the Dijon Academy's question was 'yes'. Voltaire's *Le Siècle de Louis XIV* (1751) had, after all, recently celebrated the progress of the arts, sciences and letters in the 'century' of Louis XIV (see Chapter 9 of this volume). In his prize-winning response, Rousseau recasts the question: 'Has the restoration of the Sciences and Arts contributed to the purification of Morals, or to their corruption?' (Rousseau 1751a: 5). By arguing that the sciences and arts had contributed to the *corruption* of morals, Rousseau produced his first major critique of the founding assumptions of the *Encyclopédie*.

Rousseau begins the *Discourse on the Sciences and Arts* by acknowledging the impressive achievements of the Enlightenment, especially its revelations about the universe and human nature. But he also describes the arts and sciences as a means of maintaining and sweetening the political repression of despotic government:

> While the Government and the Laws see to the safety and the well-being of men assembled, the Sciences, Letters, and Arts, less despotic and perhaps more powerful, spread garlands of flowers over the iron chains with which they are laden, throttle in them the sentiment of that original freedom for which they seemed born, make them love their slavery, and fashion them into what is called civilized Peoples. Need raised up Thrones; the Sciences and Arts have made them strong.
>
> (Rousseau 1751a: 6)

Here Rousseau criticizes the role of the arts and sciences in monarchical systems of government. The text's republican sentiments are, indeed, flagged on the title page, which announces that it was written 'Par un Citoyen de Genève', although Rousseau had yet to regain the citizenship which he had lost when he converted to Catholicism in 1728.

Rousseau implicitly associates the arts and sciences with civilized luxury. In doing so, he invokes the assumption of Enlightenment writers on both sides of the English Channel that luxury necessarily leads to physical, moral and political corruption (see Sekora 1977). In the discourse Rousseau asserts that 'our souls have become corrupted in proportion as our Sciences and our Arts have advanced towards perfection [and] Virtue has been seen fleeing in proportion as their light rose on our horizon' (Rousseau 1751a: 9). Later, in his last major reply to critics of the *First Discourse*, Rousseau declared that 'A taste for letters, philosophy, and the fine arts softens bodies and souls' (Rousseau 1753: 98). Like other republican and patriotic writers of the eighteenth century, Rousseau presents a series of historical examples to show that the luxury represented or generated by the arts and sciences enervates the bodies of men and the body politic, and so enables both to be enslaved (Rousseau 1751a: 8–10). He also offers a set of positive examples of republics, such as Sparta, that remained free and vigorous by repudiating the arts and sciences (Rousseau 1751a: 11). For Rousseau, the rustic and manly example of Sparta ought to have been emulated by all modern nations: 'Peoples, know, then, once and for all, that nature wanted to preserve you from science as a mother snatches a dangerous weapon from the hand of her child' (Rousseau 1751a: 14). Rousseau suggested that modern nations ought to have remained in a state of childhood.

In the second part of the *Discourse on the Sciences and Arts* Rousseau cites a number of major philosophers, including Thomas Hobbes (1588–1679), Baruch Spinoza (1632–77), George Berkeley (1685–1753) and Denis Diderot, accusing them of having concocted their theories not as 'lovers of wisdom' but in the manner of 'a troop of charlatans, each hawking from his own stand on a public square' (Rousseau 1751a: 25). He also attacks a 'host of obscure Writers and idle Literati . . . They smile disdainfully at such old-fashioned words as Fatherland and Religion, and dedicate their talents and their Philosophy to destroying and degrading all that is sacred among men' (Rousseau 1751a: 17–18).

The *First Discourse* thus becomes a modern jeremiad, warning readers against undermining a trinity of interlocking values – virtue, faith and patriotism. Rousseau's 'Preface to *Narcissus*' makes it clear that there is a fundamental incompatibility between the aspiration of the *philosophes* to inculcate a taste for the arts and sciences in the people and the political duties required of citizens in a well-constituted state, that is, a republic:

> In a well-constituted State all citizens are so thoroughly equal that no one may enjoy precedence over others as being the most learned or even the most skilled, but at most for being the best: though this last distinction is often dangerous; for it makes for scoundrels and hypocrites.
>
> (Rousseau 1753: 97)

By insisting that the equality of all citizens is the mark of a well-constituted state, Rousseau is decisively rejecting the compromise between philosophical Enlightenment and political absolutism which he believed at the time marked the thought of major Enlightenment figures. Yet Rousseau's criticism suggests that political virtue and Enlightenment, citizenship and philosophy, are fundamentally incompatible with one another: 'A taste for philosophy loosens all the bonds of esteem and benevolence that tie men to society, and this is perhaps the most dangerous of the evils it engenders' (Rousseau 1753: 99). In place of love of country and civic virtue as bonds of society, the philosophers of the Enlightenment have substituted self-interest (Rousseau 1753: 100).

But while Rousseau points out the *philosophes'* dangerous paradoxes, he was himself, as his detractors regularly pointed out, given to paradox. Having begun the *First Discourse* by arguing that the arts and sciences reinforce the *ancien régime*, he goes on to claim that they undermine the state (and then argues in the 'Preface to *Narcissus*' that they reinforce the social bonds of mutual interest). He argues that the sciences and the arts distort nature and corrupt society by generating a false taste in art. Paradoxically, he praises Louis XIV for establishing academies for the arts and sciences (Rousseau 1751a: 24). Rousseau claims that these institutions make possible a reconciliation between Enlightenment and virtue; their effect will be to preserve rather than destroy knowledge and morals.

While the best philosophers, like Socrates (*c.* 470–399 BC), knew their own ignorance and warned of the dangers of false knowledge, there are also original, independent thinkers whom nature intended to be philosophers (such as Bacon, Descartes and Newton) and who produce genuine knowledge (Rousseau 1753: 102). Although the *First Discourse* has been seen as an attack on Baconian ideas about science and enlightened absolutism (Cranston 1984: 25), Rousseau's recognition here that there are a few genuine philosophers who engage in the study of science for the good of all leads him to endorse the alliance between monarchy and science proposed by Bacon and taken up by Voltaire and d'Holbach. Rousseau reminds us that 'The Prince of Eloquence [Cicero] was Consul of Rome, and the greatest, perhaps, of Philosophers [Bacon], Lord Chancellor of England'. Under absolutist political systems, only such an alliance of power and wisdom can produce good Enlightenment (Rousseau 1751a: 27). Rousseau does not, then, advocate banishing the arts and sciences from the *ancien régime* but recommends a reorganization of the relation between them and political power. Instead of allowing the arts and sciences to flourish in an unregulated manner outside government control, Rousseau suggests, in a manner that recalls Plato's *Republic* and the traditional genre of advice to princes, that philosophy and political power should mutually restrain each other.

As for the rest of the population, the 'vulgar' (among whom Rousseau includes himself), they ought to be encouraged to avoid aspiring to become men of letters because it would involve seeking 'our happiness in someone else's opinion' rather than in being virtuous (Rousseau 1751a: 27). Rousseau therefore attacks the modern tendency to encourage more and more writers and readers to believe that they might participate in the dissemination of Enlightenment:

> What are we to think of those Anthologizers of works which have indiscreetly broken down the gate of the Sciences and introduced into their Sanctuary a populace unworthy of coming near it; whereas what would have been desirable

is to have had all those who could not go far in a career in Letters deterred from the outset, and become involved in Arts useful to society?

(Rousseau 1751a: 26)

Rousseau thus seems to condemn projects such as the forthcoming *Encyclopédie*, to which he himself had contributed. And while he promotes political equality, he strongly recommends that the study of the arts and sciences be restricted to those 'few men' who are capable of pursuing them without being corrupted by them. The 'republic of letters' and political republics are thus founded on different, seemingly incompatible, principles. Yet if the people are to be denied easy access to the sciences and arts, Rousseau does offer them a different kind of Enlightenment in which virtue becomes a sublime 'science' (Rousseau 1751a: 28).

THE CONTROVERSY OVER THE *DISCOURSE ON THE SCIENCES AND ARTS*

The *Discourse on the Sciences and Arts* is a short, apparently confused, and certainly derivative work (Wokler 1995: 27–30). It is nonetheless important as 'the first major statement of the philosophy of history – to the effect that our apparent cultural and social progress has led only to our real moral degradation – which Rousseau was to develop as one of the most central themes of his work' (Wokler 1995: 25). In his letter to the Abbé Raynal (1713–90), editor of the *Mercure de France*, he wrote:

I know in advance with what great words I will be attacked. Enlightenment, knowledge, laws, morality, reason, propriety, considerateness, gentleness, amenity, politeness, education, etc. To all of this I will only answer with two other words which ring even more loudly in my ear. Virtue, truth!

(Rousseau 1751b: 31)

The challenge was immediately recognized and responded to by the *philosophes* and their allies (Masters and Kelly 1992b: 23–198). One of the first responses, published in the *Mercure de France* in September 1751, was the anonymous 'Reply to the Discourse which was awarded the prize of the Academy of Dijon'. This was written by Stanislaus Leszczyński (1677–1766), King of Poland, patron of the arts and sciences, and father-in-law of Louis XV. D'Alembert, in the 'Preliminary Discourse' to the first volume of the *Encyclopédie* (1751), also responded:

even assuming we were ready to concede the disadvantage of human knowledge, which is far from being our intention here, we are even farther from believing that anything would be gained from destroying it. We would be left the vices, and have ignorance in addition.

(quoted in Gourevitch 1997: xiii)

Rousseau replied to both critics in his 'Observations by Jean Jacques Rousseau of Geneva on the Answer Made to his Discourse', which appeared in the October 1751 edition of the *Mercure de France*. Although he urges that all useless and dangerous things ought to be eliminated from the state, Rousseau insists that this does not mean that 'we should now burn all Libraries and destroy the Universities and the Academies. We would only plunge Europe back into Barbarism, and morals would gain nothing from it'. In a footnote he commends and agrees with D'Alembert (Rousseau 1751c: 50). He also makes it clear that he is not advocating abandoning science and returning to ignorance:

> Science in itself is very good, that is obvious; and one would have to have taken leave of good sense, to maintain the contrary. The Author of all things is the fountain of truth; to know everything is one of his divine attributes. To acquire knowledge and to extend one's enlightenment is, then, in a way to participate in the supreme intelligence.
>
> (Rousseau 1751c: 33)

But such enlightenment is restricted to 'a few privileged souls' who combine true learning with virtue; most of those who pursue science produce impieties, heresies, errors, absurd systems and obscene books (Rousseau 1751c: 33, 35). Rousseau offers a historical explanation: science and philosophy began to be antithetical to true religion when scholasticism attempted to wrap religion 'in the authority of Philosophy' (Rousseau 1751c: 43). But since Jesus did not 'entrust his doctrine and ministry to scholars' but to 'twelve poor fishermen', Rousseau concludes that most people ought not to dabble in science and philosophy but ought rather to follow 'the sublime simplicity of the Gospel', which is 'the only book a Christian needs, and the most useful of all books even for those who might not be Christians' (Rousseau 1751c: 40, 41, 44). Rousseau recommends the Reformation ideal of the sufficiency of the scriptures for spiritual and moral guidance. This allows Rousseau to point out that he is not recommending 'ferocious and brutal ignorance', as Stanislaus had suggested, but 'another, reasonable sort of ignorance . . . the treasure of a soul pure and satisfied with itself . . . [which] has no need to seek a false and vain happiness in the opinion others might have of its enlightenment' (Rousseau 1751c: 49). Reasonable ignorance thus fuses the religious virtue of the early Christians with the political virtue of Sparta.

Although reasonable ignorance is to be commended, it cannot be recovered once people have been spoiled by luxury and vanity: 'their hearts, once spoiled, will be so for ever; no remedy remains, short of some great revolution almost as much to be feared as the evil it might cure, and which it is blameworthy to desire and impossible to foresee' (Rousseau 1751c: 51). While a revolution might overturn political systems in which the arts and sciences are born of and generate luxury, Rousseau is not willing to prescribe such a dangerous remedy. The only possible course in such a case, once again, is to counterbalance the corrupting effects of Enlightenment with an agreeable Enlightenment that provides the people with distractions (Rousseau 1751c: 51).

Rousseau's prescription for those people who have been poisoned by the sciences and the arts is a prescription for absolutist monarchies such as France and for corrupt cities such as Paris. Later, in 1758, in his *Letter to M. D'Alembert on the Theatre*, a book that constituted his final break with the *Encyclopédists*, Rousseau attacked

D'Alembert's entry on 'Geneva' in the seventh volume of the *Encyclopédie* (1757) for suggesting that Geneva would benefit from having a theatre (Rousseau 1758). Yet, while he objects to a theatre in a virtuous state, he accepts its necessity in a corrupt one: in the preface to his juvenile play *Narcissus*, he recommends that the people (of Paris) be offered theatrical entertainment in order to keep them from doing evil (Rousseau 1753: 104).

One of the striking things about Rousseau's contributions to the controversy over the *First Discourse* is that he repeatedly accuses his critics of failing to understand his argument and of failing to offer arguments in reply. As he puts it in the 'Preface to *Narcissus*', 'I will be attacked with witticisms, and I will defend myself with nothing but arguments: but provided that I convince my adversaries, I do not much care whether I persuade them' (Rousseau 1753: 92). Concluding the 'Preface to *Narcissus*', Rousseau reflects anew on his own status as a writer and seems willing to consider that he might be among the few who are fit to pursue the arts and sciences. More clearly than in the *First Discourse*, the 'Preface to *Narcissus*' indicates that the vices of the Enlightenment arise through bad government and hence that enlightened corruption might be avoided in Europe through political, legal and moral transformations. Rousseau even implies that the rational analysis offered in his own writings might help bring about such transformations (Rousseau 1753: 101). But while Rousseau claims that his writings might be useful, he also insists that they are written for a limited audience. He imagines that his writings might 'have edified a small number of good [people]', while in the 'Preface of a Second Letter to Bordes' he says that his writings thus far have been aimed at 'those capable of understanding' and that he 'never wanted to speak to the others' (Rousseau 1753: 104; Rousseau 1761b: 110). Rousseau announces that he will continue to 'write Books, compose Poems and Music, if I have the talent, the time, the strength and the will to do so: [and] I shall continue to state openly the bad opinion in which I hold letters and those who practise them'. He insists, in a footnote, that this is not to be self-contradictory but to act as a wise physician of the state who has diagnosed the condition of his patient and selected the appropriate remedy (Rousseau 1753: 105).

ROUSSEAU'S NOVELS

Despite his claims about his intended readership in the *First Discourse*, and his attack on the popularization of the Enlightenment, Rousseau began to write texts aimed at a wider audience. In doing so, he was attempting to counteract the influence of Parisian Enlightenment over the hearts and minds of the people. In the *Letter to M. D'Alembert*, Rousseau stresses that he is not writing for 'the few but . . . the public' (Rousseau 1758: 6). In his two novels, *Julie, ou La Nouvelle Héloïse* (1761a) and *Emile, ou, De L'Education* (1762), Rousseau presented imaginative visions of future society. Both are set in rural locations. *Emile* consists of the gradual enlightenment of Emile by his tutor, who guides his pupil through an education based on a Lockean empiricist epistemology designed to allow him to become self-sufficient, relying on his own experience and practical reason rather than the authority of others or the prejudices of the fashionable world. In due course, Emile marries Sophie and they live in an isolated rural enclave, along with her family and his tutor (Rousseau 1762).

Although the most exciting aspect of *Julie* for eighteenth-century readers was that it appears to celebrate the consummated love affair between St Preux, a tutor, and his young pupil, Julie, the novel is primarily concerned with the characters' moral development, with Julie eventually rejecting St Preux in favour of marrying the older and wiser M. de Wolmar, who she respects but does not love. The second half of the novel is devoted to a detailed account of the small, imagined community of virtuous individuals that Julie and Wolmar gather round them at Clarens on the north-eastern shore of Lake Geneva. This community or extended family fashioned an alternative to Parisian society that is at once more faithful to the Enlightenment's original principles and reconciles them with piety, virtue, sincerity and republican values. Rousseau's alternative community includes philosophy and the arts and sciences, but subsumes them to the useful arts (such as horticulture), the bonds of love, the need for transparency between people, and the heroine's achievement of virtuous piety. St Preux is invited to join the community, and Julie's last request to her former lover is that he educate her children not to 'make scholars of them, [but to] make them into charitable and just men' (Rousseau 1761a: 610).

Yet *Emile* and *Julie* are didactic novels in a double sense: the former in part a treatise on education, the latter a collection of fictional and non-fictional letters on the same topic and other philosophical subjects. The novel's subtitle claims that it consists of 'Letters of Two Lovers Who Live in a Small Town at the Foot of the Alps, Collected and Published by Jean Jacques Rousseau' (Rousseau 1761a: 1). The prefaces of the novels meditate on the nature and effect of novels. If the theatre is both a source of and an antidote to corruption in great cities such as Paris, Rousseau suggests in the first preface that novels play a similar double role with regard to whole peoples: 'Great cities must have theatres; and corrupt peoples, novels. I have seen the morals of my times, and I have published these letters. Would I had lived in an age when I should have thrown them into the fire!' (Rousseau 1761a: 3)

It is possible to see the second preface to *Julie*, which consists of a dialogue between two characters indicated by the letters 'N' and 'R', as an imaginary dialogue between Rousseau (posing as the editor 'R') and Diderot (see Jackson 1992: 104–41). Rousseau had finally broken with Diderot in 1758, believing that he had joined the *philosophes*' 'plot' against him (see Rousseau 1782: 416–17). The dispute between Rousseau and the *philosophes* had arisen not only because Rousseau had written against their convictions but also because he had acted on the consequences of his arguments by eschewing patronage and abandoning Paris in favour of semi-rural retirement. Diderot's play *Le Fils naturel* (*The Natural Son*; 1757) includes an attack on solitaries – especially in the assertion that 'Only the wicked man is alone' (Act IV, scene 3) – that Rousseau took personally (Rousseau 1782: 382). The dialogue between 'R' and 'N' is a response to this attack (Rousseau 1761a: 8, 9, 14). In the first preface Rousseau advises the reader that if

[he] is willing to undertake the reading of these letters . . . he must tell himself in advance that their writers are not French, wits, academicians, philosophers; but provincials, foreigners, solitary youths, almost children, who in

their romantic imaginations mistake the honest ravings of their brains for philosophy.

(Rousseau 1761: 3)

In the second preface 'R' implies that *Julie* offers a positive alternative to French Enlightenment philosophy:

> Two or three simple but sensible youths discuss among themselves the interests of their hearts . . . Filled with the single sentiment that occupies them, they are in delirium, and think they are philosophizing . . . They talk about everything; they get everything wrong; they reveal nothing but themselves, they make themselves endearing. Their errors are more worthy than the knowledge of Sages . . . finding nowhere what they are feeling, they turn in on themselves; they detach themselves from the rest of Creation; and inventing among themselves a little world different from ours, there they create an authentically new spectacle.
>
> (Rousseau 1782: 11)

Although these childish letter-writers may be mistaken about their 'philosophizing', their simple sincerity makes them endearing and the enclave they create for themselves at Clarens constitutes 'an authentically new spectacle'. Regardless of the editor's condescension in the prefaces, the second half of the novel makes it clear that this authentically new spectacle is presented as a model of human society that functions as a serious alternative to that of Parisian Enlightenment.

'R' also stresses that *Julie* is not aimed at the worldly readers of great cities but at provincial readers:

> When it comes to morality, no reading, in my view, will do worldly people any good . . . The further one gets from the bustle, from great cities, from large gatherings, the smaller the obstacles become. There is a point where these obstacles cease to be insurmountable, and that is where books can be of some use. When one lives in isolation, since there is no hurry to read to show off one's reading, it is less varied and more meditated upon . . . Many more novels are read in the Provinces than in Paris, more are read in the country than in the cities, and they make a much greater impression there.
>
> (Rousseau 1782: 13)

Given the susceptibility of provincial readers, it is all the more important that they read novels that encourage them to live their lives virtuously. But the majority of the novels produced in Paris corrupt provincial readers, luring them to Paris in order to imitate the corrupt characters they have read about. The exodus from the countryside to capital cities is taking place all over Europe and 'propels Europe . . . towards her ruin'. There is therefore a need for novels that inculcate good citizenship in provincial readers by promoting a love of rural life that allows them to see new meanings in their lives. 'R' imagines that *Julie* might be the novel to do this (Rousseau 1782: 16). *Julie*, then, is not just a novel about an imagined rural community of beautiful souls that forms a positive alternative to Parisian Enlightenment; it also attempts to constitute an imagined community of rural readers who will imitate the 'happy couple' they read about – not Julie and St Preux, but Julie and Wolmar.

ROUSSEAU'S READERS

In an essay on Rousseau's eighteenth-century readers Robert Darnton reveals that *Julie* was indeed read by just such a husband and wife as Rousseau envisages in the second preface. Jean Ranson (1747–1823), a merchant from La Rochelle, became fascinated by Rousseau and his writings and shaped his life and opinions by what he read; he and his wife raised their children according to the principles outlined in *Emile* (Darnton 2001: 217, 235–42). As perhaps the best-selling novel of the eighteenth century, *Julie* spread its message throughout Europe, reaching areas and classes that the *philosophes* failed to reach:

> At least seventy editions were published before 1800 – probably more than for any other novel in the previous history of publishing. True, the most sophisticated men of letters, sticklers for correctness like Voltaire and Grimm, found the style overblown and the subject distasteful. But ordinary readers from all ranks of society were swept off their feet.
>
> (Darnton 2001: 242)

What is interesting is the way readers responded to *Julie*: 'They wept, they suffocated, they raved, they looked deep into their lives and resolved to live better, then they poured their hearts out in more tears – and in letters to Rousseau, who collected their testimonials in a huge bundle' (Darnton 2001: 242). Thus the novel's imagined community of letter-writing characters brought into being an imagined community of letter-writing readers focused on Rousseau himself. What their letters reveal is that *Julie* 'inspired [Rousseau's] readers with an overwhelming desire to make contact with the lives behind the printed page – the lives of the characters and his own' (Darnton 2001: 244). This impulse demonstrates that readers 'believed and wanted to believe in the authenticity of the letters' (Darnton 2001: 233). Above all, what readers wanted to say to Rousseau was that 'his message had got across' (Darnton 2001: 244). The message they derived from *Julie* was not the virtue of love but the love of virtue: 'They wanted to tell him how they identified with his characters, how they, too, had loved, sinned, suffered, and resolved to be virtuous again in the midst of a wicked and uncomprehending world. They knew his novel was true because they had read its message in their lives' (Darnton 2001: 246). Reading *Julie* thus enabled readers to reread their own lives: 'Again and again the readers returned to the same theme. Jean Jacques had made them see deeper into the meaning of their lives' (Darnton 2001: 247). Based on the evidence of the letters that readers of *Julie* sent to Rousseau, Darnton suggests that Rousseau effected a general transformation in the way that readers responded to texts: 'Rousseau taught his readers to "digest" books so thoroughly that literature became absorbed in life' (Darnton 2001: 251).

The example of Jean Ranson indicates how Rousseau 'could touch lives everywhere' (Darnton 2001: 252).

For Darnton, the response to *Julie* is a measure of how Rousseau fabricated 'romantic sensitivity' in a whole generation and hence paved the way for the Romantic rejection of the Enlightenment at the end of the eighteenth century. For Hulliung, by contrast, Rousseau's later writings can be seen as fashioning 'a dazzling one-man alternative enlightenment that reached an exceptionally wide audience' (Hulliung 1994: 4).

It seems to me that both these conclusions contain an element of truth. The rural community that is imagined in *Julie*, and that so touched the imaginations of its readers, does constitute an alternative Enlightenment. Yet this alternative, with its focus on authenticity, sincerity, virtue and sympathy, might, indeed, be called a 'Romantic Enlightenment', centred not in Paris or London but in the virtuous hearts of ordinary readers.

REFERENCES

Berlin, Isaiah (ed.) (1956) *The Age of Enlightenment: The 18th Century Philosophers*, New York: New American Library.

Cranston, Maurice (1984) 'Introduction', in Jean Jacques Rousseau, *A Discourse on Inequality*, London and New York: Penguin.

Darnton, Robert (2001) *The Great Cat Massacre, and Other Episodes in French Cultural History*, London and New York: Penguin.

Derrida, Jacques (1967) *Of Grammatology*, trans. Gayatri Chakravorty Spivak (1976) Baltimore and London: Johns Hopkins University Press.

Diderot, Denis (with Jean Le Rond D'Alembert) (ed.) (1751–65) *Encyclopédie, ou Dictionnaire Raisonné des Sciences, des Arts et des Métiers*, 17 vols, Paris (vols 1–7) and Neufchastel: Samuel Faulche (vols 8–17).

Gay, Peter (1967) *The Enlightenment: An Interpretation: The Rise of Modern Paganism*, London: Weidenfeld & Nicolson.

—— (1972) *The Enlightenment: An Interpretation: The Science of Freedom*, London: Weidenfeld & Nicolson.

Gourevitch, Victor (1997) 'Introduction', in Jean Jacques Rousseau, *The Discourses and Other Political Writings*, ed. and trans. Victor Gourevitch, Cambridge and New York: Cambridge University Press.

Hampson, Norman (1968) *The Enlightenment: An Evaluation of its Assumptions, Attitudes and Values*, London and New York: Penguin.

Hulliung, Mark (1994) *The Autocritique of the Enlightenment: Rousseau and the Philosophes*, Cambridge, Mass., and London: Harvard University Press.

Jackson, Susan, K. (1992) *Rousseau's Occasional Autobiographies*, Columbus: Ohio State University Press.

Kelly, Christopher, Masters, Roger D. and Stillman, Peter G. (eds) (1995) *The Confessions and Correspondence, Including the Letters to Malesherbes*, trans. Christopher Kelly in *The Collected Writings of Rousseau*, vol. 5, Hanover, NH, and London: University Press of New England.

Kramnick, Isaac (ed.) (1995) *The Portable Enlightenment Reader*, New York and London: Penguin.

Masters, Roger D. and Christopher Kelly (eds) (1992a) *Discourse on the Origins of Inequality (Second Discourse), Polemics, and Political Economy*, trans Judith R. Bush, Roger D. Masters, Christopher Kelly and Terence Marshall in *The Collected Writings of Rousseau*, *op. cit.*, vol. 3.

—— (eds) (1992b) *Discourse on the Sciences and Arts (First Discourse) and Polemics*, trans. Judith R. Bush, Roger D. Masters and Christopher Kelly in *The Collected Writings of Rousseau*, *op. cit.*, vol. 2.

Rousseau, Jean Jacques (1751a) *Discours sur les sciences et les arts*, ed. Victor Gourevitch in Gourevitch (1997) *op. cit.*

—— (1751b) 'Letter to Monsieur l'Abbé Raynal', ed. Victor Gourevitch in Gourevitch (1997) *op. cit.*

—— (1751c) 'Observations by Jean Jacques Rousseau of Geneva on the Answer Made to his Discourse', ed. Victor Gourevitch in Gourevitch (1997) *op. cit.*

—— (1753) 'Preface to *Narcissus*', ed. Victor Gourevitch in Gourevitch (1997) *op. cit.*

—— (1755) *Discours sur l'origine et les fondements de l'inégalité parmi les hommes*, ed. Roger D. Masters and Christopher Kelly in Masters and Kelly (1992a) *op. cit.*

—— (1758) 'Letter to M. D'Alembert on the Theatre', ed. and trans Allan Bloom in (1960; 1968) *Politics and the Arts: Letter to M. D'Alembert on the Theatre*, Ithaca: Cornell University Press.

—— (1761a) *Julie, ou La Nouvelle Héloïse*, ed. and trans. Philip Stewart and Jean Vaché in (1997) *The Collected Writings of Rousseau*, *op. cit.*, vol. 6.

—— (1761b) 'Preface of a Second Letter to Bordes', trans. and ed. Victor Gourevitch in Gourevitch (1997) *op. cit.*

—— (1762) *Emile, ou, De L'education*, ed. and trans. Allan Bloom (1979) New York: Basic Books.

Rousseau, Jean Jacques (1782) *Confessions*, ed. and trans. Christopher Kelly, Roger D. Masters and Peter G. Stillman in (1995) *The Collected Writings of Rousseau*, *op. cit.*, vol. 5.

Scott, John T. (ed. and trans.) (1998) *Essay on the Origin of Languages and Writings Related to Music in The Collected Writings of Rousseau*, *op. cit.*, vol. 7.

Sekora, John (1977) *Luxury: The Concept in Western Thought, Eden to Smollett*, Baltimore and London: Johns Hopkins University Press.

Voltaire (1755), 'Letter from Voltaire to Rousseau' in Masters, Roger D. and Christopher Kelly (eds) (1992) *Discourse on the Origins of Inequality (Second Discourse), Polemics, and Political Economy, The Collected Writings of Rousseau*, vol. 3, 102–104.

Wokler, Robert (1975) 'The Influence of Diderot on the Political Theory of Rousseau: Two Aspects of a Relationship', *Studies on Voltaire and the Eighteenth Century*, 132: 55–111.

—— (1995; 2001) *Rousseau: A Very Short Introduction*, Oxford and New York: Oxford University Press.

CHAPTER THIRTY-SIX

BURKE AND THE RESPONSE
TO THE ENLIGHTENMENT

Frances Ferguson

Perhaps the most remarkable aspect of the Enlightenment was that it very clearly introduced ideas into struggles for political power. When writers traced the origins of the American and French revolutions to the inspiration of Voltaire, Rousseau and others, they were recognizing that politics had become idea-driven to an unprecedented degree. The revolutions that established American independence from Britain and overthrew the French monarchy claimed that their legitimacy stemmed from human reason and its efficacy in discovering the natural rights to which every person could lay claim. For the philosophers, and for the revolutionaries who appealed to them, those rights were universal. In their view the bare capacity for reason — without regard to questions of social class or even national identity — authorized individuals to hold and voice opinions about political justice. Politics became an international project, as individuals felt free and more than free to express their views on the political struggles of other nations. Indeed, reason seemed almost to require that freedom-loving Englishmen recognize the claims of the American colonies for independence, or that Americans support the French revolutionaries' assertion of the rights of the majority of the population against the French monarchy and aristocracy. The premium that the Enlightenment placed on reason in conferring rights did not just give a new authority to public opinion; it also made public opinion international.

BURKE'S POSITION IN THE REVOLUTIONARY
CLIMATE

Edmund Burke (1729–97) fully participated in the newly internationalized debates, first as a defender of the American colonies against Britain. Yet, even though Burke allied himself with the forces of freedom in that cause, he was later to become anathema to the political thinkers who aligned themselves with political liberty. They took his defence of the cause for agreement with the radical arguments used in its favour. Burke, in fact, refused to discuss the abstract justification for the rebellion, confining himself to arguments against the insensitive treatment of the colonists by successive governments. This was an early sign that over the course of his career,

Figure 36.1 *Edmund Burke*, engraving (*c.* 1830) by William Holl (1807–71). By permission of the National Library of Australia.

he would develop into one of the staunchest defenders of the notion of social and political culture as a conservative force. Particularly in *Reflections on the Revolution in France*, he described culture in a fashion that would become extremely important for conservative thinkers in the future. Culture, for Burke, involved all the things that one could not choose about one's society – ongoing institutions such as the Anglican Church or a legal system organized around the ancient English constitution of unwritten laws. It included all the elements of an ongoing society. In his view, culture was as forcible as nature. It was, indeed, as James Chandler (1984) has pointed out, a 'second nature'. Moreover, if the first step in the argument in defence of culture was to recognize that no one could choose the culture in which they lived, the second step was to claim that individuals should particularly prize their culture as a special inheritance. Burke, by the end of his career, had diverted a debate about universal rights into one about relevance of national traditions and present circumstance. He commented on France in order to provide a contrast with England, and offered a highly articulated conservative patriotism. He did not merely encourage the English to avoid '[aping] the fashion they have never tried', but argued that they should come to be acutely conscious of the love they ought to bear for their country (Burke 1790: 111).

The immediate English context for Burke's public comments on the French Revolution was his sense that a case needed to be made against those who wanted England to imitate the French in making their government more fully representative and less property-based. He was incensed by the *Discourse on the Love of Our Country*, preached by the dissenting minister Richard Price (1723–91), before the meeting of the London Revolution Society on 4 November 1789 in commemoration of the Glorious Revolution of 1688/9. Price argued that, just as that revolution had yielded a model for the American and French revolutions, so those revolutions could show the British the way to improve their own claims to freedom. Price was not alone in his encomiums to the French Revolution (Price 1789: 195–6). There were general celebrations for the fall of the Bastille (14 July), and British political leaders, such as Charles James Fox (1749–1806), praised the French Revolution in Parliament.

Reacting to such praise and the assumption that the same principles were appropriate to, and were being implemented in, different societies, Edmund Burke ardently defended the national, the local and the customary. In 1790 he published his *Reflections on the Revolution in France*, in which he responded to Richard Price and attacked the Society for Constitutional Information and the Revolution Society, and prompted Mary Wollstonecraft (1759–97), Thomas Paine (1737–1809) and James Mackintosh (1764–1832) to spirited rebuttal (Wollstonecraft in *A Vindication of the Rights of Men*, Paine in *The Rights of Man* and Mackintosh in *Vindiciae Gallicae*). The new enlightened politics, they thought, made individuals citizens of the world, and gave them a stake in the actions of societies other than their own. In *Reflections* Burke demurred from the enthusiasm for the French Revolution that inspired Price and its British and American sympathizers. He challenged what he described as a new orthodoxy among both the French revolutionaries and their defenders. The book's importance – and its abiding interest – did not lie simply in its indictment of French revolutionaries and their international supporters abroad. Instead, *Reflections* deployed all of Burke's considerable rhetorical skills – the talents that the poet William Wordsworth (1770–1850) referred to in *The Prelude* as the 'Genius of Burke' – to write a spirited defence of the customs and institutions of his native country. Since the French revolutionaries and their sympathizers saw public opinion as a new and powerful political force that could be harnessed in the Revolution, Burke aimed to develop a readership which would join with him in resisting the French contagion. He courted its assent by glorifying the symbolism of Britain's political power.

To put the matter in this way, however, does not capture the ingenuity that Burke brought to his task. In the *Reflections* Burke defended the rights of property, affectionate ties and religion against those who adopted the perspective of universal reason. Burke represented the *Reflections* less as a political pamphlet than as a personal letter (albeit a personal letter of unusually great length). In November 1789 Charles-Jean-François Depont, whom Burke identifies as a 'very young gentleman at Paris' in his prefatory remarks, had written to Burke to ask for his assurance that the French were worthy of liberty and that they knew how to distinguish liberty from licence and legitimate government from despotic power. Burke had initially replied by saying that he had his doubts but that he was ignorant of much of what had occurred and could not venture to say much. Within a matter of months, however, he had begun to attack the British sympathizers of the Revolution and openly criticize the revolutionary principles.

In presenting the *Reflections* as if it were a private letter even as it swelled to hundreds of pages, Burke was able to establish an air of intimacy with a substantial readership. Even though he had already been making speeches in Parliament attacking the Revolution, he implied that his readers were privileged to have access to his views. In writing to the 'very young gentleman at Paris', Burke puts himself in a position to explain Britain and its symbolic commitments to someone who stands in need of a full account (Burke 1790: 84). He thus begins by correcting his correspondent's misapprehensions. You may well have imagined, he suggests, that I might approve of the French Revolution because you thought that the Constitutional Society and the Revolution Society represented all public opinion, but they do not represent mine. You may well have imagined that the Constitutional Society is an influential group, but no one 'of common judgment, or the least degree of information' takes them seriously (Burke 1790: 87).

BURKE'S CRITICISM OF RATIONAL ABSTRACTION

Burke is particularly offended by anonymous publications which, to the revolutionaries and their sympathizers, may look like the expression of the principles of liberty. For him, an unsigned document substitutes abstraction for the reality of politics: 'Circumstances (which with some gentlemen pass for nothing)', he writes, 'give in reality to every political principle its distinguishing colour, and discriminating effect' (Burke 1790: 90). Throughout his work, Burke offers variations on his theme of the importance of particular circumstances and traditions. By identifying his correspondent as a young Frenchman, he continually creates occasions for engaging in political debate while maintaining a generous tone towards his own interlocutor. Burke ends the *Reflections* by saying that he has 'candidly' told his young correspondent his sentiments, and then immediately observes, 'I think they are not likely to alter yours. I do not know that they ought. You are young; you cannot guide, but must follow the fortune of your country' (Burke 1790: 376). He thus makes a double point: that politics is not primarily based on principles and argument but rather on the kind of intuitive distinctions that people make as members of a culture, and that the views of individuals are seldom determinative in the political world, in which most people 'cannot guide, but must follow the fortune' of their country (Burke 1790: 376). By the end of *Reflections* Burke has disguised the fact that his own emphasis on the precise context of any political ideas prevents application of his analysis to the French situation. He claims that his external viewpoint confers special authority for his views, insisting that his opinions result from 'long observation and much impartiality' (Burke 1790: 376).

A CONSERVATIVE INTERPRETATION OF 'HUMAN NATURE'

Burke offers a substitute for the French revolutionaries' enlightened insistence upon a rational human nature. Enlightenment thinkers might imagine that reason is universal, he suggests, but argues that a more important practical assumption is that human nature is everywhere the same, which was a commonplace among Enlightenment thinkers. They, however, fail to take into account the nature of human beings as political animals, who define themselves in terms of their commitments to their families, their religion and their country. Burke focuses the discussion on assignats, the paper currency issued by the revolutionary government; for him, they represented an inflated currency with no substantial backing, and he treated them as emblematic of the entire revolutionary government. He also produces a catalogue of the consequences of the Revolution:

> Laws overturned; tribunals subverted; industry without vigour; commerce expiring; the revenue unpaid, yet the people impoverished; a church pillaged, and a state not relieved; civil and military anarchy made the constitution of the kingdom; every thing human and divine sacrificed to the idol of public credit, and national bankruptcy the consequence; and to crown all, the paper securities of new, precarious, tottering power, the discredited paper securities of impoverished fraud, and beggared rapine, held out as a currency for the support of an empire.
>
> (Burke 1790: 126)

Burke, however, ignores the material conditions that contributed to revolutionary zeal. (The French people had, during the last years of the reign of Louis XVI, experienced considerable hardship as a result of a series of bad harvests. Marie Antoinette's indifference to the suffering of the common people exacerbated feelings of hostility towards the monarchy.) Instead, he describes the French as rebelling 'against a mild and lawful monarch, with more fury, outrage, and insult, than ever any people has been known to raise against the most illegal usurper, or the most sanguinary tyrant' (Burke 1790: 126). 'These dreadful things', as Burke calls the events of 1789, are treated as if they are all the more dreadful for having been completely unnecessary; indeed the revolution was simply the result of 'rash and ignorant counsel in time of profound peace' (Burke 1790: 126). For him, the acts of the revolutionaries are simply a result of 'unforced choice, this fond election of evil' (Burke 1790: 127).

Having dismissed the legitimacy of the economic and legal issues in whose name the revolutionaries fought, Burke resorts to *ad hominem* criticism, saying that only the character of the persons involved in the National Assembly can explain choices that 'would appear perfectly unaccountable' (Burke 1790: 127). The National

Assembly 'fondly' elects 'evil', Burke claims, because it is composed of persons of modest capacity. While the 'title and function' that the Assembly appropriates for itself may sound as though it represents the 'virtue and wisdom of a whole people collected into a focus', the individuals who bear those titles in no way live up to them (Burke 1790: 127). Moreover, it is impossible that they could. They simply lack the capacities to be as wise and virtuous as the people would like for them to be: 'no name, no power, no function, no artificial institution whatsoever, can make the men of whom any system of authority is composed, any other than God, and nature, and education, and their habits of life have made them. Capacities beyond these the people have not to give' (Burke 1790: 128).

Burke argues that the problem with the Assembly is that it is directed by 'new men' who have no sense of the past and believe that they can overrule nature and experience. Addressing his correspondent directly, he speaks of his 'surprize' at learning that 'a very great proportion of the Assembly, a majority, I believe, of the members who attended [were] practitioners in the law' (Burke 1790: 129). These 'practitioners' were not judges, 'leading advocates' or 'renowned professors', he continues. Instead, they were 'the inferiour unlearned, mechanical, merely instrumental members of the profession' and persons who had previously had careers as 'fomentors and conductors of the petty war of village vexation' (Burke 1790: 129–30). Drawing a vivid picture of the low esteem in which they are held by the French people generally, he observes that they are men who have not been 'taught habitually to respect themselves' or had reason to think of themselves as having any 'previous fortune in character at stake' (Burke 1790: 130).

From one standpoint, of course, the heavy representation of 'practitioners in the law' in the Assembly might seem to be an obvious way of acknowledging individuals who may lack aristocratic rank but have developed professional credentials in the emerging meritocracy. Their credentials might be said to lie in their individual abilities rather than in their claim to hereditary property. Indeed, just such an argument motivated Wollstonecraft, Paine and Mackintosh when they eloquently criticized the aristocracy. In their view, it was perfectly obvious that a governmental system that was organized around property did not serve the interests of society in general, because it had no way of screening out men of mean capacities who had happened to inherit substantial tracts of land or a throne. If a meritocracy ought to make the abilities of the most talented available for the public good, these defenders of the Revolution argued, it also should avoid concentrating power in the hands of the untalented.

BURKE'S UNREVOLUTIONARY ACCOUNT OF THE GLORIOUS REVOLUTION

Burke argues against representation based on merit rather than family status not merely by heaping personal scorn on the credentials of the 'new men' who have become central to the new government in France. He also offers up a description of British history that is designed to illustrate that the most crucial feature of government is its ability to preserve orderly lines of succession. As Burke glosses the story of the Glorious Revolution of 1688, it is difficult to discern that religious tensions continually stoked political conflict in England. It is harder still to make out that James II had turned out judges who were likely to disagree with him, and appointed in their place new ones likely to agree, had named Roman Catholics to head some of the Oxford colleges, and had raised the ire of the clergy by demanding that they read from every pulpit the declaration of indulgence in which he granted full religious liberty to his subjects. Moreover, Burke passes over the fact that these various religious and political irritants came to a head when the line of succession looked clearer when the Queen gave birth to a son and heir. Certainty about succession, indeed, exacerbated the tensions, as the Protestants who felt oppressed by James's rule came to recognize that they could no longer hope to outlast a Catholic monarchy, and both political parties united in inviting William of Orange to support what they took to be the time-honoured religion and laws of England.

In Burke's account there is no mention of the fact that James had lost even the support of his own army, that a convention Parliament had pronounced that his flight amounted to abdication, and that the same Parliament had offered the crown jointly to William, who was not in the direct line of succession, and his wife Mary, who was. If he had discussed such features of England's Glorious Revolution, it might have been easy to see why the members of the Constitutional Society and the Revolution Society had seen a precedent for making kings answerable to the will of the people, and why Richard Price had said to the Revolution Society that the English king was 'almost the *only* lawful king in the world, because the *only* king who owes his crown to the *choice of his people*' (Burke 1790: 96; cf. Price 1789: 186). For what had the Glorious Revolution been if not a dramatic internal political shift that transferred the ultimate decision-making authority from the King to the Parliament? Yet Burke quotes Price's remark contemptuously, and also disputes his claim that the principles of the Glorious Revolution have given the English people three fundamental rights: to choose their governors; 'to cashier them for misconduct'; and 'to frame a government' for themselves (Burke 1790: 99).

Burke's arguments against Price's account of the Glorious Revolution and its heritage are twofold. He first asserts that most Englishmen in the present do not want, and would resist, the rights that the Revolution Society invokes on their behalf. Second, he provides a highly creative interpretation of English history. Skipping over the political controversies of the Glorious Revolution almost entirely, Burke makes momentous historical events appear the mildest possible solution to a vexing practical conundrum about the line of succession to the crown.

Although he heaps scorn on his antagonists for their use of principle, when convenient he himself resorts to principle and writes, 'If the *principles* of the Revolution of 1688 are any where to be found, it is in the statute called the *Declaration of Right*' (Burke 1790: 100). He eventually concedes that 'if ever there was a time favourable for establishing the principle, that a king of popular choice was the only legal king, without all doubt it was at the Revolution', but only by way of arguing that that principle had been rejected rather than embraced at the moment when it was available for a decision (Burke 1790: 101). Indeed, the burden of Burke's discussion of the Glorious Revolution is to insist that the words of the Declaration of Right apply in his time, not just in 1688. In his reading, the Declaration of Right does not merely suggest that an election would in 1688 have been 'utterly destructive of the "unity, peace, and tranquillity of this nation"'; it also, he thinks, indicates that electing sovereigns would always disrupt national harmony (Burke 1790: 103). The story of the Glorious Revolution becomes the story of orderly succession, not the rise of the notion that even kings must seek and have popular support. In his account, governments ought to recognize that their central role is to maintain their own continuity, to make it possible for persons to feel that their circumstances are never open to their choice. Thus, their absolutely central task is to provide for orderly succession from one monarch to another, and to keep 'a doubtful title of succession' from 'too much [resembling] an election' (Burke 1790: 103).

Through the course of this discussion, Burke manages to make elections look as though, far from being an expression of the public will, they abrogated popular sentiment and ceded the law to 'the will of a prevailing force' (Burke 1790: 105). Praising Lord Somers (1651–1716), who drafted the Declaration of Right, Burke calls attention to the adroitness with which 'this temporary solution of continuity [was] kept from the eye' in 1688, and Somers and his parliamentary colleagues 'threw a politic, well-wrought veil over every circumstance tending to weaken the rights, which in the meliorated order of succession they meant to perpetuate . . . that they might not relax the nerves of their monarchy, and that they might preserve a close conformity to the practice of their ancestors' (Burke 1790: 102–3). The Declaration of Right, in other words, introduced into the political situation of 1688 an inspired double-speak: James's lack of support and flight to France were not evidence that the English were repudiating hereditary succession, but evidence that they were embracing it (Burke 1790: 103). Thus, Lord Somers had continually justified the joint sovereignty of William and Mary, not as a departure from orderly succession but as a perfect example of it. The brilliance of his statecraft lay, for Burke, in his having minimized the crisis altogether and reinstated a sense of public security by constantly appealing to ancient precedents 'strongly declaratory of the inheritable nature of the crown' and embracing William and Mary as if they clearly had the best of all available titles to the throne (Burke 1790: 102). They were, in the terms that Somers offered, not new monarchs but monarchs with the strongest possible claim to precedent.

TRADITION AND THE APPEAL TO 'CHIVALRY'

With such gestures as this, Burke establishes his own credentials for deference to tradition and those who helped to establish it. He had complained that Price had demonstrated an improper understanding of the nature of the Church by introducing politics into the pulpit, and that the English defenders of the French Revolution were trying to 'quit their proper character, to assume what does not belong to them' (Burke 1790: 94). While this criticism was an *ad hominem* attack on those who espoused 'democratic and levelling principles', Burke meant to suggest that those individuals had it in their power to destroy a society's faith in itself (Burke 1790: 96). In one of his most powerful lines of argument, Burke addresses the question of the reasonableness of civil society itself, and affirms that government is improved by illusion. In a wildly sentimental description of Marie Antoinette, whom Burke regularly refers to merely as 'the queen', he traces her various movements on having been ousted from the palace and marched along the streets of Paris (Burke 1790: 169). He continually describes her as someone whose humanity is revealed – but at a considerable cost not just to her but to all the members of society. That no one rushed to Marie Antoinette's defence, he insists, is a sign of social decline: 'I thought ten thousand swords must have leaped from their scabbards to avenge even a look that threatened her with insult. – But the age of chivalry is gone. –That of sophisters, oeconomists, and calculators, has succeeded; and the glory of Europe is extinguished for ever' (Burke 1790: 170).

Burke's nostalgia for the age of chivalry may sound melodramatic, but it allows him to focus on Marie Antoinette rather than Louis XVI. He singled out the conspicuously weaker of the royals and argued in the most dramatic fashion that the revolutionaries exposed her weakness: 'On this scheme of things, a king is but a man; a queen is but a woman; a woman is but an animal; and an animal not of the highest order. All homage paid to the sex in general as such, and without distinct views, is to be regarded as romance and folly' (Burke 1790: 171). Chivalry involves more than mere courtesy. It also, as Burke expands on its importance, comes to seem like civilization itself – as opposed to the regular assertion of brute force. Chivalry involves all the impulses that lead men to defer to women rather than to demonstrate that they are stronger; it distorts 'real' power relations in the interest of a social generosity that Burke laments by saying, 'Never, never more, shall we behold that generous loyalty to rank and sex, that proud submission, that dignified obedience, that subordination of the heart, which kept alive, even in servitude itself, the spirit of an exalted freedom' (Burke 1790: 170).

Chivalry, in Burke's treatment, even turns out to be an instrument for achieving a kind of equality: chivalry 'was this, which, without confounding ranks, had produced a noble equality, and handed it down through all the gradations of social life. It was this opinion which mitigated kings into companions, and raised private men to be fellows with kings' (Burke 1790: 170). Chivalry, for him, includes 'all the pleasing illusions, which made power gentle, and obedience liberal, which harmonised the different shades of life, and which, by a bland assimilation, incorporated into politics the sentiments which beautify and soften private society' (Burke 1790: 171). The problem with the 'new conquering empire of light and reason', then, is that it hopes to explode 'as a ridiculous, absurd, and antiquated fashion' all the ideas that are emotional – the moral imagination, which the heart owns, and the understanding ratifies, as necessary to cover the defects of our naked shivering nature, and to raise it to dignity in our own estimation' (Burke 1790: 171).

THE MORAL IMAGINATION

Burke dismisses the perspective of Enlightenment politicians and thinkers as short-sighted, calculating and over-reliant on the role of reason. His refrain that 'moral certainty' differs from rational certainty and demonstrable proof underlines a standard distinction made by French and English writers of the seventeenth century and adopted by many of his contemporaries. Societal obligations on his account cannot properly be made contractual and explicit, because the very idea of 'the engagement and pact of society, which generally goes by the name of the constitution' requires that the public openly admit their mutual obligations (Burke 1790: 105). Thus, he denies that England needs the kind of explicit constitution that the French had adopted, and argues that it has a stronger, more binding constitution, the unwritten one of custom and precedent that enables the English 'to derive all we possess as *an inheritance from our forefathers*' (Burke 1790: 117).

Yet if he stresses the way in which the English constitution is stronger for being inexplicit, he goes so far as to imagine that the rationalist position is inimical to moral conduct itself. The politics of revolution, he thinks, 'temper and harden the breast, in order to prepare it for the desperate strokes which are sometimes used in extreme occasions' (Burke 1790: 156). Political rationalists persuade themselves that the abstract political principles under which they march may require murderous deeds, and even if they never act on any of their potential schemes, 'the mind receives a gratuitous taint; and the moral sentiments suffer not a little, when no political purpose is served by the depravation'. The very thought of immoral action leads to 'stopping up' the avenues to the heart (Burke 1790: 156).

In stressing the moral emotions Burke not only denounces the political spectacles that he accuses the revolutionaries of having staged – in holding up Marie Antoinette to public ridicule – but also brings the standards of fiction and theatre to bear on reality. While reason might never be able to check itself, he argues, the theatre can be a 'school of moral sentiment', and a better school than 'churches, where the feelings of humanity are . . . outraged' as Richard Price has outraged them by celebrating the principles of the French Revolution and ignoring its human costs (Burke 1790: 176). 'Poets, who have to deal with an audience not yet graduated in the school of the rights of men, and who must apply themselves to the moral constitution of the heart, would not dare to produce such a triumph [as that in which Marie Antoinette and Louis XVI were forced to march] as a matter of exultation' (Burke 1790: 176).

Emphasis on the arguments of the emotions and the morality of the heart links the early and late phases of Burke's career. For, although Burke's denunciation of the French Revolution has plausibly looked like a contradiction of his earlier support for the American Revolution, the emotional aspects of power occupied him through-out. For it had been Burke who had in 1757 published *A Philosophical Enquiry into the Origin of Our Ideas of the Sublime and Beautiful*, in which he had analysed even aesthetic experience in terms of emotions about power. The sublime, he thought, included everything that people responded to when they felt that they perceived a power greater than their own in a person (such as a ruler or a deity), an animal (such as a wolf or a horse) or a physical site (such as a range of mountains). The beautiful, he thought, includes all that 'we love' and 'love for submitting to us' (Burke 1759: 113). By the time of the *Reflections*, he had found a way of claiming that even the recognizable pleasures of the world of the beautiful had a sublime, awe-inspiring aspect – in the thought of the 'great mysterious incorporation of the human race', in which 'the whole, at one time, is never old, or middle-aged, or young, but in a condition of unchangeable constancy, moves on through the varied tenor of perpetual decay, fall, renovation, and progress' (Burke 1790: 120). In that later scheme, individuals do not measure themselves against other individuals or objects as they were seen to do in the *Enquiry*. Instead, individuals continually measure themselves through their obligations to other persons, and find a use even for prejudice, to make 'a man's virtue his habit' and 'his duty . . . a part of his nature' (Burke 1790: 183).

REFERENCES

Burke, Edmund (1757) *A Philosophical Enquiry into the Origin of Our Ideas of the Sublime and Beautiful*, ed. J. T. Boulton (1968) Notre Dame, Ind.: Notre Dame University Press.

—— (1790) *Reflections on the Revolution in France and on the Proceedings in Certain Societies in London Relative to That Event*, ed. Conor Cruise O'Brien (1982) Harmondsworth: Penguin Books.

Butler, Marilyn (ed.) (1984) *Burke, Paine, Godwin, and the Revolution Controversy*, Cambridge: Cambridge University Press.

Chandler, James (1984) *Wordsworth's Second Nature*, Chicago: University of Chicago Press.

Freeman, Michael (1980) *Edmund Burke and the Critique of Political Radicalism*, Oxford: Blackwell.

Furniss, Tom (1993) *Edmund Burke's Aesthetic Ideology: Language, Gender and Political Economy in Revolution* (1993) Cambridge: Cambridge University Press.

Kramnick, Isaac (1977) *The Rage of Edmund Burke: Portrait of an Ambivalent Conservative*, New York: Basic Books.

Mackintosh, James (1791) *Vindiciae Gallicae: Defense of the French Revolution*; facs. edn (1989) Oxford: Woodstock.

Paine, Thomas (1792) *The Rights of Man*, ed. Gregory Claeys (1992) Indianapolis: Hackett.

Price, Richard (1789) *Discourse on the Love of Our Country*, in D. O. Thomas (ed.) (1991) *Price: Political Writings*, Cambridge: Cambridge University Press.

Wollstonecraft, Mary (1792) *A Vindication of the Rights of Men*, in vol. 5 of (1989) *The Works of Mary Wollstonecraft*, ed. Marilyn Butler and Janet Todd, 7 vols, London: Pickering & Chatto.

CHAPTER THIRTY-SEVEN

THE FEMINIST CRITIQUE OF ENLIGHTENMENT

Karen O'Brien

Did the Enlightenment have anything to offer women? How far did thinkers of the time address the rights and needs of women, and to what extent can modern feminism trace its origins to those ideas? More importantly, can women embrace the kinds of feminism offered? These questions preoccupied women writers of eighteenth-century Europe, and they continue to preoccupy and divide historians and critics today. All were and are agreed that the new ideas fomented by Enlightenment thinkers changed the way people thought about the nature, status and role of women. Yet the implications of these ideas for female equality (the key demand of modern feminism) have never been clear. Some would contend that the achievement of civil and political equality in many modern democracies can be traced back directly to Enlightenment liberal political theories. Others have found in that same liberalism the origins of contemporary forms of female subjection. The debate about the feminist potential and masculine bias of those ideas began within the Enlightenment; indeed, some would go so far as to argue that its discourse actually grew out of seventeenth-century debates about gender equality (Stuurman 1997). The purpose of this chapter is certainly not to resolve these arguments, but to show how such eighteenth-century writings engendered both contemporary and present-day critiques, and how these, in turn, reveal the paradoxical legacy of the Enlightenment.

This chapter will be divided into three sections corresponding with three distinct forms and phases of feminist critique of Enlightenment ideas in Europe. In each section, the twentieth- and twenty-first-century issues arising from the eighteenth-century critique will be addressed. As the structure of the chapter implies, modern feminist responses to Enlightenment mirror closely the concerns of eighteenth-century commentators, and many of the key co-ordinates of feminist debate today are taken from this earlier map. In modern democratic settings the issues raised by Enlightenment writers – such as the need to recognize, simultaneously, both female equality and biological difference, and both female individuality and the family dimension of women's lives – have become, if anything, more pressing. To a significant degree, the Enlightenment created the terms within which women's social and political positions are still debated, particularly in connection with civil and political rights, and questions relating to women's 'nature', their role in history, their intellectual equality with men, and the social implications of their sexual difference.

LIBERALISM AND FEMINISM

A crucial text for Enlightenment thought in Britain was John Locke's *Two Treatises of Government* (1690), which made a compelling case for a rights-based model of citizenship. Locke characterized the state as a contract, voluntarily made between equal individuals, in which the price of protection of person and property is obedience to political authority. Natural rights are exchanged for civil and political rights, provided government does not tyrannize its citizens. Locke's work had enormous influence, particularly later in the eighteenth century, upon revolutionaries and reformers arguing that the British state failed to respect the rights and property of its subjects. In the 1790s British supporters of the French Revolution transformed the Lockean language of individual rights as part of a powerful critique of the un-reformed British state. This language entered feminist discourse when Catharine Macaulay and Mary Wollstonecraft, both ardent supporters of the French Revolution, promoted ideas of feminine equality. Throughout the eighteenth century, both male and female writers argued for rights and voluntary consent in civil matters, such as marriage and property entitlements, but it is the belated demand for equal political rights, which can be seen as the root of modern liberal feminism. Neither writer made this demand the central feature of her work; indeed, Wollstonecraft never wrote the second part of her *Vindication of the Rights of Woman*, in which she said she would give specific proposals for reforming the 'laws relative to women' (Wollstonecraft 1792: vol. V, 70). Yet Wollstonecraft's feminist work is animated by her belief in what she elsewhere called the 'natural and imprescriptible rights of man' (Wollstonecraft 1794: vol. VI, 115), just as Macaulay's *Letters on Education* are quietly indignant at the 'total and absolute exclusion' of women from 'every political right' (Macaulay 1790: 210). In France, Olympe de Gouges pointed out in her *Les Droits de la femme* that the Revolutionary Declaration of the Rights of Man and Citizen had not been applied to women, and demanded political representation and civic education for women (Gouges 1791).

If women were slow to derive a theory of female citizenship from Locke, it is easily explained by the fact that even in the most enlightened parts of Europe, men's political rights were limited (although their civil rights were more extensive). Locke does not state whether women are party to the contract. There are certainly grounds for reading into this silence an implicit denial of a civil identity for women. For Carole Pateman, in her influential study *The Sexual Contract* (1988), this precluded female citizenship by means of a new model of patriarchy, one which has persisted to this day: 'Modern civil society is not structured by kinship and the power of the fathers; in the modern world, women are subordinated to men *as men*, or to men as a fraternity.' In her reading of Locke, women do not participate in the male public sphere, but enter, via the marriage contract, a private sphere of personal subjection, a subjection which women owe *naturally* to men (Pateman 1988: 3, 52–3). Pateman's work is powerful both as an account of the anti-feminist implications of Enlightenment contract theories (from Locke to Rousseau), and as an indictment of the limitations of modern liberal feminism. De Gouges, Wollstonecraft and Macaulay argued that female equality can best be achieved by applying the same arguments for male civil and political rights to the female case; it can also be said that such a project will fail if the masculine bias

Engraved by Ridley from a Painting by Opie .

M^{RS}. WOLLSTONECRAFT.

Figure 37.1 *Mary Wollstonecraft*, engraved by William Ridley (1796) after a painting by John Opie. By courtesy of the National Portrait Gallery, London.

of its philosophical underpinnings is not recognized. Since the 1960s, feminists have highlighted the difficulties of extending the Enlightenment notion of the free and equal individual male citizen to women; this involves a superficial ascription of male characteristics to women and distorts biological and social differences, as well as political and civil requirements. Furthermore, it fails to take into account the consequences of these tendencies for the private and public spheres.

It is striking how early and how forcefully Lockean liberal individualism was subjected to trenchant feminist criticism. Very few advocates of female equality and education, in the late seventeenth or early eighteenth centuries, identified themselves politically with the party most committed to contract theory, the Whig Party, and many more (for example, Aphra Behn, Sarah Fyge Egerton and Mary, Lady Chudleigh) actively embraced the more traditional political ideologies of the opposing Tory or Jacobite parties (Barash 1996). This is a conundrum for modern commentators, because Tories and Jacobites generally emphasized the status of the monarch as father of the nation, the need for unquestioning obedience to his authority, and the traditional and inherited (rather than contractual) nature of political obligation. Yet these were the political views espoused by one of the most incisive feminist writers of the period, Mary Astell, a writer who may be said to have inaugurated the feminist critique of the Enlightenment. Her work *Some Reflections on Marriage* (first published 1700) mounts a blistering attack on the tyranny and arbitrary power, in law and in practice, of married men over their wives. The preface to the third edition asks, in an implicit rebuke to her contemporary Locke, 'If all Men are born free, how is it that all Women are born slaves?'(Astell 1706: x). Astell exposes the limits, gender-specificity and hypocrisy of contractarian thought. She warns that 'She who Elects a Monarch for Life, who gives him an Authority she cannot recall however he misapply it' had better not delude herself that she has any rights or redress just because she entered voluntarily into the marriage contract (Astell 1706: 32–3). In reality, voluntary contracts in both the marital and political domains give no protection against tyranny, 'for Covenants between Husband and Wife, like Laws in an Arbitrary Government, are of little Force, the Will of the Sovereign is all in all' (Astell 1706: 39). The best solution, in both domains, is traditionally sanctioned and justly exercised authority on the part of the ruler, and what she calls 'passive obedience' on the part of the subject or wife. Or, better still, a woman should not marry at all.

Astell vents her anger at the hopeless position of English wives, subsumed as they were in law by their husbands' civil status. She does not comfort her readers with the thought that a state offering theoretical rights of choice and resistance to men will have anything to offer women. Like Carol Pateman nearly three hundred years later, she is suspicious of the separation of society into public and private spheres which Enlightenment political theory appeared to usher in, since this formally excluded women from the public sphere and enabled men to rule over them in private. By writing of gender relations in party-political terms, Astell's text works against this separation. In this respect, she resembled a number of women writers of the period whose feminist observations sat awkwardly with, or openly criticized, liberal aspects of Enlightenment thought.

The most prominent of these was Lady Mary Wortley Montagu, author of the *Turkish Embassy Letters*, in which she recorded her visit to Turkey in 1716–18 as the wife of the British ambassador. They were published posthumously in 1763 as part of a larger collection of letters, with a preface by Mary Astell. Unlike Astell, Lady Mary was, through family and marital ties, a Whig, but like Astell she used the public language of rights, obedience and resistance to capture her own contradictory position as a politically unfree woman in a politically progressive society. Her time in Turkey gave her a wonderful opportunity to explore these themes of freedom and subjection while developing her own extraordinary literary talents. The Ottoman Empire was little known and still less understood by European travellers; most treated it as a prime example of political subjection and female sexual exploitation, although indignation did not deter male writers from fantasizing about the secret depravity of the Oriental harem. By contrast, Lady Mary's letters are remarkable for her sympathetic understanding of an alien culture, and, in particular, for their insight into the lives of Turkish women. Ignoring the traditional Western clichés about Eastern women, she was able to write at first hand about the harem, the bathhouses and shops. She did not deny that, in Turkish society, women were far more segregated from men than in her own world, but this segregation, she insisted, is actually the source of their relative freedom:

> 'Tis also very pleasant to observe how tenderly he [Aaron Hill, the author of an earlier account of the Ottoman Empire] and all his brethren voyage-writers, lament on the miserable confinement of the Turkish ladies, who are perhaps freer than any ladies in the universe, and are the only women in the world that lead a life of uninterrupted pleasure, exempt from cares, their whole time being spent in visiting, bathing or the agreeable amusement of spending money and inventing new fashions.
>
> (Montagu 1763: vol. III, 29)

The same vein of ironic celebration runs through her detailed descriptions of the women's bathhouse, the private apartments of aristocratic Turkish ladies, and of the secret sexual assignations of married Turkish women, made easier by the use of the veil. It was an article of faith among all French and British Enlightenment writers that the free mixing of men and women in public spaces gave women opportunities and freedoms unknown to the segregated women of Eastern societies. Lady Mary's purpose is to jog her readers out of their stereotypical views of the East, and, in the process, to reconsider the public and private meanings of freedom and subjection. In her view the Ottoman regime was certainly despotic (in the sense that no laws limited the absolute power of the Sultan), yet the women experienced a latitude of private freedom not enjoyed by British women. As an English lady, she came from a political regime framed by constitutional laws, yet she is resigned to the English duty of 'passive obedience' to her husband (using the Tory party-political catchphrase of her day). Lady Mary's *Turkish Embassy Letters* thus criticize some liberal Enlightenment ideas by showing the asymmetries between private and public freedoms in difference cultures and social spaces.

Like Mary Astell, Lady Mary had no delusions about the freedom of British women, despite the social opportunities to mix with and influence powerful men afforded to aristocratic women like herself. Her own father had tried to make her marry a man she loathed, leaving her no option but to elope with an unsatisfactory man who subsequently forbade her to publish her Turkish letters.

Enlightenment writers continued to use the idea of the despotic East as a means not only of demonstrating but also of making the case for greater freedom in the West, associating the question of female liberation with arguments about national and racial difference. The politician and writer George Lyttelton, in his *Letters from a Persian*, argued that English women should be encouraged to cultivate their minds because, unlike in Persia, where 'a Woman has not Occasion for any Thing but Beauty, because of the Confinement in which she lives', they are 'admitted to a familiar and constant Share in every active Scene of Life' (Lyttelton 1735: 157). A similar, but more sophisticated, case was made in Montesquieu's highly popular novel, *Lettres persanes* (1721). Montesquieu contrasts the violent subjection of women of the Persian harem (through letters to their husbands) with the sexual and social yet ultimately politically meaningless 'freedom' of wealthy French women.

The entanglement of questions of gender equality in issues of racial and national difference certainly persists in feminist debate today; one need only think of the deep contentiousness of the argument, made by some Islamic women, that the veil gives them freedom from the sexual objectification suffered by their Western counterparts. For Enlightenment writers, as to a lesser extent for modern commentators, these issues were also implicated in still larger questions of historical progress. They tended to see non-Western societies as representing an earlier phase of history, and their own society as the prototype of global modernity. Few would argue today that Eastern societies represent a stage in human development, which liberal Western societies have been through and surpassed, although Enlightenment habits of thought do surface in casual references to the 'advanced' state of the West, and of Western women, in relation to the more 'backward' East. We are all heirs to the Enlightenment tendency to measure degrees of male and female liberty in relation to an implicit historical model. Enlightenment thinkers insisted upon the need to view women's nature, role and freedom historically; modern feminist thought still tries to steer between an Enlightenment emphasis on universal rights and appreciation of historical and cultural context.

ENLIGHTENMENT HISTORY AND ITS FEMINIST CRITICS

Montesquieu, in his *Lettres persanes* and in his seminal *De L'Esprit des lois* (1748), explores the position of women in relation to different geographical areas, historical periods and types of political regime. He changed the central question of eighteenth-century feminist debate from 'What is women's worth?' to 'How does historical change affect the position of women?' Enlightenment commentators were far more engaged with this historical issue than with questions about the innate 'nature' of women, at least until the beginning of the nineteenth century, as is explained by Jane Rendall (Chapter 16 of this volume). Montesquieu influenced Scottish Enlightenment writers such as David Hume, Adam Smith, William Robertson, Henry Home, Lord Kames and John Millar, all of whom made the historical evolution of women's position a prominent part of their analyses of the progress of civilization through difference economic, social and political stages. John Millar, a pupil of Adam Smith, dedicated the long opening chapter of his *Origin of the Distinction of Ranks* (1771; 1779) to the subject of 'The Rank and Condition of Women in Different Ages', while his Scottish contemporary William Alexander published around the same time his *History of Women, from the Earliest Antiquity to the Present Time* (1779). From these writers, as well as from French and German contemporaries, notably Antoine Léonard Thomas (1772) and Christoph Meiners (1788–1800), something like a consensus emerged. It was agreed that women are physically less strong than men, and for this reason primitive societies subjugate and segregate them, giving them no role in society and no rights. As societies evolve politically and economically, there is more leisure, more legal security, and more complex forms of commercial interaction between people (involving shopping, consumer choice and taste), and opportunities emerge for women to assert themselves as distinct beings. Women can use their sexual appeal (without fear of abduction or rape) to negotiate a more favourable social position for themselves. As they come to enjoy far more interaction with men outside the home, they acquire influence and power. Modern, commercial societies, in this analysis, promote female freedom, self-expression, sexuality and power; conversely, it is possible to ascertain the relative backwardness of other countries, such as Turkey, simply by examining how they treat their women.

Enlightenment history of the progress of women gained enormous currency not only in Britain and France, but also in Germany, and, until the very end of the century, informed a widespread popular orthodoxy that women in modern times were far better off than they had ever been before (Hull 1996). With hindsight, one can discern some complacency in most of these Enlightenment histories of women (which excluded demands for political rights for women), but there was also a vigorous polemic against male violence towards women, against the exclusion of women from the social sphere, and against the idea of an inferior female nature. For these reasons, perhaps, those who criticized this model of history did not jettison historical argument as a means of understanding and promoting better rights for women (as, for example, did nineteenth-century feminists such as J. S. Mill and Harriet Taylor). No women writers adopted uncritically Enlightenment versions of the history of women, but some chose to make their case on historical ground. Chief among these, in Britain, were Catharine Macaulay and Mary Wollstonecraft.

It was a bold and unusual step for a woman to enter the male domain of historical writing in the eighteenth century, yet Macaulay's eight-volume *History of England* (1763–83) achieved considerable critical and popular success in its day. The *History* is a radical republican account of England's seventeenth- and early eighteenth-century past which documents the country's all too brief experiment with genuine liberty (the Commonwealth of 1649–53), its reversion to despotism under Cromwell, and its failure to make any progress since then. Macaulay's work, when seen in the context of Enlightenment historical writing, is a partial rejection of current ideas of progress, and implicitly of the idea of the progress of women. She demonstrates that the idea of progress needs to be understood not in terms of the growth of commerce, the constitutional regulation of the monarchy, the increased social role of women (although she favoured all of these), but in terms of the progress of liberty. For Macaulay, liberty is an idea of which she has as much right to speak as any man, since it transcends the gender, class and historical limitations placed upon those who crusade for its cause: 'The invidious censures which may ensue from striking into a path of literature rarely trodden by my sex', she remarked in the preface to the first volume, 'will not permit a selfish consideration to keep me mute in the cause of liberty' (Macaulay 1763–83: vol. I, x).

Wollstonecraft engaged in a more direct critique of Enlightenment histories of the progress of civilization, while consolidating the link established by Macaulay

Figure 37.2 *The Nine Living Muses of Great Britain*, Richard Samuel. These portraits of the leading bluestockings of the day show them in the characters of the daughters of Zeus in the Temple of Apollo, each presiding over a different art. The picture, exhibited at the Royal Academy in 1779, shows Elizabeth Sheridan, the singer, standing in the centre playing a lyre. The artist Angelica Kauffmann is seated to the left at an easel and the writers Elizabeth Carter and Anna Letitia Barbauld stand behind her. On the right are grouped Charlotte Lennox, the historian, Catherine Macaulay (holding a parchment), Hannah More, Elizabeth Montagu and the playwright and novelist Elizabeth Griffith (with a tablet). By courtesy of the National Portrait Gallery, London.

between feminism and republicanism. Her *Vindication of the Rights of Woman* re-opens some fundamental questions: Has the progress of civilization brought about progress for women? From the point of view of human rights and liberty, can there be said to have been much progress at all? To both questions, her answer is a resounding negative, and she deplores the degenerate condition of modern women with their empty heads, willing submissiveness and overly sexual ways of dealing with men. To the question as to whether civilization has progressed since Roman times, Wollstonecraft answers that it has only done so lop-sidedly with no benefits for women: 'women, in general, as well as the rich of both sexes, have acquired all the follies and vices of civilisation, and missed the useful fruit' (Wollstonecraft 1792: vol. V, 129). The limited power which women possess owes nothing to their rational faculties or moral conduct, and everything to the 'distinction of sex', by which she means the over-feminine, over-sexualized behaviour which society expects of them. Many Enlightenment writers argued that greater sexual differentiation, or distinction of sex, was itself a sign of historical progress, and that, conversely, primitive men gave women little chance to express their sexual identity (through dress, conversation or shared social activities, etc.). For Wollstonecraft, 'this distinction is . . . the foundation of the weakness of the character ascribed to woman', and women would gain more power by becoming as similar to men as possible (Wollstonecraft 1792: vol. V, 126). Her critique of Enlightenment notions of modern woman, as flirtatious and powerful only through indirect means, thus proceeds from a broader critique of the modern world, which, for her, is corrupt, aristocratic and unfree.

Wollstonecraft did not write an alternative history of civilization, as Macaulay had done (although she did write a history of the French Revolution), but she may have been impressed by Condorcet's project for such a history, his *Esquisse d'un tableau historique des progrès de l'esprit humain* (1795). Condorcet expanded the model of history as a series of developmental stages into a narrative of the progress of the human mind and of universal human rights. Yet, despite its radical intentions, the *Esquisse* demonstrates the difficulty of recasting Enlightenment history to satisfy feminist concerns. Although Condorcet elsewhere promoted women's education and political emancipation (Condorcet 1790), his outline of universal progress leaves older Enlightenment histories of women undisturbed. European readers would have to wait for Engels's *Origin of the Family, Private Property and the State* (1884) for an Enlightenment-style universal history in which the 'world-historical defeat of the female sex' would be charted through successive stages of economic development.

The problem of integrating women's history into national and global historical narratives remains. For modern feminist historians, examining women as the barometers of social progress, as Enlightenment historians did, is to deny their creative role. Yet to endeavour to explore women's activity under the historical conditions of male domination is often to produce a static image of history in which change happens very slowly, if at all. Some modern historians opt to create a separate historical account of women, but most retain an Enlightenment commitment to an integrated gender history that nevertheless recognizes the distinctive experiences of women.

THE RESPONSE TO ROUSSEAU

In some additional respects we have returned to an Enlightenment view of the relationship between women and social progress, particularly in our tendency to equate the relative sexual freedom of women with the level of civilization, a view which deeply informs modern Western perceptions of developing countries. Though a yardstick of feminism today, sexual freedom was a more complex issue for eighteenth-century feminist writers. We have seen how Wollstonecraft criticized women's sexual manipulation of men as a legitimate route to power in a tone which sounds, at times, positively prudish. Both she and Macaulay, in her *Letters on Education*, bravely attacked the double standard through which women were encouraged to overwhelm men with the full force of their femininity, and yet were ruthlessly punished by society if they were found to have transgressed sexually. Yet, to a modern feminist way of thinking, these writers can also sound conservative in their insistence that women should restrain their desires and become moral agents for the improvement of society as a whole. They sought liberation for women, not on the basis of greater freedom of desire, but by means of rational and moral elevation, and they criticized the Enlightenment history of women for its instrumental and hypocritical treatment of female sexuality. In this, they were also engaged in a complicated and troubled dialogue with the Enlightenment's most influential critic, Jean Jacques Rousseau. Paradoxically, it was Rousseau, no advocate of women's rights or education, who provided late eighteenth-century feminist writers with the intellectual framework and vocabulary to generate a radically new account of female consciousness. He enabled women writers to articulate a public role for themselves, even as they accepted his prescriptions for the withdrawal of women from the social to the domestic sphere. And it was Rousseau's fiction which authenticated female desire outside the normal boundaries of marriage, in works which also, paradoxically, moralized private family life.

In several influential works (the *Discourse on the Origin of Inequality*, 1755; *Emile*, 1762) Rousseau argued that women are fundamentally estranged from their true nature and feelings by modern civilization, and that, moreover, civilization itself is not a progressive process so much as a distortion of human reason by human competitiveness. In *Emile* Rousseau argues that the inauthenticity of modern man can be partly remedied by a process of 'natural' and sequestered education, but he applies the remedy only to men. Feminist writers, such as Wollstonecraft and Macaulay, were indignant at Rousseau's insistence upon female subordination to men and his restriction of women's role to that of domestic support-staff for the public activities of men. But they also found compelling his analysis of female inauthenticity, and his account of the way in which women's moral identity had become submerged in the culture of politeness and gallantry. A number of these writers – including Choderlos de Laclos, the author of the novel *Les Liaisons dangereuses*, itself a powerful depiction of the abuse of female sexual power in French aristocratic society – adapted Rousseau. In his essay *Des Femmes et de leur éducation* (written in the 1780s) Laclos argued that the modern 'social woman' is a distortion of femininity, a symptom of the decadence of the *ancien régime*, and the product of centuries of involuntary enslavement. What was needed, he argued, was a mental emancipation of women through an *Emile*-style system of education (Steinbrügge 1995: 83–9). Other writers, such as Louise D'Epinay, in her *Conversations D'Emilie* (1784), had considerable public success in adapting for women Rousseau's model of education.

Some accepted, others were troubled by, Rousseau's view of the two sexes as profoundly different yet complementary in terms of the kinds of tasks a regenerated society would need them to perform. In both nineteenth-century Britain and France, there were many women who credited Rousseau with raising their status as mothers and as the moral instigators and regulators of male public action (Ozouf 1995). Other admirers could not accept Rousseau's devaluation of the Enlightenment ideal of the mixed social sphere, but were nevertheless overwhelmed by his ability to speak to and about women through his fiction. Germaine de Staël, the most celebrated female

European writer of the early nineteenth century, in her first published work, *Lettres sur les écrits et le caractère de J. J. Rousseau* (1788), confessed herself seduced by *La Nouvelle Héloïse* (1761), even though she defended the social visibility and influence of women. In Rousseau's novel the heroine Julie succumbs to her passion for her lover, a passion which is purified but not effaced by her rehabilitation later in the novel as the wife of another man and a mother. Rousseau's portrait of the female psychological make-up appeared to many women writers both convincing and revolutionary. De Staël's *Corinne* (1809), Mary Hays's *Memoirs of Emma Courtney* (1796) and Wollstonecraft's *The Wrongs of Woman* (1798) owe a great deal to *La Nouvelle Héloïse*, not only because of their sympathetic portrayal of unconventional female passion, but also because, like Rousseau, they seek to articulate ways in which such passion might become socially meaningful in a reformed society. Despite differences of political outlook, Rousseau, De Staël, Wollstonecraft and Hays are united in their view of the moral shallowness of Enlightenment accounts of female desire, and of the capacity of a female point of view to transform the understanding of the social order. Rousseau's portrayals of passionate women such as Julie and the gracious, sexually unconventional Mme de Wolmar in the *Confessions* (1782) inspired nineteenth- and twentieth-century French feminists, from Manon Roland and George Sand to Simone de Beauvoir, who emphasized the need to find a fuller female identity by living, not in the opinion of others, but through individual passion and love.

Rousseau envisaged a complementary relationship between men and women who inhabited different spheres and performed different roles. This idea derived from a long tradition of republican thought and played its part in the French revolutionary debates about the status of the *citoyenne*. Olympe de Gouges's *Les Droits de la femme* drew a number of replies by male republicans who argued, following Rousseau, that women had exercised a pernicious influence on the public life of the *ancien régime*, and that it was time for the revolutionary state to make use of their benign influence in the domestic sphere (Offen 2000: 58). In Britain, as in France, there was greater emphasis upon the public function of cohesive and virtuous private family life, and upon the role of women as the domestic anchors of the social order. This was reinforced by an increased stress, in medical, psychological and moral discourse, upon the innate differences between men and women. The new political economy, inaugurated by Adam Smith's *Wealth of Nations* (1776), contributed to these trends by endorsing implicitly the withdrawal of (middle-class) women from the workplace. The most socially effective division of labour, Smith implied, would entail a domestic role for women as housekeepers and consumers. Women writers reacted to this polarized redefinition of male and female roles in a variety of ways. A few – notably Priscilla Wakefield in her *Reflections on the Present Condition of the Female Sex* (1798), Charles Théremin in his *De La Condition des femmes dans les républiques* (1799) and Theodor Gottlieb von Hippel in his *On Improving the Status of Women* (1792) – argued for equality of economic opportunity for women. Others – particularly British evangelical Christian campaigners and writers, such as Hannah More – argued for a distinct, socially useful role for women as educators, writers and philanthropic activists (Rendall 1985: 73–107). Women writers as diverse as Wollstonecraft, Maria Edgeworth and the conservative, never overtly feminist More were united in their insistence that women's power should owe nothing to their sexual attractiveness, and that virtuous, rational conduct is the only true source of female merit.

The emphasis on female virtue became in Victorian times something of an obsession. Pious and chaste women, it was argued, were better qualified as arbiters of their country's policies and actions than the immoral, aristocratic men who dominated its political life (Mellor 2000: 19), and in the nineteenth century this view encouraged women to take leading roles in charities, schools, missionary work, anti-slavery and temperance campaigns. Recent historians and critics, rejecting older arguments about the patriarchal nature of the newly gendered, separate spheres of early nineteenth-century Europe, have made the case for this 'domestic revolution' as 'the successful effect of Enlightenment feminist work' (Bannet 2000: 218). This overstates the case by constructing a seamless narrative of progress out of the complex Enlightenment dialogue about the nature and position of women. Enlightenment writers, having deprived women of effective arguments for more genuine equality, had rationalized their public activity by emphasizing their distinctive virtues; they had shown that female difference was an effect of the progress of civilization, although Rousseau had argued that such difference is something both innate and socially necessary. Evangelical British women writers adopted Rousseau's model but supplemented it with a pious, patriotic and economic case for a division of labour, in which women would play a distinctive, socially beneficial role, for which they would receive a rigorous but different education (More 1799). British women were able to capitalize far more effectively than their French counterparts on the new thinking. After the defeat of French revolutionary feminist aspirations (which in de Gouges's case ended with the guillotine), a number of writers under the Napoleonic regime, notably the aristocrat Alexandre Ségur, sought to articulate a model of female patriotism in which women are celebrated for their bravery as wives and mothers, like Rousseau's Julie dying to save her child (Ségur 1803). With the restoration of the monarchy, French women were left with very few means with which to articulate a public role for themselves beyond the guardianship and promulgation of Catholic values. Yet there persisted in France, to a much greater extent than in Britain after the evangelical revival, a legacy of Rousseau which forged an association between political liberation, female desire and genuine self-fulfilment. Well into the twentieth century, this shaped the character of French feminism. It helps to explain why French feminism often seems comparatively at ease with the sexual side of femininity, whereas British and American feminism is still heir to the conflict, embedded in the work of Mary Wollstonecraft, between the desire to be rationally identical to men and the need to express and celebrate difference from them (Ozouf 1995).

Twenty-first-century genetics and neuroscience are now revealing new, innate differences in the biological composition of men and women. Those differences are not those identified by late eighteenth-century theorists of female 'sensibility' (see Chapter 16 of this volume). Nevertheless, they represent a challenge to feminism not unlike that posed by the new thinking about gender in the late eighteenth century, and in meeting this challenge, there will certainly be a continuing role for Enlightenment views of femininity.

REFERENCES

Alexander, William (1779) *The History of Women from the Earliest Antiquity to the Present Time*, 2 vols, Edinburgh.

Astell, Mary (1706) *Some Reflections on Marriage*, 3rd edn, London.

Bannet, Eve Tavor (2000) *The Domestic Revolution: Enlightenment Feminisms and the Novel*, Baltimore: Johns Hopkins University Press.

Barash, Carol (1996) *English Women's Poetry, 1649–1713: Politics, Community and Linguistic Authority*, Oxford: Clarendon Press.

Condorcet, Marie-Jean-Antoine-Nicholas Caritat, Marquis de (1790) 'Sur L'Admission des femmes au droit de la cité', *Journal de la Société de 1789*, 3.

—— (1795) *Esquisse d'un tableau historique des progrès de l'esprit humain*, Paris.

Epinay, Louise d' (1784) *Conversations d'Emilie*, Paris and Liège: Plombeaux.

Gouges, Olympe de (1791) 'Les Droits de la femme', in Darline Gay Levy, Harriet Branson Applewhite and Mary Durham Johnson (eds) (1979) *Women in Revolutionary Paris, 1789–95*, Urbana: University of Illinois Press.

Hippel, Theodor Gottlieb von (1792) *Über die bürgerliche Verbesserung der Weiber*, trans. Timothy F. Sellner (1979) as *On Improving the Status of Women*, Detroit: Wayne State University Press.

Hull, Isabel V. (1996) *Sexuality, State and Civil Society in Germany, 1750–1815*, Ithaca: Cornell University Press.

Laclos, Choderlos de (1979) 'Des Femmes et de leur éducation', ed. Laurent Versini in (1979) *Oeuvres complètes*, Paris: Gallimard.

Locke, John (1690) *Two Treatises of Government*, ed. Mark Goldie (1993) London: Everyman.

Lyttelton, George (1735) *Letters from a Persian to his Friend at Ispahan*, London.

Macaulay [Graham], Catharine (1763–83) *The History of England from the Accession of James I to that of the Brunswick Line*, 8 vols, London: J. Nourse and others.

—— (1790) *Letters on Education, with Observations on Religious and Metaphysical Subjects*, London: C. Dilly.

Meiners, Christoph (1788–1800) *History of the Female Sex: A View of the Habits, Manners and Influence of Women, among All Nations, from the Earliest Ages to the Present Time*, trans. F. Shober (1808) 4 vols, London.

Mellor, Anne K. (2000) *Mothers of the Nation: Women's Political Writing in England, 1780–1830*, Bloomington: Indiana University Press.

Millar, John (1779) *The Origin of the Distinction of Ranks in Society*, 4th edn (1806) Edinburgh.

Montagu, Mary Wortley (1763) *Letters of the Right Honourable Lady M-y W-y M-3: Written during her Travels in Europe, Asia and Africa*, 3 vols, London.

Montesquieu, Charles Secondat de (1721) *Lettres persanes*, ed. Paul Vernière (1975) Paris: Garnier.

—— (1748) *De L'Esprit des lois*, ed. Robert Derathe (1973) 2 vols, Paris: Garnier.

More, Hannah (1799) *Strictures on the Modern System of Female Education*, 2 vols, London: T. Cadell and W. Davies.

Offen, Karen (2000) *European Feminisms 1700–1950*, Stanford: Stanford University Press.

Ozouf, Mona (1995) *Les Mots des femmes: essai sur la singularité française*, Paris: Fayard.

Pateman, Carole (1988) *The Sexual Contract*, Cambridge: Polity Press.

Rendall, Jane (1985) *The Origins of Modern Feminism: Women in Britain, France and the United States, 1780–1860*, Basingstoke: Macmillan.

Rousseau, Jean Jacques (1755) 'Discours sur l'origine et les fondements de l'inégalité parmi les homes', ed. Bernard Gagnebin in *Oeuvres complètes* (1959–64) 3 vols, Paris: Bibliothèque de la Pléiade.

—— (1761) *La Nouvelle Héloïse*, in *Oeuvres complètes* (1959–64) *op. cit.*

—— (1762) *Emile, ou De L'Education*, in *Oeuvres complètes* (1959–64) *op. cit.*

Scott, Joan Wallach (1996) *Only Paradoxes to Offer: French Feminists and the Rights of Man*, London and Cambridge, Mass.: Harvard University Press.

Ségur, Alexandre Joseph (1803) *Les Femmes, leur condition et leur influence dans l'ordre social chez différents peoples anciens et modernes*, 3 vols, Paris.

Staël-Holstein, Germaine Necker, Baronne de (1788) *Lettres sur les écrits et le caractère de J. J. Rousseau*, Paris.

—— (1807) *Corinne; ou L'Italie*, London.

Steinbrügge, Lieselotte (1995) *The Moral Sex: Woman's Nature in the French Enlightenment*, trans. Pamela E. Selwyn, Oxford: Oxford University Press.

Stuurman, Siep (1997) 'Social Cartesianism: François Poulain de la Barre and the Origins of Enlightenment', *Journal of the History of Ideas*, 58: 617–40.

Théremin, Charles (1799) *De La Condition des femmes dans les républiques*, Paris.

Thomas, Antoine Léonard (1772) *Essai sur le caractère, les moeurs et l'esprit des femmes dans les différens siècles*, Paris: Moutard.

Wakefield, Priscilla (1798) *Reflections on the Present Condition of the Female Sex; with Suggestions for its Improvement*, London.

Wollstonecraft, Mary (1792) *A Vindication of the Rights of Woman*, ed. Marilyn Butler and Janet Todd in vol. 5 of (1989) *The Works of Mary Wollstonecraft*, 7 vols, London: Pickering & Chatto.

—— (1794) *An Historical and Moral View of the French Revolution*, ed. Marilyn Butler and Janet Todd in vol. 6 of (1989) *The Works of Mary Wollstonecraft*, *op. cit.*

CHAPTER THIRTY-EIGHT

AN ENLIGHTENMENT CRITIQUE OF THE *DIALECTIC OF ENLIGHTENMENT*

———•◆•———

Howard Williams

INTRODUCTION

There is a widespread sense that the Enlightenment has been a disappointment. Looking back from the vantage point of the beginning of the twenty-first century, it appears as though this diverse project of the late sixteenth, seventeenth and eighteenth centuries awakened many more expectations than it was able to fulfil. Indeed, there appears from our present vantage point not only to be a strong reaction against the Enlightenment, conceived as a unitary phenomenon, but against the whole notion of having expectations of the human race in general or (however expressed) of society as a whole. Social projects have fallen foul of pessimism about the capacities of the human species and apparent boredom with our collective fate has taken hold. It is true to say that this may be no more than a mood, perhaps a mood engendered by the collapse of centralized socialism in Russia and its former satellites. The period of the Cold War was, after all, a time of high tension and it is natural that after such persistent and acute tension there might follow a period of sober reflection and reassessment. But the proponents of the anti-Enlightenment thesis would thoroughly dispute the idea that their critique represents no more than a passing phase. For many of them, it inaugurates a new phase which many commentators have described as the period of 'postmodernism'.

There are two major sources of this disappointment or disenchantment with the Enlightenment. The first is the neo-Marxist critique of Theodor Adorno and Max Horkheimer of the Enlightenment and its collapse into the contemporary culture industry. The second is the – largely French – postmodernist school of philosophy which has taken to task modernist thinking (including that of neo-Marxists like Adorno and Horkheimer) for its unjustified progressivist assumptions. I shall be concerned with the first here, but the two are clearly connected. They are connected in their origins, since many of the postmodernists were neo-Marxists of a similar kind before their conversion; and they are connected in their content, since both cast a negative light on much modernist thought. Here I want to present some redeeming thoughts on the Enlightenment by comparing Horkheimer and Adorno's views with the expectations of their fellow-German philosophers Kant and Mendelssohn. In 1784 these latter two thinkers outlined their views on Enlightenment and expressed what their personal expectations of the process were. In particular, I want to draw attention to the contrast between Horkheimer and Adorno's total commitment to neo-Hegelian dialectic and Kant's more narrowly conceived methods.

Adorno and Horkheimer's argument about the inherent tensions within the Enlightenment project is couched in terms that reflect their own philosophical backgrounds. Both were greatly influenced by German philosophical methods, especially by neo-Hegelian dialectical methods of argument that were a feature not only of German philosophy in the 1930s but also of the Marxism espoused by members of the Frankfurt school. Their methods are synthetic and so set on comprehending totalities; consequently, a detailed analysis of the components of their argument is often very difficult. They are aiming at concreteness and completeness. They are averse to casting their thoughts as reflections about society because, for them, society itself is already a reflective process. They see themselves as not thinking about society, but rather as expressing what social agents already think about themselves.

THE *DIALECTIC OF ENLIGHTENMENT* EXPLAINED

As the title of their celebrated book suggests, the thesis of Horkheimer and Adorno owes a great deal to the dialectical thinking of Hegel and Marx. Adorno seems to have been fascinated by the dialectical method and it represents one of the most important focuses of his own philosophy. This is perhaps most evident in his later work *Negative Dialectic*, though, of course, the argument and structure of *Minima Moralia* is self-evidently dialectical in form.

The unity of opposites which is one of the key themes of Hegel's and Marx's method is greatly in evidence in *Dialectic of Enlightenment*. Another theme that is also evident is the notion, drawn from Heraclitus' philosophy, that everything is becoming or in a process of constant change. The first theme leads to the claim that the Enlightenment, 'the positive', is intimately linked with closed totalitarian societies, 'the negative'; and the second theme leads to the claim that the ongoing process of Enlightenment of itself gives us its opposite – darkness and the rule of myth. What is evident also as an influence of Hegel's (and to some extent also of Marx's) dialectic is the assumption that humankind is in the grip of a world-historic process over which it has no control. The impotence of the individual in the face of cosmic forces that threaten his existence is perhaps the most startling claim of Horkheimer and Adorno's book. In Hegel this cosmic force takes the shape of *Geist* or Spirit, whose course governs human history; and in Marx's political theory it is the social process of production of capital that takes on this role. In *Dialectic of Enlightenment* it is not clear whether it is the Marxist supposition or the Hegelian idealist supposition that is dominant. On the one hand, the notion that it is not too late for the individual (critical) thinker to do something about the fatal course of the Enlightenment would imply a tendency in the direction of the Hegelian supposition; but, on the other, the supposition that the Enlightenment creates a mass social form of existence that is oppressive would imply a tendency in the Marxist direction. The issue about the

Hegelian or Marxist direction of Horkheimer and Adorno's thought is not one that is easily resolved. They veer strongly in the Hegelian direction in the emphasis they put on the role of ideas, but they also veer markedly in the Marxist direction when they emphasize that radical political action (of a wholly unspecified kind) may make a difference.

These Hegelian–Marxist dialectical tropes are apparent in the way that Horkheimer and Adorno pose their problem in the *Dialectic of Enlightenment*. One of the consequences of the development of modern society is, they argue, 'the self-oblivious instrumentalization of science' (Horkheimer and Adorno 1947: xxi). The Enlightenment made scientific thought the touchstone of truth in the modern world but the public was let down by the manner in which science was harnessed to the needs of industry. Instead of science being the instrument of human emancipation, it became the instrument of the aggrandizing development of the market economy. Science became detached from the pursuit of truth and was reduced to problem-solving for the capitalist enterprise. But the difficulties of modern society run deeper than this seduction of science, for even those 'trends opposed to the accepted scientific mode' have been 'affected by the total process of production' (Horkheimer and Adorno: xii). One of the first premises of Hegelian dialectic is that 'the true is the whole' and it seems that no one is able to escape the influence of the totalizing tendencies of modern production. For Adorno and Horkheimer, critical social thinking has been absorbed within the technological process itself. The ideas of critical thinkers adorn in handsomely covered books the coffee-tables of the well-to-do in society, and so are absorbed as trinkets of the effete civilization they would seek to undermine.

Modern civilization is the outcome of the critique of pre-modern social life presented by the Enlightenment. But these critical social trends, true to the Hegelian–Marxist dialectic, 'suffer what triumphant thought has always suffered' (Horkheimer and Adorno 1947: xii). In the Marxist manner the ruling thoughts of an epoch are always the thoughts of the ruling class. Thus, as the critical ideas of the ideologues of the Enlightenment came to power, they ceased to be critical. Or, as Hegel would put it, the innovative and critical ideas of one historical period inevitably become the dogmas and received truths for later generations. Equally, for Adorno and Horkeimer, 'the philosophy which put the fear of death into infamy in the eighteenth century, despite all the book-burnings and piles of corpses, chose to serve that very infamy under Napolean' (Horkheimer and Adorno 1947: xii). Enlightenment thought became the servant of earthly masters rather than the measure of truth. The consequences are dire, for 'the metamorphoses of criticism into affirmation do not leave the theoretical content untouched, for its truth evaporates' (Horkheimer and Adorno 1947: xii).

The all-embracing view drawn from Hegelian–Marxist dialectic leads Horkheimer and Adorno to advocate desperate measures. In their view there are very few resources available in contemporary philosophy and culture with which to resist the stupefying effect of the absorption of Enlightenment thinking: 'There is no longer any available form of linguistic expression which has not tended toward accommodation to dominant currents of thought' (Horkheimer and Adorno 1947: xii). So how do we get out of the open prison that is modern society? In Horkheimer's and Adorno's view most contemporary intellectuals voluntarily comply with conditions of social censorship. In wanting to make their products marketable and thereby conform to notions of style and presentation that meet with the requirement and tastes of their age, the need for external censorship is lessened. The prevailing form of philosophy that believes in the 'strict limitation to the verification of facts and probability theory' (Horkheimer and Adorno 1947: xiii) sees to it that no lavish, subversive systems of thought see the light of day. For Horkheimer and Adorno there seems no escape: we are trapped within a once-progressive system of thought that has become its opposite, paving the 'way for political error and madness' (Horkheimer and Adorno 1947: xiii).

Horkheimer and Adorno are neither voluntarists nor determinists. Enlightenment thinking is a process that combines both elements, and, seen from a determinist perspective, it is itself to blame for the lamentable condition into which the human race has fallen. Wearing their voluntarist hats, they believe that it still can be – and has to be – redeemed, but they find themselves in a paradoxical situation. The paradox is expressed most strongly in their comments in the preface to the new edition of *Dialectic of Enlightenment* that 'today critical thought (which does not abandon its commitment even in the face of progress) demands support for the residues of freedom, for tendencies toward true humanism, even if these seem power-less in regard to the main course of history' (Horkheimer and Adorno 1947: ix–x). Although the phenomenon they are investigating is the 'self-destruction of the Enlightenment', they are 'wholly convinced . . . that social freedom is inseparable from enlightened thought'. They see as their task the discovery and elucidation of the 'recidivist element' within the Enlightenment which they designate as the 'destructive aspect of progress'. So they see themselves as engaging in a quasi-Kantian task of subjecting 'the modern theoretical faculty' (Horkheimer and Adorno 1947: xiii) to a systematic critique.

Kant conceived of his *Critique of Pure Reason* as an attempt to rein in the over-ambitious speculations of his metaphysical colleagues. He believed that the claims of reason in the theoretical sphere were greatly inflated and could be justifiably limited. Adorno and Horkheimer seek to engage in a similar critique, but in their case their objective is to encourage philosophers into greater ambition in going beyond ordinary experience. In this strategy we can see quite clearly the Hegelian–Marxist supposition that there is always within the positive a negative. The unthinking compliance of the twentieth-century individual with domination and barbarism is, for Horkheimer and Adorno, implicit within the positive critique of oppressive order inaugurated by Enlightenment thinkers. The apple is not suddenly bad: modern civilization has from the beginning had a rotten core. They want to take this dialectic one stage further by attempting to discover within the flawed totality of the Enlightenment those elements that may yet lead to emancipation.

For Horkheimer and Adorno the framework of rationality within which modern civilization functions is wrong. Social activity and the process of production focus upon the mastery of nature in too authoritarian and single-minded a manner. Their critique of the Enlightenment is 'intended to prepare the way for a positive notion of enlightenment which will release it from entanglement in blind domination'. To Horkheimer and Adorno, thinkers like Kant, Sade and Nietzsche 'mercilessly elicited the implications of the Enlightenment'. In doing so they brought out both

Figure 38.1 *Immanuel Kant*, engraved by Johann Friedrich Bause (1791) after a drawing by V. H. F. Schnorr. By permission of the Staatliche Graphische Sammlung, Munich.

the positive and negative sides of the movement. The bad side, which was not so evident at its inception, was the 'submission of everything natural to the autocratic subject'. This, in their view, 'finally culminates in the mastery of the blindly objective and natural' (Horkheimer and Adorno 1947: xvi).

So Horkheimer and Adorno set themselves the task of recovering the emancipatory potential of the movement, and seek to do this without drawing too extensively from Enlightenment thinkers themselves. In their view, the original exponents of Enlightenment are too steeped in its errors and false ambitions to provide a wholly trustworthy resource for the present. They are part of a bad past that has to be rejected. Its critics have to look primarily to themselves and new, radical contemporary trends to ground their new thought. This accounts for the strong interest shown by Horkheimer and Adorno in the avant-garde, atonal music and new forms of personal and social expression. Here they share the supposition of later postmodernist thinkers that a completely fresh start has to be made.

THE MYTH OF THE *DIALECTIC OF ENLIGHTENMENT*

Horkheimer and Adorno see as one of the main aims of the Enlightenment the debunking of myth; they regard it as a process of 'the disenchantment of the world'. As they put it, 'In the most general sense of progressive thought, the Enlightenment has always aimed at liberating men from fear and establishing their sovereignty' (Horkheimer and Adorno 1947: 3). However, the tragedy is that the historical development of Enlightenment thinking has led to the reinstatement of myth at the centre of the human world. They attribute this tragedy to the excessive ambition of Enlightenment thought. Enlightenment philosophers were blind to the limitations and dangers of their own project. They succumbed to an excessive optimism about the power of thought over nature and followed Bacon in thinking that 'the human mind, which overcomes superstition, is to hold sway over a disenchanted nature'. In the conflict between nature and the human species reason becomes the tool with which nature is brought under our control. 'Knowledge, which is power, knows no obstacles: neither in the enslavement of men nor in compliance with the world's rulers.' Reason, in its efforts to subdue the world, is itself overwhelmed by computation and technique; instead of referring to our critical capacity to orientate ourselves in a reality that is always not wholly of our choosing, reason becomes identified with natural science. In the modern, enlightened world what 'men want to learn from nature is how to use it in order wholly to dominate it and other men. Ruthlessly, in spite of itself, the Enlightenment has extinguished any trace of its own self-consciousness' (Horkheimer and Adorno 1947: 4).

The debunking of ancient and pre-modern myth only makes way for its own:

> Myth turns into enlightenment, and nature into mere objectivity. Men pay for the increase of their power with alienation from that over which they exercise power. Enlightenment behaves toward things as a dictator toward men. He knows them in so far as he can manipulate them.
>
> (Horkheimer and Adorno 1947: 5)

The Enlightenment myth is that everything can be turned into a number. For each thing that is a number can be exchanged for all other things that have been converted into a number. In order to account for nature, science requires uniformity. Reality becomes calculable and so manageable once it is reduced to the form of an easily divisible and multipliable number. 'Number becomes the canon of the Enlightenment' (Horkheimer and Adorno 1947: 6), reflecting the rise of commercial society and the emergence of industrial production. Bourgeois society is dominated by the exchange of equivalents. The circulation of commodities and the pursuit of profit are its dominating aims. The market which mediates this process reduces everything to its price.

However, in reducing the essence of the Enlightenment to the capitalist society to which it partly gave rise, Horkheimer and Adorno misrepresent the historical Enlightenment. Just as the ancient and pre-modern societies that were displaced by modern capitalism were not in every respect hostile to the aims of human emancipation, so not all the proponents of the Enlightenment were blind to the limitations of modern commercial society. In debunking the myth, Horkheimer and Adorno are themselves responsible for creating a new myth: that all Enlightenment thinkers are irreducibly bourgeois and blind to the negative tendencies implicit in the uncritical championing of science. The most apparent aspect of this new myth is that the Enlightenment was a unified movement that had one central theme. Less apparent, but equally misleading, is that those who championed Enlightenment were optimists who saw no limits to the advancements they recommended and no obstacles and drawbacks to the broadening of horizons they embraced.

Among Enlightenment thinkers, Kant fares reasonably well in the unrelenting critique of Horkheimer and Adorno. He is applauded for going beyond the usual dogmas of the movement and for presenting an understanding of scientific knowledge that was ultimately of no interest to the twentieth-century positivist followers of the Enlightenment. It was rejected because it cast science in too critical a light, simply as one (albeit powerful) form of human awareness (Horkheimer and Adorno 1947: 85). Horkheimer and Adorno even find in Kant's transcendental idealism a prefiguring of the twentieth-century culture industry in which the objects of knowledge are partially shaped by our conceptual apparatus.

Kant was a critic of the empiricist view presented by Locke and Hume that our ideas were formed solely by what we took in through our senses. For Kant, experience was a combination of what came to us from outside (via our senses) and what we ourselves contributed through our knowledge-forming faculties. Human perception and understanding were as much responsible for what we see in the world as the supposed 'external reality' outside ourselves. Horkheimer and Adorno see a more sinister implication to this theory of knowledge. Here, 'intuitively, Kant foretold what Hollywood consciously put into practice: in the very process of production, images are pre-censored according to the norm of the understanding which will later govern their apprehension'. Hollywood and the modern culture industry as a whole represent a more vigorous and systematic realization of the Kantian view of experience: the world is shaped for us by the perception and understanding of the movie-making process. 'Even before its occurrence, the perception which serves to confirm the public judgement is adjusted by that judgement.' What, for Kant, must take place in the conciousness of every individual for an object or an event to be observed is, in Horkheimer and Adorno's view, transformed in the modern world into a social process of commercial, unwitting self-censorship. The critique of reason paves the way for one monopolistic public reason. For it is Kant's prescience that makes him into an unwitting tool of the dialectic of Enlightenment. In providing the rules for the systematic ordering of our knowledge in the *Critique of Pure Reason* he displays not a timeless truth but the scientific priorities of bourgeois man. With Kant, 'reason constitutes the court of judgement of calculation, which adjusts the world for the ends of self-preservation and recognises no function other than the preparation of the object from mere sensory material in order to make it the material of subjugation' (Horkeimer and Adorno 1947: 84).

Kant's moral philosophy is judged no less harshly. His conclusions in that area are, according to Horkheimer and Adorno, undermined by his own theoretical philosophy. Kant's attempt

> to derive the duty of mutual respect from a law of reason finds no support in the *Critique*. It is the conventional attempt of bourgeois thought to ground respect, without which civilisation cannot exist, upon something other than material interest and force; it is more sublime and paradoxical than, yet as ephemeral as, any previous attempt.
>
> (Horkheimer and Adorno 1947: 85)

Kant's insistence on goodness consisting in doing duty for duty's sake appears utterly foolish in the light of the dominance of material interests in capitalist society. His moral philosophy serves only to highlight the distance between true civilization and the monstrous world that his own adherence to Enlightenment in his theoretical philosophy helps bring about.

But is Kant this sanguine (or foolish) about scientific knowledge and the process of Enlightenment? Horkheimer and Adorno read the *Critique of Pure Reason* as a total vindication of the scientific method and spirit, whereas it was in fact conceived as an attempt to set limits on an overambitious metaphysics and a dogmatic application of science to the world. It is as though Horkheimer and Adorno have absorbed the analytical side of Kant's *Critique* without paying attention to its negative, dialectical side. Far from presenting a picture of an all-conquering scientific reason, Kant presents a picture of theoretical reason hopelessly trapped by its own internal contradictions. The metaphysics of his day did not demonstrate the triumph of rational thought but rather its limitations. Kant did not think that science held the key to human life in its totality. Theoretical reason in his system takes second place to practical reason (Neiman 1994). Answering the question 'What ought I to do?' is the highest priority for reason. Whereas seeking an answer to the question 'What can I know?' leads the critical philosopher to place limits on the ambitions of reason. In seeking to answer the first question it is appropriate to allow the ambitions of reason free rein.

Horkheimer and Adorno depict Kant as forcibly subsuming the whole of reality under the system of the transcendental ego. In this epistemological equalization they detect the spirit of modern industry that seeks to produce everything with a uniform quality. They misrepresent Kant's philosophy, however, in depicting his theory of knowledge in this way. In the first *Critique* Kant wanted to show how scientific knowledge arose as part of a subjective process of cognition within the human individual. This process could not occur without there being a stimulus from outside, but scientific knowledge was not the thoroughgoing comprehension of this outside stimulus. Finite human beings can only know things as they are appropriated through our sensing capacities and intellectual faculties. The outside stimulus, or the 'thing in itself', remains always beyond our understanding. The human individual knows only appearances or 'phenomena'. So Kant's epistemological enterprise is to show the limits of human reason and so to curb the pretensions of science. Science can explain what we observe because for something to be observed, means that it has already conformed (as a phenomenon) to our inbuilt principles of cognition. There is no telling that this is how the thing (or reality) is constituted in itself. It might justifiably be said that the thing 'in itself' is a kind of fiction, just a sign to say that we do not know how reality is finally constituted.

However, despite this largely symbolic significance, Kant was very serious about the boundaries the concept placed on what we can know. We can indeed account for things and events as they occur discretely in time and space, but we cannot account for them in their totality. From natural science, as Kant understood it, we can draw no ultimate theoretical conclusions about the nature of the universe and human life. The dialectic of pure reason shows the inconclusiveness and impotence of theoretical reason when it is drawn into disputes where it has no competence. Speculative reason cannot determine whether, for instance, the world has a beginning in time, and is limited as regards space (first antinomy); nor can it determine whether or not there is freedom (third antinomy). As Howard Caygill notes, 'The "solutions" to the antinomies, developed at great length and subtlety, consist in showing how they arise from reason's failure to comprehend its own limits; that is, its mistaking appearances for things in themselves' (Caygill 1995: 77).

Clearly, then, human reason is not the measure of everything. On those points on which theoretical reason most urgently requires answers, none is available. The resolution of the antinomies of pure reason is simply that they cannot be resolved. Some things always remain a mystery. In Horkheimer and Adorno's terms, the universe does not lose its allure and enchantment.

Only in the context of practical or moral philosophy does Kant claim that reason has supreme authority. We are justified in seeking a synthesis in our moral life because this concerns an inner world over which we do have some influence. Although we cannot always be sure that we act according to the moral principles that we set ourselves, we can be sure that we have intellectually and motivationally adopted them. Reason's total authority is sanctioned within the limits posed by the categorical imperative. In determining the maxims according to which we will act we should always conceive of our maxims in such a way that they can form part of a universal law that everyone must observe. In other words, we should not adopt maxims we cannot envisage and expect all others to adopt as well. For instance, following this rule, we could not resolve always to treat strangers badly because it is neither a maxim we should like others to adopt in relation to us, nor one that others would like us to adopt in relation to them. As it is a further explicit requirement of the categorical imperative that we never treat others solely as means, and we envisage ourselves as always potentially forming a dominion of ends with others, enlightened reason cannot, with Kant, lead to totalitarianism.

Horkheimer and Adorno depict the Enlightenment as an overwhelming ideological force that removed everything in its path. They see it as an active intellectual and social process, as a subject that makes itself felt through particular thinkers and political events. This contrasts sharply with the way in which Kant conceives of Enlightenment. For him, it is a process that has its starting point in the individual; it is a movement away from the status of a minor or 'self-incurred immaturity' (Kant 1784: 54). Enlightenment requires us to make a choice. The individual has to decide to counter the laziness and cowardice that is implanted in every human being. Because of this laziness and cowardice it 'is all too easy for others to set themselves up' as our guardians (Kant 1784: 54). Admittedly, for Enlightenment to take root, it is best for it to become a social process. To this extent, Kant does anticipate the Marxian call for social transformation. It is easier for us to raise ourselves from a condition of ignorance and superstition if others are doing the same, too. But there is no doubting for Kant that it is an active process radiating outwards from individuals. It is alien to his conception that Enlightenment be seen simply as a mass social development sweeping the individual along with it.

Enlightenment is a difficult and uncertain process which takes time:

> it is difficult for each separate individual to work his way out of the immaturity which has become almost second nature to him. He has even grown fond of it and is really incapable for the time being of using his own understanding, because he was never allowed to make the attempt. Dogmas and formulas, those mechanical instruments for rational use (or rather misuse) of his natural endowments, are the ball and chain of his permanent immaturity. And if anyone did throw them off, he would still be uncertain about jumping over even the narrowest of trenches, for he would be unaccustomed to free movement of this kind.
>
> (Kant 1784: 54–5)

No one can simply leap out of their previous immaturity. As part of our nature, our lack of standing and independence can only slowly be cast off. The Marxist revolutionary path does not appeal to Kant. He thinks it will not work: 'A revolution may well put an end to autocratic despotism and to rapacious or power-seeking oppression, but it will never produce a true reform in ways of thinking' (Kant 1784: 55). Just as there is no immediate path out of our immaturity, so there is no linear process of improvement. Because of the difficulty and complexity involved in exercising our independence, we can easily slip back into our previous paths. Kant foresaw that Enlightenment might well end for some in despair. He seems also to have anticipated that this would be connected with the instrumentalization of reason, the 'dogmas and formulas, those mechanical instruments for rational use (or rather misuse) of . . . natural endowments.' They are 'the ball and chain of . . . permanent immaturity' (Kant 1784: 55). In taking to task Kant's philosophy as one reflecting the Enlightenment it should be borne in mind that Kant did not consider that 'at present' he lived 'in an enlightened age'. On the contrary, he considered himself to be living in 'an age of Enlightenment' (Kant 1784: 58) where the promise was yet to be fulfilled.

Whereas Horkheimer and Adorno predominantly present the contemporary individual as the victim of an insufficiently complete process of Enlightenment, Kant emphasizes most strongly the individual's own culpability for his or her lack of enlightenment. If Kant has to attribute a sense of guilt to anyone for their unenlightened condition, it is likely he would blame it on the persons themselves. Individual regress, and so social failure, is a constant possibility with Kant. With Horkheimer and Adorno it is civilization itself which is guilty of the failure to fulfil the promise of Enlightenment. They cast the individual too much as the victim of events. For Kant, radical evil arose from the wrong choices of finite individuals. Human individuals have a propensity to evil that they have to seek always to counteract. Kant wants to put individuals in a position to press forward with their enlightenment, but for Horkheimer and Adorno it is Western society that has to be put back on track. Horkheimer and Adorno conceive of the individual as passive and social processes as active, whereas Kant sees the individual as active and social processes as the outcome of individual choice. Ultimately there is more hope in Kant's outlook than there is in Horkheimer and Adorno's bleak civilizational vision. Although, for Kant, there is a potentially negative side to enlightenment: since we cannot hope to learn to walk without support immediately, there are no grounds for pessimism and fatalism. We have always to rise to the challenge, and where we fail seek to restart the process. With Horkheimer and Adorno, the failure seems so entrenched in society that it is difficult to know where we might begin.

Kant's contemporary, Moses Mendelssohn, also advised caution against taking too sanguine a view of enlightenment. In his view, enlightenment, culture and education are profoundly interrelated concepts (Mendelssohn 1989: 461). He believed that they were concepts new to the German language and best known only from books. That they were terms not used by the wider public did not, in his view, mean that they could not be applied to the German people. Mendelssohn saw the terms as applying to modifications of social life, attaching to the hard work and striving of individuals to improve their circumstances. Enlightenment and culture are, he thinks, component parts of education (*Bildung*). He sees enlightenment as having to do with the theoretical side of things and culture with the practical. Enlightenment is a capacity to weigh up rationally the things of human life. A particular language gains enlightenment through the human and natural sciences. Culture, in contrast, comes to a language through social intercourse, verse and rhetoric. Mendelssohn maintains that 'man as man does not require culture but he needs enlightenment' (Mendelssohn 1989: 462). Enlightenment provides us with the knowledge through which we can enhance our practice. It is a stepping-stone for culture but not one we need necessarily use.

So Mendelssohn stresses that enlightenment and culture need not necessarily develop in harmony. It is possible to have culture without enlightenment and an advanced condition of enlightenment with a less marked development of culture. Where the enlightenment of a people progresses separately from culture, this can lead to difficulties. A deficiency in culture where enlightenment advances may lead to corruption. The increase in knowledge which occurs through enlightenment may lead to abuse. Enlightenment may occur unevenly among social classes, so culture may take a long time to root. For Mendelssohn, it is possible to 'misuse' enlightenment and where this occurs it leads to hard-heartedness, 'egoism, irreligion and anarchy' (Mendelssohn 1989: 464). He sees no necessary connection between enlightenment and progress. Indeed, although Mendelssohn is an enthusiast for enlightenment and its harmonious combination with culture he sees no sure formula for success for the human race in either. Improvement, for him, can be a signal for later decline, and he warns, in conclusion, that an 'educated nation recognises in itself no other danger than the excess of its national happiness' (Mendelssohn 1989: 465). Enlightenment is indeed a way forward but it can also pave the way for an even greater decline: the more refined its perfection, the more detestable its ruin. Temporary optimism gives way to pessimism in Mendelssohn's long-term view of enlightenment.

Although Kant was not able to read Mendelssohn's essay before publishing his own, it seems that the latter's discussion does reflect some of Kant's unease at regarding enlightenment as an unequivocal good. The concept has to be carefully defined and distinguished from similar concepts for it properly to represent a measure of human improvement. It seems unlikely, though, that Kant would have expected enlightenment in the sense he understood it to lead to hard-heartedness, egoism, irreligion and anarchy. Their prevalence would suggest that enlightenment had failed properly to take root. He views culture as a good deal more problematic. An advance in culture can bring with it the prospect of many more vices. Culture is inseparable from inequality and so gives rise constantly to competitive stirrings fuelled by envy and greed. So, for him, as for Mendelssohn, the relationship between enlightenment and culture is a problematic one. Indeed, according to Kant, Rousseau had demonstrated 'that there is an inevitable conflict between culture and the nature of the human race as a physical species each of whose individual members is meant to fulfil his destiny completely' (Kant 1786: 227).

CONCLUSION

In this brief survey I have tried to show how Horkheimer and Adorno's famous thesis about the self-destructive tendencies of the Enlightenment is itself limited. Engaging and challenging as it is, it nonetheless portrays the Enlightenment in too stark and one-sided a way. I have briefly attempted to demonstrate how this is so by looking at some of the main themes of the philosophy of Kant, one of their chief adversaries in their analysis. Arguably, Kant's dialectic of theoretical reason subsumes Horkheimer and Adorno's dialectic. Their ambitious speculations might be seen as part of the extravagant use of theoretical reason Kant sets out to counter. Also Kant's views on Enlightenment are a good deal different from what we might expect from Horkheimer and Adorno's account, and indeed, along with the speculations of Mendelssohn, present sharp warnings about the possible deficiencies of Enlightenment. From this perspective, the Enlightenment is not simply an event that has occurred in the past, but is a continuing process that, if it is true to itself, encompasses its own criticism.

REFERENCES

Caygill, Howard (1995) *A Kant Dictionary*, Oxford: Blackwell.

Adorno, Theodor and Horkheimer, Max (1947) *Dialektik der Aufklärung*; trans. John Cumming (1979) as *Dialectic of Enlightenment*, London: Verso Editions.

Kant, Immanuel (1784) *An Answer to the Question: 'What is Enlightenment?'* and (1786) *Conjectures on the Beginning of Human History*, both in (1970) *Kant's Political Writings*, ed. with an introduction and notes by H. Reiss, trans. H. S. Nisbet, Cambridge: Cambridge University Press.

Mendelssohn, Moses (1989) *Schriften ueber Religion und Aufklaerung*, ed. Martina Thom, Berlin: Union Verlag.

Neiman, Susan (1994) *The Unity of Reason: Rereading Kant*, Oxford: Oxford University Press.

CHAPTER THIRTY-NINE

POSTMODERNISM AND THE ENLIGHTENMENT

Susan Wilson

'WHAT IS ENLIGHTENMENT?'

This question provides the title for seminal essays by Immanuel Kant (1724–1804) and Michel Foucault (1926–1984). Kant's essay (1784) addressed a question which had emerged out of a heated debate among contemporary German intellectuals: why had only minimal political changes resulted from more than forty years of enlightened absolutism under Frederick the Great? (Schmidt 1996: 3) Shaken by the traumatic experience of the Holocaust in the middle of the twentieth century, Max Horkheimer and Theodor W. Adorno argued in *Dialectic of Enlightenment* (1947) for an intrinsic relationship between enlightened reason and the political atrocities of industrialized societies, an argument which had already underpinned Hegel's *Phenomenology of Spirit* (1807). Foucault's essay (1984) was equally motivated by the wish to understand the political background to philosophical reasoning.

Two questions were paramount for postmodern thinkers: the first was whether there can be a single, coherent and reasoned account of all aspects of thought and experience; the second concerned the identification of the factors that would need to be considered in such an account. Of particular concern was a subsidiary question: were there features of such philosophical thinking that either appealed to or had been exploited by the governments, totalitarian or otherwise, under which these discussions had taken place? Furthermore, relativity theory and quantum theory confronted twentieth-century thinkers with the ultimate refutation of the position of the neutral observer of scientific experiment. Large-scale social, cultural and intellectual changes during the period of regeneration after the Second World War also contributed to a need for a radical break with philosophical traditions; the term 'postmodernism' signalled this desire for rupture with everything that had gone before. Yet, in order to account for their own philosophical premises, postmodern thinkers had to come to terms with the foundations of the period that they claimed to supersede. 'What is Enlightenment?' therefore became an urgent question. However, it was frequently framed by reductive assessments of the differences between then and now, with the result that a complex landscape of eighteenth-century controversies and rival claims was simplified into a supposedly homogeneous period:

that of the Enlightenment. The attempt to define this period's essence tended to target Kant as the culprit who had defended the existence of autonomous critique. For Foucault, Kant's essay had established belief in numerous mistaken premises even while it had failed to answer the question of its title, which Foucault asks anew: 'What, then, is this event that is called the *Aufklärung* and that has determined, at least in part, what we are, what we think, and what we do today?' (Foucault 1984: 32).

RATIONAL AUTONOMY AND THE UNIVERSAL SUBJECT

For Kant, the ability to use reason as a matter of choice is the epitome of human achievement. The freedom of the individual to exercise his own innate capacity for rational thought, of 'thinking for himself', is, for Kant, 'every man's vocation' – and it is also the key to enlightenment. The human dignity of each member of the 'great unthinking masses' (Kant 1784: 2) is best promoted by their progressive self-development into autonomous rational individuals capable of forgoing the 'tutelage' (Kant 1784: 1) incurred by unexamined dogma or authority. But this 'step to competence', Kant notes, 'is held to be very dangerous by the far greater portion of mankind'. 'Resolution and courage' are necessary adjuncts to autonomy:

> Enlightenment is man's release from his self-incurred tutelage. Tutelage is man's inability to make use of his understanding without direction from another. Self-incurred is this tutelage when its cause lies not in lack of reason but in lack of resolution and courage to use it without direction from another. *Sapere aude!* 'Have courage to use your own reason!' – that is the motto of enlightenment.
>
> (Kant 1784: 1)

From these beginnings, Kant envisages 'progress in general enlightenment', for such development is 'the proper destination' of 'human nature' itself (Kant 1784: 4). Enlightenment is in progress, according to Kant's judgement in 1784, even if mankind cannot yet be designated 'enlightened':

> If we are asked, 'Do we now live in an *enlightened age?*' the answer is, 'No,' but we do live in an *age of enlightenment*. As things now stand, much is lacking which prevents men from being, or easily becoming, capable of correctly using their own reason in religious matters with assurance and free from outside direction.
>
> (Kant 1784: 5)

After the death of Frederick II of Prussia in 1786, many freedoms, particularly with regard to religious practices and the separation of Church and state, were again curtailed. These hostile political circumstances could not, however, alter Kant's view of human nature and he continued to maintain that Enlightenment was our inevitable, if distant, destination.

Kant's whole philosophical system revolves round an autonomous and timeless – or, as he calls it, transcendental – conception of the self. As Robert Solomon describes it, 'the reflecting self does not just know itself, but in knowing itself knows all selves, and the structure of any and every possible self . . . The underlying presumption is that in all essential matters everyone, everywhere, is the same' (Solomon 1988: 6).

Kant was criticized by his contemporaries for the peculiar vocabulary in which he expressed his philosophical views, especially as he began from fairly orthodox premises. He accepted the view, going back to Aristotle, but more recently prominently advocated by John Locke and David Hume in Britain, that the human mind and its activities can be analysed at three levels, or in terms of three interlocking processes: the basic sensory level, at which a constant stream of sensory stimuli are received into the mind; a second stage, of the imagination, which begins to process these transient stimuli; and a crucial, third level of the understanding or intellect, which identifies and classifies stimuli. The understanding achieves this by means of the 'categories': these are sorting mechanisms, which enable us to grasp the nature of our original sensations or impressions by ordering them and helping us recognize their similarities to and differences from earlier remembered sensations. Without this work of the intellect, we would have no understanding of sensory stimuli. The work of the intellect enables us to understand our sensory experiences, anchored as they are in the dimensions of space and time (Kant 1781/7: A20/B34, 66; Kant 1783: §§36, 65); but, at the same time, the intellect interposes itself between us and what is, or might be, really present in reality if it were not organized and thus also obscured by our own enquiring minds.

The division of the empirical realm into objects or events is thus a procedure carried out by human understanding under the guidance of its own concepts, rather than an organization pre-established in nature. The understanding subdivides sensory impressions into different categories and places them in abstract classes; in this way we make sense of the continuously diverse nature of sensory experience which Kant calls the 'manifold of intuition' (Kant 1781: A105, 135). Coherent experience depends on this synthesizing capacity of the understanding.

For Kant, human beings can have knowledge only of their own impressions of objects, not of the objects themselves. In the 'Copernican Revolution' Kant argues that the human subject actively imposes form upon nature rather than passively registering it, and he concludes that 'the order and regularity in the appearances, which we entitle *nature*, we ourselves introduce' (Kant 1781: A125, 147). The cognitive apparatus of all human beings organizes their sensory experiences in an identical manner. Each normal human being therefore constructs a version of 'external reality' that is shared by everyone else.

Kant's 'transcendental idealism' (Kant 1781/7: A28/B44, 72) postulates the existence of an a priori, and therefore universal, structure of the human mind which underlies the identity of 'each one of us around the globe and throughout history' (Solomon 1988: 4). In principle, everyone possesses such a 'transcendental self' and has the right to use its powers of reasoning. This 'universalism', as Terry Eagleton argues, was 'one of the greatest emancipatory ideas of world history', for with it '[t]he exotic new thesis was abroad that you were entitled to freedom, autonomy, justice, happiness, political equality and the rest not because you were the son of a minor

Prussian count but simply on account of your humanity' (Eagleton 1996: 112–13). However, such universalism also depended upon a 'ferocious abstraction' (Eagleton 1996: 113). No cultural, social, bodily or emotional experience could be permitted to interfere with the operation of rationality, which alone constitutes what it is to be human. Kant's references to the 'transcendental self', which exists outside time, also partly explains why his account of the human condition seems to ignore its historical and cultural aspects.

Kant's universal subject has also been accused of establishing the white male as its norm. His prejudiced attitude demonstrates itself, for instance, when he claims that the exercise of rationality can be detrimental to women's essential identity:

> Laborious learning or painful pondering, even if a woman should greatly succeed in it, destroy the merits that are proper to her sex . . . A woman who has a head full of Greek . . . or carries on fundamental controversies about mechanics . . . might as well even have a beard; for perhaps that would express more obviously the mien of profundity for which she strives.
>
> (Kant 1764: 581)

Such passages demonstrate that the theory of the 'universal' subject can imply insidious views about gender difference. It could also be conjoined with racial preju-dice; Kant regrettably pronounced that 'The Negroes of Africa have by nature no feeling that rises above the trifling.' The difference between these 'two races of man', the white and the black, is 'fundamental . . . and it appears to be as great in regard to mental capacities as in colour' (Kant 1764: 638). For Kant, that a 'fellow was quite black from head to foot' was 'a clear proof that what he said was stupid' (Kant 1764: 639).

CRITICS OF THE ENLIGHTENMENT

The experience of the French Revolution cast a shadow over the naive optimism of the specifically Kantian version of inevitable progression towards Enlightenment. The fiercest critic of such optimism was Friedrich Nietzsche (1844–1900), who rigorously indicted eighteenth-century philosophy for subsuming its arguments into grand narratives about cultural and intellectual progress and thus supporting the aspirations of the period's political rulers. Since Enlightenment philosophers could not escape the political, social and moral implications of their contexts, Nietzsche called for an open admission that knowledge and power were inseparable.

For Nietzsche 'truth' itself was an item of human and political provenance. In 1886 he contended that '[i]t is no more than a moral prejudice that truth is worth more than appearance; it is even the worst-proved assumption that exists' (Nietzsche 1886: §§34, 65). To attempt objectivity, to aspire to look at the world from no particular perspective, was, in Nietzsche's estimation, equivalent to *not* looking at the world at all. If 'one deducted the perspective', no 'world would still remain over'; so Nietzsche argued that the 'being' of the world 'is essentially different from every point' (Nietzsche 1901: 305–6). It is only from a perspective that one can see the world, and that perspective will delimit what is seen.

Nietzsche's perspectivism implies that 'There are no facts'; we must make do with 'what is relatively most enduring': 'our opinions' (Nietzsche 1901: 327). In the face of 'ugly truths', authoritarian and absolute in their certainty, 'the belief *that there is no truth at all* is a great bath and relaxation'; for Nietzsche, the proto-postmodernist, 'Nihilism is our kind of leisure' (Nietzsche 1901: 325, n. 45).

Another response to some of the badly reasoned and prejudiced statements of Enlightenment philosophy has been to incorporate previously excluded groups into a genuinely universal notion of the rational and autonomous human subject. Such a strategy of continuity and correction, urged most cogently by Jürgen Habermas (1929–), aims to continue and ultimately 'complete' the project of Enlightenment and human emancipation.

By contrast, however, many postmodern theorists direct their critique at the basic building-blocks of Enlightenment thought by questioning the ideas of rationality, autonomy and the very possibility of establishing universal truths. Heavily influenced by Nietzsche, Foucault denies the possibility of any 'ideal discourse that is both ultimate and timeless' (Foucault 1969: 70). Foucault sought to develop a postmodern method of philosophizing instead. His project is not to refute Enlightenment ideas but 'to excavate their concrete human (psychological, social, political) origins'. In Foucault's analysis, 'ideas neither descend from a timeless heaven nor are grounded in the necessities of "nature", but develop out of the imaginations and intellects of historical human beings' (Bordo 1994: 220). As Foucault asserts in his version of 'What is Enlightenment?', we must now decide 'what place is occupied by whatever is singular, contingent, and the product of arbitrary constraints' in those notions offered to us in Enlightenment philosophy as 'universal', 'necessary' and 'obligatory' (Foucault 1984: 45).

The Enlightenment is 'a privileged domain for analysis' for Foucault because it encompasses 'a set of political, economic, social, institutional, and cultural events on which we still depend in large part'. We are ourselves, as Foucault cautions, 'beings . . . historically determined, to a certain extent, by the Enlightenment'. Analysis of Enlightenment thought will, then, determine the self-knowledge of contemporary thought. Where Kant sought a priori necessity, Foucault will trace 'the contingency that has made us what we are' (Foucault 1984: 42, 43, 46) and prove that we may have been made differently. Foucault's analysis of the Enlightenment project is thus 'genealogical in its design and archaeological in its method':

Archaeological – and not transcendental – in the sense that it will not seek to identify the universal structures of all knowledge . . . but will seek to treat the instances of discourse that articulate what we think, say, and do as so many historical events. And this critique will be genealogical in the sense that it will not deduce from the form of what we are what it is impossible for us to do and to know; but it will separate out, from the contingency that has made us what we are, the possibility of no longer being, doing, or thinking what we are, do, or think. It is not seeking to make possible a metaphysics that has finally become a science; it is seeking to give new impetus, as far and wide as possible, to the undefined work of freedom.

(Foucault 1984: 46)

Foucault offers a 'critique of what we are' – a critique of what the Enlightenment has made us (Foucault 1984: 50). His aim is transformation, but also continuation, of the 'work of freedom' urged by the Enlightenment itself. Foucault's critique could not be more fundamental; he will contest the right of any discourse to consider itself simply 'true' or self-evidently 'rational'. Foucault even goes so far as to claim that 'rationalities' themselves are plural and transitory (Foucault 1966: xxii). By defining reason as the product of historical factors, Foucault highlights one of the most prominent assumptions of postmodern philosophy.

THE DISCURSIVE FORMATION

Foucault's strategy consists 'in seeing historically how effects of truth are produced within discourses which in themselves are neither true nor false' (Foucault 1977: 118). There is, Foucault asserts, 'an epistemological space specific to a particular period' within which 'ideas could appear, sciences be established' (Foucault 1966: xi, xxii). It is only within that space, also referred to by Foucault as the 'epistemological field', *episteme* or 'discursive formation', that statements may be interpreted as 'true'. To be 'true', however, does not require correspondence with the real, but rather conformity to the rules of a specific discursive formation. The 'real', Foucault argues, is not itself separable from the discourses that examine it. The 'silent, self-enclosed truth' of madness, for example, is suppressed precisely as it is subjected to analysis by the medical discourse that seeks to define it (Foucault 1969: 32).

The discursive formation constitutes its own objects and transforms them over time. We must 'substitute for the enigmatic treasure of "things" anterior to discourse, the regular formation of objects that emerge only in discourse' (Foucault 1969: 47). Among all the possible 'things' that have emerged from discourses that purport to be merely descriptive, one in particular has attracted Foucault's attention. The rational, autonomous human subject, the hero of Kant's emancipatory narrative in 'What is Enlightenment?', is, in Foucault's account, an invention brought into being only by Enlightenment thinking itself.

THE DISAPPEARANCE OF MAN

The first step in Foucault's undoing of Kant's Copernican Revolution is to deny the autonomy of the human subject. Kant's 'knowing subject', through the forms of intuition and the categories of the understanding, was responsible for imposing order on nature; Foucault's subject must cede this organizational mastery to a diffuse 'discursive practice' (Foucault 1966: xiv).

Kant's lawgiver is now jostled by the rules of discursive formations. 'I should like to know', Foucault asks, whether 'subjects . . . are not determined in their situation, their function, their perceptive capacity, and their practical possibilities by conditions that dominate and even overwhelm them.' It is within this Foucauldian and postmodern 'discursive revolution' that the autonomous human subject of Enlightenment thought is made vulnerable to obsolescence, like any other 'object' formed by an allegedly superseded discourse. Provocatively, Foucault looks forward to the demise of 'man': 'It is comforting . . . and a source of profound relief to think that man is only a recent invention, a figure not yet two centuries old, a new wrinkle in our knowledge, and that he will disappear again as soon as that knowledge has discovered a new form' (Foucault 1966: xiv, xxiii). Foucault aims to liberate us from the definition of who we are which has been imposed by our Enlightenment heritage, a task which is crucial for his archaeological project. Like other postmodern philosophers, he undermines not merely the qualities of the human subject, its endowment with reason and its progress towards autonomy, but also the authenticity of its existence.

LYOTARD: THE POSTMODERN CONDITION

Like Foucault, Jean-François Lyotard (1924–98) charts the 'decline of universalist discourses', those 'metaphysical doctrines of modern times', which propose 'narratives of progress, of socialism, of abundance, of knowledge' (Lyotard 1983: xiii). Interventions such as Kant's 'What is Enlightenment?' are, in Lyotard's account, coercive and authoritarian in their universalism, even when their expressed intent is that of universal emancipation. Lyotard warns against any accounts – which he calls 'metanarratives' or 'grand narratives' – that claim to be all-embracing. To ensure integrity, liberty and emancipation, he advocates the telling of numerous, varied and localized 'little' narratives – his ideal is the *petit récit*.

Like Nietzsche, Lyotard seeks to establish an ethics of difference by advocating disagreement and dissent. For Lyotard, 'invention is always borne of dissension' (Lyotard 1979: xxv). He uses the technical metaphor of a 'language game' to refer to the highly complex conventions and practices which define the communications between interlocutors. These language games are heterogeneous and the resulting 'postmodern condition' is one of potentially irreducible disagreement. Language games may encounter an impasse in the guise of a *différend*:

> As distinguished from a litigation, a differend [*différend*] would be a case of conflict, between (at least) two parties, that cannot be equitably resolved for lack of a rule of judgment applicable to both arguments. One side's legitimacy does not imply the other's lack of legitimacy. However, applying a single rule of judgment to both in order to settle their differend as though it were merely a litigation would wrong (at least) one of them (and both of them if neither side admits this rule).
>
> (Lyotard 1983: xi)

Here, Lyotard argues, the notion of rational consensus 'does violence to the heterogeneity of language games' (Lyotard 1979: xxv). The world of the *petit récit* must dispense with truth and a shared rationality to guarantee its pluralism.

BAUDRILLARD: THE HYPERREAL

Jean Baudrillard (1929–) proposes a theory of 'simulation' which 'threatens the difference between the "true" and the "false", the "real" and the "imaginary"'. For him, 'the era of simulation is inaugurated by a liquidation of all referentials' (Baudrillard 1981: 3, 2), an act by which reality itself ceases to exist. Postmodernity, according to Baudrillard, is an 'era of simulacra and of simulation'; reality has been lost to 'the image' which evolves through four successive phases:

- it is the reflection of a profound reality;
- it masks and denatures a profound reality;
- it masks the *absence* of a profound reality;
- it has no relation to any reality whatsoever: it is its own pure simulacrum.

(Baudrillard 1981: 6)

In the fourth phase, the image no longer relates to any objectively existing reality; instead, the image generates its own 'hyperreality':

> Simulation is no longer that of a territory, a referential being, or a substance. It is the generation by models of a real without origin or reality: a hyperreal. The territory no longer precedes the map, nor does it survive it. It is nevertheless the map that precedes the territory – *precession of simulacra* – that engenders the territory.

(Baudrillard 1981: 1)

Like Foucault, Baudrillard posits a subject that is not a 'referential being' but a 'model . . . without origin or reality' (Baudrillard 1981: 1).

PARADOXES IN POSTMODERNISM

However, there are also those who accuse postmodernism of 'bad philosophy on every count' (Norris 1992: 191). The charges that postmodernism brings against the Enlightenment project can be turned against postmodernism itself (Eagleton 1996: 28). We must ask whether Foucault's account of the 'history of truth' can simply be 'true' itself or whether the contingency of his own discourse is implied by his own conclusions. Equally, is Lyotard's account of the diversity of linguistic forms and practices itself an all-embracing account or metanarrative? And is Baudrillard's theory of simulation its own pure simulacrum?

It is the postmodern critique of truth and reason that causes such self-reflexive paradoxes in its own operation. We can see both cause and effect very clearly in Hilary Lawson's introductory remarks to a collection of essays entitled *Dismantling Truth: Reality in the Post-modern World* (1989). The 'reality' of the postmodern world is, apparently, as follows: 'If we are certain of anything, it is that we are certain of nothing. If we have knowledge, it is that there can be none. Ours is a world awash with relativism. It has seeped into our culture, it threatens to become our faith'

(Lawson 1989: xi). Here, we exchange belief in truth for belief in the truth of relativism. Via relativism we know that there is no truth to be known. If postmodernism means to declare that *it is true that there is no truth*, then it becomes self-defeating. Truth, in this instance, is dispensed with in favour of self-contradiction.

DERRIDA: CONTINUITY OF ENLIGHTENMENT REASON

It is no clearer how postmodernism can dispense with reason as an obsolescent adjunct of a merely fictional Enlightenment narrative without also revoking its own rational status. In fact, Jacques Derrida (1930–), whose work has frequently been taken to exemplify a branch of postmodernist discourse, makes a compelling case against the possibility of a postmodern break with Enlightenment reason. As Norris emphasizes:

> Derrida's arguments depend at every point on the conceptual resources of an age-old philosophical tradition which effectively determines the form and possibility of reasoned argument in general. They presuppose (among other things) the 'if . . . then' structure of deductive or syllogistic reasoning; the existence of *criteria* for judging the validity of (more or less rigorous) deconstructive readings; and the use of terms like 'origin', 'proper', 'legitimate', 'necessary' and so forth, terms which – on a simplified view of deconstruction – should have no place in Derrida's vocabulary. But that is to misunderstand the very nature of his critical engagement with the concepts that organize philosophical discourse.
>
> (Norris 1990: 199)

If one wishes to deploy reasoned arguments, even against the history of Enlightenment reason, one cannot deny the validity of reason itself. To understand Derrida's 'critical engagement' with 'reason', and with postmodernism, we will examine his 'unhappy consciousness' (Derrida 1964: 31) that Foucault's early study, *Madness and Civilization: A History of Insanity in the Age of Reason* (1961), cannot itself avoid being a part of that which it condemns, that is, 'the language of the jailer . . . the language of classical reason' (Derrida 1964: 37).

Foucault's history was not to be of psychiatry or medicine, or any discourse on the side of '*sovereign reason*'. Instead, he set out to explore the experience of madness itself prior to its restatement 'through the merciless language of non-madness' (Foucault 1961: xi). Foucault's subject-matter is, then, the silencing of madness in the age of reason:

> [T]he constitution of madness as a mental illness, at the end of the eighteenth century, affords the evidence of a broken dialogue, posits the separation as already effected, and thrusts into oblivion all those stammered, imperfect words without fixed syntax in which the exchange between madness and reason was made. The language of psychiatry, which is a monologue of reason about madness, has been established only on the basis of such a silence.

I have not tried to write the history of that language, but rather the archaeology of that silence.

(Foucault 1961: xii)

Foucault's attempt to write 'a history of untamed madness, of madness as it carries itself and breathes before being caught and paralysed in the nets of classical reason', is, Derrida affirms, 'the most audacious and seductive aspect of his venture'. But, as Derrida continues, 'it is also . . . the *maddest* aspect of his project'. Foucault intends to present 'madness speaking about itself', but can only promote, plan, communicate and execute this aim 'from within the very language of classical reason itself' (Derrida 1964: 34). To do otherwise, to refuse reason, is, as Foucault insists himself, to endure enforced silence; 'it is the "absence of the work," as Foucault profoundly says' (Derrida 1964: 43).

In contrast to this 'absence', Foucault's 'archaeology of . . . silence' must imply 'a logic, that is, an organized language, a project, an order, a sentence, a syntax, a work'. Foucault may 'stack the tools of psychiatry neatly, inside a tightly shut workshop' but this gesture does not 'end all complicity with the rational or political order which keeps madness captive' (Derrida 1964: 35). The discourse that has defined and interned madness comprises the whole of Western reason:

All our European languages, the language of everything that has participated, from near or far, in the adventure of Western reason – all this is the immense delegation of the project defined by Foucault under the rubric of the capture or objectification of madness. *Nothing* within this language, and *no one* among those who speak it, can escape this historical guilt . . . which Foucault apparently wishes to put on trial. But such a trial may be impossible, for by the simple fact of their articulation the proceedings and the verdict unceasingly reiterate the crime.

(Derrida 1964: 35)

Foucault's work and the other varieties of postmodernism we have examined remain parts of the contemporary 'adventure of Western reason' even as they criticize its routes and aspirations. To reject 'Western reason' in its entirety is merely to embrace what we understand by irrationality (and self-confessed irrationality has lost the argument with reason before it begins. We must seek instead for a way to 'question the principle of reason without thereby giving way to an irrationalism devoid of critical force' (Norris 1987: 17). It is Derrida who proposes a solution: 'the revolution against reason', he argues, 'can be made only within it' (Derrida 1964: 36).

CONCLUSION

Insofar as the 'order of reason' inherited from the Enlightenment continues to define the intelligible, the logical and the cogent for us, our philosophical discourses cannot do without it:

The unsurpassable, unique, and imperial grandeur of the order of reason, that which makes it not just another actual order or structure (a determined historical structure, one structure among other possible ones), is that one cannot speak out against it except by being for it, that one can protest it only from within it; and within its domain, Reason leaves us only the recourse to stratagems and strategies.

(Derrida 1964: 36)

In 1964 Derrida could cite Foucault's history of madness as an example of the self-defeating structure of works intent on pushing their critique of Enlightenment reason so far as to recommend jettisoning that discourse as a whole. However, by 1984, in his own essay, 'What is Enlightenment?', Foucault also comes to identify 'permanent' features of the Enlightenment 'ethos':

I have been seeking to stress that the thread that may connect us with the Enlightenment is not faithfulness to doctrinal elements, but rather the permanent reactivation of an attitude – that is, of a philosophical ethos that could be described as a permanent critique of our historical era.

(Foucault 1984: 42)

Neither Enlightenment thought nor postmodernism can be exempted from this 'permanent critique' which is the ethos of one and the inheritance of the other. Postmodernism is merely the latest, and undoubtedly not the last, attempt to enlighten us about the strengths and weaknesses of the philosophical traditions of the Enlightenment.

REFERENCES

Baudrillard, Jean (1981) *Simulacres et simulation*; trans. Shelia Faria Glaser (1994) as *Simulacra and Simulation*, Ann Arbor: University of Michigan Press.
Bordo, Susan (1994) 'Feminism, Foucault and the Politics of the Body', in Ricardo Miguel-Alfonso and Silvia Caporale-Bizzini (eds) *Reconstructing Foucault: Essays in the Wake of the 80s*, Amsterdam: Rodopi.
Derrida, Jacques (1964) 'Cogito et l'histoire de la folie'; trans. Alan Bass (1978) as 'Cogito and the History of Madness', in *Writing and Difference*, London: Routledge.
Eagleton, Terry (1996) *The Illusions of Postmodernism*, Oxford: Blackwell.
Foucault, Michel (1961) *Folie et déraison: Histoire de la folie à l'âge classique*; trans. Richard Howard (2001) as *Madness and Civilization: A History of Insanity in the Age of Reason*, London: Routledge.
—— (1966) *Les Mots et les choses*; trans. Alan Sheridan (1970) as *The Order of Things: An Archaeology of the Human Sciences*, London: Routledge.
—— (1969) *L'Archéologie du savoir*; trans. A. M. Sheridan Smith (1972) as *The Archaeology of Knowledge*, London: Routledge.
—— (1977) 'Vérité et pouvoir'; trans. Colin Gordon (1980) as 'Truth and Power', in Michel Foucault *Power/Knowledge: Selected Interviews and Other Writings 1972–1977*, ed. Colin Gordon, Brighton: Harvester Press.

—— (1984) 'Was ist Aufklärung?'; trans. Catherine Porter as 'What Is Enlightenment?', in Paul Rabinow (ed.) *The Foucault Reader: An Introduction to Foucault's Thought*, London: Penguin.

Habermas, Jürgen (1988) *Nachmetaphysisches Denken: Philosophische Aufsätze*; trans. William Mark Hohengarten (1992) as *Postmetaphysical Thinking*, Cambridge: Polity.

Hegel, Georg Wilhelm Friedrich (1807) *Phänomenologie des Geistes*; trans. A. V. Miller (1977) as *Phenomenology of Spirit*, Oxford: Oxford University Press.

Horkheimer, Max and Adorno, Theodor W. (1947) *Dialektik der Aufklärung*; trans. John Cumming (1973) as *Dialectic of Enlightenment*, London: Allen Lane.

Kant, Immanuel (1764) *Beobachtungen über das Gefühl des Schönen und Erhabenen*; trans. John T. Goldthwait (1995) as *Observations on the Feeling of the Beautiful and the Sublime*, in Isaac Kramnick (ed.) *The Portable Enlightenment Reader*, London: Penguin.

—— (1781/7) *Kritik der reinen Vernunft*; trans. Norman Kemp Smith (1933) as *Critique of Pure Reason*, 2 edns (A text, 1st edn; B text, 2nd edn), London: Macmillan.

—— (1783) *Prolegomena zu einer jeden künftigen Metaphysik*; trans. Lewis White Beck (1950) *Prolegomena to Any Future Metaphysics*, Indianapolis: Bobbs-Merrill.

—— (1784) 'Was ist Aufklärung?'; trans. Lewis White Beck (1995) as 'What Is Enlightenment?', in Isaac Kramnick (ed.) *The Portable Enlightenment Reader*, London: Penguin.

Lawson, Hilary (1989) 'Stories about Stories' and 'Stories about Representation', in Hilary Lawson and Lisa Appignanesi (eds) *Dismantling Truth: Reality in the Post-modern World*, London: Weidenfeld & Nicolson.

Lyotard, Jean-François (1979) *La Condition postmoderne: Rapport sur le savoir*; trans. Geoff Bennington and Brian Massumi (1984) as *The Postmodern Condition: A Report on Knowledge*, Manchester: Manchester University Press.

—— (1983) *Le Différend*; trans. Georges Van Den Abbeele (1988) as *The Differend: Phrases in Dispute*, Manchester: Manchester University Press.

Nietzsche, Friedrich (1886) *Jenseits von Gut und Böse: Vorspiel einer Philosophie der Zukunft*; trans. R. J. Hollingdale (1990) as *Beyond Good and Evil: Prelude to a Philosophy of the Future*, London: Penguin.

—— (1901) *Wille zur Macht*; trans. Walter Kaufmann and R. J. Hollingdale (1968) as *The Will to Power*, London: Weidenfeld & Nicolson.

Norris, Christopher (1987) 'Against Postmodernism: Derrida, Kant and Nuclear Politics', *Paragraph*, 9: 1–30.

—— (1990) *What's Wrong with Postmodernism: Critical Theory and the Ends of Philosophy*, New York: Harvester Wheatsheaf.

—— (1992) *Uncritical Theory: Postmodernism, Intellectuals and the Gulf War*, London: Lawrence & Wishart.

Peñalver, Patricio (1994) 'Archaeology, History, Deconstruction: Foucault's Thought and the Philosophical Experience', trans. Ricardo Miguel-Alfonso in Ricardo Miguel-Alfonso and Silvio Caporale-Bizzini *Reconstructing Foucault: Essays in the Wake of the 80s*, Amsterdam: Rodopi.

Schmidt, James (1996) *What is Enlightenment? Eighteenth-century Answers and Twentieth-century Questions*, Berkeley: University of California Press.

Solomon, Robert C. (1988) *Continental Philosophy since 1750: The Rise and Fall of the Self*, Oxford: Oxford University Press.

Taylor, Victor E. and Winquist, Charles E. (eds) (2001) *Encyclopedia of Postmodernism*, London: Routledge.

GLOSSARY

Absolutism A type of government associated with absolute monarchy which claimed that the concentration of power in the government of an absolute monarch represented the best interests of the state and was also willed by God. The general tendency was towards the rationalization and centralization of power, but in practice absolute monarchs could not govern effectively without the co-operation of the privileged.

Ancien régime A term used to describe the old regimes of Europe, notably that in France prior to the French Revolution. They were characterized by an emphasis on social hierarchy, privileges and liberties, rather than rights and liberty, and were usually governed by monarchs and always by elites. This term, first used by French revolutionaries to describe the Bourbon regime which they had replaced, implies that the life of all regimes described in this way was limited, and that modernizing forces would transform them by either reform or revolution.

Anglomanie Continental fashion for English culture, ideas and styles of the 1730s and 1740s.

Aristotelianism/Aristotelian philosophy Philosophy of the ancient Greek thinker Aristotle (384–322 BC), the only complete system of philosophy to reach the Western Middle Ages from ancient times and consequently the dominant philosophy in European universities until the seventeenth century.

Arminianism A liberal theological outlook associated with the Dutch theologian Jacobus Arminius (1560–1609). In the tradition of Erasmus, he distinguished between essential and non-essential doctrine. Although grace was ultimately a gift of God, unlike strict Calvinists he believed it was open to all men (not just the elect). He favoured tolerance and an emphasis on practical Christianity. Although banned in 1618/19, and remaining so until the end of the Dutch Republic in 1795, it continued to form an important tradition in Dutch Protestant Christianity. Arminius and his followers also influenced latitudinarianism in England, and, through John Wesley's Arminian views, the Methodist movement. See **Remonstrant** and **Dutch Reformed Church**.

660

Atomism   Ancient Greek system of philosophy in which all things were explained in terms of invisibly small, indivisible particles, or atoms, combining and recombining to constitute all bodies. Revived during the Renaissance thanks to rediscovery of ancient writings by Epicurus (342–271 BC) and Lucretius (*c.* 95–55 BC).

Baconianism   Used here to designate the philosophy and methodology developed by the Royal Society after 1660, based on the proposals for reform of natural philosophy propounded by Francis Bacon.

Biblical 'Jubilee'   A year of rest to be observed by Israelites every fiftieth year in which slaves were freed (Leviticus 25).

Boehmist   A follower of Jakob Boehme (1575–1624), a mystic who believed that God is within man: 'in Man all of creation lies; heaven and earth with all essences including God Himself lies in man'. He rejected the idea of an external material world, for the world is not a being, but a becoming. Boehme embraced religious diversity and favoured tolerance.

Cambridge Platonists   A group of seventeenth-century English thinkers, among whom Ralph Cudworth (1617–88) and Henry More (1614–87) were the most prominent. They sought refuge in the inner light of the spirit as a source of religious toleration and reconciliation.

Cameralism   Theory of government influential in the eighteenth-century Germanic world that stressed the centrality of the absolutist state in managing the economy and reforming society.

Cartesianism   Philosophy of René Descartes (1596–1650), which was the most influential version of the **mechanical philosophy**.

Categorical imperative   The view expressed by Immanuel Kant (1724–1804) 'that I ought never to act except in such a way that I can also will that my maxim should become a universal law'.

Commonwealthmen   A group of eighteenth-century radical thinkers who derived their inspiration from the period of the English Commonwealth of the seventeenth century (1649–1660). They were republican in sentiment, critical of the Glorious Revolution (1688/9), favoured more frequent Parliaments and a wider franchise, and, although proponents of free speech and toleration, were fiercely anti-Catholic.

Corpus Hermeticum   A compendium containing Neo-Platonic, Judaic and mystical writings intended for an elite of believers, as a substitute for Christianity.

Cosmopolitanism   Those who claim to be citizens of the world and who stress the universal nature of man and of his rights in contrast to those, such as Rousseau, who attacked 'cosmopolites' as those who 'boast of loving everyone in order to have the right to love no one'. Proclamation of cosmopolitan values gave Enlightenment thinkers in the various countries a sense of belonging to a collective enterprise.

Deists Those who believed that the universe was designed by a creator whose laws were rational and uniform, and that true religion required no assistance from scriptural revelation.

Determinism The doctrine that whatever happens is the inevitable consequence of preceding events, including physical, psychological and environmental causes, that are entirely independent of the human will. In a weaker version it is merely the view that every event has a cause.

Dissenters Those who did not conform to the Church of England. The civil disabilities to which they were in theory subject were a source of grievance and caused many Dissenters in the late eighteenth century to support religious and political reform.

Dutch Reformed Church The Calvinist Church which developed in the Netherlands in the mid-sixteenth century. From the outset, it was closely associated with the Dutch revolt from Catholic Spain (1572–1648), when it was adopted as the 'public Church', effectively becoming an established Church. Particularly following the Twelve Years' Truce of 1609, it became riven by fierce theological and political disputes between the **Arminians** or **Remonstrants** and the orthodox Calvinists, Gomarist or Counter-Remonstrants. In 1618–19 at the National Synod at Dordrecht, the Calvinists triumphed, ensuring that the Dutch Reformed Church became more strictly Calvinist in theology than before. There followed a period in which Arminians were persecuted, although soon they began to enjoy a *de facto* toleration.

Edict of Nantes An edict of 1598 of Henry IV (who had converted from Protestantism to Catholicism in order to become French King) by which French Protestants were accorded religious toleration. It also included specific privileges enabling Huguenot areas to protect themselves. These were whittled away over the following decades. In 1629 by the Peace of Alais the Huguenots lost those privileges but retained the right to religious toleration. The ultimate aim of the state was the conversion of the Huguenots to Catholicism, and the civil and religious rights of Huguenots continued to suffer erosion. Finally, an aggressive policy of conversion to Catholicism during the reign of Louis XIV led to the revocation of the edict in 1685 by the Edict of Fontainebleau. Huguenots lost all their legal rights and they were not recognized in law until 1787.

Empiricism The theory that truth is grounded in sensory experience; often contrasted with **rationalism.**

Enlightened absolutism/despotism A form of absolutism influenced by the ideas of Enlightenment thinkers. A tendency rather than a clear-cut programme of reform.

Epistemology The theory of the origin, nature and limits of knowledge.

Erastian The supremacy of the civil authority in ecclesiastical and civil matters.

Experimental philosophy Designation used by English natural philosophers to distinguish their version of the **mechanical philosophy** (supposedly based on experimental grounds) from the **Cartesian** version (based on rationalist claims).

Fideist   One who takes the view that religious belief cannot be grounded in reason but in faith. Often associated with scepticism which demonstrates the limitations of reason.

Freethinking   Rational reflection on matters of religion, rejecting orthodox theology and the supremacy of revelation.

Hermeticism   Views associated with writings datable to AD 100–300, primarily associated with astrology, alchemy and other occult sciences.

Holy Roman Empire   The legacy of the Christian Roman Empire and Charlemagne's Frankish Empire. It never succeeded in attaining unity, although from medieval times a Habsburg had always been emperor. The title was not, however, hereditary. The emperor was elected by seven electors, three ecclesiastical (the archbishops of Mainz, Trier and Cologne) and four lay (the electors of Saxony, Bohemia, Brandenburg and the Palatinate). These enjoyed great prestige, but there was no clear hierarchy of power in the empire, which remained a complex of overlapping powers and jurisdictions. The lack of unity is underlined by the fact that there was no imperial treasury and no effective defensive organization.

Hospital   A place where the poor, old and sick were looked after, but not primarily a centre of medical attention.

Induction/inductive reasoning   Inferences and predictions lacking the certainty of mathematics because they are based on experiment and observation.

Inquisitions   Institutions set up by the Roman Catholic Church at key points in its history to exterminate heresy, beginning in the twelfth century and continuing through to the nineteenth century, marked by their willingness to use torture to obtain information and to use the death penalty against heretics.

Jansenism   An austere movement within the Roman Catholic Church inspired by the *Augustinus* (1640) of Cornelius Jansen (1585–1638) which expounded the Augustinian doctrine that man's salvation can be achieved only through grace.

Junker   A member of the Prussian landed aristocracy.

Kabbalism   An esoteric system which claimed to reveal the meanings of doctrines in Jewish sacred texts.

Latitudinarianism   Form of Anglicanism based upon minimal doctrinal requirements, intended to form an acceptable faith for all Christians.

Laws of nature   Used loosely since ancient times to refer to any regularities in natural phenomena, but radically transformed by Descartes to signify three specific statements about the way bodies move. These formed the basis of **Cartesian mechanical philosophy** but were refined and replaced by Newton's three laws of motion in his *Principia mathematica* and became the subsequent basis for mechanics until the advent of relativity and quantum theories in the twentieth century.

Libertin This had two main senses: the first, a philosopher who felt able to think freely in the privacy of his study; the second, a person who did not conform to the sexual mores of society.

Linnean taxonomy A widely adopted rigid classification of the natural world in terms of genus and species proposed by the Swedish botanist Carolus Linneaus (1707–78) which contrasted to the looser descriptive classifications of nature, notably by the Comte de Buffon (1707–88).

Materialism A philosophical view according to which all things can be explained by reference to physical properties and relations. Some maintained that matter could think.

Mechanical philosophy Philosophical system in which all physical phenomena were explained in terms of contact interactions between invisibly small particles of matter in motion.

Mennists/Mennonite Evangelical sect, followers of Menno Simons (1492–1559), opposed to taking oaths, holding public office or performing military service.

Metaphysics Literally 'before physics': refers to general doctrines about the nature of reality which underwrite physical precepts. So, some physical claims about the movement of bodies would be valid in a metaphysical system in which space is said to be an absolute entity with its own real existence, but would be invalid in a metaphysical system in which space is said to be merely a relational phenomenon, defined only in terms of the location of bodies but with no real existence of its own.

Methodology Philosophy of correct method or procedures to use in science (or **natural philosophy**) to arrive at the truth.

Millennialism The doctrine that through human and providential progress there would be the inauguration of a thousand years of peace before the Second Coming of Christ and the last judgement. This progressive interpretation of the coming of the Millennium was sometimes conflated with a millenarian interpretation, in which, following catastrophic events, Christ returns to earth to inaugurate the Millennium, at the end of which there would be the last judgement.

Monism A term invented by Christian Wolff (1679–1754) to refer to the doctrine that the whole of reality is an indivisible and unchanging metaphysical system, in contrast to the dualism of mind and matter.

Natural philosophy Traditional term (deriving from ancient times) for the study of the natural world and its workings. Increasingly replaced by a wider range of terms, which reflected the development of the modern sciences, with their emphasis on experimental method.

Neo-classicism A style which emerged from the 1750s, in reaction to **rococo**, affecting all the arts, taking its primary inspiration from Greek and Roman ideals, forms and ornamentation.

New philosophy   General name used to refer to a number of rival **natural philosophies**, all intended to replace Aristotelianism. Often used, in the seventeenth century, to refer to **mechanical philosophy** or **experimental philosophy**.

Newtonian/ism   Even before Newton's death in 1727 many admirers who often had no understanding of his mathematics or even the details of his account of the laws of the universe proclaimed their adherence to 'Newtonianism'. His methods of investigation and argument were believed to displace the views of Descartes, which had dominated European scientific thinking from the second half of the seventeenth century. Newtonianism was felt to have unlocked the secrets of nature and for many theologians provided unassailable evidence of God's beneficent design.

Pantheism   The view, particularly associated with Spinoza, that all things are aspects of a divine substance, and that God and nature are indivisible.

Pantisocracy   From the Greek *pan-socratia*, an all-governing society. Refers to a scheme of the 1790s for an English settlement on the banks of the Susquehanna in Pennsylvania. It was envisaged that the community would be self-governing and there would be equality between the sexes and shared property. Coleridge hoped it would be an experiment in human perfectibility.

Parlements   The sovereign law courts of France, dating from medieval times, the most important being the *Parlement* of Paris. Legislation needed to be registered in the *Parlements* before being enacted. Refusal to register legislation was used as a means of opposing royal policy and furthering the constitutional claims of the *Parlements*. These judicial institutions should not be confused with the British Parliament.

Pelagian   Doctrine which denied original sin and affirmed free will; condemned as a heresy by the Catholic Church in 416.

Philosophe   Used here primarily to denote the leading thinkers of the French Enlightenment.

Phlogiston   All combustible substances were thought to contain this invisible weightless substance which dispersed on burning. The theory, which explains many phenomena, was current for much of the eighteenth century but was disproved by the discovery of oxygen.

Physico-theology   Natural theology, founded upon the facts of nature and the evidence of divine intelligence, and their harmonization with the truths of revelation.

Physiocracy   Economic theory that saw agriculture as the basis of national prosperity, and that stressed free trade as the precondition for greater agricultural productivity.

Pietism   Religious reform movement within the Protestant Churches, stressing inward spirituality over mere conformity, and promoting private religious discussion. Often politically radical and persecuted by established Churches.

Polybian A model of government derived from Polybius (*c.* 205–*c.* 125 BC) which aimed to create a balance between monarchy, aristocracy and democracy – the one, the few and the many – as a means of creating a virtuous and self-sustaining republic.

Primitivism The view that civilization has been in decline since the earliest and most perfect period of mankind.

Pyrrhonism This post Aristotelian doctrine argues that, because nothing can be certainly known, the wise man achieves piece of mind by suspending all judgement. As applied to historical knowledge, pyrrhonists cast doubt on the possibility of accurate knowledge of the past.

Quietism A religious movement, primarily Roman Catholic, associated with the Spanish theologian Molinos (1640–97), and with Madame Guyon (1648–1717) and Archbishop Fénélon (1651–1715) in France. Its key feature was abandonment to God, and the practice of a passive, non-judgemental Christianity.

Rationalism A philosophical system which reaches its conclusions by a process of abstract ratiocination based on a set of initial premises or axioms (which are themselves usually held to be obviously or undeniably true). Often modelled on Euclidian geometry, a successful rationalist system.

Real presence The theological view, primarily Roman Catholic, concerning the actual presence of the body and blood of Christ in the sacrament. See **transubstantiation**.

Remonstrant A statement of **Arminian** teaching drawn up in 1610 which emphasizes free will and the possibility of salvation for all. Remonstrants formed an Arminian party within the **Dutch Reformed Church** which was banned at the Synod of Dordrecht (1618–19). Remonstrantism continued as a dissenting tradition outside the Church and was not finally recognized until 1795.

Rococo An elegant decorative style which emerged from late baroque in the 1690s and affected design, painting, sculpture and architecture.

Salonnières Women, usually aristocratic, who organized the social gatherings, the salons, for *philosophes*.

Scholastic philosophy Supposedly characteristic version of **Aristotelianism** developed from the thirteenth century onwards by medieval and Renaissance schoolmen. In fact, more reflexive, diverse and powerful than leading figures in the **Scientific Revolution** or the Enlightenment cared to admit.

Science Term used in ever broader ways from the late seventeenth century. Initially it meant 'knowledge' and was confined to formal mathematical deductions. By the late eighteenth century, many new areas of investigation, including the life sciences, had displaced mathematics from the centre of their investigation: the common theme was emphasis on experiment and observation.

Scientific Revolution Term now used to denote the major shift in the understanding of nature which occurred in the seventeenth century, notably through the achievements of Galileo and Newton.

Socinianism Religious movement taking its name from the Italian Faustus Socinus (1539–1604). He argued that the Bible gave no warrant for the doctrine of the Trinity, although he accorded Christ divine status. Socinus settled in Poland, where Socinianism made considerable headway. The essence of his teaching was contained in the Racovian catechism of 1605, which was translated and widely distributed throughout Europe. Socinians were noted for their rational discussion of the biblical text and for their repudiation of the doctrines of original sin and predestination. In the eighteenth century Socinians increasingly distanced themselves from notions of the divinity of Christ. Throughout this period they were regarded as dangerous heretics and subversives, and many suffered from persecution.

Spinozism Heretical doctrines associated with Baruch Spinoza (1632–1677), including the view that there was no distinction between God and nature; that God was impersonal, His will inscrutable, and not revealed in the Bible. 'Spinozist' was normally used pejoratively.

Theism The term was first used to denote the opposite of atheism. It came to be used later in a philosophical sense as representing a belief in a transcendent and personal God.

Transubstantiation Roman Catholic doctrine that at the Eucharist the bread and wine after consecration become the body and blood of Christ.

Unitarians Dissident religious group who rejected belief in the Trinity and increasingly stressed the humanity of Christ. During the Enlightenment associated with political radicalism. See **Socinianism**.

Vitalism The view that living beings can be explained only by a third force other than the mechanical and chemical organization of the body: namely, vital spirits. In medicine in the tradition of Paracelsus (*c.* 1493–1551), the health of the body depended on those spirits.

Voluntarist The term covers two separate views: first, that God governs the universe by the exercise of His sovereign will, although this may not be intelligible to mankind; second, the secular view that, by the exercise of their will, individuals can shape their future.

NAME INDEX

Page entries in **bold** show Plates. Page entries followed by 'n 'refer to endnotes

SUBJECT INDEX